AF505558

DALÍ/DUCHAMP

DALÍ

DUCHAMP

ROYAL ACADEMY OF ARTS
THE DALÍ MUSEUM

First published on the occasion
of the exhibition
'Dalí/Duchamp'

Royal Academy of Arts, London
7 October 2017 – 3 January 2018

The Dalí Museum,
St Petersburg, Florida
5 February – 27 May 2018

This exhibition has been co-organised by
the Royal Academy of Arts, London, and
The Dalí Museum, St Petersburg, Florida,
in collaboration with the Fundació
Gala-Salvador Dalí, Figueres, and the
Marcel Duchamp Archive.

Royal Academy exhibition supported by

WHITE & CASE

Supported by Jake and Hélène Marie Shafran

The exhibition in London has been made
possible by the provision of insurance
through the Government Indemnity
Scheme. The Royal Academy of Arts
would like to thank HM Government for
providing Government Indemnity and the
Department for Culture, Media and Sport
and Arts Council England for arranging the
indemnity.

Exhibition and Catalogue Concept
Dawn Ades and William Jeffett

ROYAL ACADEMY OF ARTS
Artistic Director
Tim Marlow

Exhibition Curators
Dawn Ades
William Jeffett
Sarah Lea, Royal Academy of Arts

Consultant Curator
Montse Aguer Teixidor, Director of the
Dalí Museums, Fundació Gala-Salvador
Dalí, Figueres

Curatorial Assistants
Rebecca Bray
Jasmine Fenn

Exhibition Organisation
Flora Fricker
assisted by Belén Lasheras Díaz

Photographic and Copyright
Co-ordination
Susana Vázquez Fernández

THE DALÍ MUSEUM
Director
Hank Hine

Exhibition Curators
Dawn Ades
William Jeffett
Sarah Lea, Royal Academy of Arts

Consultant Curator
Montse Aguer Teixidor, Director of the
Dalí Museums, Fundació Gala-Salvador
Dalí, Figueres

Exhibition Organisation
Dirk Armstrong
Shaina Buckles Harkness
Allison Cruse
Joan Kropf
Peter Tush

Exhibition Catalogue
Royal Academy Publications
Beatrice Gullström
Alison Hissey
Rosie Hore
Carola Krueger
Peter Sawbridge
Nick Tite

Translation from the French
(Cécile Debray): Caroline Beamish

Translation from the Spanish
(Pilar Parcerisas): Graham Thomson

Design: Patrick Morrissey/Unlimited

Picture research: Sara Ayad

Colour origination: DawkinsColour
London

Printed in Wales by Gomer Press

British Library Cataloguing-in-Publication
Data
A catalogue record for this book is
available from the British Library

ISBN 978-1-910350-47-8 (hardback PLC)
ISBN 978-1-910350-86-7 (The Dalí Museum)

Distributed outside the United States and
Canada by ACC Publishing Group,
Woodbridge

Distributed in the United States and
Canada by ARTBOOK | D.A.P., New York

Editorial Note
Measurements are given in centimetres,
height before width before depth.

ILLUSTRATIONS
Page 7: cat. 28
Page 9: detail of cat. 78
Page 14: detail of cat. 14
Page 20: detail of cat. 140
Page 34: detail of cat. 43
Page 48: detail of cat. 42
Pages 54–55: detail of cat. 19
Page 56: detail of cat. 27
Page 106: detail of cat. 72
Page 152: detail of cat. 145

Front cover
Left: Horst P. Horst, *Portrait of Dalí*, 1943
(cat. 40; detail). Silver gelatin print,
25.4 x 20.3 cm. Horst Estate. Image Rights
of Salvador Dalí reserved. Fundació
Gala-Salvador Dalí, Figueres, 2017

Right: Man Ray, *Marcel Duchamp as
Rrose Sélavy*, 1921 (detail). Gelatin silver
bromide glass negative, 12 x 9 cm.
Centre Pompidou, Musée national
d'art moderne/Centre de création
industrielle, Paris

Back cover
Top: Salvador Dalí and Edward James,
Lobster Telephone, 1938 (cat. 61).
Telephone, steel, plaster, rubber, resin
and paper, 18 x 30.5 x 12.5 cm.
West Dean College; part of the
Edward James Foundation

Bottom: Marcel Duchamp,
Fountain, 1917 (1964 edition; cat. 102).
Porcelain, 36 x 48 x 61 cm.
Galleria Nazionale d'Arte Moderna
e Contemporanea, Rome

CONTENTS

6 FOREWORD
8 ACKNOWLEDGEMENTS

10 SALVADOR DALÍ, TENOR SAX
MARCEL DUCHAMP, DRUMS
ED RUSCHA

14 INTRODUCTION
DAWN ADES AND WILLIAM JEFFETT

20 REPRESSION IN PAINTING
CÉCILE DEBRAY

26 READYMADES, SCULPTURES, OBJECTS:
'A HAPPY BLASPHEMY'
WILLIAM JEFFETT

34 SYSTEMATISING CONFUSION:
DUCHAMP AND DALÍ, 'WRITERS'
GAVIN PARKINSON

40 PHOTOGRAPHY AND FILM
DAWN ADES

48 A CHESS GAME
PILAR PARCERISAS

CATALOGUE
56 IDENTITY
68 GENDER AND PUBLIC PERSONAE
82 ANTI-ART AND MODERN ART
98 THE IRONIC, THE COMIC AND THE ABSURD
104 THE SURREALIST BULLFIGHT

106 EROTICISM
114 EROTIC OBJECTS
140 ÉTANT DONNÉS
144 THE ENIGMA OF WILLIAM TELL
150 THE TRAGIC MYTH OF MILLET'S ANGELUS

152 SCIENCE AND RELIGION
160 THE BRIDE STRIPPED BARE BY HER
BACHELORS, EVEN
168 PERSPECTIVE
172 MEASUREMENT
178 OPTICAL ILLUSIONS

194 CHRONOLOGY
MONTSE AGUER TEIXIDOR
AND CARME RUIZ GONZÁLEZ

206 THE DALÍ THEATRE-MUSEUM AS A READYMADE
MONTSE AGUER TEIXIDOR
AND CARME RUIZ GONZÁLEZ

210 EXHIBITIONS FEATURING WORKS BY
DALÍ AND DUCHAMP
212 ENDNOTES
216 SELECT BIBLIOGRAPHY
218 LENDERS TO THE EXHIBITION
219 PHOTOGRAPHIC ACKNOWLEDGEMENTS
220 INDEX

FOREWORD

To assemble the critical works of two essential artists of the twentieth century requires an exhibition theme of the most compelling nature and the collaboration of key institutions globally. The Dalí Museum and the Royal Academy of Arts were driven by the excitement of putting together two artists who are arguably the antipodes of twentieth-century art: Dalí the pictorialist and Duchamp the progenitor of conceptual art. The challenge in placing their work in a context demonstrating mutuality as well as difference is nothing less than a revision of fundamental assumptions about the art of this era.

We are fortunate to have the support of those institutions holding the work and enabling research into Dalí and Duchamp; the commitment as collaborating partners made by the Fundació Gala-Salvador Dalí and the Marcel Duchamp Archive has been essential and we extend our boundless appreciation to Montse Aguer Teixidor and Antoine Monnier of those institutions, as well as to Tim Marlow, Artistic Director of the Royal Academy, for his vision in championing this project. Our museums recognise proudly the confidence and support of our governing boards in enabling this exhibition.

Through key works – including Duchamp's *Large Glass* and Dalí's *Christ of St John of the Cross* – a similar artistic and philosophical aspiration is evidenced. A remarkable discovery prompted by the works in this exhibition is that the two artists' projects equally strive to liberate the mind of the viewer. Dalí's use of multiple images and Duchamp's seminal work of unresolvable visual and verbal constructions each propose a world of proliferating and unfixed possibility. Both identified a fracture in the premises of modernism and took on the enormous task of resetting the course of art. If it may be said that Duchamp broke down the barriers between art and life, Dalí in a similarly bold manner reset the parameters of art to correspond with the discoveries of psychology and physics. Our highest hope is that younger audiences will see past the categories imposed in the past and understand the singularity of impulses within this body of work.

In this task we have been greatly aided by the acute scholarship of Dawn Ades and William Jeffett, who have curated the exhibition with Sarah Lea. The additional contributors to our catalogue, Montse Aguer Teixidor, Cécile Debray, Pilar Parcerisas, Gavin Parkinson, Carme Ruiz González and Michael R. Taylor, provide essential insights. We are also delighted to have the reflections of Ed Ruscha Hon RA, whose own work so compellingly advances the proposals of both artists.

Special thanks are due to all those involved in the curation and organisation of the exhibition at the Royal Academy of Arts and The Dalí Museum. We also thank Royal Academy Publications for producing this catalogue. The Royal Academy is grateful to White & Case LLP and Jake and Hélène Marie Shafran for their support, which has enabled us in our project.

Christopher Le Brun PRA
President, Royal Academy of Arts

Hank Hine
Director, The Dalí Museum,
St Petersburg, Florida

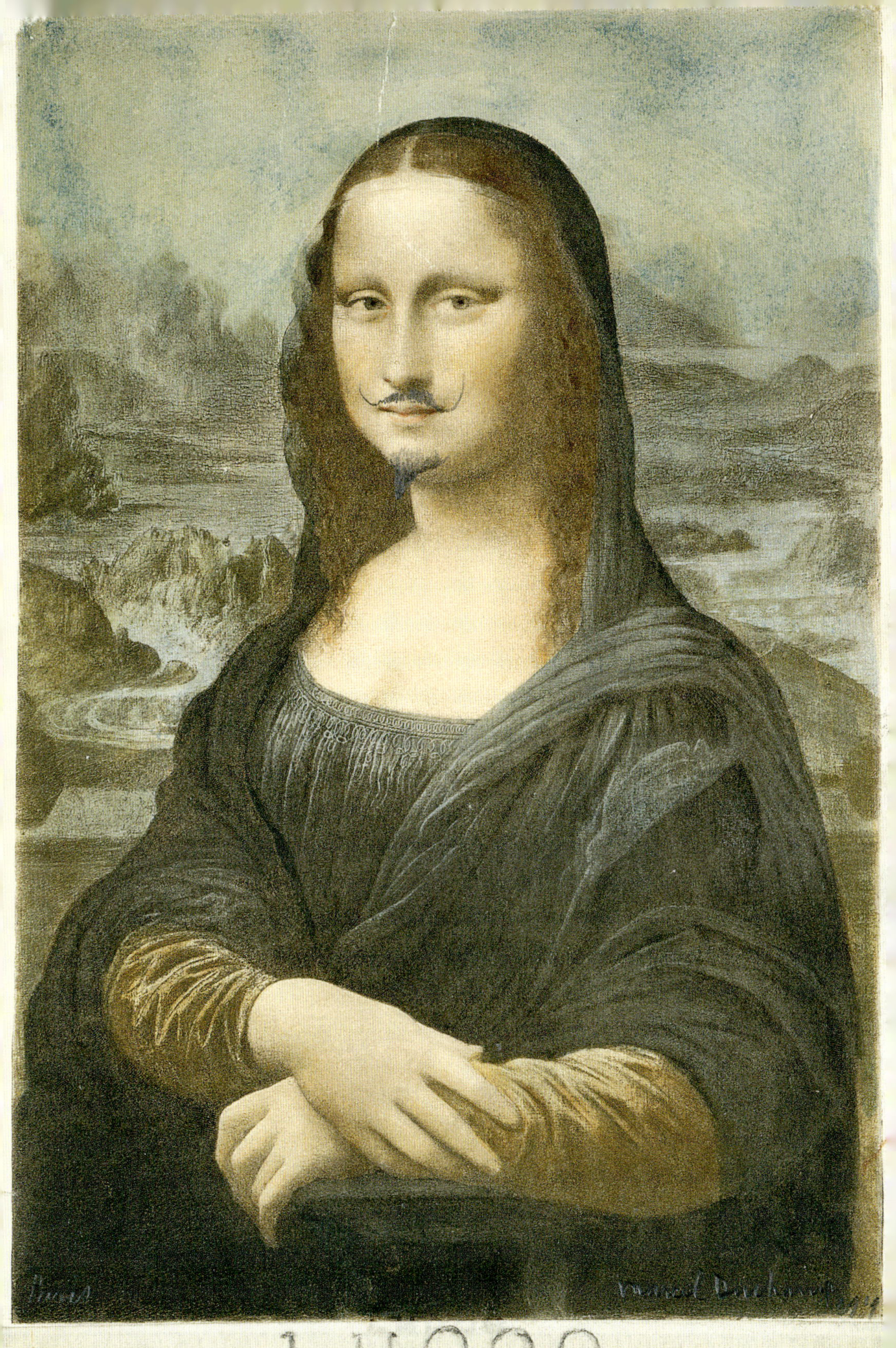

L.H.O.O.Q.

ACKNOWLEDGEMENTS

The curators and organisers of the exhibition would like to thank the following individuals for their invaluable assistance during the making of the exhibition and its catalogue:

Tim Adès, C. d'Afflitto Collection, Florence, Matthew Affron, Damarice Amao, Mercedes Aznar, Simon Baker, Neil Ballantyne, Valentina Bandelloni, Timothy Baum, Steve Bello, Bernard Blistène, Achim Borchardt-Hume, Manuel Borja-Villel, Emmanuel Boussard, Adam Boxer, Susanna Brown, My Bundgaard, Olivier Camu, Clarenza Catullo, Jacques Caumont, Clément Chéroux, Cristiana Collu, Andrew Cowan, Cécile Degos, Isabelle Diu, Adele Donati, Duncan Dornan, Patrick Elliott, Christopher Etheridge, David Fleiss, Marcel Fleiss, Paul Franklin, Matthew Gale, Jennifer Gough-Cooper, Daniel Griffiths, Keith Hartley, Joan Hernández Casellas, Steven High, Kathleen Hill, Julius Hummel, Guillaume Ingert, Julie Jones, Adina Kamien-Kazhdan, Sean Kelly, Paol Kemp, Sandra Kisters, Juan José Lahuerta, Françoise Le Penven, Jean-Jacques Lebel, Anne Lemonnier, Adrian Locke, Jon Lopez, Jenny McComas, Rosa María Malet, Stefano Marson, Guite and Diego Masson, Fiontán Moran, Iris Müller-Westermann, Juliet Murphy, Francis Naumann, Hikaru Nissanke, Ann-Sofi Noring, Alison Norton, Emma O'Driscoll, Didier Ottinger, Rosario Peiró Carrasco, Magnus af Petersens, Anabelle Kienle Poňka, Paula Ramírez Jimeno, Marie Ritzler, Craig Robins, Megakles Rogakos, Timothy Rub, Joanna Rutter, Natalie Seroussi, Pepe Serra Villalba, Richard Sieber, Pippa Stephenson, Karen Stewart, Francesco Stocchi, Jonas Storsve, Andrew Strauss, Ann Temkin, David Thompson, Oliver Tostmann, Winnie Tyrrell, David Usborne, Helen Valentine, Ioanna Vryzaki, Sheena Wagstaff, Adam Waterton, Astrid Welter, Oliver Wick, Pete Woronkowicz and Denys Zacharapoulos

Special thanks are due to A Practice for Everyday Life, Désirée de Chair, Séverine Gossart, Margaret Metras, Antoine Monnier, Jacqueline Matisse Monnier, OMMX

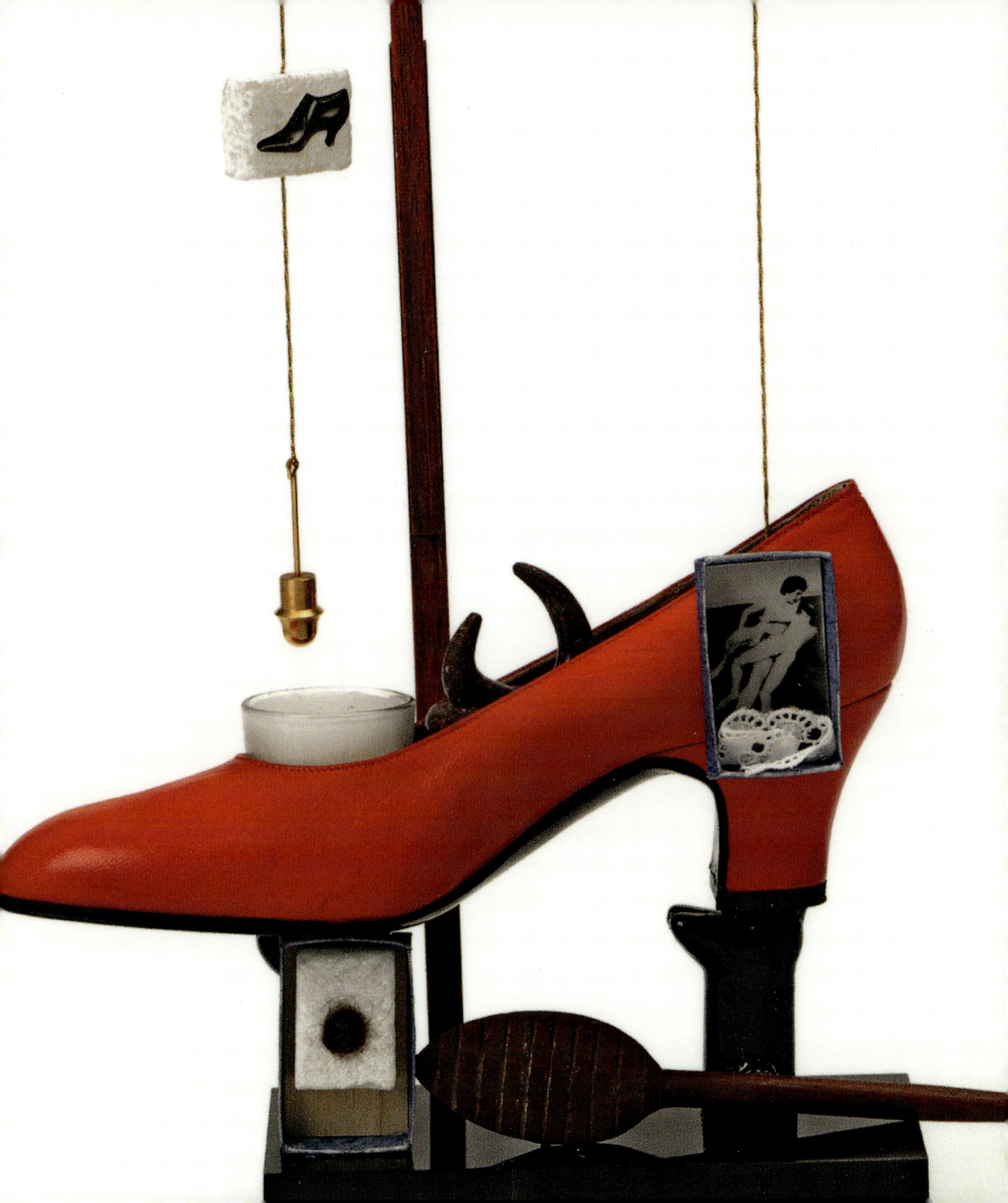

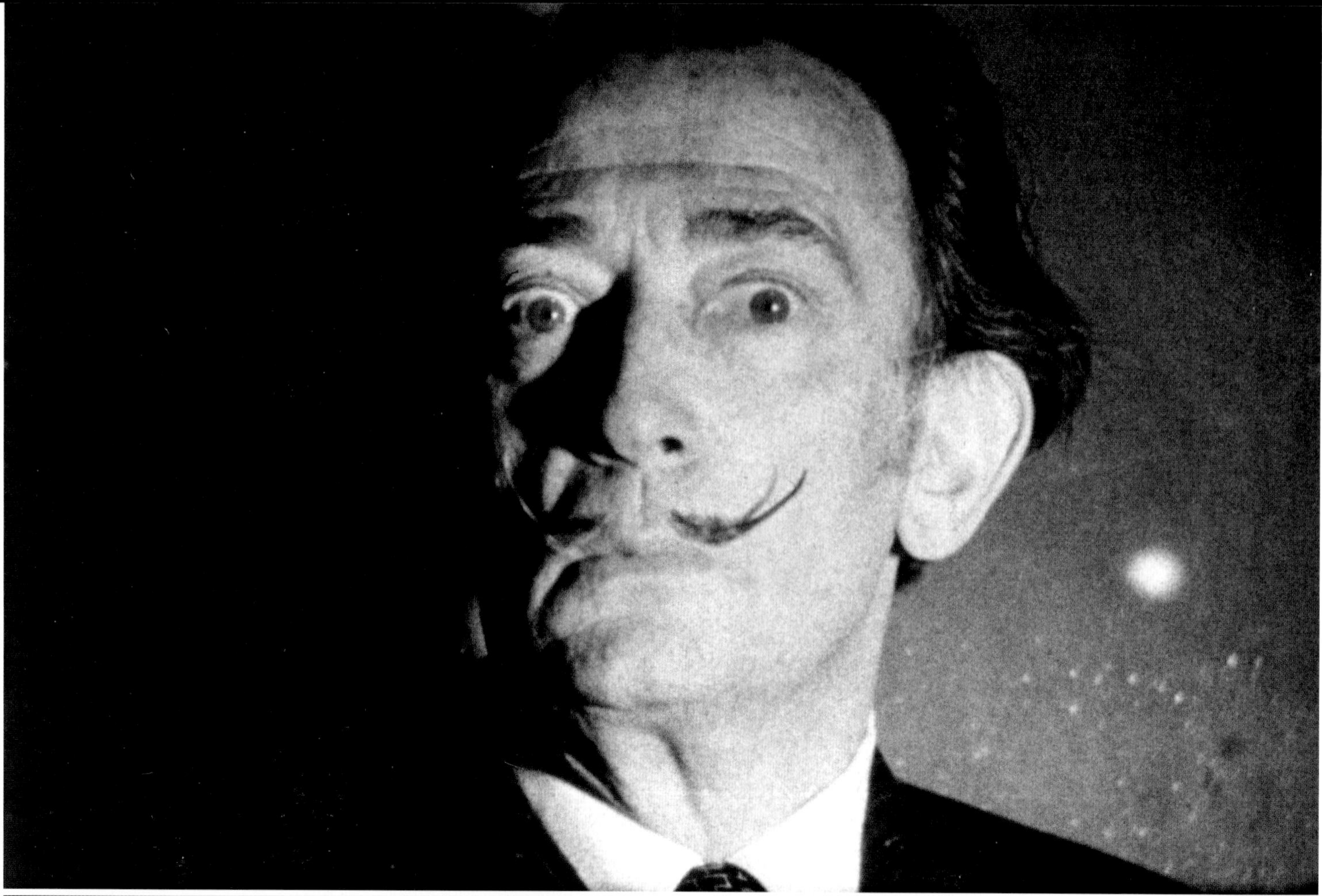

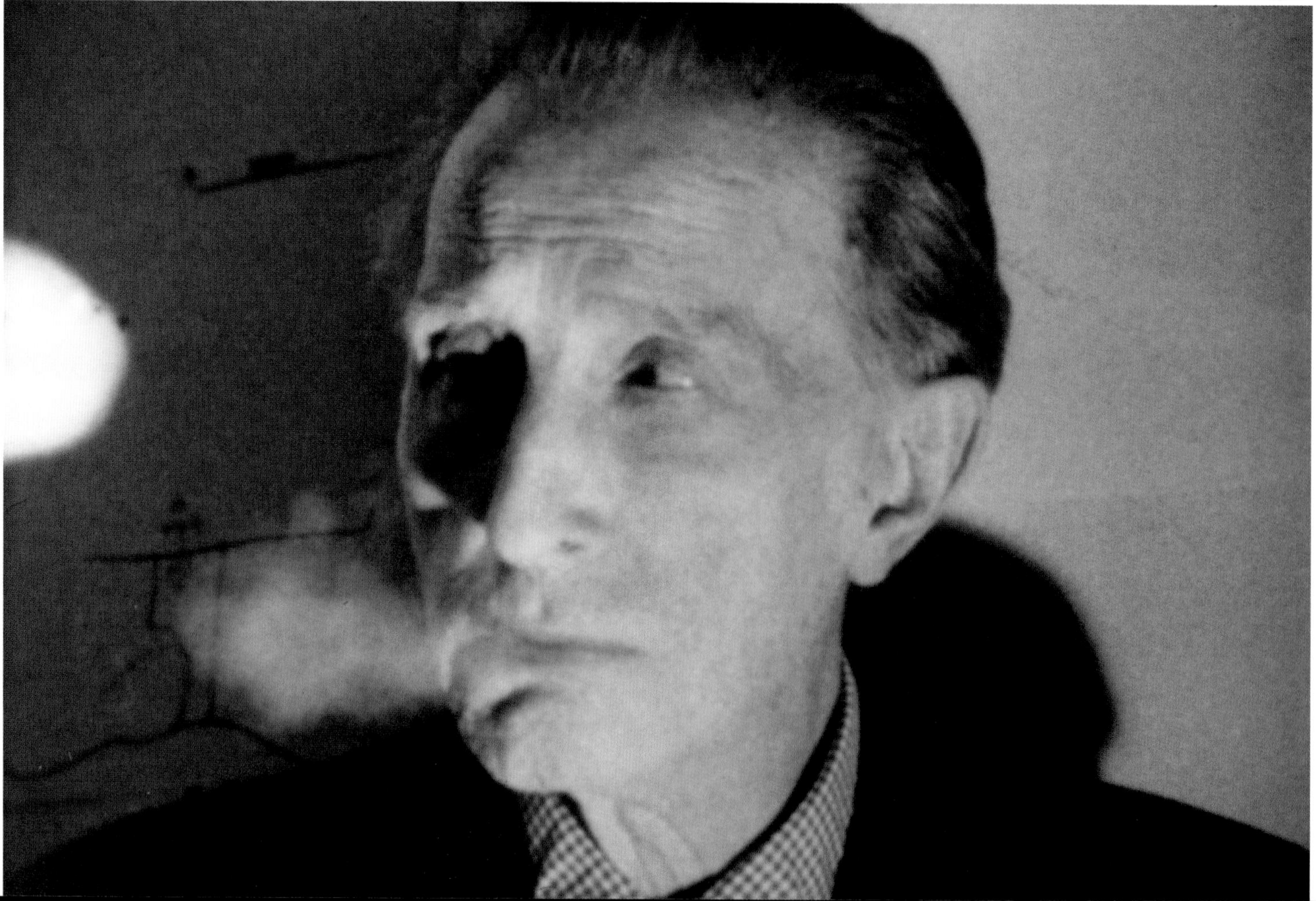

SALVADOR DALÍ, TENOR SAX
MARCEL DUCHAMP, DRUMS
ED RUSCHA

The question might be: how could two completely and utterly different human beings be so aligned with the course and dynamics of the twentieth century? These two artists breathed the same air, saw the same things, stood on the same ground, listened to the same political discourse and ate the same basic foods. Both blew our hair back with their creations. This happened during a stretch of time of great world struggle, and eventually we see the magnitude of their combined works.

The curator Walter Hopps introduced me to Marcel Duchamp in 1963 during the installation of his retrospective at the Pasadena Art Museum. He wore a suit and tie and was smoking a cigar in the galleries, which was permitted in those days. He was friendly and warm and I noticed that he held his cigar between his thumb and his forefinger, which was a very European gesture. Another time, I saw him holding the cigar between his forefinger and his middle finger, which I saw as a very American trait. That led me to believe that he was embracing an American custom and thus had embraced America.

He held in balance those elements that were haphazard versus those that were very carefully thought out, all the while declaring that the viewer of the art was also part of the final product, and that extended to the critic who likened his masterpiece, *Nude Descending a Staircase, No. 2*, to 'the explosion of a shingle factory'.[1] His vision that the viewer completes the necessary cycle to make the art official and resolved is nothing short of profound.

Thundering tons of polemics and critique regarding his creations have followed Duchamp throughout his whole life and after. We can be exhausted by these discourses to the point of just wanting to look at his works for what we see, and be done with all the words about them.

If Duchamp missed attending the Governor's Ball or some such other event he would make up for it by creating something equally or more elegant in his studio. This leads to the assumption of time well spent in his life. Some of his friends commented that he lived every second wisely. The simple act of smoking a cigar, his mind racing faster than the clock ticks, shows us a smile on his face as he exhales, a job well done.

A panel discussion took place in 1949 at the San Francisco Museum of Art involving Duchamp, the architect Frank Lloyd Wright and others. Ever the gentleman, Duchamp responds to Frank Lloyd Wright in this way:

WRIGHT I'm sure [Duchamp] doesn't himself regard [the *Nude Descending a Staircase*] a great picture now; I am sure he doesn't.

DUCHAMP I beg your pardon, sir.

WRIGHT I regard Mr Duchamp as an honest man; and I am glad that he still swears by his original mistakes.

DUCHAMP On the other hand, forty years have gone by, and time, after all, is an important factor in the decision whether a thing is good or bad.

WRIGHT That's what I imagined you felt when you did the so-called 'Nude Descending the Stair Case' [*sic*].

DUCHAMP Now, when you made your first architecture, did you know whether it was going to be a good thing –

WRIGHT No, my first was kindergartenish, and I was learning to walk.

DUCHAMP So was I.

WRIGHT That's what I assume … now that you walk, Marcel Duchamp, do you still regard it as a great picture?

DUCHAMP More so.

WRIGHT I am in no such position regarding my first efforts.[2]

Frank Lloyd Wright disturbed most of the panellists, among them the composer Darius Milhaud, by calling modern art degenerate. He was particularly critical of modern artists' use of primitive art as a stylistic source. Duchamp took exception to Wright's remarks:

DUCHAMP Why do you call it degeneracy? You seek in the primitive what might be good to take.

MILHAUD And healthy.

WRIGHT Would you say that [homosexuality] was degenerate?

DUCHAMP No, it is not degenerate.

WRIGHT You would say that this movement which we call modern art and painting has been greatly … in debt to homosexualism?

DUCHAMP I admit it, but – not in your terms.

WRIGHT To me it is significant.

DUCHAMP I believe that the homosexual public has shown more interest or curiosity for modern art [than] the heterosexual: so it happened but it does not involve modern art itself.[3]

Fig. 1
Andy Warhol, *Screen Test: Salvador Dalí*, 1966. 16mm film, black and white, silent, 3 minutes 7 seconds at 16 frames per second. The Andy Warhol Museum, Pittsburgh

Fig. 2
Andy Warhol, *Screen Test: Marcel Duchamp*, 1966. 16mm film, black and white, silent, 4 minutes 4 seconds at 16 frames per second. The Andy Warhol Museum, Pittsburgh

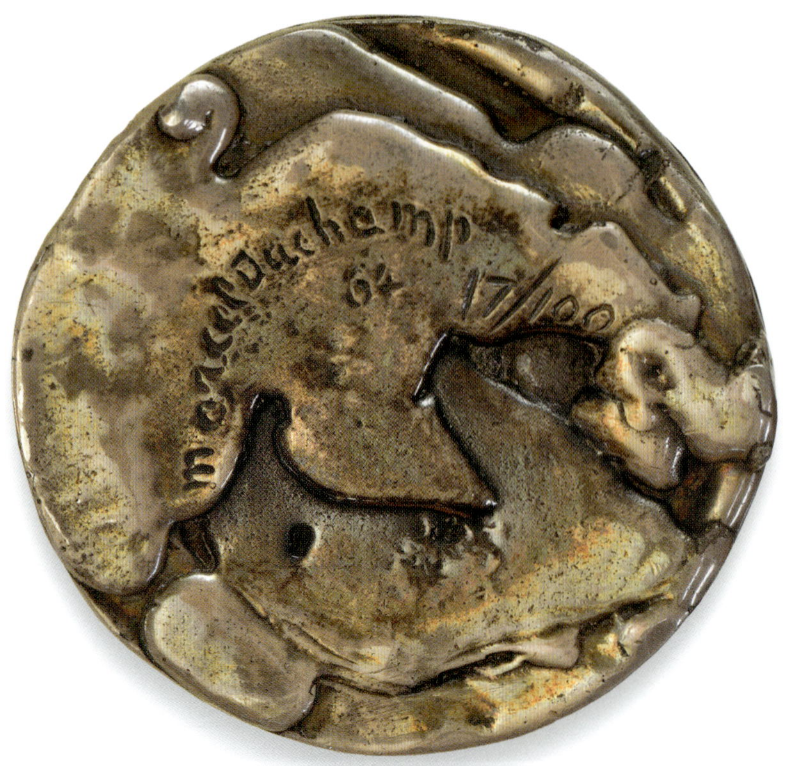
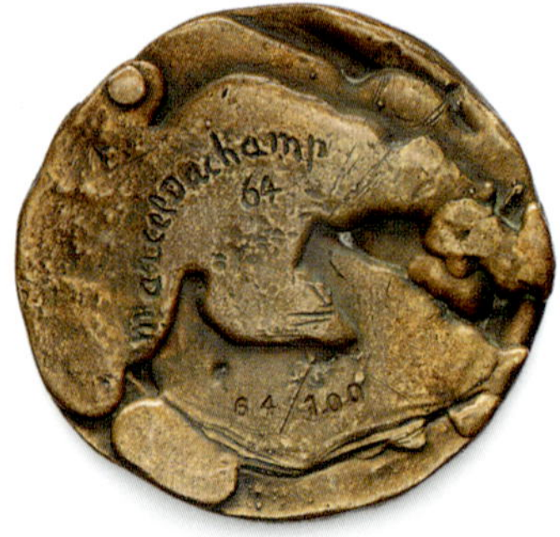
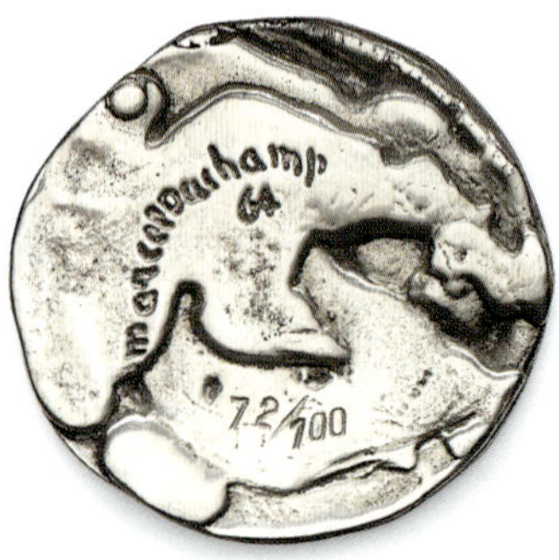

Duchamp later added: 'The very fact that modern art is so much liked and disliked is sufficient proof of its vitality.'[4]

The artist George Herms made a comment to consider: 'The great gift Duchamp gave all artists, I feel, is if you take the word *painter* and change one letter it becomes *pointer*. As a teacher I try to emphasise that this is a beautiful world we live in and it's as important to point out what is already in existence and beautiful as it is to come up with a product. That's the gift I would like to thank Duchamp for.'[5]

No stranger to multiple editions of objects, Duchamp produced several throughout his lifetime. My attention is drawn to *Sink Stopper* of 1964. I concentrate on the underside rather than the topside of the work, with its free-form, unplanned mould marks and edition signatures (figs 3–5). They contrast subtly from one to the next with their variations. Duchamp, with his total concentration towards his creations, must have fretted over, savoured and rhapsodised over the differences and similarities of the 'forgotten' side of his *Sink Stopper*.

I met Salvador Dalí in 1972 at the St Regis Hotel in New York City. I was taken there by my friend Ultra Violet (Isabelle Dufresne), who was, at that time, somewhat of a muse to the wild-man artist from Spain. There were maybe a dozen other people visiting him at the same time. As if to make an attention-getting presentation, he picked up the room phone and in a slow and very measured voice yelled out 'R-R-R-R-R [like a jackhammer] R-R-R-Room Serveece' and ordered champagne. A homeless man from the street was brought in and announced that he made art out of garbage, which Dalí seemed to have great appreciation for, then the doorbell rang and a very old man appeared in the entryway. He began to approach our group painfully slowly, taking 30 seconds to advance one foot. Finally, Dalí, impatient with the progress of his friend and publisher, embraced the man, who was in his very late nineties, and said: 'Come meet Mr Skira … before he dies!'

It might have been Dalí's habit to make up false names for people he had just met. In any case, mine was 'Mr Genestre'. On leaving, he gave me a sort of benediction with his thumb between my eyes like a priest would do. Four days after my return to Los Angeles, a nasty boil appeared on the exact spot of the benediction.

Dalí introduces himself to us as a divine creature set upon this earth for us to be confounded, rather like a Muhammad Ali of an earlier age.

He was extremely adept at ad-hoc split-second book signing and chicken-scratch creations. I came across a drawn-on cloth book cover that Dalí allegedly made in 1965 (fig. 6). It was a short series of swift lines with his signature at the top. It had swashbuckling, Zorro-like swinging strokes and my gaze would not deviate from a detail that has two perfectly placed, overlapped lines with no evidence of any over-bulge,

Fig. 3
Marcel Duchamp, *Sink Stopper*, 1964/1967 (verso). Cast bronze multiple with incised signature and date on the reverse, numbered 17/100, d. 6.5 cm.
Ed Ruscha Collection

Fig. 4
Marcel Duchamp, *Sink Stopper*, 1964/1981 (verso). Cast bronze multiple with cast-in signature and date on the reverse. Numbered 64/100 (Schwarz, 608b), d. 6.2 cm.
Private collection

Fig. 5
Marcel Duchamp, *Sink Stopper* 1964/1981 (verso). Polished stainless-steel cast multiple, with cast-in signature and date on the reverse. Numbered 72/100 (Schwarz, 608b), d. 6 cm.
Private collection

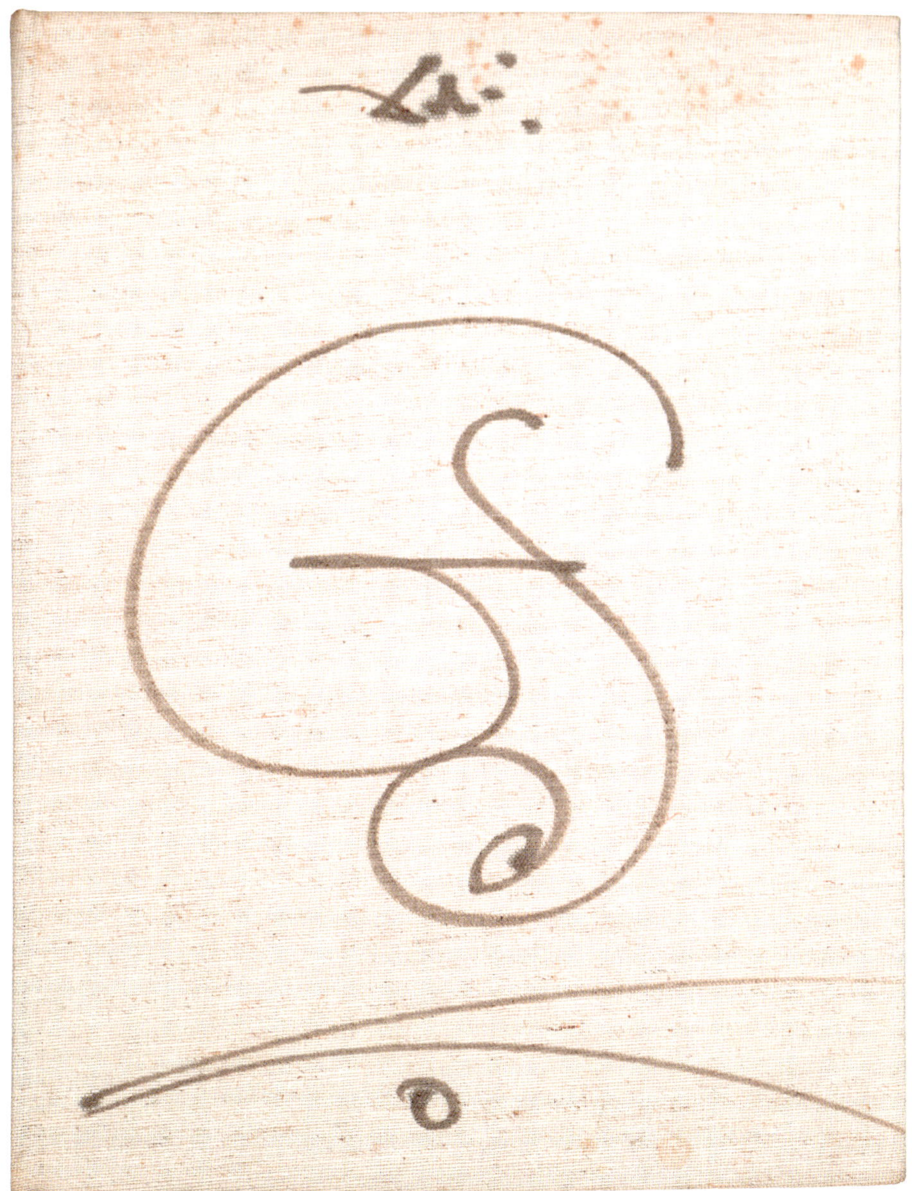

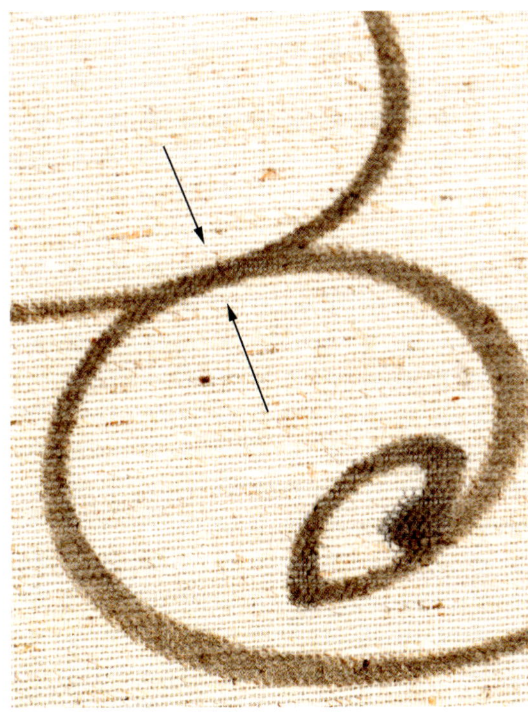

above or below, where the lines lie atop one another (fig. 7). I don't consider this to be mastery of craft, but more the result of a rascal's dive-in attitude combined with silly luck. Nonetheless, it's a compelling doodle.

Both artists made forays into erotic and phallic-like imagery. So much so that during a less enlightened period they might have been written off as perverts. Their message regarding this could be seen as having decades to mature, which is to our advantage since art is meant to open new avenues of experience.

The use of carefully chosen titles for artworks was extremely important to Dalí and Duchamp, as if giving a work a title was like adding a totally new colour to the palette. We are given an extra dimension when we combine the title with the work.

Both were self-referential to great degrees. Witness their mutual love of posing for pictures and sometimes altering those pictures for effect. A gentle wave of narcissism flows through the lives of both artists.

For all this, I would have felt an eager need to invent them had they not already existed. Attempting to understand their work fully is like searching for bones in ice cream – they might be in there but they are never to be found.

Finally, to our fortune, these two artists of the Jazz Age are brought together under one roof in this exhibition, throwing multitudes of sweet musical notes our way.

Fig. 6
Hand-drawn front cover of Gaston Diehl,
The Moderns: A Treasury of Painting Throughout the World, 1961.
Ed Ruscha Collection

Fig. 7
Detail of the cover of Gaston Diehl,
The Moderns, 1961.
Ed Ruscha Collection

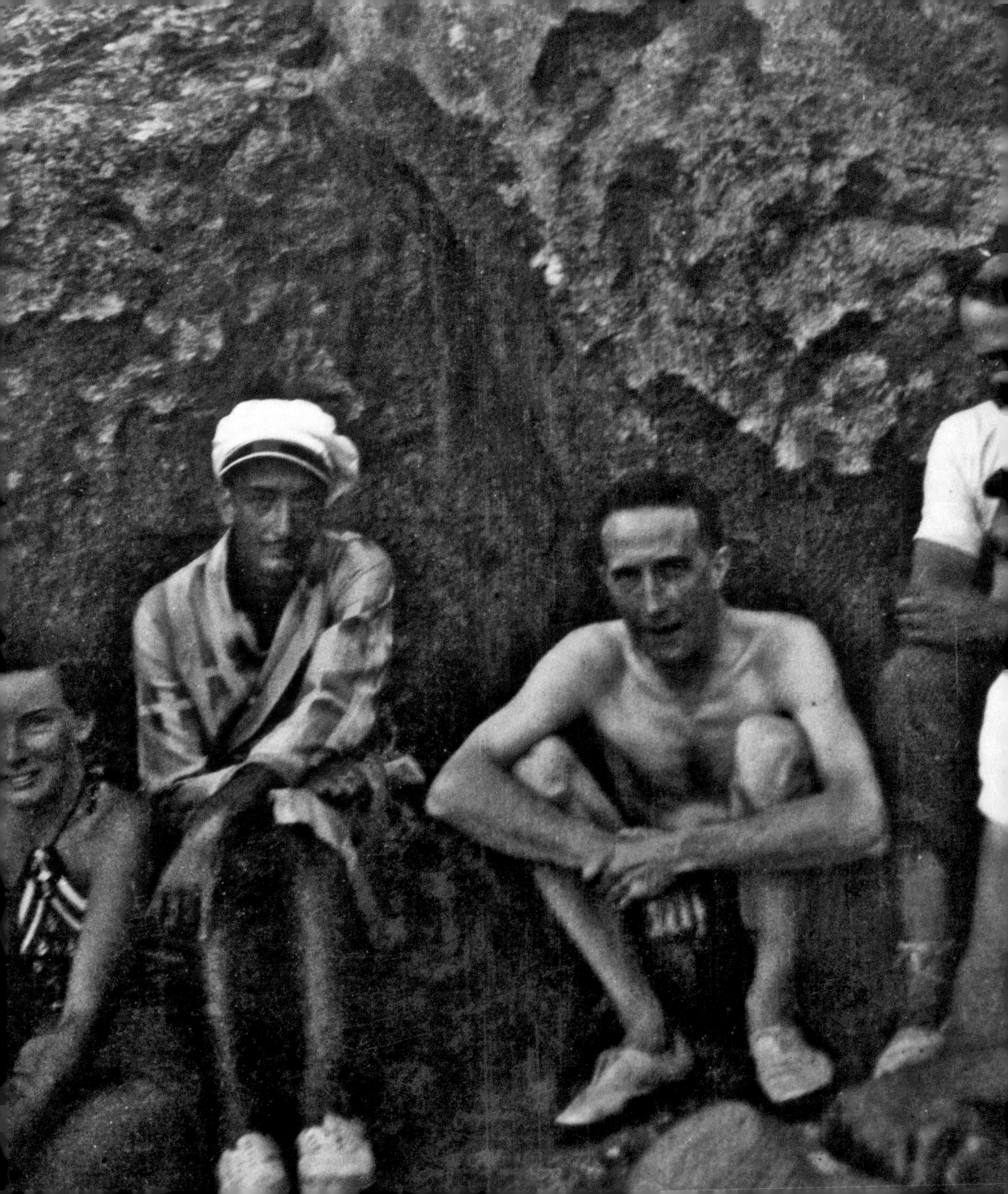

INTRODUCTION
DAWN ADES AND WILLIAM JEFFETT

Marcel Duchamp (1887–1968) and Salvador Dalí (1904–1989), two of the most famous twentieth-century artists, are seen as opposites in almost every respect. Duchamp renounced painting and invented the 'readymade', whose production he limited, while Dalí continued to paint prolifically. Dalí courted notoriety and became the first artist-celebrity, while Duchamp preferred to go underground, and apparently withdrew from art to play chess. Duchamp is now regarded as the hermetic father of conceptual art, while Dalí is seen as the defender of painting, dedicated to the continuation of an artistic tradition to which Duchamp had dealt a death blow. These diametrically opposed positions have assumed the status of myth.

It is therefore a surprise to discover that the two men were not only close friends but shared attitudes to art and life that infuse their work at every turn, bringing up unexpected and exhilarating connections and parallels. This book investigates the aesthetic, philosophical, personal and even political links between them, giving a fresh view of their respective *œuvres* and radically revising their familiar positions in the history of twentieth-century art. Comparisons, collaborations and contrasts are explored across a wide range of media, in connection with the many common themes that run through their work.

Duchamp and Dalí shared an uncompromising belief in the individual, were sceptical of modern art and reflected with absolute clarity on their positions. As Dalí wrote in his 1959 article on Duchamp,[1] '*L.H.O.O.Q.* can be taken quite adequately as the epitaph of modern painting', which, he continued, he himself could not be accused of practising.

Dalí held Duchamp in high esteem, while Duchamp defended Dalí against his detractors. The friendship puzzled and irritated several of their respective supporters. Richard Hamilton and John Cage, regular summer visitors to Duchamp at Cadaqués, tried to avoid invitations to meet Dalí. Cage said in a 1973 interview, 'He was friendly with Dalí. Isn't that strange? … I was astonished to see that Marcel took a listening attitude in the presence of Dalí. It almost appeared as if a younger man were visiting an old man, whereas the case was the other way round.'[2] Edward James, Dalí's patron in the late 1930s, was sensitive to an implied unfavourable comparison: 'During lunch when you were speaking at length of your esteem for your friend Marcel Duchamp, the fact that you were underlining that he had such a good nature that you never quarrelled with him could have been by chance and not by design….'[3]

The friendship began in Paris in the context of Surrealism, a movement of which Dalí was an enthusiastic member and Duchamp a courted but slightly remote affiliate, and lasted until Duchamp's death. Duchamp had in a sense been inherited by the Surrealists from the Dada movement, in which Dalí was too young to have participated, although he led his own anti-art putsch in the late 1920s in Catalonia. He joined the Surrealist movement in the summer of 1929.

Surrealism was not, at least to begin with, primarily concerned with art, and had absorbed some of Dada's anti-art attitudes but without the veto on creativity and experiment. Duchamp preferred to say 'an-art', meaning no art at all, rather than anti-art. Later,

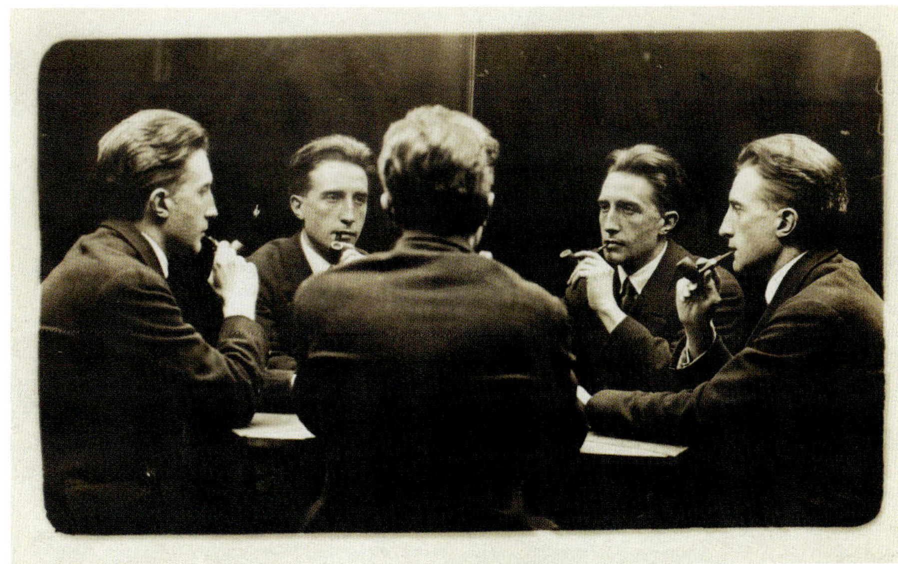

Fig. 8
Multiple portrait of Marcel Duchamp, 1917 (cat. 1)
Gelatin silver print, 8.7 x 14 cm
Centre Pompidou, Paris. Musée national d'art moderne/Centre de création industrielle

Opposite: detail of cat. 14

he admitted that he was 'Nothing else but an artist....'[4] His ambition was to not have to earn his living from painting. Very early he sensed the inevitable danger of having to repeat yourself if you are dependent on selling your pictures. His liberation, as he thought of it, came in 1912, after the experience of having his painting *Nude Descending a Staircase* (fig. 37) rejected by the Salon des Indépendants. Albert Gleizes, head of the Hanging Committee, had requested Duchamp's brothers, also painters, ask him to withdraw the work or change its title. Duchamp decided from then on never to belong to a group, and to try to earn a living in other ways than by painting.[5] Not only did he not want to repeat himself, he was averse to following the trends and the '-isms' of the time, Cubism and Futurism among them. Apart from one commissioned painting in 1918 (*Tu m'*), he made his last oil on canvas in 1914. As Paul B. Franklin has put it: 'Determined to redefine art, art making, and the identity of the artist, he publicly cultivated the role of the "anartiste" and spent his time ruminating on a question that he first posed in a note of 1913: "Can one make works that are not works 'of art'?" His response to this query – the readymades – radically altered the aesthetic landscape.'[6]

The first was a bicycle wheel mounted on a stool, his first work actually to move, as well as his first use of already existing manufactured materials. *Bicycle Wheel* (cat. 77) is an ironic comment on the Futurists' vain pursuit of representing movement and speed in two dimensions, and possibly also refers to Alfred Jarry's text 'The Passion Considered as an Uphill Bicycle Race'.[7] Like *Bottle Rack* (cats 58, 106), the first pure readymade (i.e. a mass-produced object that Duchamp chose), it was never exhibited, and Duchamp left both in his Paris studio when he sailed to New York in 1915. From there he wrote to his sister Suzanne, telling her the term he had coined for these objects and adding that he had chosen a few more: 'I've bought some objects in the same taste and treat them as "readymade", you know enough English to understand the meaning of "tout fait" (readymade) that I give these objects.'[8] He then asks her to take *Bottle Rack* as a present – 'I'm making it a "readymade", from a distance' – and to inscribe it inside the lowest ring. Unfortunately, his sister had already cleared out his studio and disposed of it and *Bicycle Wheel*.

Apart from an exhibition in New York in 1916, at which nobody noticed his 'readymades', which Duchamp later said were exhibited in the umbrella stand, the first public outing for a readymade was the complex incident of *Fountain* (cat. 102) in 1917. Duchamp was already famous in contemporary art circles in New York because of a furore surrounding *Nude Descending a Staircase* at the Armory Show in 1913, and was on the jury for the forthcoming first Independents Exhibition in New York, which was welcomed in the first issue of *The Blind Man*, a little magazine he produced with his friends Henri-Pierre Roché and Beatrice Wood. New York was about to

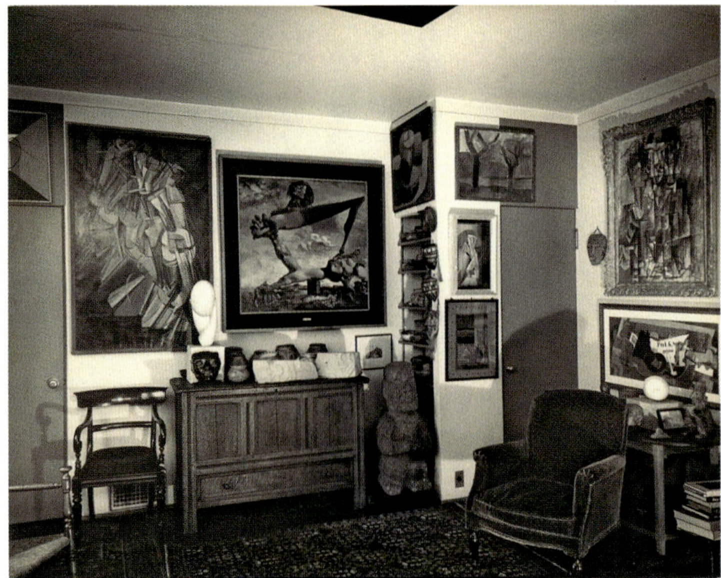

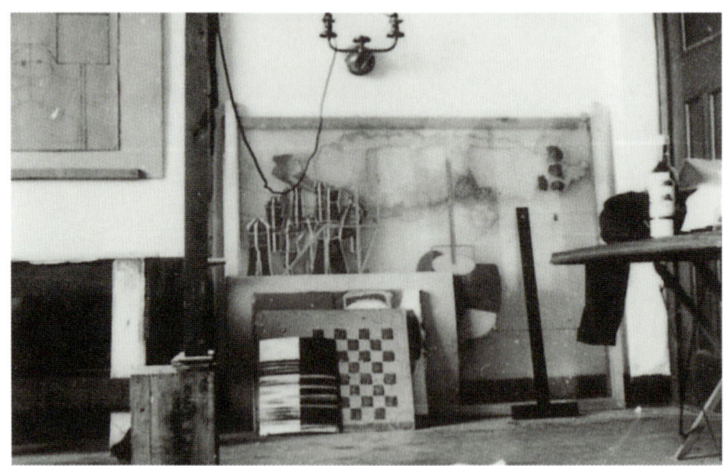

rival Paris as a hub of modern art! Anyone on payment of six dollars could enter! Under the pseudonym 'R. Mutt' a porcelain urinal was submitted. After a row between members of the Hanging Committee, it was refused, and apparently hidden behind a partition. The incident was masterminded by Duchamp, though he was careful to disguise his identity.[9] Along with friends including Wood he retrieved the urinal and took it to Alfred Stieglitz's studio, where it was photographed. The second and final issue of *The Blind Man* (cat. 101) publicised the affair with the photograph 'Fountain by R. Mutt – The exhibit refused by the Independents' and an unsigned text, 'The Richard Mutt Case', actually written by Wood. This text, the only public statement about the readymade, explained that it was of no importance whether Mr Mutt had made the work with his own hands or not: HE CHOSE IT. By giving it a new title and point of view he had 'created a new thought for that object'.[10]

The readymades occupy a *terrain vague* that is neither art nor utility. This is one of the reasons they were so valuable for the 'Surrealist object with

Fig. 9
The library and art collection in the home of Mr and Mrs Walter Arensberg, New York, 1945. Duchamp's *Nude Descending a Staircase (No. 2)* is visible to the left, beside it is Dalí's *Premonition of Civil War*. Photograph by Fred R. Dapprich. Condé Nast Collection

Fig. 10
Marcel Duchamp's studio at 33 West 67th Street, New York, 1917–18. Photograph attributed to Henri-Pierre Roché. Gelatin silver print, 6.2 x 3.8 cm. Philadelphia Museum of Art. Gift of Jacqueline, Paul and Peter Matisse in memory of their mother, Alexina Duchamp, 1998

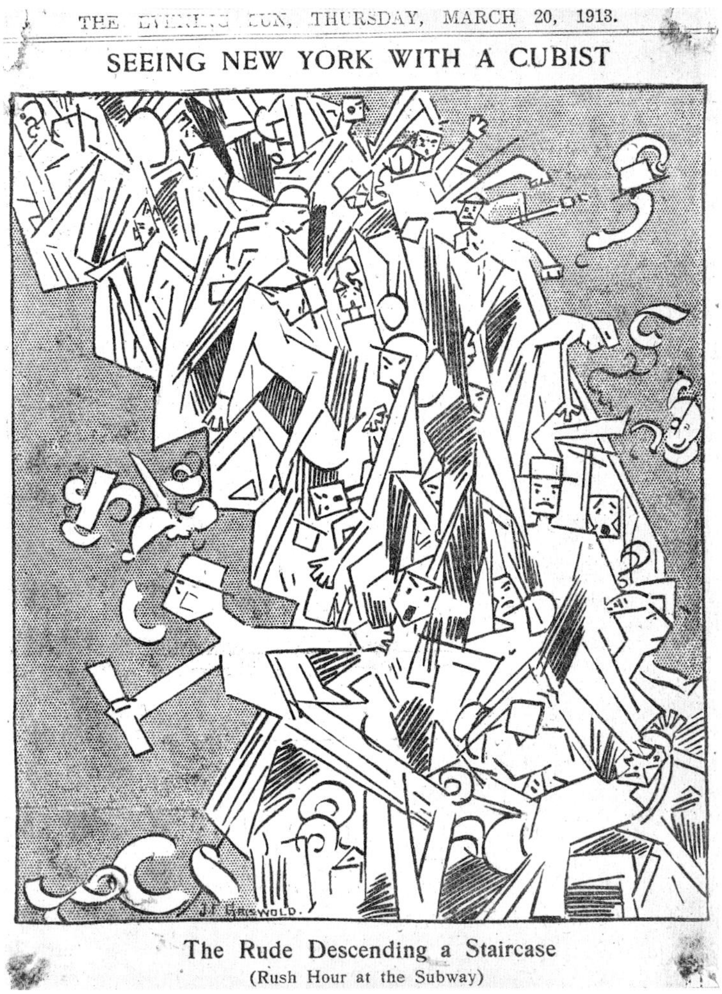

others.'[11] Although Duchamp 'does little more than play chess nowadays', Breton admired his 'marvellous intelligence', the play between indifference and personal choice ('signing a factory-made object'), his unfinished glass painting 'around which the most fabulous legends are being woven' and the puns signed Rrose Sélavy (the female alter-ego Duchamp invented in 1920), and clearly regarded him as a beacon in a bleak world.

Dalí, while the young leader of the Catalan avant-garde in the 1920s, was impatient with the stagnation of culture and art in Catalonia, and published the anti-art *Yellow Manifesto* in March 1928 with his friends the critics Sebastià Gasch and Lluis Montanyà. Denouncing 'all literature, all poetry and all philosophy' as well as sentimental old-fashioned art and architecture, the manifesto called for root and branch reform: 'THERE IS: the cinema, sport, popular music, automobile and aeronautic trade shows … "the phonograph, which is a little machine / the camera, which is another little machine" … A MULTITUDE anonymous – and antiartistic – collaborates, with its daily efforts, on the affirmation of the new age.'[12] Acknowledging diverse tendencies, including Futurism, Dada and L'Esprit nouveau, and announcing a 'Post-Machinist State of Mind', the manifesto ends with an eclectic list entitled 'Great artists of today', including Picasso, Ozenfant, Miró, Le Corbusier, Tzara, Éluard, Aragon, Stravinsky and Breton. With the *Yellow Manifesto* and many other writings, Dalí flung himself into debates about art, enthusiastically embraced the 'assassination of painting' famously announced by Miró,[13] and praised 'anti-artistic' as opposed to 'art' films, photography for its liberation from the hand, and the poetry of the 'standardised object': telephone, pedal-sink, refrigerator, bidet. His own painting reached a zenith of aggression and innovation with the extraordinary almost empty canvases of 1928, to which he attached extra-pictorial materials and found objects; he then seems temporarily to have abandoned the practice in favour of film and writing, before returning to it in a quite different mode in *The First Days of Spring* (cat. 59).

Duchamp abandoned work on *The Bride Stripped Bare by Her Bachelors, Even*, also known as *The Large Glass* (fig. 81), in 1923, leaving it 'definitively unfinished', and thereafter apparently devoted himself to chess, with the occasional foray into making something or devising an exhibition installation. The myth that he had virtually suspended his artistic activity continued until his death. But his friend William Copley was convinced that he perpetrated this myth 'as the most direct way to ensure himself the privacy he needed to continue working in the light of what was already becoming an exaggerated reputation'.[14]

Dalí and Duchamp are both mentioned in the final issue of *La Révolution surréaliste* (December 1929). Dalí's admission to the group is celebrated, details from his latest paintings are reproduced and

symbolic function', which, launched by Dalí in 1931, was to be made using strictly everyday things. Like the readymade, the Surrealist object could also invite touch, and move or promise to move, with the purpose of arousing desire and with a flamboyant subversion of the utilitarian. It thus reflects back on the readymades and 'assisted readymades', i.e. those in which Duchamp had intervened, such as *Why Not Sneeze Rose Sélavy?* (cat. 105), helping to reveal the extent to which they relate to the body and have sexual and erotic overtones.

Duchamp was unaware of Dada during his 'anti-art' activities in New York in 1917, although he and Man Ray later produced one issue of *New York Dada* (cat. 32), in a slightly bantering tone. He kept his distance from Dada in Paris but his influence, mysteriously widespread, was recognised in 1922 by André Breton, the future leader of Surrealism, who described in the Paris Dada review *Littérature* his unique position whereby 'the most recent groups more or less take his name as an authorisation, without our being able to say how much he ever sanctioned this, and from which we see him detach himself with complete freedom, even before a particular cluster of ideas – whose originality largely derives from him – has taken on that systematic cast that eliminates

Fig. 11
J. F. Griswold, 'Seeing New York with a Cubist: *The Rude Descending a Staircase* (Rush Hour at the Subway)', published in *The New York Evening Sun*, 20 March 1913.
The Museum of Modern Art Archives, New York. *Armory Show Scrapbook* (1913), compiled by Harriet S. Palmer. MA172/ MMA 20.504

he appears among the other members of the group in the photomontage *Je ne vois pas...* (cat. 148). Dalí's 'master impulse' towards Surrealist experiment through his paranoiac-critical method and his 'exceptional interior "boiling"' were later singled out for praise in Breton's text *What Is Surrealism?*[15] Duchamp is mentioned only once in *La Révolution surréaliste*, in a despairing tone, when Breton complains in his 'Second Manifesto' that Duchamp had abandoned his 'position' in favour of chess: 'Free Duchamp was not to give up the game he was playing in the vague vicinity of the war years, for an interminable game of *chess* which may give a strange idea of a mind loath to serve but also – always the execrable Harrar – seeming afflicted with a generous dose of scepticism insofar as it refuses to say why.'[16] Duchamp had of course ensured, by refusing to join the movement, that he was completely free to 'give up the game', but his insistence on the pre-eminence of individuality clashed with the Surrealist need for cohesion and belief in a collective. Breton was right about Duchamp's scepticism.

Duchamp had been impressed by reading the Classical sceptics while he was a librarian at the Bibliothèque Sainte-Geneviève in Paris before the First World War. He became familiar with the thought of the Greek philosopher Pyrrho of Elis as interpreted by Sextus Empiricus from the library's copy of the French translation *Les Hipotiposes; ou, Institutions Pirroniennes de Sextus Empiricus* (1725).[17] In 1945 Duchamp is reported to have said, 'There is no solution, because there is no problem',[18] an observation that seems to come straight out of Pyrrho.

Dalí, too, later embraced scepticism, and many of his later paintings and other activities draw the category of art into question, although often he employs the tools of painting to do so. And this is what Dalí means when in 1963 he writes that Duchamp 'categorically refuses to take part in the artistic brawl'.[19] Dalí's connection to scepticism came through his reading of the Renaissance philosopher Michel de Montaigne, whom he mentions twice in his book *50 Secrets of Magic Craftsmanship* and whose essays he illustrated in 1947. Montaigne devotes an extensive discussion to Pyrrho of Elis' ideas in the famous chapter in his *Essays* devoted to the Catalan theologian Raymond Sebond. Such sceptical modes of thought, centred on indifference, doubt and suspension of judgement, could be summarised, Montaigne states, in the following terms: 'If you can picture an endless confession of ignorance, or a power of judgement which never, never inclines to one side or the other, then you can conceive what Pyrrhonism is.'[20]

Dalí and Duchamp shared a sceptical position regarding not only art, but also politics, which exacerbated problems, particularly in Dalí's case, in their relationship with the Surrealist movement. Although they shared the Surrealists' resistance to propaganda art and to the Communist Party's insistence on proletarian literature,[21] neither was prepared to subscribe to the Surrealists' attempts to find an alternative collective social and political action.

Duchamp criticised the Surrealists because, as he put it, 'Without being downright on one side or the other, in terms of "ordinary" politics, [they] sought, on the contrary, to create by themselves a "new" political formula....'[22] Dalí, unlike Duchamp, did sign Surrealist manifestoes and participated fully in Surrealist games and experimental activities throughout the 1930s, but he was not prepared to sign up to the new group, 'Contre-attaque', that was formed by Breton and Bataille at the end of 1935 to confront the threat of fascism: 'I have great sympathy and admiration for the steps you are taking, which unfortunately I can only see as interesting from an experimental point of view. Quite honestly, I cannot take an active and militant part because I DO NOT BELIEVE IN IT.'[23] Dalí reiterated his lack of interest in politics in his autobiography *The Secret Life of Salvador Dalí*: 'Politics have never interested me,'[24] he said, conveniently forgetting, as Robert Radford has remarked, his earlier involvement in the Bloc Obrer I Camperol, the Workers' and Peasants' Bloc.[25] Herein, perhaps, lies an explanation, if not a justification, for his willingness to return to a Spain under the dictatorship of Franco after the war, and Duchamp's lack of concern at spending his summers at Cadaqués at a time when other artists, Picasso among them, would not set foot in the country on principle. The trauma of the Spanish Civil War – whose causes he vividly described in *The Secret Life* – exacerbated Dalí's resistance to politics. Moreover, Dalí had been desperate to return to his Catalan home, 'the only place in the world where I feel loved'.[26] Duchamp, indifferently peripatetic, and Dalí, prepared to compromise in order to return home, placed the individual first: 'Every one for himself, as in a shipwreck', as Duchamp put it.[27]

Exactly when the two first met is unknown. Both showed in Aragon's important March 1930 exhibition of collage, 'La Peinture au défi' ('A Challenge to Painting'; cat. 147), at the Galerie Goemans in Paris, although it is not clear if either was present at the opening. Duchamp was among the audience at the premiere of Luis Buñuel and Dalí's film *L'Âge d'or* in Paris on 28 November 1930, seated close to Dalí and Gala.[28] Duchamp and Gala, who became Dalí's companion in 1929, had known each other since Dada days in Paris, when she was married to Paul Éluard. In mid-August 1933 Duchamp and his companion Mary Reynolds rented a small house at Cadaqués near Dalí's house at Portlligat (fig. 12). If their choice for a summer vacation was not necessarily dependent on Dalí – Cadaqués had been a destination for artists before the war: Picasso and Fernande for example, spent the summer of 1910 there – they certainly saw him and Gala almost daily.[29] Photographs of their expeditions and parties on the beach (cats 18–21) confirm their convivial and frequent meetings, one of which was the occasion for Dalí's text

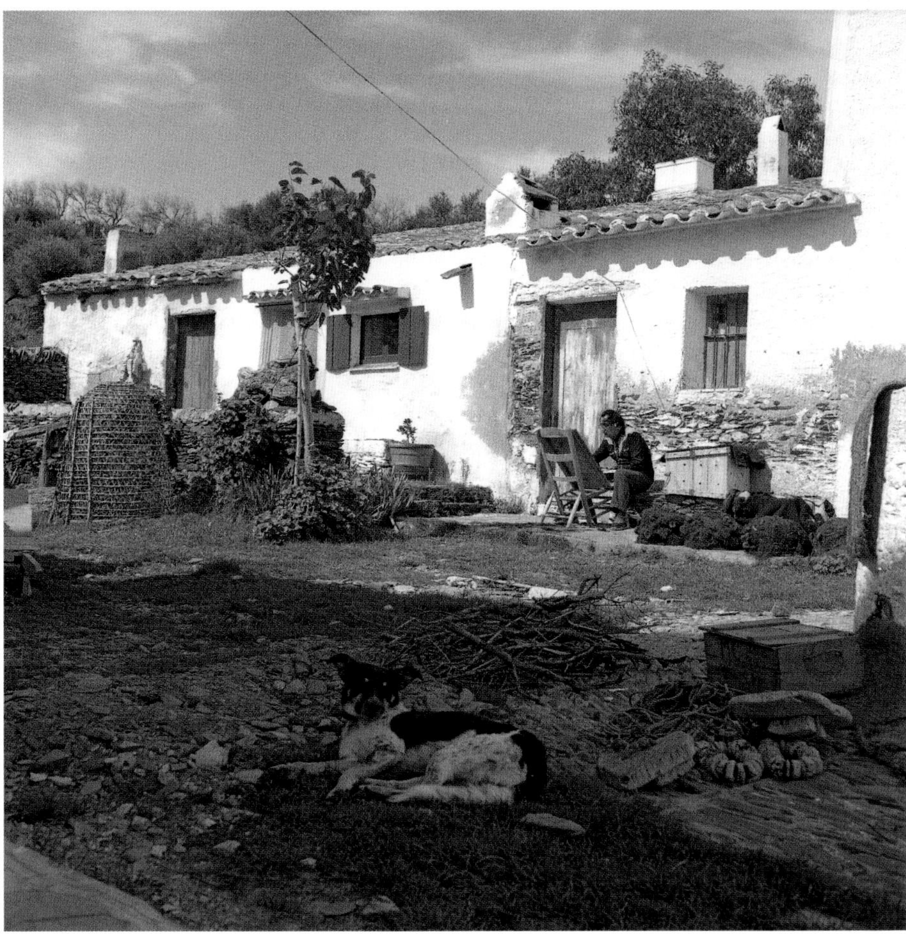

Both artists combined an anti-retinal attitude, not only, paradoxically, with a passion for optical devices and illusions, but also with an interest in technique. As Duchamp remarked, 'I introduced again some very elaborate decisions about details, even in the readymades. The fact that it was not made with my hands didn't stop me from finding other ways of applying my meticulous technique to them. You see, I suppose, in spite of myself I'm a meticulous man.'[31] From 1935 he was preoccupied with making a miniature portable museum of 'approximately all my works', the *Boîte-en-valise* (*Box in a Suitcase*; cat. 62), which involved intricate technical issues. In some ways Dalí, no less than Duchamp, was a 'cerebral inventor' preoccupied with 'technical problems'.[32] In 1948 he published *50 Secrets of Magic Craftsmanship*, for which he pillaged treatises on technique, and in 1973 his *10 Recipes for Immortality* (cat. 123). This was a sumptuously produced box, shaped like a suitcase, in homage to Duchamp's *Boîte*, containing meticulously made paper pop-up sheets demonstrating exercises in perspective in two and three dimensions. Perhaps the most emphatic evidence of Dalí's esteem for Duchamp ('...our own Marcel Duchamps, the great Marcel Duchamps who today greatly influences our epoch...') is his own Theatre-Museum at Figueres (pp. 206–07), which contains specific references to Duchamp, not only to the coal-sack ceiling Duchamp had devised for the 1938 International Surrealist Exhibition in Paris but also to his last work, *Étant donnés* (fig. 76). In its concept, moreover, the Theatre-Museum parallels Duchamp's portable museum, in that it gathers together and devises ('curates') the mode of display of his own works.[33]

'Je mange Gala' ('I eat Gala'; cat. 66). Barcelona was also on Duchamp's agenda for the trip, as he helped Dalí engage Man Ray to take the photographs destined to illustrate Dalí's article on art nouveau architecture planned for the forthcoming issue of *Minotaure*.

Duchamp often expressed his dissatisfaction with modern art, complaining that since Courbet, through the Impressionists, the Fauves and even the Cubists, painting had addressed itself only to the retina. 'Previously, it had had other functions: it could be religious, philosophical, moral. If I had the opportunity to take an anti-retinal attitude, it didn't change much; the whole century has been completely retinal, except for the Surrealists who tried to get away from it a bit.'[30] Dalí's paintings in their own way counter the purely retinal. In the 1930s he developed a personal iconography elaborated from such myths as William Tell, and in 1933 he wrote a 'psychoanalytical essay', 'Interprétation Paranoïaque-critique de l'image obsédante, *L'Angélus* de Millet', which forms the 'base text' for many of his paintings at the time, in the way that classical mythology or the Bible once did for art (these latter sources Dalí was to revive in his own way in his late works). There is thus an interesting parallel with the Notes Duchamp wrote in relation to his *Large Glass*, which should be consulted together (cat. 124).

The five essays in this book look at the mediums used by Dalí and Duchamp in their work. The three plate sections that follow explore themes that offer connecting threads between the two artists' works. The first, Identity, sets the scene and raises questions about their respective relationships with painting and modern art. The second, Eroticism, a major preoccupation for both artists, acts as the link between the Surrealist object and the readymades. Desire is configured through touch or sight, through the imagination and memory, in objects that include the promise of movement or an invitation to manipulation, drawings that speak to tactile or ocular pleasures, paintings of sexual anxieties and a group of works related to Duchamp's immobile, secretive masterpiece *Étant donnés*. The third brings together a range of works, including experiments in optics and kinetics, optical illusions and propositions inspired by the scientific discoveries of the twentieth century, which substituted the old certainties of space, physical mass and time for realities hidden from our immediate senses, such as the atom and the notion of the space/time continuum.

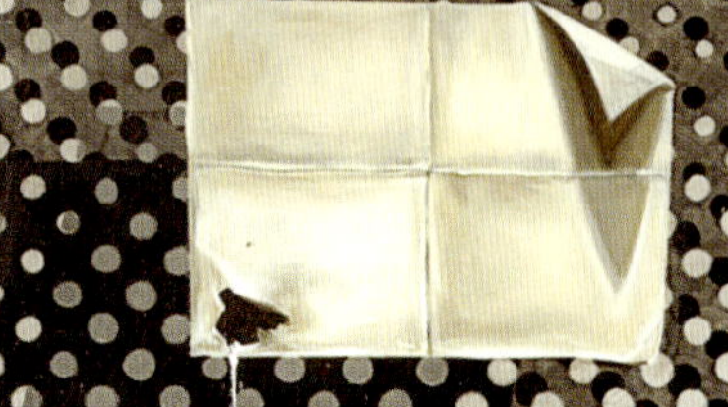

REPRESSION IN PAINTING
CÉCILE DEBRAY

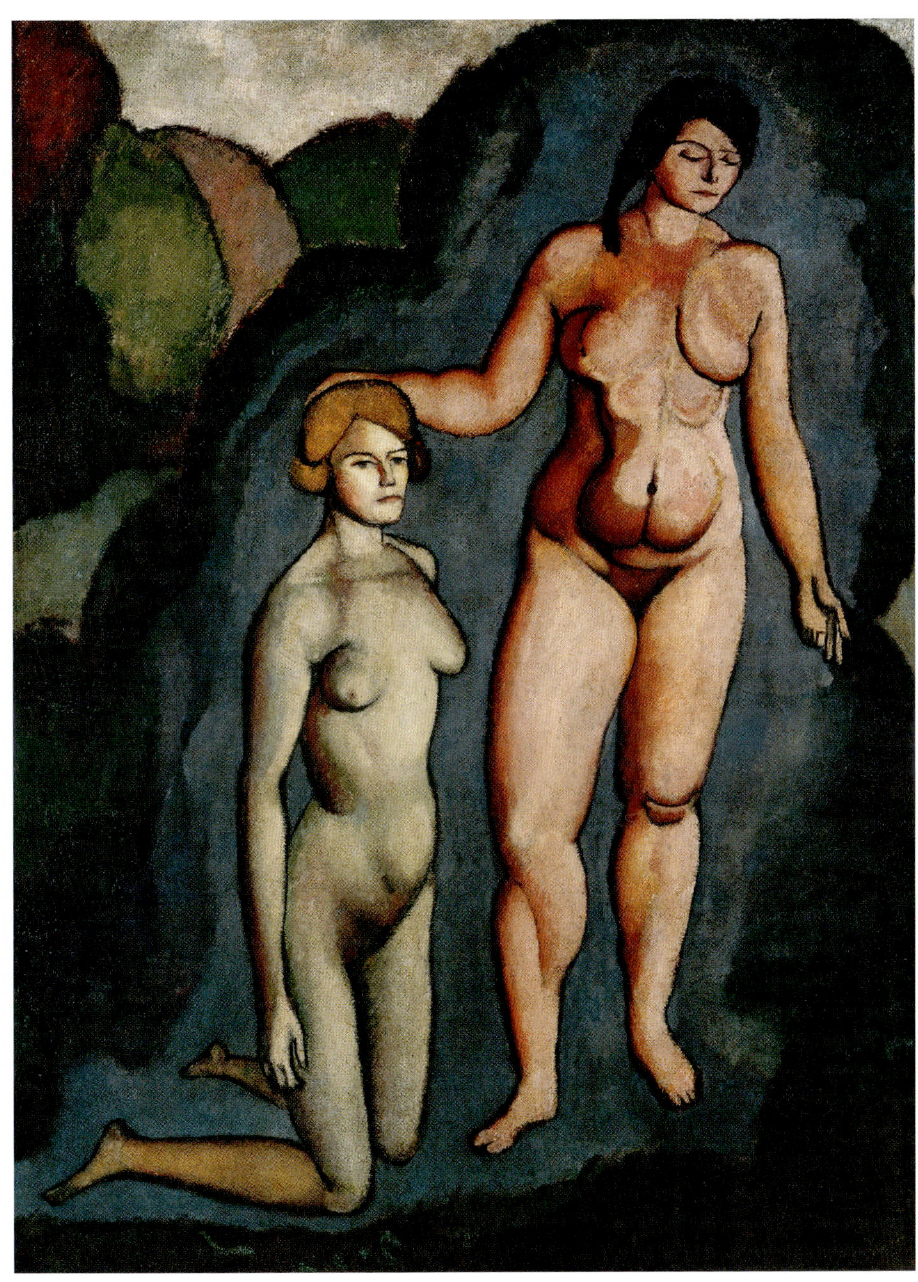

Fig. 13
Marcel Duchamp, *The Bush*, 1910–11.
Oil on canvas, 127.3 x 91.9 cm.
Philadelphia Museum of Art.
The Louise and Walter Arensberg
Collection, 1950-134-51

Opposite: detail of cat. 140

At the heart of the attribute that might identify Duchamp or Dalí either as an artist or as an 'anartist' lies the question of painting. Having consciously rejected painting in 1923, Duchamp described himself thereafter as an 'anartist'; he named Dalí as the only true painter of the twentieth century.

Both began as painters, but both later attempted to change the pictorial landscape in very different, indeed conflicting, ways. Duchamp began his subtle dematerialisation of painting with the complex, hermetic invention, *The Bride Stripped Bare by Her Bachelors, Even* (*The Large Glass*; fig. 81);[1] Dalí, on the other hand, used his paranoiac-critical method to create a style of modern painting, popular and universal, that aimed to harness impulses and contemporary myths in the way the cinema had done. As well as *The Large Glass*, Duchamp created another enigmatic piece, concealed throughout the artist's lifetime, *Étant donnés* (fig. 76). Dalí produced a large body of work.

When the two artists met in 1930, Duchamp had long since abandoned painting and had become a tutelary figure for the Surrealists. Dalí had arrived in Paris in 1929 and had been welcomed into André Breton's circle; he was experiencing his first success with works that were later to become – noisily and durably – the major manifestations of Surrealist painting. Duchamp was an unassuming but powerful thinker, Dalí a prolific and publicity-hungry painter. Despite these contrasts, a certain attraction and complicity immediately drew them to one another, and Duchamp, the elder of the two, took great trouble to intercede with Breton on several occasions on behalf of the young Catalan when Dalí's political stance became less than ambivalent. Symptomatically, Dalí's first break from the Surrealists was caused by a painting: this was his submission to the Salon des Indépendants in 1934 of *The Enigma of William Tell* (fig. 79), a very large canvas depicting William Tell, a castrating father-figure in Dalí's iconography, wearing the features of Lenin. Lenin is portrayed as the patriarchal and authoritarian emblem of Communism. To have exhibited such a painting at the exact moment when the far-right leagues were demonstrating in Paris (6 February 1934) aroused Breton's fury; he saw it as a counter-revolutionary stance that betrayed a readiness to accept Hitlerian Fascism. Many years later, Duchamp acted as intermediary with Pontus Hultén, director of the

Moderna Museet, Stockholm, when the museum acquired the painting. He stated at that time: 'Personally I find this picture one of the most important of the good period.'[2] These words of praise are unequivocal. Duchamp regarded it as an historic painting, a work that marked the Surrealists' 'Dalí trial'; it revealed Dalí's insubordination and his refusal to conform to the movement's political engagement. In 1936 Duchamp, that most Dada of all artists, the creator of *L.H.O.O.Q.*, reconnecting with his earlier vision of non-anecdotal painting, advocated the total freedom of the artist and emphasised the threat to art posed by Fascist or Communist ideology: 'Painting is now dedicated the world over to propaganda – to subject-matter [...] It is as true in Europe as in America – even more so – that people's minds are concentrated on politics, including the artists'. Both Fascism and Communism are bent on regimenting people, robbing them of their individuality. It is no atmosphere in which creative art can thrive. The zest, the joy, is gone.'[3]

While Duchamp re-affirmed his philosophy of indifference, Dalí for his part was fascinated by the irrational – if not outrageous and sado-masochistic – character of the 1930s and by the rise of totalitarianism, transposing it into a series of canvases on William Tell, Lenin, Hitler and war, among other subjects.[4] His pictorial output was supported by a series of texts: 'Le Grand Masturbateur',[5] 'I defy Aragon',[6] 'Vive la guerre! Le surréalisme et Hitler'.[7] According to his first notions of Surrealism, heavily influenced by psychoanalysis (Freud then Lacan), Dalí's paintings are intended as an 'incursion into the perilous, forbidden realms of the subconscious', the 'human brain [having] the ability to adopt at will any given kind of madness, in other words, a normal man in a certain frame of mind can think in exactly the same way as a mental patient, a paraplegic, a paranoiac, someone with delusions of grandeur etc. Objectivisation, the act of according reality to this unreal world of the mind, constitutes the surreal world.'[8]

In addition to the subversive element of a painting, it is exactly this 'objectivisation' of the surreal, the non-anecdotal, the dream-like, of *The Enigma of William Tell*, and of Dalí's painting in general, that might have appealed to Duchamp – the smooth neutrality of Dalí's style having no subjective content and nothing expressively pictorial.

In 1965, returning to his own experience as a painter, Duchamp resorted to a French idiom: 'In French, there is an old expression, *la patte*, meaning the artist's touch, his personal style, his "paw". I wanted to get away from *la patte* and from all that retinal painting. The painting around me was completely retinal. Forget about anecdote, forget about emotion in the subject – that was the idea.'[9]

He thereby stigmatises any notions surrounding the plastic, aesthetic or 'retinal' qualities of painting: 'since the advent of Impressionism, visual production stops short at the retina. Impressionism, Fauvism, Cubism, Abstraction are all retinal types of painting. Physical preoccupations – reaction of colours etc. banish reactions of the grey matter to the background.'[10] 'Reactions of the grey matter', a photographic metaphor, would include the phenomena of extra-retinal radiations, 'electric light circles', the question of 'fluids', the X-rays of early scientific and psychic photography that had made such an impression on him in 1910, somewhat surprisingly echoing Man Ray's comments on Dalí: 'He maintained that his painting was a kind of colour photography. He would anyway have preferred to photograph his ideas and considered his work as a form of anti-painting.'[11] Dalí was trying to produce 'the surreal' in order to entrap it, using some very accomplished sleight of hand. Duchamp, on the other hand, was from the outset inventing 'meta-realism' in his paintings, the combination of a mixture of influences from Matisse and Symbolism: '*The Bush* [fig. 13] was painted at a time when I was searching for an evasion from naturalistic painting as expressed by the Impressionists and the Fauves. In that painting, without a definite "plot", I was looking for some *raison d'être* in a painting other than the visual experience – the *Bush* and the two nudes in relation to one another seemed at that time to satisfy the desire I had to introduce some anecdote without being "anecdotal" … in other words I did not, in that painting, illustrate a definite theme, but the disposition of the three elements evoked for me the possibility to invent a theme for it, afterwards.'[12] In addition, Duchamp was insistent on the importance of the title in his search for a modern, open, allegorical form: 'This painting marks a change of direction, towards another type of Fauvism, one not based solely on distortion. The drawing of the figures is stylised and the colours are at once contrasted and merged. The presence of a non-descriptive title appears here for the first time. In fact, henceforward I would always give the title an important role, considering it to be an invisible colour.'[13] This alliance between image and text (the title), whose source can be found in the work of Symbolist poets and writers such as Laforgue, Mallarmé, Roussel, initially gave birth to Duchamp's dreamlike poetic pieces, such as *Young Girl and Man in Spring* (fig. 14) or the rectified readymade *Pharmacy* (cat. 57),[14] and then, very shortly afterwards, the meta-text (the Notes – the *Green Box* and the *White Box*) accompanies a wide-ranging reflection on motion, optics, perspective, language, chemistry and mathematics transported into an erotic setting – a bride stripped bare by her bachelors – by means of the diagrammatic, abstract composition of *The Large Glass*.

In addition to the erotic vision shared by the two artists – Duchamp was to say at the end of his life: 'Eroticism was a theme, even an "ism" of everything I was doing at the time of *The Large Glass*. It kept me from being obligated to return to already existing

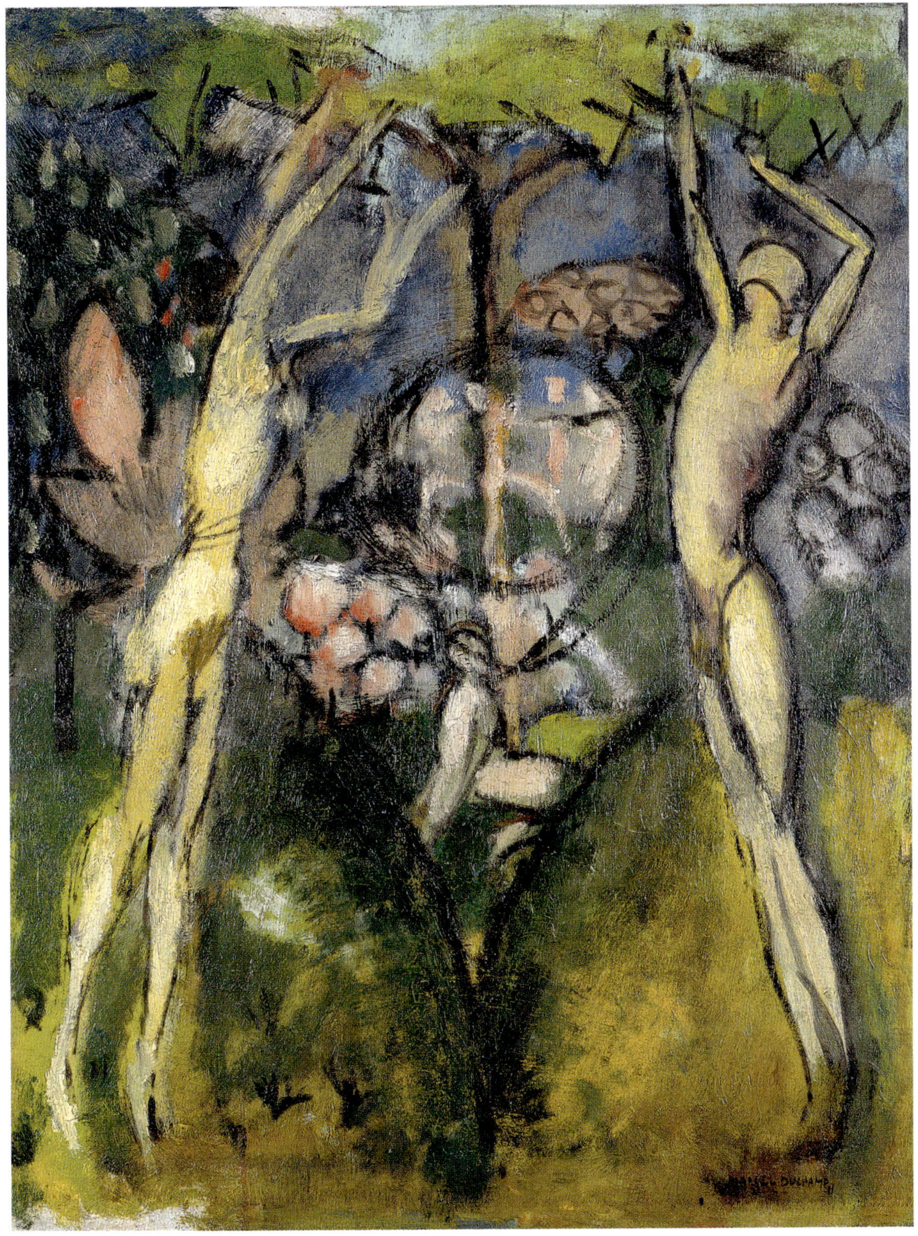

Like his older colleague, Dalí was interested in scientific progress. He was an avid reader of popular-science publications and was aware of the development of the image, scientific or otherwise, by such technological inventions as the electron microscope, scanners and the hologram. Unlike the young Duchamp, when faced with the work of Albert Londe, the pioneer of early medical photography, Dalí did not interpret this as rendering painting obsolete but viewed it instead as the reassertion of realism in painting, of the significant power of reality and its representation via the opportunity to depict and reveal the world's psychic dimension.

In *The Large Glass*, Duchamp reaches the outer limits of representation and painting. 'The glass, being translucent, could provide maximum efficacy to the rigidity of the perspective; it also removed any trace of *patte*, personal style, or of materials. I wanted to change, to try a new approach.'[17] He recalls the original intention behind his *Large Glass* project: 'I wanted to distance myself from the physical act of painting. I was definitely more interested in re-creating ideas in painting. [...] I wanted to relocate painting in the service of the mind.'[18] If the gradual phasing out to be observed in this work leads to the disappearance of painting and of the artist from 1923, it does not actually signal a total break with art on Duchamp's part. The artist always denounced – particularly in his scatological and Dada acts, such as *L.H.O.O.Q.* (cat. 28) or *Fountain* (cat. 102) – the tyranny of good taste and aestheticism. One might wonder also whether, to judge by the malicious pleasure he takes in praising eccentric, unfashionable artists such as the American Louis Michel Eilshemius, he is not defending the colour values of Dalí's paintings as a deliberately provocative example of 'bad taste'. Dalí, going against the prevailing modernism, lavishes praise on the conventional and detailed *pompier* painting of Ernest Meissonier (fig. 15): '[to acquire] the supreme audacity today to fear neither Meissonier nor making a lively, *pompier* painting'.[19] In Duchamp's case, this professional precision and attention to detail is associated with the disappearance of expressiveness from his work – borrowed as much from engineering or mechanical drawing as from the oil paintings of Cranach the Elder. Later in life, Duchamp attributed his reaction against 'retinal' painting to the discovery of the mythological paintings of Arnold Böcklin (fig. 16) during the summer of 1912 when he was in thrall to Cubism. He was overwhelmed by the eroticism and the comic and unique grandiloquence of the Swiss painter's work: 'In Böcklin I discovered a reaction against realism, against what I term "retinal" painting – I was already planning to react against it. Impressionism, Pointillism, Fauvism all augmented this reaction. [...] Böcklin was the person who made this possible. I looked at it but I did not copy it. Not that I was totally convinced by Böcklin. But there was something there. He is one of the sources of Surrealism. Absolutely.'[20]

Fig. 14
Marcel Duchamp, *Young Girl and Man in Spring*, 1911. Oil on canvas, 65.7 x 50.2 cm. The Vera and Arturo Schwarz Collection of Dada and Surrealist Art, Israel Museum, Jerusalem, B03.0071

theories, aesthetic or otherwise'[15] – the esoteric, scientific nature of the large piece, gestated over about ten years and now the object of innumerable analyses, was bound to fascinate Dalí, who sought out and revealed all sorts of hidden meanings and images, in reality as in his painting. It seems reasonable to suppose that the re-evaluation he proposed in his preface to the catalogue of the exhibition, held at the Centre Georges Pompidou in 1979, of his youthful work *Basket of Bread* (1926; cat. 51) betrays this fascination: 'the most esoteric and the most surrealist of all the paintings I have produced so far. [...] In my paintings, where things intertwine, according to my most recent paranoiac-critical research, it turns out that the structures of the basket, seen through the electronic microscope, correspond exactly to the structures of mercury.'[16]

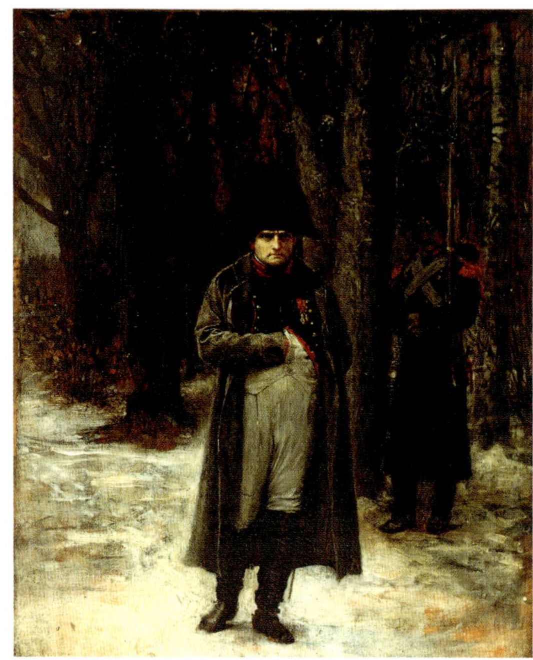

In the crude excesses and the eroticism of Böcklin's subjects Duchamp undoubtedly found a kind of representational obscenity that attracted him, and at a later date Dalí had no difficulty in accepting it either. Dalí commandeered Millet's famous painting *The Angelus* (fig. 17), featured on innumerable chocolate boxes, to explore his own oedipal fantasies regarding the sexuality of the parents, and the dead child/brother, like some residual, buried image of childhood: 'I remember that *The Angelus* moved me very particularly when I was a child. After my intellectual and artistic education, the painting became embroiled in utterly discredited and

ineffectual hierarchies of spiritual activity and was forgotten; the same happened to the examples of wonderful Modern Style architecture that I am also attempting to rehabilitate after a long and shameful suppression.'[21]

At the International Exhibition of Surrealism held in New York in 1960–61, organised jointly by André Breton, José Pierre, Edouard Jaguer and Duchamp (who was present), the latter – against the advice of the others – invited Dalí to exhibit his large painting *Madonna* (cat. 140). In the eyes of the veteran Surrealists, this repossession of Raphael's *Sistine Madonna*, rehoused in an enormous ear, inspired by photographs of the recently elected Pope John XXIII published in *Paris Match*,[22] and described by Jaguer as a 'monumental crust of consecrated bread',[23] embodied the acme of the academic, reactionary style of the artist whom Breton, in 1939, had expelled on grounds of his 'sympathies for Roman Catholicism and the Fascism of Madrid'.[24] Was Duchamp, through Dalí's painting, reliving his submission of *Fountain* in 1917 to the first Independents Exhibition in New York, of which he was a founder member? Was he undermining the opinion of a group of enlightened amateurs by testing their open-mindedness when faced with a porcelain urinal, reified into a work of art? Another parallel can be found in the cynicism and political nihilism of the film *L'Âge d'or* (1930), in which Buñuel and Dalí mocked the humanitarian ideas of the liberal thinkers of the League of Nations.

Dalí's *Madonna* consists of a canvas with a pointillist or pixelated surface, a reference to Seurat shared by Dalí and Duchamp, who were both attracted by optical tricks. At this time, Dalí devoted an article to Duchamp, identifying his youthful *The King and Queen Surrounded by Swift Nudes* (cat. 46) as a piece that

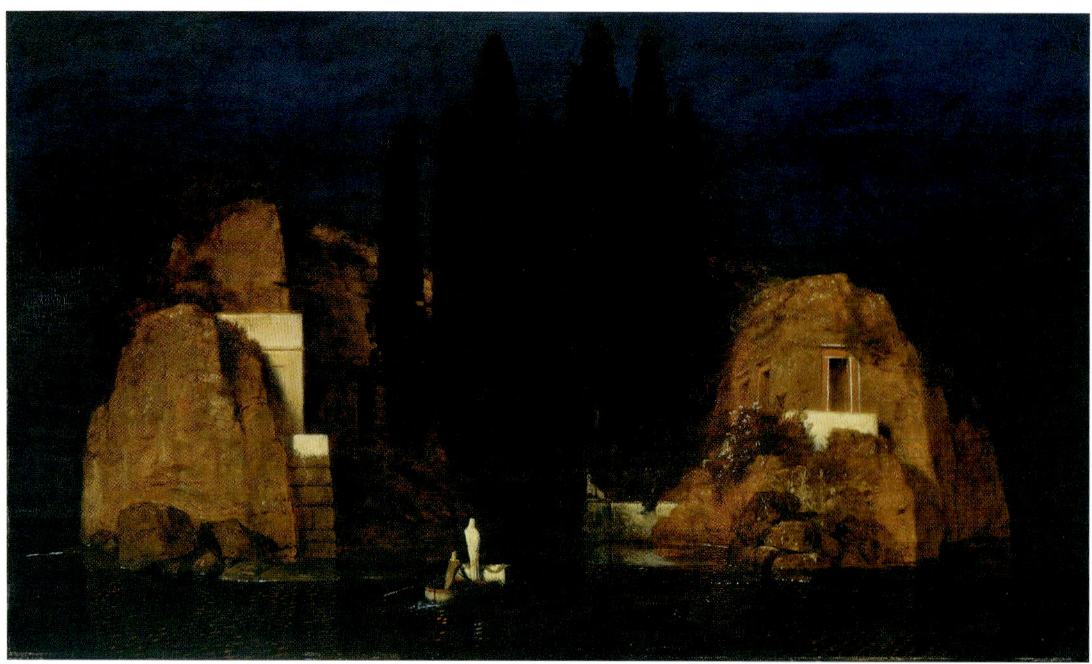

Fig. 15
Ernest Meissonier, *Portrait of Napoleon*, 1863. Oil on wood panel, 14 x 11.2 cm. Fundació Gala-Salvador Dalí, Figueres

Fig. 16
Arnold Böcklin, *Island of the Dead*, 1880. Oil on wood, 73.7 x 121.9 cm. Metropolitan Museum of Art, New York. Reisinger Fund, 1926. Inv. 26.90

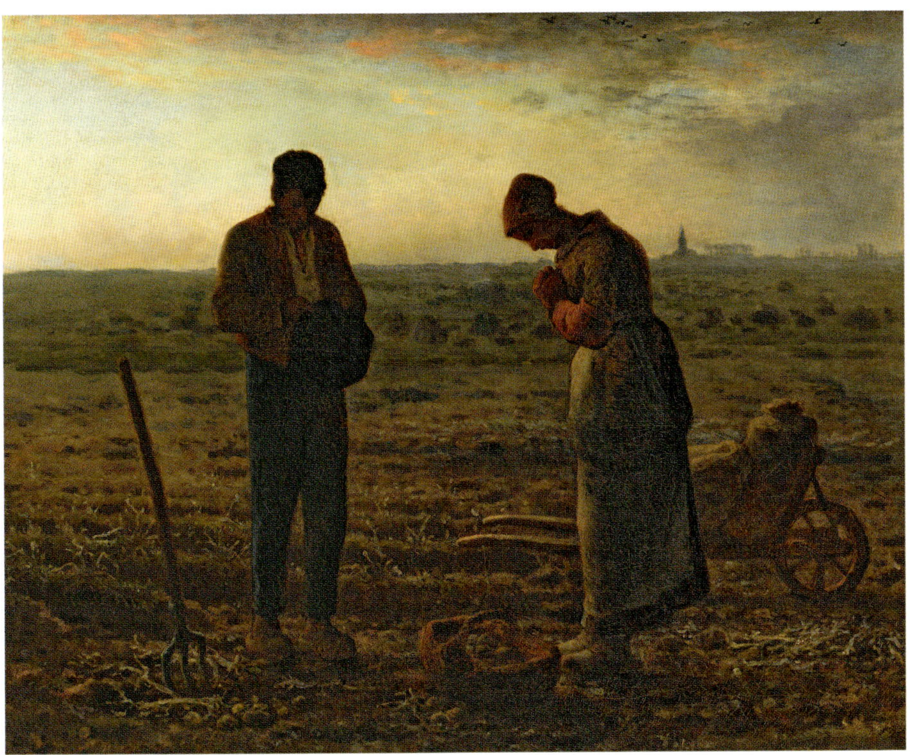

presaged his own work. He saw it as anticipating quantum physics, describing Duchamp as an 'aristocratic anarchist' who had escaped from the 'imminent collective failure of modern painting'.[25] Duchamp's own comments on this painting, however, direct us instead towards a reflection on the process of conceptualisation that is closer to certain poetic and abstract forms than to Dalí's realism: 'There is a little more in chess than in mathematics as far as beauty is concerned, if you want to call it – Beauty in chess is more plastic (takes physical shape) than in mathematics. In mathematics "square is possibility of square". In chess when you speak of a beautiful achievement in a problem it comes out of abstract thinking and ends in a physical shaping of a king doing this or a queen doing that. As if it were giving life to an abstract thing. Queen or King become animals that behave according to abstract thinking but you see a queen doing this – you feel a queen do this – you touch her... while mathematical beauty is always in the abstract. Architectural beauty is not mathematical beauty.'[26]

Evidence of the profound reciprocal influence between the two artists was in fact revealed by the discovery, after Duchamp's death in 1968, of his last work, *Étant donnés*. Created in great secrecy over twenty years, between 1946 and 1966, it muddies the image of Duchamp the iconoclast once and for all. The late works, such as his series of erotic casts or engravings after the Old Masters (cats 68–69, 71, 79–81, 87), produced partly in Cadaqués, where Duchamp regularly stayed near Dalí and Gala, belong to the slow emergence of *Étant donnés*. Having from the 1950s based his art on the principle of double images, anamorphosis, Dalí deflected his realism towards stereoscopic and holographic procedures, increasingly seeking illusion through the suggestion of a third dimension. At the same moment, Duchamp resumed his investigation into the third and fourth dimensions in his first anaglyptic and stereoscopic works, but his approach was the exact opposite: he was seeking illusionistic embodiment rather than schematic dematerialisation. It is difficult not to spot subtle hints of his exchanges with Dalí – in the voyeuristic and stereoscopic device of the grotto of greenery in which a female form lies with legs spread; it contains a number of obsessional elements from Duchamp's own iconography (the waterfall, the Bec Auer gas lamp, the hairless genitalia). Dalí's universe, with its recurrent themes – the rotting donkey, the ants, the fried eggs, the figure of the castrating father, Gala, the rocks of Portlligat, himself as Christ – plus his extroverted enjoyment of the image (whence his late celebration of Catholicism with its aesthetic of incarnation), and in view of the identification of obscenity and beauty – all seem to have conspired together to free Duchamp from repression.

Fig. 17
Jean-François Millet, *The Angelus*, 1857–59. Oil on canvas, 56 x 66 cm. Musée d'Orsay, Paris

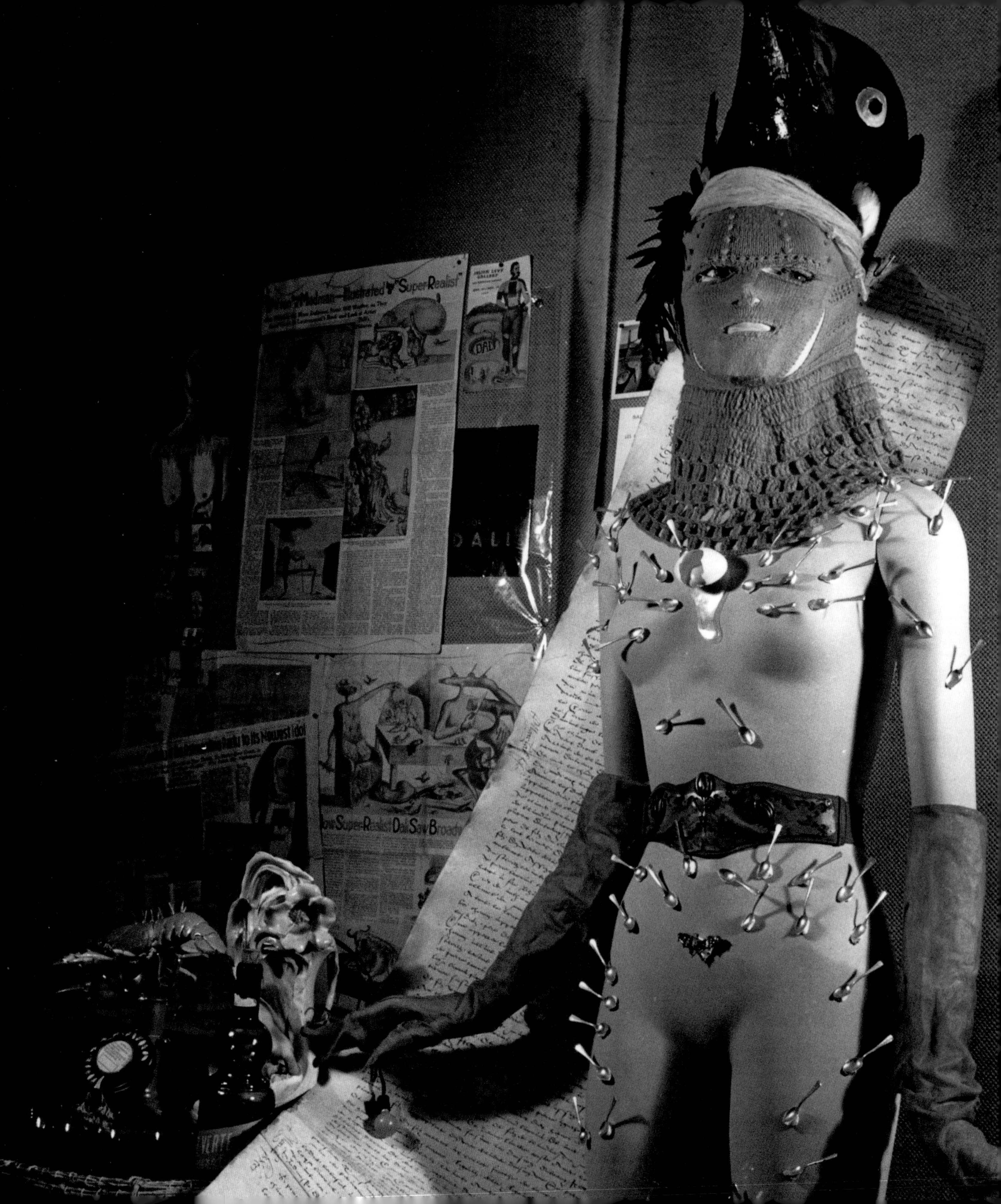

READYMADES, SCULPTURES, OBJECTS: 'A HAPPY BLASPHEMY'

WILLIAM JEFFETT

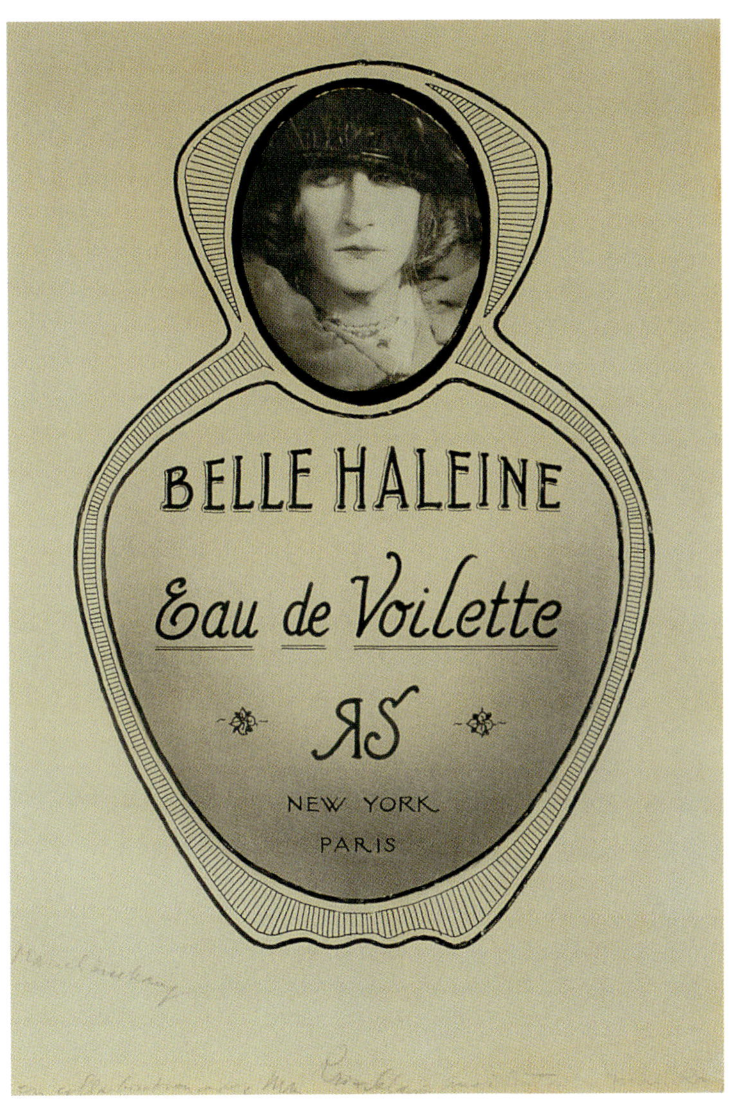

Opposite: Fig. 18
Salvador Dalí, *Mannequin*,
'International Exhibition of
Surrealism', Galerie Beaux-Arts, Paris,
1938. Photograph by Denise Bellon.
Fonds Photographique
Denise Bellon, Paris

Above: Fig. 19
Marcel Duchamp in collaboration with
Man Ray, *Belle Haleine: Eau de Voilette*
(*Beautiful Breath: Veil Water*), 1920/21
(inscribed in 1964). Imitated rectified
readymade, collage, 29.6 x 20 cm.
Private collection

It may seem perverse to open a catalogue on the works of two artists who flouted the traditional categories of painting and sculpture with essays on 'mediums'. However, it is precisely in the ways that these traditional mediums and their associated terminologies were challenged and superseded that some of the most exciting and far-reaching experiments in twentieth-century art can be understood. If the 'challenge to painting' was to an extent made and received within that tradition, the challenge posed by the three-dimensional experiments represented by the readymades and the Surrealist object moved beyond the parameters of sculpture altogether and into a world of construction, materials and spaces hitherto foreign to it.

It is true that collage had disturbed the distinction between the two- and the three-dimensional and, with its introduction of extra-pictorial and readymade elements into two-dimensional works, had shattered the unity and identity of painting, as Aragon argued in his essay for the 1930 exhibition of collages, 'La Peinture au défi' ('A Challenge to Painting'), at the Goemans Gallery in Paris. This was the first exhibition in which Duchamp and Dalí coincided: Duchamp was represented with two versions of *L.H.O.O.Q.* (1930, Centre Georges Pompidou, and cat. 28), *Pharmacy* (cat. 57), *Eau de Voilette* (fig. 19) and *Monte Carlo Bond* (cat. 38), and Dalí with *The First Days of Spring* (cat. 59). Dalí's use of collage, Aragon says, defies interpretation: the bits of pasted print look painted while the painted parts resemble collage. Dalí employs his extraordinary facility to mock 'the despair of the painter in the face of the inimitable'. The 'incoherence' of *The First Days of Spring* is characteristic of collage, Aragon writes, implying that its truncated narrative inheres in the jumble of mediums – paint, stencil, photograph, print – before concluding: 'Dalí is associated with the anti-pictorial spirit which ... today invades painting.'[1] The difficulty of accounting for the collages in conventional terms is a positive quality for Aragon, as a Surrealist.

Regarding Duchamp's five works in the Goemans Gallery show, Aragon opposes the apparent negation of Duchamp's and Picabia's Dada activities with the positive notion of the 'personality of choice', an idea first picked up by Breton from the 'Richard Mutt Case' of 1917 (cat. 101). Aragon doesn't distinguish between the two-dimensional readymade *Pharmacy* and the urinal (which he mistakenly describes as signed by

Arthur Cravan). So the question arises, are there distinctions to be made between the two-dimensional and the three-dimensional readymades, and if so, what are they? In Duchamp's many later comments on his choices for his readymades in interviews, there are constants and variations. As discussed in the Introduction, the first readymades were experiments, created in the privacy of the studio. Duchamp described *Bicycle Wheel* (cat. 77), an ironic 'Futurist' sculpture, as a gadget. Still more of a construction, or what he later called an 'assisted readymade' – the detached wheel mounted on a stool resembling a sculptor's support – *Bicycle Wheel* introduced movement, which was to be important for the concept of the Surrealist object. When Duchamp spun it in his studio, he said, it gave him pleasure, like watching a fire in a fireplace.[2] The first pure readymade, *Bottle Rack* (1914; cats 58, 106), was a then-familiar domestic object, mass-produced, selected and purchased by Duchamp, and unaltered except for the addition of an inscription. A point he reiterates is that the basic condition for choosing a readymade was that he should remain aesthetically indifferent to the object. It was a way, he said, of getting rid of taste, as well as of dispensing with the '*patte*', the painter's hand. *Pharmacy*, of course, is a two-dimensional readymade, a kitsch calendar image chosen by Duchamp – who added the red and green dots that introduce an optical dimension – and as such it is 'mass-produced art'. Most of his other readymades were mass-produced utilitarian objects and are thus much more ambiguous in terms of status. And as the possibilities were endless, a new question arose, prompting a note: 'Limit the no. of readymades yearly (?)'[3] Is there any way, Duchamp was once asked, that a readymade can be considered a work of art? He replied:

> That is the very difficult point, because art first has to be defined. All right, can we try to define art? We have tried, everyone has tried, and every century there is a new definition of art. I mean that there is no one essential that is good for all centuries. So if we accept the idea that trying not to define art is a legitimate conception, then the readymade can be seen as a sort of irony, or an attempt at showing the futility of trying to define art, because there it is, a thing that I call art. I didn't even make it myself, as we know art means to make, hand make, to make by hand. It's a hand-made product of man, and there instead of making, I take it ready-made, even though it was made in a factory. But it is not made by hand, so it is a form of denying the possibility of defining art.[4]

Liberated from the fixed ideas of what makes a work a work of art, and from standard ideas of the appropriate medium, Duchamp, between working on *The Large

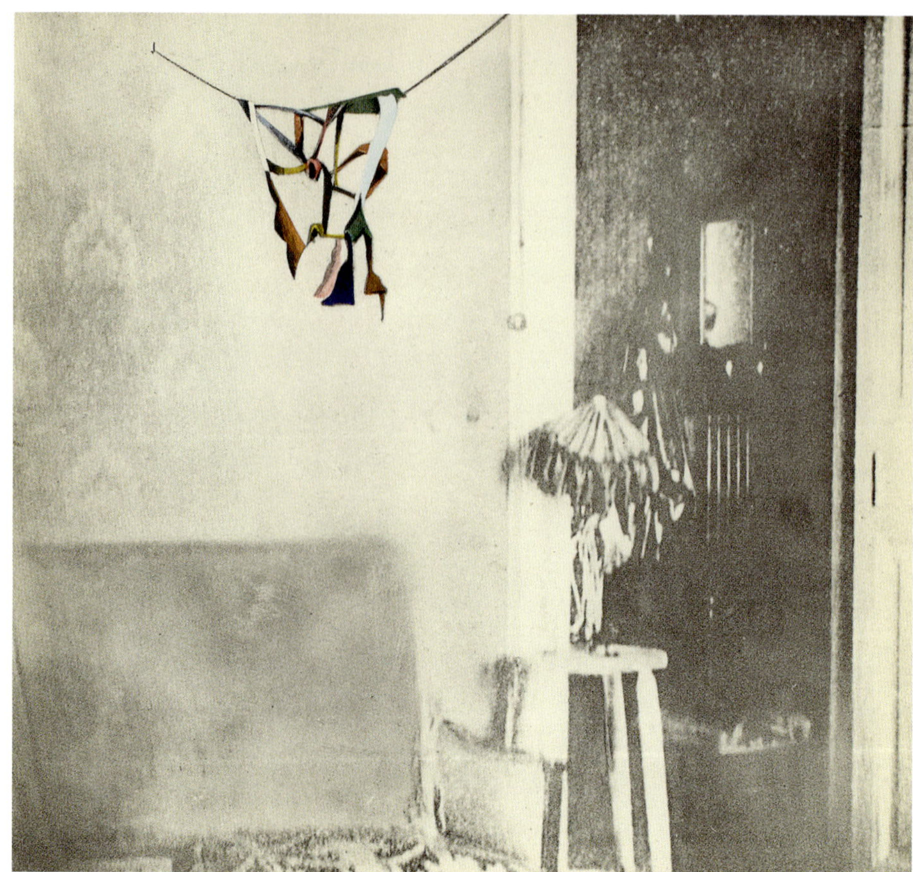

Glass and occasionally choosing a readymade, experimented with materials. In 1918, on the eve of leaving New York for Buenos Aires (the United States having finally entered the First World War), he made a sculpture from multi-coloured rubber bathing caps. 'I cut them into little irregular strips, stuck them together, not flat, in the middle of my studio (in the air) and attached them with string to the various walls and nails in my studio. It looks like a kind of multi-coloured spider's web.'[5] This was, literally, sculpture in an expanded sense. He took the work with him to Argentina and when he came to assemble the ingredients for his portable museum, the *Boîte-en-valise* (cat. 62), he drew in and coloured the suspended rubber web on a photograph of his room in Buenos Aires and named it *Travelling Sculpture* (fig. 20). Escaping not just conventional materials but also the placing of objects in space, photographs of his New York studio in *c*. 1918 show 'Ready mades' including *Fountain* (cat. 102) suspended from the ceiling (figs 22, 23).

Nonetheless, each readymade, concentrated and minimal as it is, has a specific character. *Bottle Rack*, though nominally a mere utilitarian apparatus, can be read, when the wine bottles are absent, as a fetishistic object presenting spike-like, phallic forms, even recalling African Nkisi sculptures.[6] Similarly, the infamous *Fountain* is more than a transgression of the category of the craft aspect of an artwork: in its

Fig. 20
Marcel Duchamp, photograph of *Travelling Sculpture* (1918; original lost; rubber bathing caps, dimensions variable); reproduction coloured 1940 for the *Boîte-en-valise* (cat. 62), 16.6 x 17.3 cm. Collection Hummel, Vienna

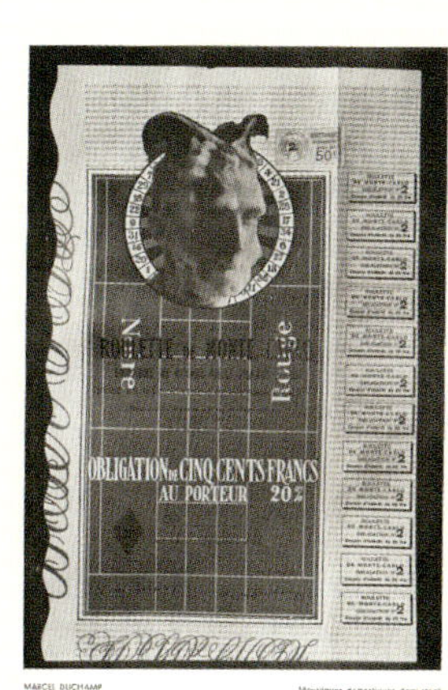

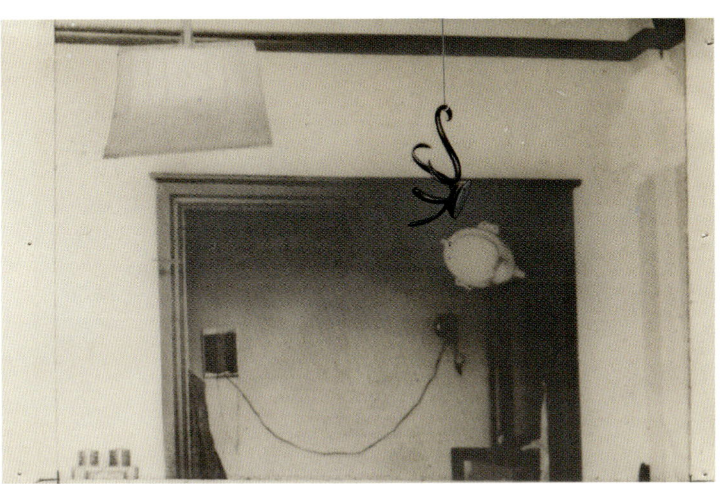

Fig. 21
Salvador Dalí, 'Derniers modes
d'éxcitation intellectuelle pour l'été'
('Latest Intellectual Excitement for the
Summer'), published in *Documents 34:
Intervention Surréaliste*, new series,
no. 1, June 1934, pp. 32–33.
Private collection

Fig. 22
Marcel Duchamp, photograph of
Duchamp's studio at 33 West 67th Street,
New York (taken *c*. 1917–18), showing
Ready-made (Hat Rack) (1917); retouched
enlargement produced in 1940 for the
Boîte-en-valise (cat. 62). Gelatin silver
print, 18.2 x 12.5 cm.
Marcel Duchamp Archive

Fig. 23
Marcel Duchamp's studio at 33 West 67th
Street, New York, 1917–18. Photograph
attributed to Henri-Pierre Roché.
Gelatin silver print, 6.2 x 3.8 cm.
Philadelphia Museum of Art. Gift of
Jacqueline, Paul, and Peter Matisse
in memory of their mother, Alexina
Duchamp, 1998

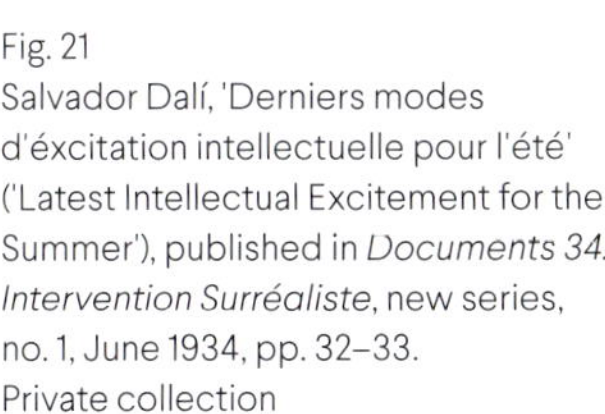

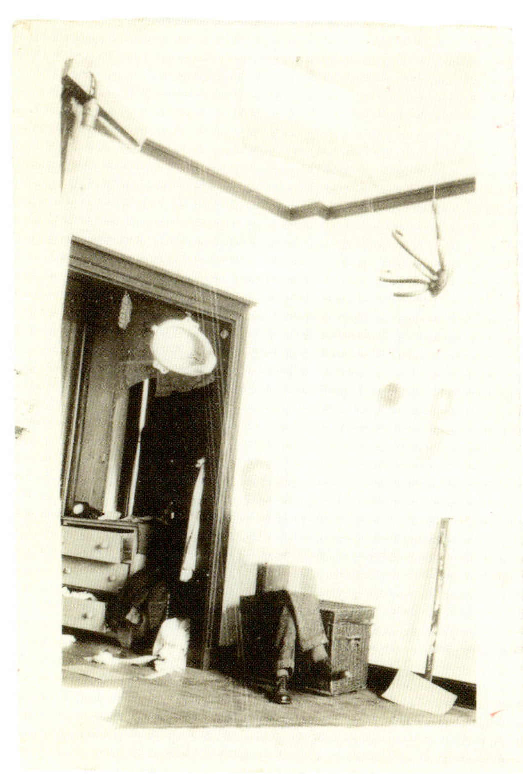

inversion on a base it takes on the qualities of sculpture and, because of its position and title, conceptually implies the idea of water or piss irrigating the viewer, figuratively and literally. So Duchamp did more than piss on the category of art – he challenged the viewer's safe distance from the work with the immediacy of bodily fluids. Moreover, *Fountain* points not only to masculine anatomy: it can equally be read as a representation of the female genitals, as in a 1914 note: 'One has only, for *female* the urinal and one *lives* by it.'[7]

In the 1930s the Surrealists proposed the problem of the object as a primary concern. The world could only be understood to the extent that one could perceive it, and this could only be done inside it, from the limited point of view of the human body inhabiting a real space. Our experience of space was optical but, more importantly, tactile and immediate. Philosophers of the neo-Hegelian persuasion spoke of a concrete existence in the real world, just as did Surrealist writers. The philosopher Jean Wahl wrote: 'Concrete existence is always existence before a work or in an action or before a being, an existence in relation with something other than the self.'[8] Breton spoke of the 'Crisis of the Object', proclaiming that 'the thought processes which created all of these objects moved steadily from the abstract towards the concrete'.[9]

In 1934 Dalí offered a definition, 'Sculpture: Moulding done by hand of the "concrete" irrationality and of the imaginative world in general.' This text was accompanied by an illustration of Duchamp's *Monte Carlo Bond* (fig. 21).[10] And in 1932 he observed that 'the object will come to be "borne out" by its own "real constitution" … The "lyrical enigma" has just acquired … a real "materialistic constitution".'[11] So thought would become real. Speaking in a similar vein, Duchamp explained later on that 'I want to grasp things with the mind the way the penis is grasped by a vagina.'[12] Though a later statement, this concern was not new: as early as 1914 Duchamp wrote in a note '… tactile grasp image (like a penknife in one's fist)'.[13]

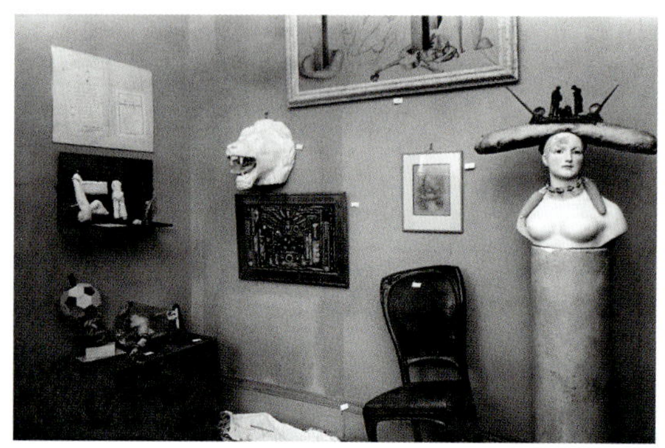

The June 1933 Surrealist Exhibition at the Galerie Pierre Colle in Paris included a number of objects. Duchamp's *Pharmacy* was surrounded by works by Dalí, most notably, as regards the object, *Board of Demented Associations*, *Atmospheric Chair*, *Atmospheric Spoon* and *Retrospective Bust of a Woman*. *Atmospheric Chair* was an art-nouveau chair with its legs cut down so that it sat at an unusable angle, and *Retrospective Bust of a Woman* was an elaborate assemblage object (fig. 24) made up of a porcelain bust, a baguette and an inkwell that included the motif of Millet's *Angelus*. The presence of both within this exhibition is more than a coincidence, when we consider that shortly thereafter, in August 1933, Duchamp and Man Ray were visiting Dalí at Cadaqués and Barcelona with the intention of assisting him in the preparation of the photographs for his next article in *Minotaure*. The resulting photographs of architectural details amounted to photographic symbolic objects, their tight, close-up framing serving to separate each object from its overall context. This was also the case with the photographs Brassaï took of Dalí's 'involuntary sculptures', reproduced opposite his text (cat. 83).[14]

In 1934 Dalí held a celebrated solo exhibition at the Galerie Jacques Bonjean in Paris, comprising 32 paintings, and notably two 'Sculptures', both in plaster, and four 'Objets Surréalistes'.[15] Of the sculptures, *Hysterical and Aerodynamic Female Nude* (1934; reconstructed 1973),[16] was a sculptural anamorphosis of a plaster reproduction of a work by the neoclassical sculptor James Pradier; in the work Dalí translated pictorial distortion into three dimensions. The other plaster, *Spectre ornamental de l'érection*, is now lost, as are the four objects, which had similarly provocative titles, and according to the catalogue were made of such ephemeral and edible materials as chocolate, eggs and milk.

In the May 1936 'Exhibition of Surrealist Objects' at the Galerie Charles Ratton in Paris (fig. 26), Dalí's *Aphrodisiac Jacket* was displayed hanging on the wall near Duchamp's *Why Not Sneeze Rose Sélavy?* (cat. 105) and *Bottle Rack*, both displayed in a vitrine, the jacket's crème-de-menthe shot glasses and woman's brassiere echoing the phallic pattern of spikes on the bottle rack and the enigmatic corporeal reference to the thermometer sticking out of the bird

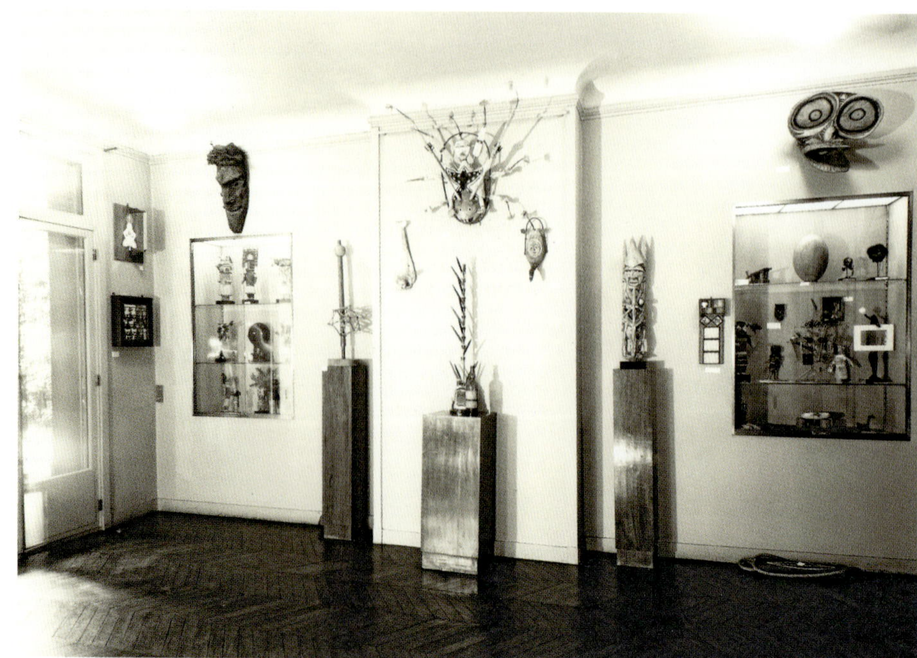

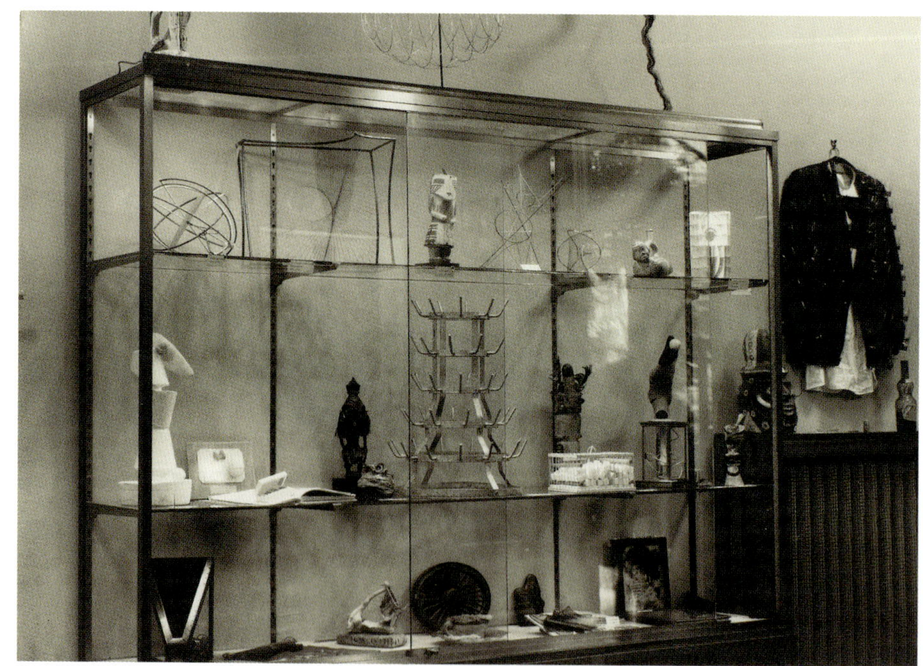

cage in *Why Not Sneeze Rose Sélavy?*. The exhibition represented a shift of context, giving the objects on display the possibility of ethnographic interpretations. Dalí's *Monument to Kant* (fig. 25) is set on a found marble base with a plaque referring to Kant and supporting an armature of numerous writing pens in a kind of delirium of writing overwhelming the rational systems proposed by the philosopher. Like his other, especially bizarre and erotic *Object* – an assemblage including a woman's shoe, a foot mould and a figurine representing two copulating figures – displayed in another vitrine (fig. 27), the *Monument to Kant* suggested more than the erotic and pointed to the

dark realms of perversion and fetishism. The work's overall shape rhymed with the Oceanic totems displayed alongside it, and directly attacked Kant's *The Critique of Judgement* (1790) by transgressing the philosopher's separation of aesthetic experience from conceptual thought. The exhibition also included Duchamp's *The Brawl at Austerlitz* (1921; Staatsgalerie Stuttgart), a miniature window on a plinth, which was displayed close to a Picasso guitar construction, as if to demonstrate the origin of the Surrealist object in the practices of collage, assemblage and construction.

A special 1936 number of *Cahiers d'art* (cat. 107) dedicated to the Object gave prominence to Dalí's works in this exhibition and additionally included the text 'Honour to the Object', Dalí's complement to Breton's 'Crisis of the Object'.[17] Similar emphasis was given to Duchamp's work, which was generously deployed alongside Gabrielle Buffet's substantial text devoted to Duchamp, 'Cœurs volants', equally the title of Duchamp's heart-shaped design on the cover of the magazine.[18] Though Buffet addressed Duchamp's work overall, from *The Large Glass* to the readymades, illustrating *Why Not Sneeze Rose Sélavy?* and *Bottle Rack*, her comments on the transgressive role of his practice are notable: Duchamp was seeking the 'Anti-masterpiece' and 'Duchamp's humour is a happy blasphemy: this usurpation of the privileges of the masterpieces by the pun destroys the masterpiece's prestige, better than any thesis.'[19]

For both Duchamp and Dalí, the object was linked to language. Aragon had emphasised the linguistic dimension of collage and object: 'We see these painters [Duchamp and Picabia] really employ objects like words.'[20] In the case of Duchamp, the use of puns in his titles and the act of signing objects were important to his sceptical undermining of the preciousness of painting and, more generally, the concept of the work of art. Many of his Notes concerning potential works are written in the infinitive, such as *faire* ('to make') or *chercher* ('to look for'): 'Chercher un Readymade qui pèse un poids choisi à l'avance';[21] instructions to himself which, as he later said, he never carried out.[22] For Dalí, language was equally important; indeed his titles are often excessively long and provocative. For both, wordplay was essential and the object offered a mechanism with which to undermine both language and pictorial representation. For the anthropologist Claude Lévi-Strauss, objects such as *Bottle Rack* 'explode the relationship between signified and signifier'.[23]

In an extension of their radical approach to the world of things, Duchamp and Dalí played central roles in the transformation of exhibitions from simply containers for objects into works and events in their own right: 'installations'. Notable in this is the 1938 'International Exhibition of Surrealism' in Paris. Although Breton and Éluard were the organisers, Duchamp and Dalí were credited with the display: Duchamp as 'générateur-arbitre' and Dalí as a 'conseiller spécial'. Dalí presented the famous *Rainy Taxi* at the entrance to the exhibition, itself a kind of elaborate Surrealist object, and both designed mannequins for the

Opposite, top left: Fig. 24
'Surrealist Exhibition', Galerie Pierre Colle, Paris, 1933. Photograph by Man Ray. Philadelphia Museum of Art. 125th Anniversary Acquisition. The Lynne and Harold Honickman Gift of the Julien Levy Collection, 2001-62-797

Opposite, top right: Fig. 25
'Exhibition of Surrealist Objects' at the Galerie Charles Ratton, Paris, 1936. In the centre is Dalí's *Monument to Kant*. Photograph by Man Ray. Centre Pompidou-MNAM-Bibliothèque Kandinsky

Opposite, bottom right: Fig. 26
'Exhibition of Surrealist Objects' at the Galerie Charles Ratton, Paris, 1936. In the case are Duchamp's *Bottle Rack* and *Why Not Sneeze Rose Sélavy?* and on the right above the radiator is Dalí's *Aphrodisiac Jacket*. Photograph by Man Ray. Centre Pompidou, MNAM-CCI, Paris

Right: Fig. 27
'Exhibition of Surrealist Objects' at the Galerie Charles Ratton, Paris, 1936. Photograph by Man Ray. Centre Pompidou, MNAM-CCI, Paris

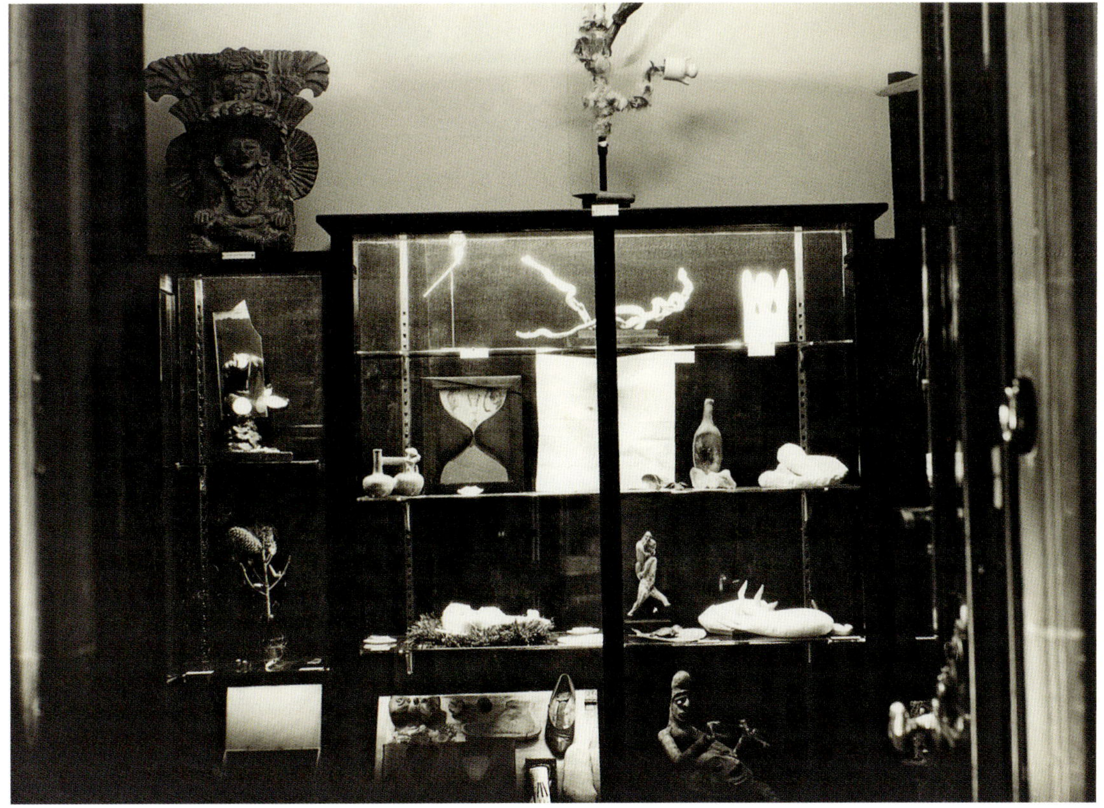

Surrealist street (figs 18, 28, 29). Duchamp staged the *Coal-sack Ceiling* (fig. 30), creating a grotto or mine-like space, and Dalí, according to Duchamp, was responsible for the 'pool' surrounded by rushes on the gallery floor. Although Dalí was generously represented in the exhibition by paintings and drawings, the first version of his *Lobster Telephone* (cat. 61) was his sole Surrealist object. Duchamp similarly showed numerous works, including among them *Pharmacy*, *The Brawl at Austerlitz* and a *Bottle Rack*, although the latter was listed simply as 'Readymade'.

The catalogue of the exhibition was Breton and Éluard's *Abridged Dictionary of Surrealism*. In it the entry devoted to the 'readymade' defined this as an 'ordinary object promoted to the dignity of an art object by the simple choice of the artist'.[24] Even more telling was the entry on 'Object', which states that Duchamp's readymades date from 1914 and 'constitute the first Surrealist objects'.[25] Breton's 1924 call for the fabrication of dream objects in his 'Introduction to the Discourse on the Paucity of Reality' was then invoked,[26] and the entry gives great attention to Dalí's concept of an Object of Symbolic Function, defining it as an 'object which lends a minimum of mechanical function and which is based on phantasms and representations susceptible of being provoked by the realisation of unconscious acts'.[27] The entry was illustrated by a photograph of a performance by Dalí, in which he staged elements of Millet's *Angelus*.

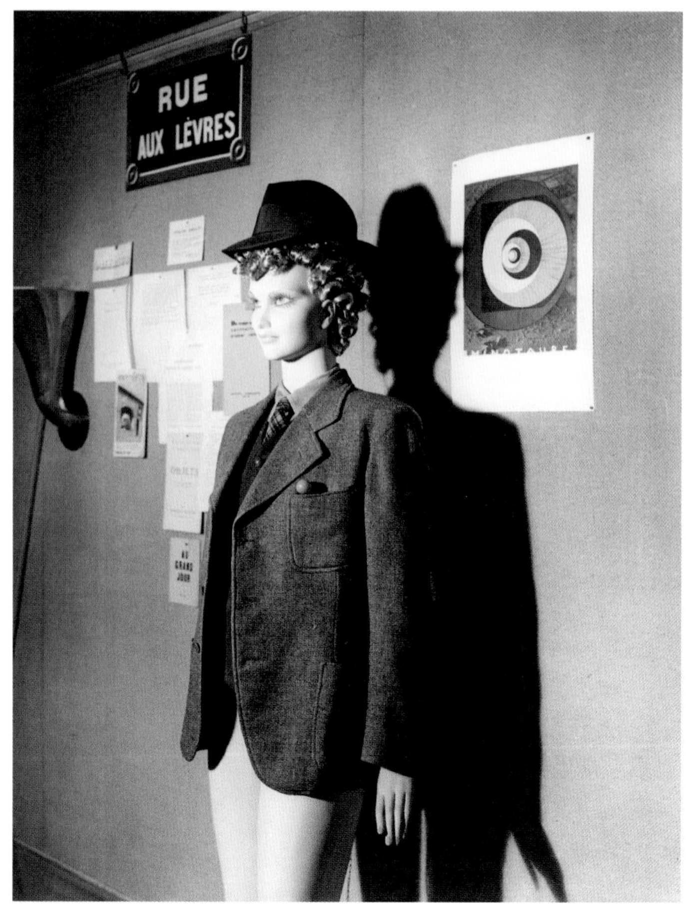

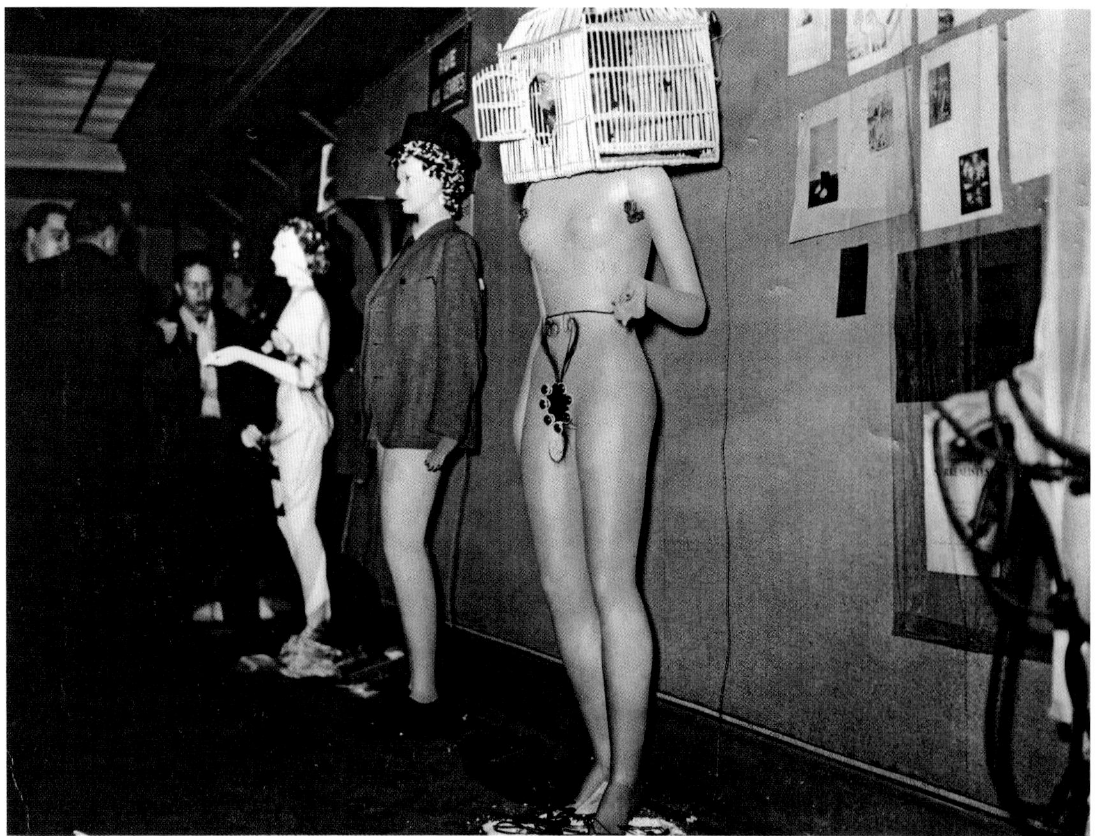

Above: Fig. 28
Marcel Duchamp, *Mannequin (Rrose Selavy)*, *Rue aux Lèvres*, 'International Exhibition of Surrealism', Galerie Beaux-Arts, Paris, 1938.
Photograph by Man Ray.
Man Ray Photographic Library, Paris, 1333

Left: Fig. 29
Mannequins for the Surrealist Street, 'International Exhibition of Surrealism', Galerie Beaux-Arts, Paris, 1938.
Duchamp's Mannequin *Rrose Selavy* is in the middle of the row, the *Rue aux Lèvres*. Duchamp himself is on the far left, facing away from the camera.
Private collection

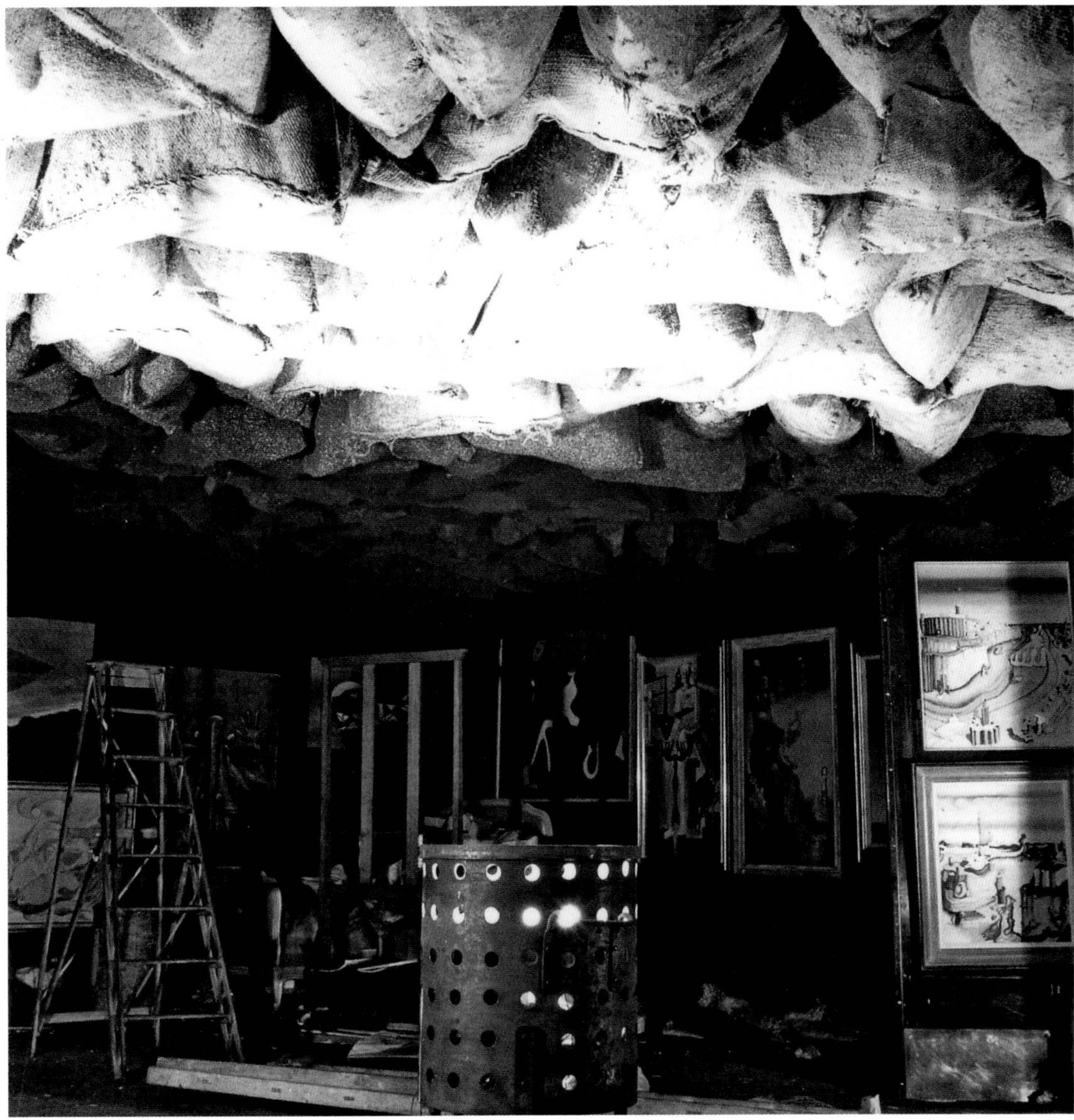

Duchamp challenged the rational categories of aesthetic judgement and taste, as understood by classical philosophy, especially that of Kant. Dalí similarly, as we have seen, challenged Kant's division of cognitive modes of thought and separation of the aesthetic from the cognitive in his *Monument to Kant*, with its emphasis not on the image but on the mechanism of writing (the fetishistic deployment of writing pens). Thomas McEvilley and others have pointed out that the source of Duchamp's defiance of Kant lay in his interest in the scepticism of Pyrrho of Elis, as discussed in the Introduction.[28] Dalí alluded to this scepticism when he wrote, 'Duchamp did not believe it necessary to pursue modern painting to its final consequences',[29] and in his preface to Duchamp's interviews he predicted the flooding of the world with readymades to the point that they would cease to exist as a category: 'Then Originality will become the artistic Work, produced convulsively by the artist by *hand*.'[30] Duchamp's project was not so much one of

negation as of contradiction: it 'suspended' judgement[31] and rejected the categories of good or bad taste.[32] Thus he told Schwarz that '…my position is the lack of a position'.[33]

Dalí's performance, though much more exaggerated than Duchamp's restrained approach, sought a similar destabilisation of categories. This is what he meant when he referred to abstract painters as 'backward Kantians' and elsewhere that 'Kant's philosophy is already moving away from the horizon like a disastrous cloud of hail….'[34] By 'Kantian', Dalí meant idealist. The category of art and the concept of the artist were the problems that had to be suspended. Duchamp considered himself a 'defrocked artist'[35] and the readymade 'a work without artist to make it'.[36] He rightly regarded the readymade as 'perhaps the most important idea to come out of my work'.[37] And, as we have seen, it lay at the origin of Dalí's objects. Indeed, through the object, both Duchamp and Dalí participated in a 'happy blasphemy'.

= L'ÉCHEC est MOIA -

1° Le premier qui compara les jours d'une jeune femme à une rose était un poète, le second possiblement un idiot

On a oublié que du moment Dada leur chef dans le moujiste, il disait, Dada et dit Dada et dit, Dada écrit et finissait Dada quand même et de la merde —

2 —

Broyage Broay et Boule

de Pierre CORDELIER
Poème de Danielle DEPETRIS
Dessins de Paul RICARD
Lithographies de Louis DECHAUME

Printed in France
sur les presses de l'Imprimerie de la Société RICARD

3e Trimestre 1967

SYSTEMATISING CONFUSION: DUCHAMP AND DALÍ, 'WRITERS'

GAVIN PARKINSON

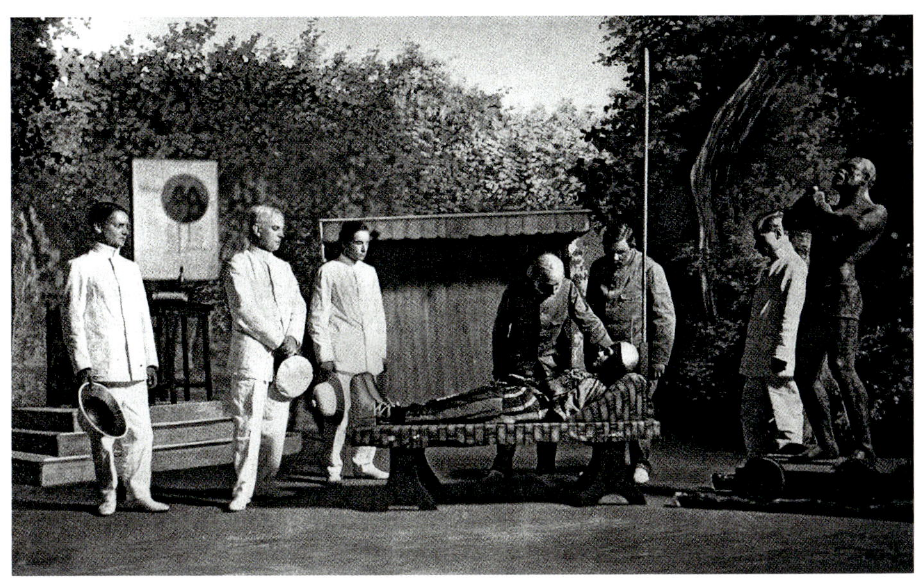

Fig. 31
Roussel's *Impressions of Africa*
performed at Théâtre Antoine, Paris, 1912.
Collection John Ashbery, Flow Chart
Foundation, New York

Opposite: detail of cat. 43

From an early age, Salvador Dalí aspired to be known and remembered as a writer as much as an artist, whereas Marcel Duchamp seems to have travelled gradually to a position of indifference towards both vocations, following a youthful enthusiasm for painting that ended in 1912, the same year that writing (that of Raymond Roussel, followed by his own) altered the path of his art irrevocably. Writing of many kinds was crucial to the art of both, enhancing it in diverse ways, even if at times the assumed profession of 'writer' or the onerous task of writing weighed heavily upon it or was experienced as a distraction, unwanted responsibility or even embarrassment.

For Dalí, at certain times, writing could take up at least as much of his day as painting. From 1941–44, for instance, 'Dalí never stopped writing', according to Robert and Nicolas Descharnes.[1] Meanwhile, Duchamp's minimalist approach to writing, from his notes to his use of text in his art to his puns and pithy appraisals of other artists – carried out from 1943 to 1949 for the catalogue of the Société Anonyme (the collection of modern art he created with Katherine S. Dreier) – apparently extended to his reluctant, delayed and rather functional letters. In one of them, addressed to the artist and writer Marcel Jean in 1958, soon after Duchamp and Dalí had renewed their lapsed friendship of the 1930s, Duchamp commented self-mockingly on the brevity of his corpus, joking about the 'book that [Michel] Sanouillet is organising

of my "writings" at [Eric] Losfeld's (!),' soon to be published as *Salt Seller: The Essential Writings of Marcel Duchamp* (1959/75) in doing so he placed a strict limit on any claim that might be made for him as a 'writer' in the ways we understand that term.[2]

However far each of them was drawn towards or put off by writing, there is no doubt that their earliest ventures into text were determined by vanguard art, yet in entirely contradictory ways. Duchamp's minimal output began in 1912 when he was painting in a style deeply indebted to Cubism but was afraid that his art and thinking were, indeed, becoming overly dependent on the contemporary avant-garde, and was wondering how to work beyond its prescriptions and even those of art itself. In May or June that year he was present at one of the few performances of Roussel's play *Impressions of Africa* (fig. 31) with Francis Picabia, Gabrielle Buffet-Picabia, Michel Leiris and perhaps the poet and critic Guillaume Apollinaire (accounts differ), commenting much later:

> It was fundamentally Roussel who was responsible for my glass, *The Bride Stripped Bare by Her Bachelors, Even*. From his *Impressions of Africa* I got the general approach. This play of his which I saw with Apollinaire helped me greatly on one side of my expression. I saw at once I could use Roussel as an influence. I felt that as a painter it was much better to be influenced by a writer than by another painter. And Roussel showed me the way.[3]

So Duchamp encountered the writings of Roussel, who propagated bizarre machines as though they were myths for the modern age and who used the pun as a device to generate narrative, at a crucial moment and in relevant company. In October that year, he travelled alongside Picabia and Apollinaire on a long and now-legendary road trip from Paris to the Jura Mountains in Switzerland. He fell ill in the car on the way back, beginning what was to become a rather frugal written *œuvre* with a set of five cryptic, poetic notes. These elaborate a personal mythology that had begun to emerge a few months earlier in the titles *The King and Queen Surrounded by Swift Nudes* (1912) and *The Passage from Virgin to Bride* (1912), and are the first textual stirrings of *The Bride Stripped Bare by Her Bachelors, Even* (*The Large Glass*) of 1915–23:

The machine with 5 hearts, the pure child,
of nickel and platinum, must dominate the
Jura–Paris road.

On the one hand, the chief of the 5 nudes
will be ahead of the four other nudes *towards*
this Jura–Paris road. On the other hand, the
headlight child will be the instrument conquering
this Jura–Paris road.

This headlight child could, graphically, be a
comet, which would have its tail in front, this tail
being an appendage of the headlight child
appendage which absorbs by crushing (gold
dust, graphically) this Jura–Paris road.[4]

This is an extract from the jottings, giving first evidence
of a casual practice through which Duchamp would
turn over his thoughts about *The Large Glass* during
its conception and construction. Among other things,
his engagement of the written *aperçu* alongside the
more familiar artist's sketch or study brought about
the mythic content of *Mariée* (Bride) and *Célibataires*
(Bachelors) through punning play on his own name
MAR/CEL in a sentence, *La Mariée mise à nu par
ses célibataires, même*, that sounds more like the
concluding line of a poem than the title of a painting.

Other projects and interventions in and beyond
art emerged from these scribbled, usually brief and
often repetitive perambulations. These included
Duchamp's idea to choose the first readymades,
which sometimes bore writing, as in the inscription
on *Comb* (1916) '3 OR 4 GOUTTES DE HAUTEUR N'ONT RIEN
A FAIRE AVEC LA SAUVAGERIE' ('Three or four drops of
height have nothing to do with savagery') and in the
title given to (and appended onto) the snow shovel
In Advance of the Broken Arm (cat. 103). Elsewhere,
Duchamp combined fragments of script in French and
English on the upper and lower surfaces of the assisted
readymade *With Hidden Noise* (cat. 108), and there are
works of the same period formed entirely from writing,
such as *The* (1915) and *Rendez-vous of Sunday 6
February 1916* (fig. 32). In all of these, the texts refuse
to make sense and can be understood collectively,
therefore, as a droll commentary on Duchamp's
struggle with a new language following his move
to New York from Paris in 1915. Many of the notes
written during the period of *The Large Glass* and
the readymades were reproduced as facsimiles and
collected in the *Box of 1914* (fig. 38), the *Green Box*
(1934; cat. 124) and the *White Box* (1966), showing the
value Duchamp placed in them but displaying barely
any similarity in their form with more conventional,
academic note-taking, even though Duchamp did
get the chance to carry out such research on the
fourth dimension, colour theory and other topics
when he took a librarian's job at the Bibliothèque
Sainte-Geneviève in Paris in 1913.

By contrast with Duchamp's attempt from 1912
onwards to situate himself outside the burgeoning
clichés of the avant-garde, to the point of questioning

art itself by drawing upon a writer like Roussel and
initiating a practice of note-taking, Dalí's voluminous
writings (see fig. 33), usually said to originate in the
late 1920s, came initially from a desire to explain and
promote his current painting. They were therefore
an attempt to access, not desert, the circles of
contemporary art, notably in his case the orbit
of Surrealism. Spanning a far wider array of genres
than Duchamp's writings – including theoretical and
philosophical forays, psychoanalytic speculations,
art historical investigations, cultural review and
commentary, manifestos, poetry, film scripts,
fiction and autobiography – Dalí's writings provide
a peculiar study in positionality from the outset.
In their acceptance of the genres of writing and in
spite of their often eccentric form, address, subject-
matter and conclusions, the texts of the 1920s and
1930s obviously partake of the non-conformist,
experimental styles of modernism and the avant-
garde, while showing an obedience in their aim at
affiliation and an effort towards acceptance by
that vanguard in a way that Duchamp's never did.[5]

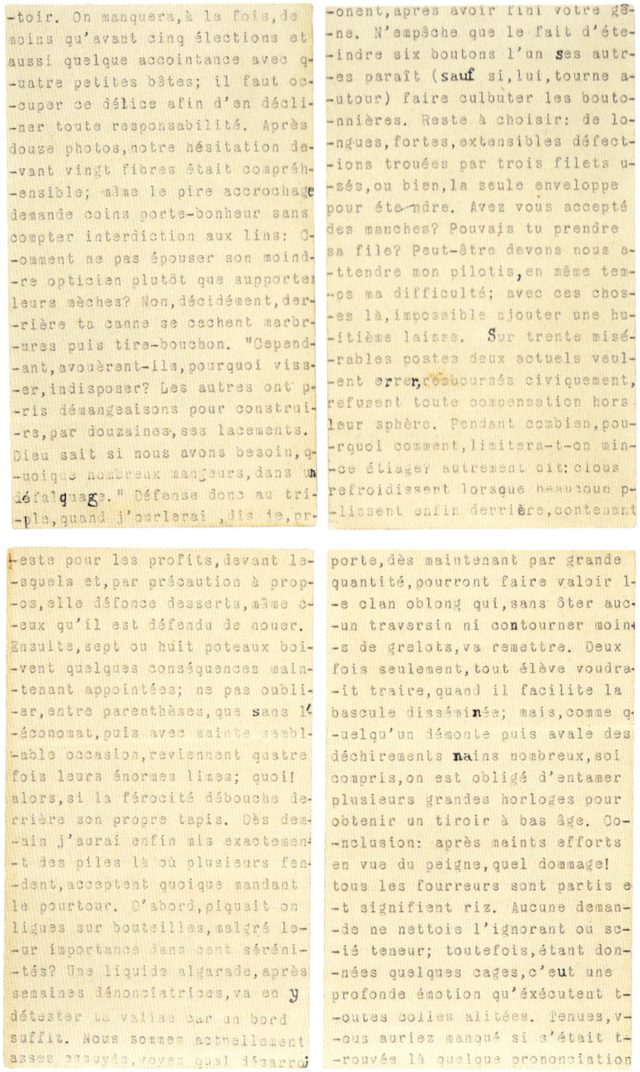

Fig. 32
Marcel Duchamp, *Rendez-vous du
Dimanche 6 Février 1916* (*Rendezvous
of Sunday, 6 February 1916*), 1916.
Typewritten text with black ink
corrections on four postcards taped
together, 28.6 x 14.4 cm.
Philadelphia Museum of Art. The Louise
and Walter Arensberg Collection,
1950-134-983

This is evident already in Dalí's wide-ranging writings from 1927 to 1929 for the Catalan art and culture review *L'Amic de les Arts* and the cultural review *La Gaceta Literaria*, which was published in Madrid as a mouthpiece for the avant-garde. Usually in Catalan or translated by Dalí from Catalan into Spanish, his contributions to these publications utilise metamorphosis, abrupt switches of scene and incongruous associations between individual objects or objects and their own attributes and materials. A combination of prose texts and poems, they are frequently scatological and sexual, or tease out a world of putrefaction and the minuscule – here, in 'Poem' of 1928, by means of individual, cordoned-off tableaux that might be montages or sketches for paintings:

> A quiet ear over a small upright wisp of smoke indicating a shower of ants over the sea.
> Near the cold boulder there lies an eyelash.
> A torn piece of flesh signalling bad weather.
> There are six breasts lost inside a square water.
> A putrefied donkey buzzing with small minute-hands representing the beginning of spring.
> There is a navel placed in some spot with its tiny white teeth like a fishbone.
> A dry crab on a cork indicating the rising of the sea.
> There is a moon-coloured nude carrying its nose.
> A bottle of Anisette lying horizontally on a hollow piece of wood, simulating sleep.
> There is an olive's shadow on a crease.[6]

Dalí assembles here small details of beach and sea similar to those glimpsed in the film he was to script in early 1929 with Luis Buñuel, *Un Chien andalou*. He was concurrently exploring such details in his pictures, already showing their surrealist proclivities in canvases like *Apparatus and Hand* (1927) and the study for *Honey is Sweeter than Blood* (1927), even before he arrived at his mature style in 1929. As well as this, 'Poem' shows Dalí, like Duchamp, steeped in poetic writing, not just through his close friendship with Federico García Lorca, which lasted from 1925 to 1928, but also through his reading of French Surrealist poets, notably Benjamin Péret, whose effortless capacity to render the ordinary extraordinary through the animation, displacement or unprecedented juxtaposition of the overlooked is strikingly similar and would soon be lauded by Dalí in *L'Amic de les Arts*.[7]

Dalí's full entrance into the Paris Surrealist group between April and June 1929 only led his writing towards further immoderation, which was fully endorsed by the Surrealists even if it sometimes caused a commotion they could have done without. The scenario for *Un Chien andalou* was reproduced in the final, twelfth issue of the Surrealists' review of the 1920s – *La Révolution surréaliste* – on 15 December 1929. That publication was succeeded by *Le Surréalisme au service de la révolution* (*SASDLR*), from 1930–33, for which Dalí was a regular contributor, publishing in all six issues. Those texts demonstrate a close examination of fantasy, obsessional neurosis and sexual pathology that had featured in the poems and prose of his two books published by Éditions Surréalistes, *La Femme visible* (*The Visible Woman*; 1930) and *L'Amour et la mémoire* (*Love and Memory*; 1931). In the second of these, for instance, we are treated to various uninhibited embellishments of the Freudian family romance:

> My sister's image
> the anus red
> with bloody shit
> the cock
> half erect
> elegantly propped up
> against
> a huge
> personal
> and colonial
> lyre
> the left testicle
> partially dipped
> in a glass
> of tepid milk
> the glass with milk
> placed
> inside
> a woman's shoe[8]

The imagery is once again redolent of the paintings, yet with anecdotal detail ('personal', 'colonial') that Dalí usually had to rely upon his titles to provide. There is also allusion to one of the Surrealist objects that he

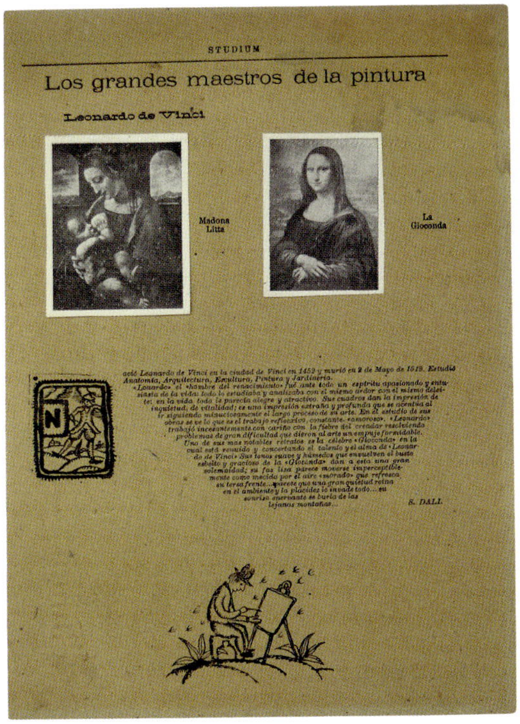

Fig. 33
Salvador Dalí
Page from *Studium*, No. 4,
1 May 1919 (cat. 2)
Book with text and illustrations by
Salvador Dalí, 31 x 22.3 cm
Collection of The Dalí Museum Archives,
St Petersburg, Florida

would fabricate (cat. 78), and his contributions to that genre and its theory in *SASDLR* are collectively among his most important to Surrealism.[9] Among his writings in that review are one of his best-known texts, 'The Rotting Donkey', which gives an early rendering of Dalí's 'paranoiac-critical theory', where the fabrication of irrational associations reminiscent of paranoia is impressed upon its audience as a reality, along with perhaps the most widely-quoted statement of his own ambition for Surrealism: 'to systematise confusion and thereby contribute to a total discrediting of the world of reality'.[10] It was also in *SASDLR* that Dalí published 'Daydream,' his notorious, precise, multi-layered and ritualistic Sadean fantasy in which our author masturbates with the aid of a soiled piece of linen while imagining sodomising a fictional eleven-year-old girl named Dulita in a stinking barn with the aid of her mother. The French Communist Party took objection and censured the text during the period of Surrealism's closeness to Communism, hauling in André Breton to explain the Surrealists' excesses and revealing Party members to be perfectly bourgeois in their public disapproval of tales of sexual transgression.

Like Dalí, Duchamp prized eroticism as a subversive instrument but Dalí's frankly shocking content and confessional, biographical or self-analytical mode of delivery, clearly informed by psychoanalysis, are entirely at odds with Duchamp's impersonal, elusive style and analytical pose and prose. This can be made evident through brief examination of their respective writings published in the circle of Surrealism in 1933, the year after they met. Duchamp's agreement to offer the Surrealists three notes for *SASDLR* from the period of *The Large Glass* that were about to be included in the *Green Box*, which appeared under the heading 'La mariée mise à nu par ses célibataires mêmes' [*sic*], heralded his return to something like artistic activity after a break of a decade following the 'incompletion' of *The Large Glass* in 1923.[11] Meanwhile the appearance of the notes on 15 May 1933 on the opening page of the penultimate issue of *SASDLR*, no. 5, shows the very high esteem in which Duchamp was held by Breton and the Surrealists (Dalí himself invited Duchamp to Cadaqués that summer). One of these notes-to-self plans what became the nine male elements or 'Malic Moulds' in the lower half of *The Large Glass* and reads in part:

By eros' matrix, we understand the group of 8 uniforms or hollow liveries
receive the
destined to give to the illuminating gas which takes 8 malic forms (gendarme, cuirassier, etc.)
The gas *castings* so obtained, would hear the litanies sung by the chariot, refrain of the whole celibate machine. But *they* will never be able *to pass beyond the Mask* = They would have been as if enveloped, alongside their

regrets, by a mirror reflecting back to them their own complexity to the point of their being hallucinated rather onanistically.[12]

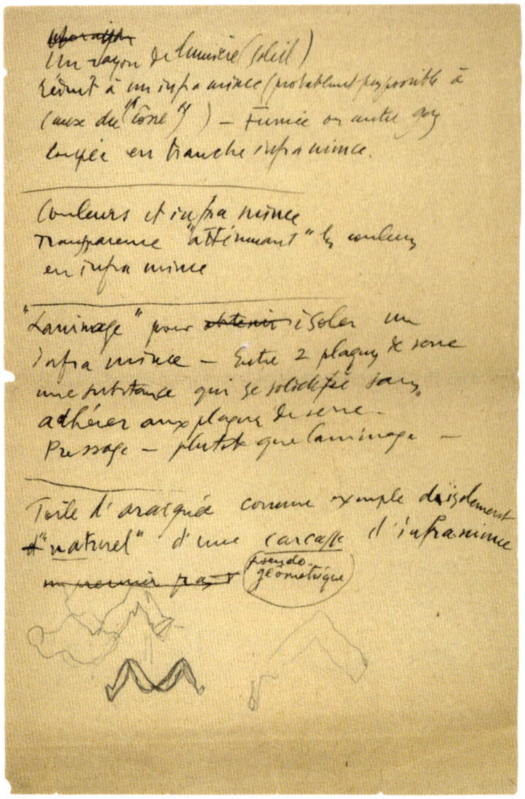

The mode of address served Duchamp's own purposes because he had already established a private mythology of 'litanies', 'chariot', 'Mask' and so on; furthermore, the hermetic terminology was attractive to the Surrealists for the ways it forged a new metaphorical language for eroticism. However, its withdrawal from the scene of tangible objects in a coherent space and time acts more as a barrier than a bridge to the 'satisfactory' reading of *The Large Glass* sought by academic rationalism.

By contrast with Duchamp's schematic, repetitive and opaque anti-itinerary of eroticism, Dalí's contribution to the same issue of *SASDLR*, 'Psychoatmospheric-Anamorphic Objects', can be read as an equally pseudo-scientific if rather more prolonged technical account, this time of the creation of the quasi-alchemical 'formless fragment[s] of molten iron of any weight and volume', which strains to make sense (or pretends to) and fails.[13] This is incomprehension through a combination of under- and over-explanation, yet like Duchamp's refusal to submit his writings to the strictures of readerly rationalism, it was welcomed by Surrealism and by Breton, whose own 'extraordinarily elusive manner of setting forth his ideas', in his books, in Margaret Cohen's words, 'translates his thematised challenge to the Cartesian subject onto the plane of style'.[14]

Fig. 34
Marcel Duchamp
'Un rayon de lumière (soleil)',
('A ray of light, sun'), autographed
note with erotic drawing,
date unknown (cat. 3)
Black ink and pencil on paper,
25.6 x 16.8 cm
Centre Pompidou, Paris. Musée
national d'art moderne/Centre
de création industrielle

This strategy can be seen at its most extreme in *The Tragic Myth of Millet's Angelus: A Paranoiac-Critical Interpretation* (1963), Dalí's full-length reading of Jean-François Millet's incredibly popular painting *The Angelus* (fig. 17), 'the most disturbing, the most enigmatic, the most dense and the richest in unconscious thoughts, ever to have existed'.[15] If it demonstrates the prolific extent to which Dalí was operating as a working author as much as an artist in the 1930s, it also goes to show by comparison how little Duchamp was interested in a career as either in that decade. His desultory and nonchalant working method is crystallised in his notes on 'infra-mince' ('infra-thin') begun around 1935 yet barely referred to in his lifetime, only coming fully to light a few years after Dalí's book came out. Where Dalí strove for a completism in *The Tragic Myth* that led him, as he had promised, to 'systematise confusion', Duchamp's partial glimpses of *infra-mince* over the course of torn bits of paper and sometimes more methodical sallies covering entire sheets are wide-ranging across mental and physical experience, yet still seem to lack a sense of, or perhaps desire for, completion, as in these few examples:

> *inframince* (adject.)/not noun – never/use as/a substantive

> Velvet trousers –/their whistling sound (in walking) by/brushing of the 2 legs is an/*infra mince* separation signalled/by sound

> *inframince* separation – better/than screen, because it indicates/interval (taken in one sense) and/screen (taken in another sense) – separation/has the 2 senses male and female –

> The warmth of a seat (which has just/been left) is *infra-mince*

> A ray of light...[16] (fig. 34)

The linguistic dance of liminality, barriers, borders and intangibles performed over ten years by the notes on *infra-mince* takes place on a terrain close to that Duchamp had earlier explored in the imagery and notes for *The Large Glass*, and might even have been inspired by it since *infra-mince* apparently emerged around the time Duchamp was preparing to return to America to repair the shattered, half-forgotten masterpiece in June–July 1936.

In the first part of the period in which Duchamp pondered the elusive *infra-mince*, Dalí continued to provide the Surrealists with written ammunition of great diversity in the review *Minotaure* (1933–39) and in his full-length books of theory and poetry *The Conquest of the Irrational* (fig. 35) and *The Metamorphosis of Narcissus* (1937). His estrangement from Surrealism at the end of that decade did not end

his writing career – far from it: the autobiography that followed soon after his departure, *The Secret Life of Salvador Dalí* (1942), is his longest single work and although it partakes of a traditional genre its frequent immersion in fantasy is hardly conventional. In the 1940s and 1950s, Dalí completed his break with Surrealism and also distanced his work from modern painting and Freudian psychoanalysis, delving into modern physics in the *Mystical Manifesto* (1951) and 'Anti-Matter Manifesto' (1958).

This scientific basis was the one upon which he wrote, finally, about his friend Marcel Duchamp, 'the aristocratic anarchist', on the occasion of the solo show at the Sidney Janis Gallery in 1959 to mark the publication of Robert Lebel's long-awaited monograph on Duchamp, whose *King and Queen Surrounded by Swift Nudes* (mistitled by Dalí) was a snapshot of the underlying structure of matter in Dalí's reading:

> In painting *The King and the Queen Traversed by Swift Nudes*, the genius of Marcel Duchamp proclaimed nothing less than the notarial act of the new intra-atomic structure of the universe, that is, the discontinuity of matter. In fact, the king and the queen can be traversed by swift nudes because matter is discontinuous. It is easy to understand that swift nudes are indivisible bodies, the corpuscles, the charged elementary particles of quantum physics...[17]

Dalí's typically idiosyncratic account of the metaphorical language of *The King and Queen Surrounded by Swift Nudes* (obviously closer to his own current preoccupations than those of Duchamp in 1912) appeared in the same year as Duchamp's collected writings edited by Sanouillet, and no doubt the 'anarchist' and 'genius' himself greeted Dalí's text with the same dry reserve he summoned in considering his new role as 'writer'.

The renewal of their friendship at that time also led to Duchamp's request that Dalí pen the preface to the book of interviews *Dialogues with Marcel Duchamp* (cat. 43). This gave Dalí the opportunity to rant against the theft by contemporary artists of the earlier anti-art of the two, and its banal replication especially by Pop. It also helped bring about the format chosen for Dalí's truly bizarre set of texts and etchings *Ten Recipes for Immortality* (cat. 123), issued in a limited edition in a mirrored suitcase in homage to Duchamp's *Boîte-en-valise* (cat. 62), a version of which Dalí owned and revered.[18] These late texts by the two elderly iconoclasts give generous further evidence that the earlier swerve performed by each from commonplace rationalism had been sustained into old age, and that the written word wielded in highly individual yet nevertheless perfectly dissimilar ways had played a vital role in this.

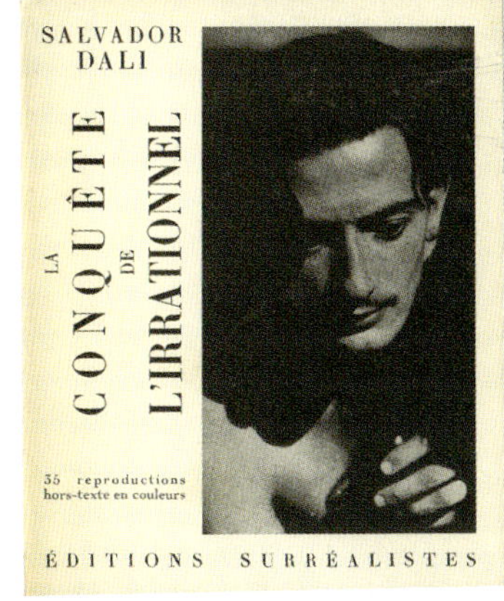

Fig. 35
Salvador Dalí, *La Conquête de l'irrationnel* (*The Conquest of the Irrational*), Paris, 1935.
Collection of The Dalí Museum Archives, St Petersburg, Florida

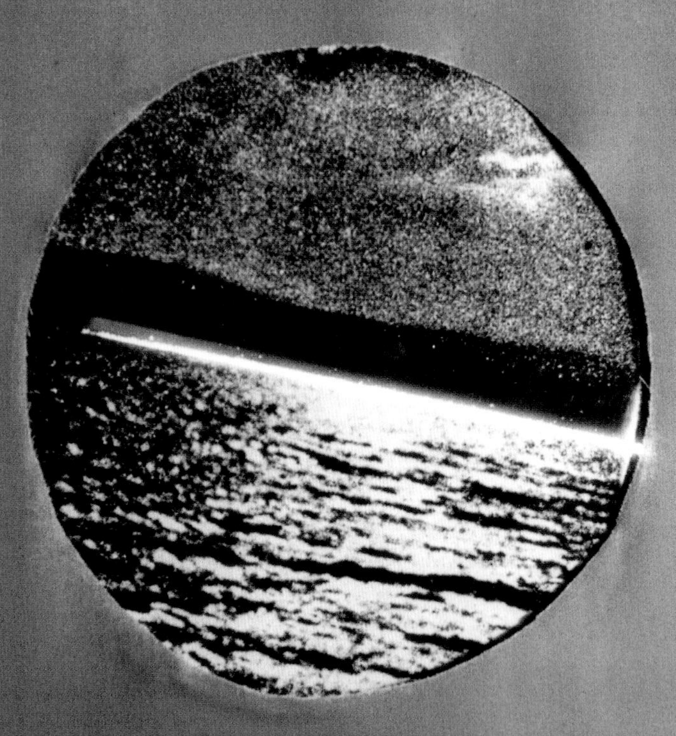

PHOTOGRAPHY AND FILM
DAWN ADES

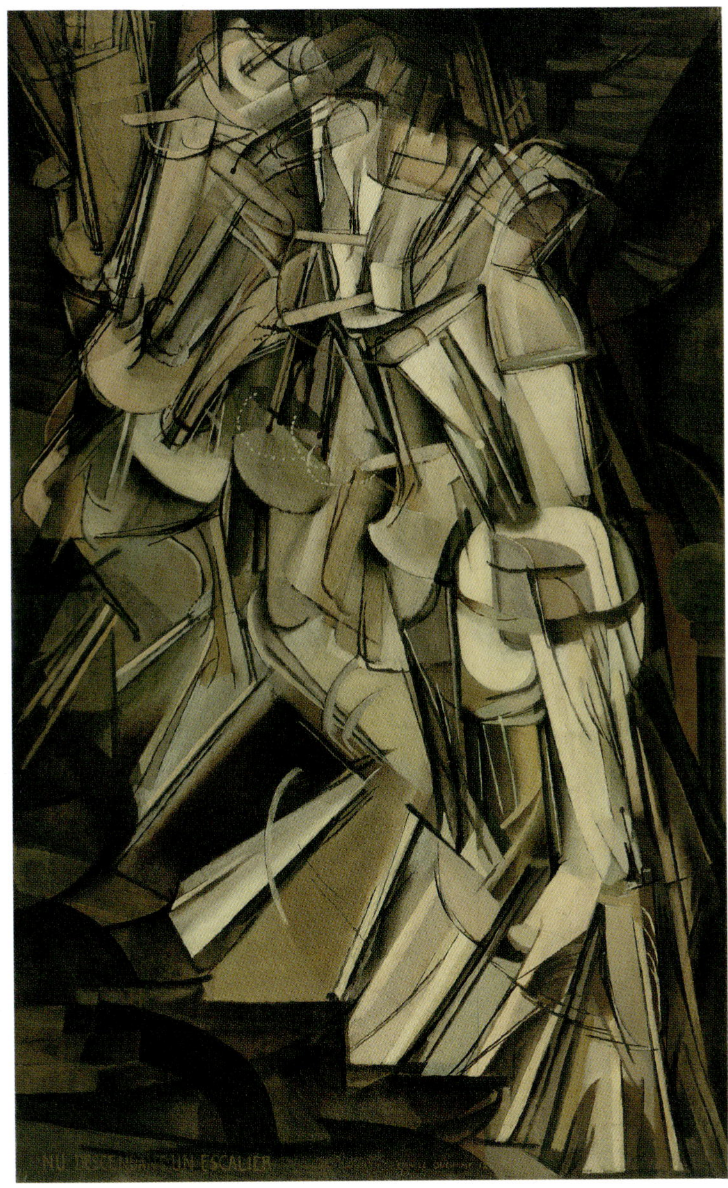

Photography and film appealed to both Duchamp and Dalí in a number of different ways, not least as alternatives and challenges to painting. Their engagement was at its most intense during the 1920s, when artists across the spectrum of the avant-gardes turned to these mediums as radical new forms of expression. Both were of the view that photography and film had superseded painting. As Duchamp wrote to Alfred Stieglitz in response to the latter's questionnaire 'Can a photograph have the significance of art?':

> You know exactly what I think about photography
> I would like to see it make people despise painting until something else will make photography unbearable – [1]

Photography no doubt was a factor in Duchamp's withdrawal from painting, as his comment indicates. But the ways he made use of it were far from straightforward. His letter to Stieglitz was written four years after he had made his last oil painting on canvas, *Tu m'* (1918; fig. 87). *Nude Descending a Staircase*, especially *No. 2* (fig. 37), was a response to the problem of motion in painting, amalgamating experiments in photographing movement (the photochronography of Marey and Muybridge) with cinema – which was still then, as Duchamp later commented, in its infancy.[2] Duchamp was undoubtedly stretching painting, pushing it beyond what it could naturally accomplish, before giving it up.

Both Duchamp's nine-foot-high glass painting, *The Bride Stripped Bare by Her Bachelors, Even* (*The Large Glass*; fig. 81), and his Notes referring to the work are shot through with photographic allusions and analogies. *The Large Glass*, on which Duchamp worked from 1915 to 1923, is not only a rejection of canvas as a support for pigment but an active engagement with photography. The glass plates themselves are huge analogues of the plates then used in cameras, and a possible allusion in one of the first notes, 'Kind of Subtitle', could be to the timing of the exposure of light on the prepared photographic plates:

> Use 'delay' instead of picture or painting; picture on glass becomes delay in glass – but delay in glass does not mean picture on glass...

Opposite: Fig. 36
Marcel Duchamp, *Green Ray*, installation in 'The Surrealist Exhibition', Galerie Maeght, Paris, 1947. Photograph by Denise Bellon. Fonds Photographique Denise Bellon, Paris

Fig. 37
Marcel Duchamp, *Nude Descending a Staircase (No. 2)*, 1912. Oil on canvas, 147 x 89.2 cm. Philadelphia Museum of Art. The Louise and Walter Arensberg Collection, 1950-134-59

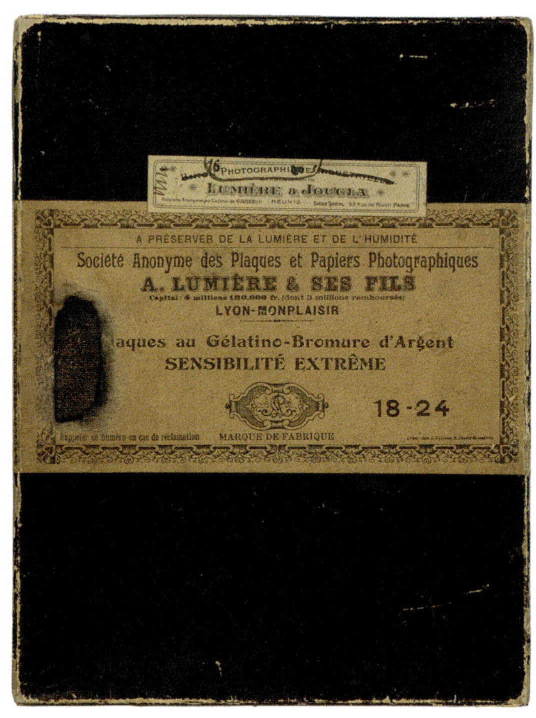

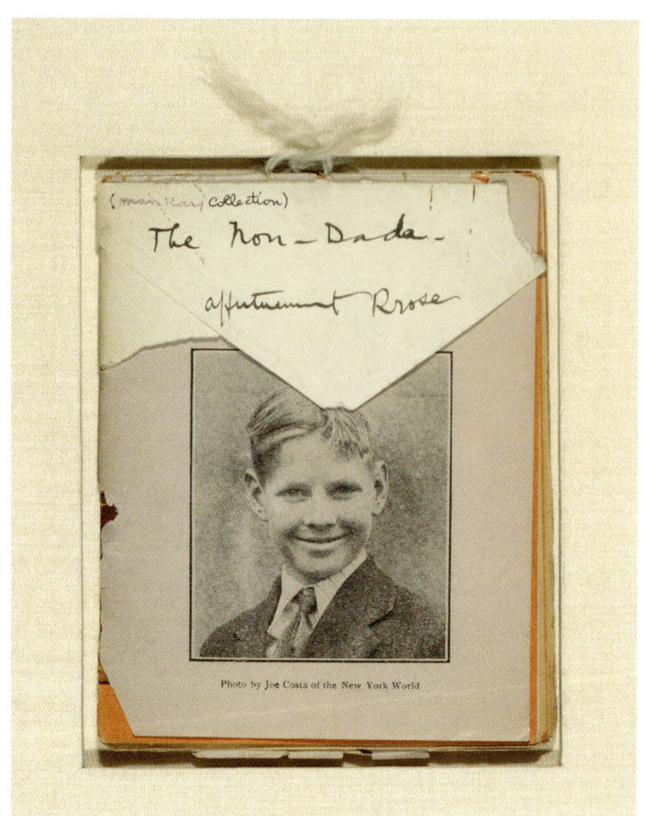

The first set of notes Duchamp assembled and published – in an edition of five – known as *The Box of 1914* (fig. 38), was placed inside cardboard containers that had originally stored photographic plates and paper fabricated by Lumière, Kodak and other manufacturers.[3] The sixteen notes were reproduced photographically, and one of the Boxes contained three gelatin-silver prints of the *3 Standard Stoppages* (cat. 133).

Although Duchamp rarely used still photography himself, relying instead on others and above all on his friend Man Ray, it was a fundamental element in his operations from 1917 on.[4] Stieglitz took the photo of *Fountain* in 1917 for reproduction in the Dada journal *The Blind Man*; Man Ray photographed *The Large Glass* and helped to give Rrose Sélavy a visible presence with two series of photographs (1921), as well as taking the images of Duchamp that figured in other identity games, such as the 'homme savon' ('soap man'), for *Monte Carlo Bond* (cat. 38).[5] On at least one occasion Duchamp adapted a readymade photograph: *The Non-Dada* was the frontispiece image for a religious pamphlet, which he annotated and signed 'The Non-Dada, affectionately, Rrose' and sent to Man Ray (fig. 39). He took the occasional photograph himself: his portrait photograph of the American painter Charles Sheeler was published in *Vanity Fair* in March 1923. Infrequently in later years works appeared that not only used photography but did so in unusual ways that took advantage of the medium's unique characteristics. Thus, as one of his

contributions to the 1947 'International Exhibition of Surrealism', Duchamp gave instructions to the architect and designer Frederick Kiesler to place behind a circular hole in the green canvas that lined the Hall of Superstitions two photographs of a seascape and a sky, separated by a neon tube that glowed green (fig. 36). *Green Ray* was dismantled at the end of the exhibition, so it is difficult fully to judge its effect, but the round 'frame' resembles a camera lens, through which the viewer would glimpse what is 'in reality' beyond, and about to be captured in the snapshot. The momentary flash of the 'green ray', a phenomenon that occurs under certain atmospheric conditions at the moment the sun sets over the sea, is in some ways analogous to the speed of the modern camera and its flash. But the two photographs have a greater resemblance to early 'combination photographs', from a time when it was not possible to photograph on a single plate both sky and land- or seascape, and when exposure times were lengthy. Another instance is a photograph of one of Duchamp's erotic objects, *Female Fig Leaf* (cat. 86), as reproduced on the cover of *Le Surréalisme, même* (fig. 40). The tiny galvanised plaster sculpture was placed upside down and photographed in such a way that it appears convex, rather than concave as it actually is.

One might see in Duchamp's uses of photography a doubling back of the medium's aims and means. Having abandoned painting, partly because, as André Breton wrote, it had been 'far outdistanced by photography in the pure and simple

Fig. 38
Marcel Duchamp, *The Box of 1914*, 1913–14. Commercial cardboard photographic supply box containing photographic facsimiles of sixteen manuscript notes and the drawing *Avoir l'apprenti dans le soleil (To Have the Apprentice in the Sun)* mounted on boards, and one photographic facsimile of the drawing *Médiocrité (Mediocrity)*, unmounted, 24.9 x 18.9 x 3.5 cm. Philadelphia Museum of Art. Gift of Mme Marcel Duchamp, 1991

Fig. 39
Marcel Duchamp, *The Non-Dada*, 1922. Printed brochure with ink inscription. National Galleries of Scotland, Edinburgh. Bequeathed by Gabrielle Keiller 1995

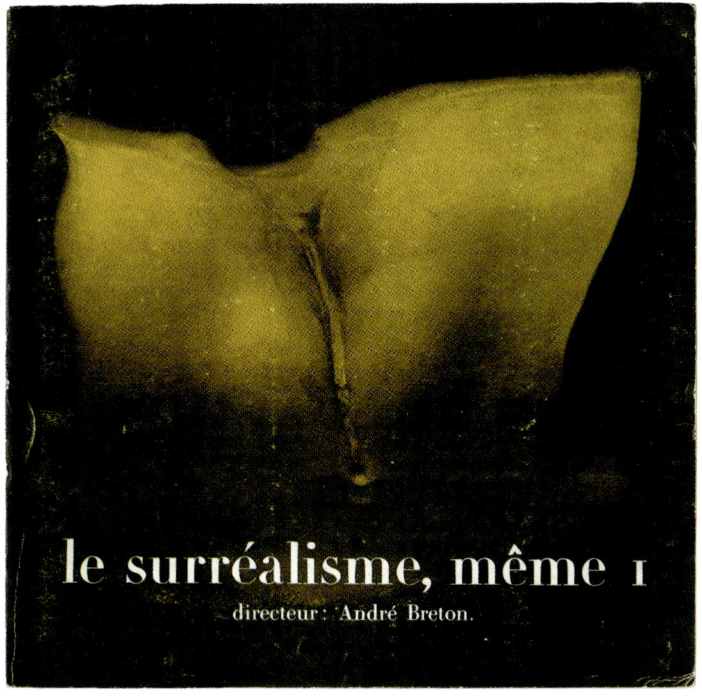

imitation of actual things', Duchamp went on, in association with Man Ray, to whom Breton's words were addressed, to demonstrate how satisfactorily it could serve 'other ends than those for which it appears to have been created'.[6] It could subvert, rather than reinforce, the 'truth' of actual things, alter existing identities and convincingly create new ones, and invade realms of the imagination that 'painting imagined it was going to be able to keep all to itself'.[7] The photograph Man Ray took (leaving the camera shutter open for an hour) of *The Large Glass* in Duchamp's New York studio, where it had lain untouched since Duchamp left for Buenos Aires in August 1918, was reproduced in the Dada magazine *Littérature* in 1922 with the caption 'Here is the domain of Rrose Sélavy / How arid it is / How fertile it is / How joyous it is / How sad it is – View taken from an aeroplane by Man Ray 1921' (fig. 41).[8] The photograph's capacity to subvert scale and confuse the texture of objects is evident: cropped so that there are no clues as to size, it converts the dust gathered on the surface of the glass into a desert landscape, the raised lines of the chocolate grinder like distant field strips. Such photographic transformations, by means of close-up, cropping, viewpoint and so on, are at the heart of the fascination the medium exerted on artists. Dalí, who had a lifelong interest in close-up, was to explore similar effects in film, notably in his 1975 TV film *Impressions of Upper Mongolia: Homage to Raymond Roussel*, where landscapes, scenes and figures emerge from a virtually abstract, colourful mass; at the end it is

Fig. 40
Cover of *Le Surréalisme, même*
(dir. André Breton, ed. Jean Schuster),
no. 1, October 1956 (cat. 4)
Journal with cover by Marcel
Duchamp, 19.3 x 19.5 cm
Collection of The Dalí Museum Archives,
St Petersburg, Florida

Fig. 41
Man Ray, *This is the Domain of Rrose Sélavy. View from an Aeroplane (Dust Breeding)*, 1921.
Littérature, New Series, no. 5,
1 October 1922

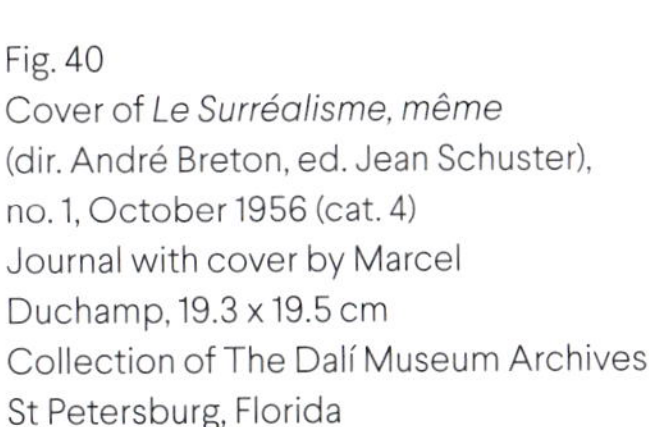

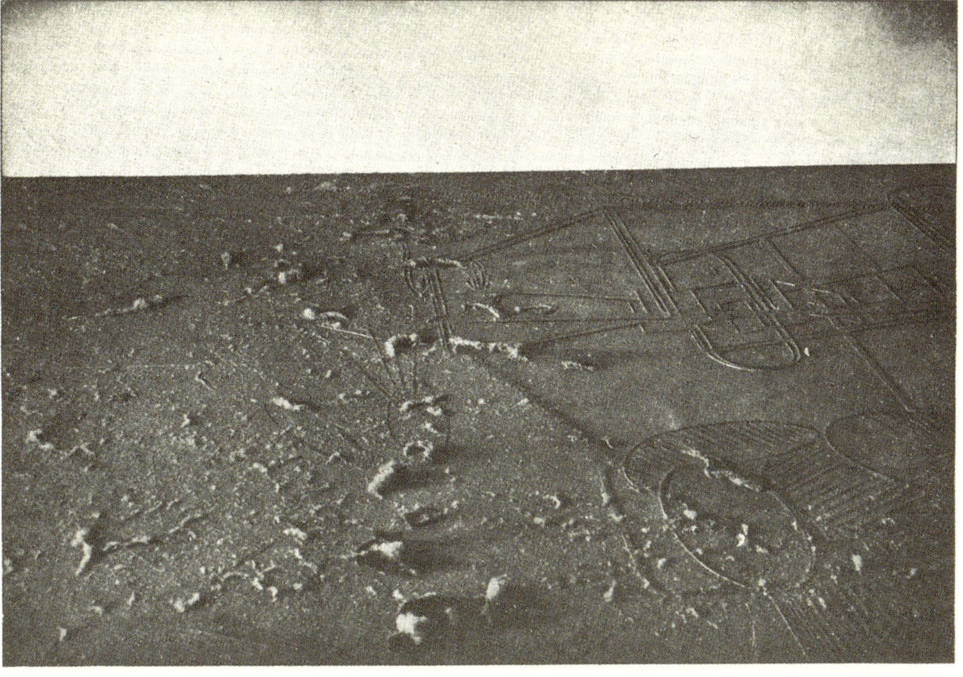

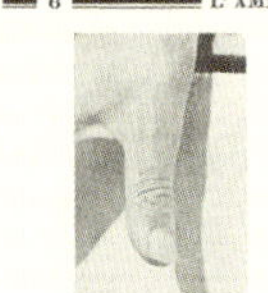
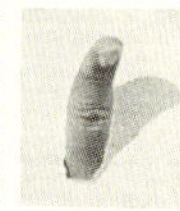
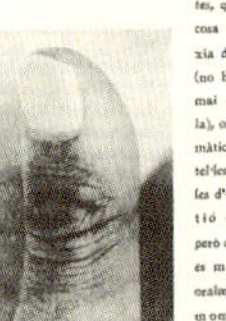

...L'alliberament dels dits...
per Salvador Dalí

...l'alliberament dels dits...

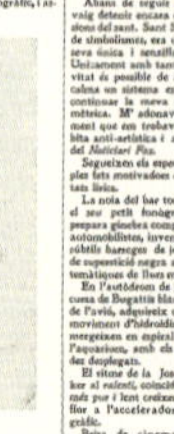

---

revealed that all was constructed 'from the close-up filming of the metallic band round a Biro, the band pitted and stained with uric acid'.[9]

Whereas Duchamp's abandonment of painting was permanent, Dalí's was only temporary, but his views about photography, film and painting were no less vehemently expressed in texts he wrote between 1927 and 1929. During this period he progressively undermined in his own work the conventions of oil painting, culminating in the anti-paintings of 1928 (cat. 56), after which he stopped painting for a time. The final issue of *L'Amic de les Arts* (31 March 1929), whose editorial board Dalí had joined in November 1927, was illustrated exclusively with photographs. No editor was named for the issue, which was the swansong of the avant-garde journal, a Dada-like finale. Dominated by Dalí, the issue looks quite different from earlier ones; modelled broadly on constructivist principles, it resembles Moholy-Nagy's Bauhaus book *Painting Photography Film* (1925/27) with black bars dividing texts and extensive use of bold fonts. One of the photographs from *Painting Photography Film* is borrowed, but re-titled as 'Eye of an Elephant' (the original was 'Eye of a marabou', with the caption 'There is extraordinary concentration in a singled-out detail'). The photograph is a cropped close-up, with the photographer reflected as a tiny figure in the cornea. *Painting Photography Film* had a profound effect on Dalí and its influence is felt throughout his texts on photography and film in the 1920s. Moholy-Nagy insisted on the ability of the photographic camera 'to *make visible* existences which cannot be perceived or taken in by our optical instrument, the eye', seeing photography as the beginning of what he called 'objective vision'.[10] 'Pure objectivity of the little camera,' Dalí wrote. It was the poetic and imaginative

---

L'AMIC DE LES ARTS 4

PUNT I APART
per Lluis Montanyà

¿No haveu provat mai, tot passejant, en una nit xafogosa d'estiu, amb alguns amics per un lloc una mica elevat dels suburbis, de destriar els sorolls de la ciutat? Sembla, de primer moment, impossible, que el brunziment continu que, malgrat de l'hora avançada, es desprèn lentament — amb una calma cansada — de la urbs, pugui ésser descompost, analitzat. Les mil remors que el formen, arriben a vosaltres com un conglomerat únic, aparentment indestriable i compacte. Fixeu-vos-hi, però, una mica. No us costarà gaire, al cap d'uns minuts d'atenció sostinguda, d'anar separant — ara l'un, ara l'altre — l'udol apagat de les sirenes del port, el fregadís dels neumàtics damunt l'asfalt dels passeigs, el ressò convergent de les veus i dels passos multiplicats dels vianants, la nota lleugerament estrident de les campanetes dels tramvies, la veu ronca i impertinent dels clacksons, el xiulet remot d'algun tren. Més aprop, el lladruc d'un ca neguitós en una casa veïna, el cant irònic dels grills que cerquen l'amor sota l'herba dels marges... I, de tant en tant, un compàs — ràpid i fugitiu — de silenci gairebé absolut.

Amb les idees, les opinions i els punts de vista personals, hom pot lliurar-se a un exercici semblant. I és molt convenient, per a la formació espiritual pròpia, de fer-ho amb certa freqüència. De procedir a una minuciosa revisió de valoracions internes. Tot sol amb si mateix. Amb una decidida voluntat de deixar de banda tota manera de pensar que no sigui autènticament pròpia, tot el pòsit d'una cultura sedimentària — d'aluvió -- que, mal que no volguem, ofega el millor de nosaltres mateixos. De destriar dintre el nostre món interior, la part original i la part subreptíciament sobrevinguda. De cercar els nostres elements vius bàsics. D'arribar a les veritats primàries, essencials, ocultes sota espesses capes de brossa. Per aconseguir-ho, cal acarar-se decididament amb el Jo, amb una absoluta independència de criteri. Situar-se per damunt de totes les èpoques, prescindir de tota teoria ultrancera i rebutjar tot partit pres favorable a cap tendència.

...Aleshores, algunes idees ben precises, han aparegut, amb una claredat extraordinària, llampecs vívissims damunt un cel gris plom.

Deixem-les descarnades, tal com es presenten, sense intentar d'ordenar-les ni de classificar-les :

DIVERSITAT ABSOLUTA DE LA LITERATURA I LA POESIA... ESTERILITAT DE TOTA LITERATURA GRATUITA... INCAPACITAT CREIXENT DE LA LITERATURA COM A VEHICLE DE POESIA... PARASSITISME SOCIAL DE L'ESCRIPTOR INDOTAT... INUTILITAT I DESTORB DE TOTA TEORIA ARTÍSTICA O LITERÀRIA «APRIORÍSTICA»... VALOR ÚNICA DE L'INDIVIDU COM A DOCUMENT I COM A ORIENTACIÓ... PREDOMINI DE LA QUALITAT INTRÍNSECA EN TOTA OBRA HUMANA... INTENSITAT POÈTICA ACTUAL DE LES ACTIVITATS AL MARGE DE TOTA VOLUNTAT ESTÈTICA... POSICIÓ DIDÀCTICA I ACTIVA DE LA VERTADERA LITERATURA...

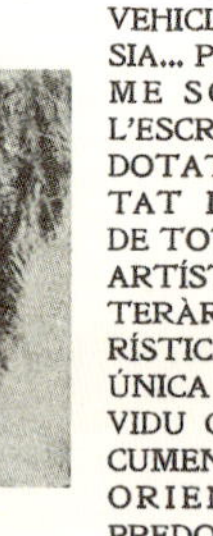

Provem, ara, de destacar-ne i comentar-ne algunes.

Hi ha dues coses molt diferents, que arriben potser a complementar-se metafísicament, però que no tenen res a veure l'una amb l'altra. Les anomenarem, per entendre'ns (sempre aquesta limitació insuportable de les paraules, que han perdut ja llur vertader sentit, que estan prostituïdes, ¡inservibles! —) L'ARTISTA i L'ESCRIPTOR. Entre ambdós està situat EL LITERAT, que no és absolutament res. L'ARTISTA, tant se val que sigui pintor, com poeta, com músic, com fotògraf, com cineasta, com que es lliuri a qualsevulga de les altres activitats espirituals creades, o que puguin crear-se en el futur. La

possibilities of this 'objective vision', however, that Dalí stressed. 'Photography slides with continual imagination over new events….' While this indicates his interest in Surrealism, Dalí is perfectly aware of the potential challenge to the Surrealist notion of automatism: 'Photographic imagination, your brain waves are faster and more agile than the murky processes of the subconscious!' Interwoven in the idea of 'Objective vision' for Dalí are poetry and the machine aesthetic: 'The photographic lens can caress the cold delicacy of white toilets.'

Early in 1929 Dalí joined Buñuel in Paris to shoot their film *Un Chien andalou* and at the same time wrote the 'Documentals' (Documentaries), a series of short dispatches from Paris to Spain. He was to start painting again later that spring, in a new and unpainterly manner (*The First Days of Spring*; cat. 59). The Documentaries are purely objective, 'anti-literary' accounts of things seen or heard, including statistics that recall passages from Louis Aragon's *Paris Peasant* (1926). All description, he writes, 'becomes immoral next to the marvellous means of photography and cinema'. Painting, he is then of the opinion, is among the innumerable 'defunct artistic means and mechanisms'. There are 30,000 painters in Paris and 20,000 cows. 'I have been in Paris twenty days,' he writes in the same text, 'I have only spoken to three people who are interested, or claim to be interested, in painting; not a single one who does not take a strong interest in cinema.'[11]

Duchamp's relatively short-lived involvement with film in the 1920s was, he always claimed, motivated by an interest in the purely optical effects that only film could realise (views expressed well before those of Moholy-Nagy). 'Cinema amused me above all for its optical aspect. Instead of making a machine that turned as I had done in New York, I said to myself: why not turn a film? It would be much simpler. I wasn't interested in making cinema as such, it was a more practical means of arriving at my optical results.'[12] Nonetheless as an admired and watched member of the avant-garde in the early 1920s, his interest in film commanded attention. The former Dadaist Hans Richter's magazine *G* (fig. 45), which highlighted experimental activity in all mediums including architecture and film, and covered approaches including Dada, Constructivism, Surrealism and all kinds of abstraction, announced that Duchamp was using his *Rotary Demisphere* to record a short film.[13]

Duchamp's experiments with film were certainly closely related to the 'optical machines', the *Rotary Glass Plates* (1920) and *Rotary Demisphere (Precision Optics)* (1925). He wrote to his sister Suzanne and brother-in-law Jean Crotti in the autumn of 1920 describing both the first of his optical machines (the *Rotary Glass Plates*) and the camera. 'I've made a "monocle". It's a thing that rotates at top speed driven by an electric motor – highly dangerous – I almost killed Man Ray with it. I hope to take some

photos of it and send them to you. I've had a "Moving Picture Camera" for six months now, but it's so expensive (the film) that I have to space out my cinematographic outpourings.'[14]

The relationship between movement and representation had fascinated Duchamp for a long time, not only in *Nude Descending a Staircase* but also the *Chess Players* (cat. 49), and had taken literal physical form in *Bicycle Wheel* (cat. 77). In the five years between acquiring his Moving Picture Camera and the film *Anémic cinéma* he experimented with various purely optical affects obtained through motion. With the mechanical contraption *Rotary Glass Plates*, the separate blades set along the axis, each painted with segments of a circle, when spun, produce the illusion of continuous concentric circles on one plane. Subsequently Duchamp reversed the effect, so that rather than achieving the illusion of circles in one plane from individual elements in depth, he devised disks bearing various forms of eccentric circles that when in rotation look like spirals and give the effect of depth from a flat surface. Apparently the first experiments with these took place at Puteaux in 1921. He wrote to his friends the Stettheimers on 1 September 1921: 'I'm trying to get some cinema effects with my camera. I hope to bring back a few feet to N.Y.'

He fixed sketches of spirals onto a bicycle wheel and filmed them with the Moving Picture Camera he had bought in New York.[15] This was still early days for the handheld movie camera, and while the model Duchamp owned is not known, the film was probably turned with a hand crank. 'A return to the hand, one might say,' he commented to Cabanne.[16]

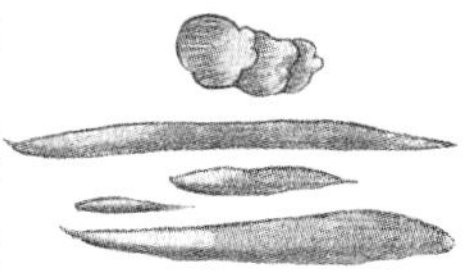

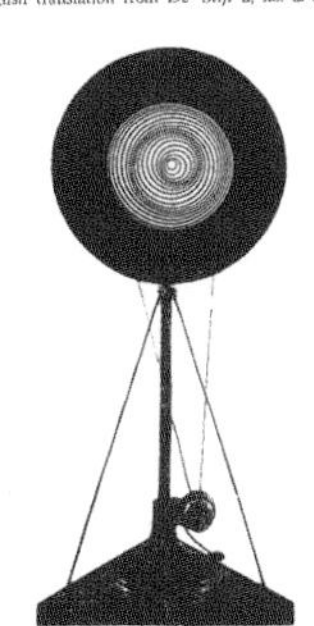

218

reason of music, the ultimate *form* . . . does not this interest you, **except as a by-product**.

Improvisors!

As I have already said, my Ballett Mécanique has under no circumstances, and at no point a single motion or movement that does not come out of *time*.

For the first time on earth *time* has been *used* under its fundamental principles in the single art in which it is fundamentally conceived . . . or better, in the single art which is fundamentally conceived out of *time*. **Time is the very stuff out of which life is made.**

([Abridged German] Translation: Heinz Umbehr.)
[English translation from *De Stijl* II, no. 12 (1925)]

Marcel Duchamp, le plus parisian, used this device — a moving disk of concentric circles that produces spirals as it rotates — to record a short film.

SHORTWAVE LIFE

Vossische Zeitung:

"The French researcher Georges Lakhovsky presented to the Académie des sciences in Paris the results of his research into the origin of life.

"He reached the conclusion that the basis of organic existence is infinite shortwaves at infinitely high frequency. The combination of an immense number of waves of various lengths — voilà, that is life. And the shorter the wave, the higher the order of the creature.

"This explains a wide variety of mysterious phenomena in the animal world, which, until now, have conveniently been called 'instinct.' For example, the reason migratory birds can orient themselves with scientific precision is, according to Lakhovsky, due to a small goniometric device built into their bodies, as it were, which is able to register certain waves that are much too long for humans to notice. The difference between one organic specimen and another — between a human being and a sparrow, say — lies in the difference in 'tuning' that results from the interplay of all the waves.

"All that remains is to build an apparatus that is able to pick up these infinitely short waves."

DIMENSION †

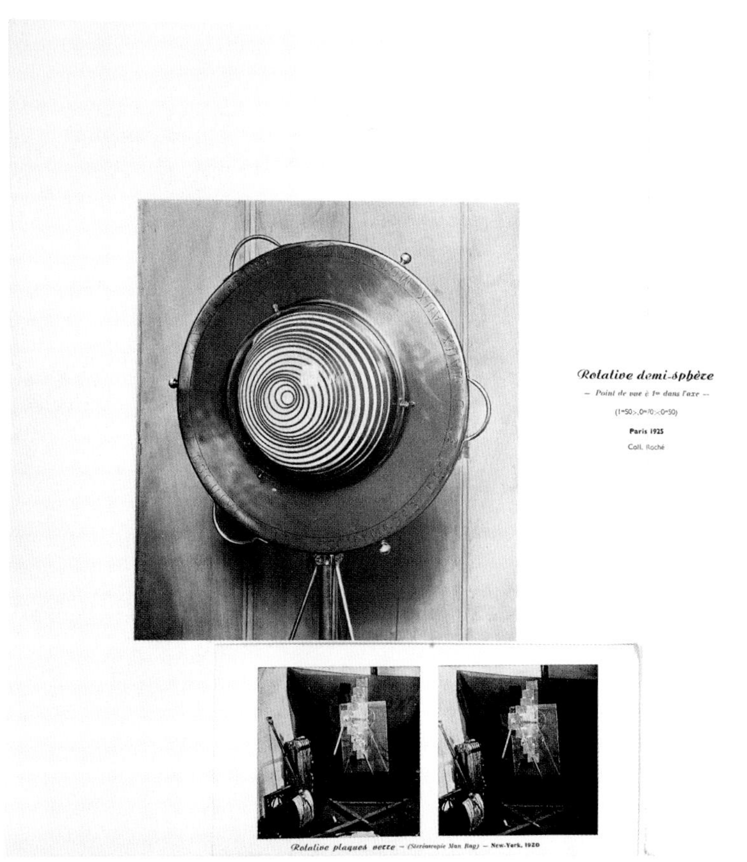

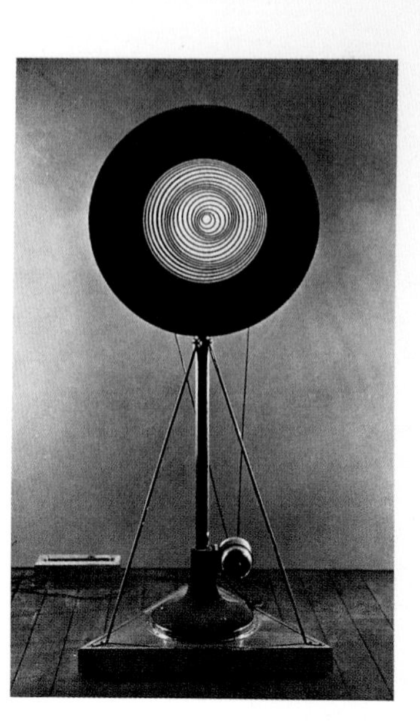

To the Arensbergs on 15 November 1921 he announced that he had made 'a bit of film, short' that he would bring with him to New York. Although still working on his *Large Glass*, and already beginning to play chess seriously, film briefly seemed to offer not only a form of expression but modest employment. 'I intend to find a "job" in cinema – not as an actor, rather as an assistant cameraman.'[17]

A failed film project featuring the second mobile construction, *Rotary Demisphere* (fig. 46), attempted to push the visual illusion of the spinning circles/spiral even further. Duchamp and Man Ray attempted to make a stereoscopic film, using two synchronised cameras filming *Rotary Demisphere* from slightly different viewpoints, one using green film, the other red, which would produce a three-dimensional effect when viewed through anaglyphic spectacles. This would therefore have doubled the illusionistic effect; we would have seen the way the black eccentric circles on the demisphere appear to pulse forwards and backwards and at the same time the sphere itself in 3D. The particular stereoscopic effect known as anaglyphic continued to interest Duchamp, and just before he died he was planning a 'handmade anaglyph' (red and green) of the chimney for his new summer home at Cadaqués. The stereoscopic film itself was ruined in the developing process and only a few frames were saved (fig. 47).

The disks and the puns that eventually formed *Anémic cinéma* were developed over the next few years. Seven sketches for concentric circles/spiral forms were produced in 1923, and eventually ten disks were used for *Anémic cinéma*, where they alternate with nine disks inscribed with puns. This, the only complete film Duchamp made, in collaboration with Man Ray and Marc Allégret, was first shown at the Fifth Avenue Cinema in New York in the late autumn of 1926. But *Anémic cinéma* – the name both pun and anagram – is more than pure optics. On one register, the disks with puns, lettered white on a black ground, operate, by analogy with silent film, as 'intertitles'. The viewer is invited alternately to read and to look.[18] But the interaction between word and image also sets up a contrast between verbal and visual illusion, the puns operating on language and rendering it unstable just as the spinning circles pulse in and out. The puns, which Duchamp began to publish as Rrose Sélavy in *Littérature*, also often relate more or less obliquely to sexual drives and the erotic. One reads: 'Avez-vous déjà mis la moëlle de l'épée dans le poêle de l'aimée?' ('Have you put the marrow of the sword in the oven of your beloved?')[19] As Katrina Martin has suggested, the disks and puns bring together 'gyratory movement and idealist desire'.[20]

Un Chien andalou remains the greatest Surrealist film and had an immediate impact in Paris, not just on the Surrealists themselves but also on the

Fig. 46
Marcel Duchamp, *Rotative demi-sphère - Point de vue à 1m dans l'axe*.
Photographs of *Rotary Demisphere* (1925; motorised optical device: painted wood/ papier-mâché demisphere mounted on a black-velvet-covered disk; copper ring fitted with a Plexiglas dome; motor, pulley and metal stand, 148.6 x 64.2 x 60.9 cm) and stereoscopic photographs of *Rotary Glass Plates* (1920); produced in 1940 for the *Boîte-en-valise* (cat. 62), 32 x 24.5 cm. Collection Hummel, Vienna

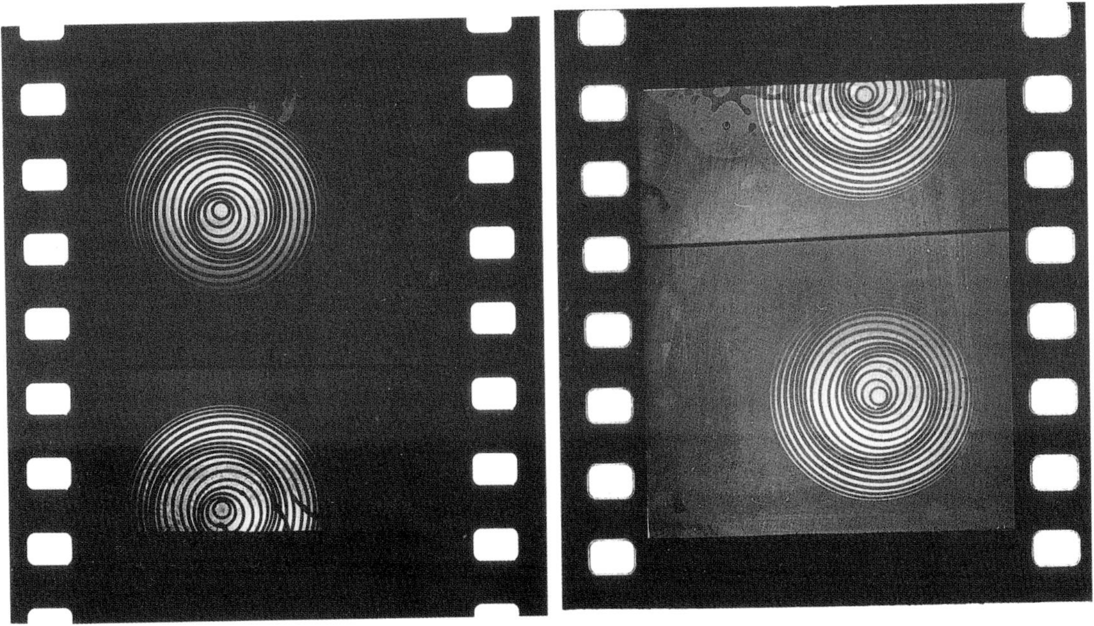

rival group gathered around Georges Bataille and the magazine *Documents*. This 'extraordinary' film, Bataille noted, 'is distinguished from banal avant-garde productions, with which one might be tempted to confuse it, in that the scenario predominates. Very explicit facts follow one another, without logical connections it's true, but penetrating so far into horror that the spectators are gripped as immediately as in adventure films. Gripped, even, by the throat: have they any idea, these spectators, where the authors of the film will stop? ... If Buñuel himself after shooting the sliced eye was ill for a week ... how can one not see how horror becomes fascinating – and also the only thing brutal enough to smash what suffocates.'[21] Bataille distinguished *Un Chien andalou* from contemporary avant-garde film – he presumably had in mind the relatively abstract films of Man Ray or the inconsequential modernism of Léger's *Ballet mécanique* – comparing *Un Chien andalou* rather to adventure films. Dalí repeatedly expressed his enthusiasm for popular cinema, for instance in 'Film-arte, film antiartístico'.[22] The first topic in a new column on 'Les Arts' in *L'Amic de les Arts* in March 1928 argued that cinema was strictly industrial and anonymous, and that its 'Anti-artistic beauty and poetry' were the 'result of absolute standardisation like the car, plane, photograph'.[23] The best ('anti-artistic') cinema so far were the two-reel comic films of Langdon, Chaplin and Keaton. These films 'Move the

masses and are considered the height of absurdity and lack of art by *putrefacts*.'[24] To the comic films Dalí added 'documentary film, type Fox News, and scientific film, of unerring emotion: plants growing, processes of fecundation, microscopy, natural history, underwater vegetation etc. etc.' It is interesting that in *Un Chien andalou* the fast-paced cutting, close-ups and unexpected juxtapositions draw on the gags in comic films but also from the kind of film proposed by Moholy-Nagy in *Painting Photography Film*. 'Dynamic of the Metropolis' is a sketch for a film about the rhythm and brutal pace of the modern city, aspirations which, Moholy-Nagy noted, were subsequently realised in Walter Ruttman's *Berlin: Symphony of a City* (1927). There are echoes of its visual dynamism in *Un Chien andalou*, with the difference that this film, which 'would not have existed without Surrealism', has a scenario rooted in cinematic facts that, like a dream, convey the reality of desires. So although it conforms fully to what Moholy-Nagy called the 'FILMIC', 'optical effects proper to the film alone', with for instance the succession of metaphorical intercutting between eye, razor, moon and cloud in the opening sequence, followed by the horrific close-up of the cut eye, *Un Chien andalou* is by no means 'purely visual'.[25] Although so different in appearance, both *Un Chien andalou* and *Anémic cinéma* explore the relationship between looking and desire in unique and purely 'filmic' ways.[26]

Fig. 47
Marcel Duchamp, *Frames from an Uncompleted Stereoscopic Film*, 1925. Film frames with holder, 9.6 x 18.5 cm. Collection Arturo Schwarz, Milan

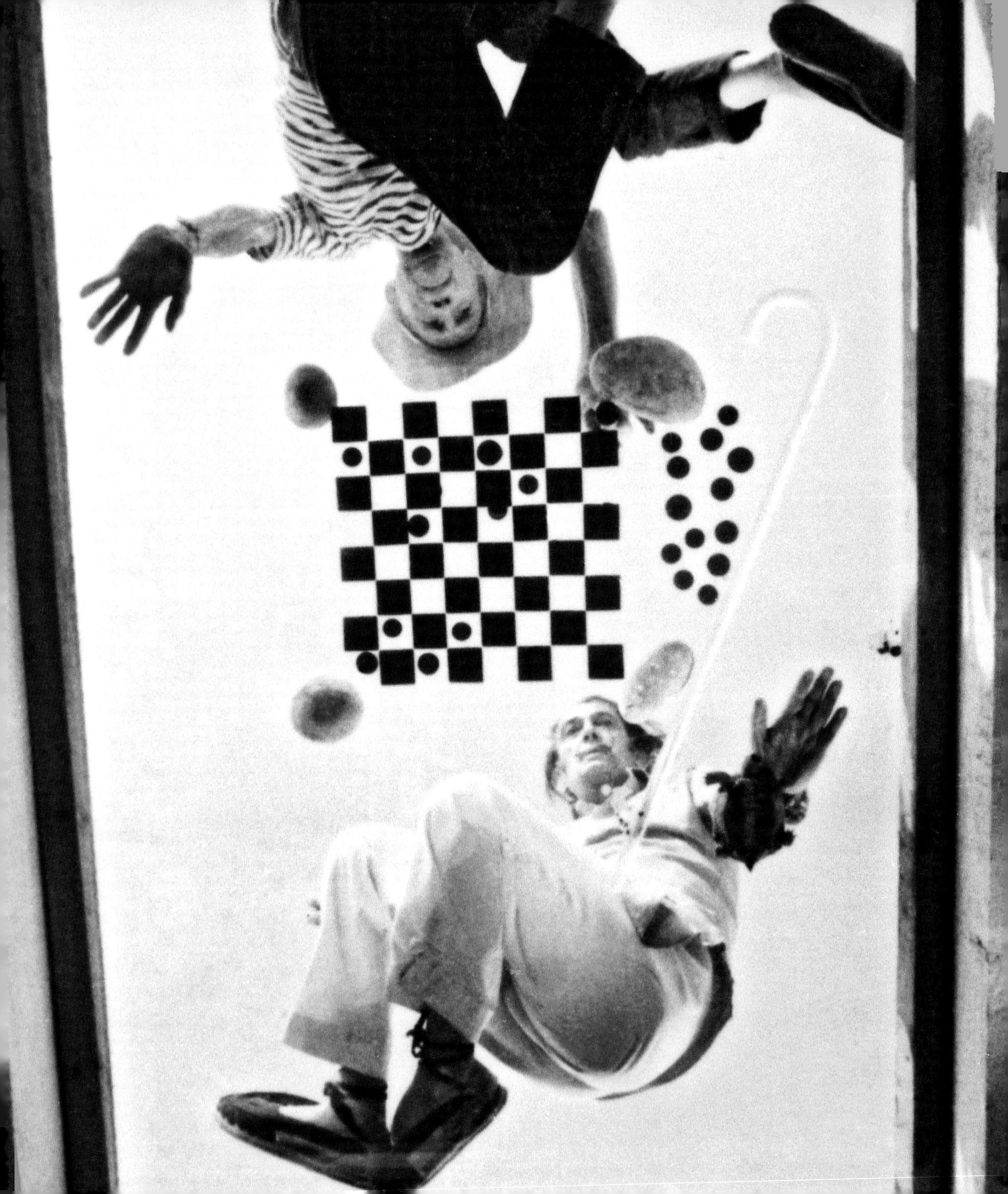

A CHESS GAME
PILAR PARCERISAS

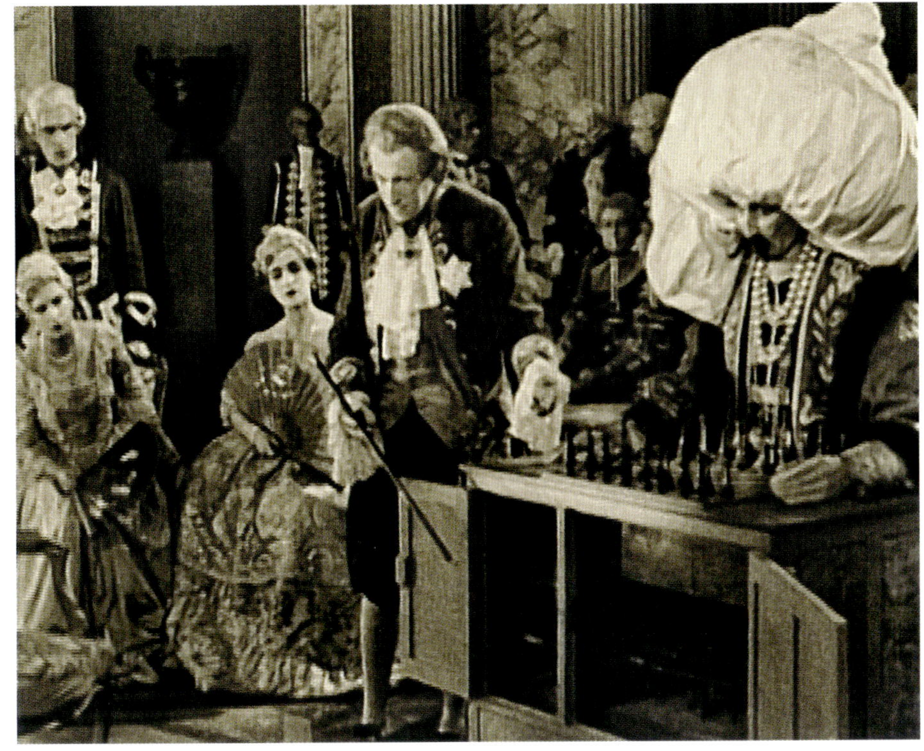

Fig. 48
Baron von Kempelen (Charles Dullin)
presents his chess-playing automaton to
the Russian Imperial Court. Still from the
film *Le Joueur d'échecs* (dir. Raymond
Bernard), 1926–27.
Photoplay Productions Ltd

Opposite: detail of cat. 42

Walter Benjamin begins his essay *On the Concept of History* with a description of the chess-playing automaton that Wolfgang von Kempelen presented to Maria Theresa of Austria in 1770, which was the inspiration for Edgar Allan Poe's story 'Maelzel's Chess Player' (1836). Known as the 'Turk', this automaton won games against Benjamin Franklin, Catherine II of Russia and even Napoleon, and was acclaimed as the first machine capable of beating a human being. Benjamin writes: 'There was once, we know, an automaton constructed in such a way that it could respond to every move by a chess player with a countermove that would ensure the winning of the game. A puppet wearing Turkish attire and with a hookah in his mouth sat before a chessboard placed on a large table. A system of mirrors created the illusion that this table was transparent on all sides. Actually, a hunchbacked dwarf – a master at chess – sat inside and guided the puppet's hand by means of strings. One can imagine a philosophic counterpart to this apparatus. The puppet, called "historical materialism" is to win all the time. It can easily be a match for anyone if it enlists the services of theology, which today, as we know, is small and ugly, and has to keep out of sight.'[1] Dialectical materialism was the machine that moved and gave meaning to history, as in a game of chess.

Automata, mostly created as entertainments to divert and amuse kings and queens, were the forerunners of the imaginary machines that appear in literary fiction as artefacts that simulate sentient human life. What we have come to know as *machines célibataires* held a special fascination for the Surrealists, and 'celibate machines' of one kind or another were created by Alfred Jarry, Edgar Allan Poe, Raymond Roussel, Lautréamont, Franz Kafka and Marcel Duchamp.

Michel Carrouges defined the *machine célibataire* as a fantastic image that transforms love into the mechanics of death, and analysed the myth of such artefacts as a union of the empire of machinism and the realm of terror.[2] The Surrealists adopted as a slogan a phrase from Lautréamont's *Les Chants de Maldoror* (1869): 'the chance meeting on a dissecting table of a sewing machine and an umbrella!'

Opening Game: Raymond Roussel

Marcel Duchamp and Salvador Dalí were great admirers of Raymond Roussel (1877–1933). In 1912 Duchamp, with Picabia and others, attended a

performance of Roussel's *Impressions of Africa*, organised by Apollinaire at the Théâtre Antoine in Paris, and acknowledged it as an influence on the conception of *The Large Glass* (1915–23; fig. 81). In 1932 Dalí sent Roussel his film script *Babaouo* with a dedication and a request that he read and consider it. Roussel, an admirer of Jules Verne, of automatons and puppetry, was a model, an inspiration in his ability to construct literary beauty through the semantic force of his vocabulary. Homonyms or homophones enable apparently similar phrases to have radically different meanings and generate fictions in and of themselves. In his posthumously published *Comment j'ai écrit certains de mes livres* (1935) Roussel explains the genesis of his method and gives as an example two sentences in which key words utterly transform the meaning of the sentence with the change of a single letter: 'Les lettres du blanc sur les bandes du vieux billard' and 'Les lettres du blanc sur les bandes du vieux pillard'.[3] In Roussel words are double-bottomed boxes whose cunning mechanism creates an endless series of imaginary combinations. Foucault situated the experience of reading Roussel in 'the "tropological space" of the vocabulary', which inaugurates a *machine célibataire* of language.[4] This Rousselian model is a key to the word games of the Surrealists, and in particular to the work of Duchamp and Dalí.

By means of the paranoiac-critical method, Dalí made the pictorial surface the tropological space of his visual vocabulary, an irrational and delirious method that doubles the image on the basis of dream or a paranoid reality. Duchamp also makes *The Large Glass* a flat, transparent 'tropological' space, like the effect created by the mirror system on the chess table of Kempelen's 'Turk'.[5]

The Cubists had seen chess as a way of getting beyond the historical illusionism of classical perspective in the pursuit of a fourth dimension. For Duchamp chess was a way of getting beyond painting as a system of representation in his pursuit of a destiny for his own life. It was 'mechanical sculpture', a *machine célibataire* in which everything takes place in the brain: 'I wanted to put painting once again at the service of the mind.'[6] 'A game of chess is a visual and plastic thing,' he said to Pierre Cabanne,[7] and continued: 'In chess there are some extremely beautiful things in the domain of movement [...] It's the imagining of the movement or the gesture that makes the beauty, in this case. It's completely in one's grey matter.'[8] To Truman Capote's question 'Why isn't my playing chess an art activity?', Duchamp replied that 'a chess game is very plastic. You construct it. It's mechanical sculpture, and with chess one creates beautiful problems; and that beauty is made with the head and hands.'[9]

In the 1920s and 1930s a number of artists and writers composed imaginary and even utopian moves and manoeuvres for the ancient game. Raymond Roussel published his 'Mat du fou et du cavalier'

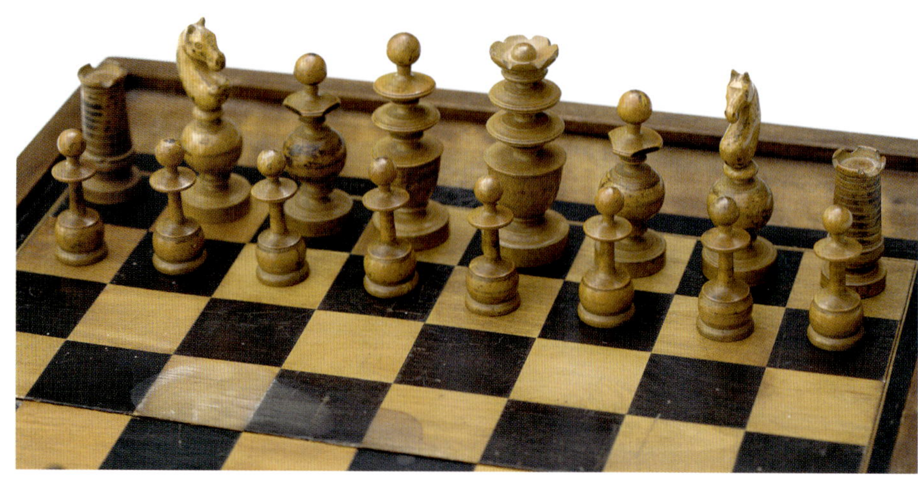

('Mate of the bishop and the knight'; 1932),[10] which was commented on by the grandmaster Savielly Tartakower, who played a match with Duchamp and is featured in Man Ray's 1933 suite of photographs *Le Monde des échecs*. In *Raymond Roussel et les échecs dans la littérature* (1933),[11] Tartakower considered the influence exerted by chess in the years when Duchamp was writing his impossible endgames. At the same time, the chess automaton described by Benjamin appeared in the plots of several novels and films. Tartakower refers to the film *Le Joueur d'échecs* (*The Chess Player*, 1927; fig. 48), directed by Raymond Bernard and based on the novel by Henry Dupuy-Mazuel,[12] which was inspired by the story of the 'Turk' in Kempelen's memoirs. This in turn provided the plot for the 1938 film by Jean Deville, also called *Le Joueur d'échecs*. Tartakower also mentions *Le Crime du fou d'échecs*

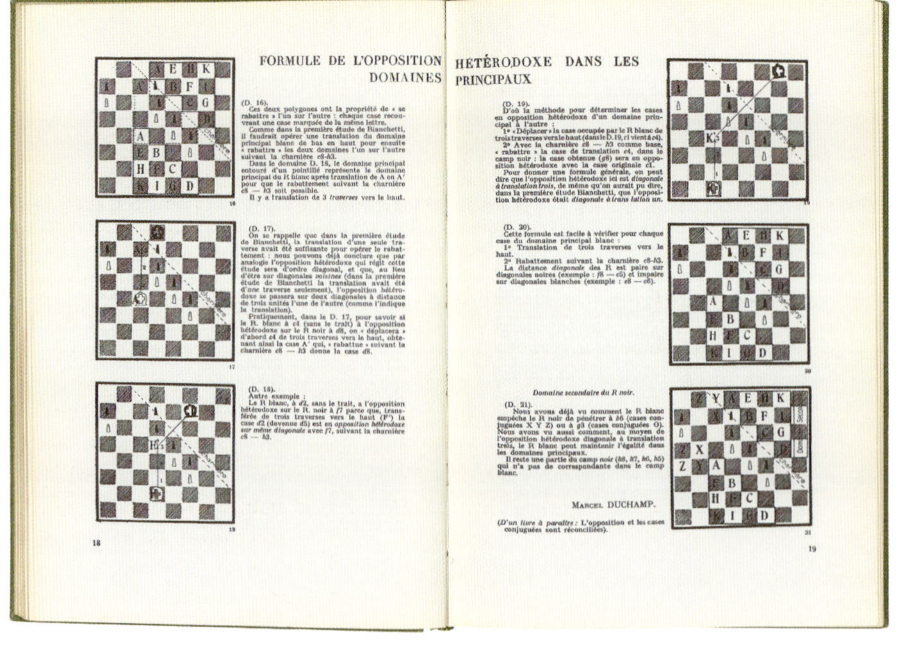

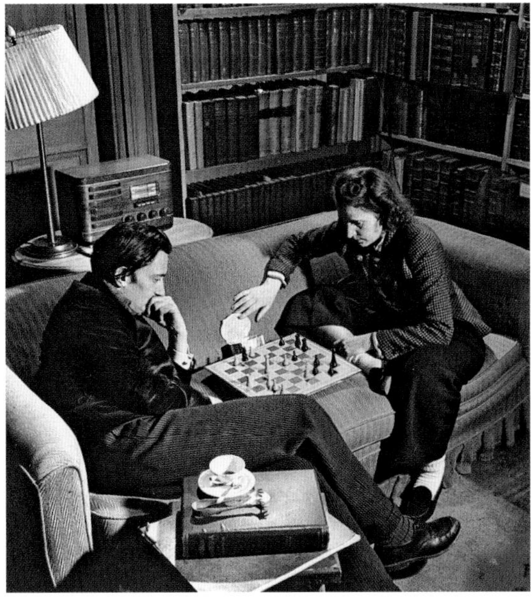

by S. S. Van Dine,[13] from 1930, and the Russian psychological novel that Vladimir Nabokov published in French as *La Défense Loujine* (1929–30) under the pseudonym W. Sirine.[14] Duchamp, Dalí and the Surrealist group would have been aware of these new books and films as they appeared in the Paris of their day. Stefan Zweig, who arranged Dalí's meeting with Sigmund Freud, also wrote *Chess Story*, also known as *The Royal Game* (1941), a novella about chess, a few months before his suicide in February 1942.

In 1932 Marcel Duchamp and Vitaly Halberstadt published their chess manual *L'Opposition et les cases conjugué*es *sont reconciliées* (fig. 50), which sets out a series of all but impossible endgames, with the presence of kings and pawns in the last stage of the match, in which the reconciliation of opposites is achieved.[15]

Middlegame: Against Picasso

In the 1940s the fervent passion for chess continued unabated. In 1940, when Gala and Salvador Dalí coincided with Marcel Duchamp at Coco Chanel's house in Arcachon, their shared refuge from the war, Dalí painted *Two Pieces of Bread Expressing the Sentiment of Love* (cat. 50), directly prompted by a game of chess between Gala and Duchamp. Two crumbling rounds of bread – one is doubled or crowned – are intercepted by a pawn that has fallen to the ground and found a place in the still-life that Dalí was painting. The presence of the pawn turns the picture into a proxy chessboard, introducing a vital tension into the *nature morte*. Are the pieces of bread perhaps the king and queen of the board? Or Gala and Dalí with an intruder, Duchamp, who arouses Dalí's jealousy, as had happened on Duchamp's first trip to Dalí's house in 1933.[16]

In the exhibition 'The First Papers of Surrealism' at the Whitelaw Reid mansion in New York in 1942,

Duchamp created links between the works hanging on the walls with yards of twine, emulating the movements of figures on a chessboard, and in 1943 he designed a portable *Pocket Chess Set*. In 1944 he and other artists installed chess in an art space with the exhibition 'The Imagery of Chess' at the Julien Levy Gallery in New York.

Duchamp had commenced the 1940s by closing his own portable museum, the *Boîte-en-valise* (cat. 62), to immerse himself in what was to be his final installation, *Étant donnés* (1946–66; fig. 76). He was gradually shutting down his already scanty artistic output and positioning himself even further, if possible, outside the competitive art world, creating the legend that he had abandoned art for chess. In the late 1940s and early 1950s the much younger Dalí faced up to Picasso, whom he depicted in terms of dynastic succession in the history of art in *Portrait of Pablo Picasso in the Twenty-first Century* (1947). In this picture the pedestal presents a double image of Velázquez combined with the head of Picasso as a monstrous ram, crowned by the rocks of Dalí's Cap de Creus: three stages of an art history in which Dalí puts himself forward as Picasso's successor. He reaffirmed this posture in his lecture 'Picasso and I' (1951), perhaps his major public offensive against his compatriot.[17]

Endgame: The End of the Western History of Art

In the late 1950s Marcel and Teeny Duchamp began to spend their summers in Cadaqués. They did so from 1958 until Duchamp's death in 1968, further strengthening their friendship with Dalí. In the art world the euphoric embrace of European Informalism and American Abstract Expressionism was cooling as new challenges emerged, and Dada and Surrealism seemed to have taken their place in history. The exhaustion of painting called for a founding anew and the beginning of a new era.

This pivotal moment in the history of art and the new questions it posed are perfectly reflected in the text that Dalí dedicated to Duchamp, 'The King and Queen Traversed by Swift Nudes',[18] its title taken from a picture Duchamp painted in May 1912, a few months after *Nude Descending a Staircase*. In the earlier Cubo-Futurist painting the chessboard king and queen are pierced by particles or corpuscles (the 'swift nudes') that pass through them like an electrical discharge, which Dalí regarded as heralding the decomposition of matter and the intra-atomic structure of the universe.

Painting had been transformed into a chessboard on which the future of art history was being played out. A photograph of Dalí and Duchamp playing on a transparent glass board (cat. 42) illustrates that development towards an endgame in the history of twentieth-century art. Taken from a low angle, the photograph foreshortens the figures, rather like the squared glass Dürer used as an aid to drawing perspective, and it is one of the unused shots from the

Fig. 49
Early French chess set used by Marcel Duchamp and his brothers (cat. 5)
Wood, 32 pieces, h. 6–10 cm
Private collection – Archives
Marcel Duchamp

Fig. 50
Marcel Duchamp and Vitaly Halberstadt, extract from *L'Opposition et les cases conjuguées sont réconciliées* (*Opposition and Sister Squares are Reconciled*), Brussels, 1932; published in *Le Surréalisme au service de la révolution* (*SASDLR*), 2, October 1930.
Collection of the Dalí Museum Archives, St Peterburg, Florida

Fig. 51
Gala and Salvador Dalí playing chess at Hampton Manor, April 1941.
Photograph by Eric Schaal.
The LIFE Images Collection

film *Autoportrait mou de Salvador Dalí* (1966) by Robert Descharnes and Jean-Christophe Averty.

In 'The King and Queen Traversed by Swift Nudes' (1959) Dalí celebrates Duchamp's gesture of putting a moustache on the *Mona Lisa* in his readymade *L.H.O.O.Q.*, and takes the title (*Elle a chaud au cul*, 'she has a hot ass') as an epitaph to modern painting. For Duchamp, the art to be bequeathed to posterity was to be assessed by its erotic quality, gauged as a temperature,[19] with Leonardo's *Mona Lisa* having the highest erotic temperature in the history of art and the masculinisation of the subject alluding to Freud's incestuous interpretation of the picture in his *Leonardo da Vinci and a Memory of His Childhood* (1910).

Dalí criticised the abstract painting of the 1950s as being derived from a bourgeois thought and a bourgeois revolution that led to the production of miles of decorative pseudo-painting: 'Now, after modern painting, a brave group has rushed at full speed to the brink of the most absolute nothingness, the condition for a pre-mystic state of mind, which

Tapié calls "another art: Kline, Tàpies, Millares, De Kooning, Mathieu".' It is here that Dalí formulates the question: 'Could we accede to a new dynasty, now, with *L.H.O.O.Q.*? I personally answer "yes".'[20]

Dalí accordingly proposed to re-found the history of art, and felt able to do so on the basis of Duchamp's Dadaist anarchism or of the *pompier* painting that he himself set out to revive.[21] In this endgame the two artists seem to be the kings on a board without pawns, in a utopian state of play worthy of *L'Opposition et les cases conjuguées sont reconciliées*: opposition and reconciliation before an endgame that must be resolved even from irreconcilable positions.

In 1967 the publisher Arthur A. Cohen asked Dalí to write a preface for the English edition of Pierre Cabanne's *Dialogues with Marcel Duchamp*, a proposal that delighted Duchamp. Dalí asked Albert Field, then a passionate cataloguer of Dalí's work, and in the St Regis Hotel in New York dictated to him the French text 'L'échecs, c'est moi' (dated January 1968),[22] with Field's English translation ('Chess, it's me') duly appearing in the Cabanne book in 1971.[23] In this text Dalí repeats himself, returning to the basic tenets of the article he had published in *Art News* in 1959. Most striking, perhaps, is the contention that Dada, Surrealism and Duchamp's readymades have been exhausted by their acceptance and popularity, and the call for artistic work to be 'produced convulsively [...] by hand', a nod to André Breton: 'Art will be made by hand or not at all.'[24]

Duchamp spent his entire life looking for the relationship between art and chess: 'If you start out playing chess when you are young, you'll still play chess when you grow old and die... It is a passion that accompanies you to your grave... It happened to me and very likely helped me to achieve what I wanted.'[25] At the end of his life he wanted to represent himself as a chess player, and he did so the year before his death with *Marcel Duchamp Cast Alive* (fig. 55), in which the bronze mask of his face looks down on the knight he designed in Buenos Aires in 1919, on a board with only three ranks.[26] Man Ray wrote on the day of Duchamp's death that his life had ended like a game of chess.[27]

For all their aesthetic differences, Dalí and Duchamp were both convinced of the need for an artistic 'machinism' that would be capable of giving rise to a new system of representation radically opposed to the movements in art generated by the bourgeois revolution, notably Impressionism and the other -isms it spawned. The painting machine in Roussel's *Impressions of Africa*, commented upon by Jean Ferry,[28] was a direct inspiration for Duchamp's *Large Glass*. Dalí was also influenced by Roussel as a source for his paranoiac-critical method, manifested in the double image. The chessboard has become a tropological space where representation can take place: a space without depth, as transparent as Dürer's glass, able to accommodate a fourth dimension.

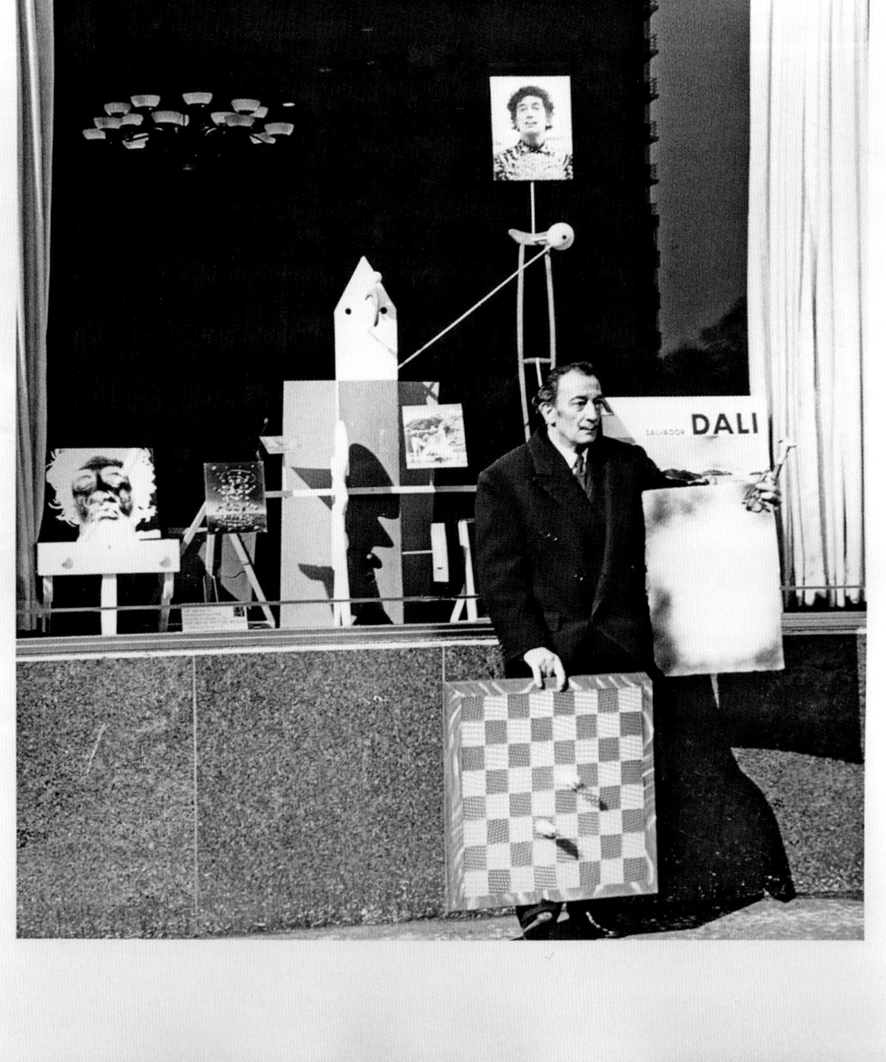

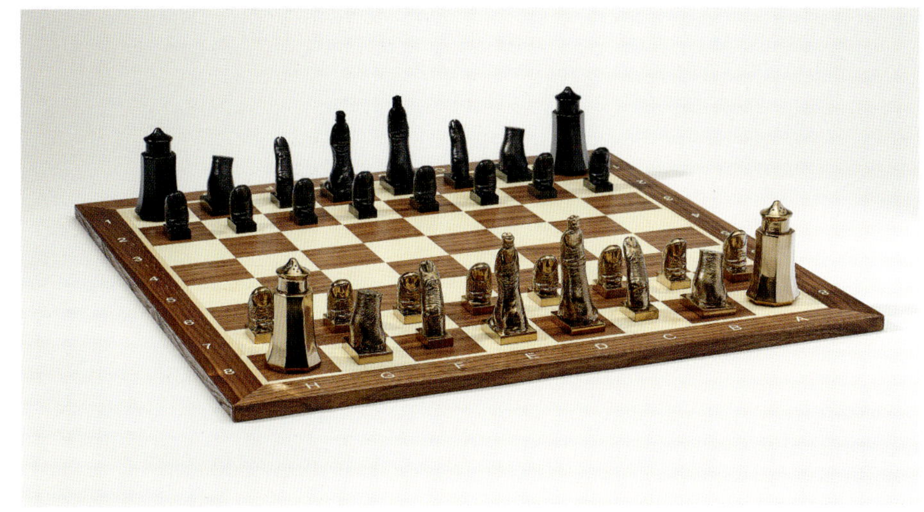

Dalí and Duchamp confronted the history of painting in a long and costly game of chess, opening new lines of development without moving from the board – a mathematical, geometric space, a machine of love and death, presided over by Gala and the Bride. In his endgame, Dalí sought to break out of Breton's old Surrealism and his own idea of putrefaction through the latest scientific theories of the disintegration of matter and Heisenberg's uncertainty principle, which contributed so much to the quantum physics that he saw in the swift corpuscles of the painting *The King and Queen Surrounded by Swift Nudes*, circulating on the board with the movements of the figures that Duchamp executed after he gave up painting. Duchamp, for his part, exchanged the art object for a gesture: the movement of chess pieces; and in another artistic gesture, in *Étant donnés* (fig. 76), transferred artistic responsibility to the spectator.[29] End of the game.

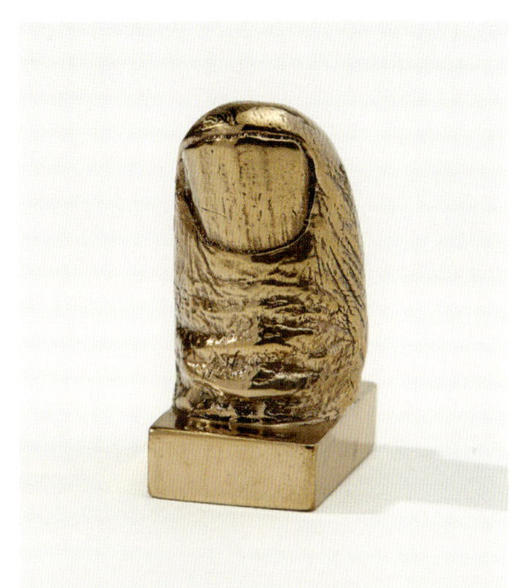

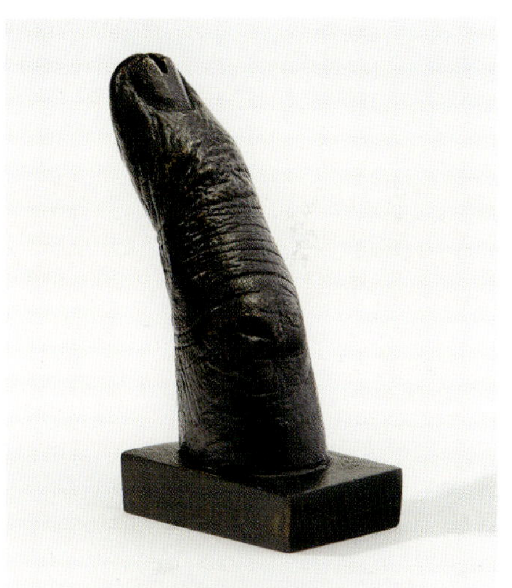

Top and centre: Figs 53a–c
After Salvador Dalí
Chess set made in homage to Marcel Duchamp, 1964; *c.* 1985 edition (cat. 7)
Edition by Barclay Gallery Ltd, for American Chess Foundation
32 pieces cast in polished light bronze and antique dark bronze. Full set, with details of individual pieces below.
Collection of The Dalí Museum, St Petersburg, Florida

Bottom left: Fig. 54
Marcel Duchamp
Note: '*Étude pour le Cavalier; Échiquier de poche 1943*' ('Study for Knight; Pocket Chess Set 1943'), 1943 (cat. 8)
Pencil on paper, 19.9 x 16.2 cm
Centre Pompidou, Paris. Musée national d'art moderne/Centre de création industrielle

Bottom right: Fig. 55
Marcel Duchamp, *Marcel Duchamp Cast Alive*, 1967. Bronze, onyx and black Belgian marble, 54.6 x 42.5 x 23.5 cm.
Cast by Editions les Maîtres, Ltd.
The Nelson-Atkins Museum of Art, Kansas City, Missouri. Acquired through the generosity of Mr and Mrs Louis Sosland, F73-53

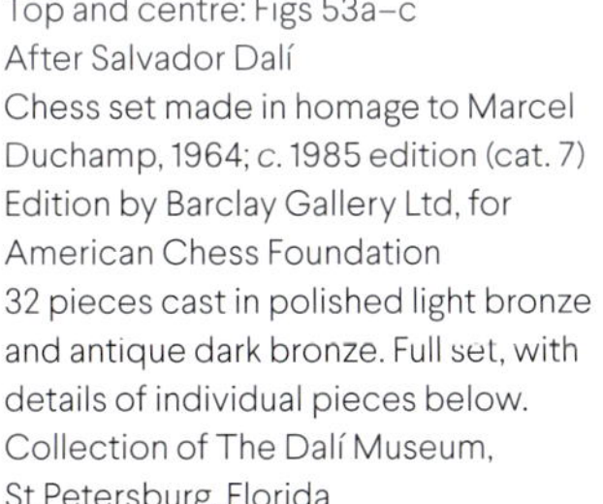

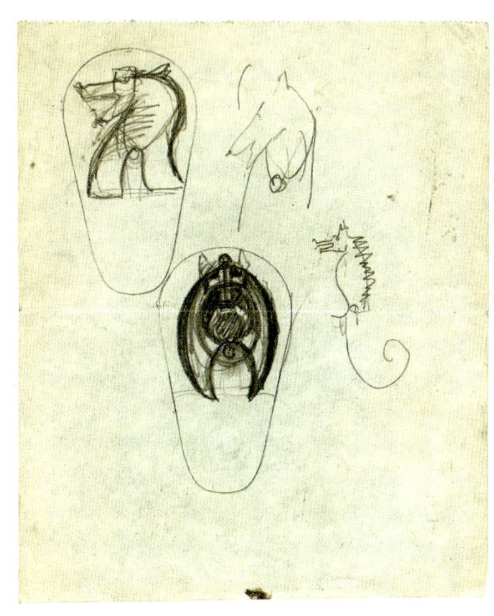

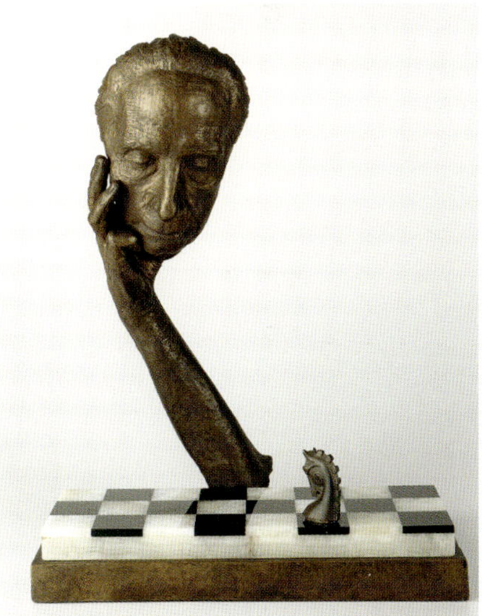

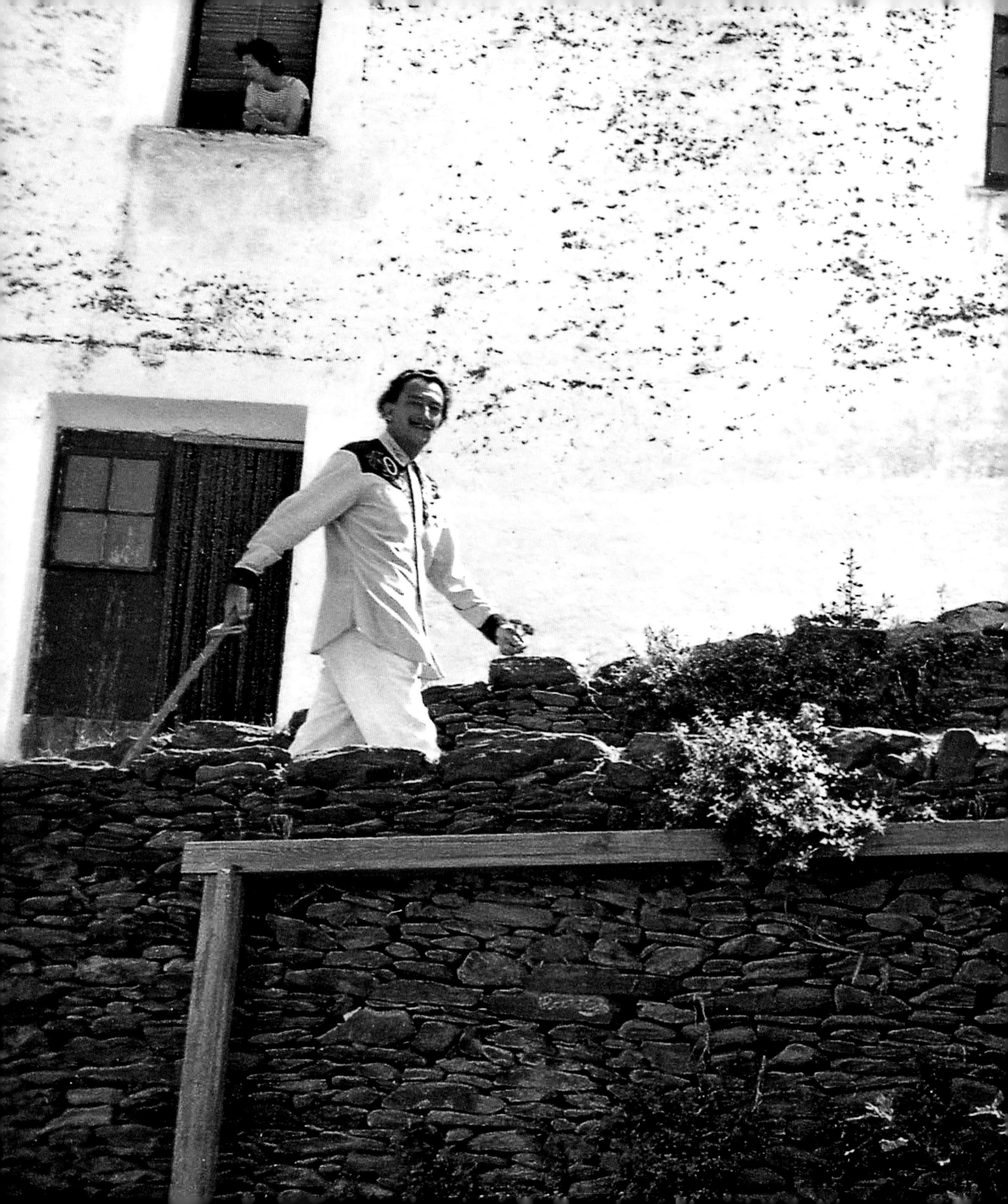

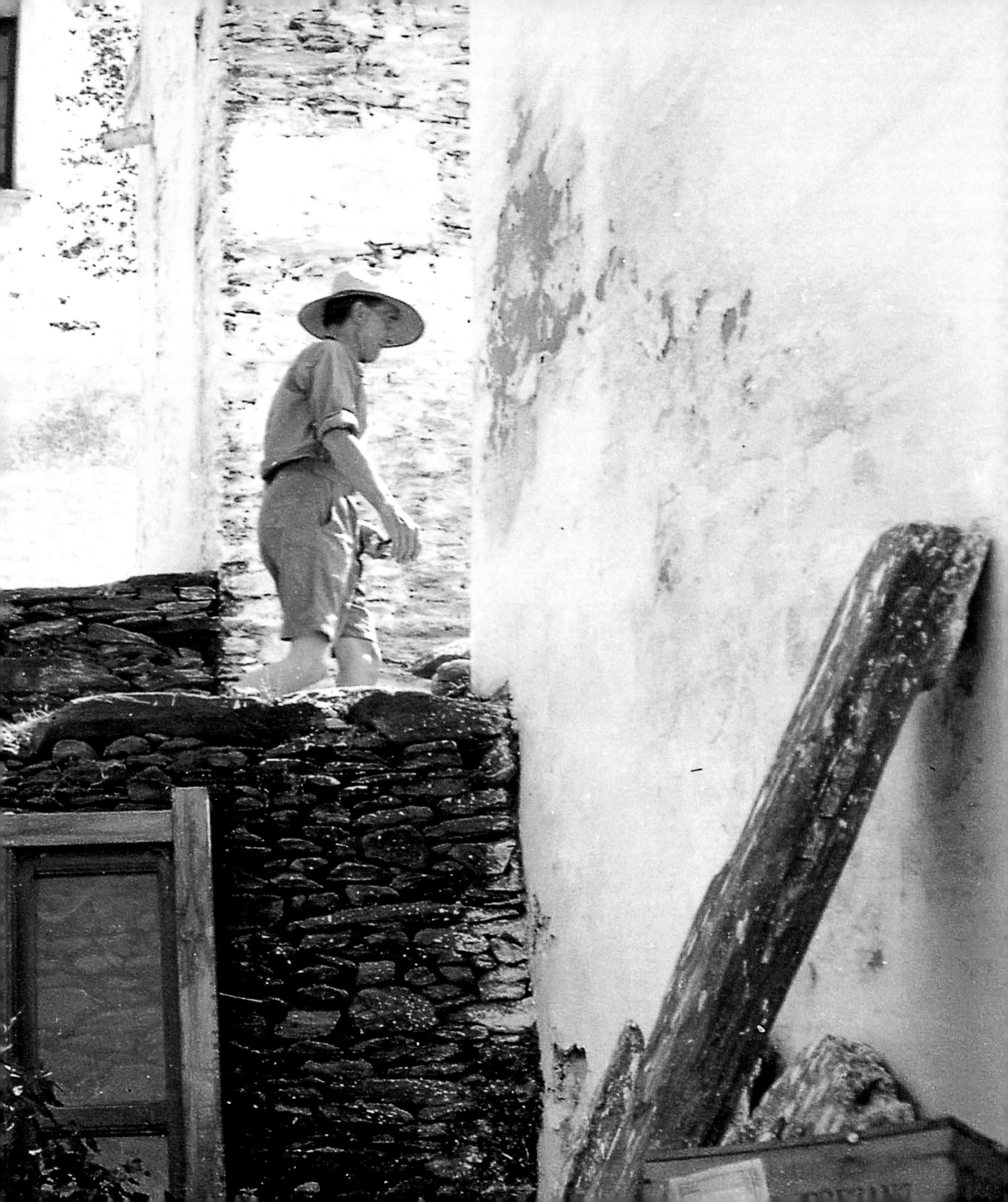

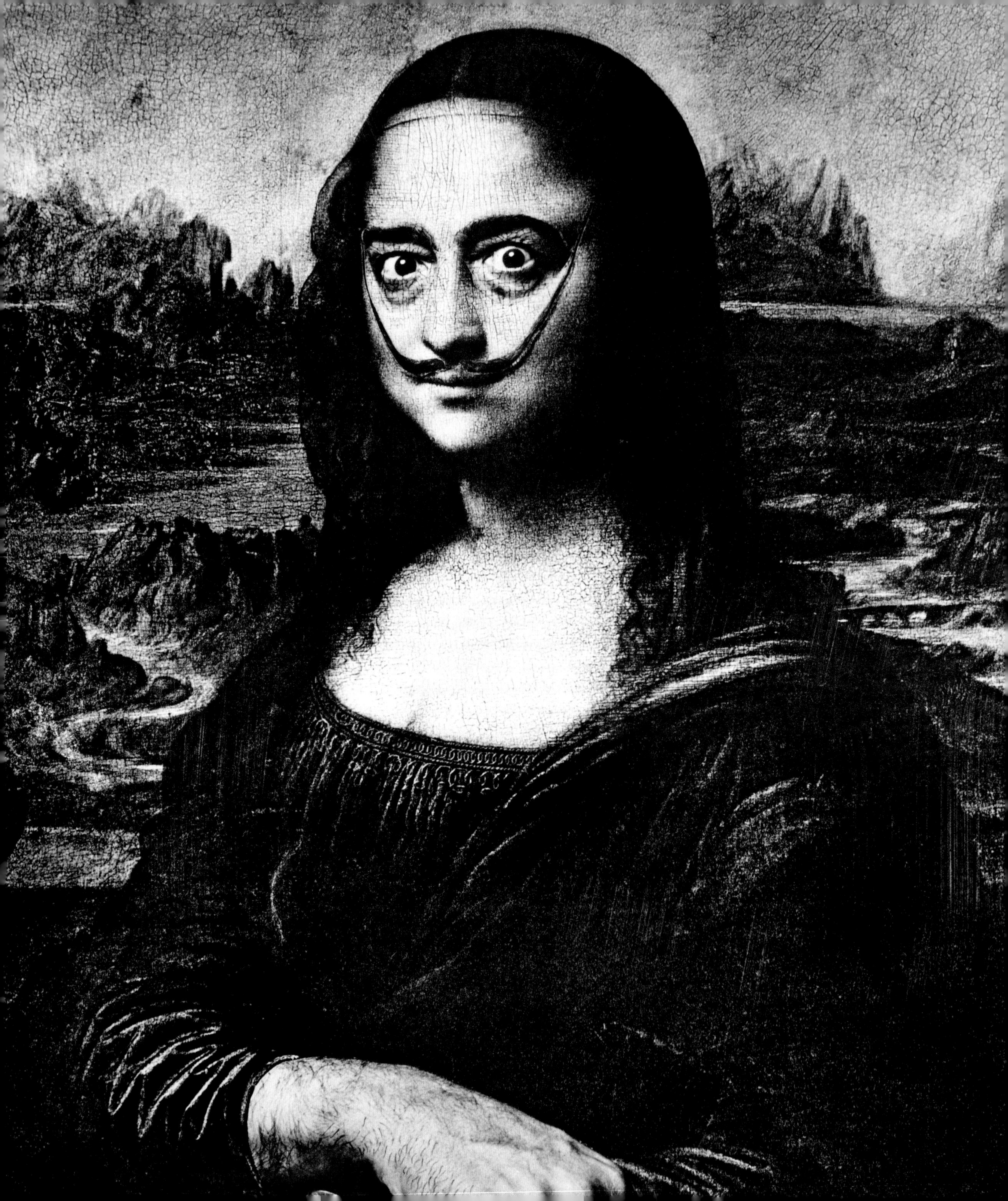

IDENTITY

IDENTITY
DAWN ADES

The long friendship between Dalí and Duchamp began in Paris in the context of Surrealism, but burgeoned at Cadaqués, where Duchamp spent his summers from 1958. He had first visited the picturesque Catalan seaside town in 1933, writing to his friend Man Ray: 'We are staying in a small but delightful house … ideal weather and charming *peseta* … Dalí is here with Gala and we see them often.'[1] Dalí had spent his summer holidays at Cadaqués as a child; his family had a holiday house there and his father used to rent a studio for him to paint in. In 1930 he bought a fisherman's cottage in the tiny village of Portlligat (cat. 9), a short walk over a headland from Cadaqués. This favoured place, frequently the setting for his paintings, is where he felt he belonged: 'I am home only here; elsewhere, I am camping out.'[2] Beyond Portlligat is Cap de Creus, the scene of many outings going back to his childhood, and of expeditions with Gala and Duchamp in 1933 and later years (cats 14–21). For Dalí Cap de Creus was a magical, mineral place, the easternmost extremity of Catalonia, where the Pyrenees descend to meet the sea.

Dalí was born and died in the nearby market town of Figueres, where his Theatre-Museum now is. From the balcony of the family house he could see the Ampurdan plain and the Bay of Roses, 'from which the calls to my vocation came to me and allowed me to escape from the bourgeois notarial universe'.[3]

This reference to the 'notarial universe' resonates with Duchamp, whose father, like Dalí's, was a notary. This important functionary has no real equivalent in Britain or the United States. Gertrude Stein, who knew both artists, believed in its significance: 'Dalí was a notary's son, in Europe the role in the arts played by sons of notaries is a very interesting one. They take the place of ministers' sons in America … They do everything they in the smaller towns run the auctions they make out all the legal papers … they give endless advice … there is always a notary's son they have a violence in freedom but are never free, that is what it is to be a notary's son. Jean Cocteau is one … the other day a lot of people were here and Marcel Duchamp and somebody said or he did that Marcel Duchamp was a notary's son oh I said that explains everything. Everything said Marcel and everybody burst out laughing but it is true it does, and Dalí is a notary's son….'[4] The two artists' portraits of their formidable fathers (cats 10, 11) were both painted at an early stage in careers lacking full paternal approval. Neither painted a solo portrait of his mother. Duchamp was 23 when he painted the portrait; he had followed his two older brothers from the family home in Rouen to become an artist in Paris in 1904 and enjoyed some success, exhibiting since 1909 at both the Salon des Indépendants and the Salon d'Automne. Dalí was 21 when he painted his father, and had resumed his studies at the Academy in Madrid having been temporarily expelled in 1923. Close at the time to the poet Federico García Lorca, he had his first one-man exhibition at the Dalmau Galleries in Barcelona in November 1925, where this portrait was exhibited.

Apart from having notaries for fathers, the two artists' family situations were different. Dalí was a much-cosseted only son, an older brother having died nine months and eleven days before his birth, with one younger sister, while Duchamp was one of six, with two older brothers and three younger sisters; four of these siblings became artists. Their father's disappointment when Duchamp's two older brothers abandoned professional medical and legal careers may have led them to change their names, Gaston to Jacques Villon, Raymond to Duchamp-Villon. However, he good-humouredly accepted their decision and Duchamp later spoke with admiration and warmth of his father's method of financial support, paying their expenses and meticulously docking the sums from their eventual inheritance. Dalí's well-documented early passion for painting was indulged, although his father allowed him to go to art school in Madrid in 1922 at the age of eighteen only on the condition that he take up an official career as an academic artist.

Neither Dalí nor Duchamp followed the prescribed route, nor did they opt straightforwardly for incorporation into the world of modern art, but asserted their independence in increasingly iconoclastic ways: perhaps the 'violence in freedom' to which Stein alluded. Duchamp made his last oil on canvas in 1918, *Tu m'* (fig. 87), although he continued to work on his glass painting until 1923. However, he had ceased to paint in a recognisably modern manner with his *Chocolate Grinder* of 1913, the same year he upended a bicycle wheel on a stool. In 1919 he graffitied the *Mona Lisa*, adding a moustache and beard to a chromolithograph of Leonardo's painting and the rude title *L.H.O.O.Q.*, 'with the idea of desecrating' this over-familiar icon (cat. 28). This was a private amusement, as were *Bicycle Wheel* (cat. 77)

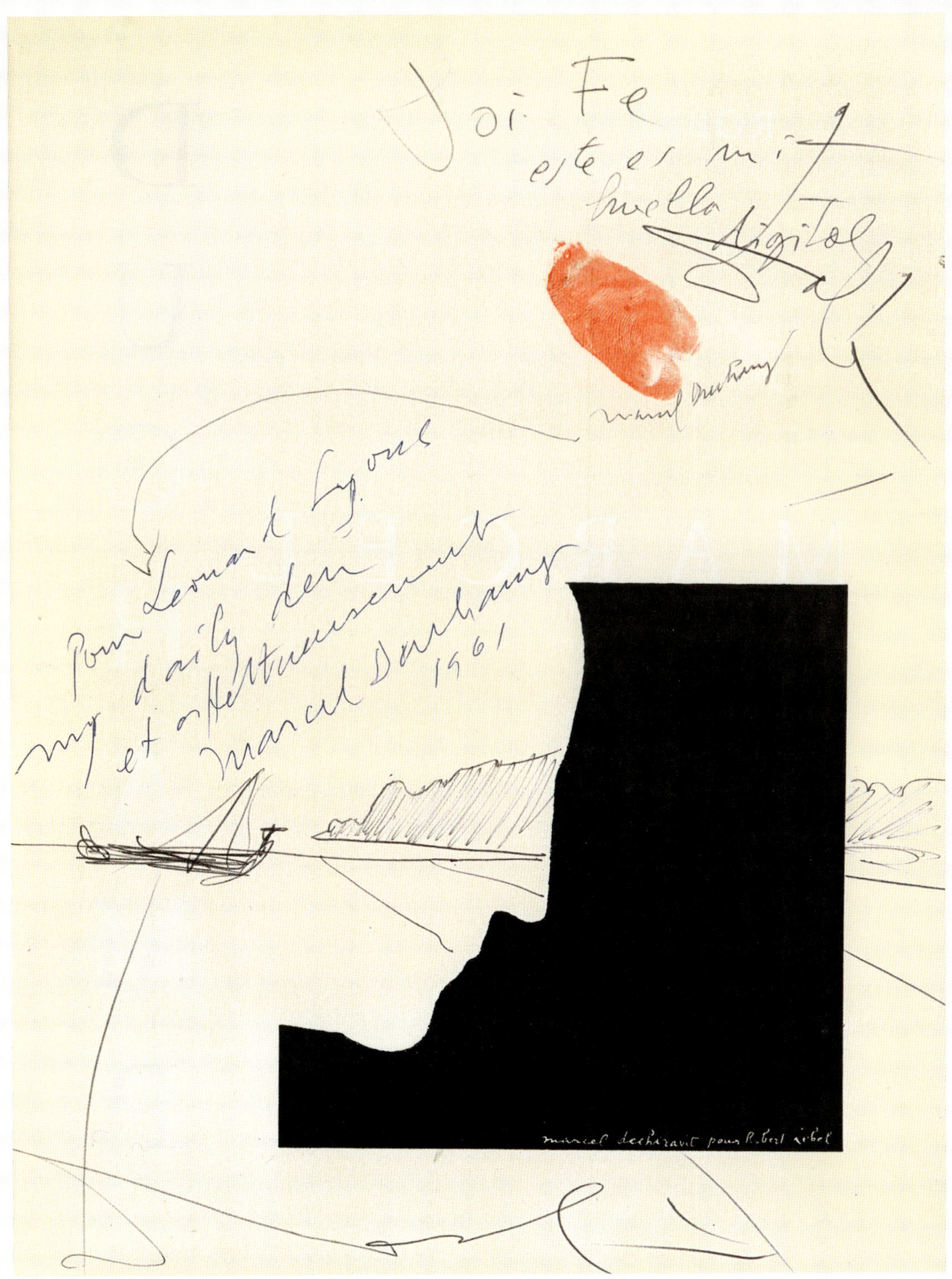

Fig. 56
Salvador Dalí and Marcel Duchamp,
Untitled (Note to Leonard Lyons), 1961.
Ink/ballpoint pen and thumbprint on
a printed book page, 31.1 x 23.5 cm.
Signed and dedicated on recto by
Marcel Duchamp.
Private collection

and *Bottle Rack* (cats 58, 106), but his friend Francis Picabia wanted to reproduce it in his Dada magazine *391*. Duchamp forgot to hand the work over before leaving for the United States in January 1920, so Picabia bought a postcard of the *Mona Lisa* and added the moustache himself, forgetting the beard, and reproduced it in *391* as 'Tableau Dada par Marcel Duchamp' (cat. 26).[5] In 1944 the original *L.H.O.O.Q.* was authenticated by Duchamp, with a notary's stamp.

In the late 1920s Dalí pushed his painting to the limits of representation, incorporating readymade materials, and seeing how far he could disguise explicitly erotic imagery in an increasingly abstract formal language. As he remarked: 'This is a passionate period because psychologically speaking [painting] is beginning to arouse everyone at the very moment its most radical assassination is being carried out.'[6] Preoccupied with questions of art and anti-art, he turned temporarily to film and photography before returning to painting with *The First Days of Spring* (cat. 59), but now in an illusionistic, anti-modernist mode, including a radical use of collage.

Both Duchamp and Dalí treated identity as potentially mutable and unfixed, open to games and masquerades, an arena for experiment. Even what would seem to be a primary identification, that of artist, became open season. Duchamp talked of his 'resistance to being an artist as artists are made of today … the word artist is a concept I try to get out of … What I am, in fact, I don't care.'[7] During the 1920s he pursued seriously his career in chess, playing in international tournaments and apparently giving up art.

Photography was a crucial tool for Duchamp and for Dalí in their respective constructions of identities, often with the connivance of Man Ray, who with Duchamp created the photographic manifestation of the latter's female alter ego, Rrose Sélavy.

I wanted to change identity and my first idea was to take a Jewish name. I was Catholic and it was already a change to go from one religion to another. I couldn't find a Jewish name that appealed to me and suddenly I had an idea: why not change sex? It's much simpler! So from there came the name Rrose Sélavy… The double R came from Francis Picabia's painting *L'Oeil cacodylate*…[8]

The change of gender is underlined by the double meanings of the name: Sélavy, *c'est la vie* ('that's life'), and the double 'R' giving *arroser la vie* ('to water life'), as well as *eros, c'est la vie* ('eros, that's life').

A white square in the last frame of Duchamp's film *Anémic cinéma* (1926) shows the autograph signature 'Rrose Sélavy', and a fingerprint, presumably Duchamp's. As identifications go, fingerprints are, or used to be, the surest, but here they play a part in Duchamp's many complex games with questions of identity, authority and authenticity. A casual thank-you note to Leonard Lyons, who published a popular column in the *New York Post*, 'The Lyon's Den', was, despite its ephemeral character, an intricate game with identity, with the two artists playing on the respective signals of fingerprint and signature (fig. 56). The note was cooked up as a gift for Lyons on the occasion of the notorious exhibition 'Surrealist Intrusion in the Enchanters' Domain'. On a detached frontispiece from Robert Lebel's book *Marcel Duchamp* (1959), which reproduced Duchamp's profile torn from a sheet of black paper inscribed 'Marcel dechiravit pour Robert Lebel', the two artists improvised dedications and alternated identities. A lipstick-red fingerprint, probably made of red ochre fingerprint dust,[9] has the signature 'Marcel Duchamp' just below it, but above is a scribble signed by Dalí asserting (with notarial confidence) 'Joi Fe' ('J'ai fait'), 'este es mí huella digital' ('this is my fingerprint'). An arrow attaches Duchamp's signature to his dedication, 'For Leonard Lyons, my daily den / and affectionately Marcel Duchamp 1961'. But this is placed as though signing a drawing that is unmistakably by Dalí, of a boat in the bay at Portlligat. The drawing, moreover, continues beyond the printed black paper so that it looks as if this has been stuck collage-like on top of it. The fingerprint, on closer inspection, bifurcates at the bottom as though it is a female torso. One of their few actual collaborations, this joint sketch is a telling sign of the two artists' friendship and mutual understanding.

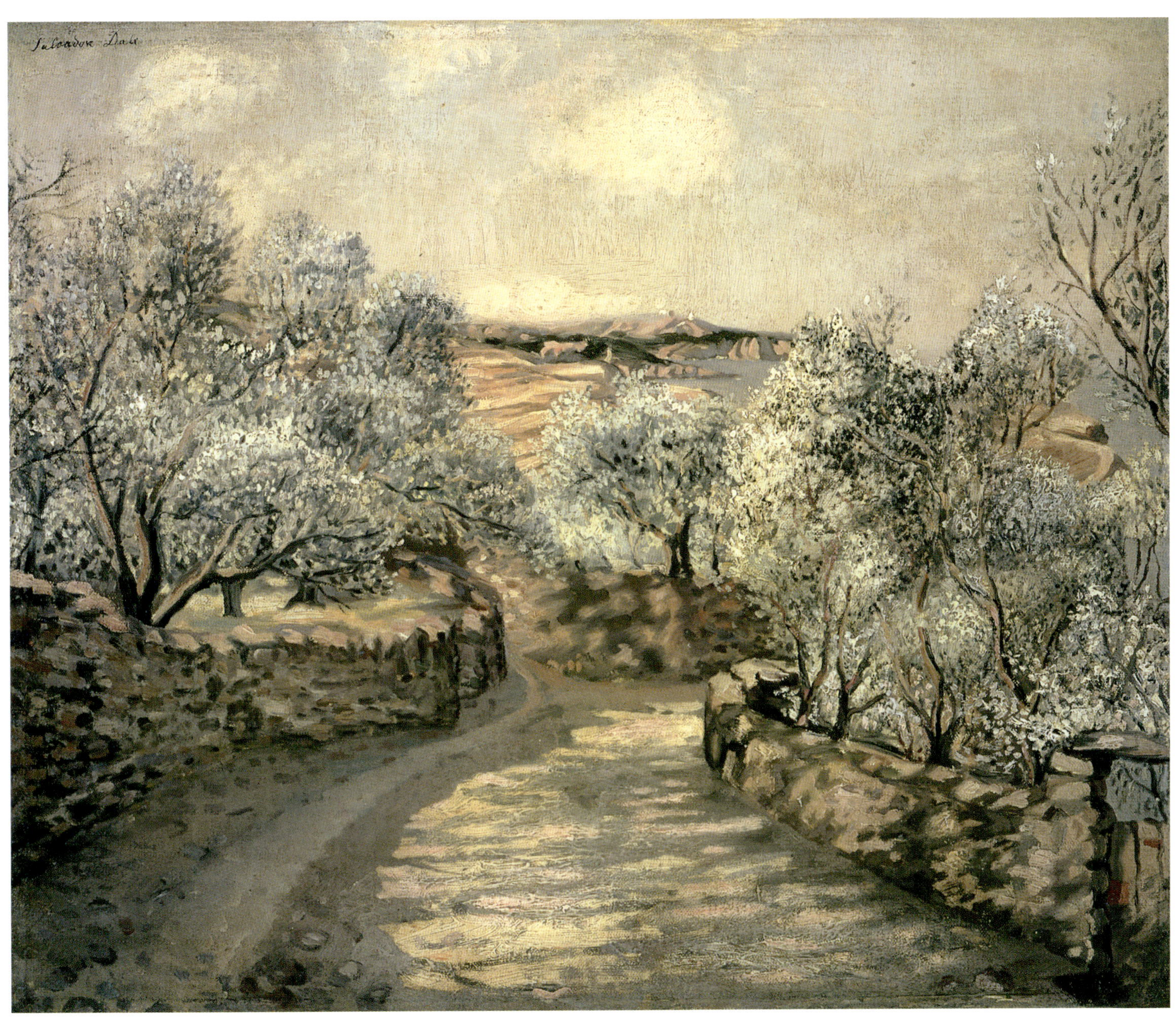

9
Salvador Dalí
The Lane to Portlligat with View of
Cap de Creus, c. 1921
Oil on canvas, 57.8 x 68 cm
Collection of The Dalí Museum,
St Petersburg, Florida

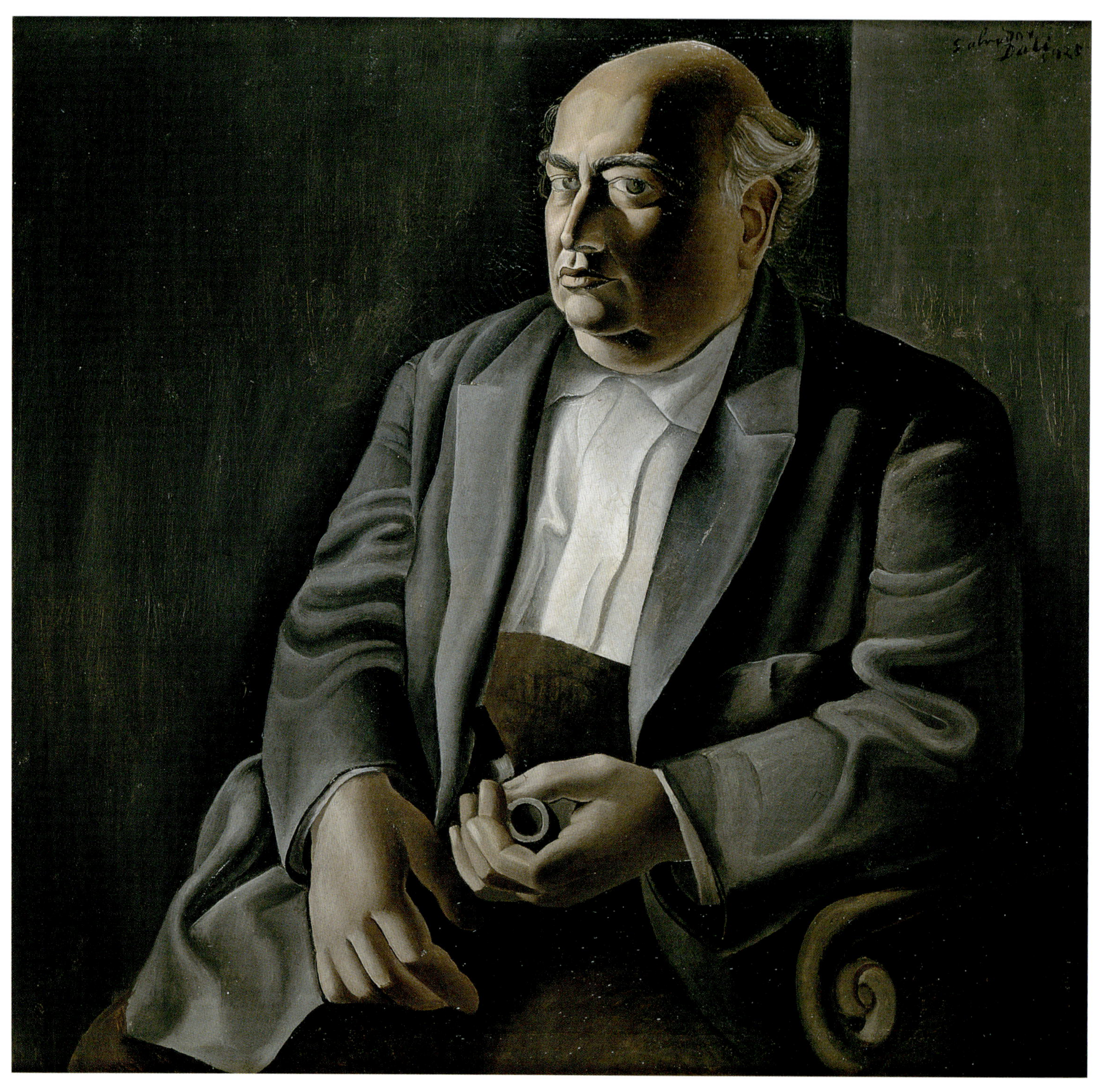

10
Salvador Dalí
Portrait of My Father, 1925
Oil on canvas, 104.5 x 104.5 cm
MNAC. Museu Nacional d'Art de
Catalunya, Barcelona

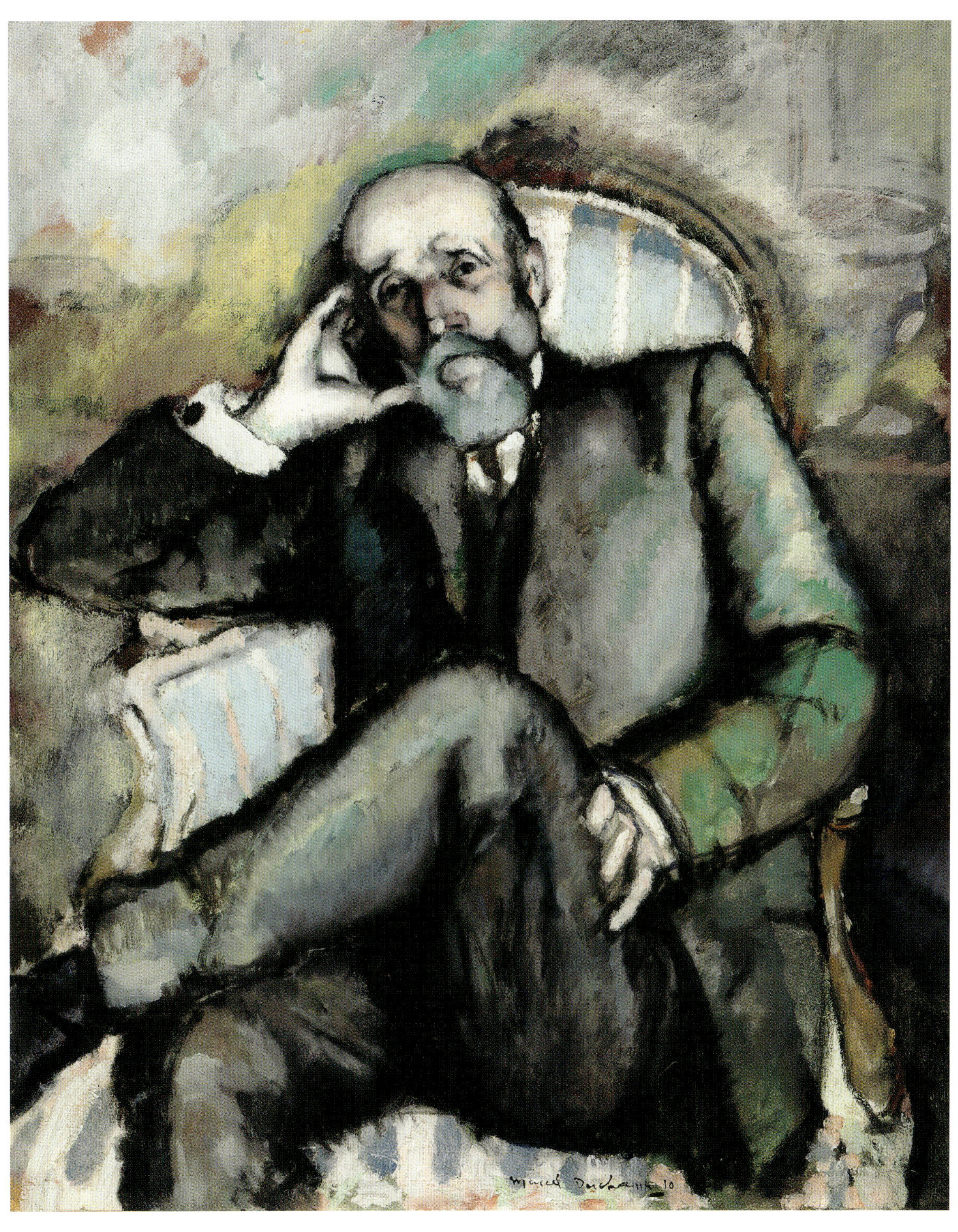

11
Marcel Duchamp
Portrait of the Artist's Father, 1910
Oil on canvas, 92.4 x 73.3 cm
Philadelphia Museum of Art: The Louise
and Walter Arensberg Collection, 1950

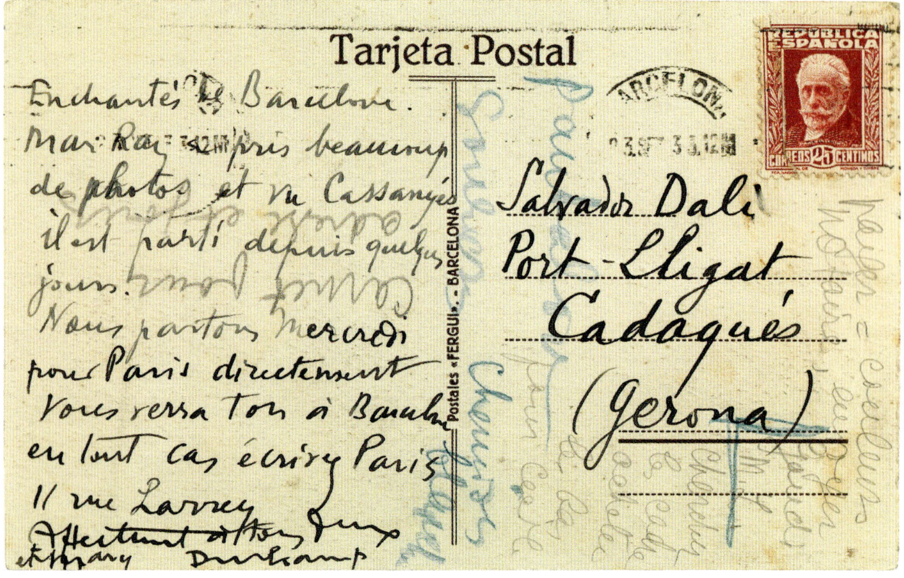

12
Postcard from Duchamp to Dalí, 1933
Fundació Gala-Salvador Dalí, Figueres

13
Postcard from Man Ray to Dalí, 1933
Fundació Gala-Salvador Dalí, Figueres

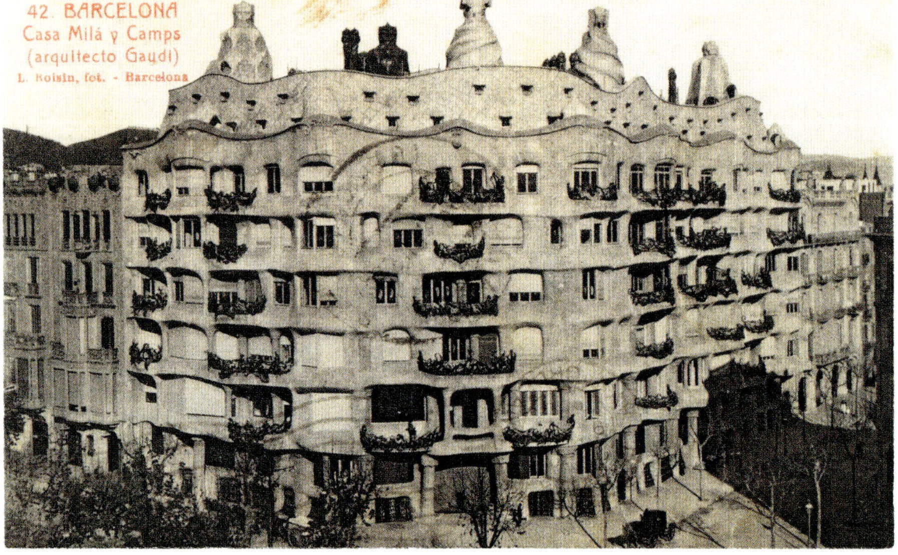

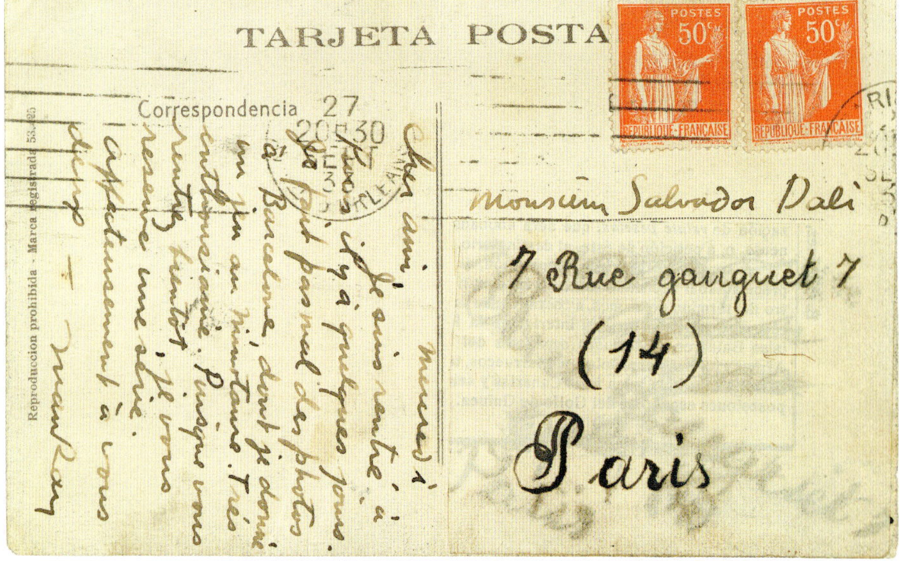

Opposite, top left: 14
Dalí, Duchamp and friends, Cadaqués,
summer 1933
Vintage gelatin silver print, 8.6 x 5.8 cm
(photographer unknown)
Emmanuel Boussard Library, London

Opposite, bottom left: 15
Dalí, Duchamp, Gala and friends,
Cadaqués, summer 1933
Vintage gelatin silver print on
Agfa-Lupex paper, 8.6 x 5.8 cm
(photographer unknown)
Emmanuel Boussard Library, London

Opposite, top right: 16
Dalí, Duchamp, Gala and friends,
Cadaqués, summer 1933
Vintage gelatin silver print on Velox paper,
4.5 x 6.5 cm (photographer unknown)
Emmanuel Boussard Library, London

Opposite, bottom right: 17
Dalí, Duchamp, Gala and friends,
Cadaqués, summer 1933
Vintage gelatin silver print on Agfa-Lupex
paper, 8.6 x 6 cm (photographer unknown)
Emmanuel Boussard Library, London

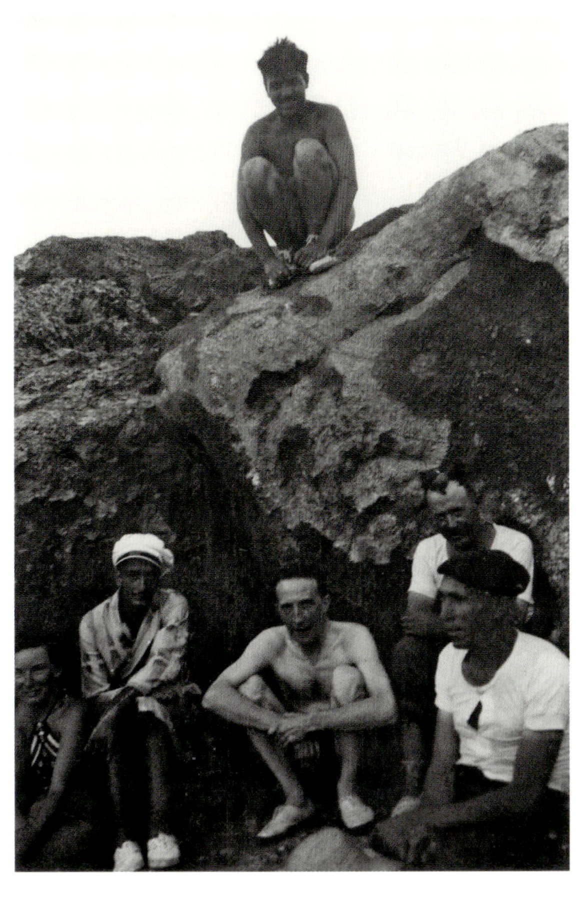

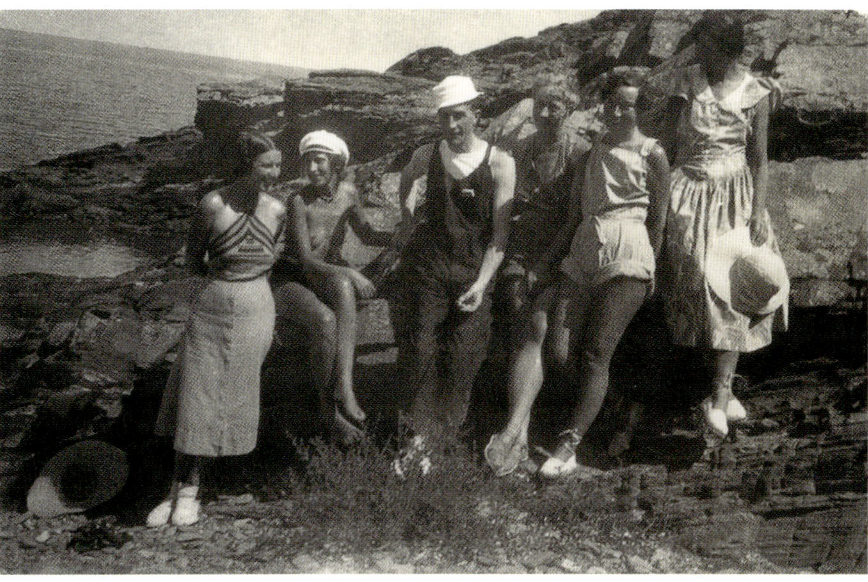

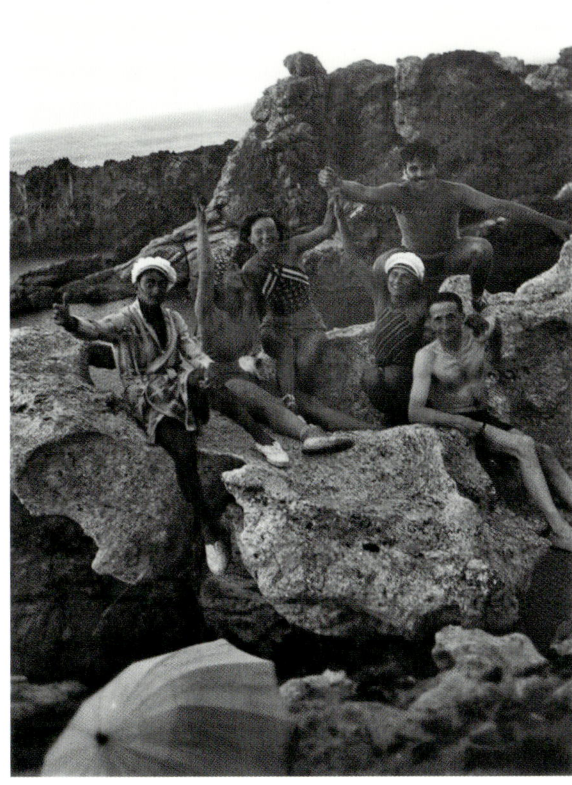

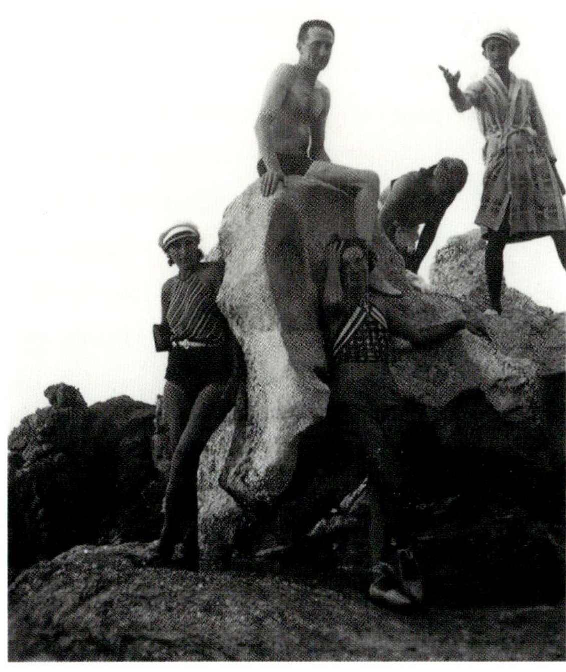

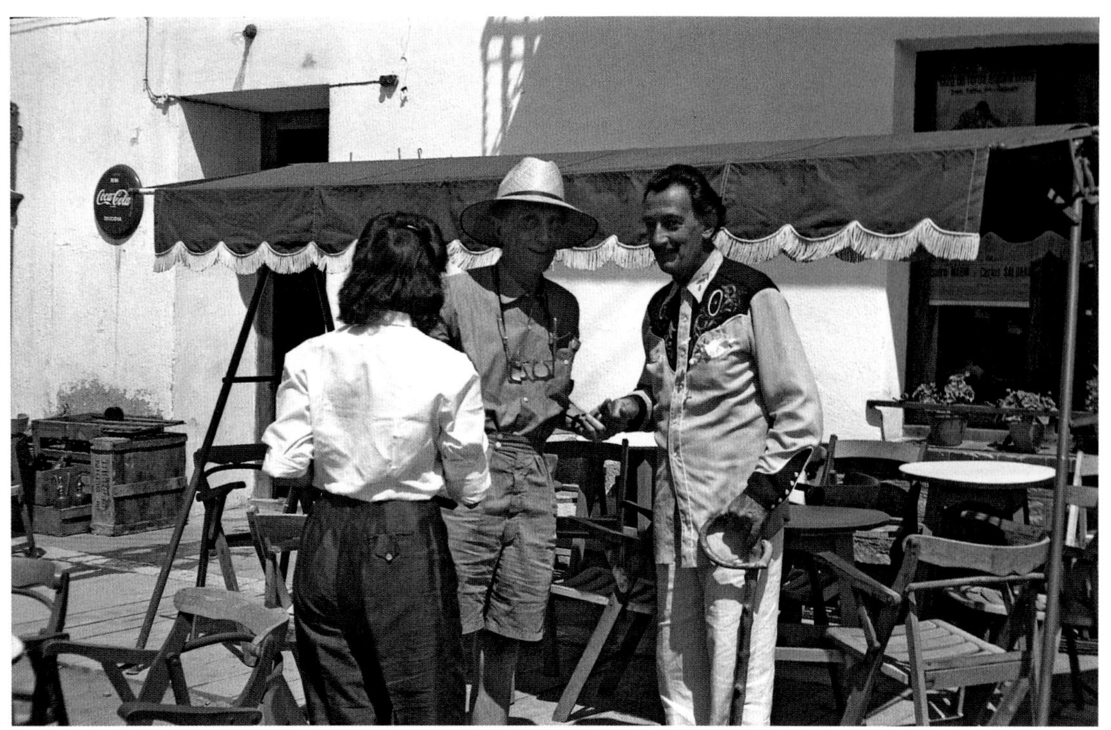

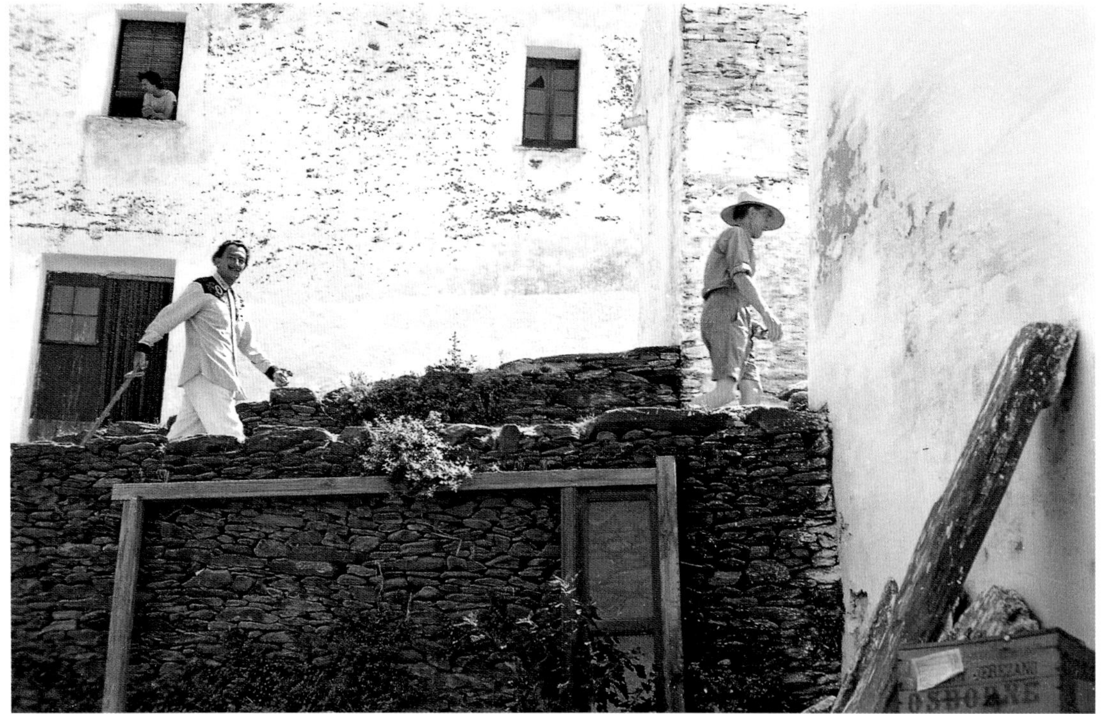

18
Robert Descharnes
Marcel Duchamp with Gala and Salvador
Dalí outside the Bar Melitón, Cadaqués,
August 1958 (printed 2004)
Photograph, 21 x 31 cm
Arxiu Pere Vehí, Cadaqués

19
Robert Descharnes
Salvador Dalí and Marcel Duchamp
walking to El Corral de Gala, August 1958
(printed 2004)
Photograph, 21 x 31 cm
Arxiu Pere Vehí, Cadaqués

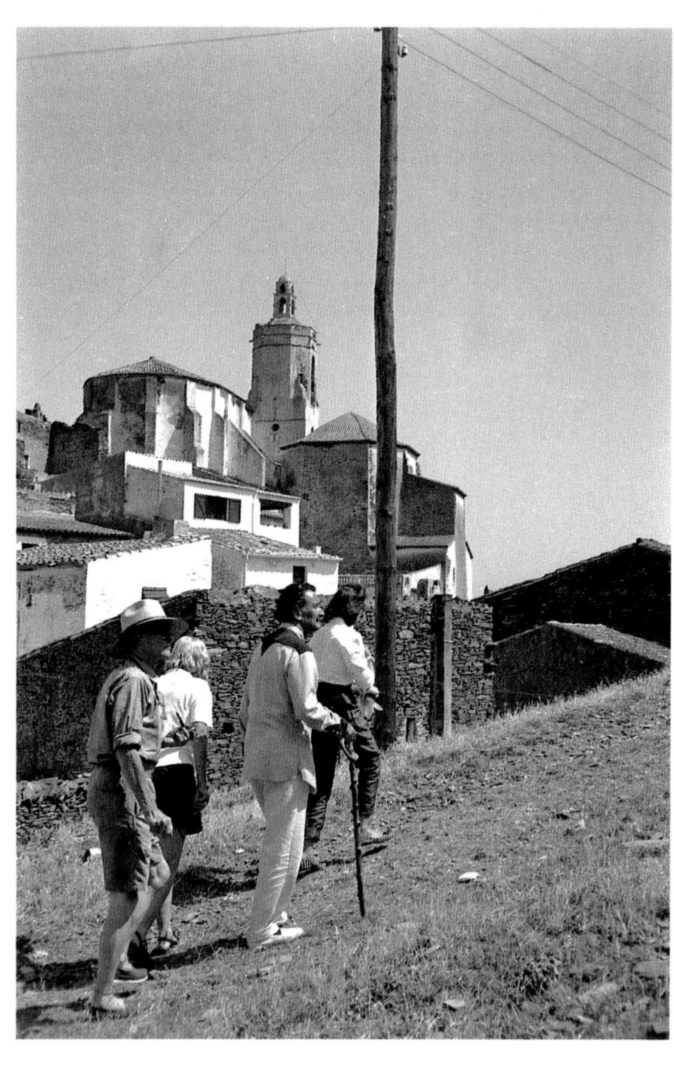

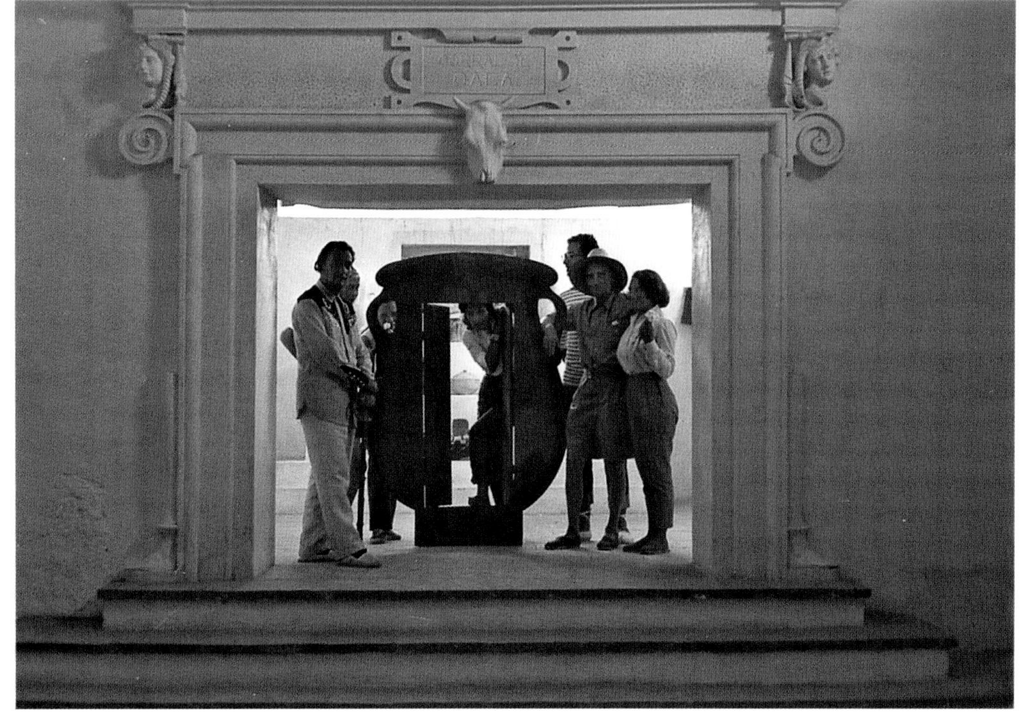

20
Robert Descharnes
Marcel and Teeny Duchamp preceded by
Gala and Salvador Dalí, on the way to El
Corral de Gala, Cadaqués, August 1958
(printed 2004)
Photograph, 31 x 21 cm
Arxiu Pere Vehí, Cadaqués

21
Robert Descharnes
In El Corral de Gala, from left to right:
Salvador Dalí, Teeny Duchamp,
Jacqueline Matisse Monnier (the
daughter of Teeny and Pierre Matisse),
Gala, Bernard Monnier, Marcel Duchamp
and Michèle Descharnes, Cadaqués,
August 1958 (printed 2004)
Photograph, 21 x 31 cm
Arxiu Pere Vehí, Cadaqués

GENDER AND PUBLIC PERSONAE
WILLIAM JEFFETT

Avant-garde experimentation led artists to reconsider all categories of subjective identity, especially those that had heretofore been considered as immutable and authentic. Both Duchamp and Dalí participated in a form of what could be called artistic dandyism. Both were the sons of prominent provincial notaries. Thus by using their own power to swear, they could re-establish and reconstruct subjective identities.

Both challenged traditional canons of masculinity and through masquerade adopted a complex approach to gender identity. They did this initially through a consideration of the male nude and specifically, at least initially, through an interest in the subject of St Sebastian.

Duchamp's treatment of the St Sebastian subject is unusual, in that he depicts a sculpture of the martyr, from the church of Saint-Martin at Veules-les-Roses in Normandy, but paints the stone as if it were flesh, revealing an awareness of historical painting and the tradition of the erotic male nude (cat. 24). His choice of subject was idiosyncratic at a time when modern artists were focusing on the landscape and studio nudes. In the 1920s Dalí, along with his friend Federico García Lorca, developed a cult-like fascination for St Sebastian inspired by the Hermitage of St Sebastian near Cadaqués. Later, Dalí repeatedly returned to an interest in St Sebastian as a subject. The exchanges of letters between Dalí and Lorca on the subject point to indeterminate identities and gender instability. In his first major text, 'Sant Sebastià', published in the review *L'Amic de les Arts* (1927), Dalí wrote: 'irony ... is nakedness; it is the gymnast which hides behind the paint of St Sebastian'.[1] It was precisely this quality of irony that both Dalí and Duchamp were increasingly to share in their respective approaches to representation.

In 1920–21 Man Ray photographed Duchamp dressed as his female alter ego, Rrose Sélavy. This image and its variants were repeated over the years. In 1921 Duchamp used the image within the collage *Belle Haleine: Eau de Voilette*, a modified design for a bottle of perfume (fig. 19). This secondary identity was more than a brief gesture or passing game, and Duchamp signed a number of works and his personal correspondence with this name. *Monte Carlo Bond* (cat. 38), for example, is signed both Rrose Sélavy and Marcel Duchamp. Again, the signature is the notarial affirmation of gender identity.

Dalí likewise presented gender in ambiguous terms and a number of his works include figures whose

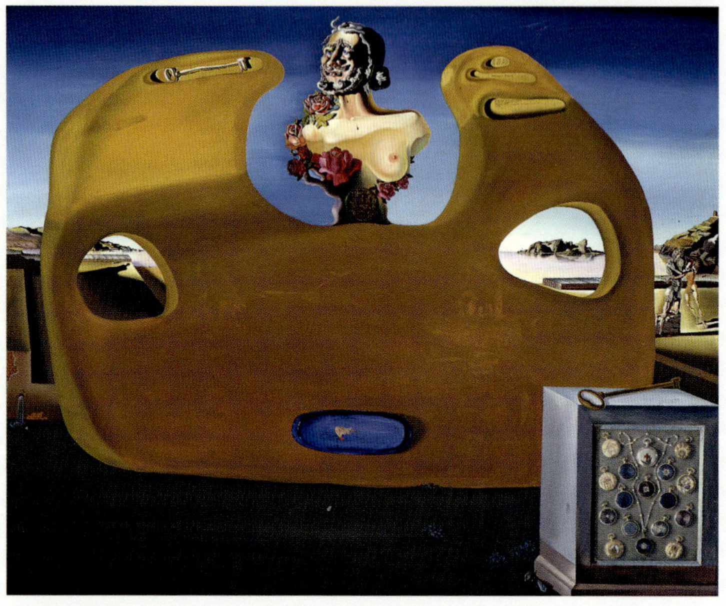

sexual anatomy reveals characteristics of both male and female, as in the object *Anthropomorphic Beach* (cat. 52) and the scandalous figures in the left foreground of *The First Days of Spring* (cat. 59). Similarly the 'William Tell' figure in the centre of *Memory of the Child Woman* (fig. 57) is both bearded and has breasts. Dalí's alter ego was Gala (fig. 59), and he signed many works 'Gala-Salvador Dalí', suggesting a more complex understanding of authorship and a fusing of the male and female into a new and androgynous mode of artistic identity.

Duchamp's interest in the image of the *Mona Lisa* in *L.H.O.O.Q.* (cat. 28) reveals gender instability, and indeed he saw in this figure masculine qualities, just as Dalí similarly, in his 1953–54 collaboration with the photographer Philippe Halsman (cat. 27), exaggerates this reading through the introduction of the bold Dalí moustache. In his article 'Why They Attack the *Mona Lisa*' (1963), Dalí evoked Duchamp and explained this 'masculinisation' in Freudian terms as 'the denigration of the Art'.[2] And Duchamp explained in a 1961 interview, 'when you look at it the *Mona Lisa* becomes a man. It is not a woman disguised as a man; it is a real man, and that was my discovery, without realising it at the time.'[3]

The two artists' shared interest in constructing artistic identity in terms of gender instability is part of their wider shared interest in projecting their

Fig. 57
Salvador Dalí, *Memory of the Child Woman*, 1931. Oil on canvas with collage, 99.1 x 55.9 cm. Collection of The Dalí Museum, St Petersburg, Florida

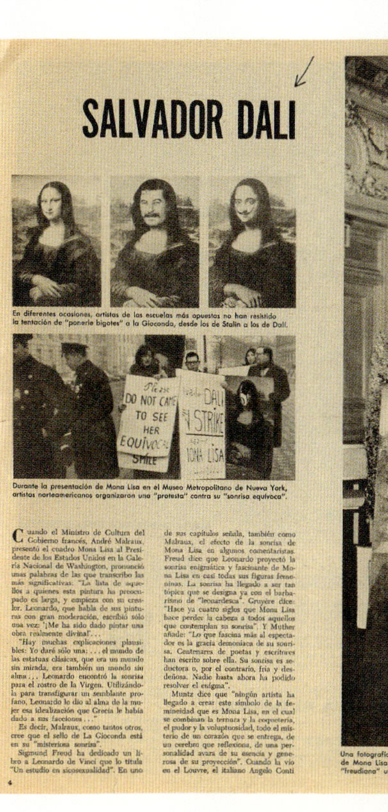

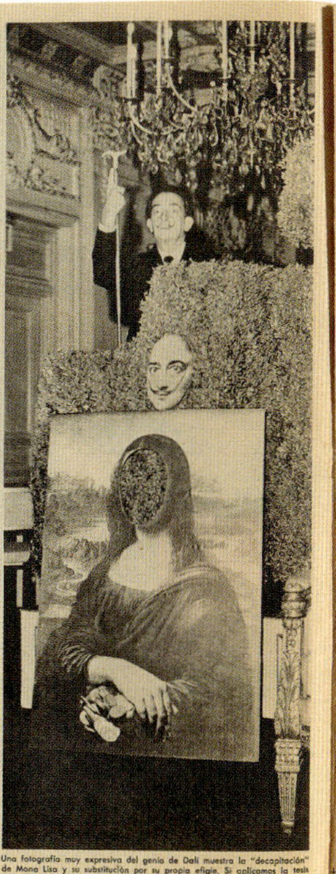

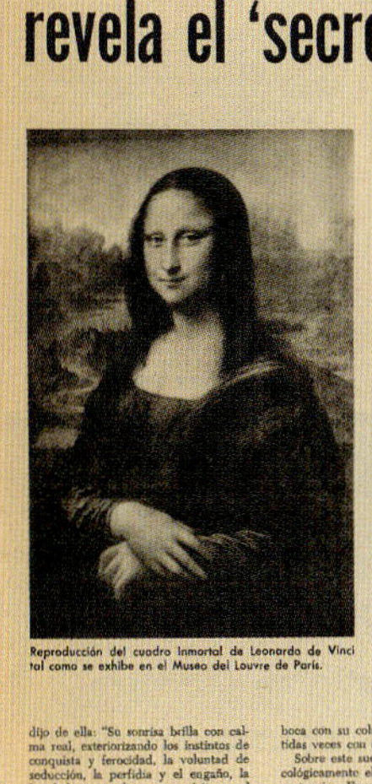

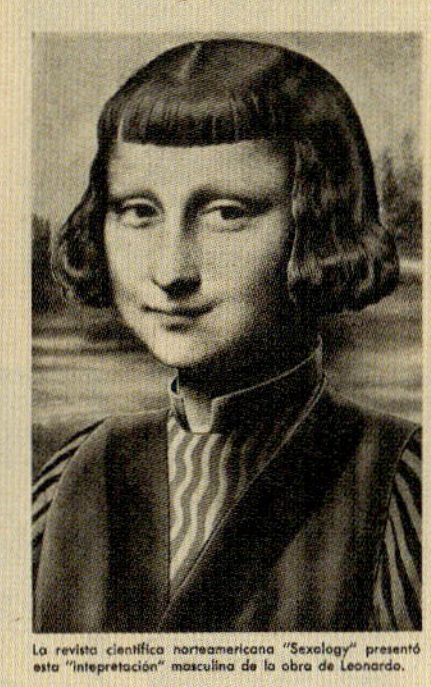

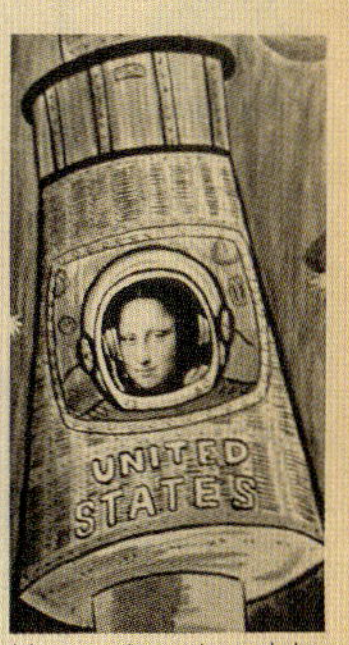

respective personae in the public sphere. And it is interesting that Duchamp came back to *L.H.O.O.Q.* in 1958 (cat. 35), while in Cadaqués, at a time when he began to spend more time with Dalí, as this was the same year that Dalí received his *Boîte-en-valise* from Duchamp.

Although Dalí is commonly seen as the showman and Duchamp as the reticent recluse, both were highly visible personalities. This visibility was largely achieved through photography, which became the medium by which their respective artistic myths were constructed. In the earlier photographs, Duchamp is seen variously as a monk, or fragmented and multiplied, or dressed as a woman, or as a chess player. In a series of images taken by Man Ray, Dalí presents himself as shrouded like a corpse (cats 92–94), thereby hiding his presence, whereas elsewhere he opted to present images of his face and, later on, ever-more-iconic moustache, thereby enacting the transformation of his self-imagery into a transgressed *Mona Lisa*. In a number of remarkable photographs we see both artists together at different, often complicit, moments in their lives, whether Duchamp is helping Dalí with his Surreal Bullfight in 1961 (see pp. 104–05) or the two are together in New York (cat. 114) in front of Dalí's *Enigma of William Tell*, a painting that Duchamp was instrumental in selling to the Moderna Museet, Stockholm, shortly thereafter. In one striking photograph by Robert Descharnes, we see them playing chess together from beneath, through a transparent pane of glass (cat. 42). Dalí no less than Duchamp was capable of making gestures towards

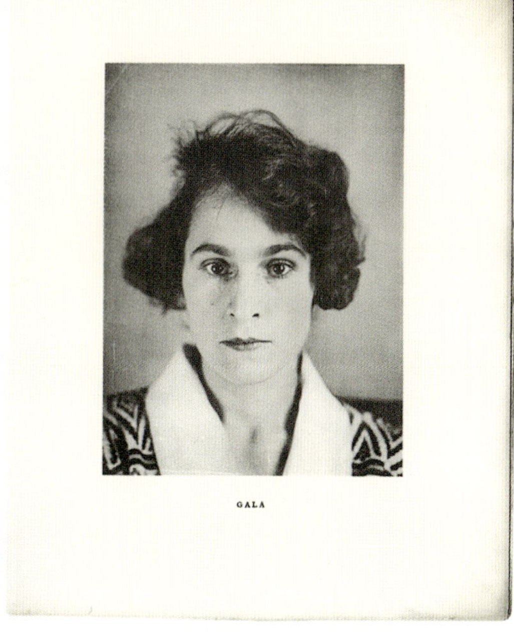

chess as a marker of identity. In these ways both offered up a public personality at the service of myth: Duchamp proposing the myth of the inactive artist–chess player defending his right to laziness, and Dalí projecting the image of the hyperactive painter-genius, never resting to reflect. Yet as the image of them playing chess together suggests, through self-imagery they each represented two sides of the same problem of artistic identity.

Fig. 58
Salvador Dalí, 'Salvador Dalí revela el "secreto" de Mona Lisa' ('Salvador Dalí Reveals the Mona Lisa Secret'), *Hablemos*, 30 June 1963 (cat. 22)
Magazine, 27.6 x 32.7 cm
Fundació Gala-Salvador Dalí, Figueres

Fig. 59
Salvador Dalí, frontispiece to *La Femme Visible*, 1931. Book, 28.4 x 22.2 cm.
Collection of The Dalí Museum Archives, St Petersburg, Florida

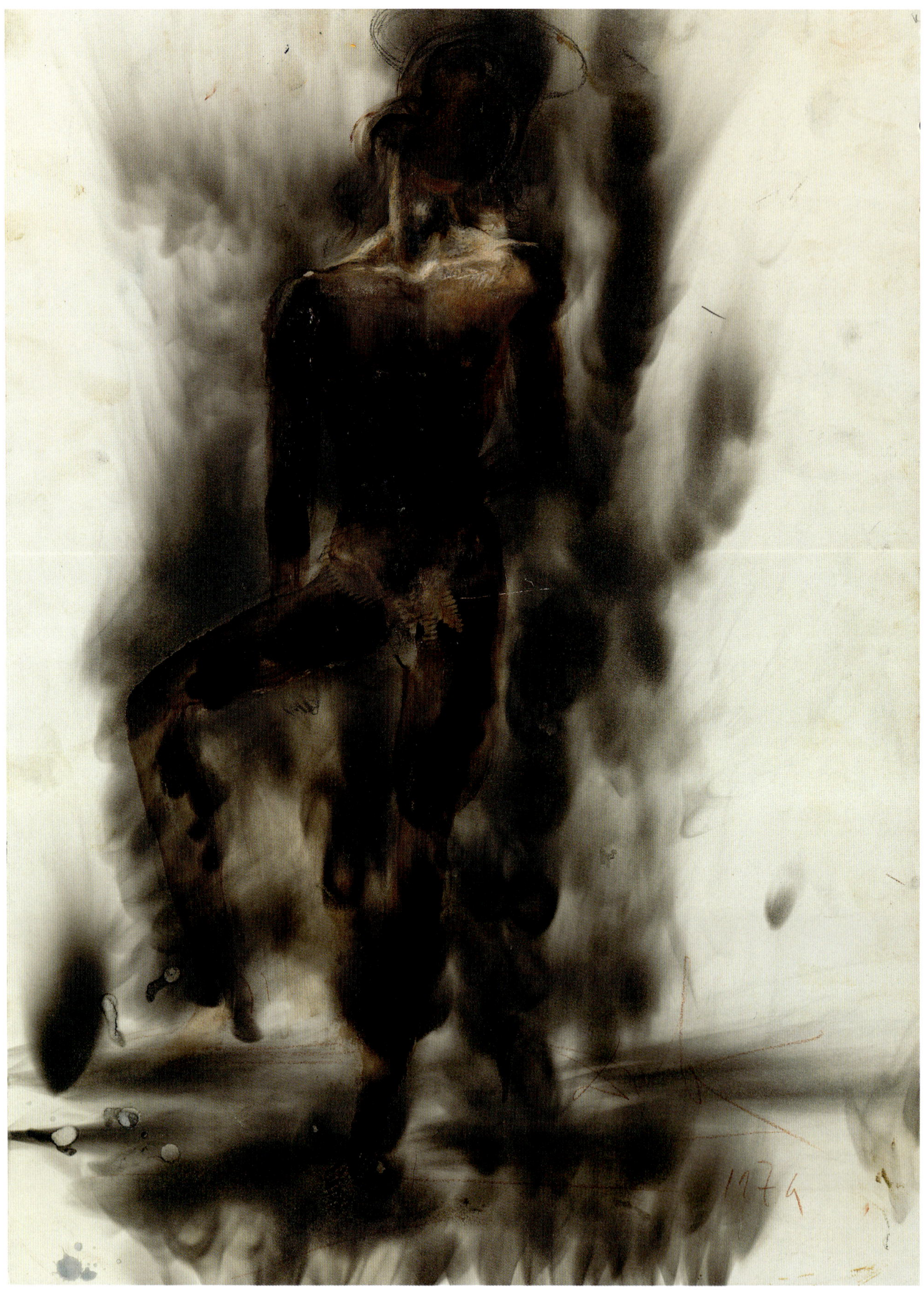

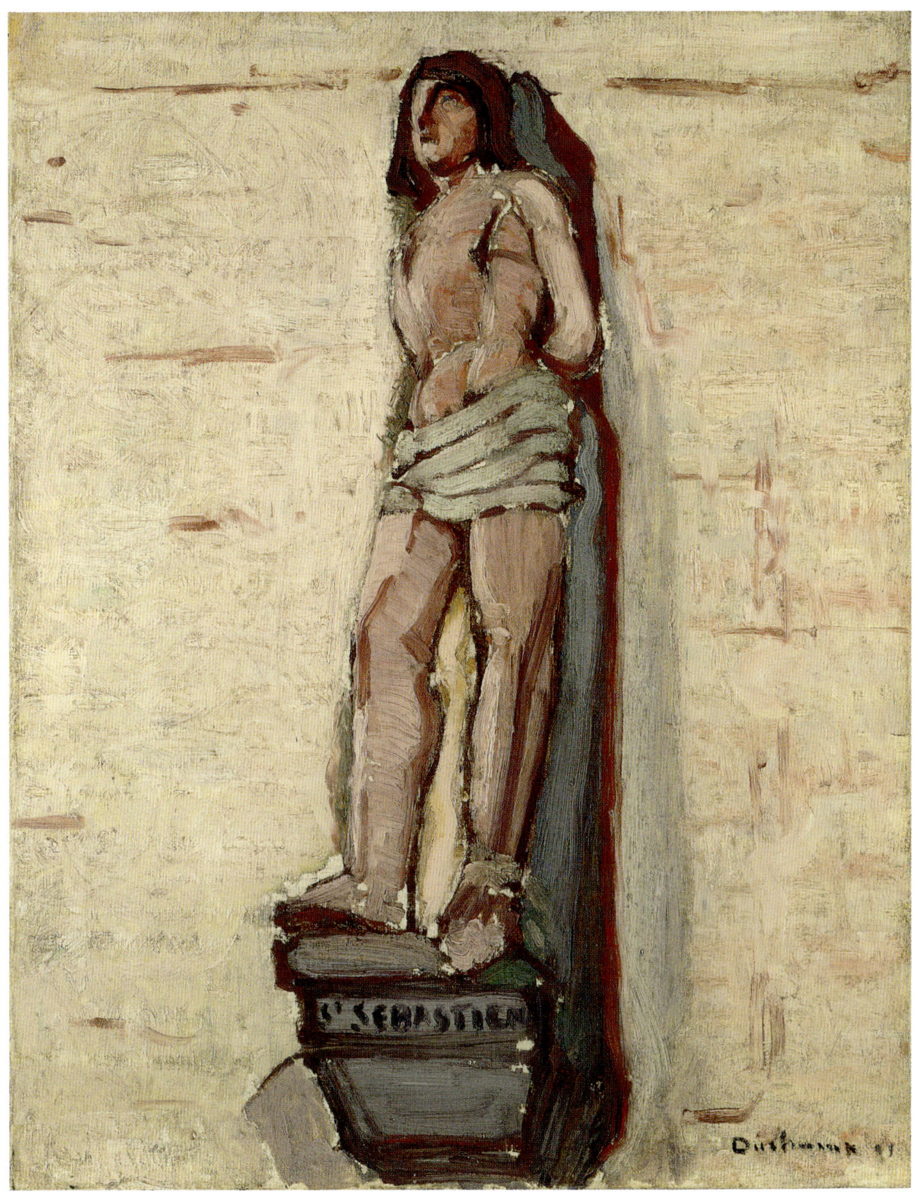

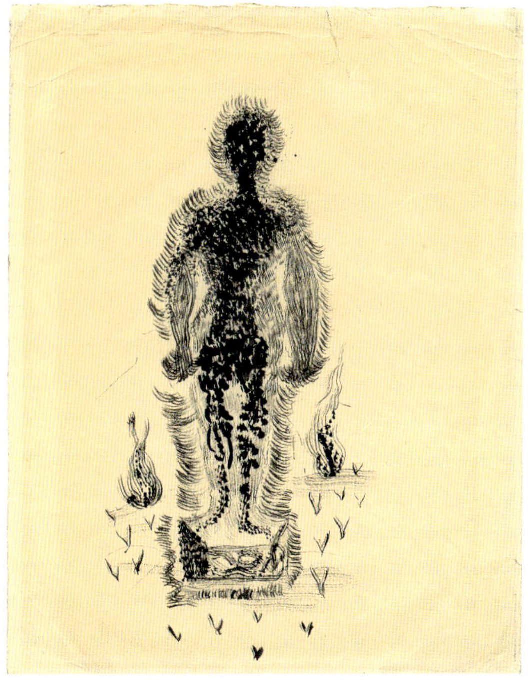

Opposite: 23
Salvador Dalí
Untitled (St Sebastian), 1974
Mixed media on cardboard with
candle smoke, 69.3 x 49.2 cm
Fundació Gala-Salvador Dalí, Figueres

24
Marcel Duchamp
St Sebastian, 1909
Oil on canvas, 61.3 x 46.4 cm
Collection of The John and Mable
Ringling Museum of Art, the State Art
Museum of Florida, Florida State
University, Sarasota, Florida

25
Salvador Dalí
Figure in Flames, 1923–25
Ink on paper, 28 x 21 cm
Collection of The Dalí Museum,
St Petersburg, Florida

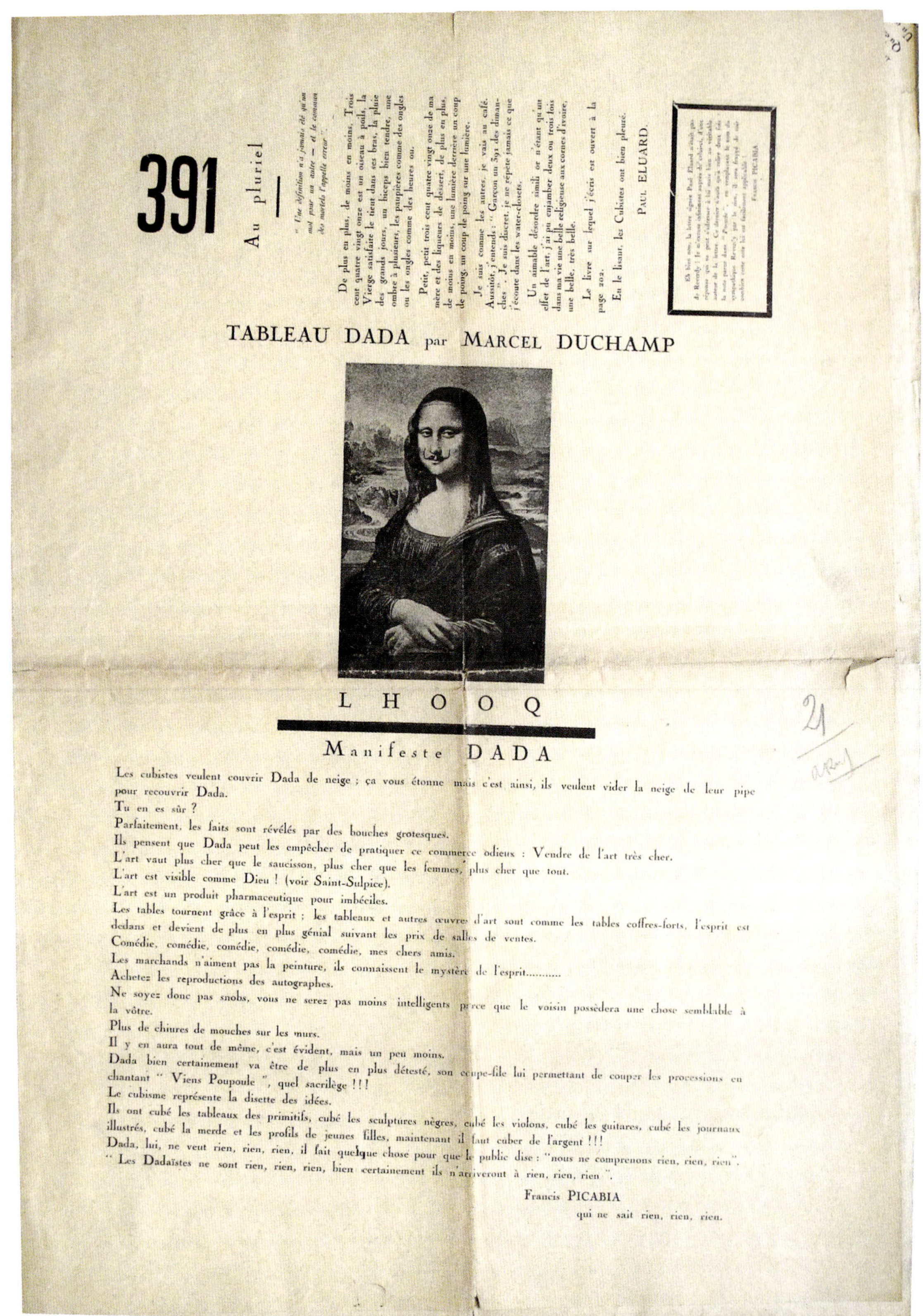

391

Au pluriel

" Une définition n'a jamais été qu'un mot pour un autre — et le commun des mortels l'appelle erreur ".

De plus en plus, de moins en moins, Trois cent quatre vingt onze est un oiseau à poils, la Vierge satisfaire le tient dans ses bras, la pluie des grands jours, un biceps bien tendre, une ombre à plusieurs, les paupières comme des ongles ou les ongles comme des heures ou.

Petit, petit trois cent quatre vingt onze de ma mère et des liqueurs de dessert, de plus en plus, de moins en moins, une lumière derrière un coup de poing, un coup de poing sur une lumière.

Je suis comme les autres, je vais au café. Aussitôt, j'entends : " Garçon un 391 des dimanches ". Je suis discret, je ne répète jamais ce que j'écoute dans les water-closets.

Un aimable désordre simili or n'étant qu'un effet de l'art, j'ai pu enjamber deux ou trois fois dans ma vie une belle religieuse aux cornes d'ivoire, une belle, très belle.

Le livre sur lequel j'écris est ouvert à la page 202.

En le lisant, les Cubistes ont bien pleuré.

PAUL ELUARD.

Eh bien non, la lettre signée Paul Eluard n'était pas de Reverdy ! Et n'aurait infiniment auprès d'éclairci, d'une réponse qui ne peut s'adresse à lui mais bien au véritable auteur de la lettre. Ce dernier n'aura qu'à relire deux fois la note parue dans " Proverbe ", en remplaçant le nom de sympathique Reverdy par le sien, il sera frappé de voir combien cette note lui est facilement applicable !

Francis PICABIA

TABLEAU DADA par MARCEL DUCHAMP

L H O O Q

Manifeste DADA

Les cubistes veulent couvrir Dada de neige ; ça vous étonne mais c'est ainsi, ils veulent vider la neige de leur pipe pour recouvrir Dada.

Tu en es sûr ?

Parfaitement, les faits sont révélés par des bouches grotesques.

Ils pensent que Dada peut les empêcher de pratiquer ce commerce odieux : Vendre de l'art très cher.

L'art vaut plus cher que le saucisson, plus cher que les femmes, plus cher que tout.

L'art est visible comme Dieu ! (voir Saint-Sulpice).

L'art est un produit pharmaceutique pour imbéciles.

Les tables tournent grâce à l'esprit ; les tableaux et autres œuvres d'art sont comme les tables coffres-forts, l'esprit est dedans et devient de plus en plus génial suivant les prix de salles de ventes.

Comédie, comédie, comédie, comédie, comédie, mes chers amis.

Les marchands n'aiment pas la peinture, ils connaissent le mystère de l'esprit...........

Achetez les reproductions des autographes.

Ne soyez donc pas snobs, vous ne serez pas moins intelligents parce que le voisin possèdera une chose semblable à la vôtre.

Plus de chiures de mouches sur les murs.

Il y en aura tout de même, c'est évident, mais un peu moins.

Dada bien certainement va être de plus en plus détesté, son coupe-file lui permettant de couper les processions en chantant " Viens Poupoule ", quel sacrilège !!!

Le cubisme représente la disette des idées.

Ils ont cubé les tableaux des primitifs, cubé les sculptures nègres, cubé les violons, cubé les guitares, cubé les journaux illustrés, cubé la merde et les profils de jeunes filles, maintenant il faut cuber de l'argent !!!

Dada, lui, ne veut rien, rien, rien, il fait quelque chose pour que le public dise : "nous ne comprenons rien, rien, rien".

" Les Dadaïstes ne sont rien, rien, rien, bien certainement ils n'arriveront à rien, rien, rien ".

Francis PICABIA
qui ne sait rien, rien, rien.

26
Francis Picabia
391, no. 12, March 1920
Journal, 55.8 x 38.2 cm
Emmanuel Boussard Library, London

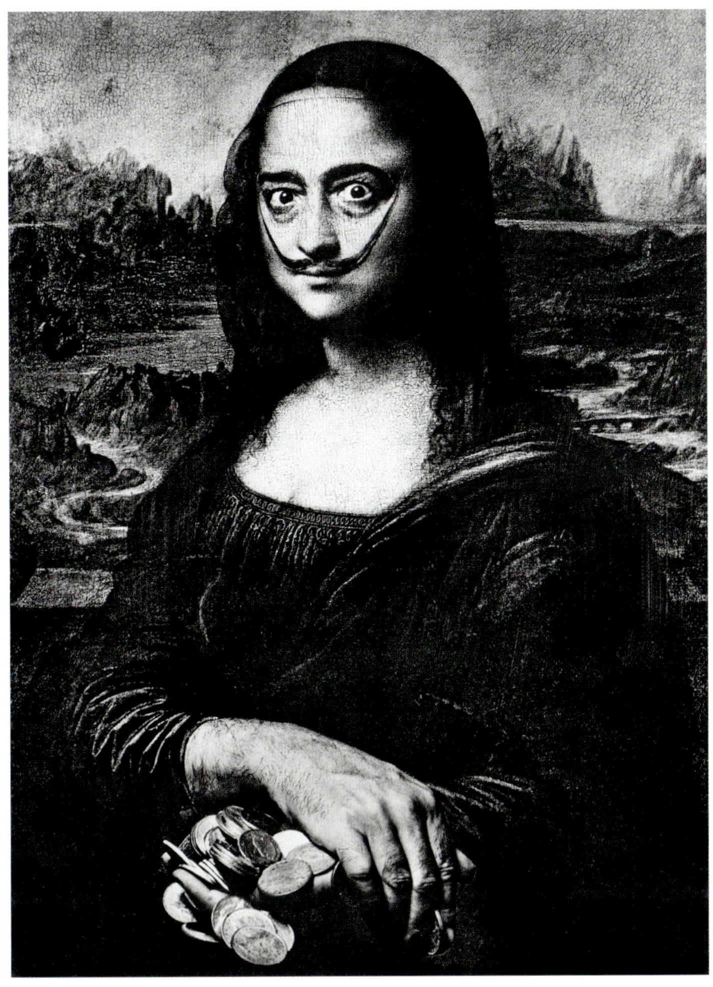

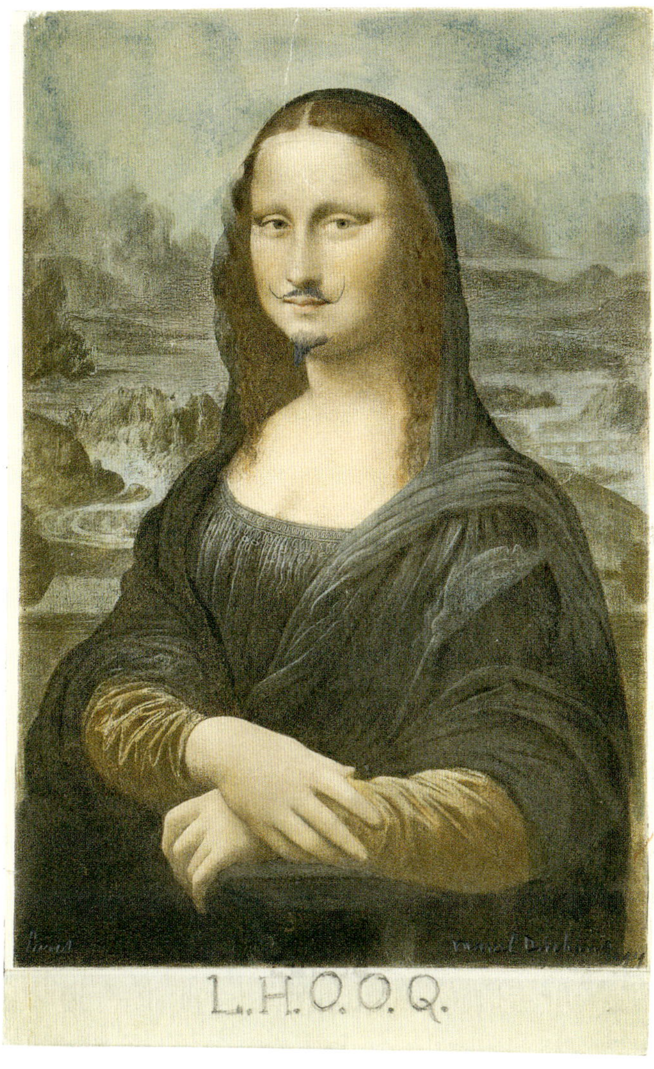

CATÁLOGO

DALÍ

1.º	La batalla de Tetuán. (Homenaje a Mariano Fortuny).	1.962
2.º	Árabes acidodesoxirribonucleicos.	1.962
3.º	50 cuadros abstractos que a dos metros se convierten en tres Lenines disfrazados de chino y a seis metros forman la cabeza de un tigre real.	1.962
4.º	Cielo hiperxiológico. (Firmado con el nombre de Gala y Lorca).	1.962
5.º	Muerte de Raimundo Lulio.	1.962
6.º	Twist en el estudio de Velázquez.	1.962
7.º	Autoretrato.	1.921
	Dibujos y acuarelas.	

FORTUNY

1.º	La batalla de Tetuán.
2.º	Un tribunal en la Alhambra. (Colección Gala Salvador Dalí)
	Academias dibujos, prestados por la Real Academia de Bellas Artes de San Jorge.

FREUD ET LA GIOCONDA

IL FALLAIT BIEN QUE UN JOUR SALVADOR DALÍ CE DECIDE A DENONCÉ PUBLIQUEMENT POURQUOI LA GIOCONDE REPRESENTAN UN "SIMBLE PORTRÈ" PEINT PAR LE PLUS COMPLICAT ET AMBIGUE DE TOUS LES PEINTRES, LEOARDO, A EU CE POUVOIR UNIQUE DANS L'ISTOIRE DE L'ART DE PROVOQUER LES PLUS DIVERSES ET TRUCULENTES AGRESIONS. EN EFFET LA GIOCONDA A SOUFFERT DEUX GENRES TIPIQUES D'AGRESIONS A L'ARCHETIPE QUELLE ET

Top left: 27
Philippe Halsman
A Paragon of Beauty from 'Dalí's Mustache', 1953–54
Print of vintage photomontage,
35.5 x 28 cm
Philippe Halsman Archive

Top right: 28
Marcel Duchamp
L.H.O.O.Q., 1919
Pencil on postcard of the *Mona Lisa*,
19.7 x 12.4 cm
Private collection
London only

Right: 29
Salvador Dalí
Manuscript for 'Freud et la Gioconda',
c. 1963
Ink on printed page, 28 x 22.3 cm
Fundació Gala-Salvador Dalí, Figueres

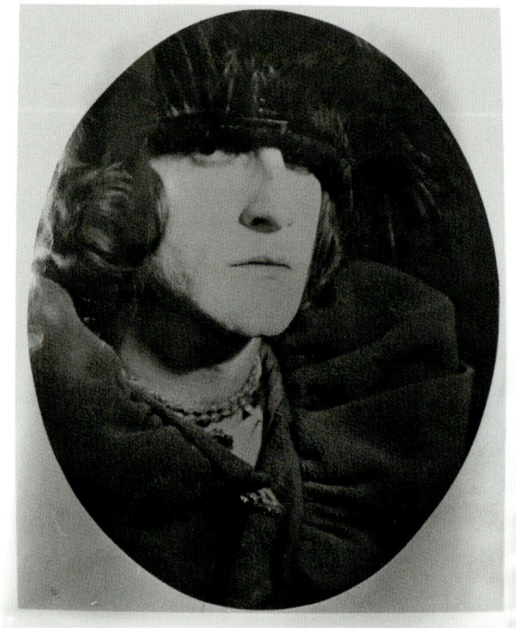

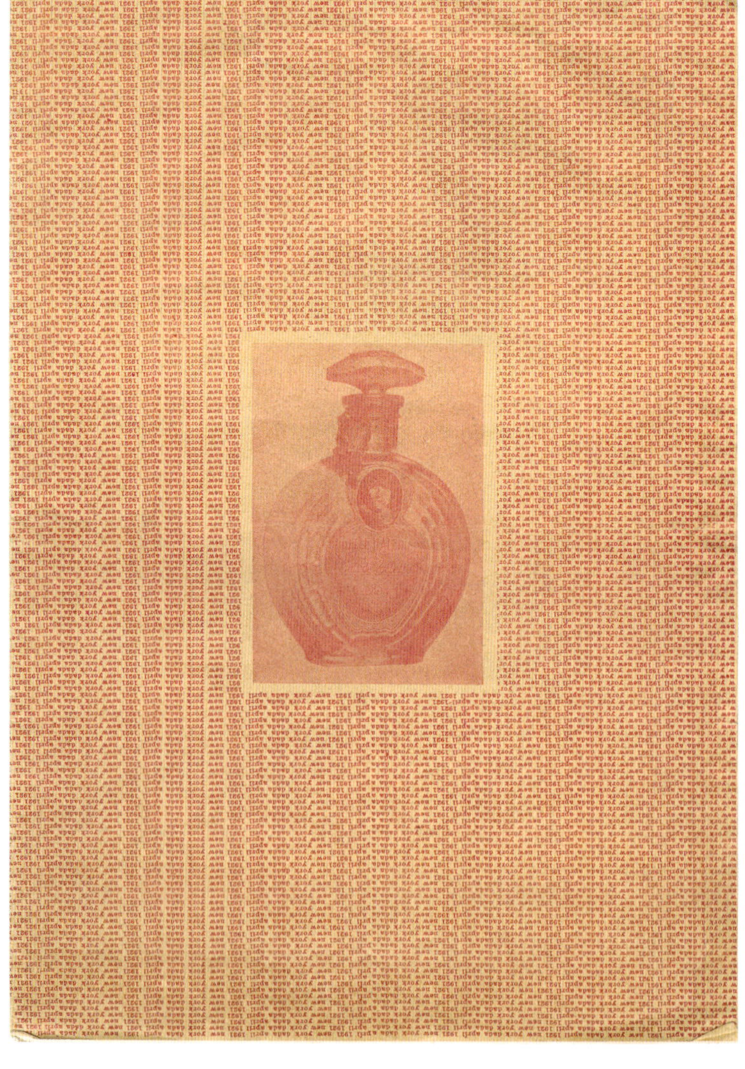

30
Marcel Duchamp
Note: '*Rrose Sélavy née en 1920 à N.Y....*'
('*Rrose Sélavy born in 1920 in NY. Jewish
name? Change of sex – Rose being the
ugliest name for my personal taste, and
Sélavy the easy pun c'est la vie [that's
life]*'), date unknown
Pencil on paper, 12.3 x 20.2 cm
Centre Pompidou, Paris. Musée national
d'art moderne/Centre de création
industrielle

31
Man Ray
Marcel Duchamp as Rrose Sélavy, 1921
Gelatin silver print, 17.5 x 12.5 cm
Private collection

32
New York Dada, 1921
Magazine facsimile, 36.7 x 25.4 cm
Private collection, London

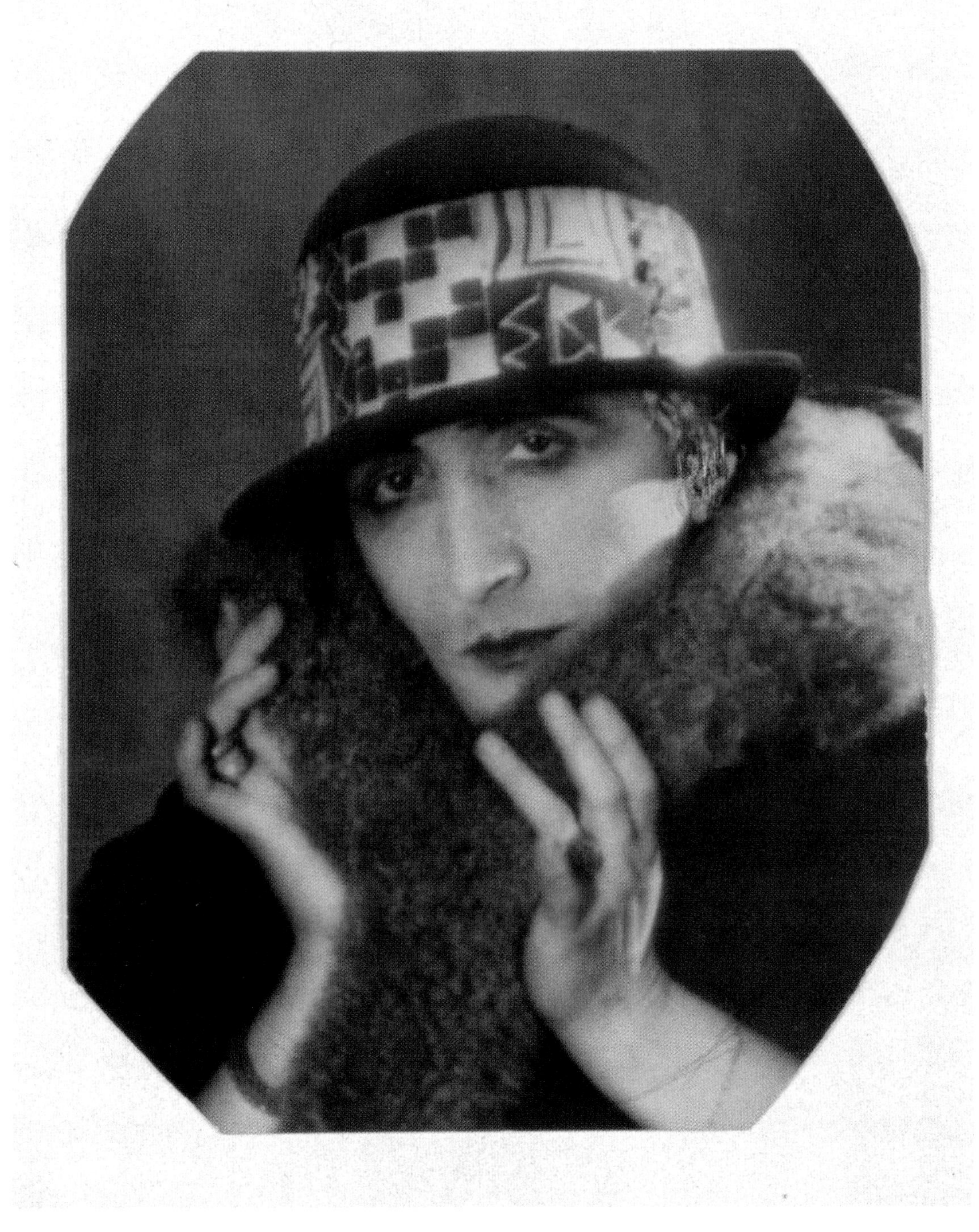

33
Marcel Duchamp
Rrose Sélavy, c. 1921
Silver gelatin print, photograph by Man
Ray retouched by the artist, 13.5 x 10.7 cm
Private collection

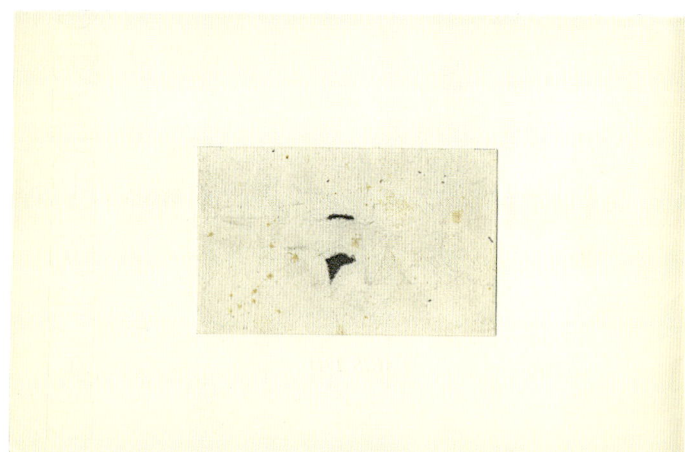

La mémoire du miroir se venge
qui fut inventée par l'homme.

Qui est cet homme?
Celui qui supprime avec des barres de glace.
Qui est cet homme?
Celui qui broie la suie
avec le moulin à cristal de la neige.

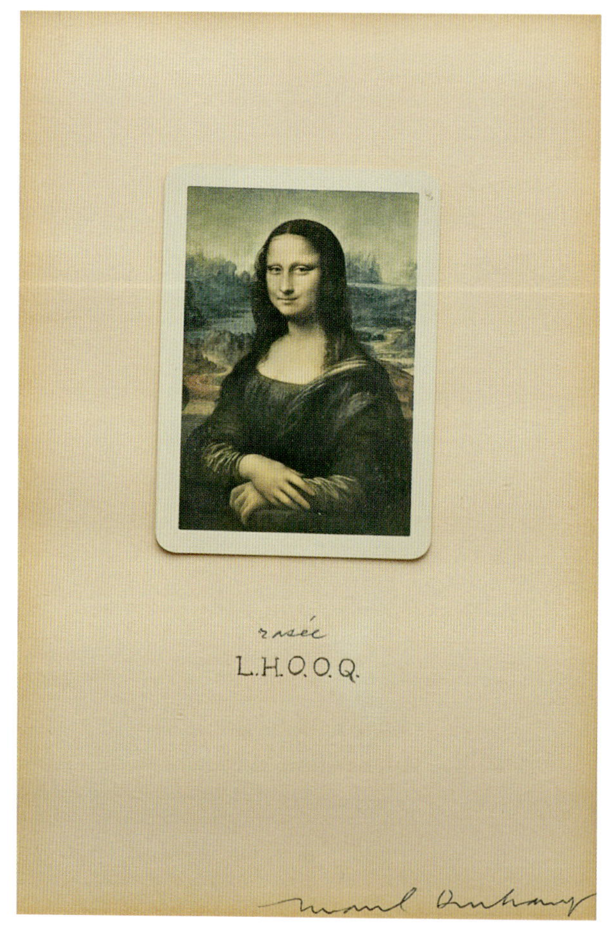

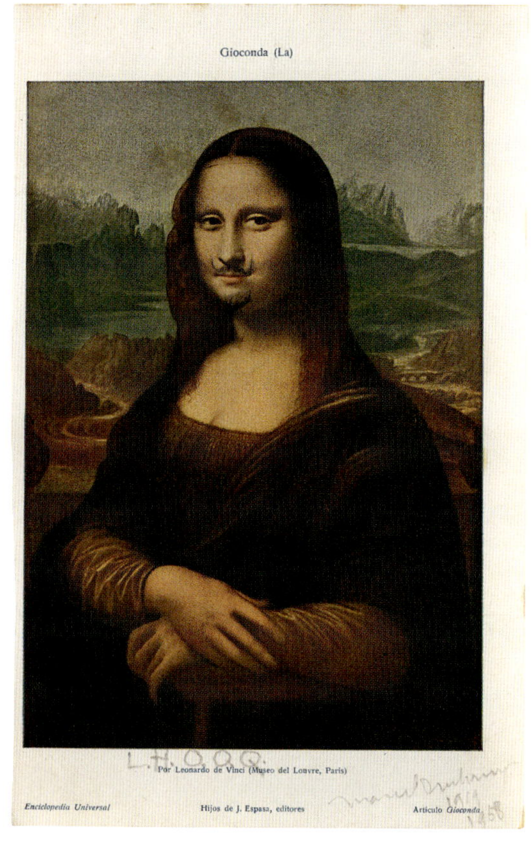

Gioconda (La)

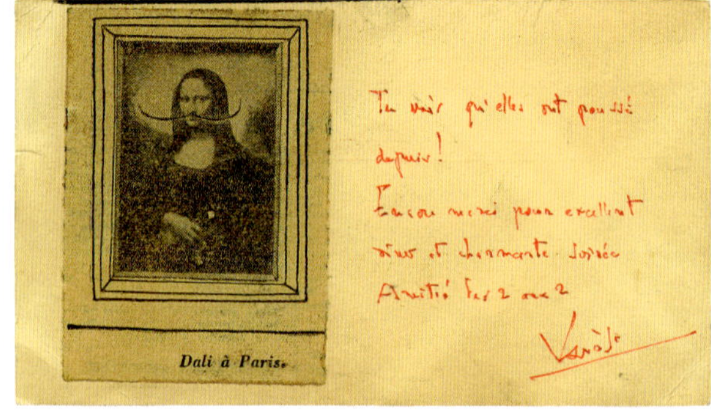

Opposite, top: 34
Marcel Duchamp
*Moustache and Beard of
L.H.O.O.Q.*, 1941
Pochoir, graphite on paper;
frontispiece for 'Marcel Duchamp',
poem by Georges Hugnet dated
8 November 1939, published Paris,
May 1941
Book, 9.7 x 14.2 cm
Collection of The Dalí Museum,
St Petersburg, Florida

Opposite, left: 35
Marcel Duchamp
L.H.O.O.Q., 1958
Moustache and goatee added to
reproduction of the *Mona Lisa*
printed in the *Enciclopedia
Universal*, 24.5 x 15 cm
Private collection, Barcelona

Opposite, centre: 36
Marcel Duchamp
*Rasée L.H.O.O.Q. (Shaved
L.H.O.O.Q)*, 1965
Reproduction of the *Mona Lisa*
(playing card), mounted on dinner
invitation, 8.9 x 6.4 cm
Private collection, courtesy
Sean Kelly, New York

Opposite, bottom: 37
Edgard Varèse
*Little Gioconda Collage:
Dalí à Paris*, 1 June 1955
Newspaper clipping mounted
on paper, 14 x 8.2 cm
Private collection – Archives
Marcel Duchamp

Right: 38
Marcel Duchamp
Monte Carlo Bond, 1924
Printed paper, gelatin silver
photograph and postage stamp;
lithograph in colour with original
photograph of Marcel Duchamp
by Man Ray on cardboard and
sandpaper, 32 x 20 cm
Private collection

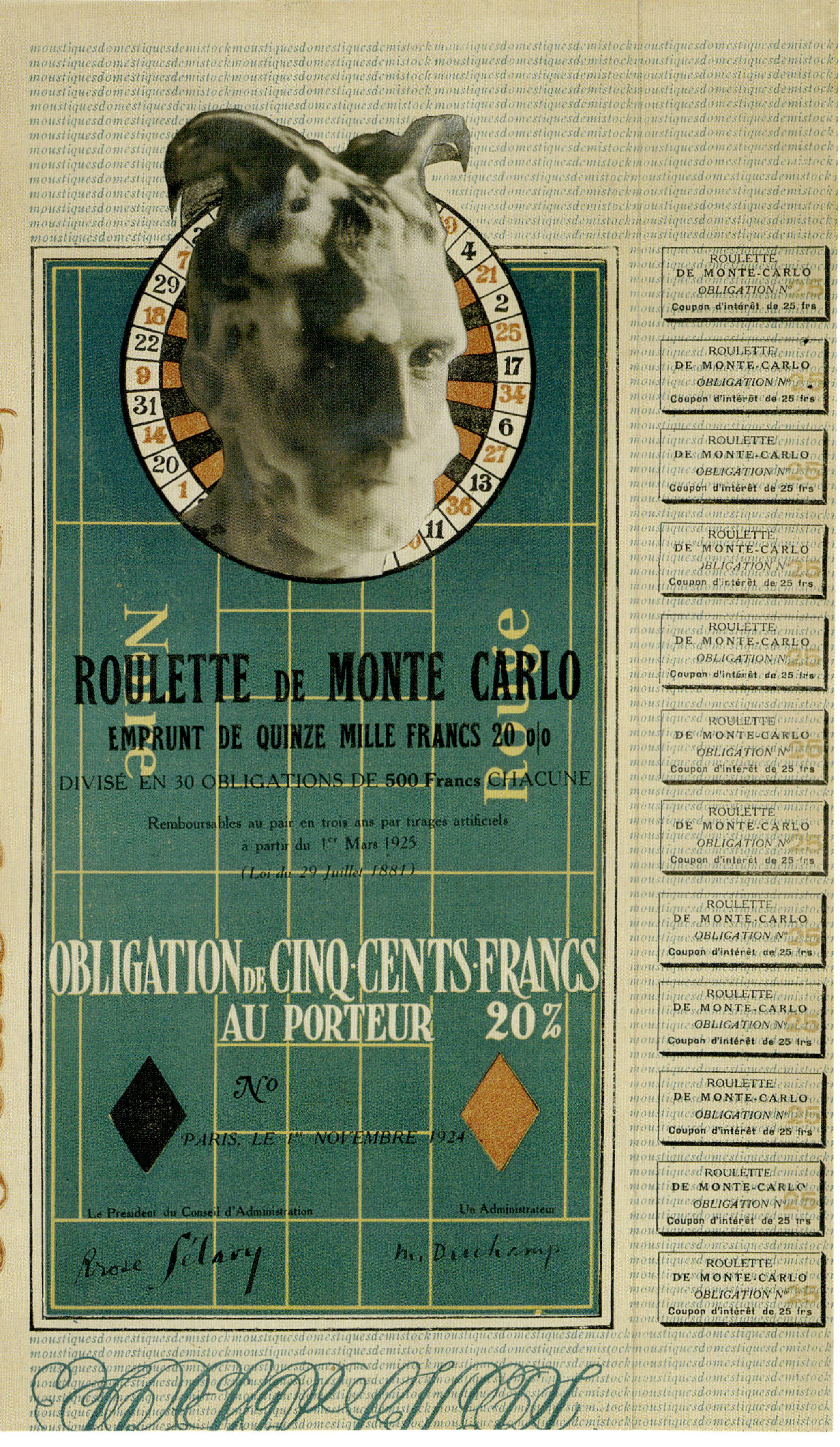

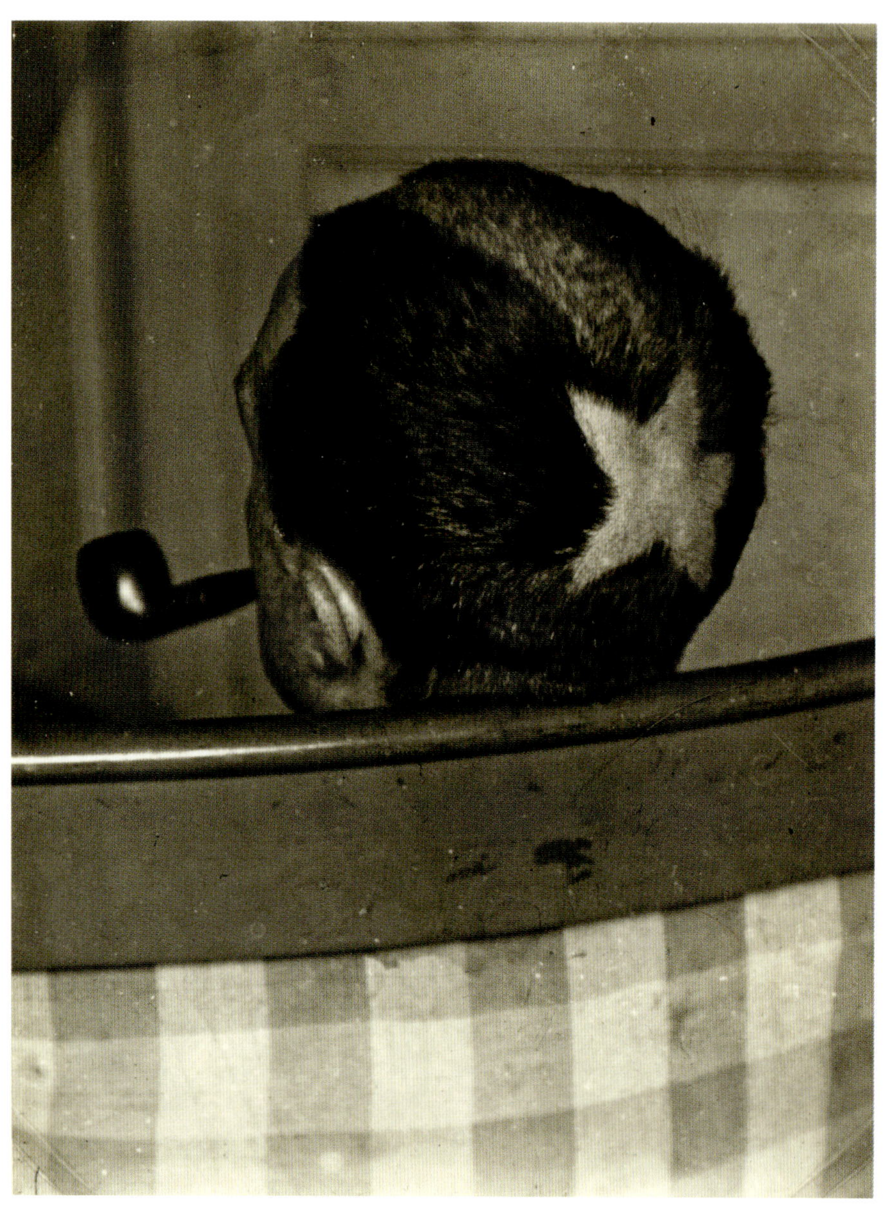

39
Marcel Duchamp
Tonsure, 1921
Photograph by Man Ray, gelatin silver print
on postcard, 12.1 x 9 cm
Private collection, courtesy:
Sean Kelly, New York

40
Horst P. Horst
Portrait of Dalí, 1943
Silver gelatin print, 25.4 x 20.3 cm
Horst Estate

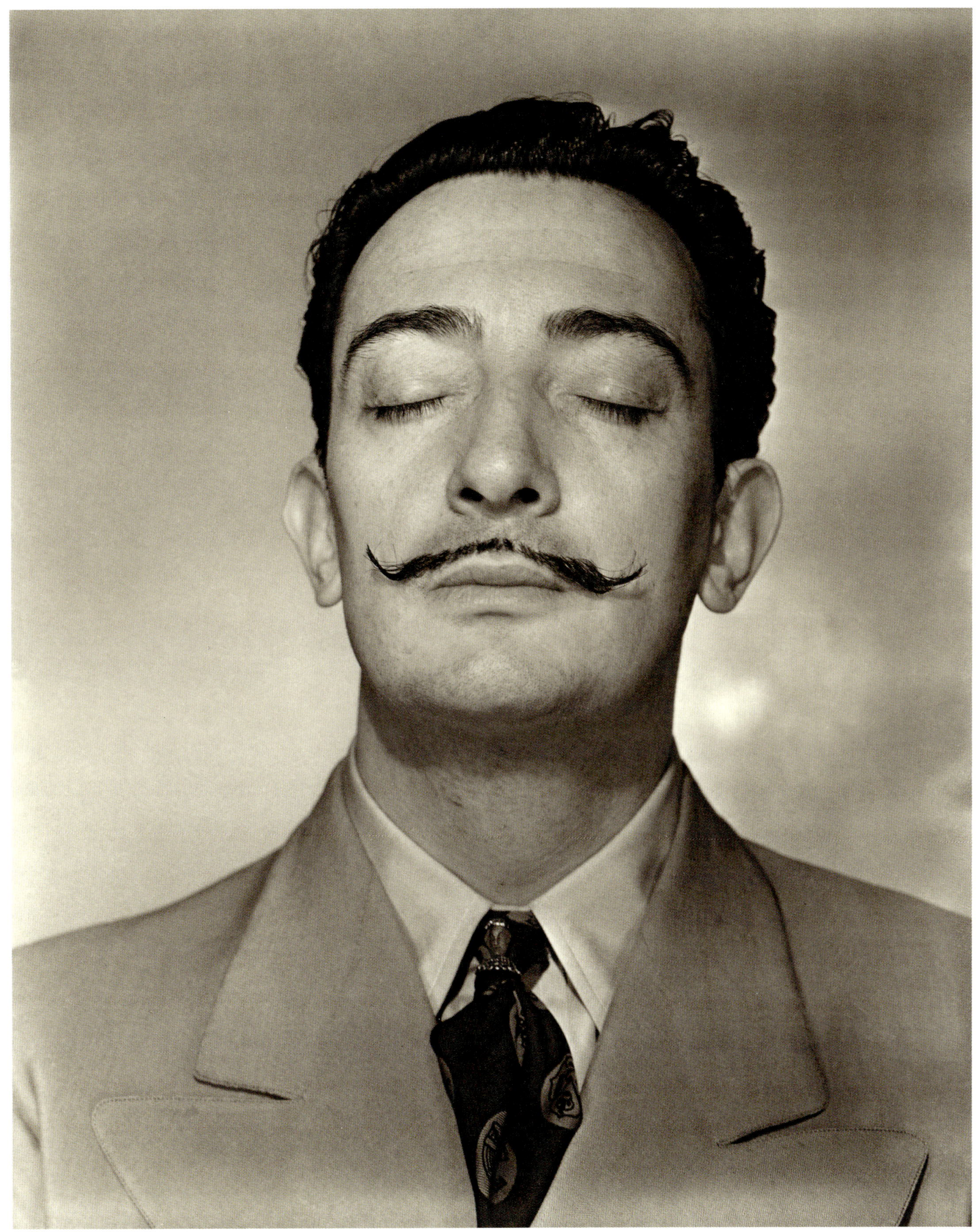

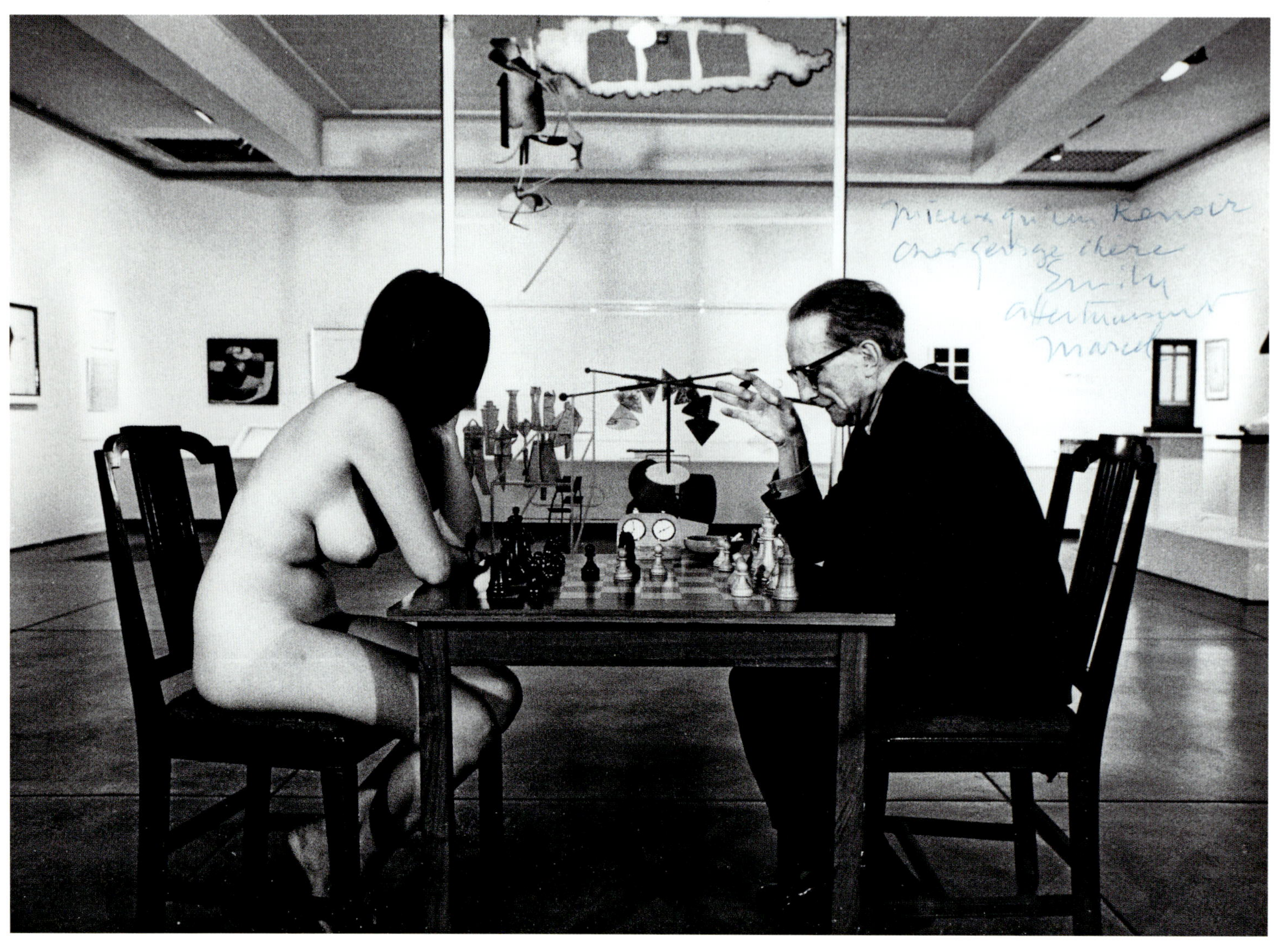

41
Julian Wasser
*Chess Match at the Pasadena Museum
between Eve Babitz and Marcel
Duchamp*, 18 October 1963
Photograph, 18 x 24.7 cm
Collection Hummel, Vienna

42
Robert Descharnes
Duchamp and Dalí playing chess during
filming for *Autoportrait mou de Salvador
Dalí* (*Soft Self-portrait of Salvador Dalí*)
(dir. Jean-Christophe Averty), 1966
(printed 2004)
Silver gelatin print, 31 x 21 cm
Arxiu Pere Vehí, Cadaqués

43
Salvador Dalí, 'L'échecs,
c'est moi' ('Chess, it's me'), *c.* 1971
Preface to Pierre Cabanne, *Dialogues
with Marcel Duchamp*, London, 1971
Fundació Gala-Salvador Dalí, Figueres

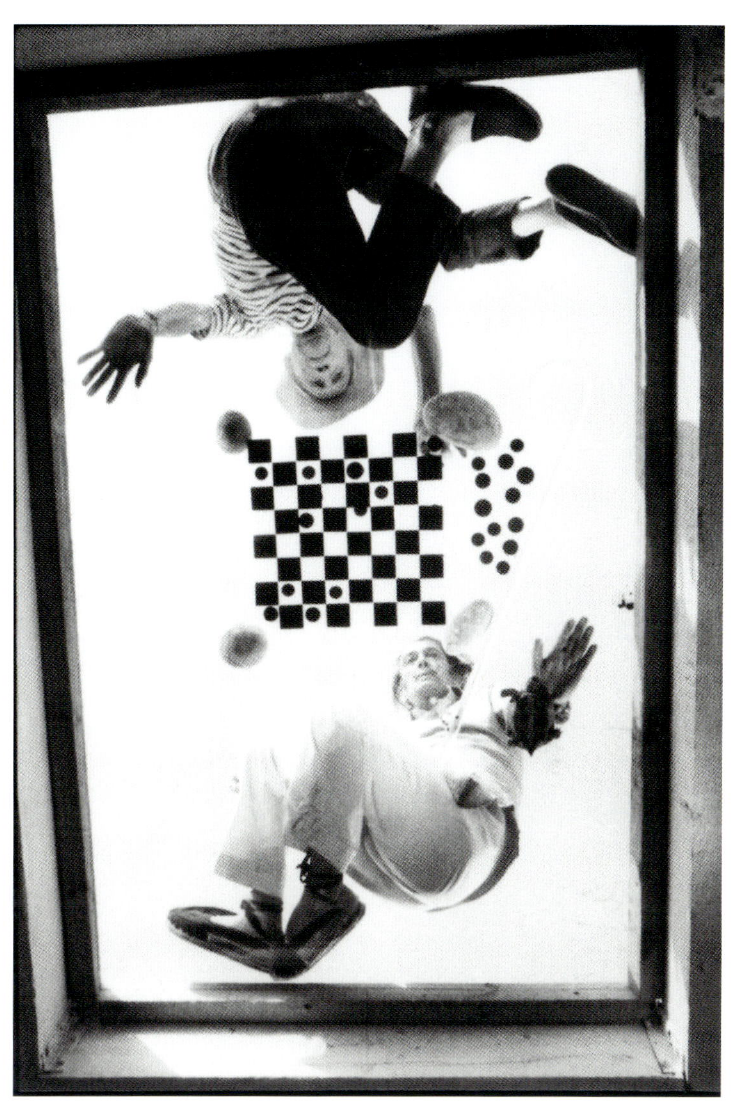

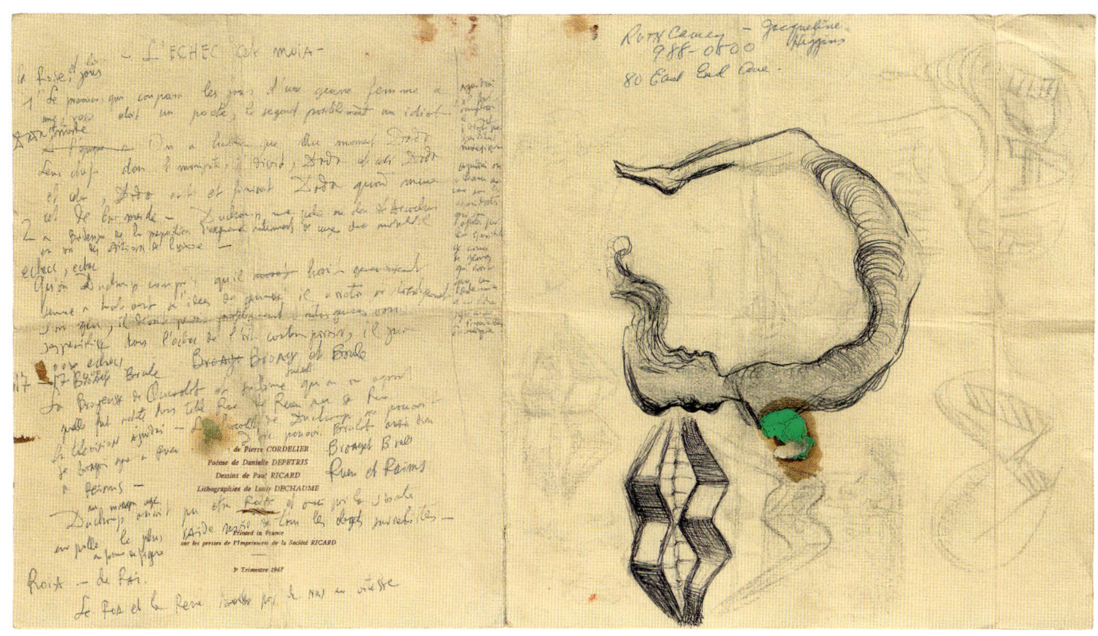

ANTI-ART AND MODERN ART
WILLIAM JEFFETT

I'm against the word anti. Because it's a bit like atheist as compared to believer. And an atheist is just as much of a religious man as the believer is, and the anti-artist is just as much of an artist as the other artist. An-artist would be much better, instead of anti-artist, AN-artist, meaning no artist at all. That would be my conception. I don't mind being an an-artist.[1]

The reaction against art that came to a head with Dada during the convulsions of the First World War took different forms and was generated from different dissatisfactions; 'Art' had become an ethical, institutional and aesthetic problem. As Tzara wrote in his Dada Manifesto, '"ART" – parrot word – replaced by DADA...ART NEEDS AN OPERATION'.[2] 'Anti-art' was a reaction against the way art was corralled into supporting the war (German soldiers marching off to the front with a volume of Goethe in their rucksacks), or against the comfortable and profitable distance even modern art took from reality ('We have enough cubist and futurist academies: Laboratories of formal ideas. Is the aim of art to make money and cajole the nice nice bourgeois?').[3] Dada manifested itself in an aggressive iconoclasm on the one hand, and on the other optimism at the possibilities of renewal through non-artistic means such as chance and non-traditional materials.

From a different direction, much of what went by the name of 'art' seemed anachronistic in the modern world, with its fine precision machines. Duchamp is reported to have commented to his companions Fernand Léger and Constantin Brancusi, while visiting the Salon de la locomotion aérienne in 1912, 'Painting is finished. Who can do better than that propeller? Tell me, can you do that?' He was, Léger said, very taken with these precise things.[4] Perhaps *Bicycle Wheel* (cat. 77) was Duchamp's response to his own challenge, an ironic comment on the Futurist embrace of the machine, which was to open up an extraordinary avenue for art in the name of non-art.

The only recognised public presentation of a readymade at the time was in the context of a much heralded exhibition of modern art in New York: the first Independents Exhibition in 1917. In connection with the exhibition, Duchamp and his friends Henri-Pierre Roché and Beatrice Wood produced two issues of a little magazine, *The Blind Man*, which seems to have been intended to short-circuit the enterprise. The first issue

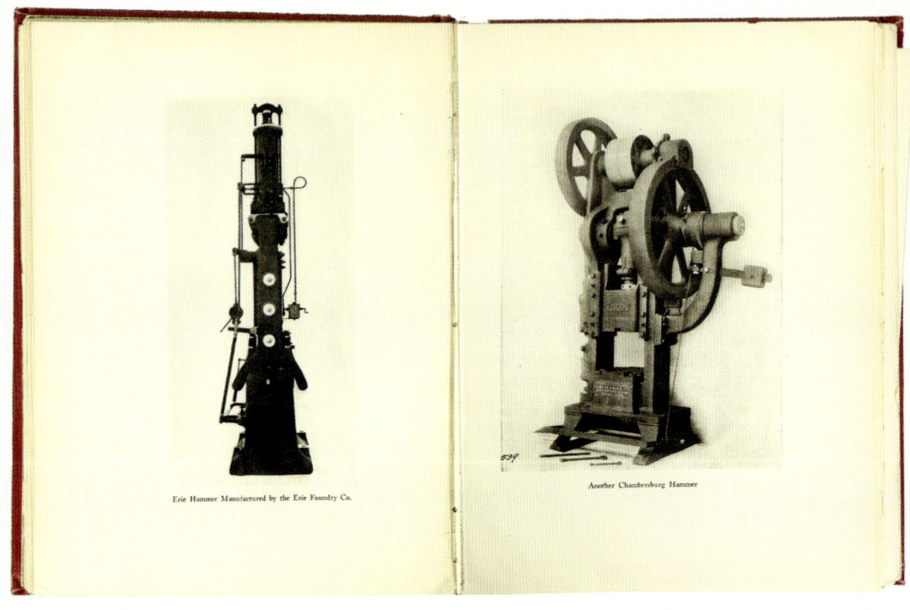

introduced the Independents Exhibition as an important milestone in the arrival of 'modern art' in the United States. 'Russia needed a political revolution. America needs an artistic one... *291* and *The Soil* have come....'[5] The second issue highlighted the 'refusal' of *Fountain* (cat. 102) by the Hanging Committee of the Independents. Apart from this iconic object's public position as emblematic of readymades, it had an immediate purpose in 1917 as a deadpan and ironic riposte to Robert Coady's little magazine *The Soil*. In this, Coady had developed his industrial aesthetic, aggressive nationalism and denunciation of the avant-garde on a grand, masculine scale with his 'Moving Sculpture' series, which featured photographs of massive machines and locomotives (fig. 60). It is not too far-fetched to imagine Duchamp's irritation at this super-macho nationalist anti-art machine rhetoric.[6] Moreover, Coady had commented mockingly on Jean Crotti's description of his wire-and-sculpture portrait of Duchamp as 'an absolute expression of my idea of Marcel Duchamp': 'How does [your absolute expression] differ from the absolute expression of a – plumber?'[7] *Fountain* managed to deal with this too: 'The only works of art America has given are her plumbing and her bridges.'[8]

A logical consequence of Dada's various forms of anti-art was to cease artistic activity altogether. By the time Dada reached Paris, this was a conclusion

Fig. 60
'Erie Hammer' and 'Another Chambersburg Hammer', plates from 'Moving Sculpture Series' in Robert Coady's journal *The Soil*, vol. 1, no. 2, January 1917. Thomas J. Watson Library, The Metropolitan Museum of Art, New York

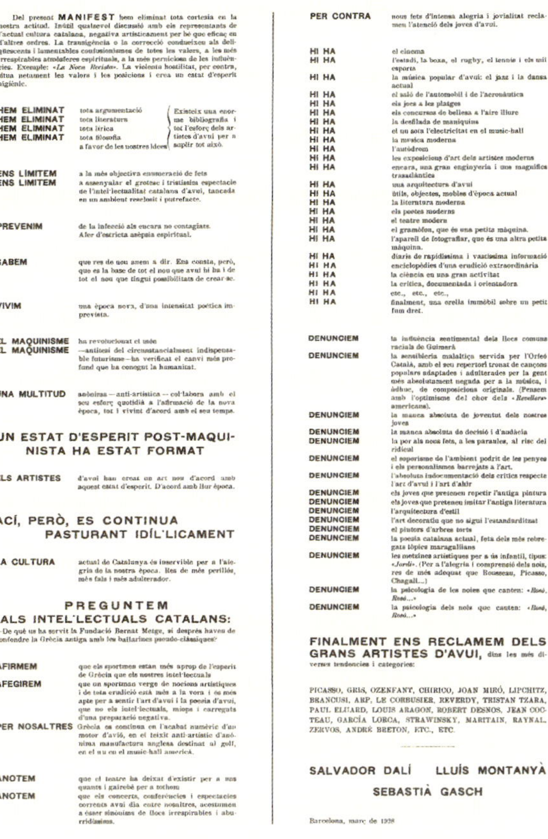

Del present **MANIFEST** hem eliminat tota cortesia en la nostra actitud. Inútil qualsevol discussió amb els representants de l'actual cultura catalana, negativa artísticament per bé que eficaç en d'altres ordres. La transigència o la correcció condueixen als deliqüescents i lamentables confusionismes de totes les valors, a les més irrespirables atmòsferes espirituals, a la més perniciosa de les influències. Exemple: «La Nova Revista». La violenta hostilitat, per contra, situa netament les valors i les posicions i crea un estat d'esperit higiènic.

HEM ELIMINAT	tota argumentació	Existeix una enorme bibliografia i tot l'esforç dels artistes d'avui per a suplir tot això.
HEM ELIMINAT	tota literatura	
HEM ELIMINAT	tota lírica	
HEM ELIMINAT	tota filosofia	
	a favor de les nostres idees	

ENS LIMITEM a la més objectiva enumeració de fets
ENS LIMITEM a assenyalar el grotesc i tristíssim espectacle de l'intel·lectualitat catalana d'avui, tancada en un ambient reclosit i putrefacte.

PREVENIM de la infecció als encara no contagiats. A fer d'estricta asèpsia espiritual.

SABEM que res de nou anem a dir. Ens consta, però, que és la base de tot el nou que avui hi ha i de tot el nou que tingui possibilitats de crear-se.

VIVIM una època nova, d'una intensitat poètica imprevista.

EL MAQUINISME ha revolucionat el món
EL MAQUINISME —antítesi del circumstancialment indispensable futurisme— ha verificat el canvi més profund que ha conegut la humanitat.

UNA MULTITUD anònima — anti-artística — col·labora amb el seu esforç quotidià a l'afirmació de la nova època, tot i vivint d'acord amb el seu temps.

UN ESTAT D'ESPERIT POST-MAQUINISTA HA ESTAT FORMAT

ELS ARTISTES d'avui han creat un art nou d'acord amb aquest estat d'esperit. D'acord amb llur època.

ACÍ, PERÒ, ES CONTINUA PASTURANT IDÍL·LICAMENT

LA CULTURA actual de Catalunya és inservible per a l'alegria de la nostra època. Res de més perillós, més fals i més adulterador.

PREGUNTEM
ALS INTEL·LECTUALS CATALANS:

— De què us ha servit la Fundació Bernat Metge, si després haveu de confondre la Grècia antiga amb les ballarines pseudo-clàssiques?

AFIRMEM que els sportmen estan més aprop de l'esperit de Grècia que els nostres intel·lectuals
AFEGIREM que un sportman verge de nocions artístiques i de tota erudició està més a la vora i és més apte per a sentir l'art d'avui i la poesia d'avui, que no els intel·lectuals, miops i carregats d'una preparació negativa.
PER NOSALTRES Grècia es continua en l'acabat numèric d'un motor d'avió, en el teixit anti-artístic d'anònima manufactura anglesa destinat al golf, en el nu en el music-hall americà.

ANOTEM que el teatre ha deixat d'existir per a uns quants i gairebé per a tothom
ANOTEM que els concerts, conferències i espectacles corrents avui dia entre nosaltres, acostumen a ésser sinònims de llocs irrespirables i aburridíssims.

PER CONTRA nous fets d'intensa alegria i jovialitat reclamen l'atenció dels joves d'avui.

HI HA el cinema
HI HA l'estadi, la boxa, el rugby, el tennis i els altres esports
HI HA la música popular d'avui: el jazz i la dansa actual
HI HA el saló de l'automòbil i de l'aeronàutica
HI HA els jocs a les platges
HI HA els concursos de bellesa a l'aire lliure
HI HA la desfilada de maniquins
HI HA el nu sota l'electricitat en el music-hall
HI HA la música moderna
HI HA l'autòdrom
HI HA les exposicions d'art dels artistes moderns
HI HA encara, una gran enginyeria i una magnífica trasatlàntica
HI HA una arquitectura d'avui
HI HA útils, objectes, mobles d'època actual
HI HA la literatura moderna
HI HA els poetes moderns
HI HA el teatre modern
HI HA el gramòfon, que és una petita màquina.
HI HA l'aparell de fotografiar, que és una altra petita màquina.
HI HA diaris de rapidíssima i vastíssima informació
HI HA enciclopèdies d'una erudició extraordinària
HI HA la ciència en una gran activitat
HI HA la crítica, documentada i orientadora
HI HA etc., etc., etc.,
HI HA finalment, una orella immòbil sobre un petit fum dret.

DENUNCIEM la influència sentimental dels llocs comuns racials de Guimerà
DENUNCIEM la sensibleria malaltiça servida per l'Orfeó Català, amb el seu repertori tronat de cançons populars adaptades i adulterades per la gent més absolutament negada per a la música i, àdhuc, de composicions originals. (Penseu amb l'optimisme del chor dels «Revellers» americans).
DENUNCIEM la manca absoluta de joventut dels nostres joves
DENUNCIEM la manca absoluta de decisió i d'audàcia
DENUNCIEM la por als nous fets, a les paraules, al risc del ridícul
DENUNCIEM el soporisme de l'ambient podrit de les penyes i els personalismes barrejats a l'art.
DENUNCIEM l'absoluta indocumentació dels crítics respecte l'art d'avui i l'art d'ahir
DENUNCIEM els joves que pretenen repetir l'antiga pintura
DENUNCIEM els joves que pretenen imitar l'antiga literatura
DENUNCIEM l'arquitectura d'estil
DENUNCIEM l'art decoratiu que no sigui l'estandarditzat
DENUNCIEM el pintors d'arbres torts
DENUNCIEM la poesia catalana actual, feta dels més rebregats tòpics maragallians
DENUNCIEM les metzines artístiques per a ús infantil, tipus «Jordi». (Per a l'alegria i comprensió dels nostres res de més adequat que Rousseau, Picasso, Chagall...)
DENUNCIEM la psicologia de les noies que canten: «Rosó, Rosó...»
DENUNCIEM la psicologia dels nois que canten: «Rosó, Rosó...»

FINALMENT ENS RECLAMEM DELS GRANS ARTISTES D'AVUI, dins les més diverses tendències i categories:

PICASSO, GRIS, OZENFANT, CHIRICO, JOAN MIRÓ, LIPCHITZ, BRANCUSI, ARP, LE CORBUSIER, REVERDY, TRISTAN TZARA, PAUL ELUARD, LOUIS ARAGON, ROBERT DESNOS, JEAN COCTEAU, GARCÍA LORCA, STRAWINSKY, MARITAIN, RAYNAL, ZERVOS, ANDRÉ BRETON, ETC., ETC.

SALVADOR DALÍ   LLUÍS MONTANYÀ
SEBASTIÀ GASCH

Barcelona, març de 1928

IMP. FILLS DE F. SABATER

considered by various writers, notably Breton and Tzara, who in 1923 both considered the possibility of simply ceasing activity.[9] For Breton, this position would be short-lived, as a nascent Surrealism opened up for him new avenues of poetic exploration.

Duchamp had spent 1918–19 intensively playing chess in Buenos Aires and his devotion to the game was such that by late 1922 he notionally had given up all forms of artistic activity in favour of a concentrated devotion to the game. And this was not a mere artistic gesture, as Duchamp really was a great chess player and competed at a very high level, playing against some of the great players of the period including the Belgian master Edgard Colle and the great Russian theoretician Eugene Znosko-Borovsky, both of whom on occasion he beat. Duchamp's chess activity was intense in the decade 1923–33, after which he ceased competitive playing.

Dalí adopted an anti-art position in the period prior to his arrival in Paris, notably in 1927–28. He frequently used the terms anti-art and anti-painting, concepts derived from Miró and Picasso. Miró had used the phrase 'assassination of painting'[10] around 1927, and this was widely reported in Catalan avant-

garde magazines such as *L'Amic de les Arts*, as well as in newspapers sympathetic to modern tendencies, including *La Publicitat*. Curiously absent from these discourses are many references to Dada, so it is not clear to what degree the young Dalí knew of works such as Duchamp's *L.H.O.O.Q.* Still, he would have been more generally cognisant of Dada and the movement's literary activity, as exhaustively considered by writers like Guillermo de Torre in the period around 1925.[11]

When Dalí set out on his anti-artistic and anti-pictorial project he also embraced mass culture, including cinema, boxing, dance halls, photography and so on. This was set out in the *Yellow Manifesto* of 1928 (fig. 61), written with Sebastià Gasch and Lluis Montanyà, in which the only direct reference to the most radical strands of Dada was mention of Tristan Tzara. One way of understanding this group's position is to see it as setting up an opposition between mass culture and art. Dalí's initial forays into anti-painting in 1927–28 challenged the autonomy of the canvas by introducing deliberately erotic images and elements such as fishermen's cork floats and ropes. In 1929, made shortly after going to Paris, his *First Days of Spring* (cat. 59) adopts the modes of commercial illustration and photography, deploying also collage, transfer images and other items to create a seamless, almost cinematic surface, at once denying subjectivity and objectively illustrating a range of symbolic and erotic readings derived from Freud's writings.

That *The First Days of Spring* was included in Aragon's exhibition of collage, 'A Challenge to Painting', at the Galerie Goemans in March 1930, is revealing. Aragon had been a Dadaist prior to his engagement with Surrealism, and here thinking of this painting by Dalí, he underscored the Catalan artist's 'anti-pictorial spirit'.[12] As for Duchamp, 'the painting process was taken so far … that the impossibility of painting imposed itself on painters. Perhaps it is unfortunate that the sterilising … influence of Marcel Duchamp did not put an end pure and simple to painting …'.[13]

Anti-art was both transgressive, seeking to destroy painting and art, and expansive, erasing the boundaries between creative activity and the immediate experience of the world, and opening the door to a greatly expanded idea of poetic activity, where anyone in touch with the marvellous reality of experience could be a poet or artist. Over the years, Dalí increasingly came to understand this aspect of Duchamp, and works like *L.H.O.O.Q.* became increasingly important for him, to the point that he incorporated similar images into his own visual practice. As for Duchamp, he remained agnostic in the face of art when he proposed 'And I go farther – by saying that words such as truth, art, veracity, or anything are stupid in themselves.'[14]

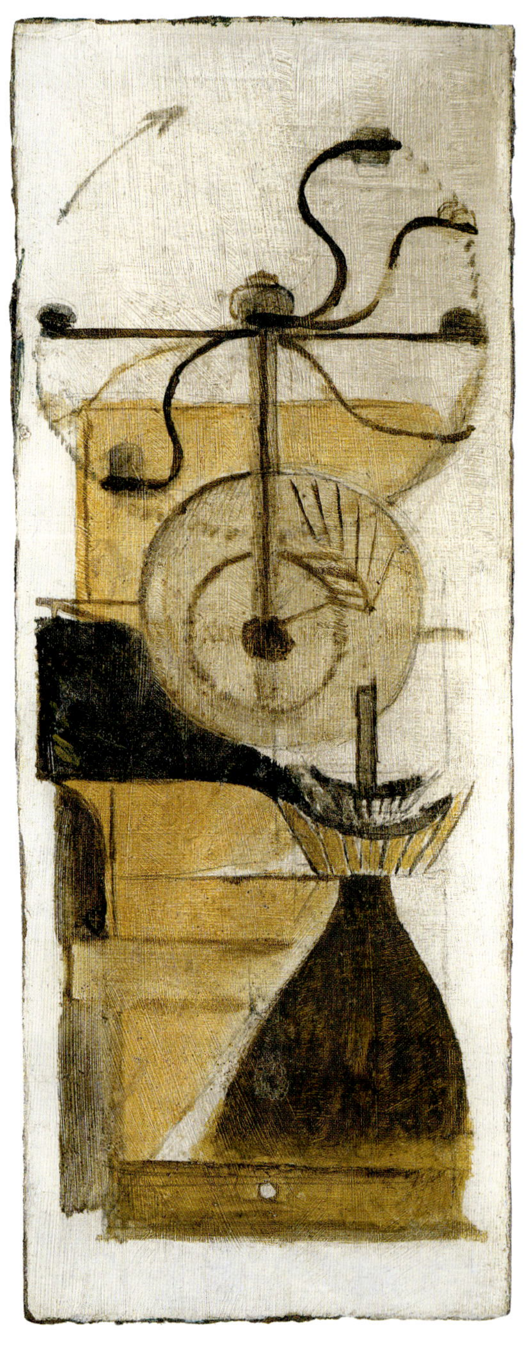

44
Marcel Duchamp
Coffee Mill, 1911
Oil and graphite on board,
33 x 12.7 cm
Tate: Purchased 1981

45
Salvador Dalí
Cubist Self-portrait, 1923
Oil and collage on cardboard on wood,
104 x 75 cm
Museo Nacional Centro de Arte Reina
Sofía, Madrid

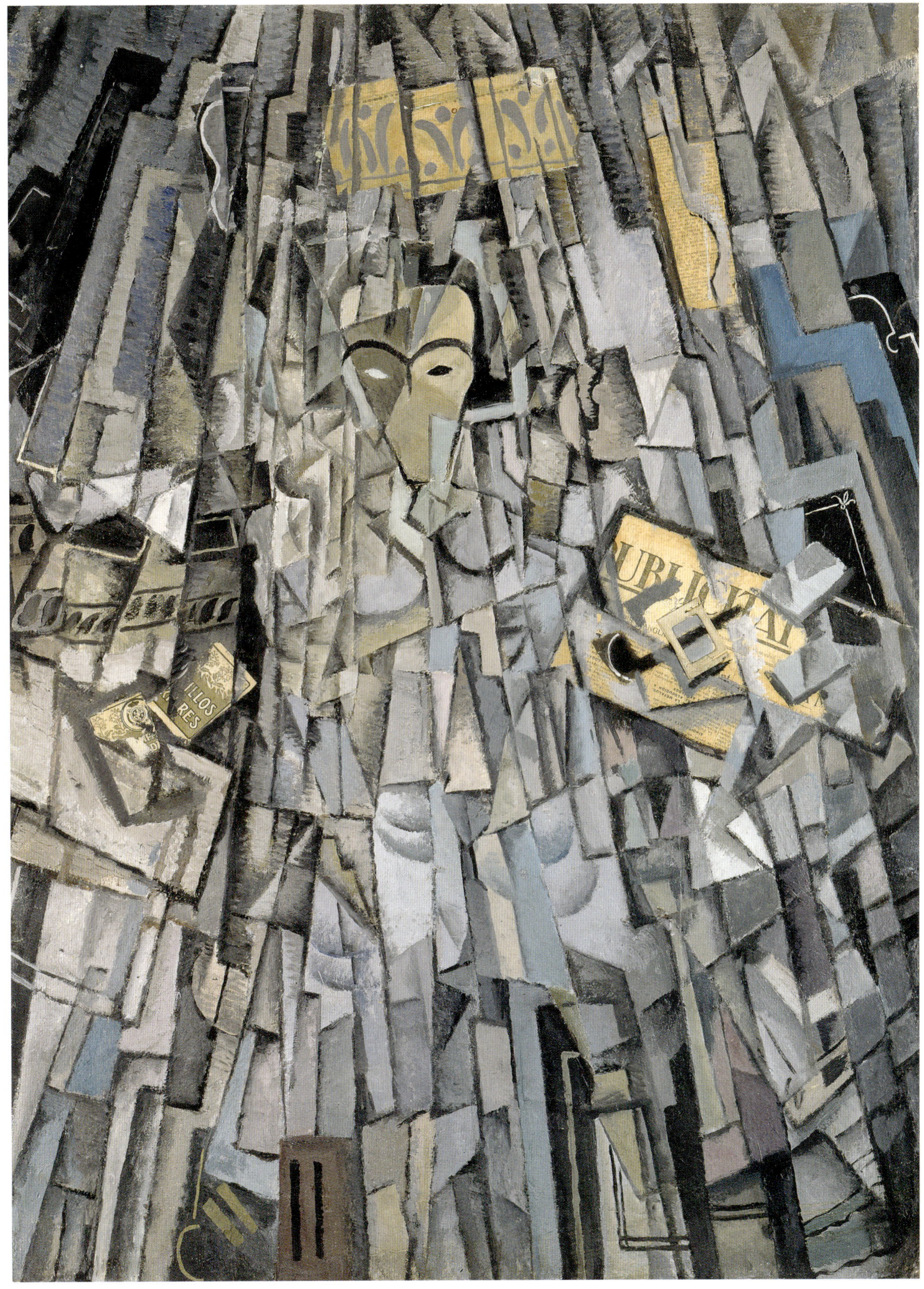

ILLOS
RES
UBLICITAT

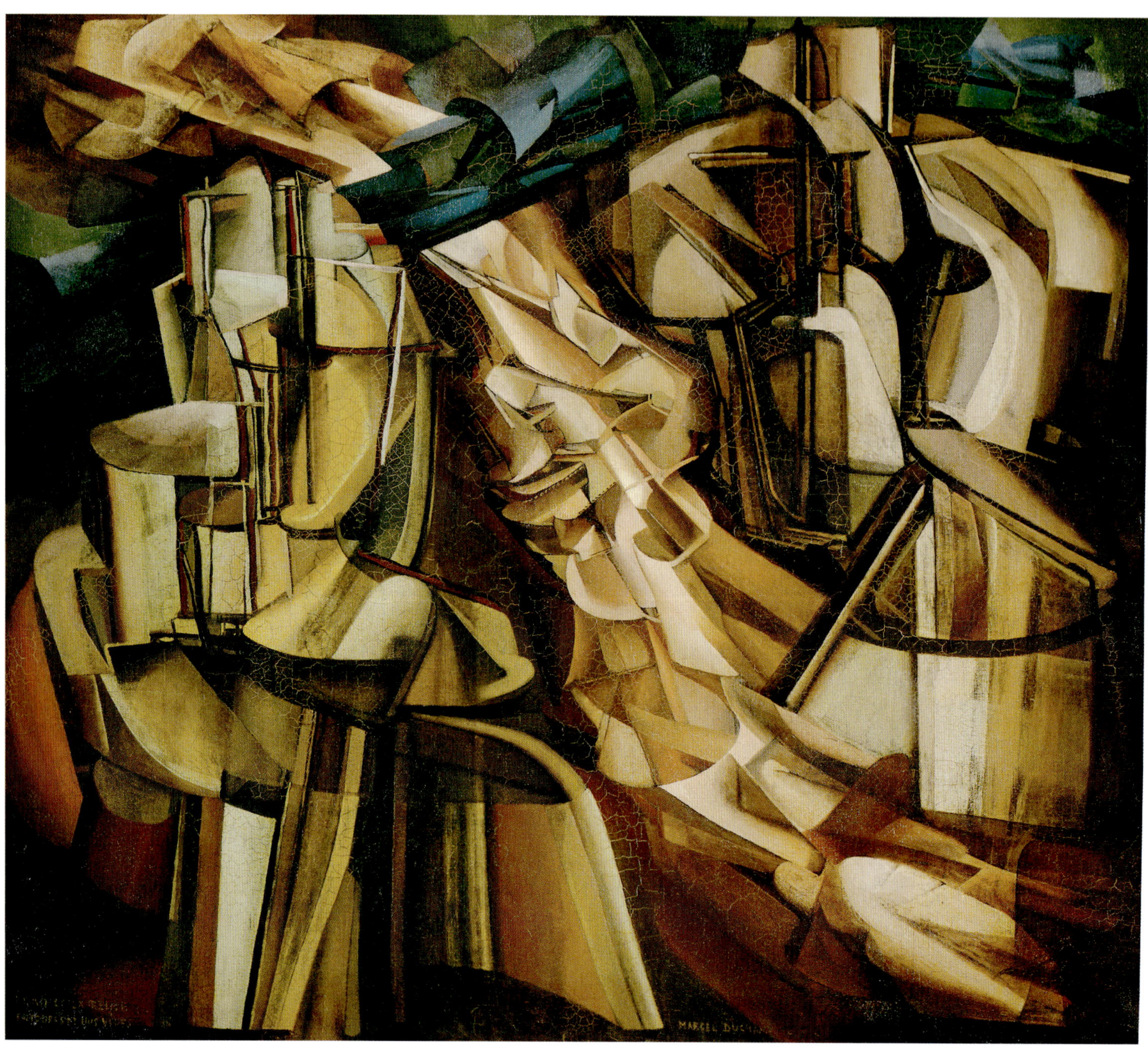

46
Marcel Duchamp
*The King and Queen Surrounded
by Swift Nudes*, 1912
Oil on canvas, 114.6 x 128.9 cm
Philadelphia Museum of Art: The Louise
and Walter Arensberg Collection, 1950

47
Salvador Dalí, 'The King and the Queen
Traversed by Swift Nudes', *Art News*,
58, April 1959
Magazine, each page 33 x 22.2 cm
Collection of The Dalí Museum Archives,
St Petersburg, Florida

By Salvador Dali

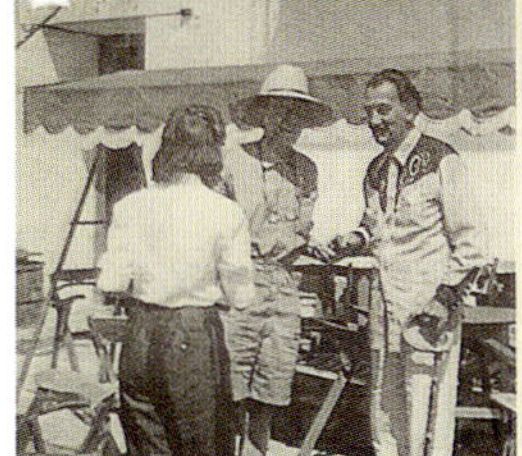

Dali and Duchamp in Spain, 1958.
Photograph Robert Descharnes

The king and the queen traversed by swift nudes

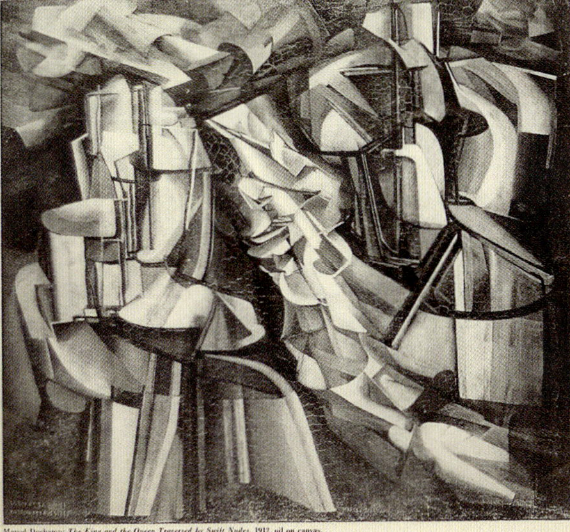

Marcel Duchamp: *The King and the Queen Traversed by Swift Nudes*, 1912, oil on canvas.
Philadelphia Museum, Arensberg Collection.

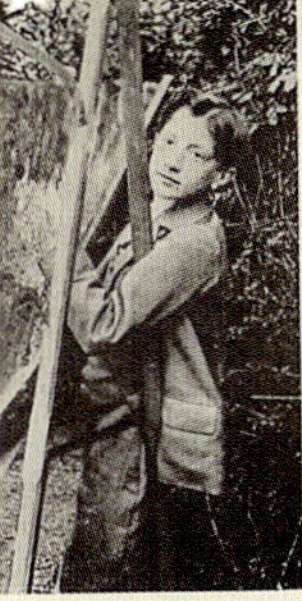
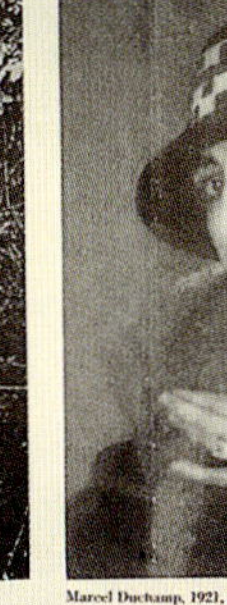

Marcel Duchamp, 1900.

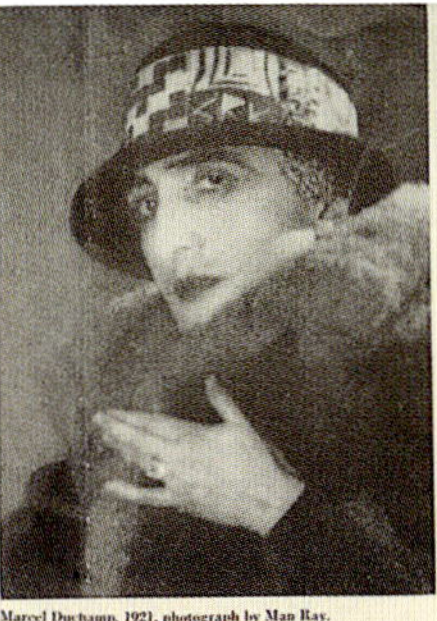

Marcel Duchamp, 1921, photograph by Man Ray.

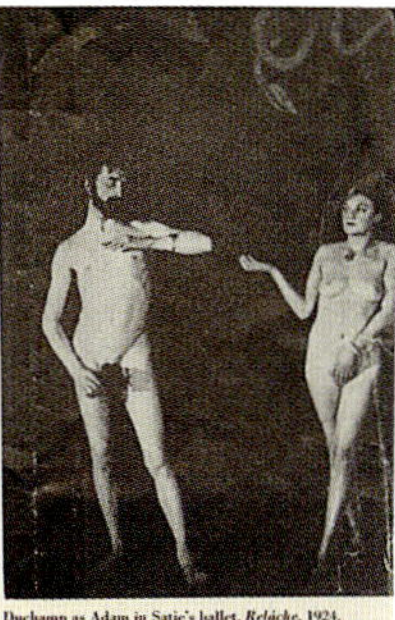

Duchamp as Adam in Satie's ballet, *Relâche*, 1924.

The master of melting watches pays homage to the master of
Nude Descending a Staircase, on the occasion
of a big Duchamp show in New York and the publication of his biography

Personally, I consider Marcel Duchamp's prophetic title alone worth miles of pseudo-decorative modern painting, and this I can affirm for the following thirteen reasons:

1 In painting *The King and the Queen Traversed by Swift Nudes*, the genius of Marcel Duchamp proclaimed nothing less than the notarial act of the new intra-atomic structure of the universe, that is, the discontinuity of matter. In fact, the king and the queen can be traversed by swift nudes because matter is discontinuous. It is easy to understand that swift nudes are indivisible bodies, the corpuscles, the charged elementary particles of quantum physics, which, with their active energy quantum, cross the finite space that, as each day passes, becomes more and more the "supreme royal space" *par excellence* and, if objections are raised, I will add "the Divine space" *par excellence*.

The speculative distance between Duchamp's princely ideas and those of my great compatriot from Tarragona, the peasant Joan Miro, is precisely the distance separating *The King and the Queen Traversed by Swift Nudes* from *Dog Barking at the Moon*; the distance between cosmic majesty and the dog of folklore.

2 Marcel Duchamp, in painting *The King and the Queen Traversed by Swift Nudes* became an aristocratic anarchist, as opposed to the inventors of anarchism, Prince Kropotkin and Prince Bakunin, who were the prototypes of anarchistic aristocrats.

3 Marcel Duchamp, having become an aristocrat because of his original Dadaist anarchism, categorically refuses to take part in the contemporary artistic brawl. He does not want to be identified with those who tirelessly continue "barking at the moon," he abandons painting, not as an act of artistic suicide, but because he continues to have swift nudes cross the king and the queen in his thoughts, while playing chess.

4 Like Louis XIV, Marcel Duchamp can say: "*L'Echec c'est moi*." [Dali's pun on "*L'Etat c'est moi*" is also a play on the triple sense of "*échec*," which in French and throughout this article means "chess," "check" and "failure."] His moral example is worthy of Socrates, but functions more Jesuitically, without suicide, for by aristocratically proclaiming his failure Duchamp alone is saved from the imminent collective failure of modern painting.

5 Marcel Duchamp paints the king's moustaches on Leonardo's queen Gioconda, the queen being the most manoeuverable and premonitory piece on the chessboard. It is well known that Leonardo's life was a continual and dramatic chess game [i.e. "a continual and dramatic game of failures"].

6 At the feet of his king, and his queen Gioconda, Marcel Duchamp wrote the famous inscription L.H.O.O.Q. [*Elle a chaud au cul*], which was the concise way for an anarchist to attest the the thermal and biological condition by which he declares his belief in hereditary continuity.

7 L.H.O.O.Q., a quasi-biochemical formula, is the kind of scatological shortcut which has always delighted kings and courtesans.

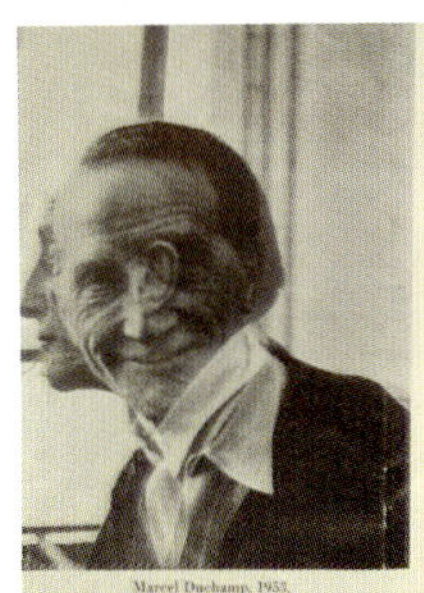

Marcel Duchamp, 1955.
Photograph by Victor Obsatz.

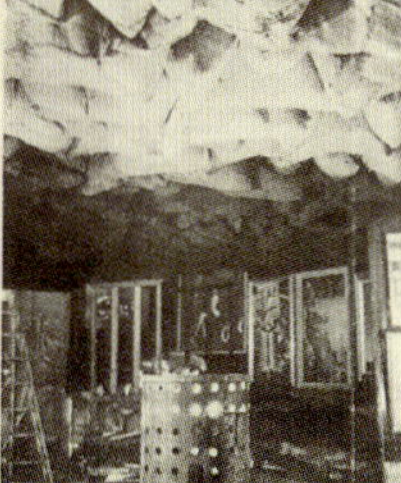

Surrealist exhibition, 1938, designed by Duchamp and Dali.

"Ready-made" *Fountain* rejected by the Independent Artists exhibition, New York, 1917.

The king and the queen traversed by swift nudes *continued*

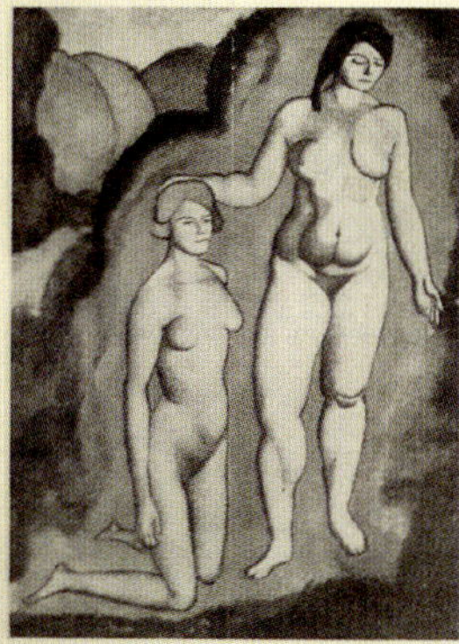

Marcel Duchamp: *The Bush*, 1911.

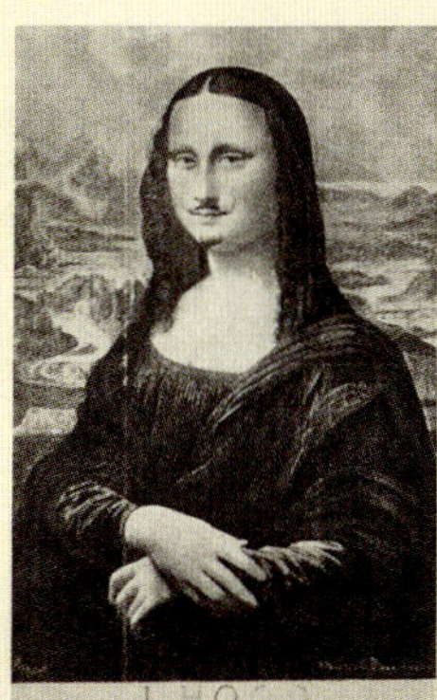

Marcel Duchamp: *L.H.O.O.Q.*, "epitaph of modern painting." 1919.

8 In *The King and the Queen Traversed by Swift Nudes*, L.H.O.O.Q. can be taken quite adequately as the epitaph of modern painting.

9 Thus Duchamp did not believe it necessary to pursue modern painting to its final consequences. Only Dali had a secret imperialist plan, but in any case I cannot be accused of practicing modern painting.

10 The Divisionism of Gaudi and Boccioni, Analytic Cubism, Duchamp's epitaph . . . nothing creative has been produced since in the history of art. From Braque to Miro, there is a reversion either to archeology or to folklore. Duchamp has the enormous advantage over all the rest of having only to look at their paintings to know what they are doing, while the others cannot know what he is doing, because he is doing nothing.

11 Already after modern painting a contagious group rushed at top speed toward absolute nothingness, this standing for a pre-mystical state of mind, what Tapié calls "*art autre*"; Kline, Tapies, Millares, de Kooning, Mathieu. Is the question that we might have access to a new dynasty here a matter of H.O.O.Q? Being here myself, I answer yes.

12 The twelfth reason why *The King and the Queen Traversed by Swift Nudes* is a sublime title is that there is no plastic, sociological, philanthropic or bureaucratic reason for such a title, whose sole and true reason is the ultra-individualistic will of a typically royal personality.

13 That is why Marcel Duchamp has spent the rest of his life filling suitcases with everything—from near or far, or rather from quite close at hand—which could concern him; with full awareness that the excrement accumulated in Louis XVI's navel should have been preserved, though not that of an anonymous elevator operator's. In the middle of the war, during a German bombardment, Duchamp and I went back and forth between Arcachon and Bordeaux filling up his famous suitcase. I remember having mentioned the possibility of bequeathing to posterity the excrement of great personalities, and that Duchamp insisted at great length on the necessity of keeping a record of the temperatures. That was failure on the historical level; the L.H.O.O.Q. of history. [Translated by Richard Howard]

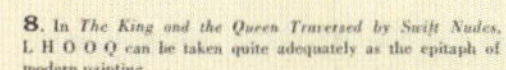

Torn-paper self-portrait, 1958, for the de-luxe publication of *On Marcel Duchamp* by Robert Lebel (Editions Trianon, New York).

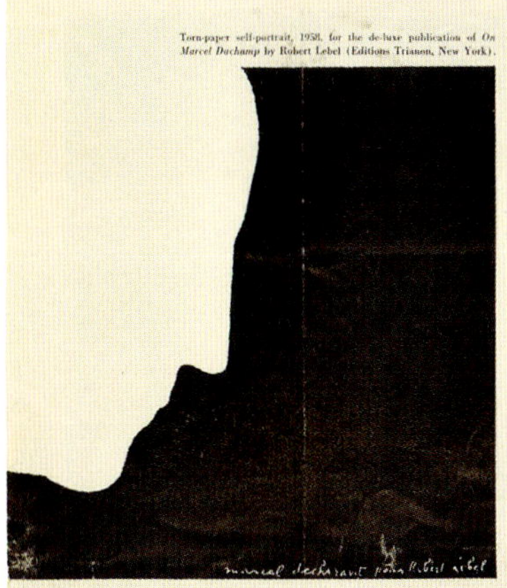

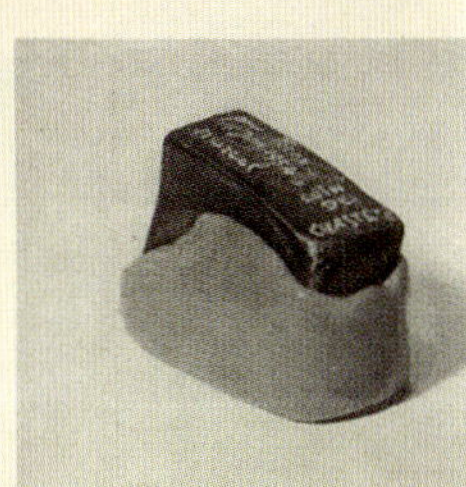

Recent ready-made: *Corner of Chastity*, 1954.

This month sees the publication of a de-luxe edition, *On Marcel Duchamp*, by Robert Lebel, designed by Duchamp, complete with box, magnet and severely limited *tirage*. In honor of the event, the Janis Gallery will exhibit a dozen major Duchamp paintings and documents from the book, and to memorialize April 1959 as Duchamp-month, one of his severest admirers assesses the Duchamp role in these pages.

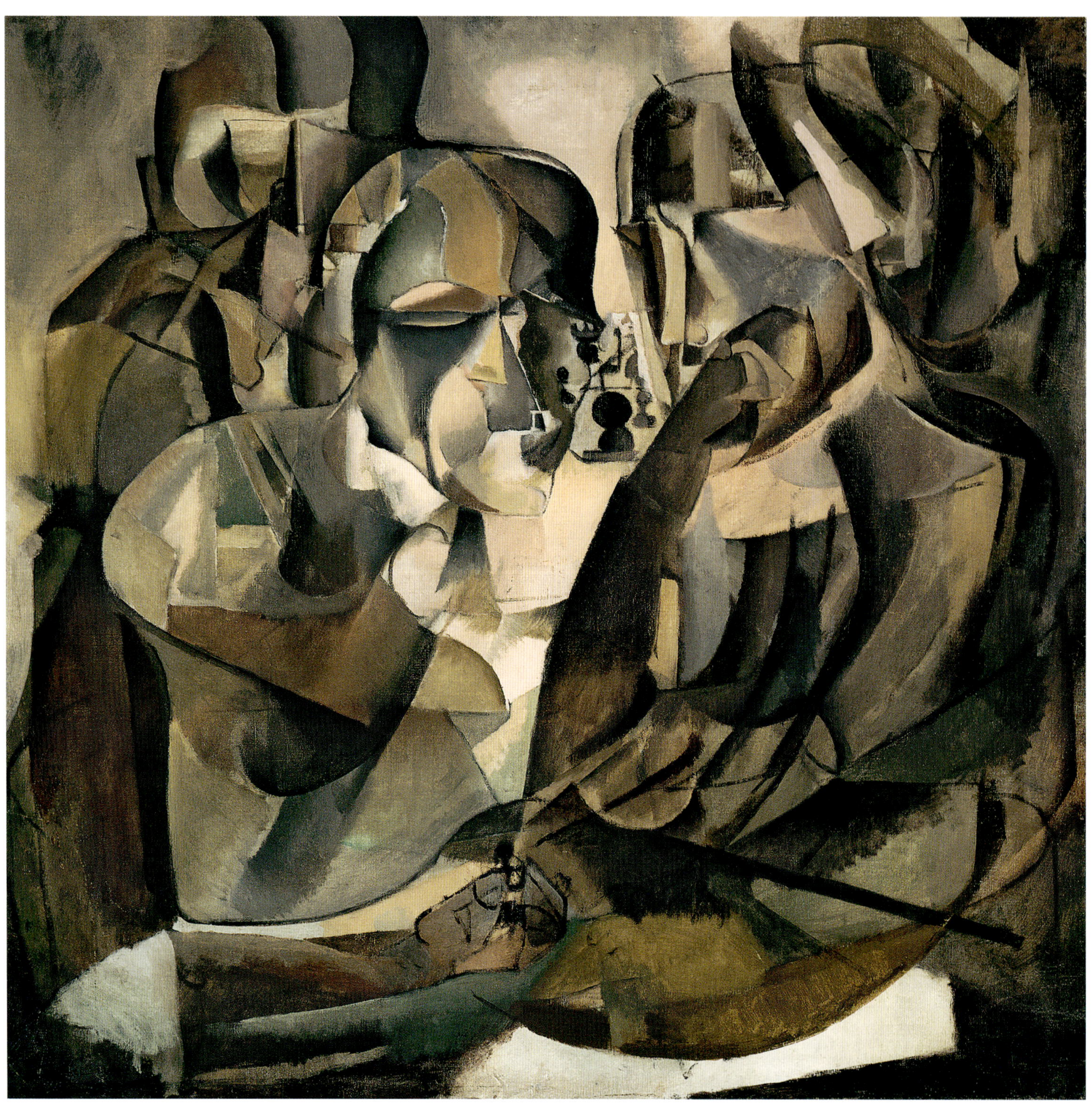

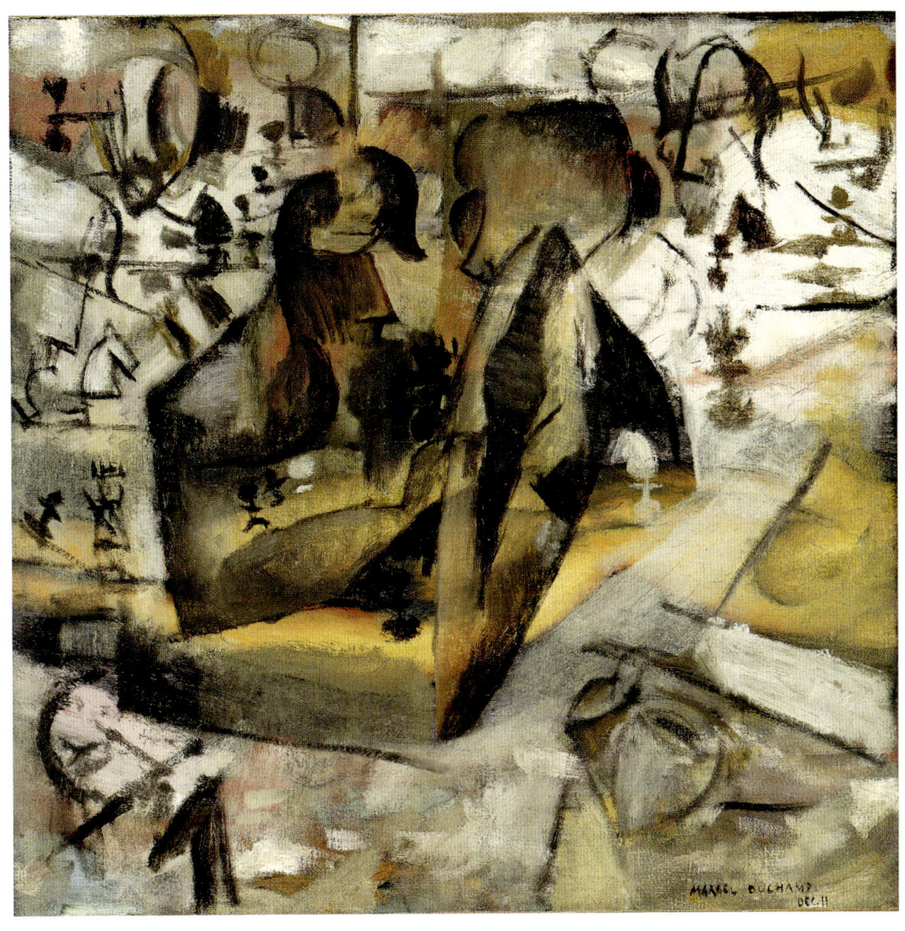

48
Marcel Duchamp
Portrait of Chess Players, 1911
Oil on canvas, 100.6 x 100.5 cm
Philadelphia Museum of Art: The Louise
and Walter Arensberg Collection, 1950

49
Marcel Duchamp
The Chess Players, 1911
Oil on canvas, 50 x 61 cm
Centre Pompidou, Paris. Musée national
d'art moderne/Centre de création
industrielle

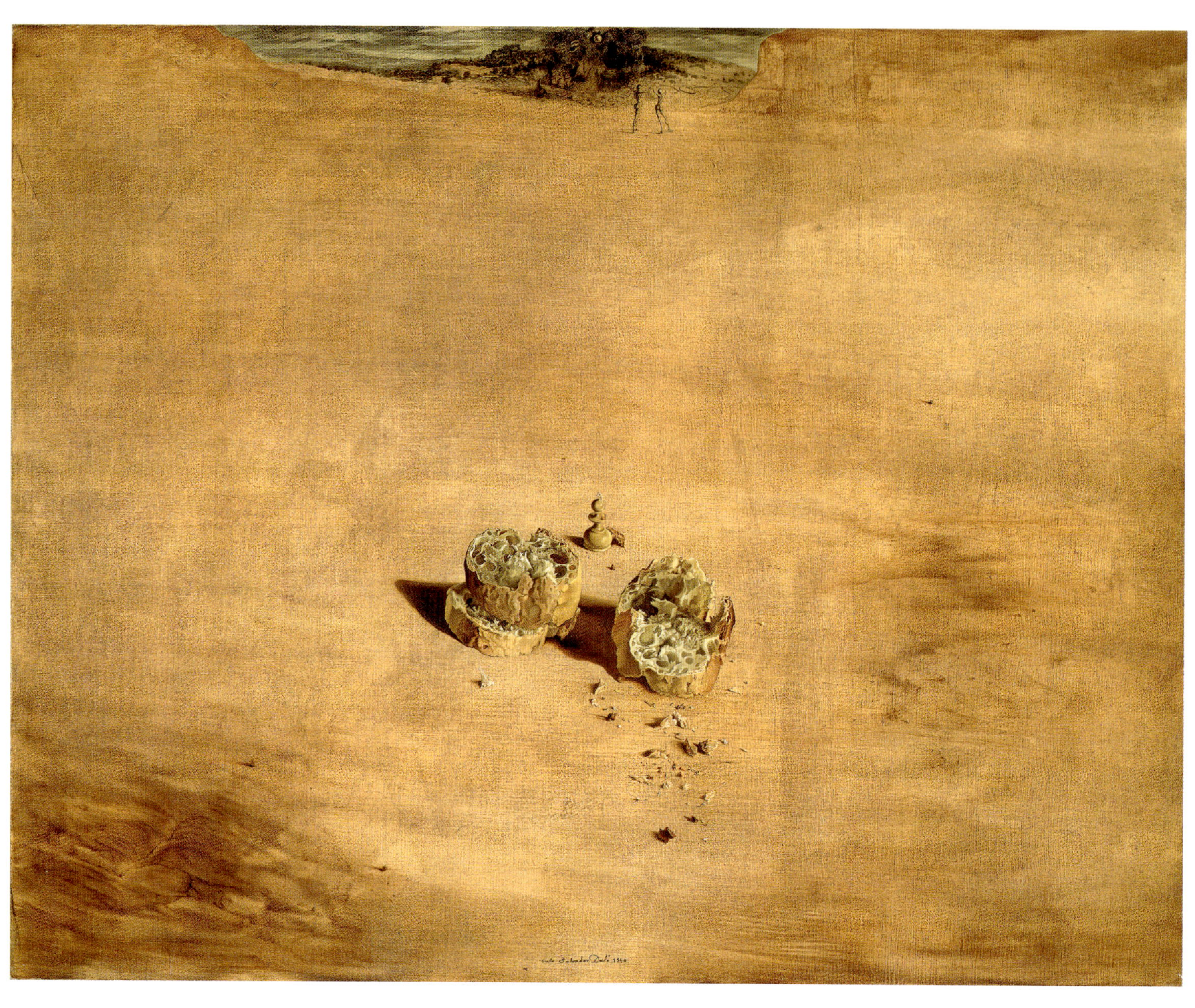

50
Salvador Dalí
*Two Pieces of Bread Expressing the
Sentiment of Love*, 1940
Oil on canvas, 81.5 x 100.5 cm
Fundació Gala-Salvador Dalí, Figueres

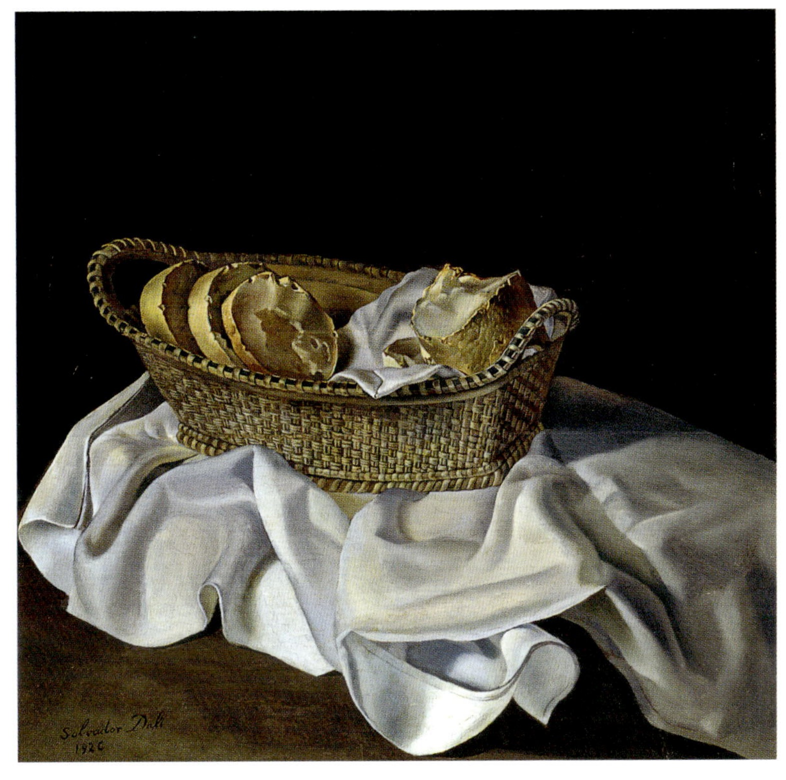

51
Salvador Dalí
The Basket of Bread, 1926
Oil on wood panel, 31.7 x 31.7 cm
Collection of The Dalí Museum,
St Petersburg, Florida

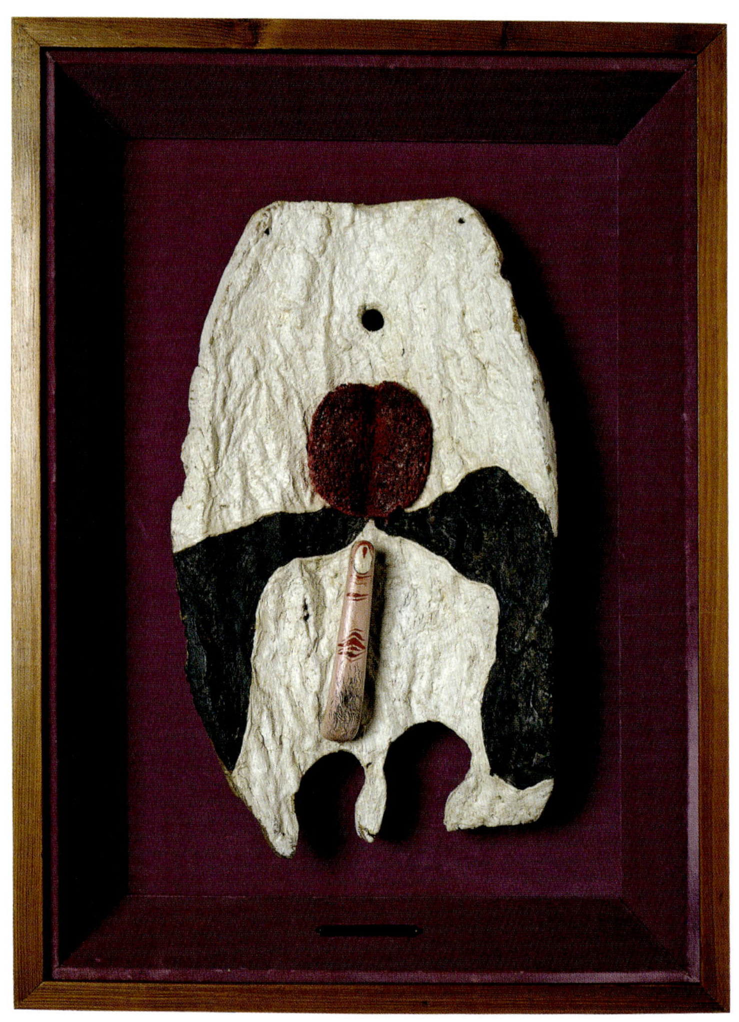

Left: 52
Salvador Dalí
Anthropomorphic Beach, 1928
(present state)
Painted cork, sponge and wood,
48.3 x 27.9 cm
Collection of The Dalí Museum,
St Petersburg, Florida

Below left: 53
Salvador Dalí
The Bather, 1927
Ink on paper, 24.1 x 30.5 cm
Collection of The Dalí Museum,
St Petersburg, Florida

Below right: 54
Salvador Dalí
Preparatory drawing for *Fishermen
in the Sun*, 1928
Drawing on paper, 20 x 18 cm
Arxiu Pere Vehí, Cadaqués

Opposite, top: 55
Salvador Dalí
Fishermen in the Sun, 1928
Oil on canvas with rope, 100 x 100 cm
Collezione Prada, Milan
London only

Opposite, bottom: 56
Salvador Dalí
Untitled, *c.* 1928
Oil on canvas, 148 x 198 cm
Museo Nacional Centro De Arte Reina
Sofía, Madrid

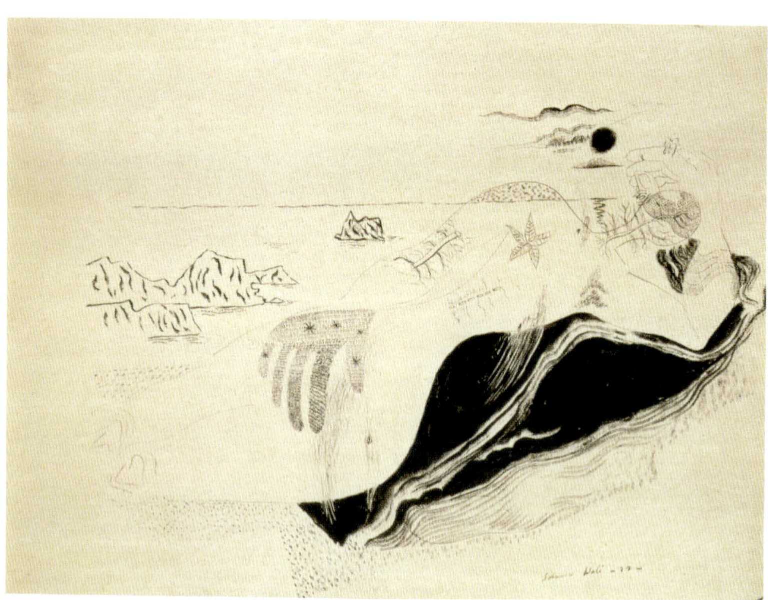

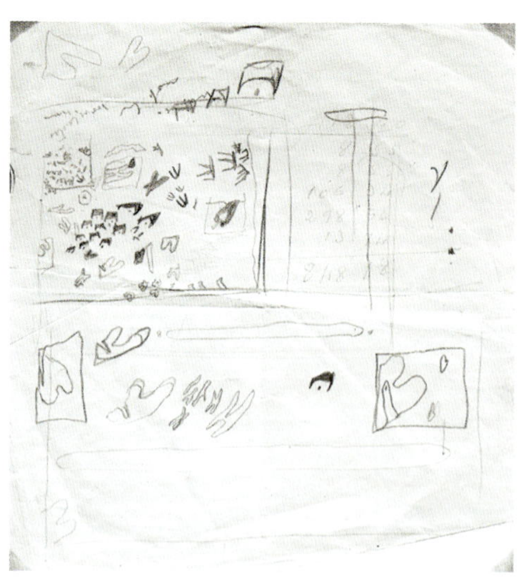

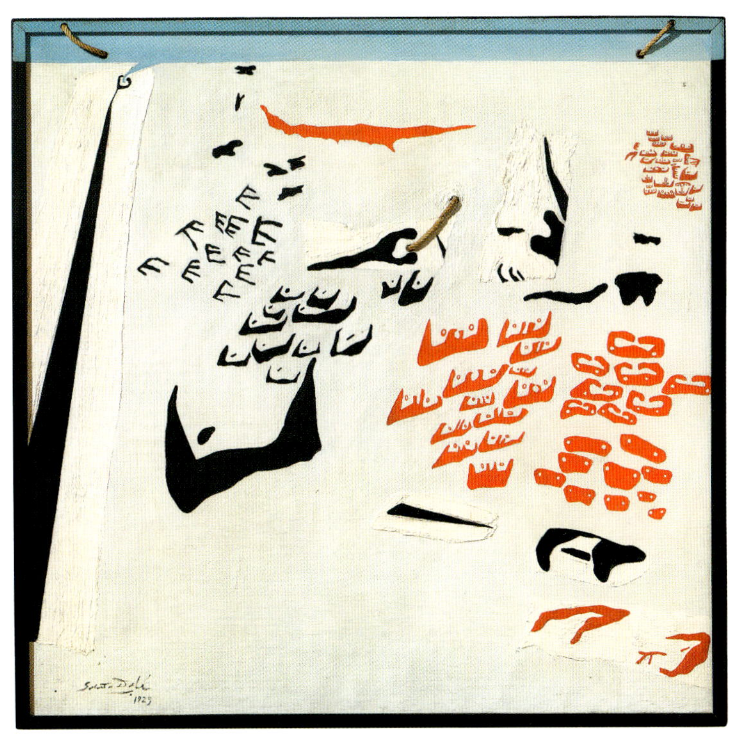

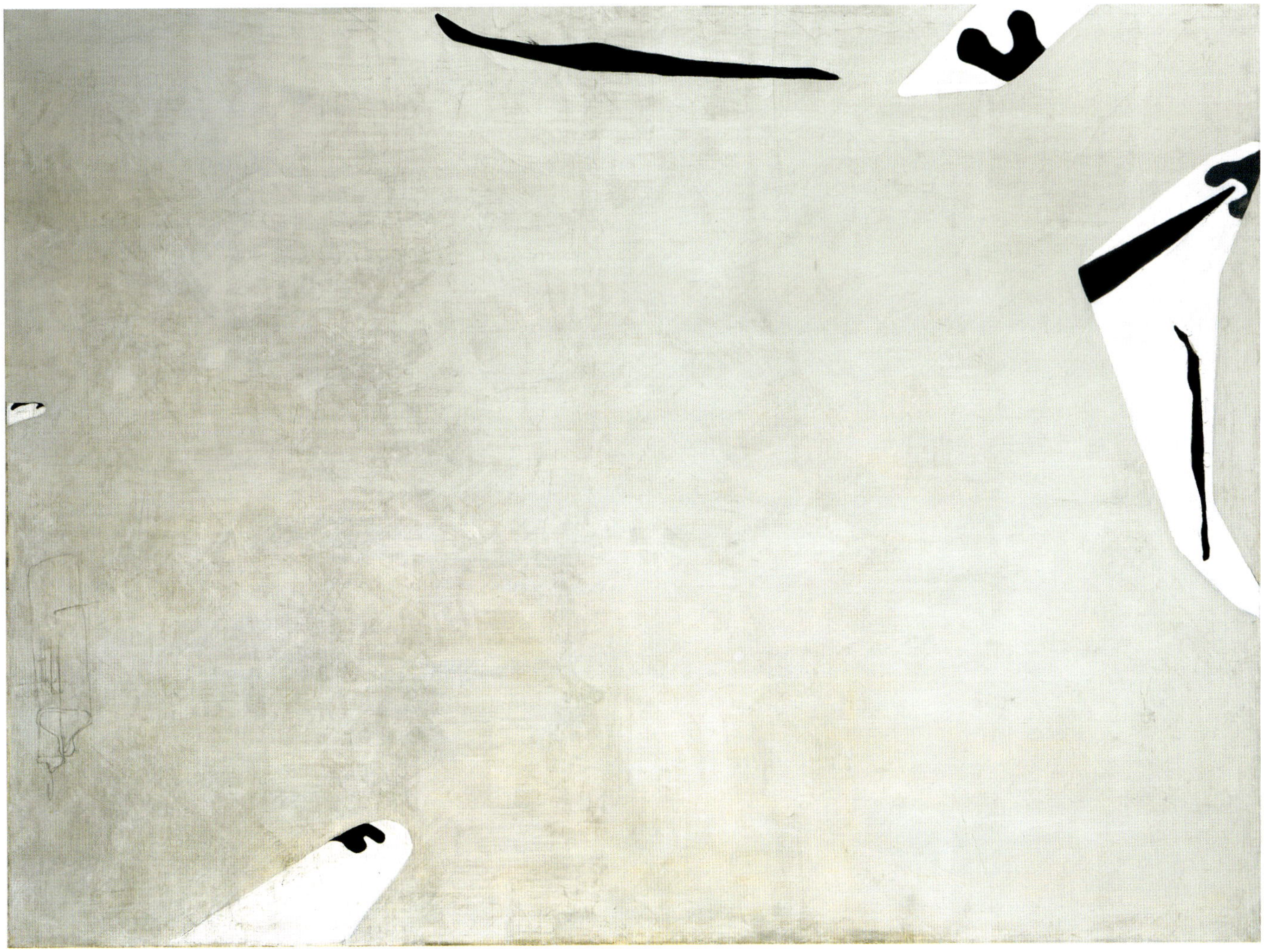

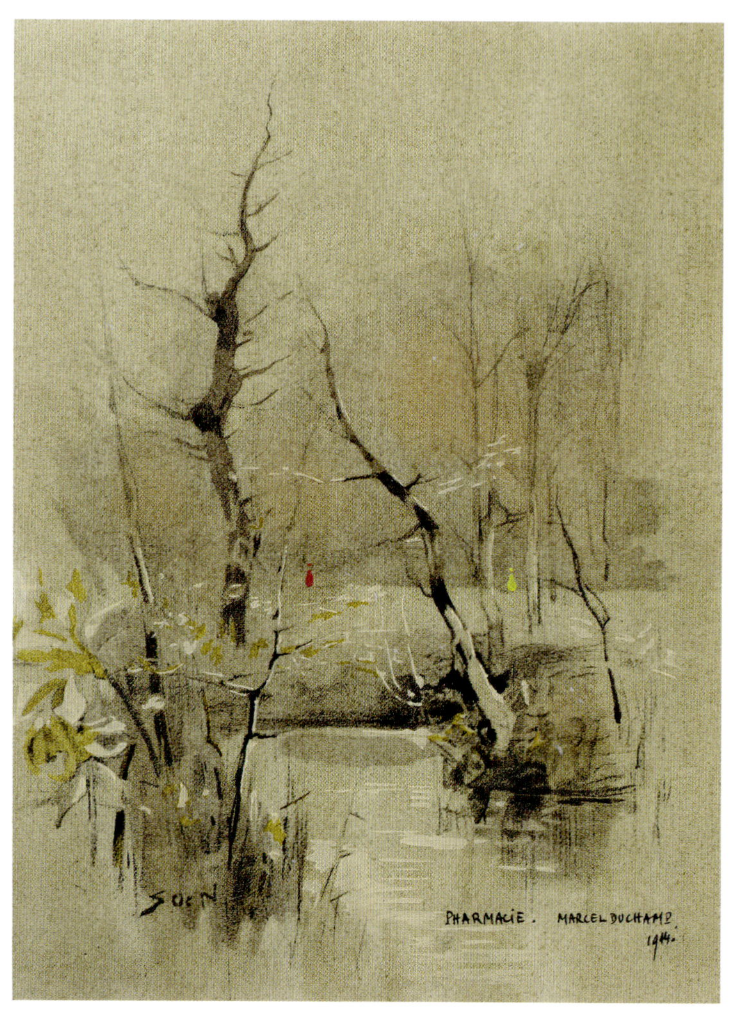

57
Marcel Duchamp
Pharmacy, 1914 (1945 edition)
Readymade: altered commercial print,
22 x 16 cm
Collection Hummel, Vienna

58
Marcel Duchamp
Bottle Rack, 1914 (*c*. 1921 replica)
Readymade: galvanised iron bottle rack,
50 x 33 cm
Private collection
London only

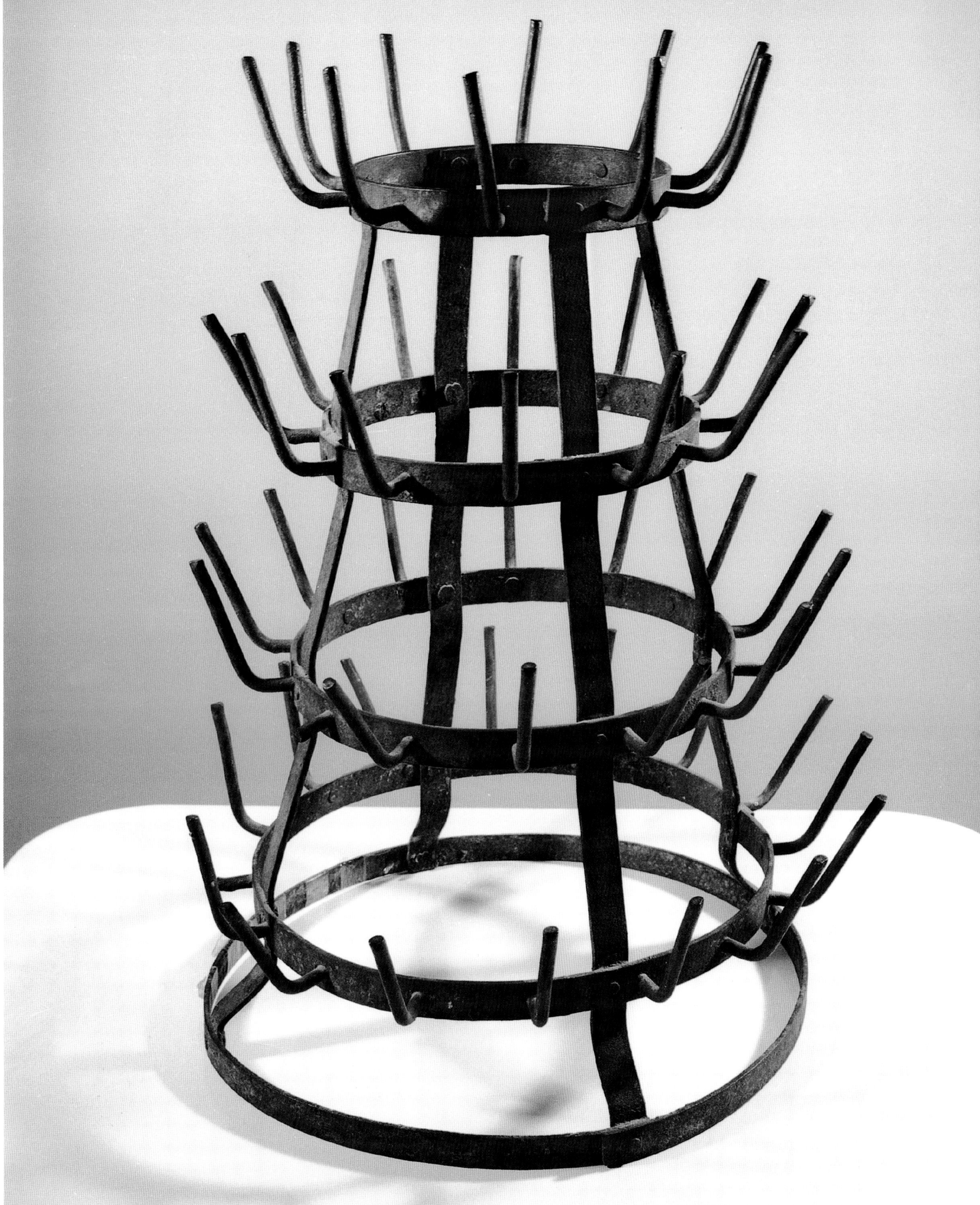

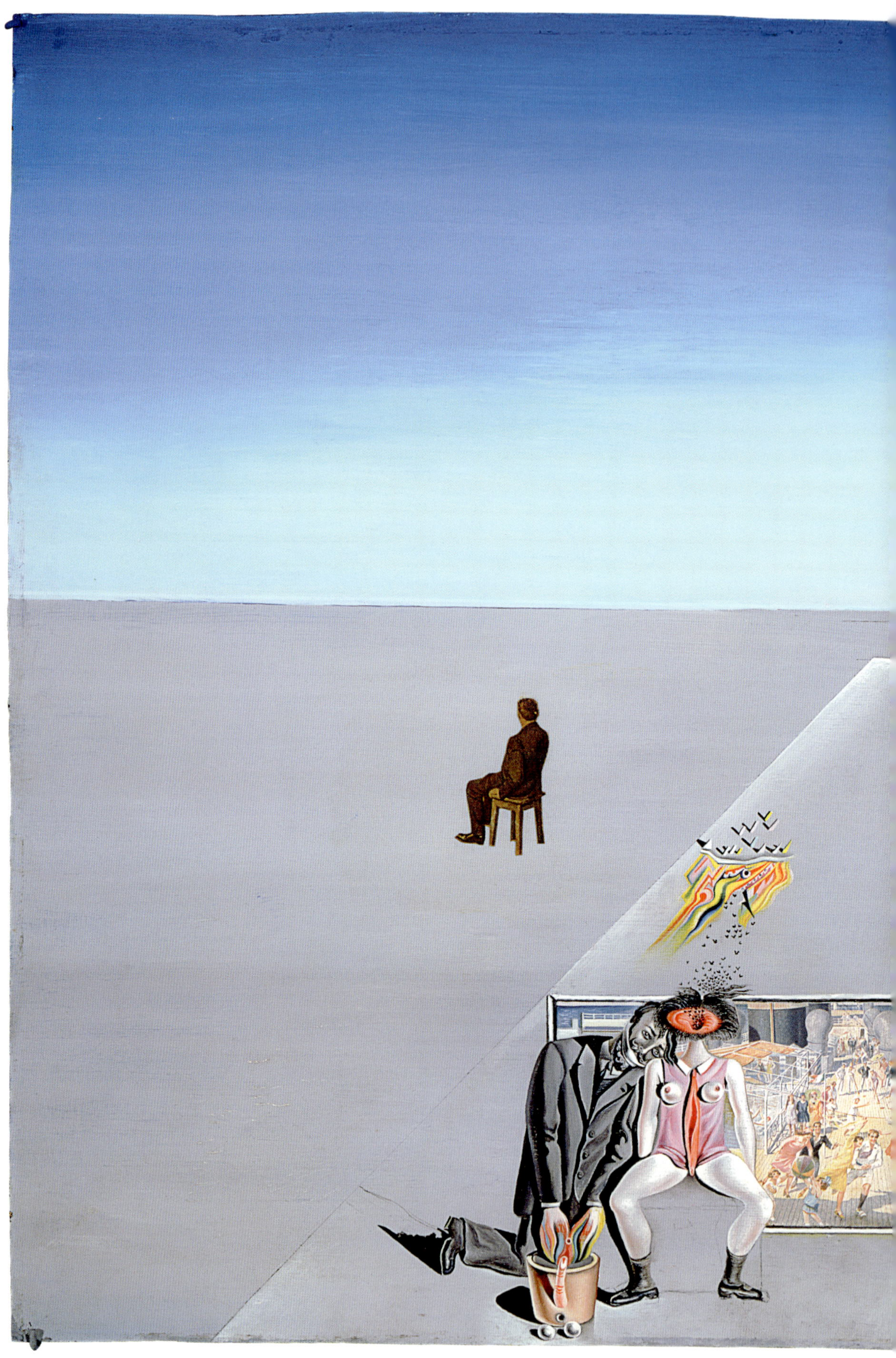

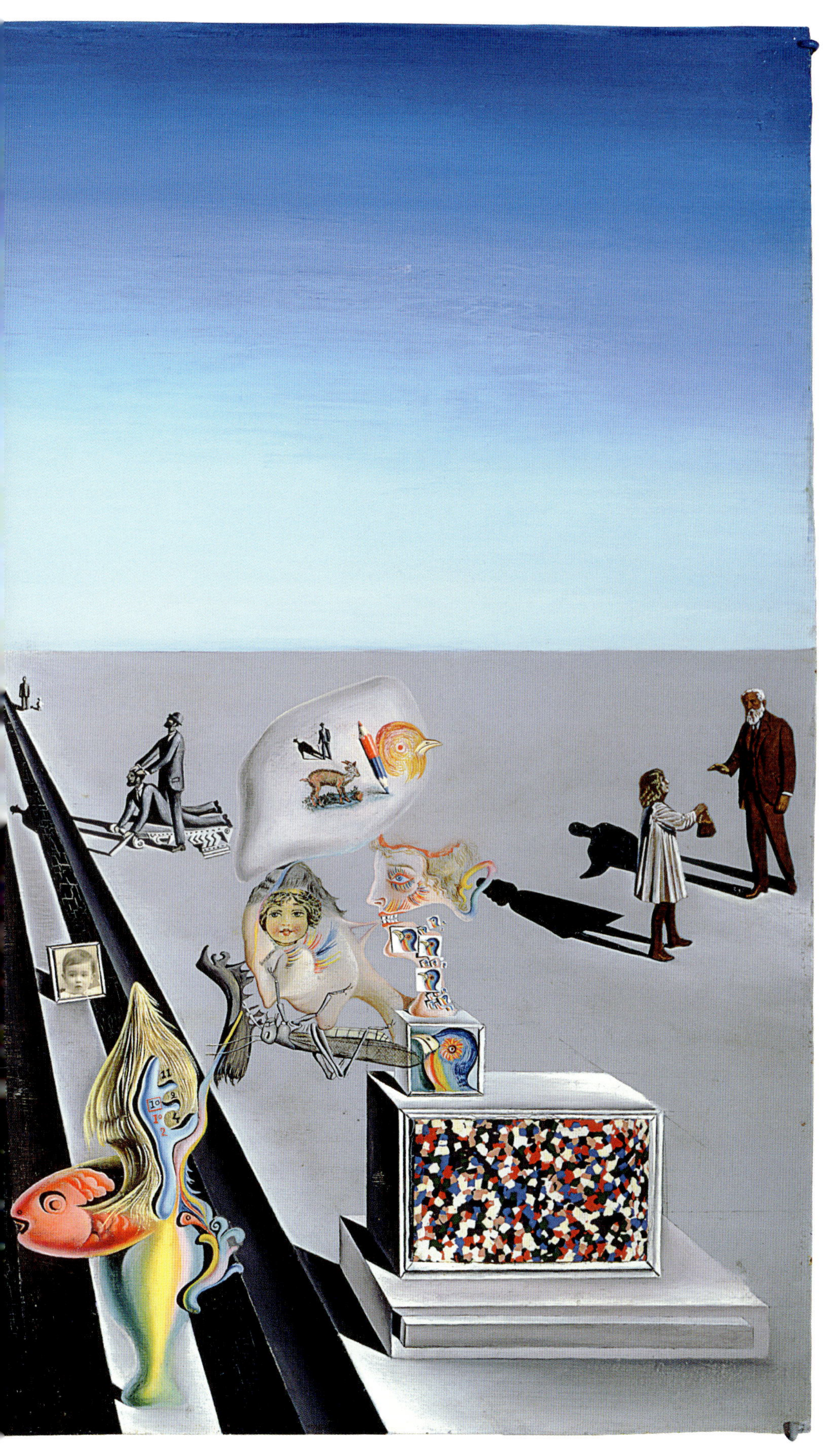

59
Salvador Dalí
The First Days of Spring, 1929
Oil and collage of paper, photograph,
postcard, linoleum and transfer decal on
wood panel, 50.2 x 65.1 cm
Collection of The Dalí Museum,
St Petersburg, Florida

THE IRONIC, THE COMIC AND THE ABSURD
GAVIN PARKINSON

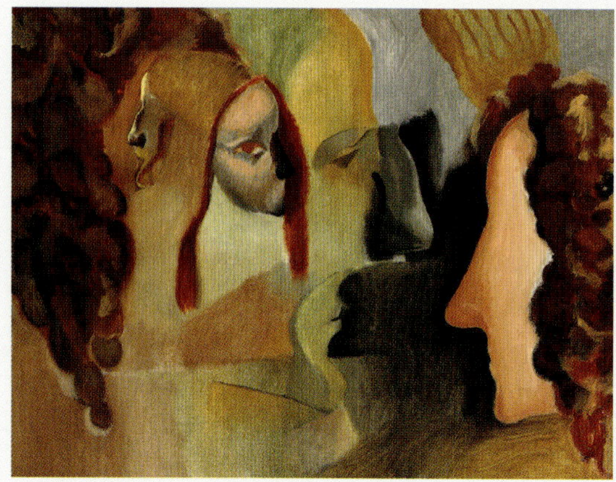

The art and writings of Marcel Duchamp and Salvador Dalí are richly leavened by diverse varieties of humour. Duchamp's tended towards an exquisite balance and precision, which often contributed to the peculiar and characteristic economies that undergird his work. Dalí employed humour far more bombastically and to a more outwardly provocative effect. However, Duchamp's milder, lighter touch conceals a seditious charge that is every bit as powerful as the more manifestly aggressive content to be found in Dalí's work. Overt cruelty, slapstick and scatology were Dalí's weapons, placed towards a similar end to Duchamp's: to discredit banal normality.

Duchamp confessed in later life that his painting *Yvonne and Magdeleine Torn in Tatters* (fig. 62) was created with the idea of '[i]ntroducing humour for the first time in my paintings',[1] adding something similar about *Sad Young Man on a Train* of the same year.[2] But it is the readymades that offer the earliest illustration of his dry sense of humour. The lean, sidelong glance at sculptural custom performed by *Bicycle Wheel* (cat. 77) would soon be matched by further deadpan gestures of the same manner such as *Bottle Rack* (cats 58, 106), but Duchamp showed neither in exhibition at the time and was still feeling his way on his new, unique path, unsure of how much humour could accomplish. Perhaps his major statement of the time in this sense was the *3 Standard Stoppages* (cat. 133), which Duchamp would later say was meant to 'discredit' science: 'mildly, lightly, unimportantly', emphasising the irony that would become one of his main resources.[3]

Duchamp's use of humour in *3 Standard Stoppages* to ridicule or mock the conventions in art

and society was to be continued in New York following his move there in 1915. In an interview of 1920, probably with Dada in mind, he insisted '[a] great deal of modern art is meant to be amusing.'[4] Duchamp had extended that mission of modernism playfully with the empty glass ampoule *Paris Air* (cat. 110) and most economically and notoriously by way of the minor but crucial additions through which he created *L.H.O.O.Q.* (cat. 28). He explored its dimensions operatically, ridiculously or both (depending on how you look at it) in what he called his 'hilarious picture' *The Bride Stripped Bare by Her Bachelors, Even* or *Large Glass* (fig. 81).[5] Humour would continue to be an insistent driving force in Duchamp's work. One of his most teasing, light-hearted gestures, the *Boîte-en-valise* (cat. 62), guarantees that every museum could potentially own a dolls' house-size 'complete works' of the artist.

The *Boîte-en-valise* was begun in Paris and while in progress would have been known to Dalí, who had been making waves in the city since 1929. But its impishness is quite at odds with the humour found in Dalí's films and paintings, hardened by elements of danger, callousness and misfortune. At times, Dalí's pictures revel grossly in their author's

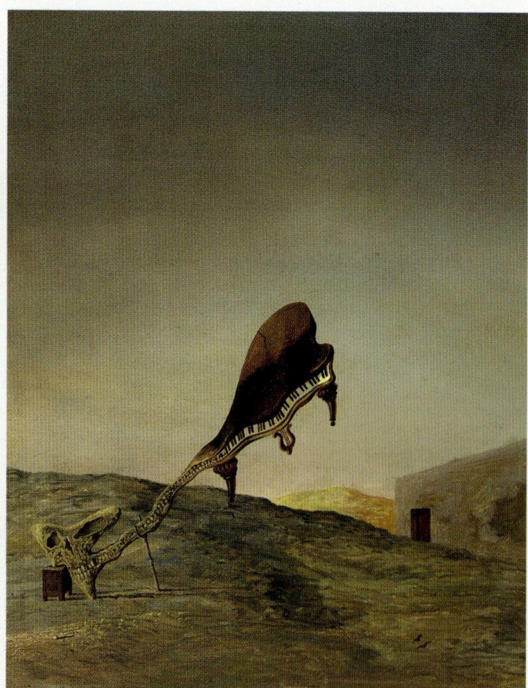

Fig. 62
Marcel Duchamp, *Yvonne and Magdeleine Torn in Tatters*, 1911. Oil on canvas, 60.3 x 73.3 cm. Philadelphia Museum of Art. The Louise and Walter Arensberg Collection, 1950-134-53

Fig. 63
Salvador Dalí, *Skull with Its Lyric Appendage Leaning on a Bedside Table which Should Have the Exact Temperature of a Cardinal's Nest*, 1934. Oil on panel, 24.1 x 19.1 cm. Collection of The Dalí Museum, St Petersburg, Florida

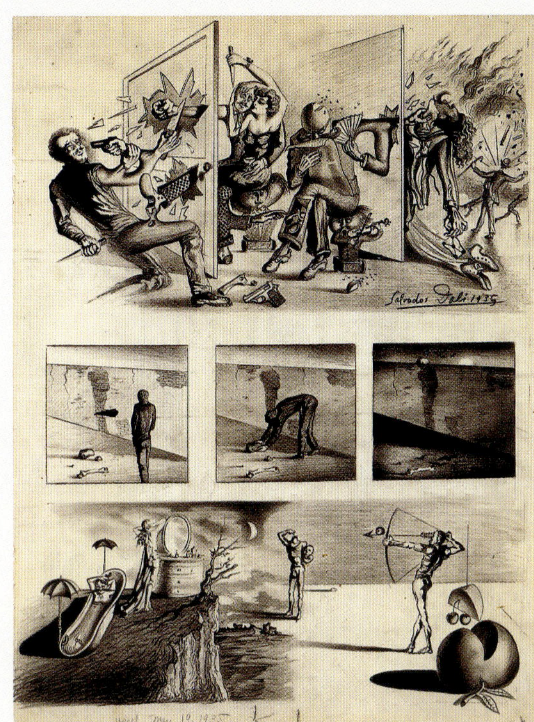

sexual proclivities and neuroses, as in *The Great Masturbator* (1929) and *The Enigma of William Tell* (fig. 79), where tragedy also seems close at hand. Elsewhere, in the *Surrealist Object Functioning Symbolically – Gala's Shoe* (cat. 78), we are invited either to play or imagine a ridiculous, fetishistic game, or carry out a bizarre scientific experiment with shoe, glass of milk and sugar cube, while the *Lobster Telephone* (cat. 61) is now such a widely aired, classic Surrealist one-liner that the joke has worn thin.

Paintings by Dalí such as *The Average Fine and Invisible Harp* (c. 1934) are richly imbued with a sense of the absurd through gigantic deformation. This is a mood enforced in titles like *Skull with its Lyric Appendage Leaning on a Bedside Table which Should Have the Exact Temperature of a Cardinal's Nest* (fig. 63), which signal a shift towards outright comedy in some of Dalí's painted and drawn work from the mid-1930s. The broader humour of popular film, comics, cartoons and caricatures seems to lie behind the drawing *Gangsterism and Goofy Visions of New York* (fig. 64), for instance. Dalí's first encounter with Harpo Marx in 1937 encouraged this trend and led to his portrait of the actor that year, as well as the

collaborative scenario under the unforgettable title *Giraffes on Horseback Salad*. Presumably it was a comedy, but it is a tragedy that it never saw completion.

Dalí's personal missives to André Breton were full of his cartoon (anti-) intellectualism, capable of convulsing the entire Surrealist group when read out aloud by their recipient.[6] For his part, Duchamp would speak in later years of humour and laughter as his 'pet tools', utilised 'for fear of dying from boredom'.[7] Breton was aware that humour played a central role in each *œuvre* and he considered both Duchampian drollery and Dalinian hilarity in his *Anthology of Black Humour* (1945). He gave priority in Duchamp's work to *3 Standard Stoppages*, the readymades and *The Large Glass*, 'signed, in protest against artistic indigence, seriousness, and vanity', along with the lame puns and sometimes remarkable and always unique economies observed by Duchamp: '[s]hould one react against the laziness of railway tracks between the passage of two trains?'[8] Breton examined Dalí's form of comic relief entirely in psychoanalytic terms, as the product of a paranoid mental state of a personality arrested in the superego. In this reading, his 'latent paranoia' allowed Dalí a remarkable interpretive range, endowing 'the external object' such as the shoe, the telephone and the bedside table 'with a symbolic life that overshadows all others and that makes it the concrete vehicle of humour'.[9]

Duchamp thought the humour behind the readymades was one 'that wasn't only intended to make people laugh … it wasn't even black humour. It was really a humour that added a note of – dare I say? – seriousness?'[10] Nevertheless, his continuing work in that vein into later life can be witnessed in the morbidly amusing *Torture-morte* (fig. 65), made in Cadaqués and perhaps shown to Dalí. This was the period in which Dalí's work was becoming almost incidental by comparison with the entertaining, frequently very funny sideshow that constituted the artist himself in television and commercial appearances. As a friend of Duchamp, John Cage was able to inspect that persona up close, which was thrown off when Duchamp and Dalí met in earnest conversation. It is something of a curiosity, then, that when they came together as a double act, the two quite different senses of humour that I have sketched here seemed to cancel each other out.

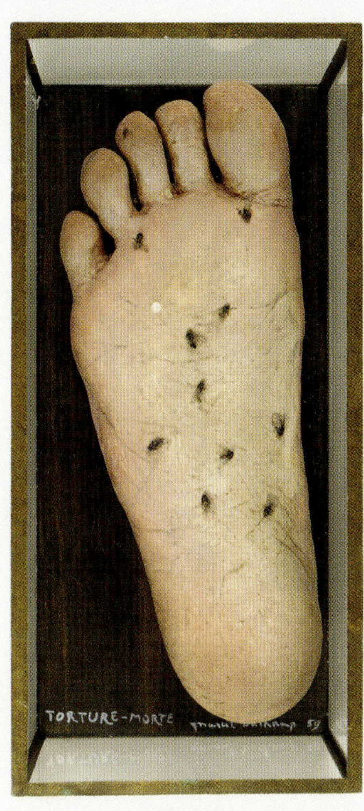

Fig. 64
Salvador Dalí, *Gangsterism and Goofy Visions of New York*, 1935.
Graphite and ink on paper, 54.6 x 40 cm.
The Menil Collection, Houston,
1974-068 DJ D

Fig. 65
Marcel Duchamp, *Torture-morte*, 1959.
Synthetic flies glued on painted plaster,
paper mounted on wood, in a glass box,
29.5 x 13.4 x 10.3 cm.
Centre Pompidou, MNAM-CCI, Paris

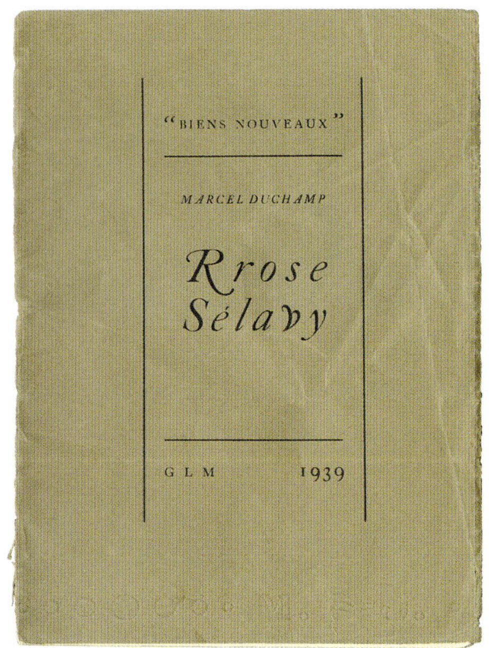
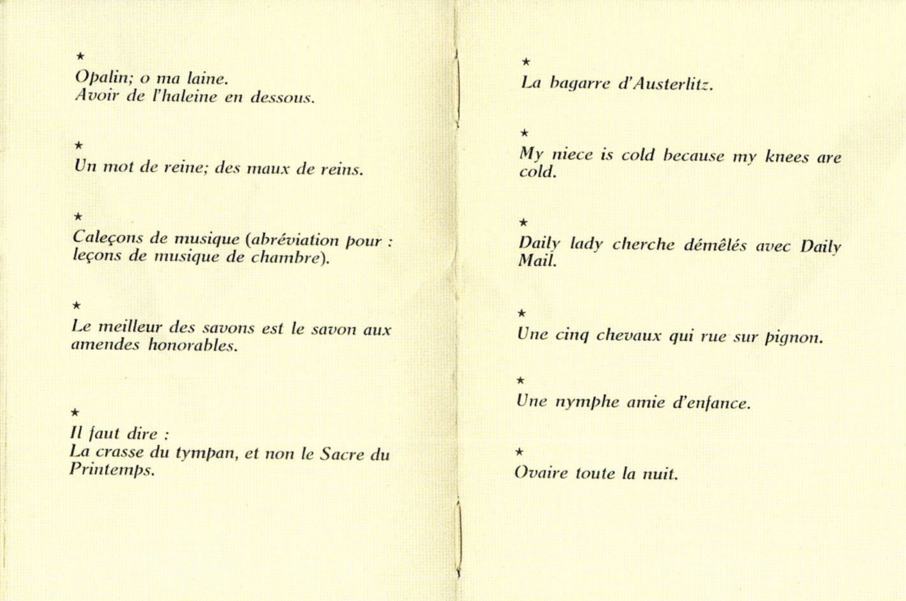

60
Marcel Duchamp
Rrose Sélavy, Paris, 1939
Booklet containing a collection of puns by
Marcel Duchamp, 16.2 x 12 cm
Collection of The Dalí Museum Archives,
St Petersburg, Florida

61
Salvador Dalí and Edward James
Lobster Telephone, 1938
Telephone, steel, plaster, rubber, resin
and paper, 18 x 30.5 x 12.5 cm
West Dean College; part of the Edward
James Foundation

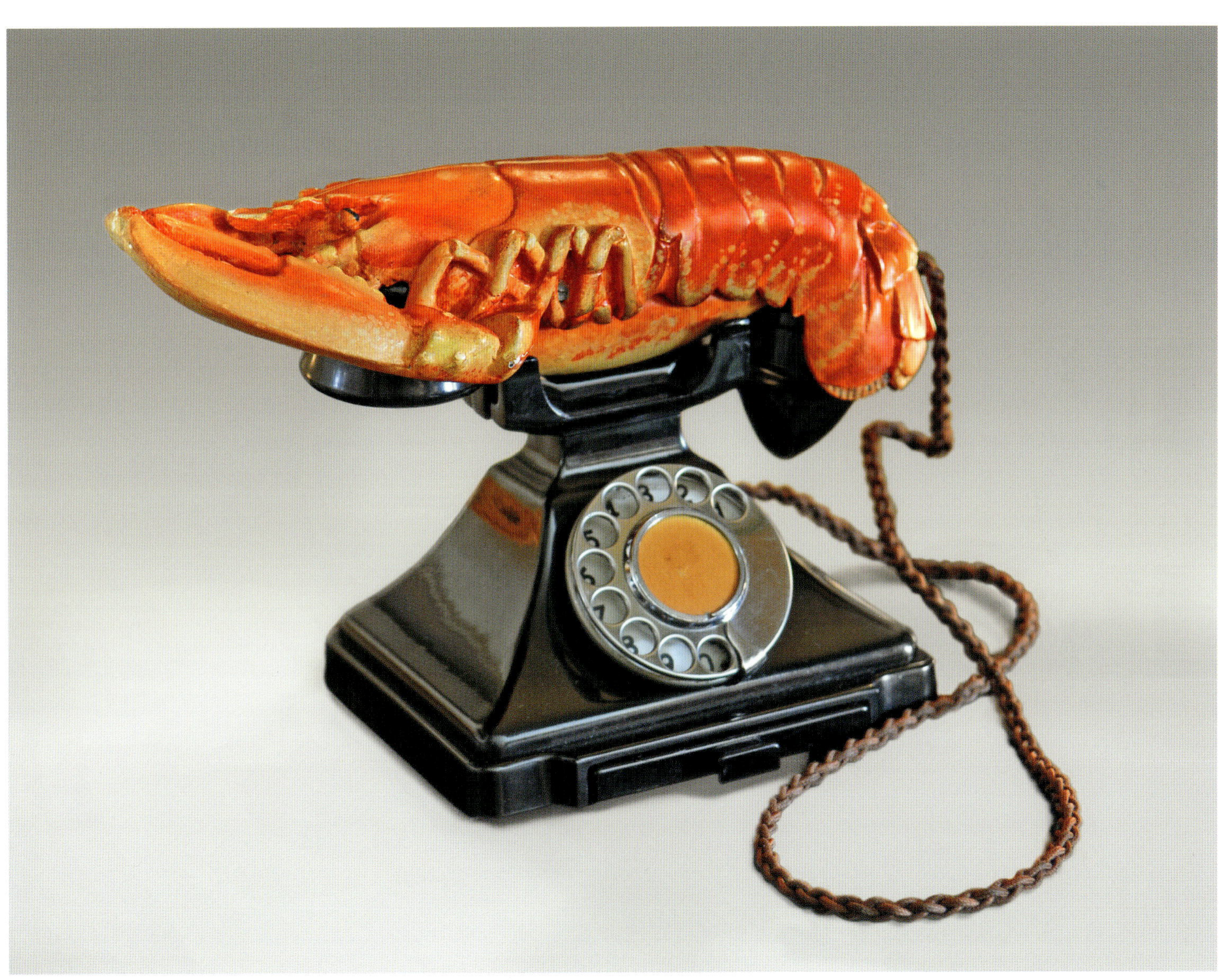

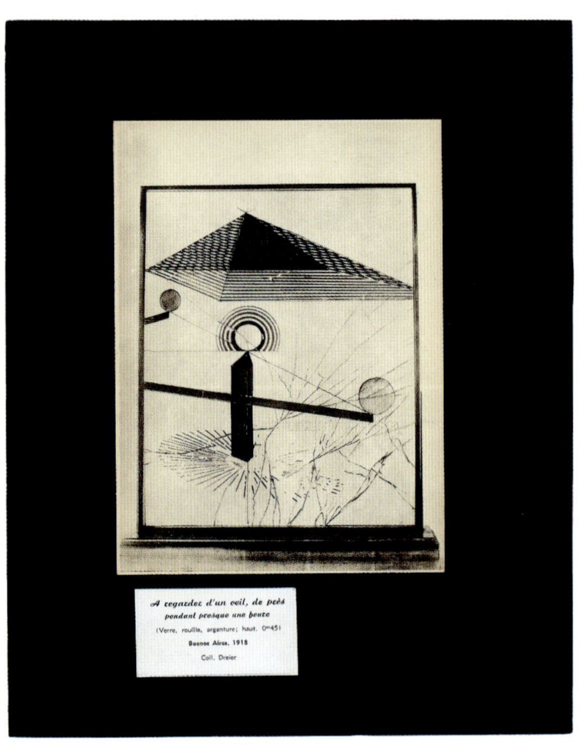

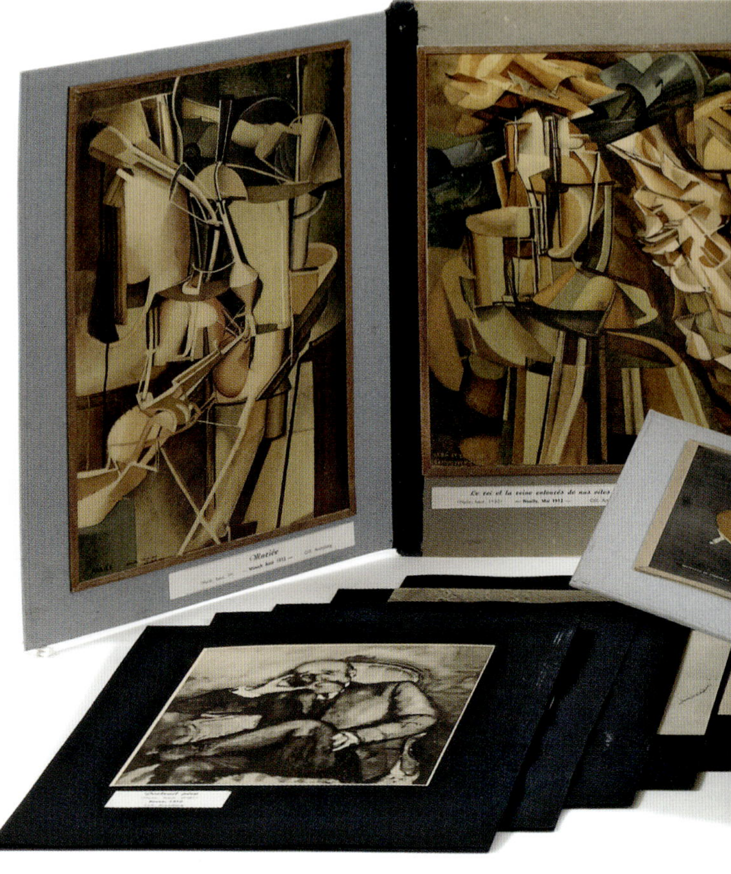

62
Marcel Duchamp
de ou par MARCEL DUCHAMP OU RROSE SELAVY
(*from or by MARCEL DUCHAMP or RROSE SELAVY*),
also known as *La Boîte-en-valise* (Series C), 1958
Linen-covered box with Ingres paper lining, 40 x 38 x 9 cm
Collection Hummel, Vienna

In 1935 Duchamp started to plan what he initially called an 'album of approximately all the things I produced', which turned into a unique 'travelling museum'. Acquiring enough reproductions of his paintings and arranging fabrication of the miniature models of the readymades (approximately 69 items in all, for an edition of *c.* 300) occupied him for about five years; the first group of 'deluxe' boxes, which had a leather outer case (*valise*), was completed in 1941. Twenty-four of these first '*Boîtes-en-valise*' exist, all with the addition of an original work of art. Duchamp succeeded, despite the disruptions of war, in getting the materials for the planned boxes shipped to New York, and over the next decades six further series of the *Boîtes* were produced with the assistance of many friends and colleagues.

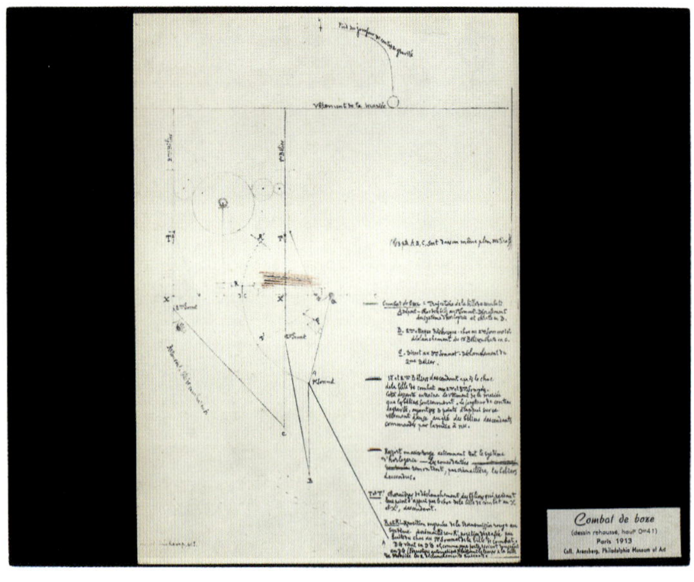

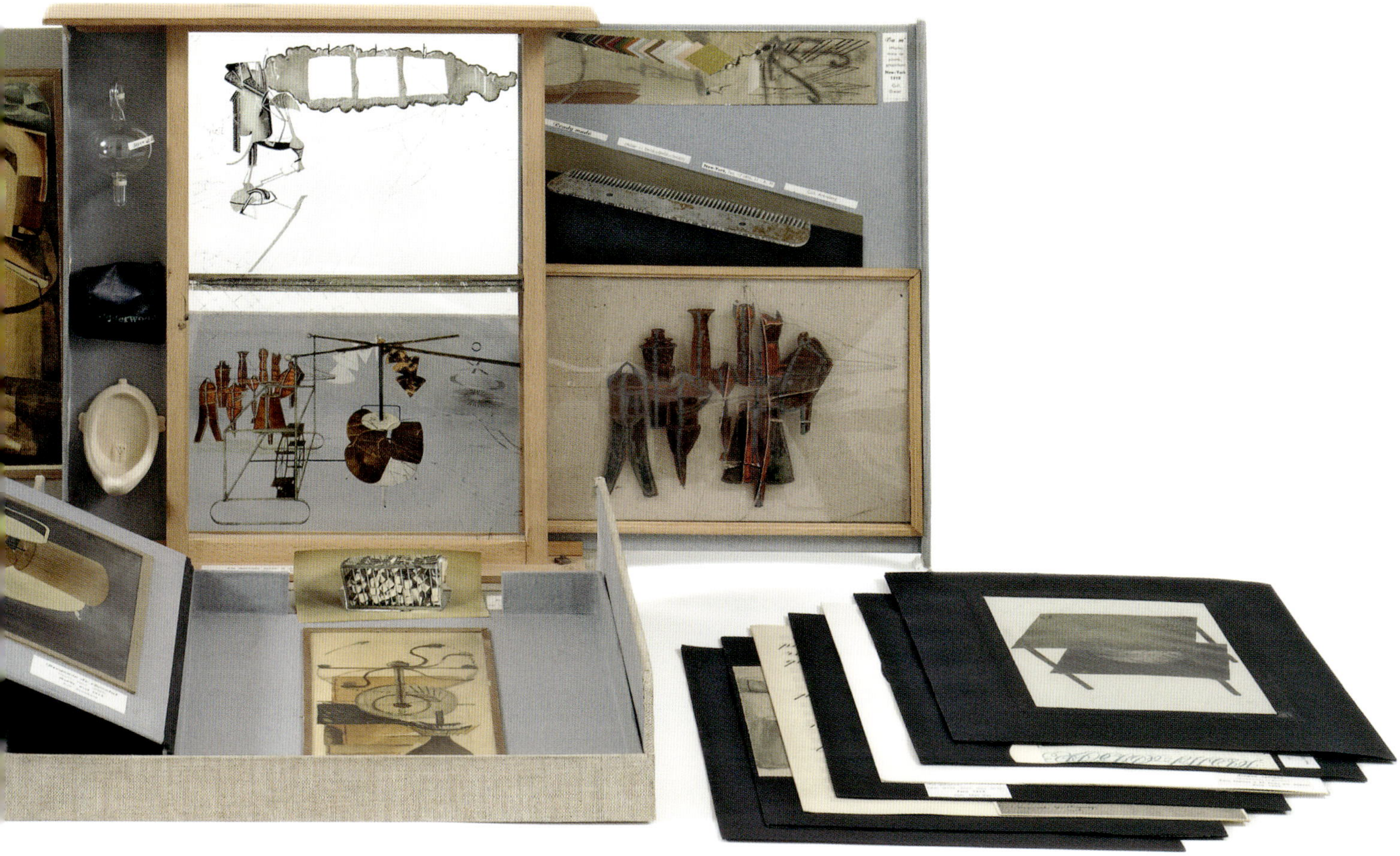

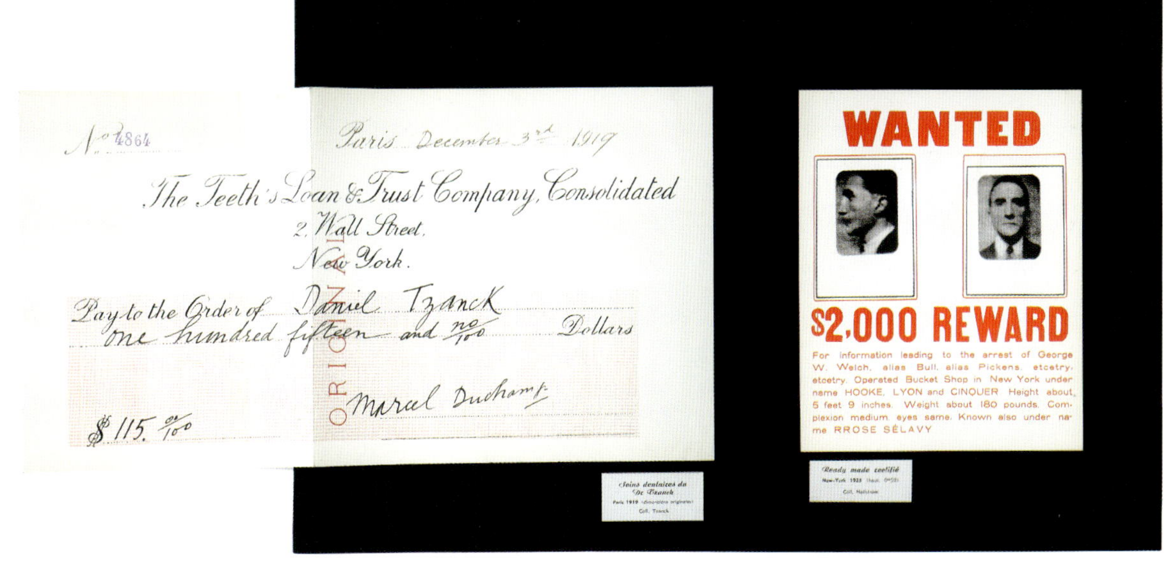
N° 4864
Paris December 3rd 1919
The Teeth's Loan & Trust Company, Consolidated
2. Wall Street.
New York.
Pay to the Order of Daniel Tzanck
one hundred fifteen and no/100 Dollars
Marcel Duchamp
$ 115. no/100
WANTED
$2,000 REWARD
For information leading to the arrest of George W. Welch, alias Bull, alias Pickens, etcetry, etcetry. Operated Bucket Shop in New York under name HOOKE, LYON and CINQUER. Height about 5 feet 9 inches. Weight about 180 pounds. Complexion medium, eyes same. Known also under name RROSE SÉLAVY

THE SURREALIST BULLFIGHT
WILLIAM JEFFETT

On 12 August 1961 Dalí was the instigator of a 'Surrealist bullfight' held at Figueres. This was organised with the help and blessing of the then Mayor of Figueres, Ramón Guardiola.[1] Dalí had conceived the idea by the early 1950s, and repeatedly mentioned it to his friend, the celebrity bullfighter Luis Miguel Dominguín.[2] Dalí's idea was to stage a traditional bullfight, and afterwards to have the carcass of the dead bull airlifted out of the ring by a helicopter, an idea he had already explored in March 1954 for the 'Fallas', the festival of San José in Valencia, for which he had made a large *papier-mâché* sculpture destined to be burned in public following its display. The Figueres *corrida* was given in honour of Dalí, and three celebrated fighters were on the 'cartel': Curro Girón, Fermín Murillo and Paco Camino. Dalí made a drawing depicting the helicopter with a dead bull suspended beneath it for incorporation into the poster announcing the spectacle. He finally obtained permission, with the help of Guardiola, to have the helicopter available for the end of the fight, but on the day high winds forced the cancellation of this part of the event.

The other component of the Surrealist bullfight was a self-destructing bull, made of plaster and paper covered in gold plates, that was filled with fireworks so that when it exploded fire would breathe from its horns and a red liquid would spew from its mouth. Duchamp helped Dalí with the staging of the event and the commissioning of the bull, which was fabricated by the Nouveaux Réalistes Niki de Saint-Phalle and Jean Tinguely. The entire event was a kind of 'happening' centred around Dalí as master of ceremonies. He made a dramatic entrance into the plaza in a Cadillac, but under the careful supervision of Duchamp, who was present in the audience and seated discreetly close to Dalí. The event was well documented in photographs taken by Robert Descharnes (fig. 69) and the explosion of the fabricated bull was filmed (fig. 66).

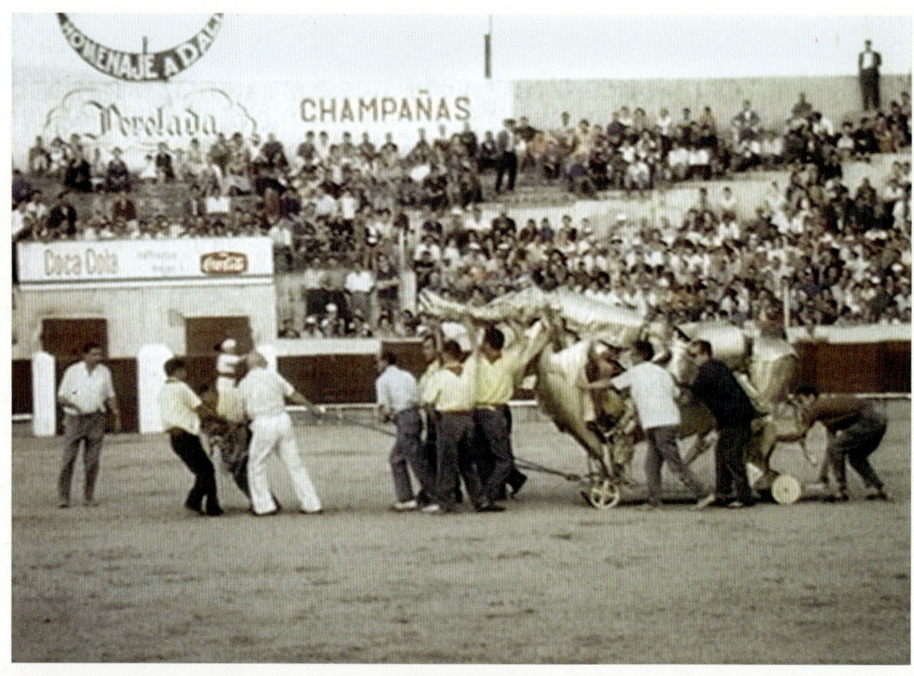

Fig. 66
Still from television footage of the Honorary Bullfight, Figueres, 1961 (cat. 63)
Ajuntament de Girona, CRDI

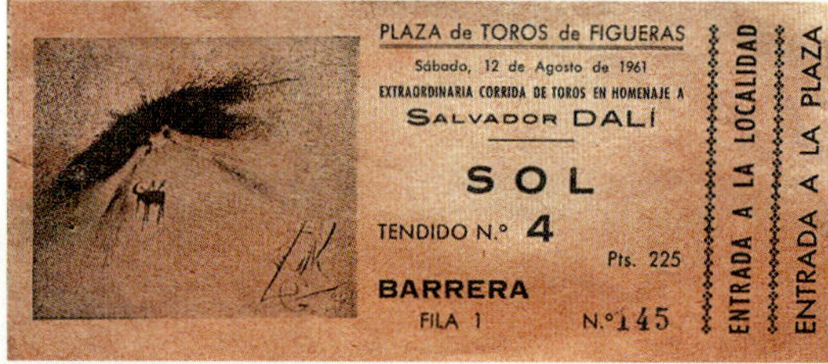

Fig. 67
Salvador Dalí
Entry Ticket for the Honorary Bullfight, 1961 (cat. 64)
Printed ink on paper, 8 x 17 cm
Arxiu Pere Vehí, Cadaqués

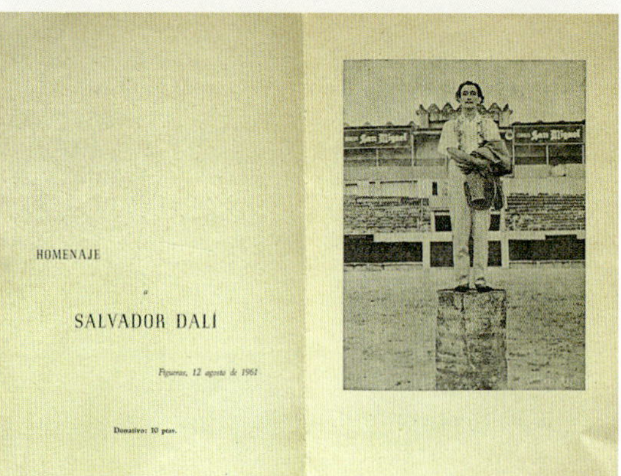

Fig. 68
Salvador Dalí
Programme of the Honorary Bullfight, 1961 (cat. 65)
Printed ink on paper, 32 x 24 cm
Arxiu Pere Vehí, Cadaqués

Opposite: Fig. 69
Dalí and Duchamp in the audience of the Honorary Bullfight, Figueres, 1961.
Photograph by Robert Descharnes

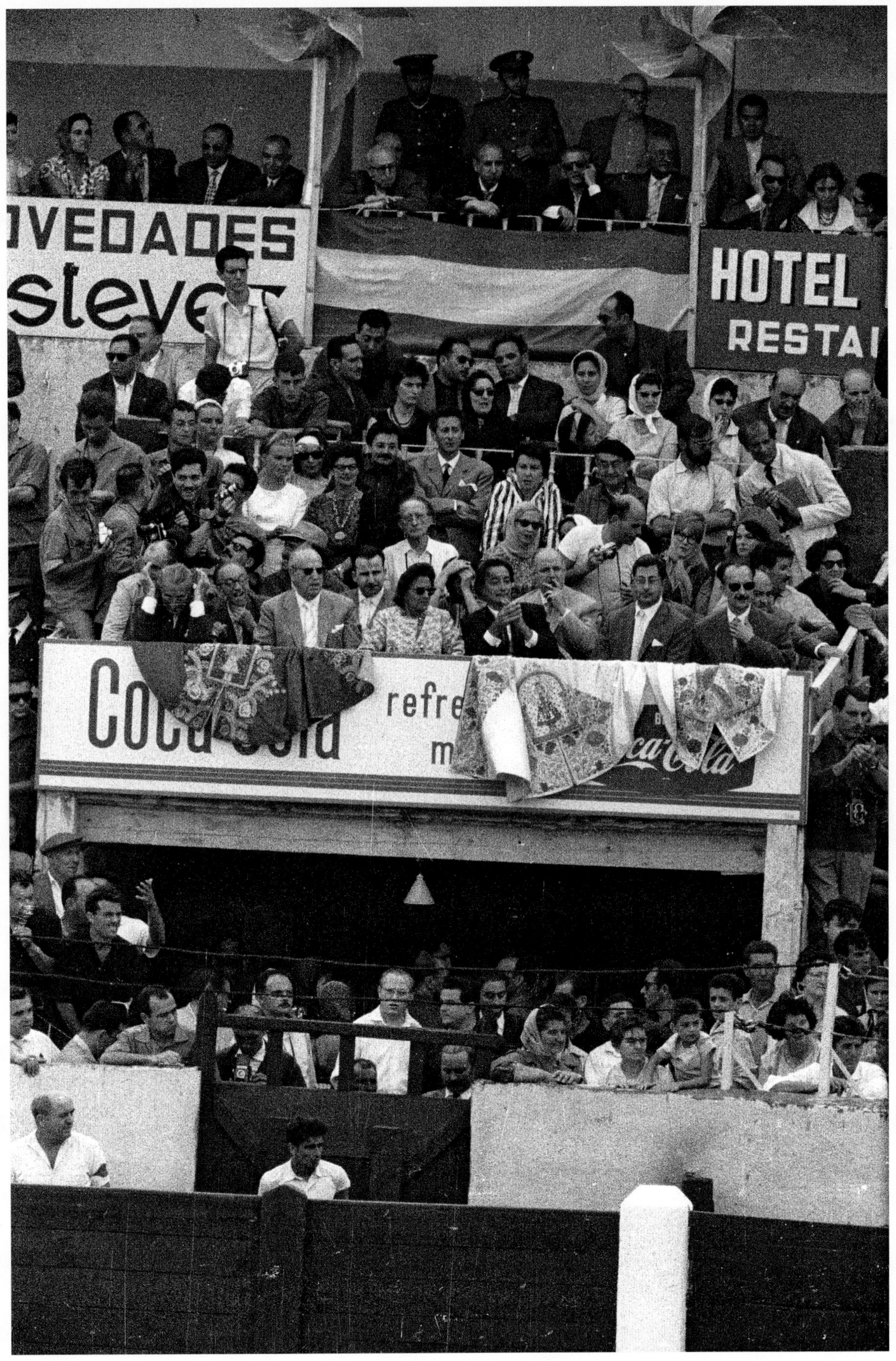
OVEDADES
steyer
HOTEL
RESTAI
Coca-Cola
refre
m
Coca-Cola

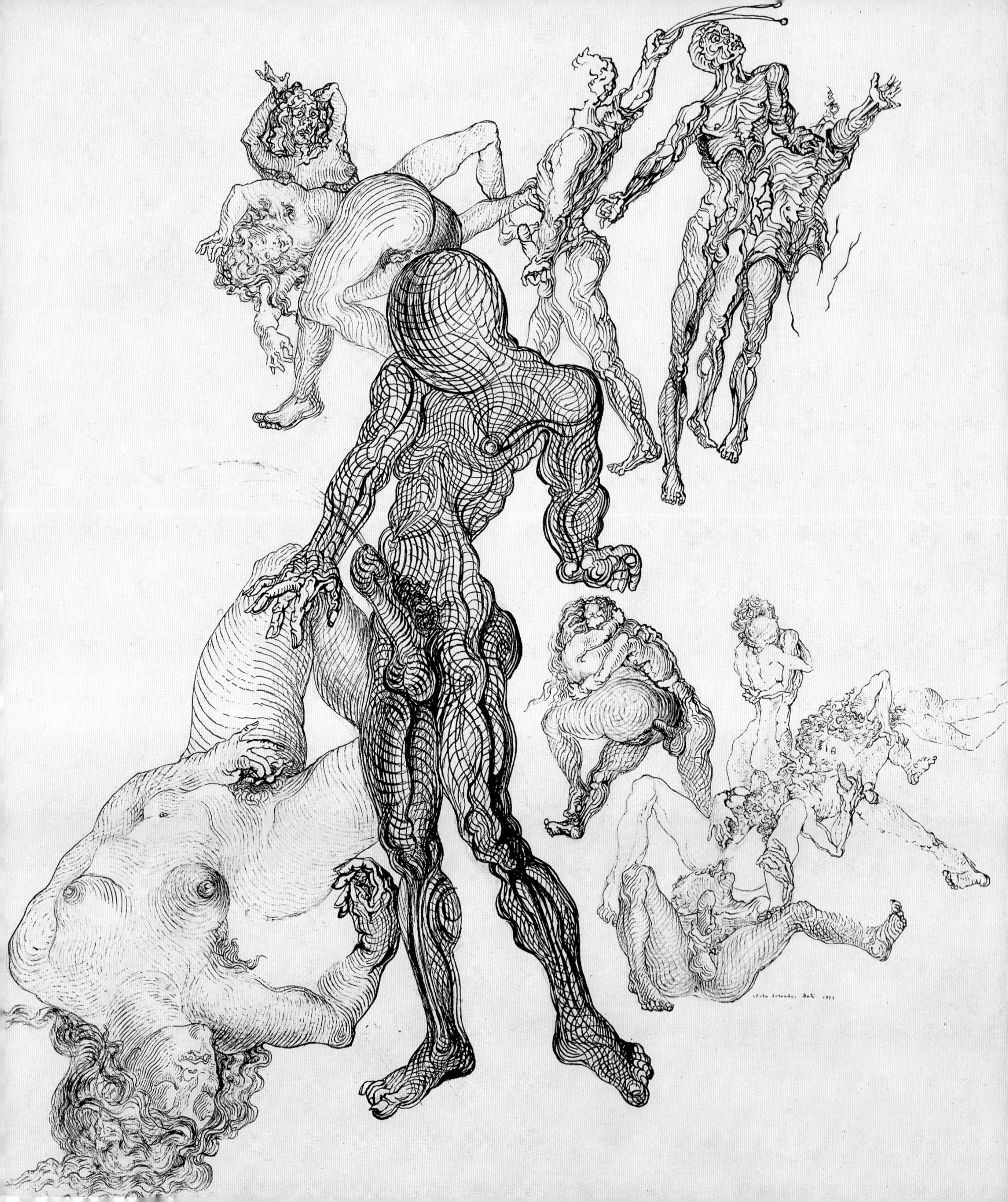

EROTICISM

EROTICISM
DAWN ADES

Eroticism pervades the work of Duchamp and Dalí. Their inventiveness in exploring and representing the erotic, visually, verbally and materially, veiled or revealed, through symbols, directly or metaphorically, is unrivalled in twentieth-century art. Duchamp said, 'I believe in eroticism a lot, because it's truly a rather widespread thing throughout the world, a thing that everyone understands. It replaces, if you like, what other literary schools called Symbolism, Romanticism. It could be another "ism" so to speak ... Eroticism was a theme, even an "ism", of everything I was doing at the time of *The Large Glass*. It kept me from being obliged to return to already existing theories, aesthetic or otherwise.'[1] Eroticism was everywhere, he felt, but no-one spoke openly about it, hindered as they were by Catholicism and social politeness.

Eroticism is trammelled neither by the sociological and physiological issues of sexuality nor by the more ideal, elevated, even altruistic question of love, though both may be involved. Rooted in the instincts, free of logic and morality, it is profoundly individual, and thus remains mysterious.

To a questionnaire on desire circulated by the Surrealists in Yugoslavia in 1932, Dalí responded, 'I have hidden desires, secret to myself, since I constantly discover myself in them ... No desire is guilty, there is a fault only in their repression – all my desires are ... vile, infamous, sordid etc. I have no so-called noble desires. The desires I consider noblest are those I consider as the most human, that is to say the most perverse.'[2] Dalí made no secret of his perverse, even pornographic, fantasies, and described or represented them in explicit detail, as in the text 'Rêverie',[3] and in 'Je mange Gala' ('I Eat Gala'), an extended 'Love poem' (cat 66). The second *chant* (song) in the unpublished drafts for this work, called 'Birth of Nutritious Perversions', describes an excursion to Cap de Creus with Gala and Duchamp, during which Duchamp got sunburned. Dalí muses on Duchamp's lobster-red face merging with the sunset on the rocks, reminding him of the grilled cutlets of the picnic awaiting them, while fantasising about consuming his beloved and, in his perverse passion, he licks the outcropping rocks while masturbating, as if deflecting his cannibalistic intentions for Gala.

In his text 'Surrealist Objects' (figs 73, 74), Dalí emphasises the 'amorous imagination' of the individual viewer, in response to the objectification of erotic desires 'through substitution and metaphor'.[4] The suggestiveness of the Surrealist objects feeds into Dalí's paintings, sometimes producing multiple metaphors. The aggressive phallic shape of one of Giacometti's dumb, mobile objects, *Disagreeable Object* (1931), itself perhaps based on banana-shaped bird figures from Easter Island,[5] or on Maori war clubs, seems to have inspired Dalí's *Catalan Bread* (cat. 82). However, Dalí drapes and shrouds his turd-like, phallic loaf, soft clock at one end and inkwell at the other, lighting it against a dark ground like a Zurbarán still-life, evading the violence of *Disagreeable Object* and troubling its erotic associations. His tiny painting *The Spectre of Sex Appeal* (cat. 67) magnetises the viewer with its image of the horror and fascination of sex. Against the faithfully depicted, hard mineral rocks of a bay at Cap de Creus, a giant decaying female body, variously bony and fleshy, hard and soft, looms over the sailor-suited child Dalí.

One of the inspirations for the Surrealist object was Breton's proposal to put into circulation objects we have dreamed of, which would help to discredit things utilitarian and rational. In this poetic text he also emphasises the need for verification, and compares the Surrealists' 'expeditions' into the world of the erotic object with human fetishism, 'which must try on the white helmet, or caress the fur bonnet'.[6]

The erotic can find expression in a variety of ways, most obviously via the gaze and the touch. The object as incarnation of desire is realised in, for instance, the fur pom-poms on Dalí's *Venus de Milo with Drawers* (cat. 89), or the velvet of *Please Touch* (cat. 87). In Dalí's drawings (cats 72–75), the different sensations of looking and touching are graphically realised: sometimes there is the objective, even remote clarity of a scene as though witnessed by a voyeur; in other examples the pencil lines are as soft and thick as flesh. He once said, 'Painting, like love, comes in through the eyes, and goes out through the short hairs of the brush.'[7]

The longest entry in the 'Lexique succinct de l'érotisme' ('Succinct Dictionary of Eroticism'), which formed part of the catalogue to the Exposition InteRnatiOnal du Surréalisme (EROS) at the Galerie Cordier in Paris in 1959–60,[8] is on *seins* (breasts), analysing their anatomical, symbolic and erotic character. Breasts as generative of pleasure figure in the screenplay of Buñuel's *Un Chien andalou* as examples of 'tactile cinema', translated in the film into the sequence where the male protagonist awkwardly

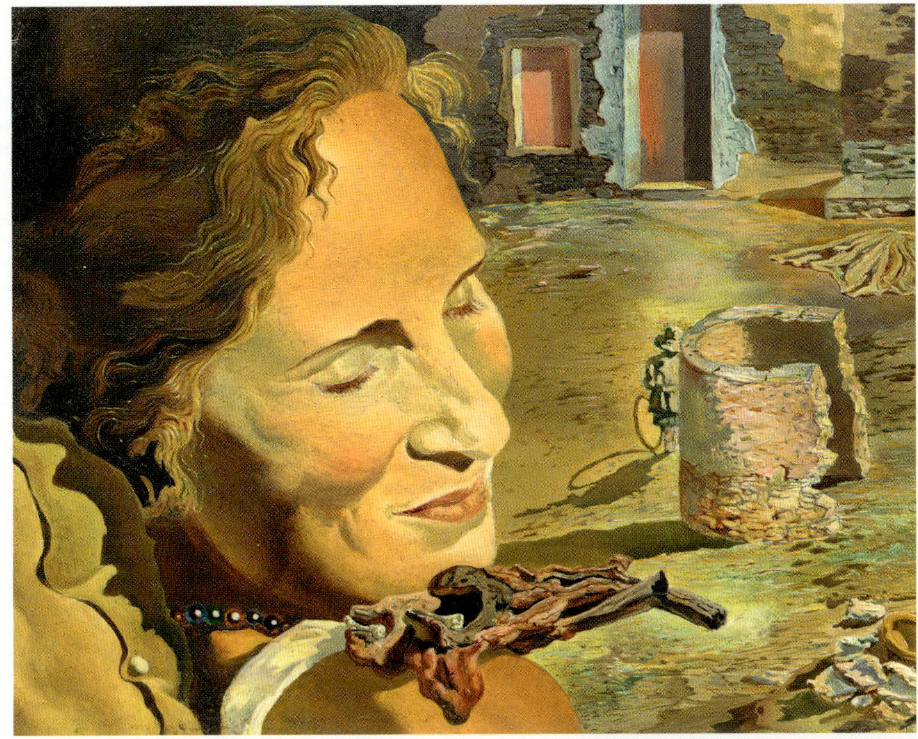

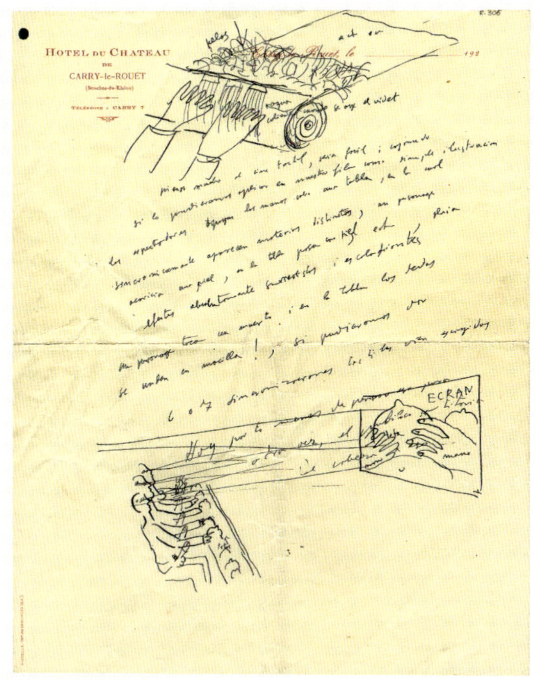

gropes a female body. In a letter to Buñuel, Dalí proposed a tactile cinema in which spectators could palpate a roller on which different textures related to the film's action succeed one another (fig. 71).[9] The catalogue for Dalí's 1936 exhibition at the Julien Levy Gallery in New York featured two breasts that have to be manipulated: the nipples are substituted by buttons that on being touched unfold into a series of postcards (fig. 72). For the International exhibition 'Le Surréalisme en 1947', Duchamp devised the catalogue cover for the 'limited' edition of 999 copies, also featuring a female breast (cat. 87).

Duchamp's scattered and fragmentary Notes often posit an erotic relation, filtered sometimes through scientific terms. His facsimile edition of a group of these Notes is entitled *The Bride Stripped Bare by Her Bachelors, Even*.[10] The eroticism of the *mariée* (bride) was neither overt nor insinuated; as the central figure in *The Large Glass*, she is described in the 'Succinct Dictionary of Eroticism' rather curiously as the object of 'intellectual lust'.[11] Duchamp created a kind of 'erotic climate', which continued until his final work *Étant donnés* (fig. 76), via the miniature sculptural miracles *Female Fig Leaf* (cat. 80), *Dart Object* (cat. 81) and *Wedge of Chastity* (cat. 79).

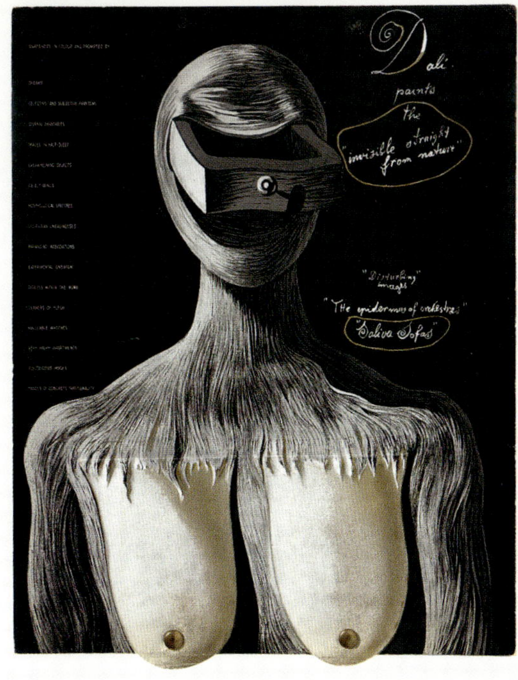

Fig. 70
Salvador Dalí, *Portrait of Gala with Two Lamb Chops in Equilibrium upon Her Shoulder*, c. 1934. Oil on wood panel, 6.8 x 8.8 cm.
Fundació Gala-Salvador Dalí, Figueres

Fig. 71
Salvador Dalí, Letter to Luis Buñuel (sent from Chateâu de Carry-le-Rouet, Bouches du Rhône), containing his sketches for a proposed project for a tactile cinema. Undated, probably February 1930.
Filmoteca Española, Madrid, A B 0106

Fig. 72
Catalogue of Salvador Dalí's exhibition at the Julien Levy Gallery, New York, 10 December 1936 – 9 January 1937.
Fundació Gala-Salvador Dalí, Figueres

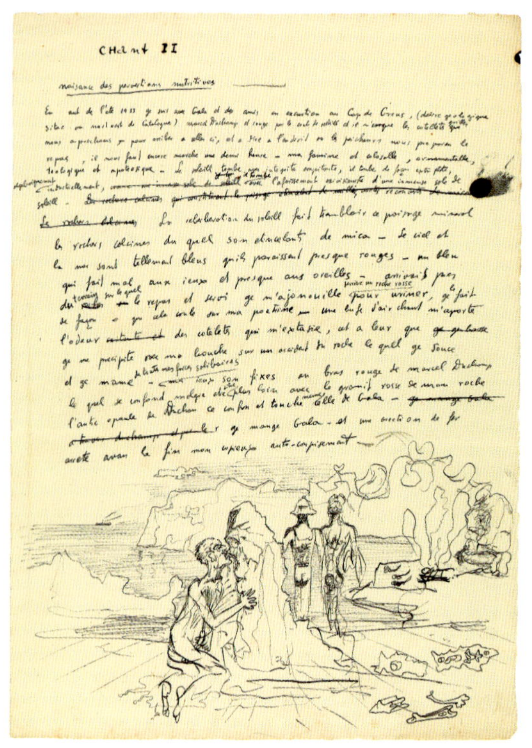

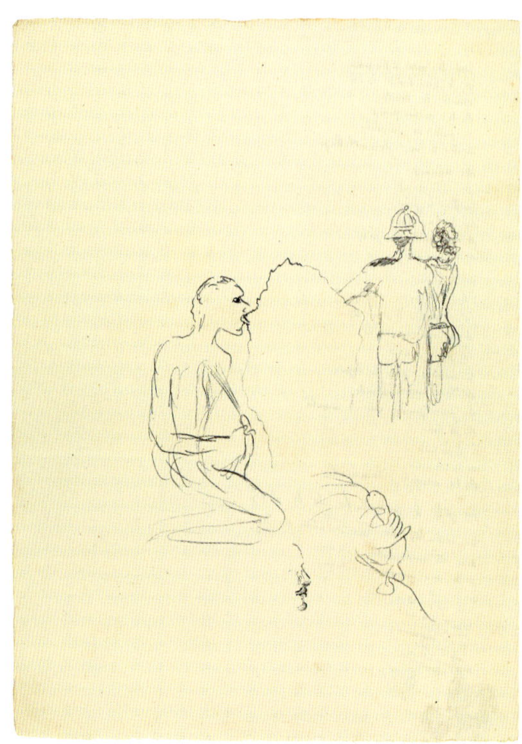

66
Salvador Dalí
Pages from the manuscript 'Je mange Gala' ('I eat Gala'); 'Chant 2: La Naissance des perversions nutritives' ('Song 2: The Birth of Nutritious Perversions'), c. 1933
Drawing with text (translation by Dawn Ades below), 32.1 x 22.5 cm
Fundació Gala-Salvador Dalí, Figueres

67
Salvador Dalí
The Spectre of Sex-appeal, c. 1934
Oil on wood on panel, 17.9 x 13.9 cm
Fundació Gala-Salvador Dalí, Figueres
London only

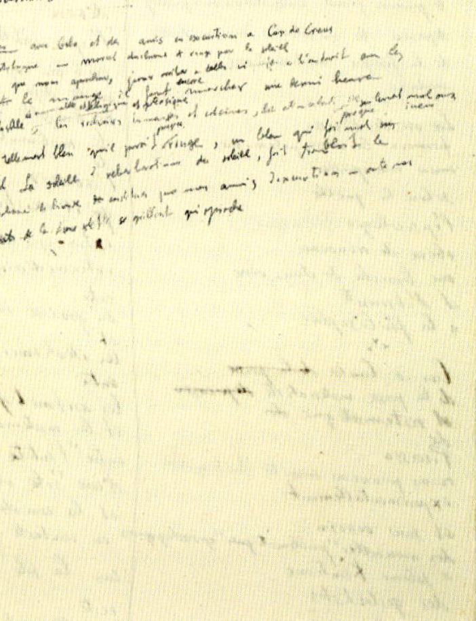

The Birth of Nutritious Perversions

In August of the summer of 1933 I am with Gala and friends on an excursion to Cap de Creus (geological delirium situated to the north-east of Catalonia). Marcel Duchamp is red because he has caught the sun and reminds me of the grilled cutlets we are approaching – to reach them, that is to say the place where the fishermen are preparing our meal, we still have to walk another half an hour. My hunger is colossal, ornamental, theological and apotheosic. The sun is setting with rippling integrity, it is falling in a streamlined way, algebraically, industrially, it is setting with the exhibitionist subsidence of an immense sun sole. The reverberation of the sun makes this mineral landscape the calcinated rocks sparkling with mica tremble – The sky and the sea are so blue that they appear almost red. A blue that hurts the eyes and almost the ears. Almost at the place where the meal is served I kneel behind a reddish-brown rock to urinate, I do so in such a manner that it flows down my chest. A breath of warm air brings me the smell of the cutlets which sends me into raptures, so then I throw myself with my mouth onto an outcrop of rock which I suck with all my salivary power – my eyes are fixed on the red arm of Marcel Duchamp which merges although it is further away with the pink granite of my rock the other shoulder of Duchamp merges with and even touches that of Gala. I eat Gala and an iron erection stops my copious peeing before it has finished.

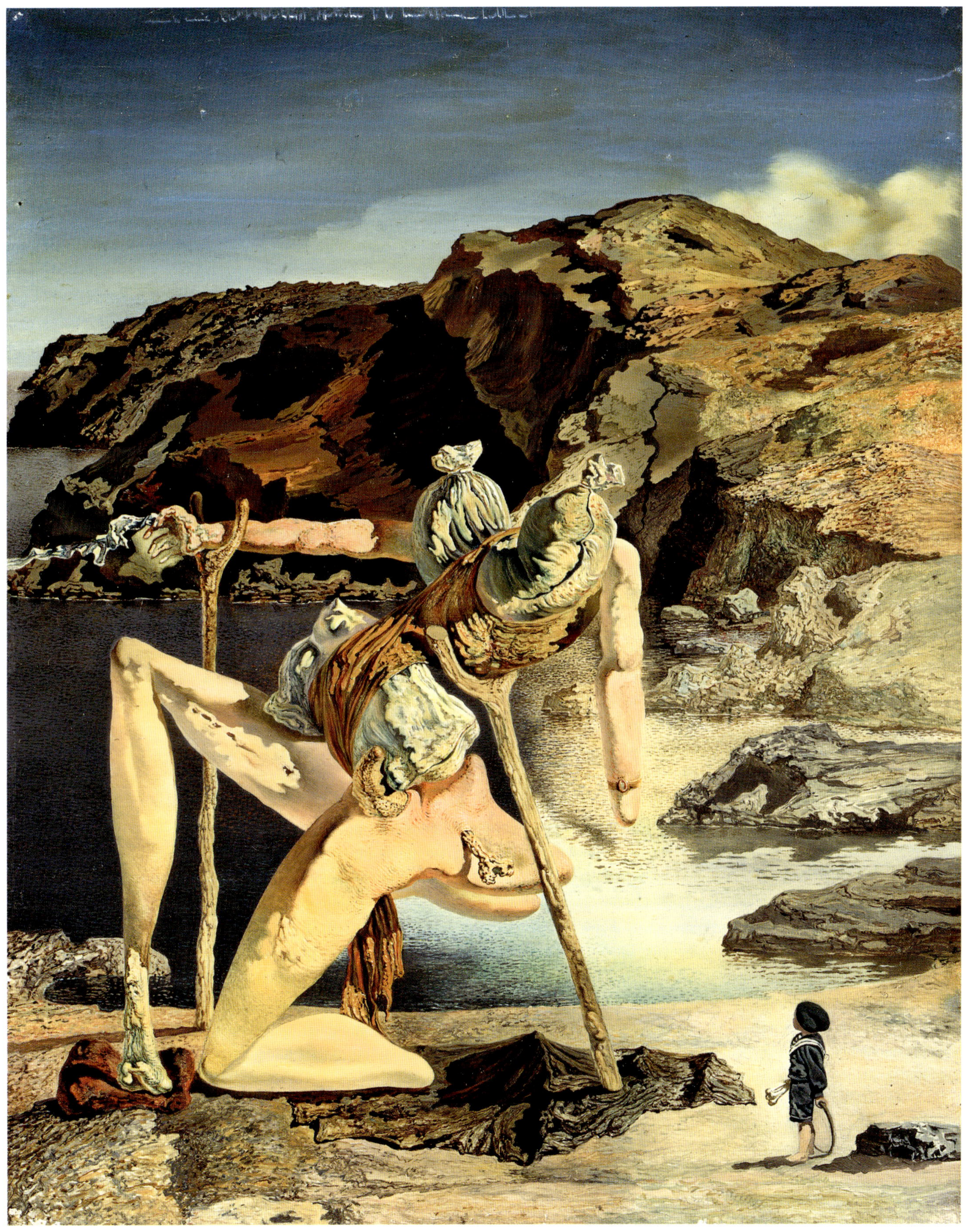

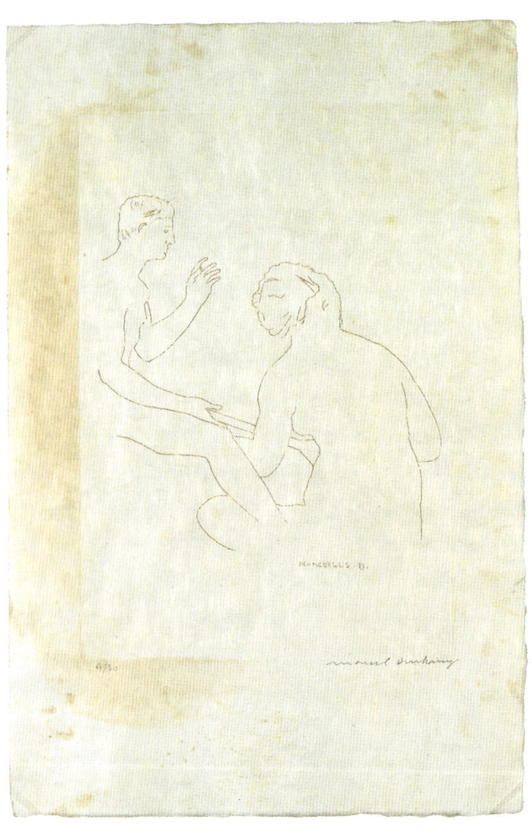 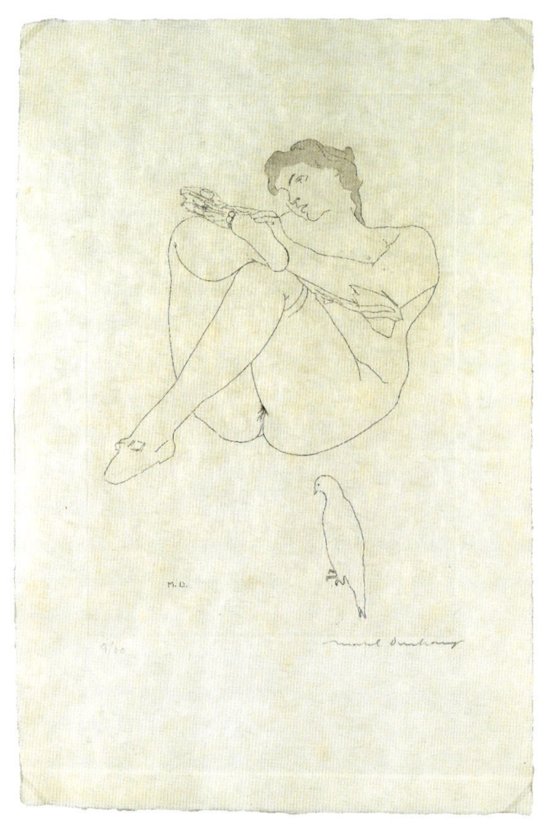

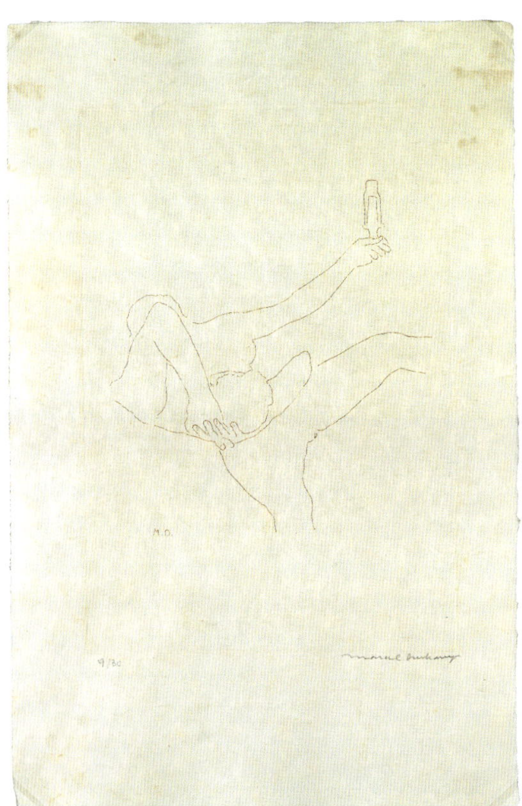 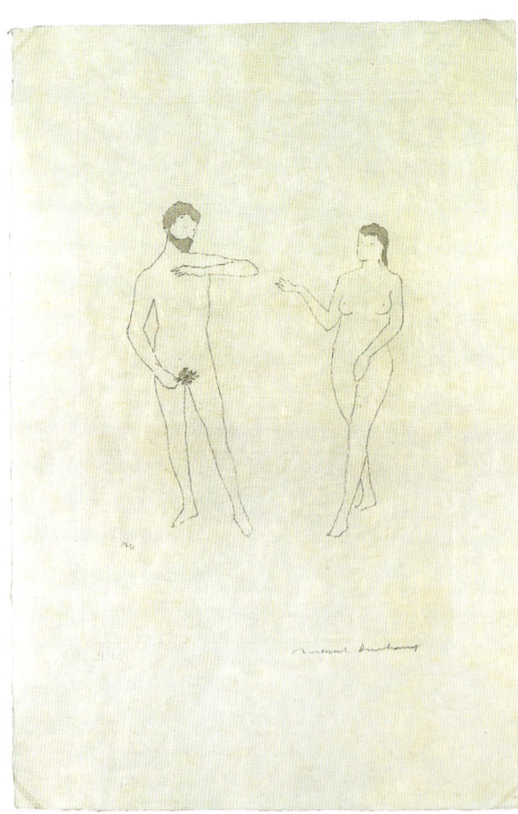

68
Marcel Duchamp
Selected Details after Ingres I, 1968
Etching, second state, printed in bistre on
Japan paper, 50.5 x 32.5 cm
Collection Hummel, Vienna

69
Marcel Duchamp
Selected Details after Courbet, 1968
Etching, second state, printed in bistre on
Japan paper, 50.5 x 32.5 cm
Collection Hummel, Vienna

70
Marcel Duchamp
The Bec Auer, 1968
Etching, second state, printed in bistre on
Japan paper, 50.5 x 32.5 cm
Collection Hummel, Vienna

71
Marcel Duchamp
*Selected Details after Cranach and
'Relâche'*, 1967
Etching, second state, printed in bistre on
Japan paper, 50.5 x 32.5 cm
Collection Hummel, Vienna

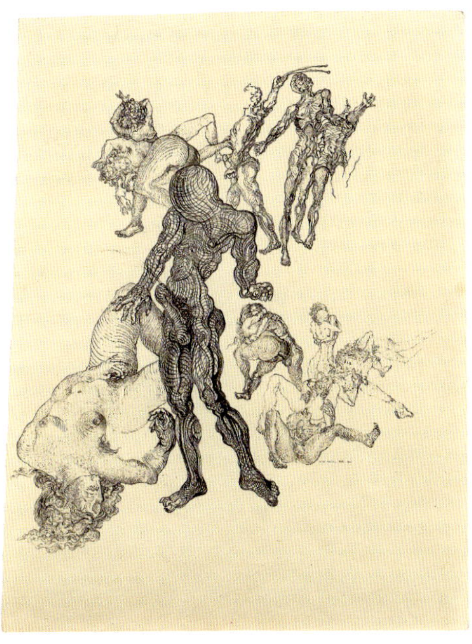

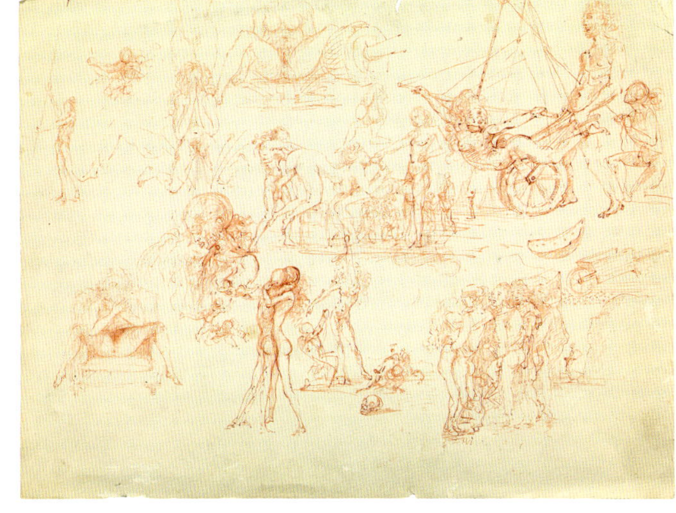

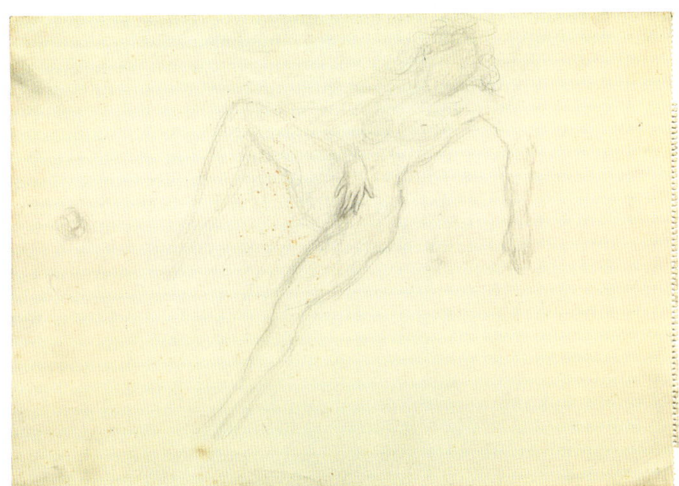

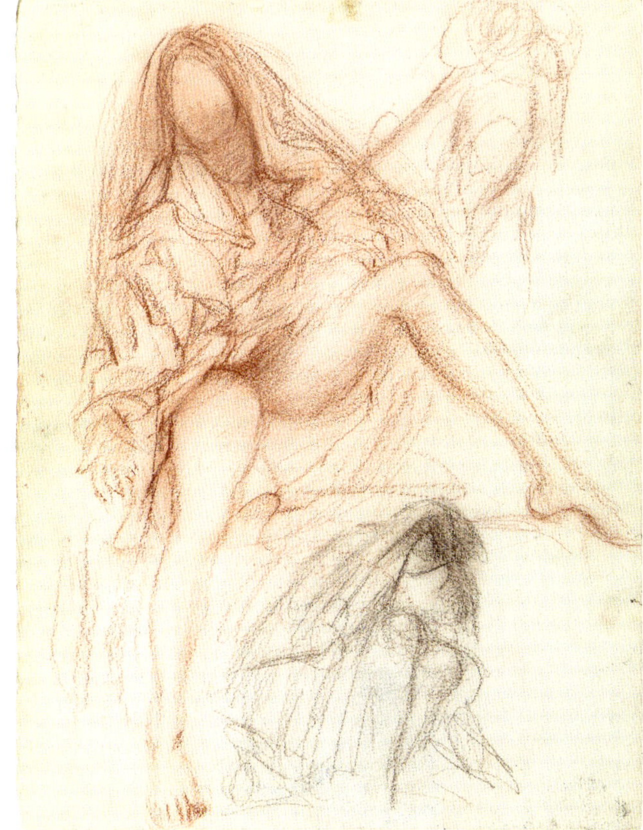

Top left: 72
Salvador Dalí
Untitled (Erotic scene), *c.* 1932
Ink on paper, 32 x 24 cm
Fundació Gala-Salvador Dalí, Figueres
London only

Top right: 73
Salvador Dalí
Untitled (Multiple erotic scenes), 1950s
Ink on paper, 27.7 x 36.1 cm
Fundació Gala-Salvador Dalí, Figueres

Bottom left: 74
Salvador Dalí
Untitled (Female nude, erotic scene),
c. 1943
Pencil on paper, 25.5 x 35.7 cm
Fundació Gala-Salvador Dalí, Figueres

Bottom right: 75
Salvador Dalí
Untitled (Erotic scene), 1960s
Conté pencil on paper, 47.5 x 35.5 cm
Fundació Gala-Salvador Dalí, Figueres

EROTIC OBJECTS
WILLIAM JEFFETT

Looked at through the lens of the Surrealist object, the erotic aspects of the readymades come into focus. At the same time the Surrealist object drew on the non-art character of the readymades to reinforce their relation to life. Duchamp's *Bicycle Wheel* (cat. 77) explored the dialectic of stasis and movement. To set it in motion required the interaction (touch) of the viewer, and once in movement it modified the viewer's optical experience. At once tactile and optical, the work presents an erotics of vision. In his writing on the Surrealist object, Dalí also emphasised the element of motion, pronouncing the object of symbolic function as depending only on the 'amorous imagination'.[1]

In 1931 he launched 'Surrealist objects', in the periodical *Le Surréalisme au service de la Révolution* (*SASDLR*; figs 73, 74). These objects were envisioned as potentially mobile, or suggesting movement, which symbolically incarnated unconscious acts thereby precipitating erotic desires and fantasies. Here he gave credit to Giacometti's recent sculpture *Suspended Ball* for the origin of the concept: 'The Objects Functioning Symbolically were envisaged following the mobile and silent object, Giacometti's suspended ball, an object that already put forward and brought together all the essential assumptions of our definition, but which still stuck to the means peculiar to sculpture.'[2] Giacometti's work remained sculpture, while the 'Surrealist object' was to be formed of found things or readymade materials. For Breton, Dalí proposed the 'fabrication of manifestly erotic, lively objects' intended to stimulate 'a particular sexual emotion'.[3] Dalí's fetishistic contribution in *SASDLR*, simply titled *Object* but now known as *Surrealist Object Functioning Symbolically – Gala's Shoe* (cat. 78), consisted of a woman's shoe and a glass of milk; suspended above the milk on a thread is a sugar cube, with a reproduction of a woman's shoe fixed to the cube, and instructions explaining that the mechanism was designed to lower the cube into the milk so that it would dissolve. Two additional sugar cubes with shoe images attached were fixed to the object's base. If this were not clear enough, the presence of a woman's pubic hairs and a small erotic photograph pointed to the full imaginary eroticism of the construction.

In addition to four objects by Dalí, Gala, Breton and Valentine Hugo, the plate section in *SASDLR* reproduced Miró's construction with outsized phallus, umbrella and bouquet of flowers, which is slyly and ironically entitled *Sculpture* – not 'object' – perhaps because it is immobile.

Duchamp's multiple *Please Touch* (cat. 87) was realised in 1947 in collaboration with his friend the artist Enrico Donati for the cover of the exhibition catalogue *Le Surréalisme en 1947*. Unambiguous and provocative, it ironically challenges the conventional distance of artworks, with their 'do not touch' labels, and replaces the optical mode of perception with one that is immediate and tactile. He took a rough model of an 'ugly bosom' in plaster to Donati, and asked him to find a way to make 999 of them. Donati managed to acquire enough rubber falsies, which were quite common at the time, through a New York wholesaler, and he and Duchamp painted them, having coloured the nipples pink with Conté crayon. Donati claimed to be responsible for the idea for the black velvet to make it look as if the breast were slipping out of a velvet dress. Donati handed the object to Duchamp saying 'Please touch', and Duchamp replied 'Prière de toucher.'[4]

Duchamp's *Étant donnés* (fig. 76) includes a torso of a nude female mannequin made out of pigskin over a plaster armature and set in a diorama representing a landscape, but this elaborate assemblage is presented in a way that imposes and then questions the primacy of the optical by distancing us from the object and the possibility of touching it, and thus positioning us as voyeurs in a peepshow. Of Duchamp's infrequent and enigmatic works that appeared between 1946 and 1956, most had some connection to this assemblage he was secretly creating. Both the parchment figure on velvet (cat. 113), and the transparent nude pricked out on Plexiglas (cat. 111) are studies for the female nude in *Étant donnés*, while *Dart Object* (cat. 81) results from a fragment of the armature used to make her breast. The mould is based on female anatomy, yet *Dart Object* is also phallic, and its eroticism challenges the art object that its punning title evokes (Art Object/Dart Object).

The other two erotic sculptures, *Female Fig Leaf* (cat. 80) and *Wedge of Chastity* (cat. 79), are also intimate, close encounters with parts of the body, the one apparently direct, the other more symbolic. *Female Fig Leaf* plays with the idea of the cast and negative shapes to represent the female genitals; an inversion of Courbet's famous *Origin of the World* (1866; Musée d'Orsay, Paris),[5] it probes the sense of

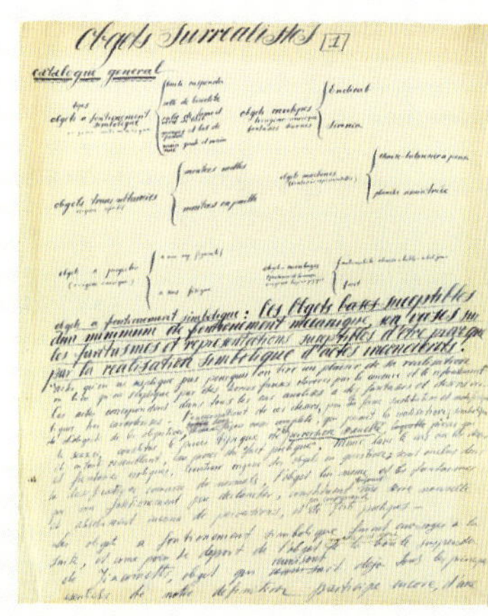

Fig. 73
Salvador Dalí, 'Objets surréalistes' ('Surrealist Objects'), published in *Le Surréalisme au service de la révolution* (*SASDLR*), no. 3, December 1931

Fig. 74
Salvador Dalí
Manuscript for 'Objets surréalistes', 1931 (cat. 76)
Ink on paper, 28.2 x 22.6 cm
Fundació Gala-Salvador Dalí, Figueres

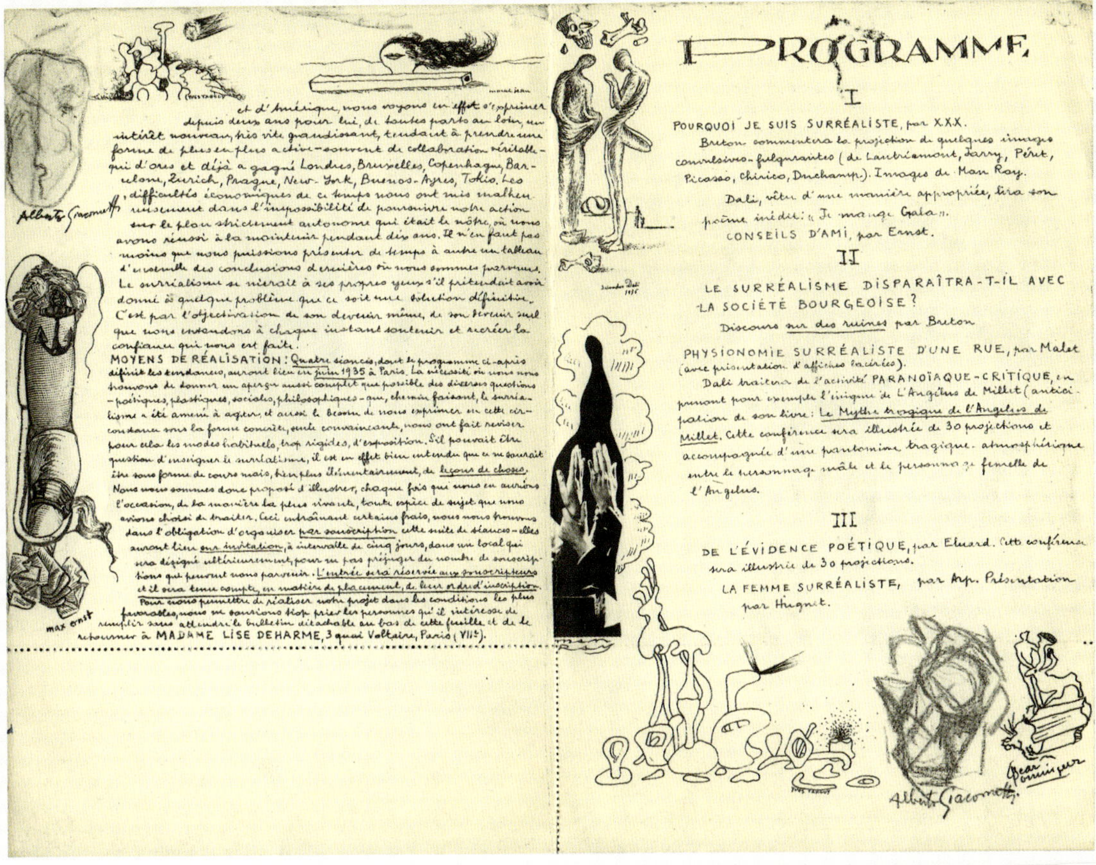

Fig. 75
Programme for the 'Systematic series of conferences on the most recent positions of Surrealism', June 1935, in which Dali was to present his unpublished poem 'Je mange Gala' (see cat. 66).
Collection of The Dalí Museum Archives, St Petersburg, Florida

touch while also misleading the eye. Appearing to be a cast, it was in fact modelled by hand, given tangible form, initially in plaster, later cast in bronze (1961). *Wedge of Chastity*, a gift from Duchamp to Teeny Matisse on their wedding day in 1954, raises the possibility of tactile interaction through its two components: the plaster wedge and the dental plastic base into which it is insertable, again translated into bronze and dental plastic in the 1960s. *Not a Shoe* (cat. 84) is the first version of the wedge in *Wedge of Chastity*.

Duchamp assisted Dalí with the technical aspects of his *Venus de Milo with Drawers* (1936), a reproduction of a plaster copy of the Venus de Milo, later cast as a bronze (1964; cat. 89) and from then on widely exhibited, first at the Galerie Charpentier in Paris, exactly when Duchamp was carefully remaking his readymades as editions with Arturo Schwarz (1964). So the work occupies two moments: the object in the 1930s (even though it was seen only in private exhibitions staged by Dalí) and a time of renewed interest in objects and multiples in the 1960s (when the work had a very public life).[6]

Dalí's object is an iconoclastic violation of the famous ancient marble, the drawers breaking into the linear purity of the surface of the sculpted body and the fur pom-poms inviting touch. Dalí's transformation of the material from marble to plaster and then to painted bronze playfully dissimulated as marble is akin to Duchamp's own playful representation of sugar cubes in marble in *Why Not Sneeze Rose Sélavy?* (cat. 105), in which the thermometer suggests corporeal warmth, setting up a series of contradictions between hard and soft, warm and cold. In Dalí's object the fur invites us to caress the breasts and torso of the otherwise aloof statue, and of course it introduces the visual pun of the Leopold von Sacher-Masoch novel *Venus in Furs* (1870). Dalí's transgressive eroticisation of a female icon of art history is shared with *L.H.O.O.Q.* (cats 228, 242), in which Duchamp not only adds a moustache and goatee to Leonardo's *Mona Lisa*, but also a punning inscription that phonetically invokes desire and sexuality.

It was movement that introduced erotic engagement and situated the figure in the realm of the real, immediate world. Thus *The King and Queen Surrounded by Swift Nudes* (cat. 46) presents two static figures based on chess pieces in relation to nude figures in motion, the nudes of the title. As Steefel suggests, referring to this painting, 'Lubricity, as Eros-motion, is the matrix of the world.'[7] For Breton, Dalí proposed the 'fabrication of manifestly erotic, lively objects' intended to stimulate 'a particular sexual emotion'.[7]

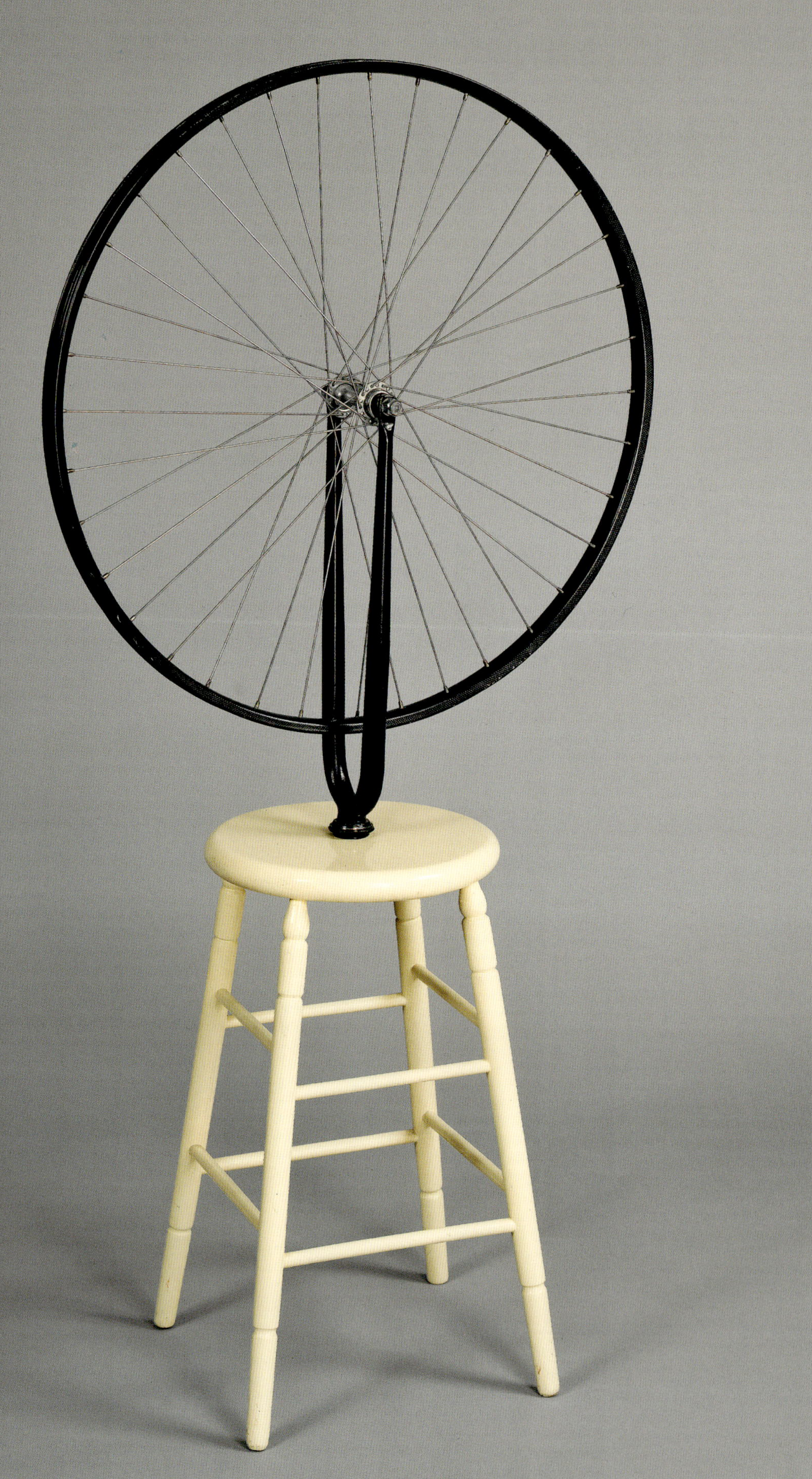

77
Marcel Duchamp
Bicycle Wheel, 1913 (1964 edition, no. 3/8)
Bicycle fork with wheel mounted on
painted wooden stool, 126 x 64 x 31.5 cm
National Gallery of Canada, Ottawa

78
Salvador Dalí
*Surrealist Object Functioning
Symbolically – Gala's Shoe* (*Objet
surréaliste à fonctionnement symbolique
– Le soulier de Gala*), 1931 (1973 edition)
Assemblage with shoe, white marble,
photographs, a glass containing wax,
a gibbet, a matchbox, hair and a wooden
scraper, 48.3 x 27.9 x 9.4 cm
Collection of The Dalí Museum,
St Petersburg, Florida

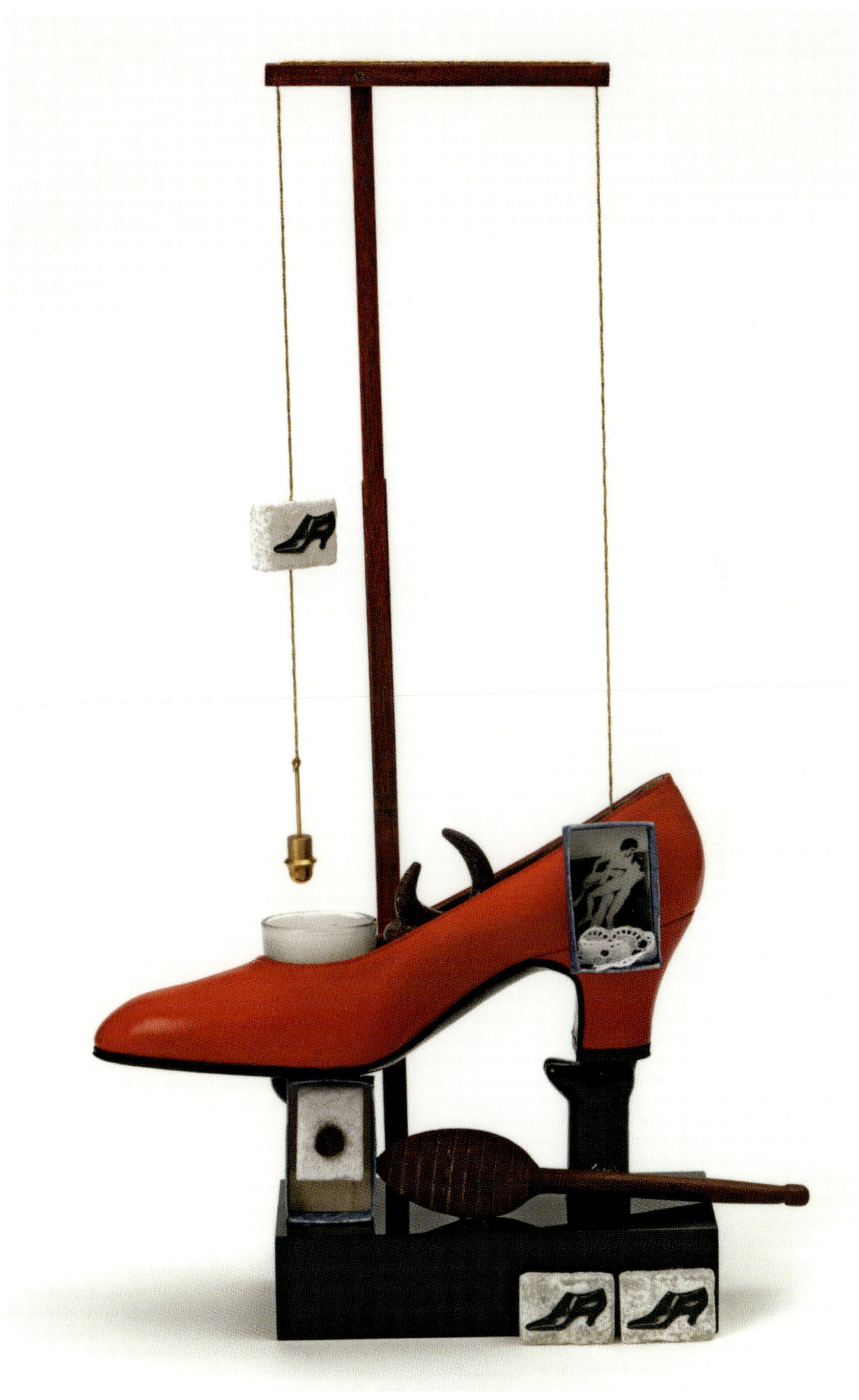

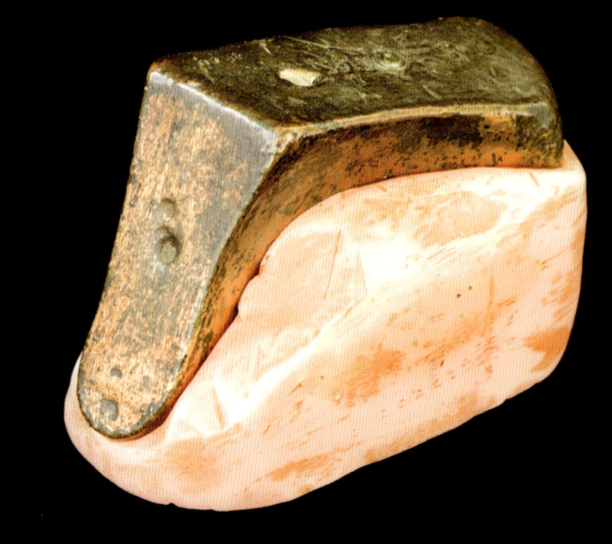
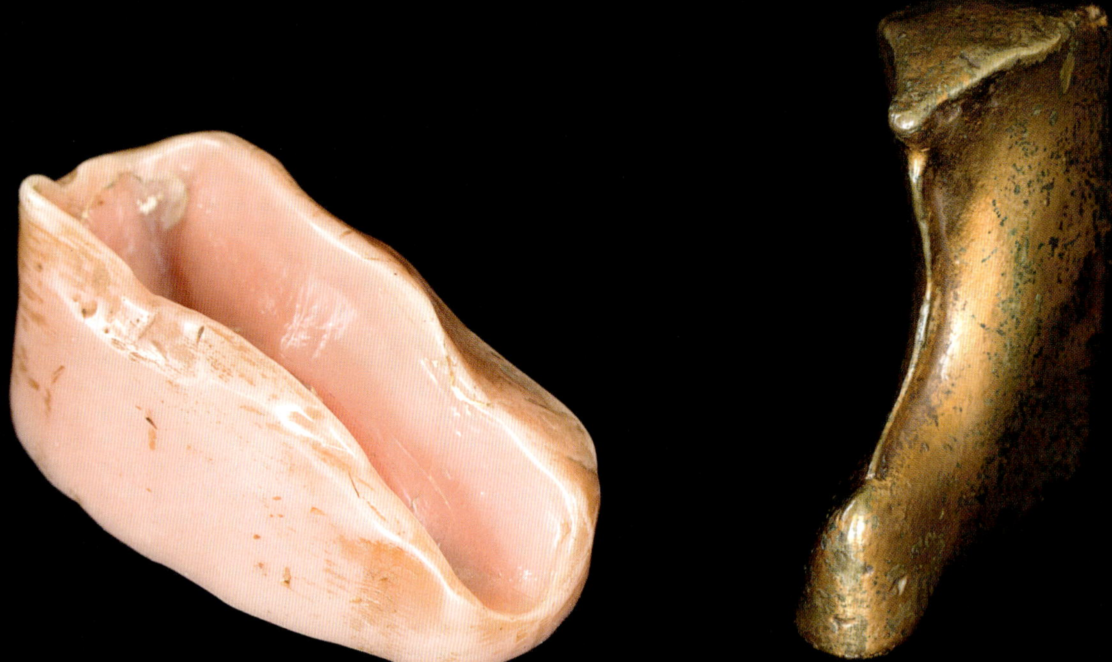

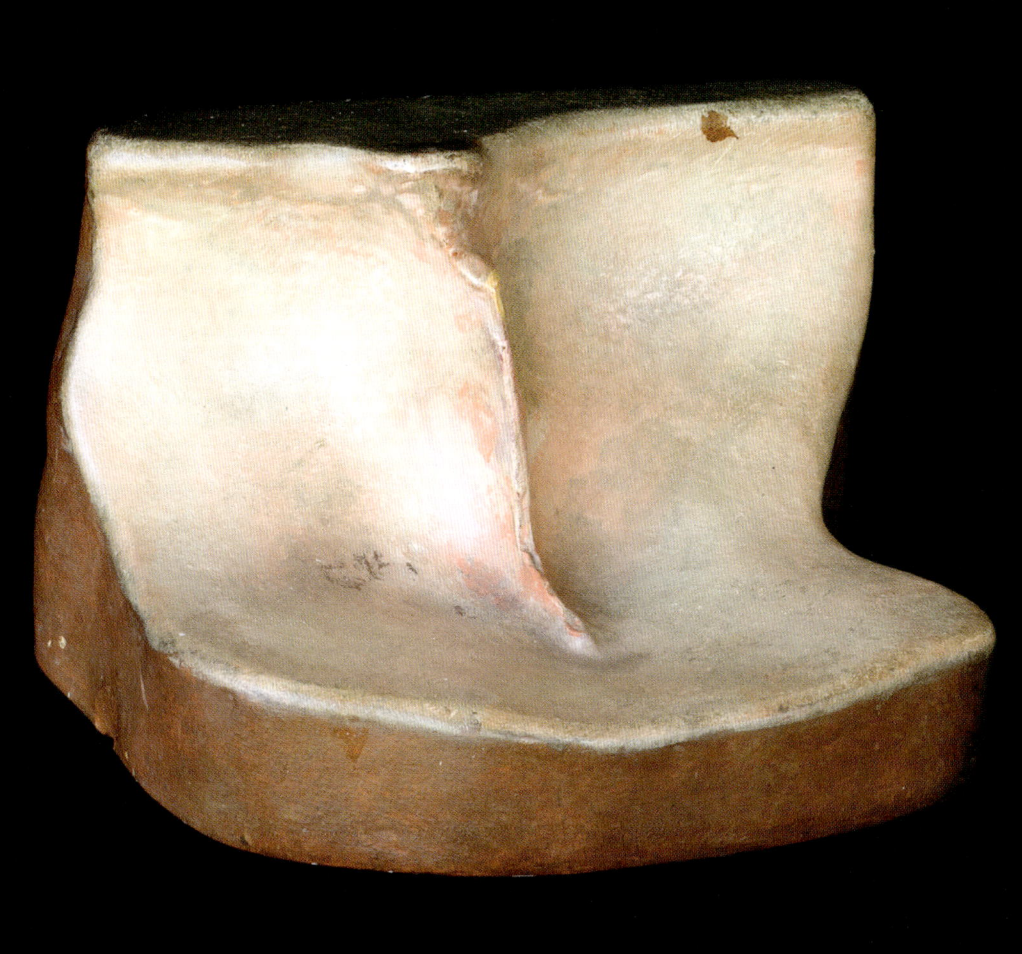

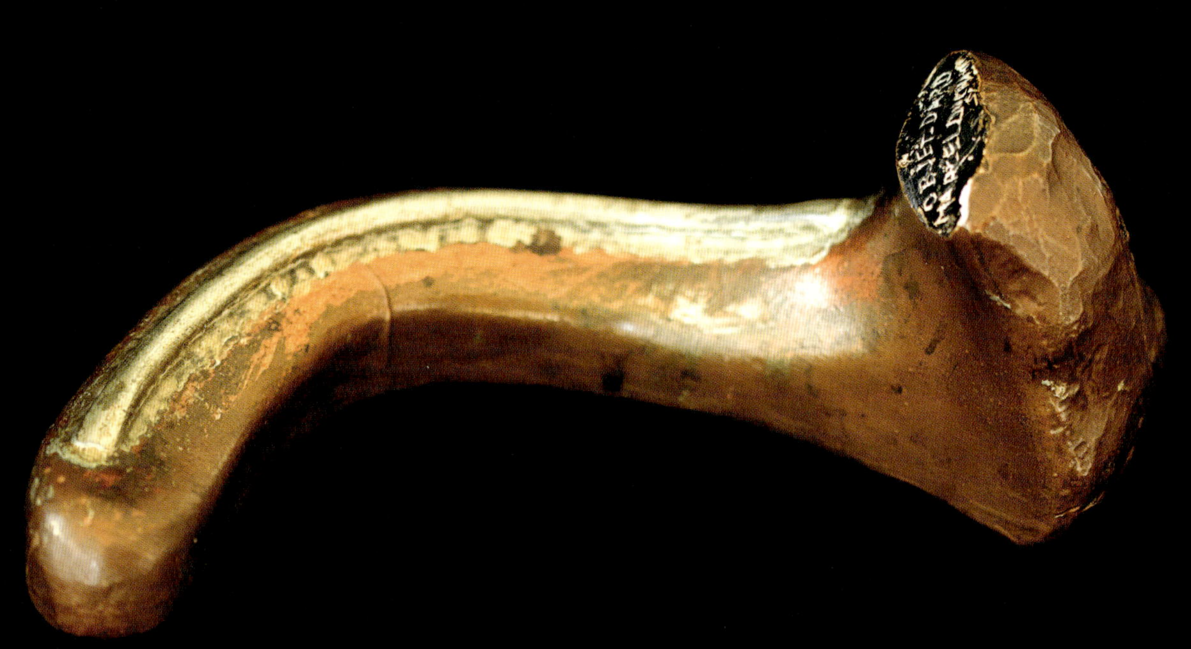

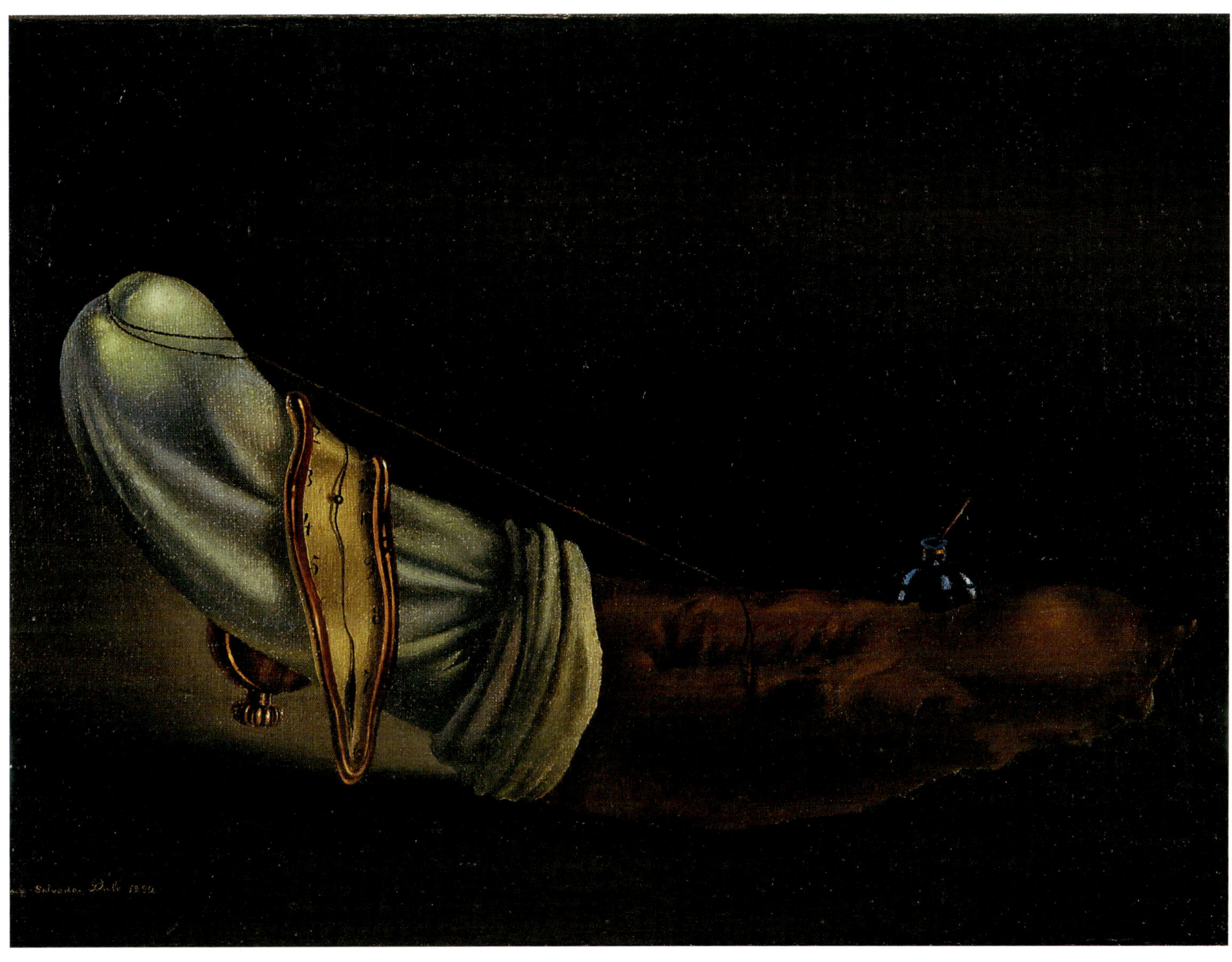

Page 118: 79
Marcel Duchamp
Wedge of Chastity, 1954 (assembled
view above, disassembled below)
Galvanised plaster and dental plastic,
5.6 x 8.6 x 4.2 cm
Private collection
London only

Page 119: 80
Marcel Duchamp
Female Fig Leaf, 1950
Painted plaster cast, 9 x 14 x 12.5 cm
Private collection
London only

Opposite: 81
Marcel Duchamp
Dart Object, 1951
Galvanised plaster with inlaid lead rib,
7.5 x 20.1 x 6 cm
Private collection
London only

Above: 82
Salvador Dalí
Catalan Bread, 1932
Oil on canvas, 24.3 x 33 cm
Collection of The Dalí Museum,
St Petersburg, Florida

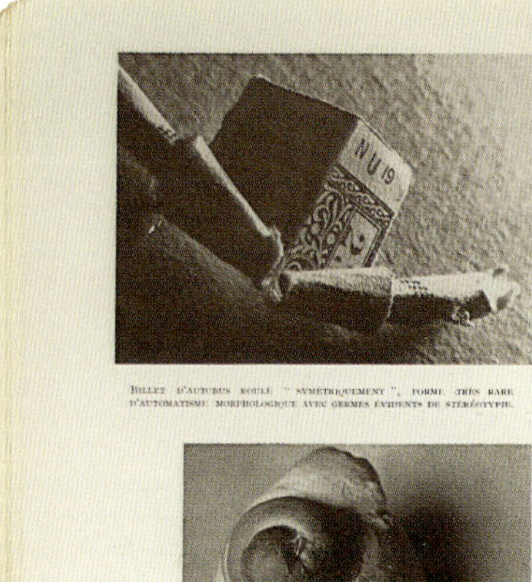
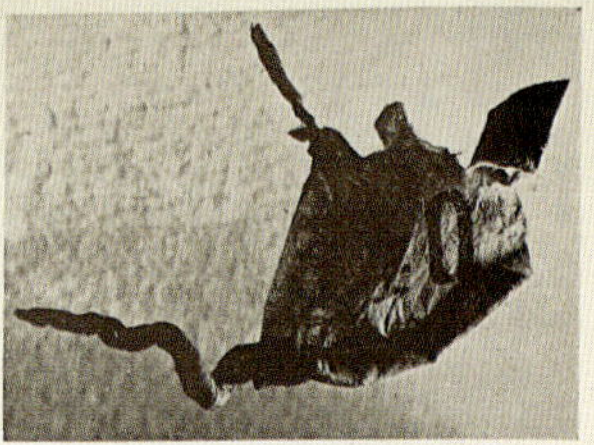
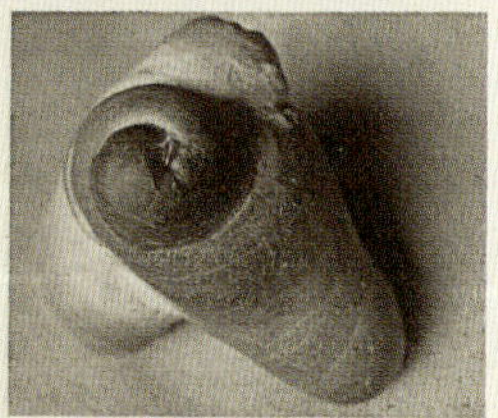
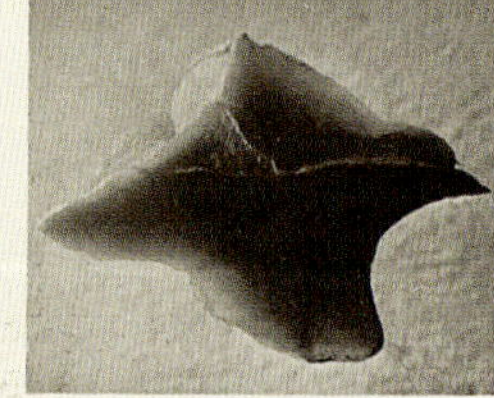
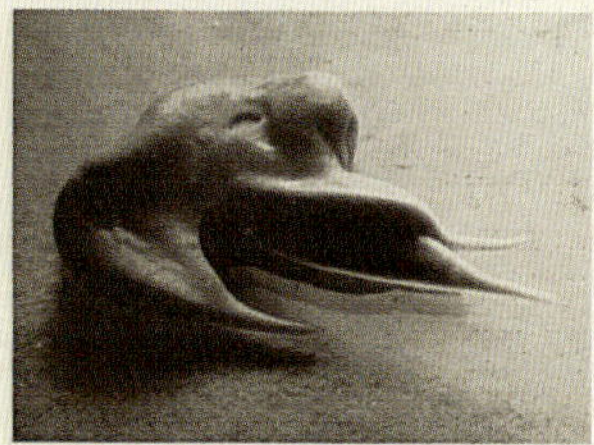
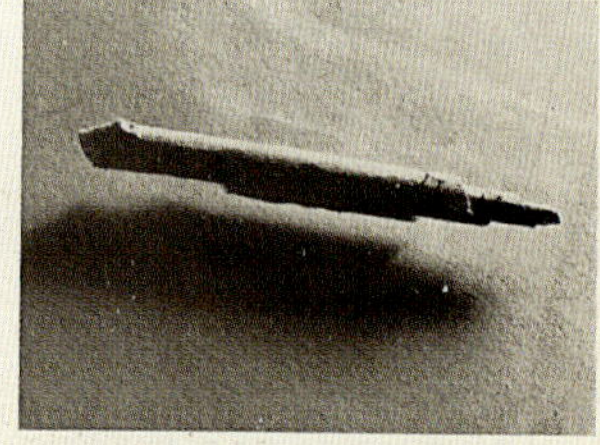

SCULPTURES INVOLONTAIRES

DE LA BEAUTÉ TERRIFIANTE ET COMESTIBLE, DE L'ARCHITECTURE MODERN' STYLE.
par
SALVADOR DALI

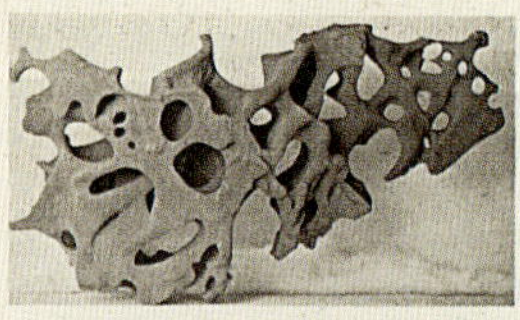
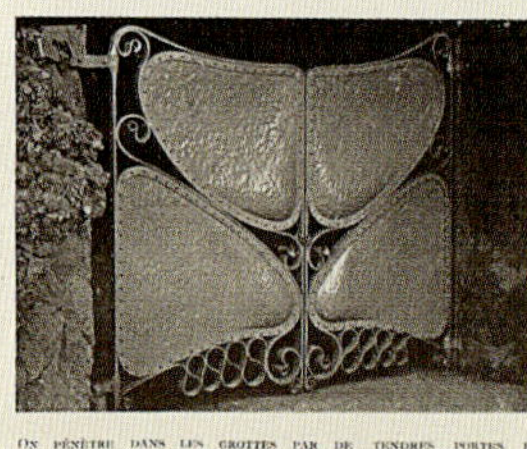

83
Spread from *Minotaure*, nos 3–4, 1933
On the right: Salvador Dalí, 'De la beauté terrifiante et comestible de l'architecture "Modern Style"' ('The Terrifying and Edible Beauty of "Modern Style" Architecture')
On the left: Dalí's 'Sculptures involontaires' ('Involuntary sculptures'), photographed by Brassaï
Journal, 30.5 x 24.5 cm
Collection of The Dalí Museum Archives, St Petersburg, Florida

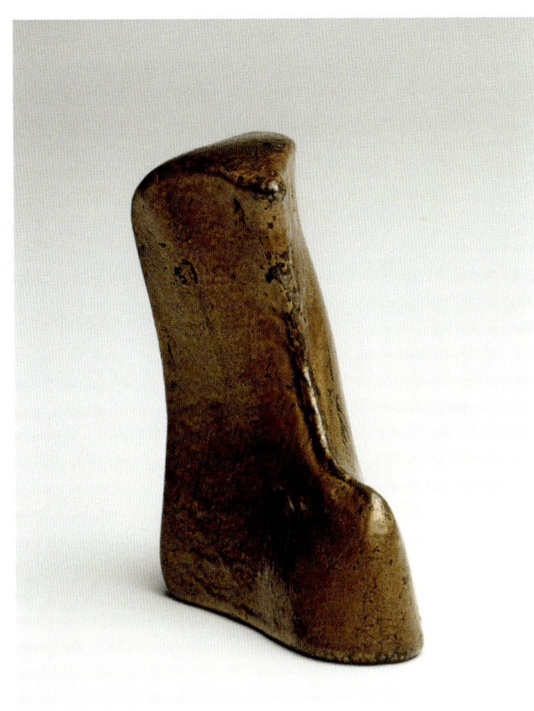

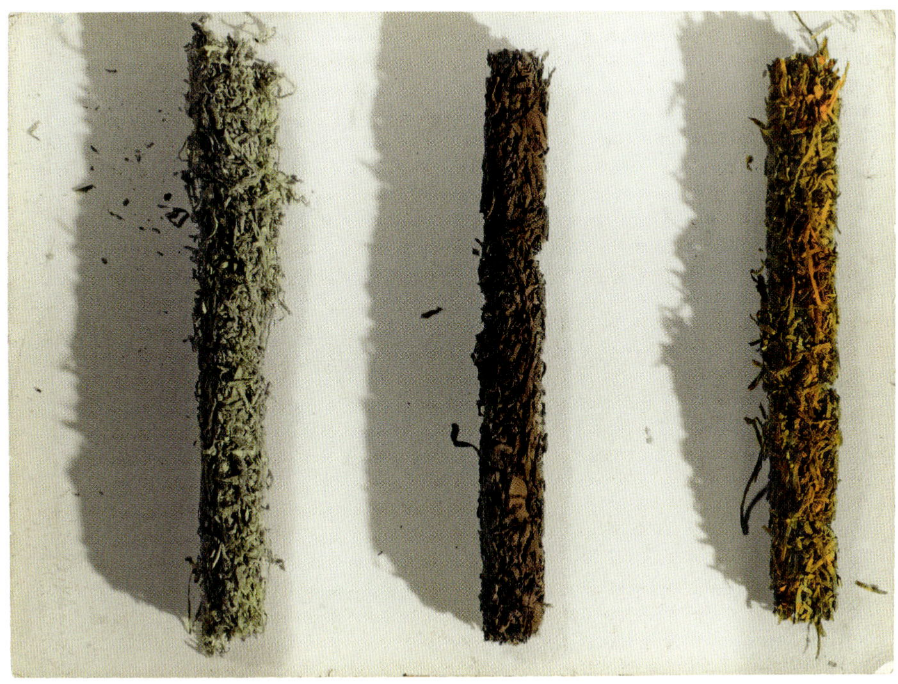

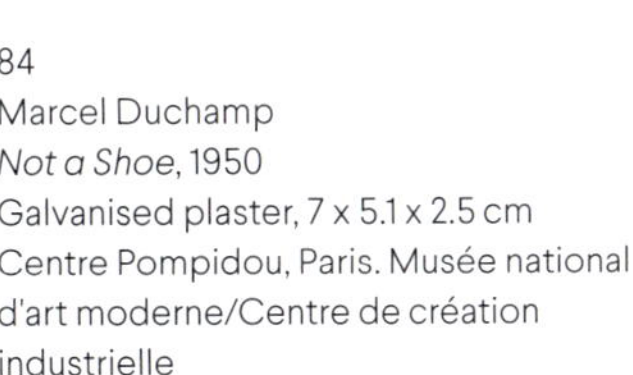

84
Marcel Duchamp
Not a Shoe, 1950
Galvanised plaster, 7 x 5.1 x 2.5 cm
Centre Pompidou, Paris. Musée national
d'art moderne/Centre de création
industrielle

85
Marcel Duchamp
Couverture-cigarettes, 1936
Gelatin silver print coloured with aniline,
30 x 40 cm
Centre Pompidou, Paris. Musée national
d'art moderne/Centre de création
industrielle

86
Marcel Duchamp
Female Fig Leaf, edition by Man Ray,
1950/1951
Plaster with green paint, 8.5 x 13 x 11.5 cm
Centre Pompidou, Paris. Musée national
d'art moderne/Centre de création
industrielle

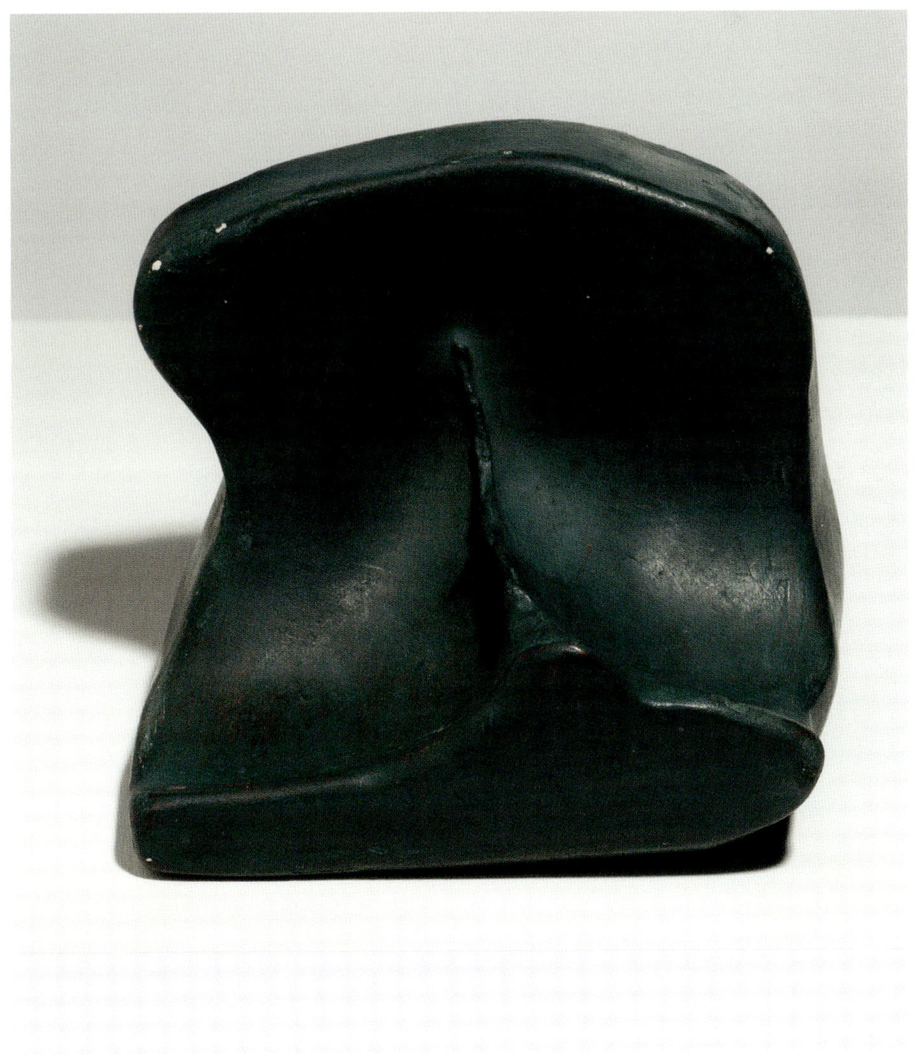

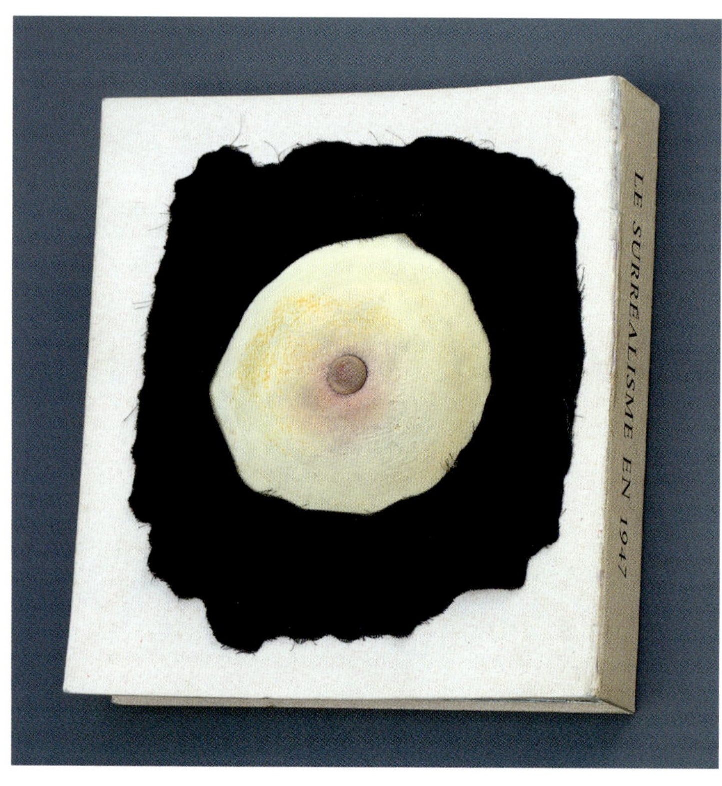

87
Marcel Duchamp
Please Touch, 1947
Cover design for *Le Surréalisme en 1947*
(exhibition catalogue)
Collage of foam rubber, pigment, velvet,
and cardboard adhered to removable
cover, 21 x 24 cm
Private collection

88
Salvador Dalí
Cover of *Minotaure*, no. 8, 1936
Collection of The Dalí Museum Archives,
St Petersburg, Florida

89
Salvador Dalí
Venus de Milo with Drawers, 1936
(1964 edition)
Bronze, fur, paint, 99 x 29.5 x 31.5 cm
Collection of The Dalí Museum,
St Petersburg, Florida
Florida only

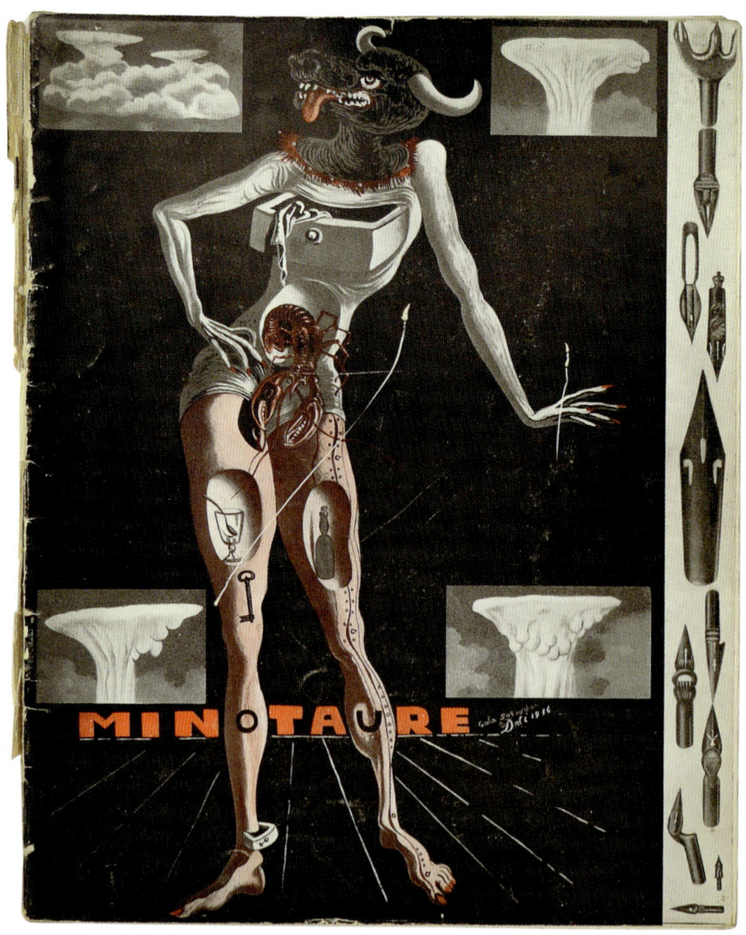

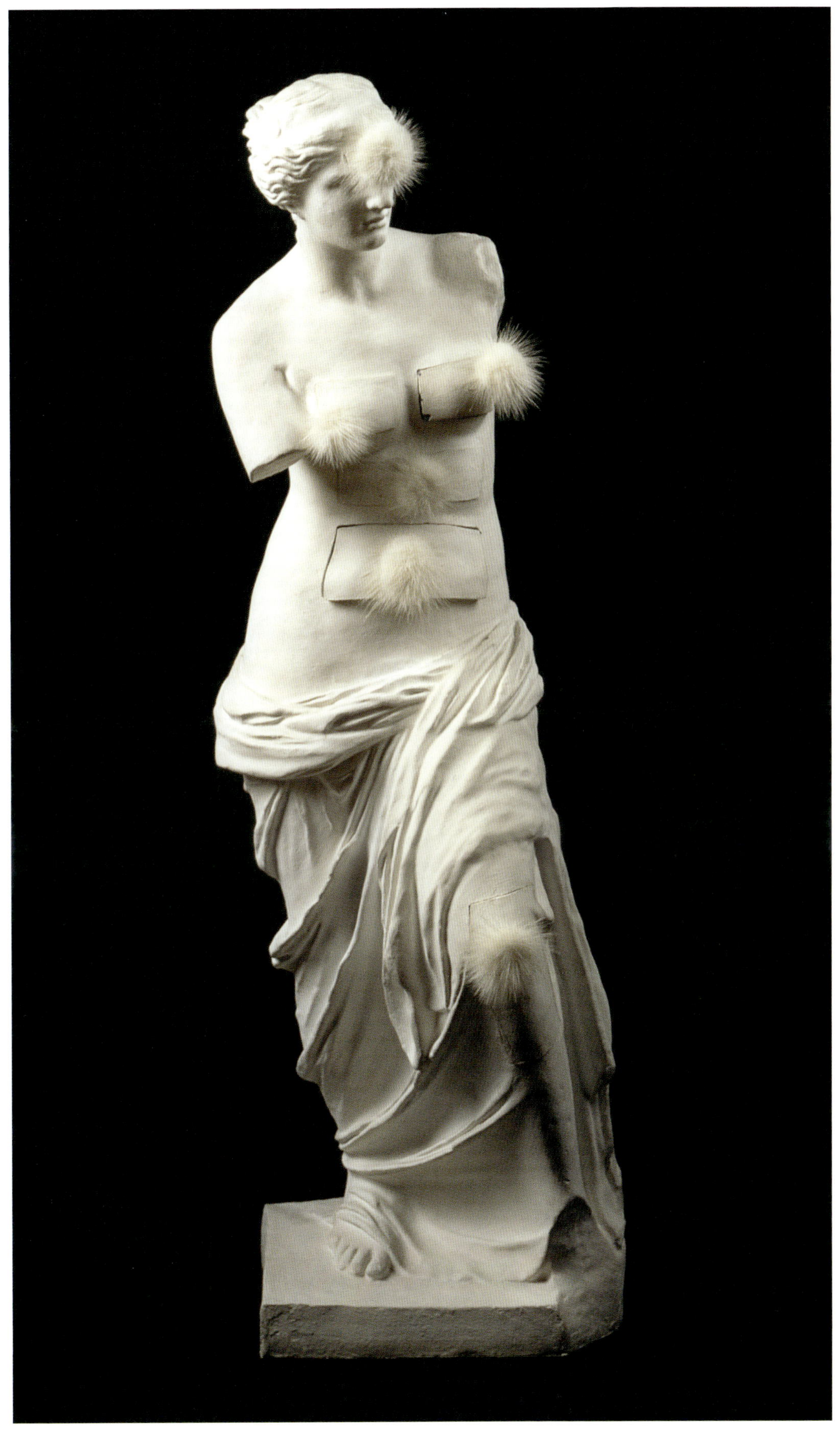

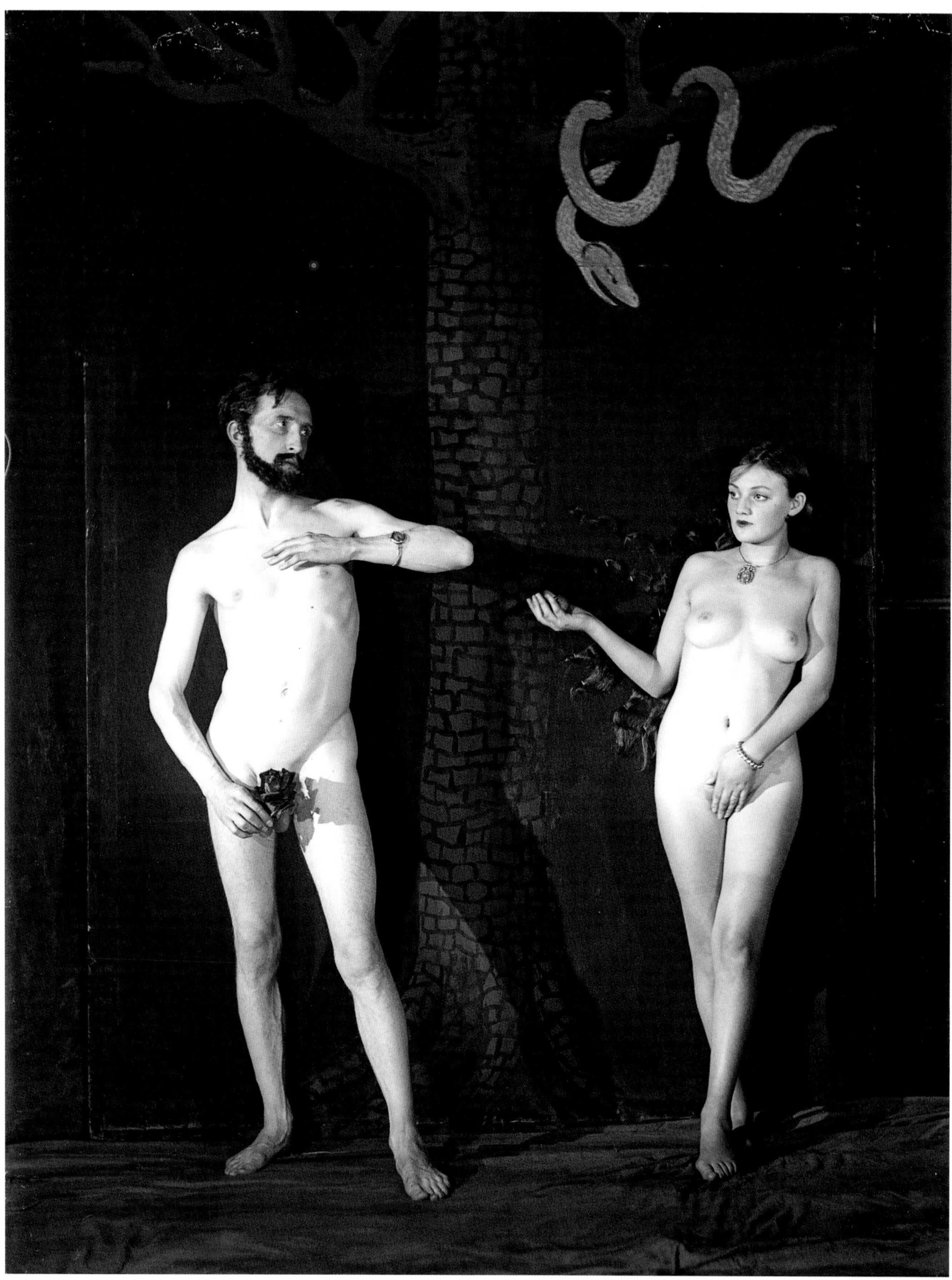

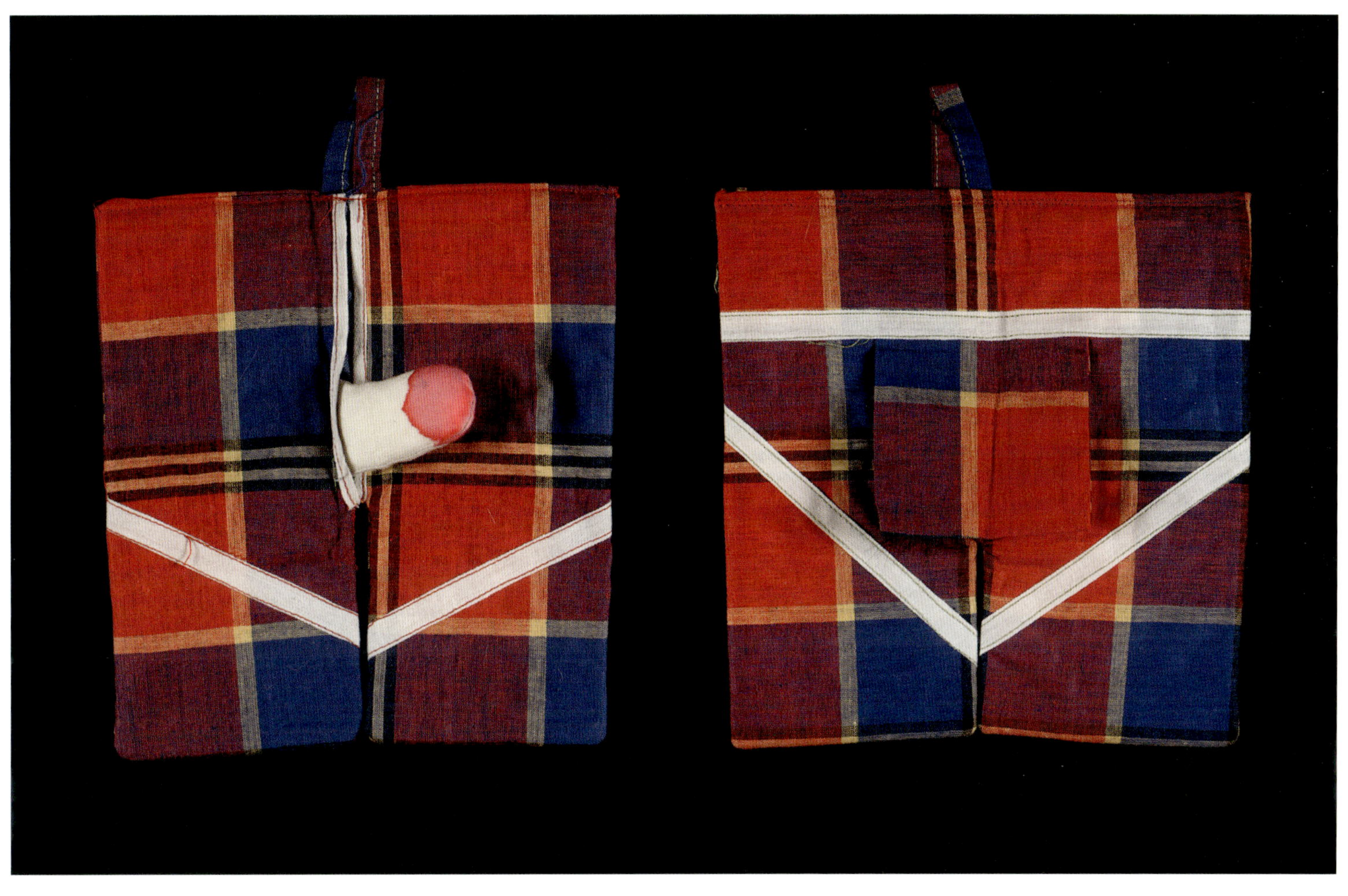

90
Man Ray
Ciné-sketch: Adam and Eve (Marcel
Duchamp and Bronia Perlmutter), 1924
Photograph (printed 2017), 12 x 9 cm
Royal Academy of Arts/Centre
Pompidou, Paris. Musée national d'art
moderne/Centre de création industrielle

91
Marcel Duchamp
'Couple of Laundress's Aprons'
from Mimi Parent, *Boîte alerte*, 1959
Two multiples of cloth and fur,
'male': 22.8 x 17.7 x 3.2 cm
'female': 24.8 x 19.8 x 2.3 cm
Tate: purchased 2000
London only

Duchamp sent two readymade tartan
potholders from New York to André
Breton in Paris for the 1959 'Exposition
Internationale du Surréalisme' (EROS),
rectified to include male and female
attributes. An edition of 20 was fabricated
for the deluxe version of the catalogue,
assembled by Mimi Parent.

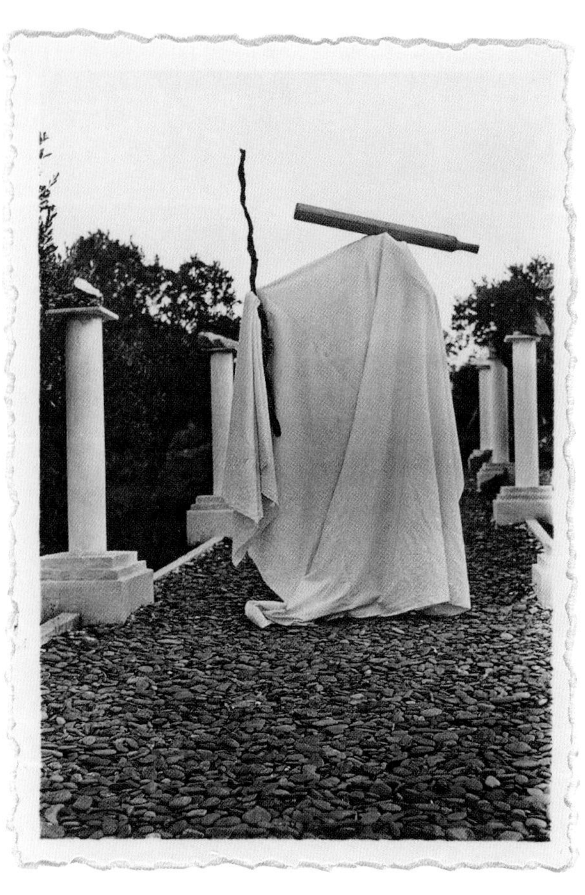
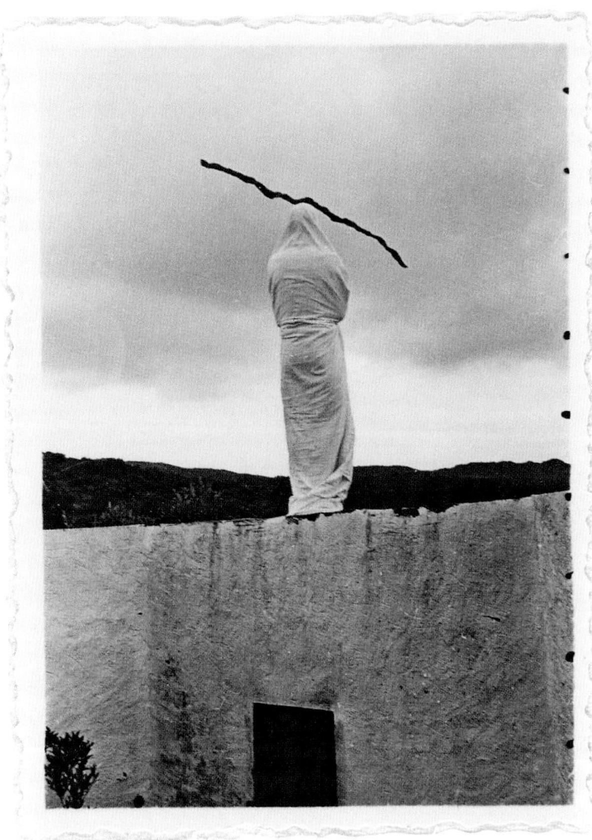
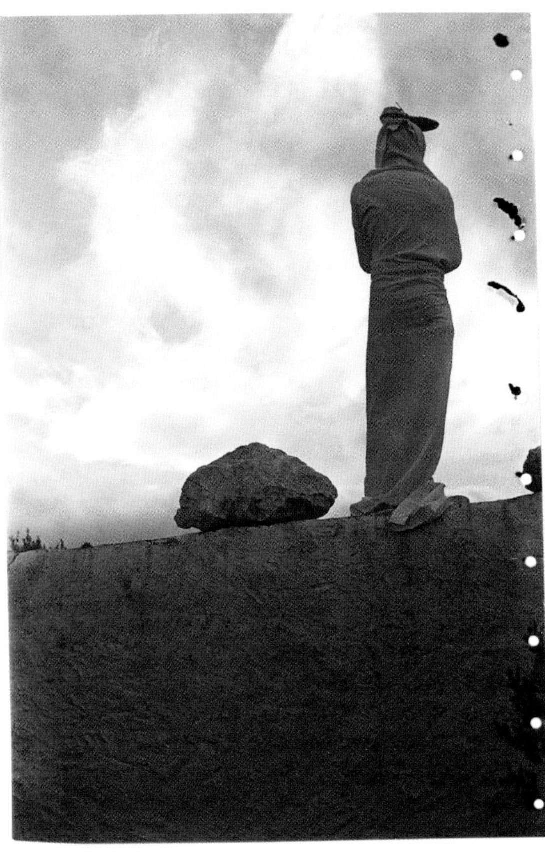
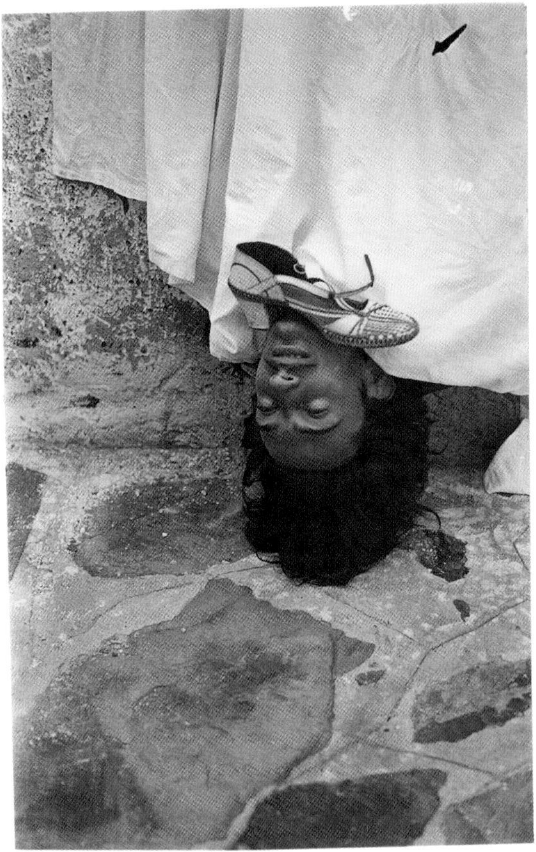

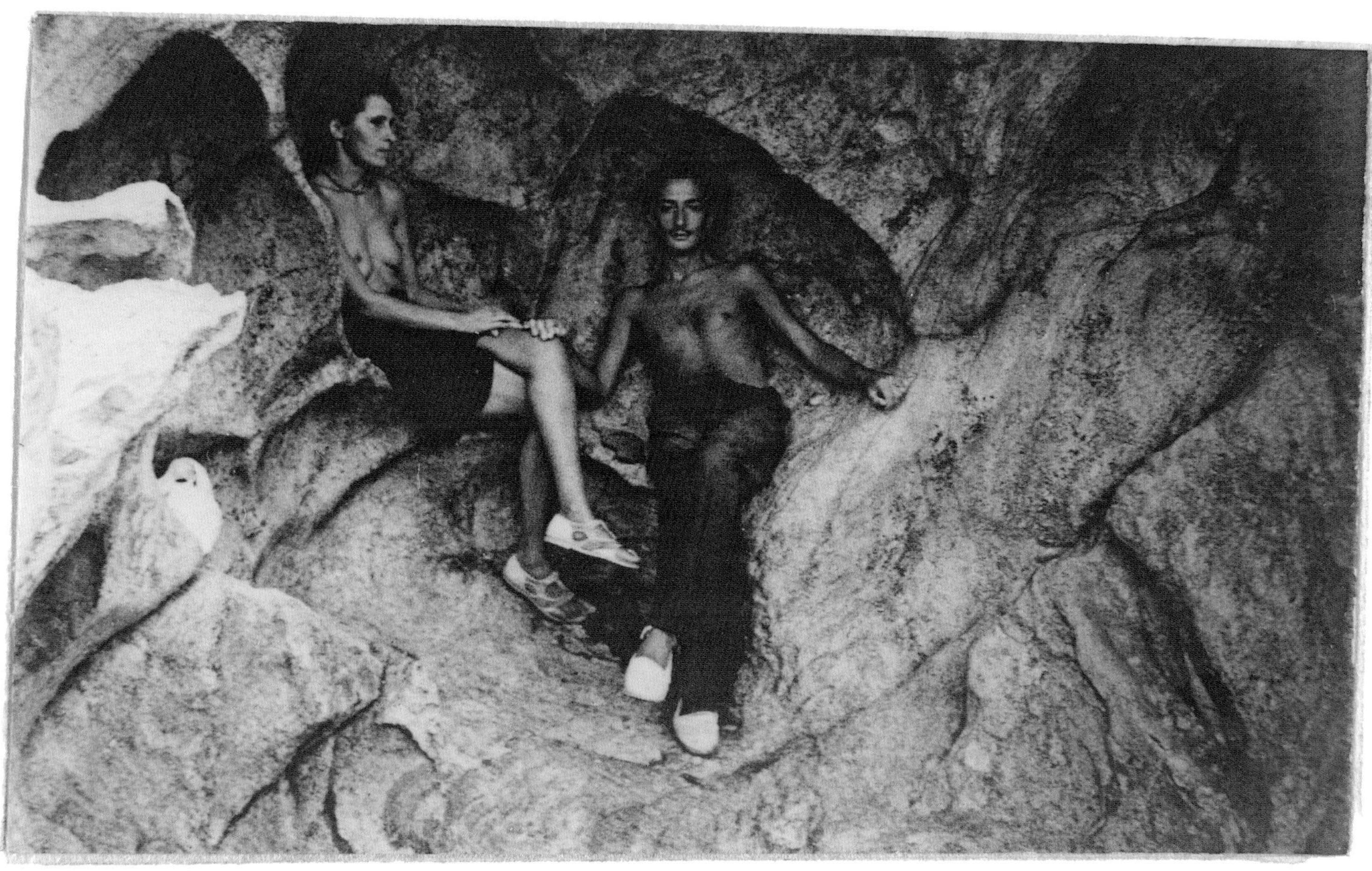

Opposite, top row and bottom left: 92–94
Man Ray
Dalí drapé series (1, 2 and 3), 1933
Silver gelatin prints, 8.5 x 5.8 cm,
8.6 x 6.1 cm, 8.8 x 5.8 cm
Centre Pompidou, Paris. Musée national d'art
moderne/Centre de création industrielle

Opposite, bottom right: 95
Man Ray
Dalí tête renversée, 1933
Gelatin silver print, 8.9 x 5.5 cm
Centre Pompidou, Paris. Musée national d'art
moderne/Centre de création industrielle

96
Man Ray
Gala and Dalí, 1933
Gelatin silver print, 3.7 x 6.2 cm
Centre Pompidou, Paris. Musée national d'art
moderne/Centre de création industrielle

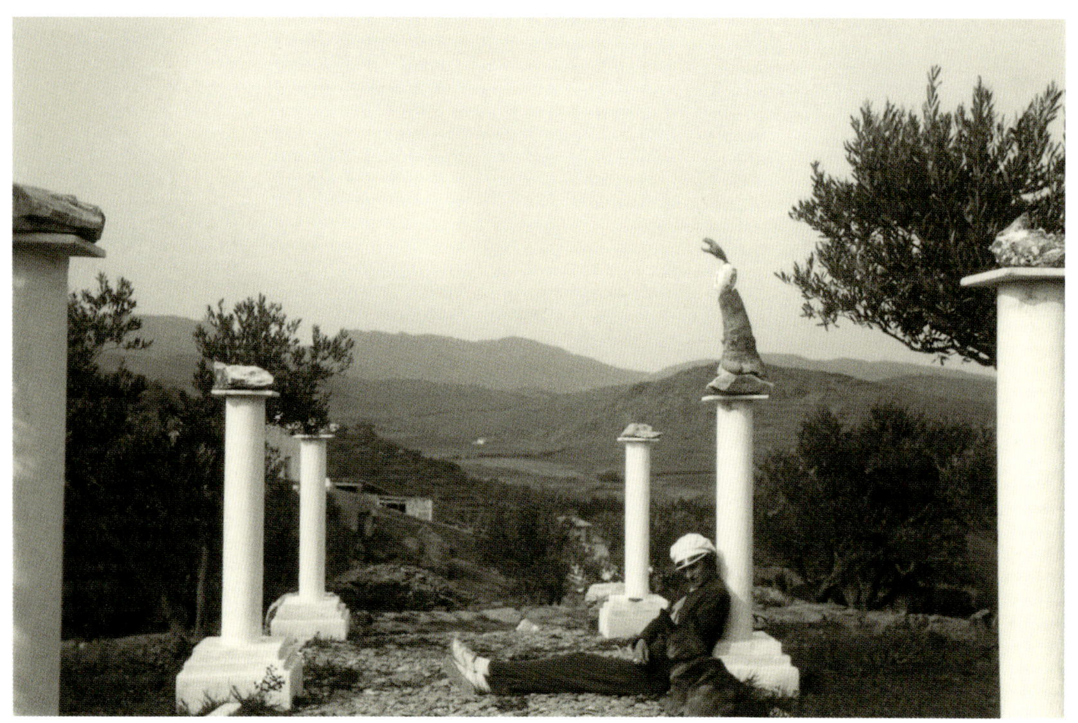

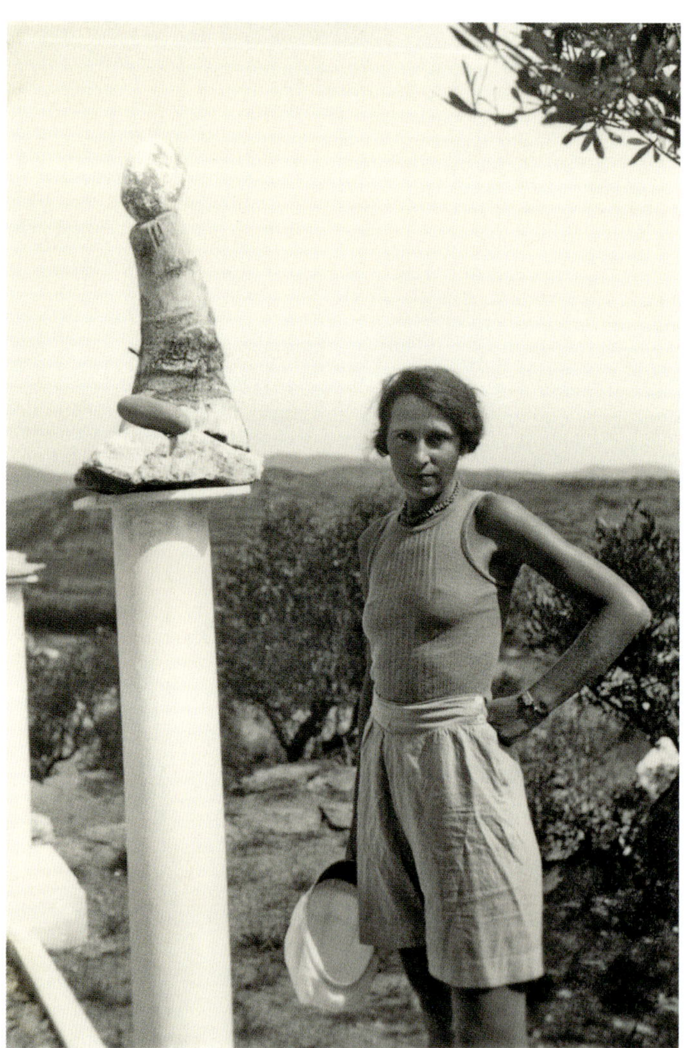

97
Man Ray
Gala with Surrealist Sculptures, 1932
Vintage gelatin silver print mounted
on cardboard, 6 x 8.5 cm
Emmanuel Boussard Library, London

98
Man Ray
Gala with a Surrealist Sculpture, 1932
Vintage gelatin silver print mounted
on cardboard, 8.5 x 6 cm
Emmanuel Boussard Library, London

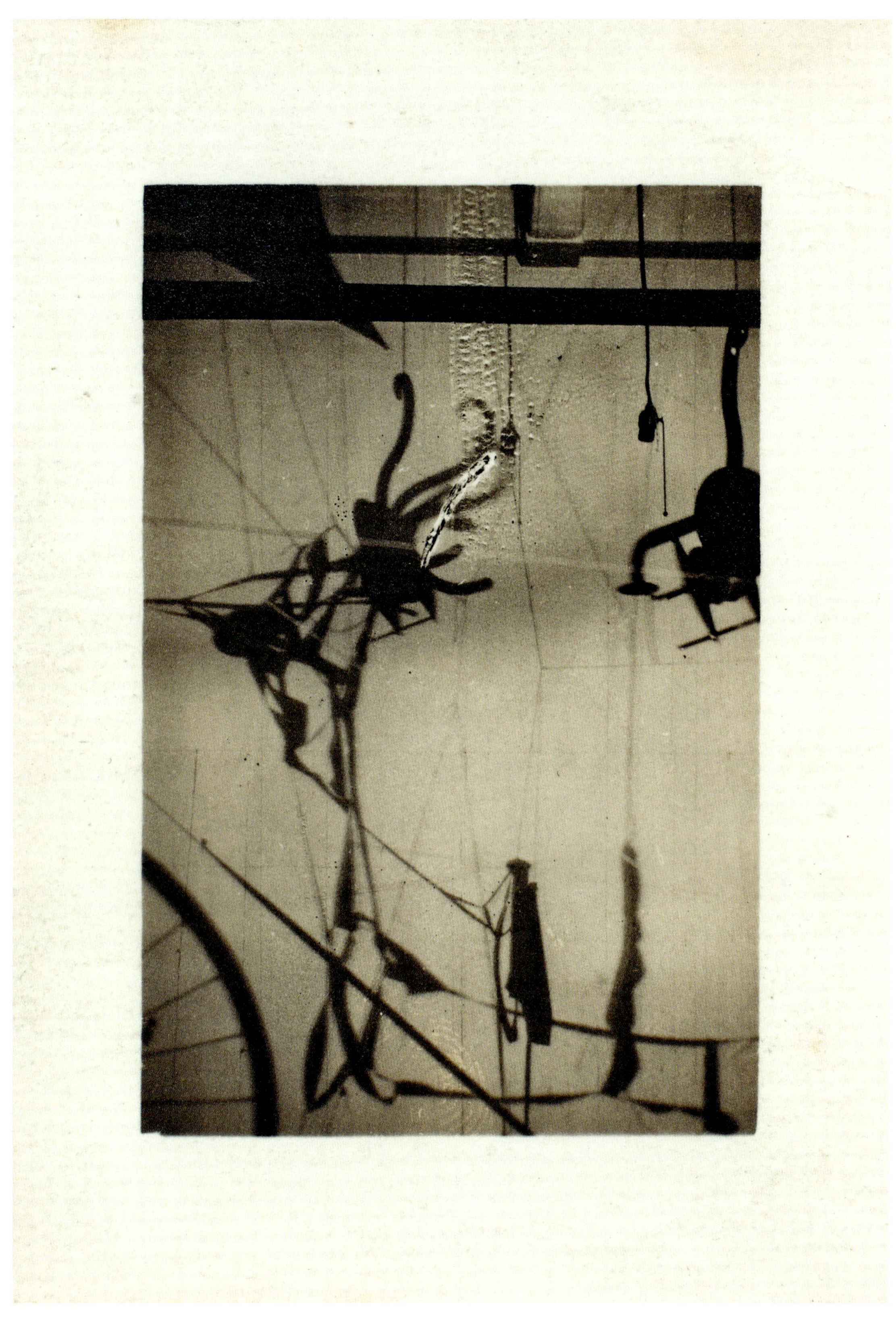

99
Marcel Duchamp
Photograph of Shadows Cast by Readymades, 1918–22
Photographic print, 8.3 x 6.1 cm
Centre Pompidou, Paris. Musée national d'art moderne/Centre de création industrielle

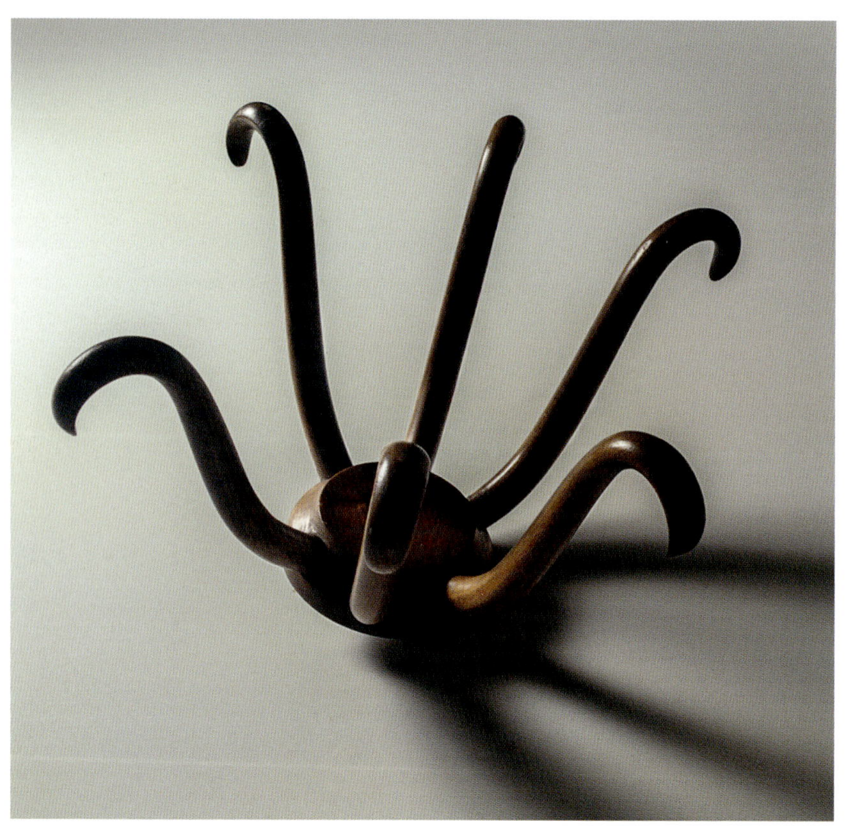

100
Marcel Duchamp
Hat Rack, 1917 (1964 edition)
Readymade: wooden hat rack,
23 x 44 x 33 cm
Galleria Nazionale d'Arte Moderna e
Contemporanea, Rome

101
The Blind Man, no. 2, May 1917
Journal facsimile (n.d.), 29 x 21 cm
Private collection, London

102
Marcel Duchamp
Fountain, 1917 (1964 edition)
Porcelain, 36 x 48 x 61 cm
Galleria Nazionale d'Arte Moderna e
Contemporanea, Rome

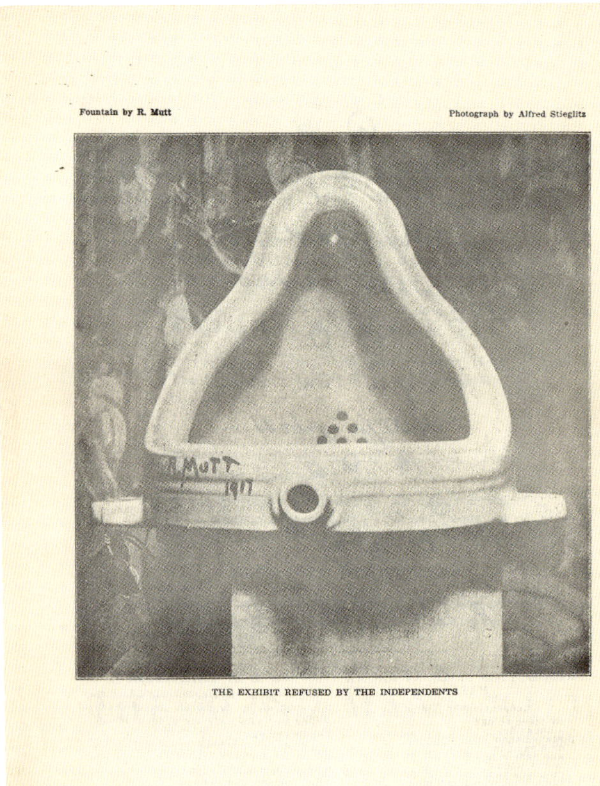

Fountain by R. Mutt

Photograph by Alfred Stieglitz

THE EXHIBIT REFUSED BY THE INDEPENDENTS

THE BLIND MAN

The Richard Mutt Case

They say any artist paying six dollars may exhibit.

Mr. Richard Mutt sent in a fountain. Without discussion this article disappeared and never was exhibited.

What were the grounds for refusing Mr. Mutt's fountain:—

1. *Some contended it was immoral, vulgar.*

2. *Others, it was plagiarism, a plain piece of plumbing.*

Now Mr. Mutt's fountain is not immoral, that is absurd, no more than a bath tub is immoral. It is a fixture that you see every day in plumbers' show windows.

Whether Mr. Mutt with his own hands made the fountain or not has no importance. He CHOSE it. He took an ordinary article of life, placed it so that its useful significance disappeared under the new title and point of view—created a new thought for that object.

As for plumbing, that is absurd. The only works of art America has given are her plumbing and her bridges.

"Buddha of the Bathroom"

I suppose monkeys hated to lose their tail. Necessary, useful and an ornament, monkey imagination could not stretch to a tailless existence (and frankly, do you see the biological beauty of our loss of them?), yet now that we are used to it, we get on pretty well without them. But evolution is not pleasing to the monkey race; "there is a death in every change" and we monkeys do not love death as we should. We are like those philosophers whom Dante placed in his Inferno with their heads set the wrong way on their shoulders. We walk forward looking backward, each with more of his predecessors' personality than his own. Our eyes are not ours.

The ideas that our ancestors have joined together let no man put asunder! In *La Dissociation des Idees*, Remy de Gourmont, quietly analytic, shows how sacred is the marriage of ideas. At least one charm-ing thing about our human institution is that although a man marry he can never be *only* a husband. Besides being a money-making device and the *one* man that *one* woman can sleep with in legal purity without sin he may even be as well some other woman's very personification of her abstract idea. Sin, while to his employees he is nothing but their "Boss," to his children only their "Father," and to himself certainly something more complex.

But with objects and ideas it is different. Recently we have had a chance to observe their meticulous monogomy.

When the jurors of *The Society of Independent Artists* fairly rushed to remove the bit of sculpture called the *Fountain* sent in by Richard Mutt, because the object was irrevocably associated in their atavistic minds with a certain natural function of a secretive sort. Yet to any "innocent" eye

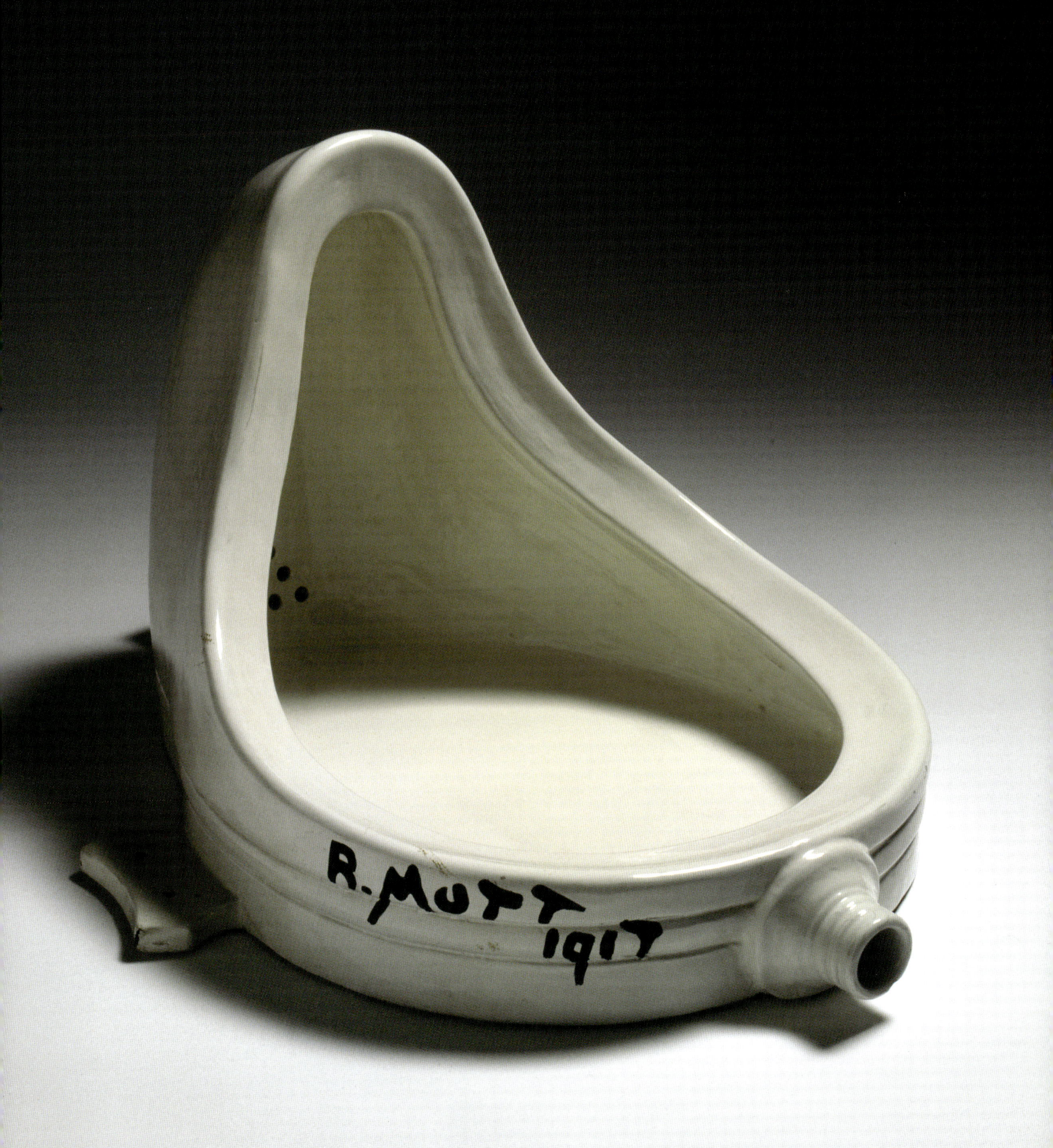

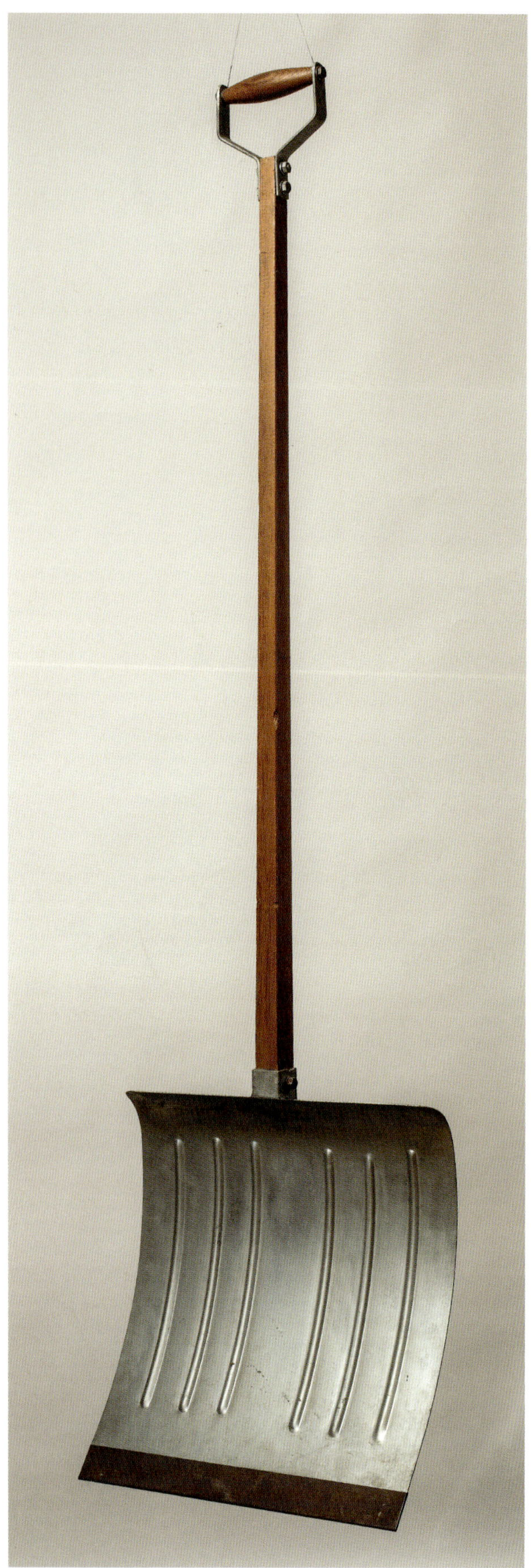

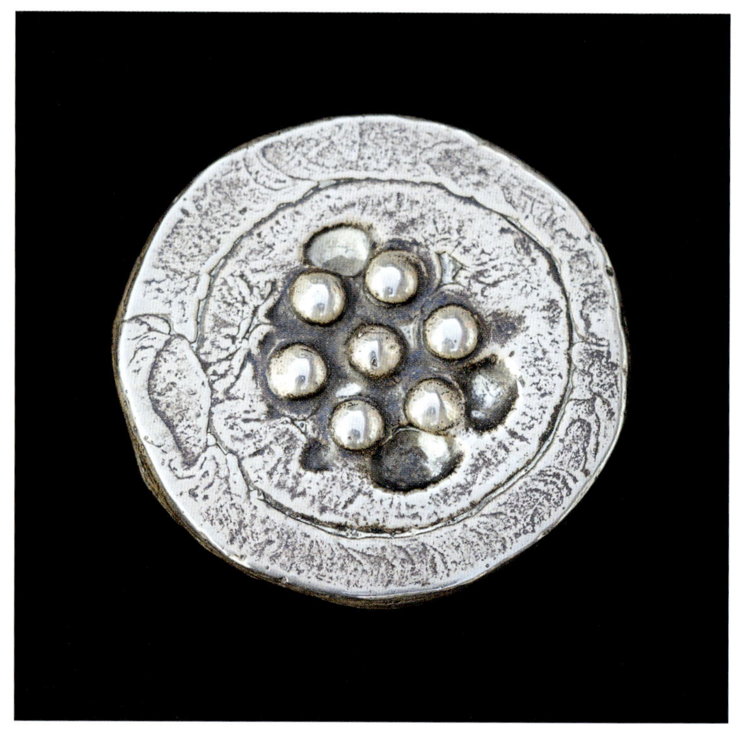

103
Marcel Duchamp
In Advance of the Broken Arm, 1915
(1964 edition)
Readymade: wood and galvanised steel
snow shovel, 132 x 34 x 15 cm
Galleria Nazionale d'Arte Moderna e
Contemporanea, Rome

104
Marcel Duchamp
Sink Stopper, 1964 (1967 edition)
Silver, 6.7 x 0.5 cm
Private collection

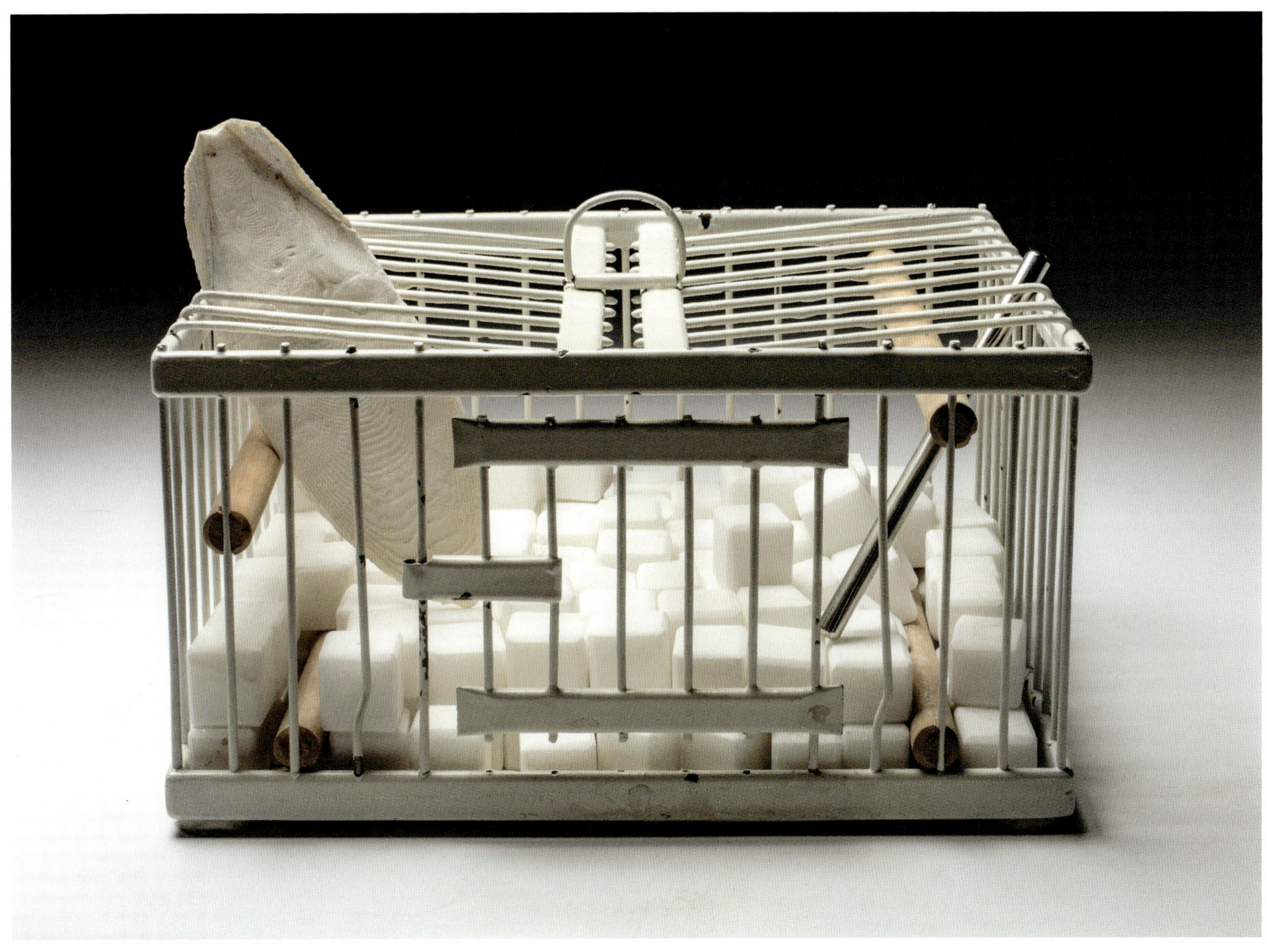

105
Marcel Duchamp
Why Not Sneeze Rose Sélavy?, 1921
(1964 edition)
152 marble 'sugar cubes', thermometer,
and cuttlefish bone in painted metal
birdcage fitted with four wooden bars,
18 x 23 x 18 cm
Galleria Nazionale d'Arte Moderna e
Contemporanea, Rome

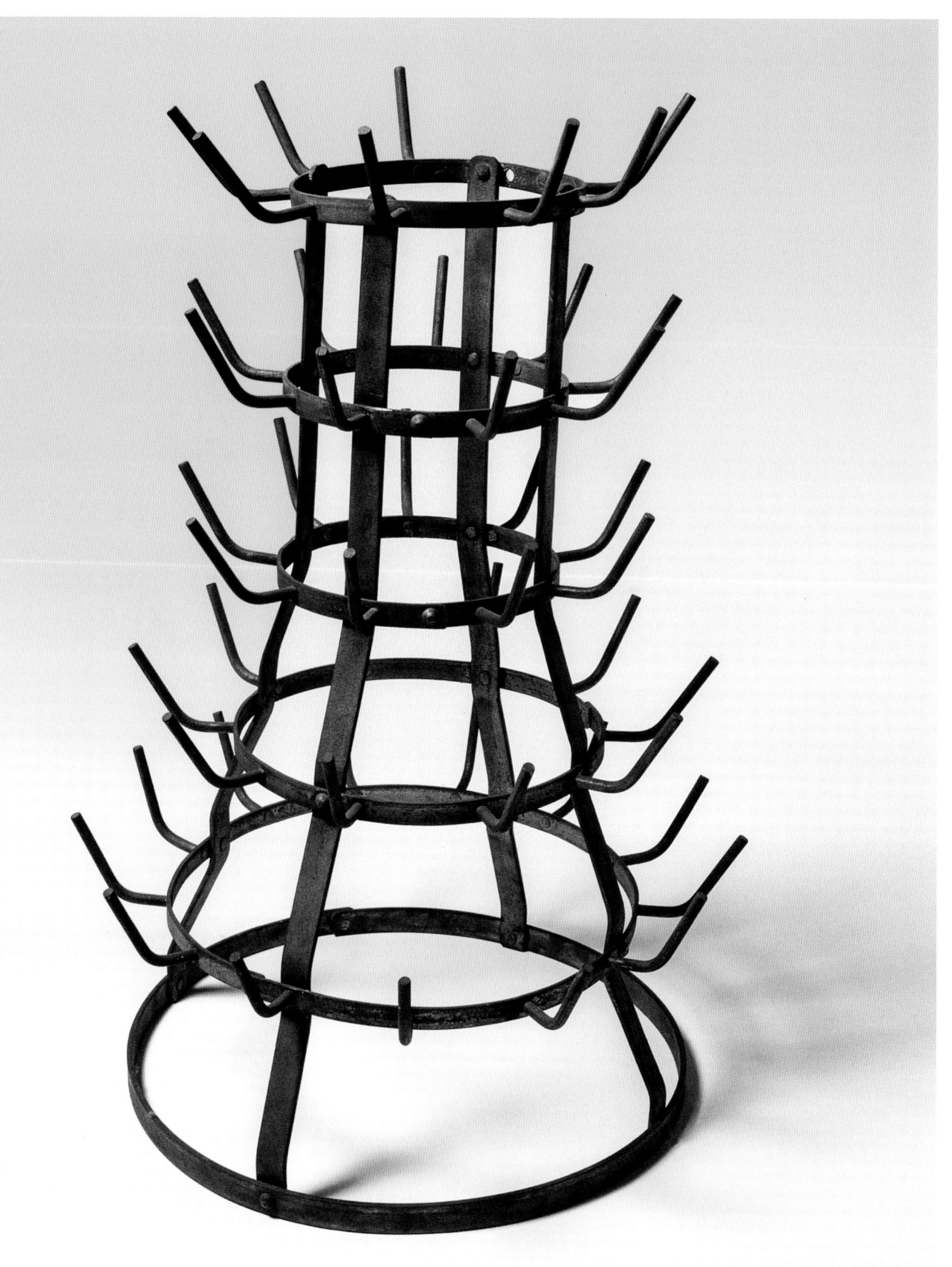

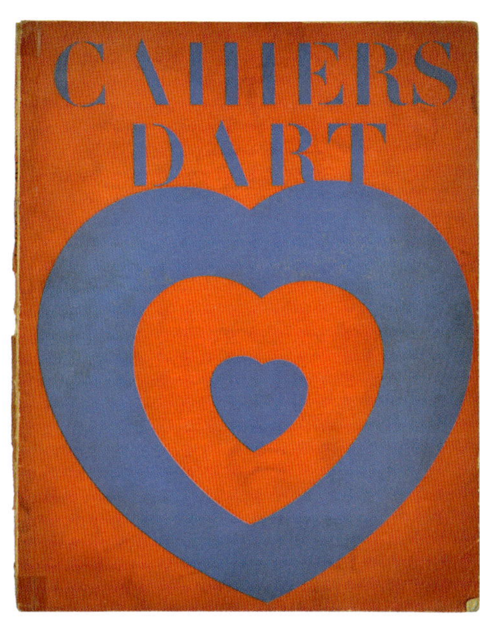

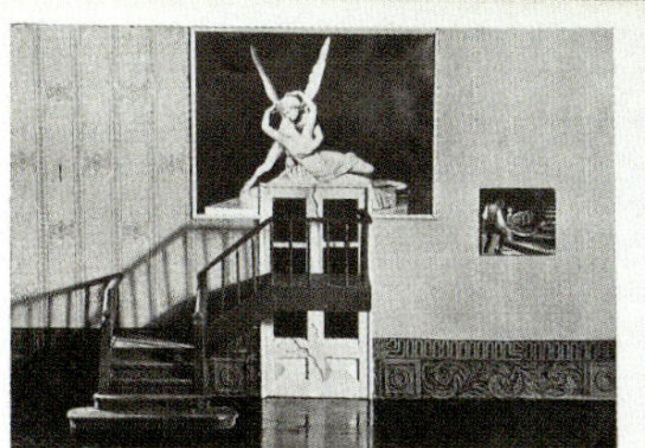

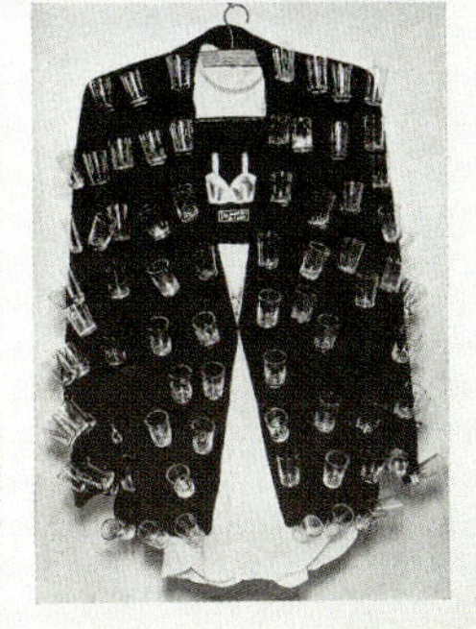

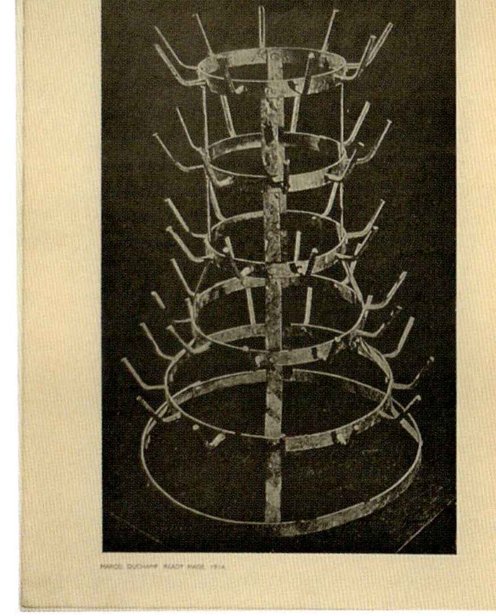

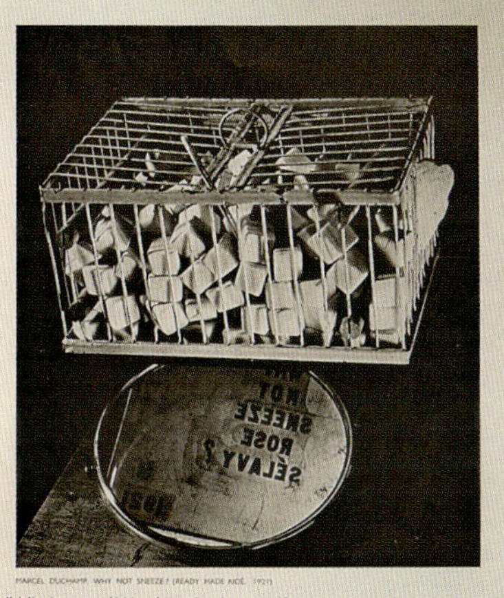

106
Marcel Duchamp
Bottle Rack, 1914 (1964 edition)
Readymade: galvanised iron bottle rack,
59 x 37 cm
Galleria Nazionale d'Arte Moderna e
Contemporanea, Rome
Florida only

107
Cahiers d'Art (Paris), XI, nos 1–2, 1936
Special issue on 'The Object', with cover
by Marcel Duchamp: *Cœurs volants*
(*Fluttering Hearts*) and articles featuring
photographs of works by Salvador Dalí
and Marcel Duchamp
Journal, 40 x 24.7 cm
Collection of The Dalí Museum Archives,
St Petersburg, Florida

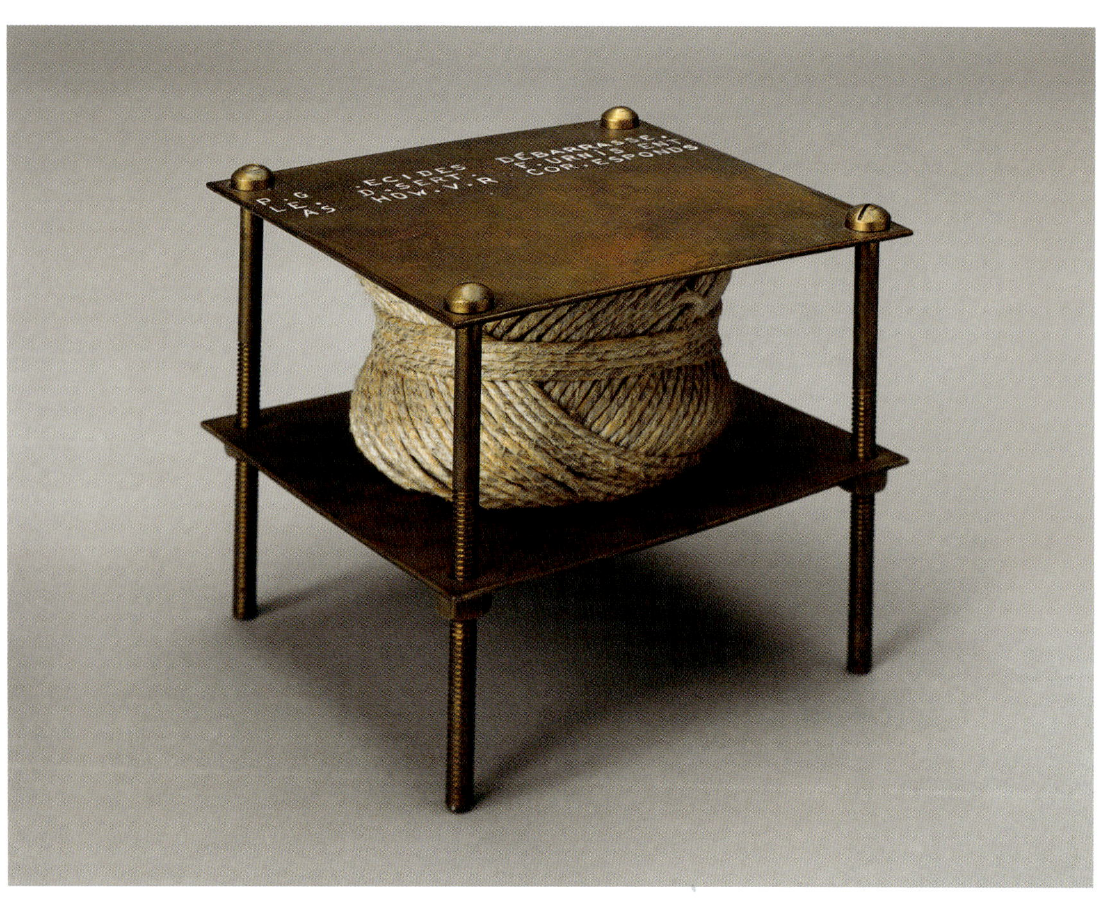

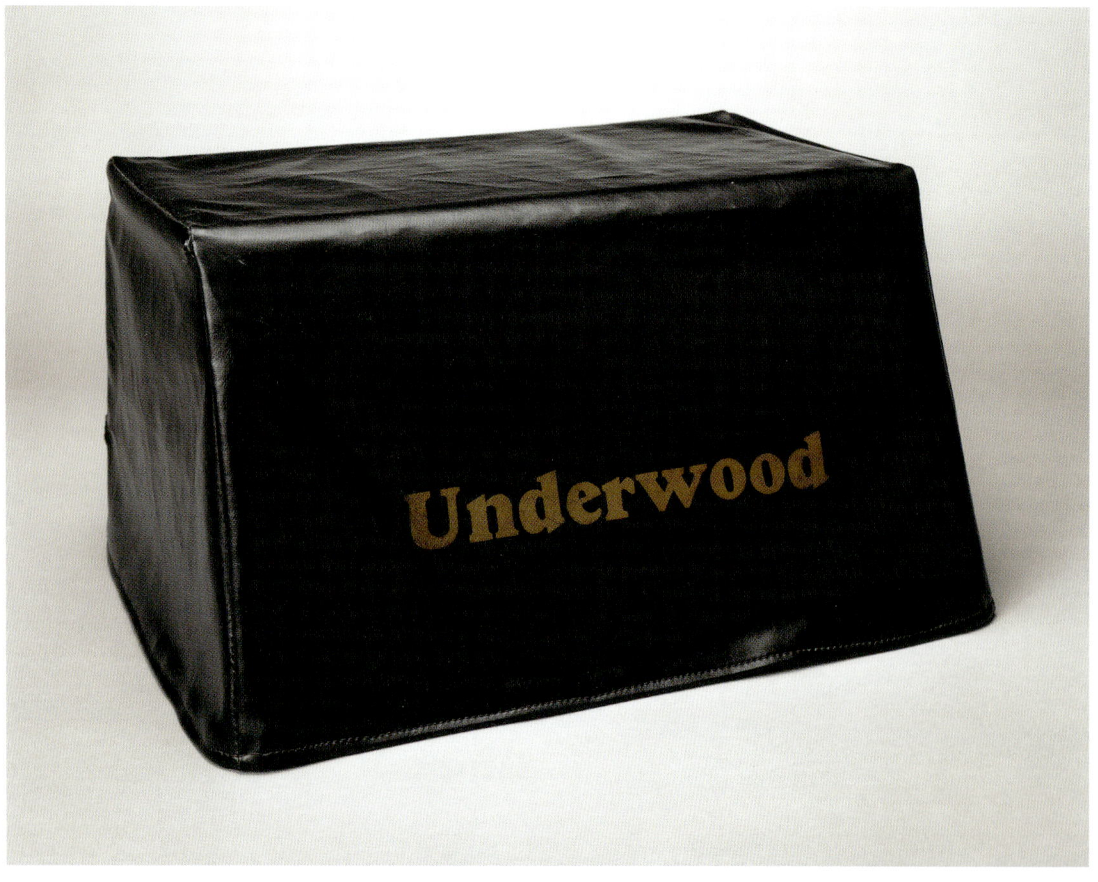

108
Marcel Duchamp
With Hidden Noise (A bruit secret), 1916
(1964 edition)
Readymade: found objects, metal, string,
11.4 x 13 x 13 cm
Collection of The John and Mable
Ringling Museum of Art, the State Art
Museum of Florida, Florida State
University, Sarasota, Florida

109
Marcel Duchamp
*Traveller's Folding Item (Underwood
Cover)*, 1916 (1964 edition)
Readymade: typewriter cover (music
stand not shown), 22.5 x 42.2 x 32.4 cm
Collection of The John and Mable
Ringling Museum of Art, the State Art
Museum of Florida, Florida State
University, Sarasota, Florida

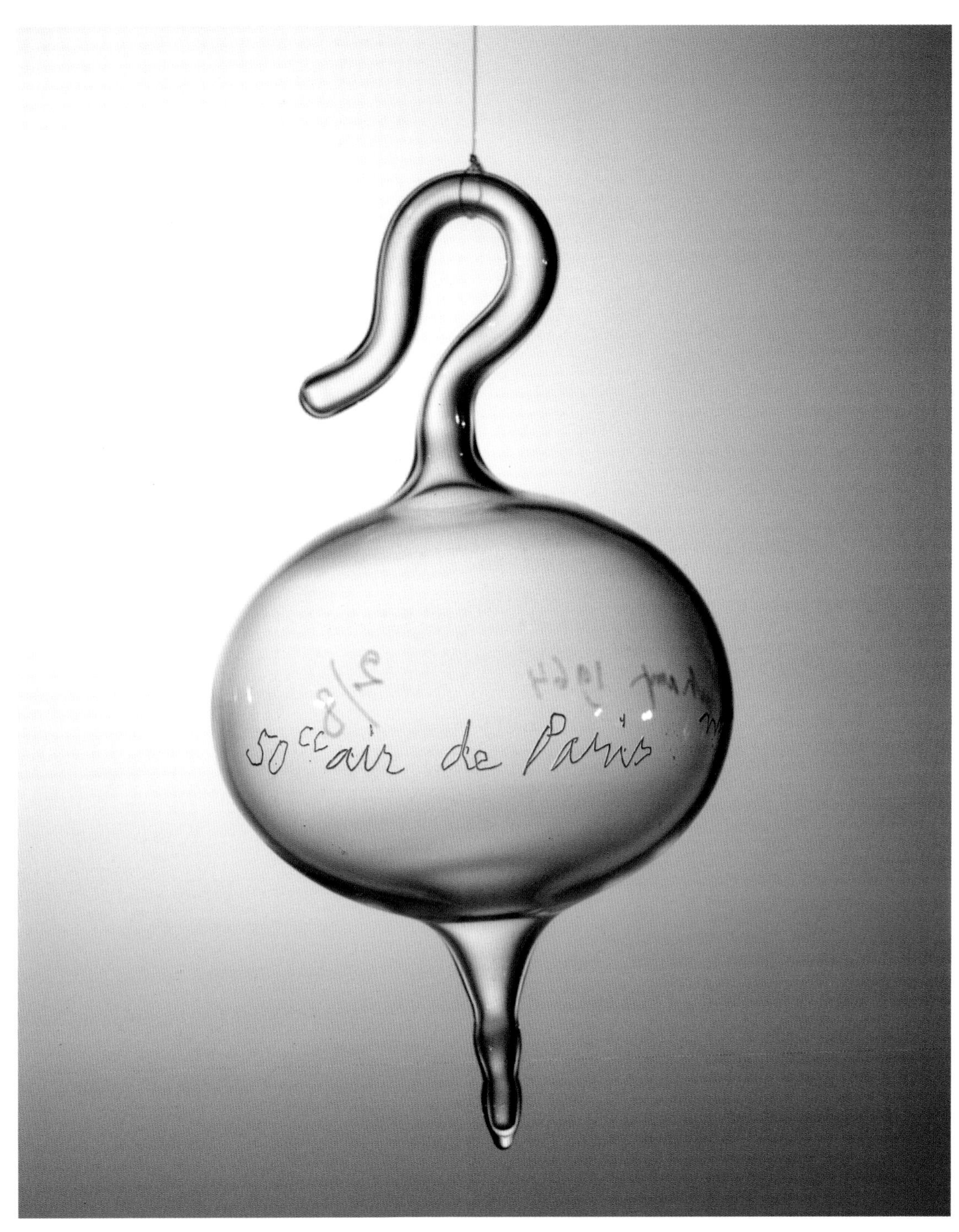

110
Marcel Duchamp
Air de Paris (*Paris Air*), 1919
(1964 edition)
50cc of Paris air in a glass ampoule,
13.3 x 6.4 cm
Collection of The John and Mable
Ringling Museum of Art, the State Art
Museum of Florida, Florida State
University, Sarasota, Florida

ÉTANT DONNÉS
MICHAEL R. TAYLOR AND DAWN ADES

No photograph can ever communicate the unique visual experience of seeing at first hand Marcel Duchamp's *Étant donnés: 1. la chute d'eau, 2. le gaz d'éclairage...* (*Given: 1. The Waterfall, 2. The Illuminating Gas...*), of 1946–66 (fig. 76). Permanently installed at the Philadelphia Museum of Art since 1969, this elaborate three-dimensional assemblage offers an unforgettable and untranslatable experience to those who peep through the two small holes in the solid wooden door. The unsuspecting viewer encounters a startling sight: a realistically constructed simulacrum of a life-size nude woman lying spreadeagled on a bed of dead twigs and fallen leaves. In her left hand, the mannequin holds aloft an old-fashioned illuminated gas lamp, while behind her, in the far distance, a lush wooded landscape rises towards the horizon. This brightly illuminated backdrop consists of a hand-painted collotype collage of a hilly landscape with a dense cluster of trees outlined against a hazy turquoise sky, complete with fluffy cotton-wool clouds. The only movement in the otherwise eerily still grotto is a sparkling waterfall, which pours into a mist-covered lake.

The pseudoscientific title of *Étant donnés* has its source in a note by the artist that was first published in 1934 in the collection of manuscript notes and diagrams known as the *Green Box* (cat. 124): 'Étant donnés 1° la chute d'eau / 2° le gaz d'éclairage'. This note, which Duchamp used as the preface to the *Green Box*, identifies two of the key elements of *Étant donnés*, namely the waterfall and the illuminating gas, both of which were also to have been included in the artist's great allegory of frustrated desire, *The Bride Stripped Bare by Her Bachelors, Even* (*The Large Glass*), of 1915–23 (fig. 81). A note in the *Green Box* reveals that the waterfall would have been represented by a water spout located above the nine Malic Moulds in the lower section, or Bachelor domain, of *The Large Glass*, whose function would be to set the Water Mill in motion. In the end, Duchamp omitted the waterfall from *The Large Glass*, fearing that a conventional landscape feature would detract from his radical intentions, but he returned to this motif in *Étant donnés*, where the flickering waterfall, powered by an unseen motor, illuminates the landscape backdrop.

Duchamp based the landscape backdrop of *Étant donnés* on a series of photographs that he took of the Le Forestay waterfall at Bellevue, a small hamlet near Chexbres, Switzerland, during the summer of 1946. These photographs formed the basis of a

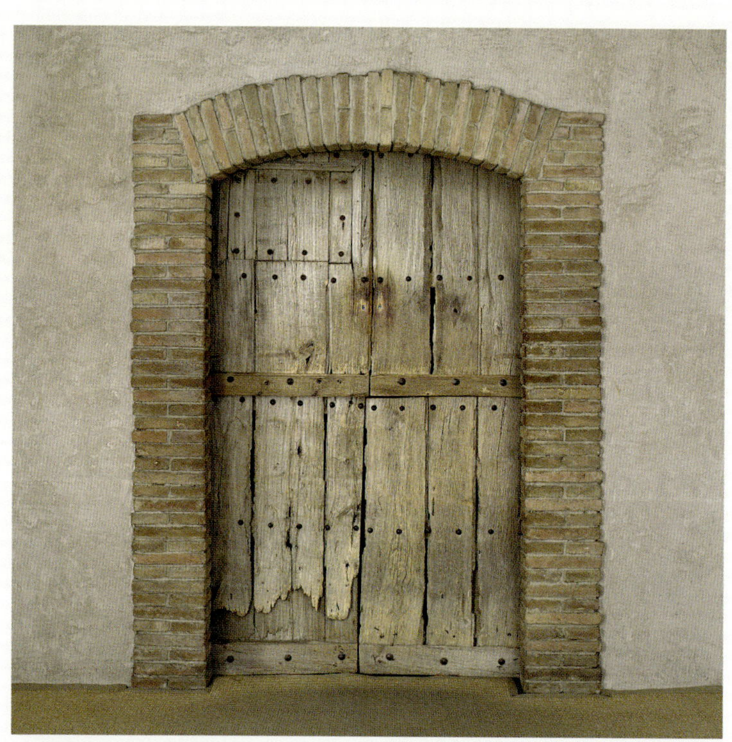

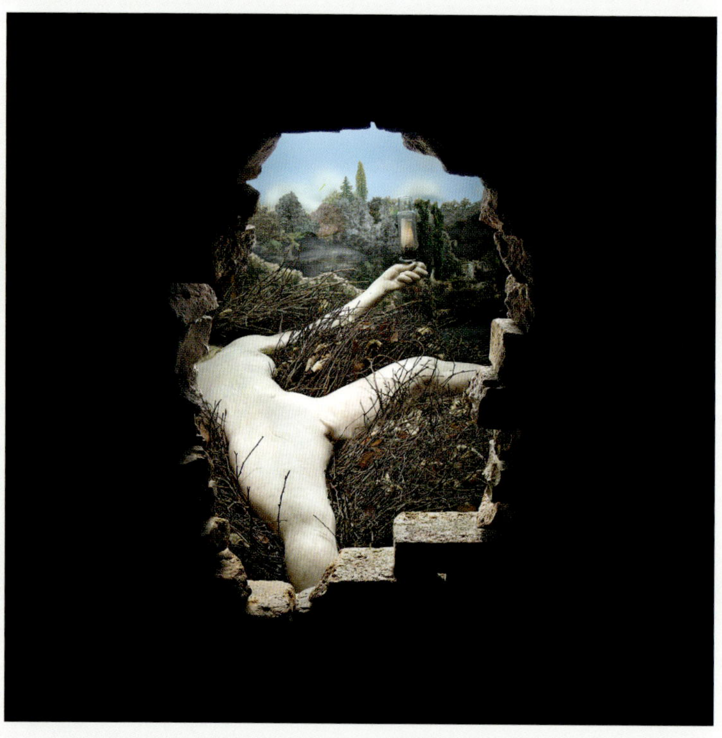

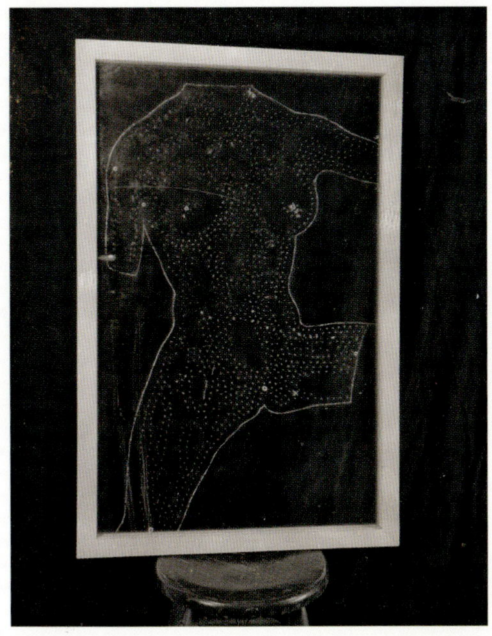
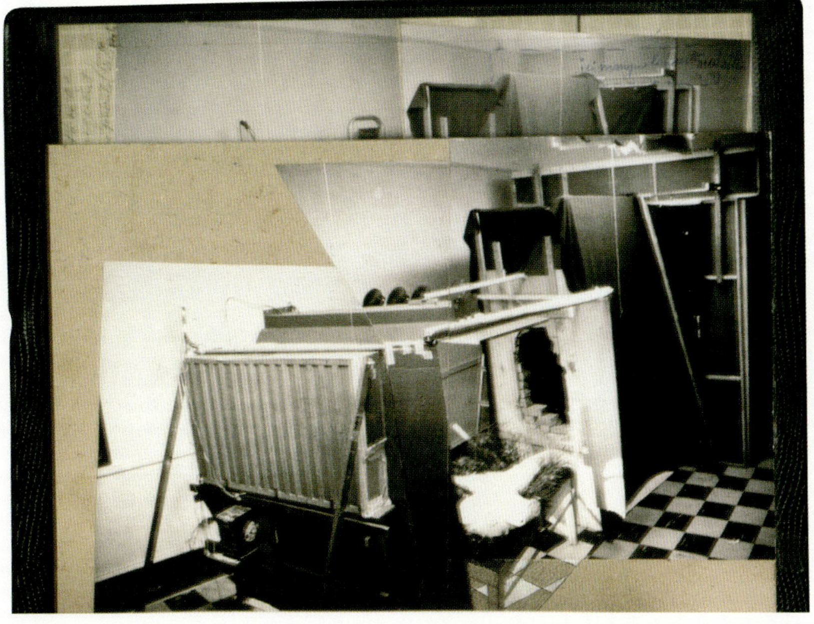

hand-painted collage that the artist assembled on plywood and took with him on his annual vacation to the Costa Brava in the summer of 1959, where he made an edition of 35 prints based on its composition, of which two examples, both made with collotype on fabric, have survived (cat. 112). An inscription in Dalí's handwriting on the verso of one of these prints – 'M Ducham [*sic*] / tirée le 1-9-59 / fini a 35 feuilles / Dalí' – confirms that Duchamp made these prints with the assistance of the Catalan artist. Dalí had a great deal of experience in printmaking, including collotype, and his Portlligat studio, located less than a kilometre from Duchamp's summer residence in Cadaqués, was well equipped to handle his friend's printing needs. Dalí's invaluable inscription supplies us with the following information: the collaborative nature of the effort, since he lists both artists' names; the size of the edition (35); and the date they were pulled (1 September 1959), and by extension the location where the prints were made, namely Catalonia, since both artists were living and working there on that date.

Among the 'studies' for the nude figure in the installation is the gouache on Plexiglas, known as 'Study for the figure in *Étant donnés*' (cat. 111). Even in his studies, Duchamp not only rarely repeated himself but explored new directions both in terms of material and conception. But as is so often the case, the question arises, what is this exactly? In his catalogue raisonné Schwarz describes this study as 'a working tool rather than an autonomous work of art'. However, a photograph, perhaps by Duchamp himself, shows the Plexiglas framed and arranged on a stool in front of a swathe of black cloth, as if testing the best way to display it. It is lit so that not only the white gouache lines and marks but also the edges of the perforated holes show up brightly against the dark. Plexiglas was a relatively new material at the time, first marketed in the

1930s. Made of acrylic, it is transparent and shatter-proof, which must have been attractive to the artist who spent eight years, between 1915 and 1923, painting and working on the two panes of glass that make up *The Bride Stripped Bare by Her Bachelors, Even*, only to have them shatter in transit in 1927 after the work was exhibited at the Brooklyn Museum.

The upright stance of the body in the study is almost identical to that of the vellum-on-velvet study (cat. 113), but unlike that tiny torso this is life-size, like the nude in *Étant donnés* itself. This previously unpublished photograph confirms that Duchamp originally intended the nude to be standing rather than reclining and adds to our understanding of the work's genesis and construction. The white paint (which looks remarkably like Tipp-Ex) outlines the torso including the truncated limbs; marks and signs denote erogenous zones – circles for vulva and breasts, then more mysterious, perhaps private, crosses and arrows. When light is shown through the holes these cast shadow-dots on the rear surface, as though Duchamp is invoking pouncing, a method of transferring a drawing to another surface – plaster for fresco, for example – in which fine powder is rubbed through pinpricks along the line of a drawing so that the design is reproduced on the surface below as a line of dots. In the case of 'Study for the figure', as *Étant donnés* itself is three-dimensional, it is not clear whether there was a practical application, or whether it was a stand-alone experiment in combining modern and ancient techniques of representation and transfer.

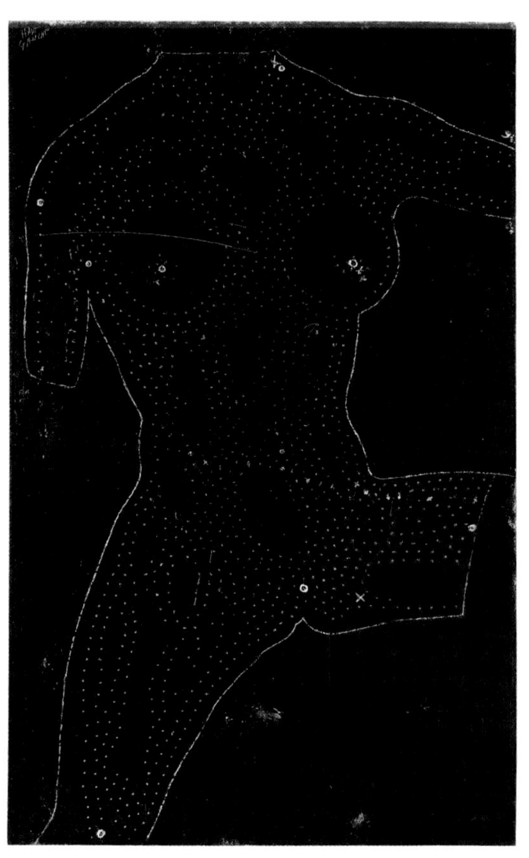

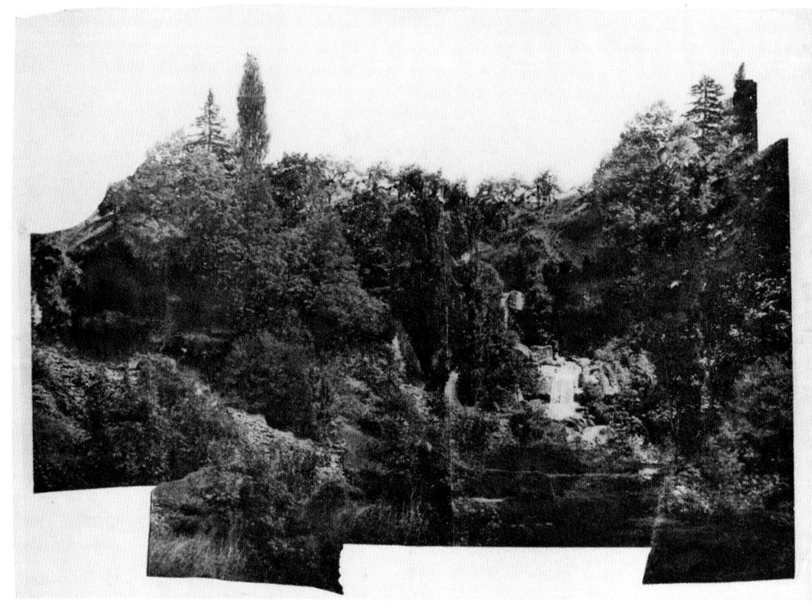

111
Marcel Duchamp
Study for the figure in *Étant donnés*,
c. 1950
Perforated Plexiglas with gouache,
91.3 x 55.9 cm
Private collection

112
Marcel Duchamp
Landscape study for *Étant donnés*, 1959
Collotype in black ink on cellulose
acetate 'silk' fabric backed with paper,
74 x 102.8 cm
Private collection

113
Marcel Duchamp
Study for *Étant donnés 1. La chute d'eau
et 2. Le gaz d'éclairage*, 1948–49
Pigment and graphite on leather over
plaster with velvet, 50 x 31 cm
Moderna Museet, Stockholm.
Donation 1985 dedicated to Ulf Linde
from Tomas Fischer

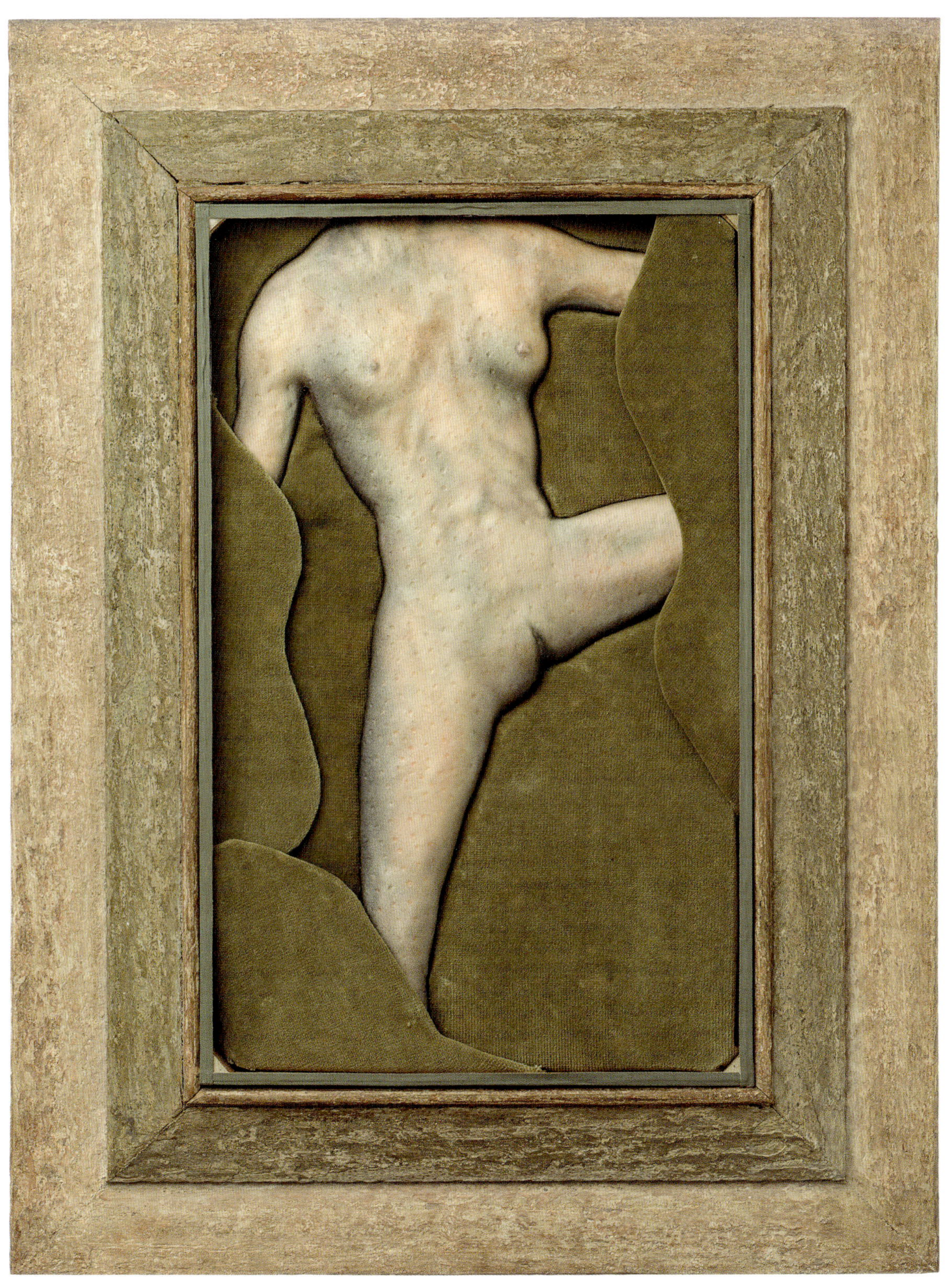

THE ENIGMA OF WILLIAM TELL
MICHAEL R. TAYLOR

The two artists' shared interest in eroticism, onanism and voyeurism was part of the reason Duchamp sought assistance from Dalí for the 1959 print edition related to *Étant donnés*. Given his exploration of the erotic thrill of peepholes in *Étant donnés* Duchamp was no doubt familiar with Dalí's 1929 painting *Illumined Pleasures*, in which a young man masturbates while looking through a peephole into a deeply recessed chamber whose forbidden sexual content, like his own presumably erect genitals, is hidden from view. Duchamp also admired Dalí's use of his paranoiac-critical method to unmask the latent content of famous paintings or sentimental folklore, as seen in his psychoanalytical re-readings of Millet's famous painting of rural piety, *The Angelus*, and of the William Tell legend.

In Dalí's version of William Tell, the innocent story of filial devotion and heroic resistance to the capricious cruelty of a foreign tyrant is dramatically transformed into an act of paternal vengeance, cannibalism and cuckoldry. The artist's interest in the legend was probably stimulated by the epic historical drama written in 1926 by the prominent Catalan writer Eugenio d'Ors, in which Tell becomes the bearer of patriotic ideals, thus imbuing the legend with a contemporary relevance to the political situation in Catalonia and its subjugation under Castilian rule. This was a political reading that Dalí's father, Salvador Dalí Cusí, a fervent Catalan nationalist, would have wholeheartedly supported. For Dalí, however, the tale of the Swiss patriot who shot an apple placed on his son's head at a distance of two hundred paces was a castration myth that could be related to his own psychosexual Oedipal drama focusing on his unresolved conflict with his overbearing, authoritarian father, who had expelled his son from the family home in December 1929 due to his adulterous relationship with Gala Éluard.

In protest at his irrevocable banishment from his father's household, Dalí defiantly shaved his head and buried his jet-black hair on the beach at Cadaqués. Shortly afterwards, the artist posed for a photograph taken by Luis Buñuel with a sea urchin balanced on his head, a clear reference to the apple placed on the head of William Tell's son; the reference is highlighted in a photomontage juxtaposing an image of Gala with Buñuel's photograph that was used as the frontispiece to *L'Amour et la mémoire* in 1931. Given his father's well-known passion for eating sea urchins, Dalí no doubt intended this surrogate apple to have cannibalistic overtones, as he later recalled in his memoirs. 'I had balanced on my head William Tell's apple, which is the symbol of the passionate cannibalistic ambivalence which sooner or later ends with the drawing of the atavistic and ritualistic fury of the bow of paternal vengeance that shoots the final arrow of the expiatory sacrifice – the eternal theme of the father sacrificing his son.'

Just as his paranoiac-critical investigation into Millet's *Angelus* was to uncover the latent eroticism of this seemingly harmless image of rural piety, so the meaning of the William Tell legend changed once Dalí's fertile and elastic imagination had unveiled the story's tragic subtext: an indecent scene revolving around a father's sacrifice of his son and seduction of his son's lover and future wife. In *William Tell and Gradiva* (cat. 118) William Tell is shown with an enormous erection as he threatens the naked Gala, who assumes the identity of Gradiva, based on the title character of the 1903 novel by Wilhelm Jensen that was the subject of a well-known psychoanalytic study by Sigmund Freud. The artist wrote poems documenting William Tell's lewd and obscene behaviour and created numerous paintings and drawings on this theme in the early 1930s, culminating in 1933 with the monumental *The Enigma of William Tell* (fig. 79), in which the Swiss hero is depicted with the features and ludicrously extended peaked cap of Vladimir Lenin, another historical father figure who for Dalí represented patriarchal authority and retribution. Given their friendship and shared delight in scandal and transgression, it is perhaps no surprise that Duchamp played an instrumental role in making sure that this controversial painting, in which Dalí asserted his commitment to freedom of thought and his complete liberation from the social and moral strictures of the Surrealist group and the Communist party, was acquired by the Moderna Museet in Stockholm in 1967. A photograph of the two artists standing in front of *The Enigma of William Tell* (cat. 114) shows them engaged in a deep discussion about the work, which Duchamp had earlier extolled to Pontus Hultén, the Director of the Swedish museum, as 'one of the most important' of Dalí's Surrealist paintings.

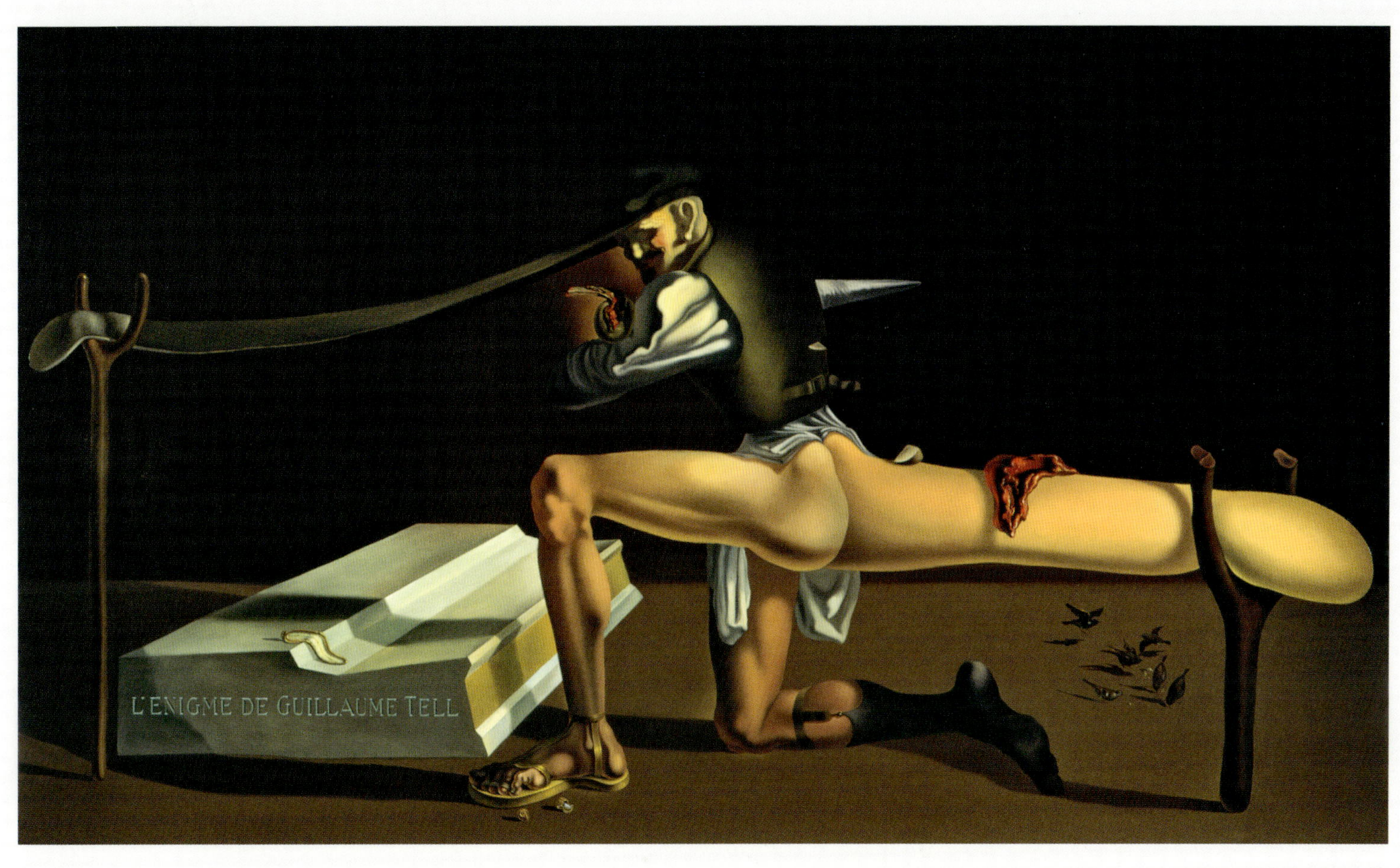

Fig. 79
Salvador Dalí, *The Enigma of William Tell*,
c. 1933. Oil on canvas, 201.3 x 346.5 cm.
Moderna Museet, Stockholm

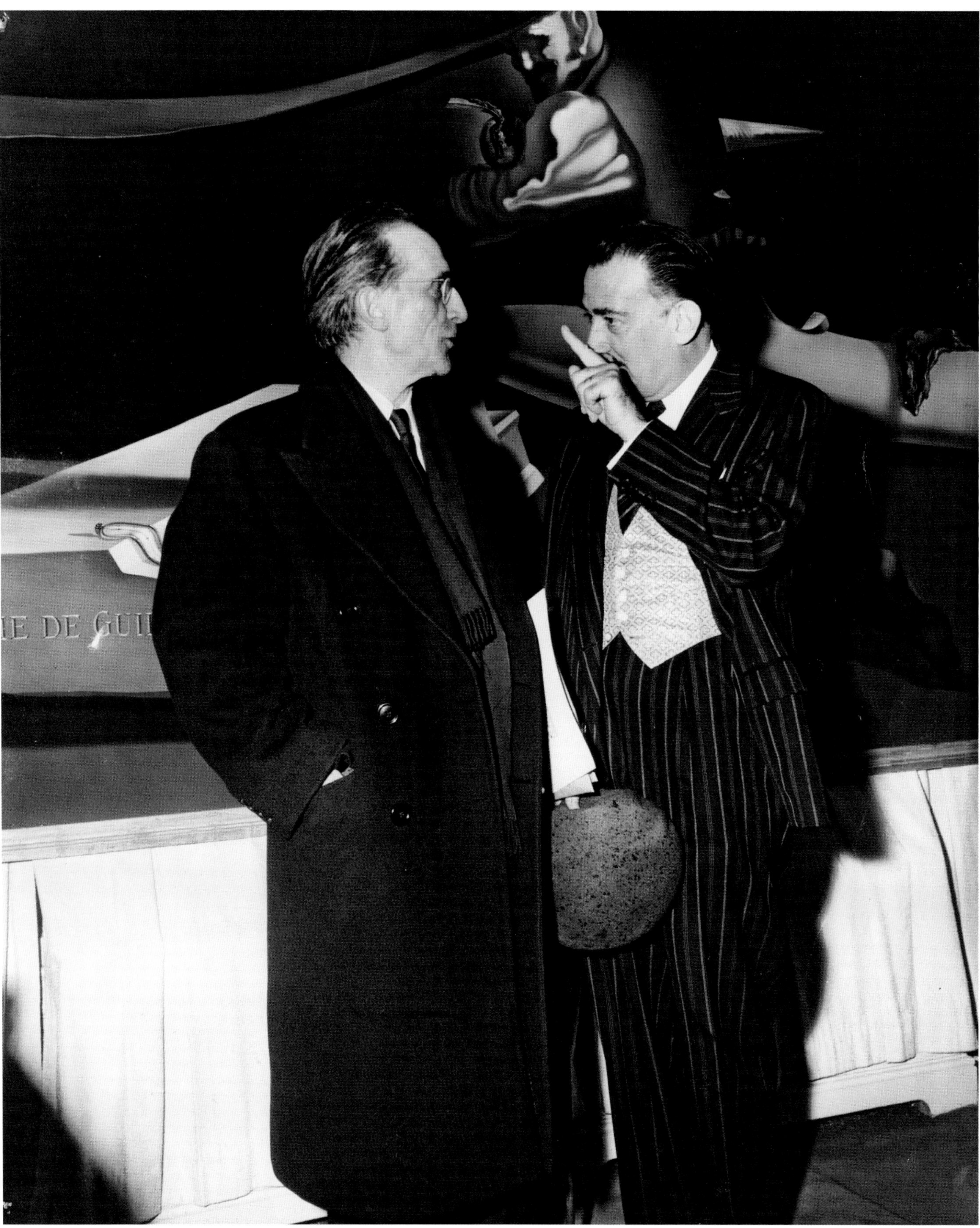

IE DE GUI

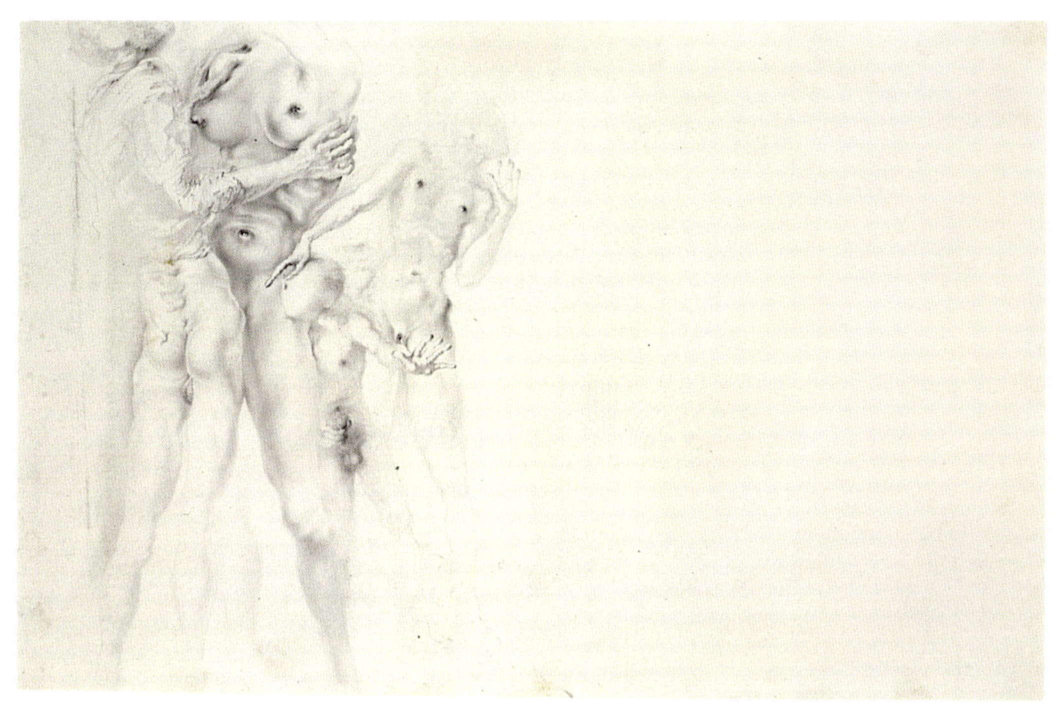

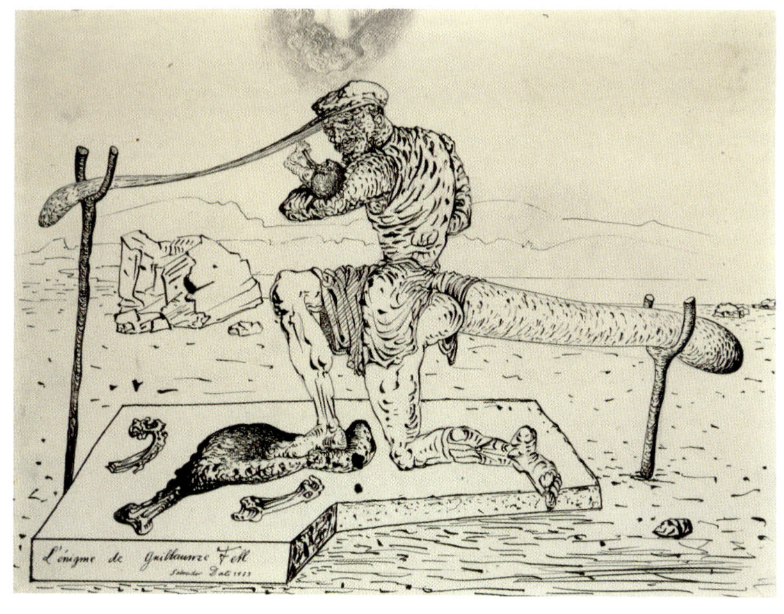

Opposite: 114
Will Weissberg
Marcel Duchamp and Salvador Dalí in
front of Dalí's *The Enigma of William Tell*
in New York, 1960
Silver gelatin print, 25.3 x 20.5 cm
Fundació Gala-Salvador Dalí, Figueres

115
Salvador Dalí
William Tell Group, 1942–43
Pencil on paper, 30.8 x 47 cm
Collection of The Dalí Museum,
St Petersburg, Florida

116
Salvador Dalí
*The Enigma of William Tell with the
Apparition of a Celestial Gala*, 1933
Ink and pencil on paper, 16.8 x 22 cm
Collection of The Dalí Museum,
St Petersburg, Florida

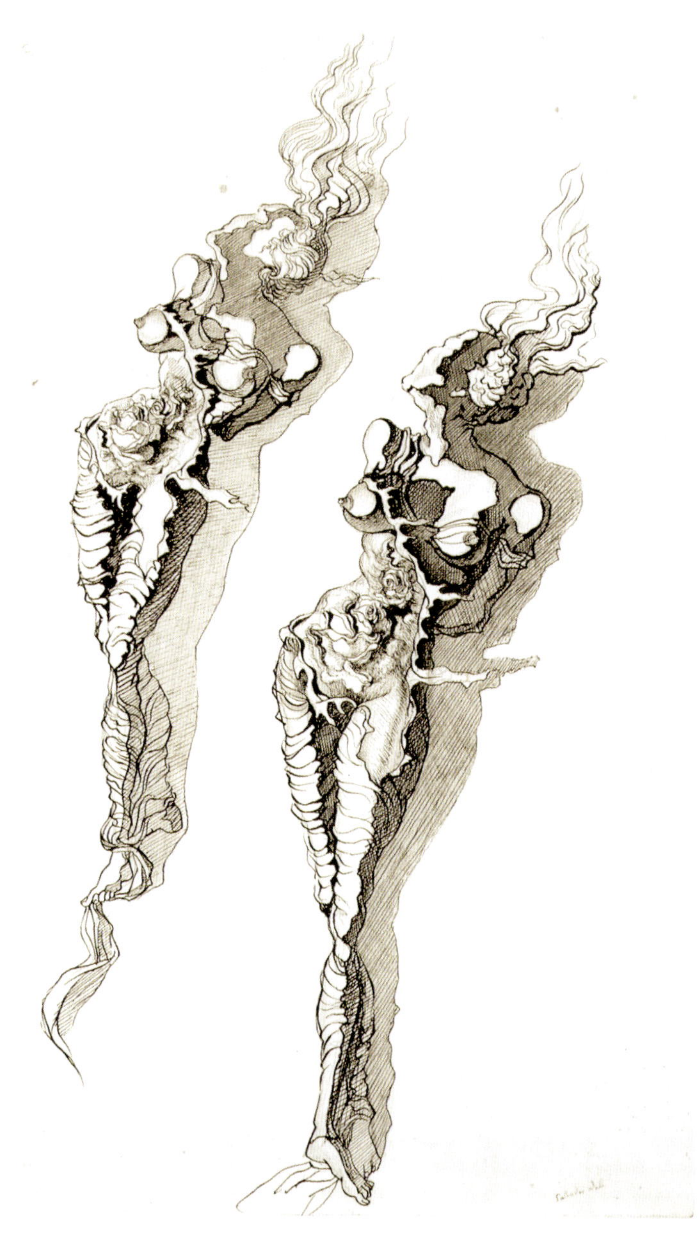

117
Salvador Dalí
Gradiva, 1930
Ink and pencil on paper, 31.1 x 22.9 cm
Collection of The Dalí Museum,
St Petersburg, Florida

118
Salvador Dalí
William Tell and Gradiva, 1932
Oil on copper, 30 x 24 cm
Fundació Gala-Salvador Dalí, Figueres

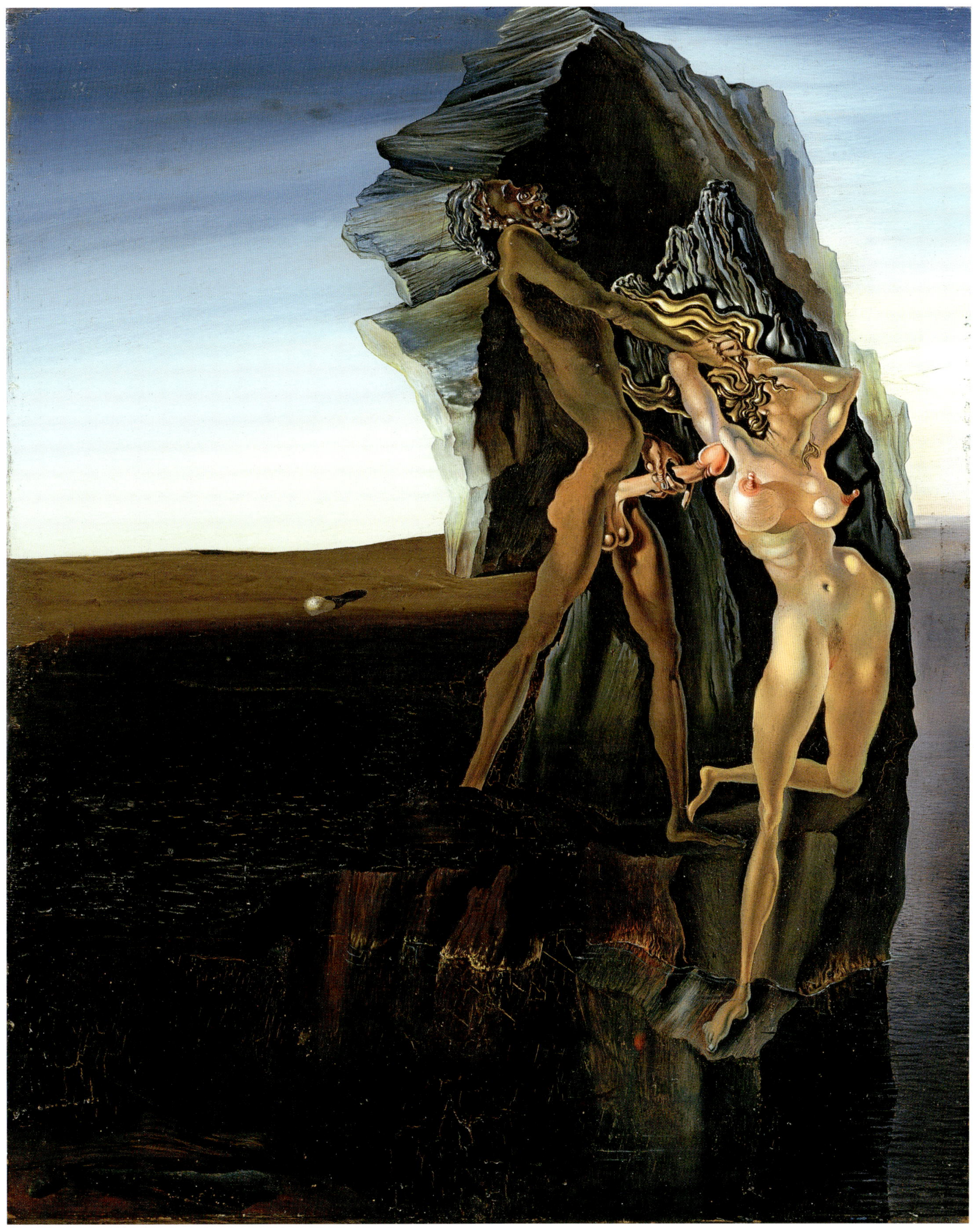

THE TRAGIC MYTH OF MILLET'S ANGELUS
MICHAEL R. TAYLOR AND DAWN ADES

In 1933 Dalí was working on his book *The Tragic Myth of Millet's Angelus, A Paranoiac-critical Interpretation* (cat. 119), which he described as a 'psychoanalytical essay'.[1] The Surrealists wanted an article from him for the glossy new journal *Minotaure*, published by Skira, and Éluard wrote to him suggesting he send the preface from his new book on *The Angelus*, but warning him: 'Il est nécessaire pour Skira que votre texte ne soit en rien porNOgraPHIque [*sic*]. Arrangez-vous...' ('It's essential for Skira that your text is not at all pornographic. See to it...'). The scars from Dalí's 1931 *SASDLR* text 'Rêverie', judged by the Communist Party to be pornographic, were still evidently raw and Éluard was probably aware of the explosive and scandalous nature of Dalí's new 'myth'. The text 'Interprétation paranoïaque-critique de l'image obsédante de *L'Angélus* de Millet', appeared in *Minotaure* in 1933, illustrated with Leonardo's *Virgin and Child with St Anne*, and Millet's *The Angelus*, *Harvesters* and *Maternal Precaution*. Dalí links the 'maternal' vulture Freud saw unconsciously 'hidden' in the gown of St Anne – interpreted by Freud in terms of Leonardo's sexuality – to his own paranoiac-critical method. Dalí's interpretation of *The Angelus* reads into it a dramatic scenario of eroticism and death, which becomes an original variant of the Oedipus myth. The innocent figures of the praying couple, through a process of association, become highly sexualised, and are subjected to an identity shift; wife and husband mutate into mother and son, the former transforming through multiple associations into a terrifying aggressor. In the final section of his book Dalí describes three successive stages of the myth. In the first, the stillness of the couple in *The Angelus* becomes a sinister immobility; the twilight that Dalí has earlier connected to the ancient eras of the Earth symbolises atavistic sensations; and the woman – the mother – has an 'expectant' attitude announcing imminent sexual aggression. In the second phase Dalí 'sees' that 'the son has coitus with his mother from behind'. The instruments of rural labour, and in particular the wheelbarrow, are interpreted as sexually charged not just through a Freudian symbolism but from the evidence of peasant lore and sayings. In the third and final phase the woman, the mother, is identified with the praying mantis, which devours the male during copulation (a footnote added later explains that this only occurs when the mantis is in the unnatural state of captivity). The idea of the female

consuming the male was threaded through the earlier 'delirious' erotic and cannibalistic associations with milk, tea cups and cherries, while the maternal was embodied in *The Angelus* in the filled sack, the ploughed earth and the basket. Dalí concludes with his impression that the frozen posture of the male, with whom he identifies himself, reveals him as 'already dead', and that the myth itself is 'the maternal variant of the immense, atrocious myth of Saturn, Abraham, the Eternal Father with Jesus Christ and William Tell himself devouring their own sons'. In *Meditation on the Harp* (cat. 120), the strange triangle of father, mother and son appears in a poignant group, the 'dead' son suppliant and calcified.

In his 1935 book *The Conquest of the Irrational*, Dalí linked *The Angelus* and the *Mona Lisa* in analytic terms according to the paranoiac-critical method, proposing that the same content could be found in both paintings.[2] That he was thinking not only of Leonardo but of Duchamp's transgressive iteration of the image is made extra clear in *The Tragic Myth of Millet's Angelus*, where he reproduces Duchamp's *L.H.O.O.Q.* facing his concluding remarks: '*The Angelus* is associated in a coherent way with the *Mona Lisa* through the Oedipus characteristic that is common to them....'[3]

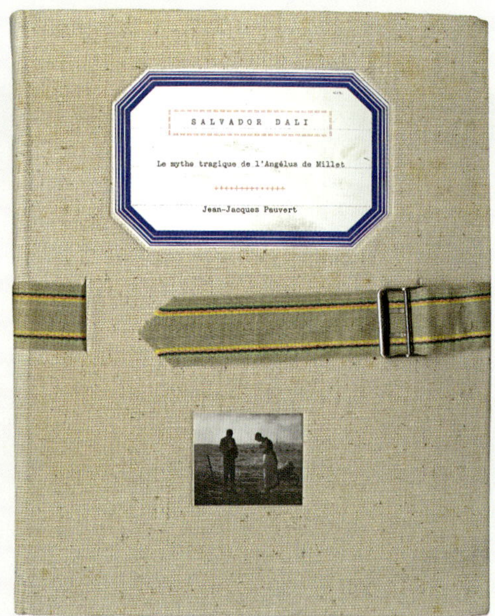

119
Salvador Dalí
Le Mythe tragique de L'Angélus de Millet: Interpretation 'paranoïaque-critique' (*The Tragic Myth of Millet's Angelus, A Paranoiac-critical Interpretation*), c. 1933–34, published 1963
Book, 27.5 x 21.7 cm
Collection of The Dalí Museum Archives, St Petersburg, Florida

120
Salvador Dalí
Meditation on the Harp, c. 1933
Oil on canvas, 66.7 x 47 cm
Collection of The Dalí Museum, St Petersburg, Florida

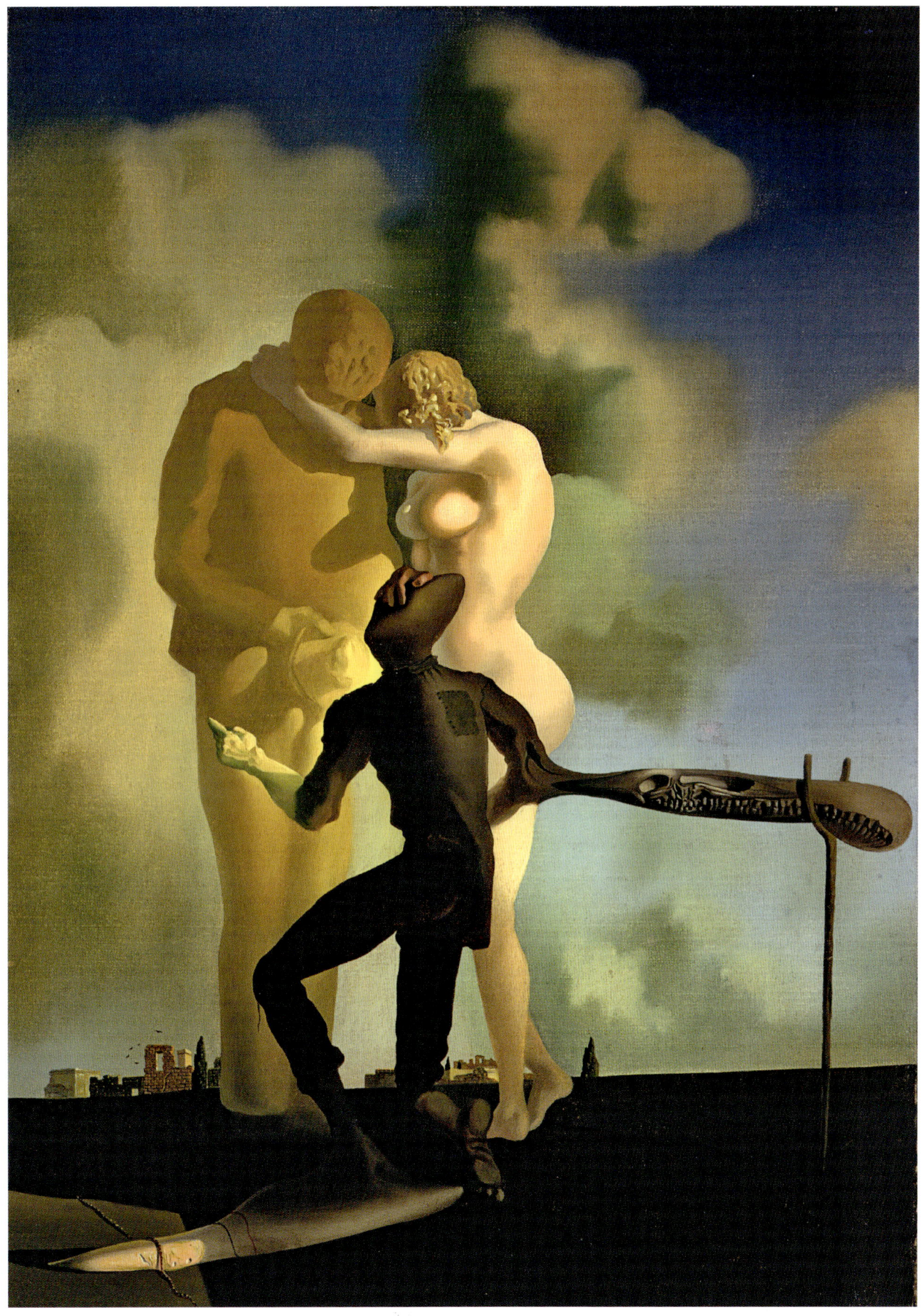

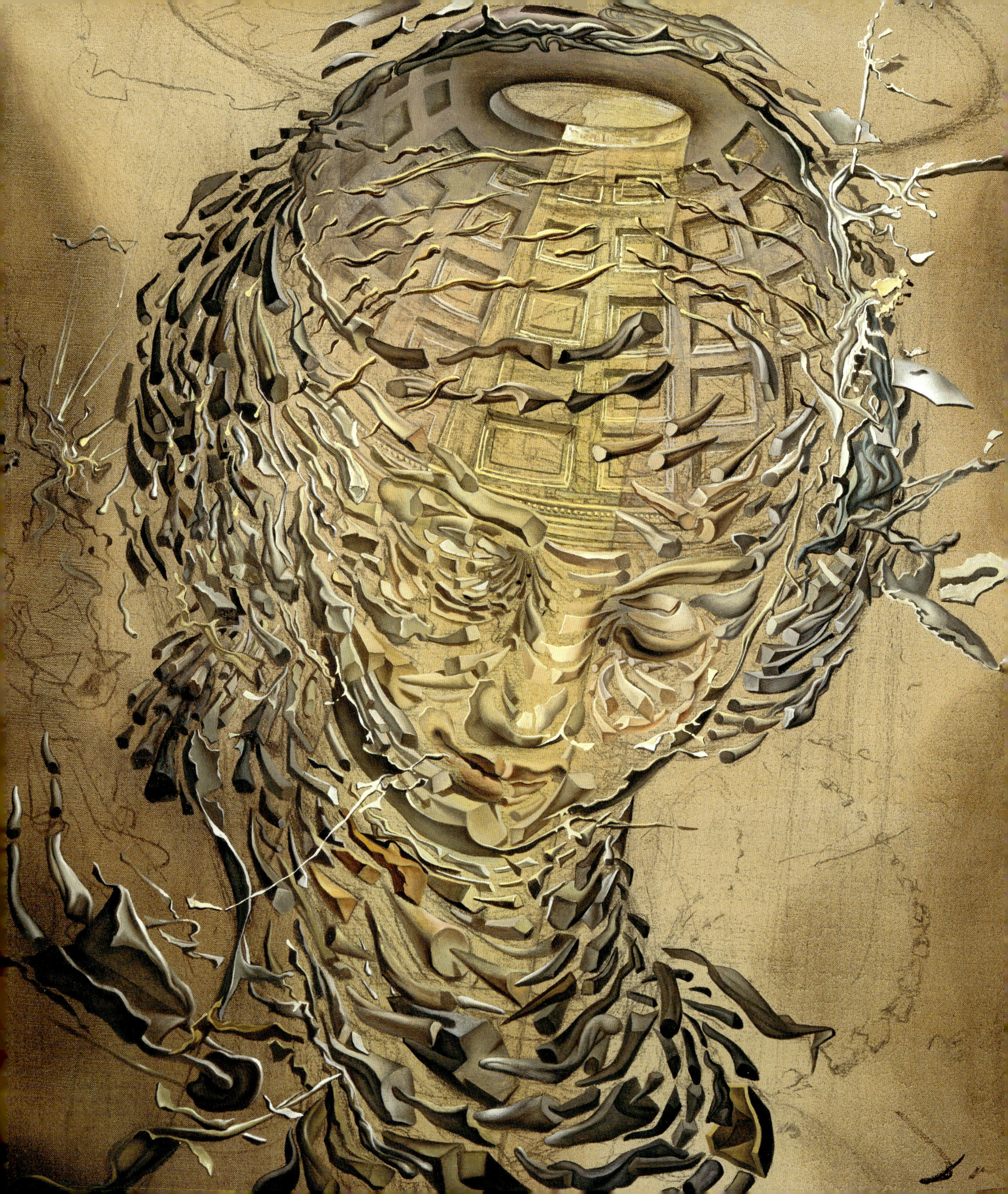

SCIENCE AND RELIGION

SCIENCE AND RELIGION
DAWN ADES

'After the self-satisfied rationalism of the nineteenth century, an ebullience of invention, of exploration beyond the realms of the visible and the rational in every domain of the mind – science, psychology, imagination – was gradually breaking down the human, social and intellectual values which up until then had seemed so solid.'[1] Gabrielle Buffet-Picabia thus succinctly summarised a seismic shift in mental attitudes in her memoir of her friend Marcel Duchamp and husband Francis Picabia.

The collapse of the old certainties in the nature of the physical universe and our place in it was accompanied by a hunger for experiment and innovation in every field, including the arts. Although many artists responded to the new theories about time and space, about energy, matter and gravity, notions of a fourth dimension, quantum theory and atomic physics, Duchamp and Dalí did so with particular intensity, and with profound consequences for their work.

Dalí followed the successive theoretical debates and scientific discoveries throughout his life, from his initial interest in psychoanalysis (sometimes described as a pseudo-science) to atomic physics and the discovery of DNA. When he died in 1989 the books beside his bed were by Stephen Hawking, Matila Ghyka and Erwin Schrödinger. In his 'Anti-matter Manifesto' of 1958 he wrote: 'In the Surrealist period I wanted to create the iconography of the interior world – the world of the marvellous, of my father Freud. I succeeded in doing it. Today the exterior world – that of physics – has transcended the one of psychology. My father today is Dr Heisenberg.'[2]

During the 1930s, while he was closely involved with Surrealism, it was by no means just psychoanalysis that preoccupied Dalí. As he put it in his important 1935 text *Conquest of the Irrational*, 'we the Surrealists ... swim between two bodies of water, the cold water of art and the warm water of science'.[3] As a student Dalí had heard Einstein lecture at the Residencia de Estudiantes in Madrid, on 9 March 1923, and whatever he might have made of relativity at the time, he was eventually to absorb the idea sufficiently to invent pictorial analogues of the relativity of time and its capacity to 'bend' space, most famously in his 1931 painting *The Persistence of Memory* (fig. 80). The concept also played a part in his development of the notion of 'Critical Paranoia', with the simultaneous appearance of multiple images. Dalí's attention to the

latest theories in quantum mechanics is evident in his remarkably early reference to Schrödinger in his 'psychoanalytical essay' *The Tragic Myth of Millet's Angelus* (cat. 119). In Dalí's prolific writings there are frequent references to science, from Einstein to Crick and Watson, to D'Arcy Thompson's study of geometry in nature, *On Growth and Form*, to the mathematicians Matila Ghyka and René Thom, and explosive generalisations about the relationship between science, nature and religion in terms of descriptions of the physical universe. René Thom's 'catastrophe theory' was, Dalí considered, the most beautiful aesthetic theory.

As Gavin Parkinson has argued, while Dalí continued enthusiastically to mine atomic physics in the post-war nuclear age, the Surrealists turned against the scientists and denounced their 'complacent research into and development of lethal weapons'.[4] Dalí's extraordinary mix, moreover, of nuclear physics and Catholic mysticism confirmed the distance separating him from his former comrades. His capacity to ingest and amalgamate distinct epistemologies is demonstrated in the following passage from his 1951 *Mystical Manifesto*: '... it being observed that ... matter is in a constant and accelerated process of dematerialisation, of disintegration, slipping out of

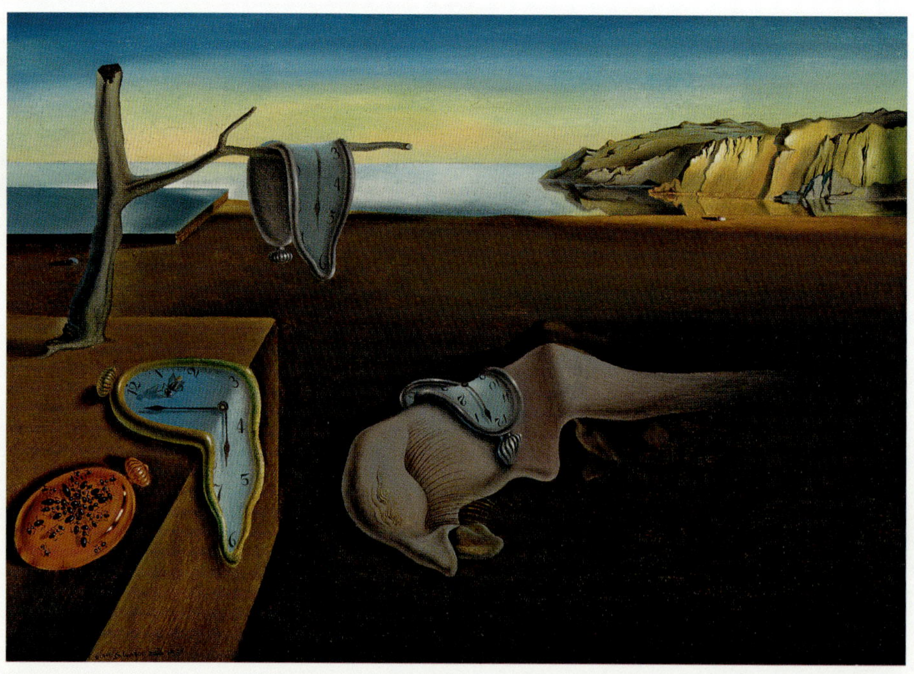

Fig. 80
Salvador Dalí, *The Persistence of Memory*, 1931. Oil on canvas, 24.1 x 33 cm. Museum of Modern Art (MoMA), New York. Given anonymously, inv. 162.1934

the hands of scientists and thus proving to us the spirituality of all substance, for the physical light of Dalí's Paranoiac-critical Activity, this too, is "wave and corpuscle" at one and the same time'.[5] The particle and wave descriptions of the effects of light photons hitting the electron were mutually exclusive, depending upon the experimental approach. Everything depended on the conditions of observation. As physicists, so far as I understand it, are still in disagreement about the behaviour of atomic processes and have settled for their undecidability, Dalí's joyous and outrageous melding of the physical and the spiritual – significantly he refers to 'wave and corpuscle' rather than 'wave and particle' – is no more and no less unprovable. 'Since 1929 I have ceaselessly studied the processes, the discoveries of the special sciences of the last hundred years. If it has not been possible for me to explore all corners of these because of their monstrous specialisation, I have understood their meaning as well as the best! One thing is certain: nothing, absolutely nothing, in the philosophic, aesthetic, morphological, biological or moral discoveries of our epoch, denies religion. On the contrary, the architecture of the temple of the special sciences has all its windows open to heaven.'[6]

It is interesting that Dalí was already urging the Surrealists in 1934 to take note of the physics of relativity and its potential spiritual role: 'I think more and more seriously that Surrealism has to evolve towards the foundation of a new materialist, anti-mystical religion, based on the progress of scientific knowledge (especially the new ideas of space, which were inaccessible not only to the Greeks but also to Christianity), a religion which would occupy the emotional imaginative void that the collapse of metaphysical ideas has produced in our era.'[7]

Duchamp's more cryptic notes are no less full of references to scientific ideas, although he refused to speculate about God. 'Carrouges' conclusion on the atheistic character of the "Bride" is not displeasing but I would just like to add that in terms of "popular metaphysics" I refuse to get involved in arguments about the existence of God – which means that the term "atheist" (as opposed to the word "believer") is of no interest to me at all ... For me, there is something other than yes, no and indifferent – the absence of investigations of this sort, for instance.'[8] Dalí once remarked that he was surprised on reading Nietzsche to discover that God was dead, having been brought up by his atheist father to believe he did not exist.

However, both masterpieces here, *The Large Glass* (cats 130, 131) and the *Christ of St John of the Cross* (cat. 132), one seemingly the epitome of objective and secular speculation about the erotic, the other the greatest religious painting of the twentieth century, contain allusions to science.

Dalí's *Christ of St John of the Cross* has been described as the 'spiritual image for the space age'.[9] Elliott King has pointed to a scientific subtext in this visionary work, in a study for the painting based on a triangle and a circle, which correspond to the triangular composition of the body.[10] His dream of the Christ of St John of the Cross had, Dalí said, 'revealed to him that Christ was "the nucleus of the atom"'; the sketch, derived from Luca Pacioli's *De divina proportione* (1509), shows a form with a hole in the centre shooting out golden rays, then refined to the geometrical triangle and circle, which symbolises the nucleus of the atom, to which Dalí gave a metaphysical meaning. 'I think of it as the very unity of the universe – the Christ.'[11]

It is striking that the most influential theories to have arisen in the latter part of the nineteenth century and in the first decades of the twentieth century, in the fields of politics, psychology and physics – those of Marx, Freud and Einstein (referred to by Duchamp as the necessary flag-name for a popular theory) – all point to hidden forces and energies that were no longer simply visible to or accessible to our immediate senses and consciousness. The idea that there were invisible forces governing our lives and our relationship with the world – traditionally belonging to the field of religion, but now given expression in very different contexts – was a challenge for artists. 'It would seem, moreover, that in every field, the principal direction of the twentieth century was the attempt to capture the nonperceptible [*sic*].'[12] This was, even, one of the principal causes of disagreement between two of the major scientists formulating quantum theory, Erwin Schrödinger and Walter Heisenberg. While Schrödinger found the visualisation of subatomic processes 'desirable and possible', Heisenberg did not: 'What Schrödinger writes about the visualisability of his theory "is probably not quite right", in other words, it's crap.'[13] Dalí blithely ignored this controversial aspect of quantum mechanics, regarding everything as potentially visualisable.

Whereas Dalí directed his science-attuned antennae towards religion and the metaphysical,

Duchamp treated his borrowings from physics with a sceptical humour in the manner of one of his mentors, Alfred Jarry. In physics this was an era of experiments 'exploring the effects of phenomena invisible to the naked eye', such as electromagnetic waves, which, 'at varying frequencies of vibration were the source of the newly discovered X-rays and "Hertzian" or radio waves'. Both in his paintings and in his notes Duchamp made extensive use of the new discoveries and the language in which they were presented. Having noted 'Make a painting of frequency', he proceeded to explore an unbelievably rich and suggestive field of double meanings in the terminology for electrons. These are 'not only swift, they are nude... (dressed in negative electricity)'.[14] *The King and Queen Surrounded by Swift Nudes* (cat. 46) was preceded by pencil sketches of 'The King and Queen Traversed by Swift Nudes' – the title Dalí mistakenly gave Duchamp's painting in his article in *Art News*.[15] 'Traverse' was a term regularly used by Ernest Rutherford and others to describe activity within the atom.[16] The Notes to *The Large Glass* published in 1934 (the *Green Box*) and in 1980 swarm with references to wireless telegraphy, alternating currents, electrical stripping and the vibrations of wave detectors. The interaction between the Bride in the upper half of the work (whose origins in the 1912 painting *Bride* owed something to the X-ray) and the Bachelors is partially governed by alternating currents. The Bride is 'splendid in her vibrations'.[17]

There are many levels of reference and meaning in *The Large Glass*, and even the possibility, despite their overwhelmingly scientific origins, of a different iconographic connection altogether: that of the Christian tradition. References vary from the deliberate if ironic allusion to the Assumption of the Virgin, as in Titian's altarpiece (fig. 83), which involves the entire composition, to more programmatic allusions based on the Notes, such as the stripping of the Bride. ('The bride reveals herself nude in 2 appearances: the first, that of the stripping by the bachelors. The second appearance that voluntary-imaginative one of the Bride.'[18]) Duchamp admitted to the multiple potential meanings of the stripping, which over and above the erotic and the electrical could even refer to the stripping of Christ.[19]

Duchamp was nearly twenty years older than Dalí and in some respects his interests in science belonged to the discoveries and interests of an earlier generation. The two artists' respective ideas about the fourth dimension, for example, reflect this difference. While Duchamp was intrigued by n-dimensional geometry, 'Dalí's fourth dimension was always time, never the fourth dimension of n-dimensional geometry or its mystical and popular accomplices'.[20] Duchamp adopted earlier notions of a fourth dimension, which was conceived to express the infinite, though he did so with a sceptical tone. He explained his pseudo-logic for the projection, in *The Large Glass*, of an invisible fourth dimension: 'by a purely intellectual analogy I considered that the fourth dimension could be the projection of a three-dimensional object, in other words any three-dimensional object ... is a projection of a four-dimensional thing that we don't know. It's a bit of a sophism, but after all it's possible. That's what I based the Bride on, in *The Large Glass*, as a projection of a four-dimensional object.'[21]

Concurrently with their commitment to the anti-retinal and their fascination with depicting the invisible, both Duchamp and Dalí pursued what seems to be the exact opposite: the ambiguities of perception and the powers of optical illusion. The paradoxical links between their obsession with the 'nonperceptible' and with optical illusion are explored in, for example, Dalí's Paranoiac-critical method.

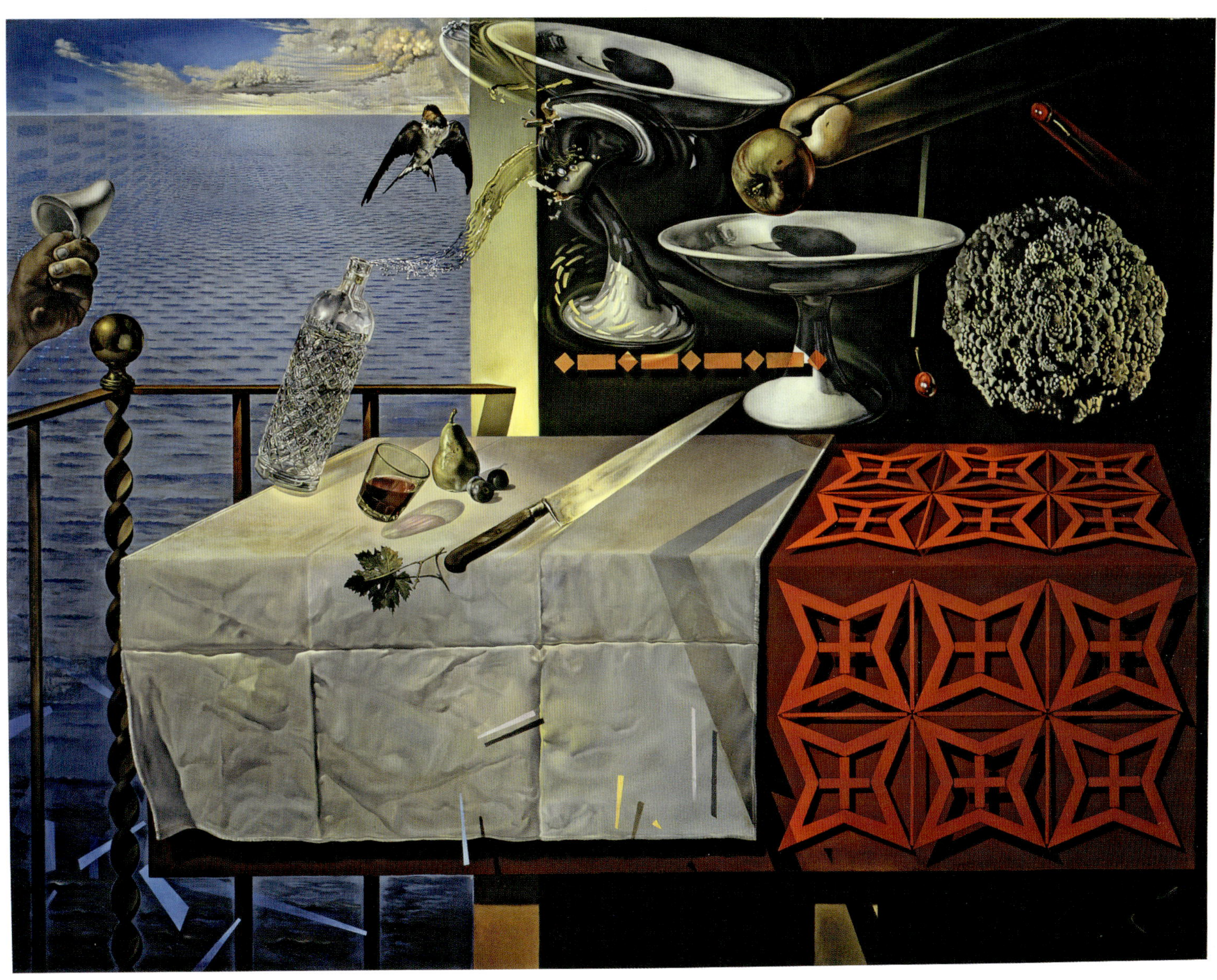

121
Salvador Dalí
Still Life – Fast Moving (Nature Morte Vivante), c. 1956
Oil on canvas, 125 x 160 cm
Collection of The Dalí Museum,
St Petersburg, Florida

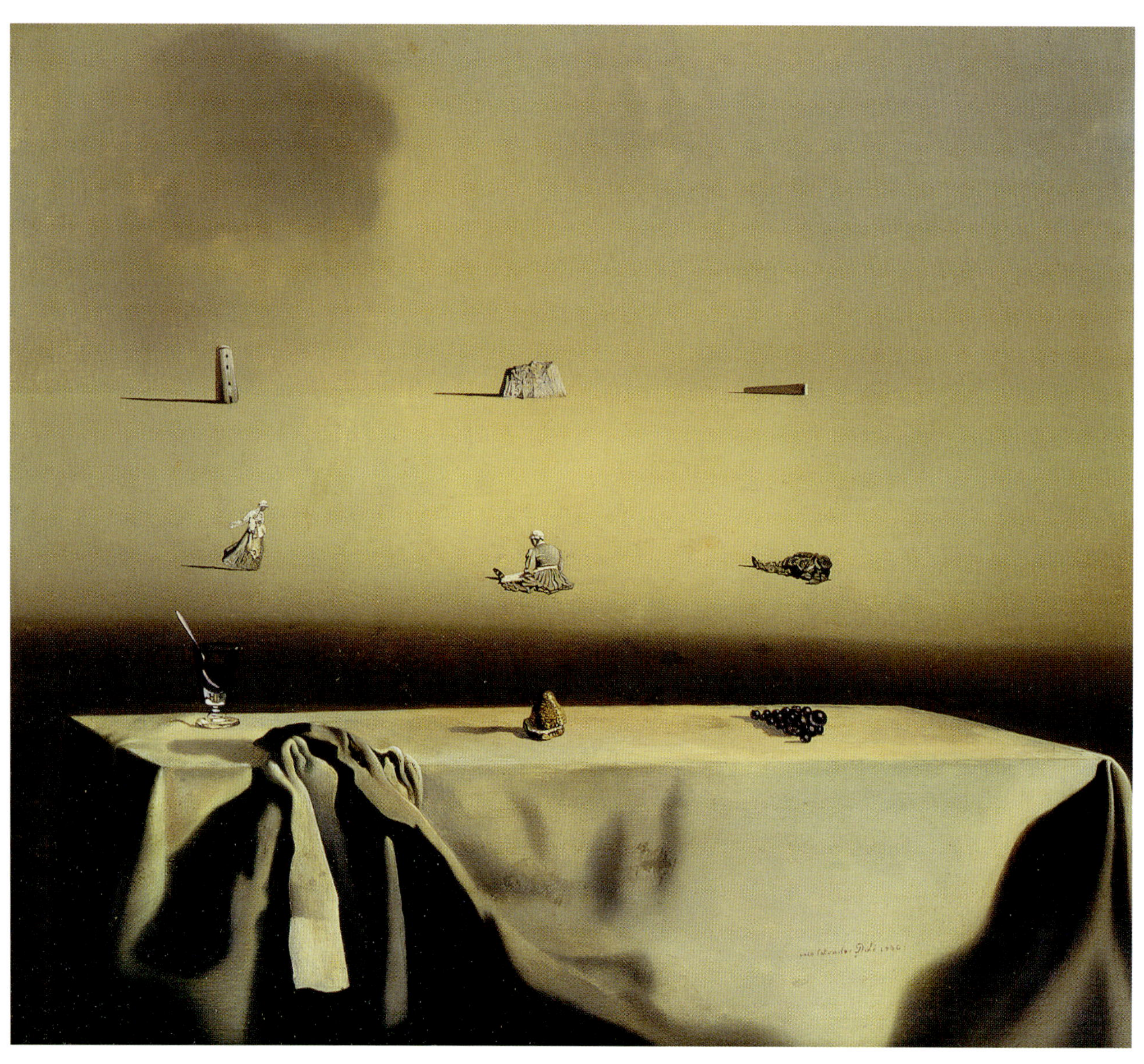

123
Salvador Dalí
10 Recipes for Immortality, 1973
Clockwise from top: Collector's box in
mixed media: acrylic with metal hardware,
64.8 x 58.4 x 11.1 cm; *Immortality
of Genetic Imperialism*, 1973,
drypoint etching with heliogravures,
33 x 77.5 x 55.9 cm; *Anamorphosis
of Anamorphoses and all is
Hologrammorphosis*, 1973,
drypoint etching with heliogravures,
14 x 33 x 25.4 cm; *Immortality of Castor
and Pollux*, 1973, drypoint etching with
heliogravures, plastic protector,
43.2 x 57.8 x 0.6 cm; *Stereoscopic
and Stereochemical Immortality
of Monarchy*, 1973, drypoint etching
with heliogravures, 37.5 x 80 x 39.4 cm
Collection of The Dalí Museum,
St Petersburg, Florida

122
Salvador Dalí
Morphological Echo, 1936
Oil on wood panel, 30.5 x 33 cm
Collection of The Dalí Museum,
St Petersburg, Florida

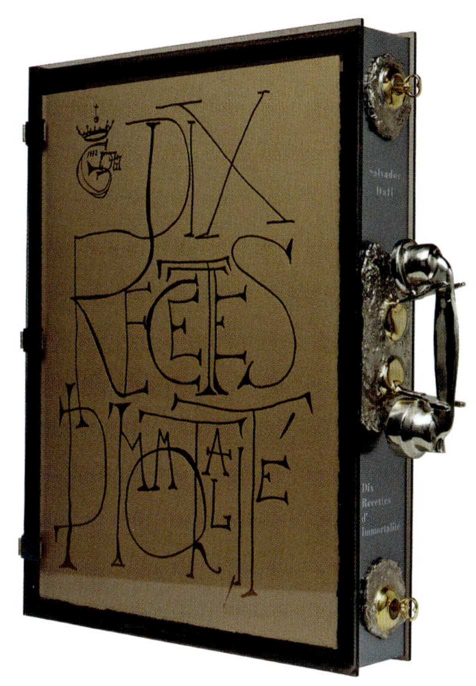

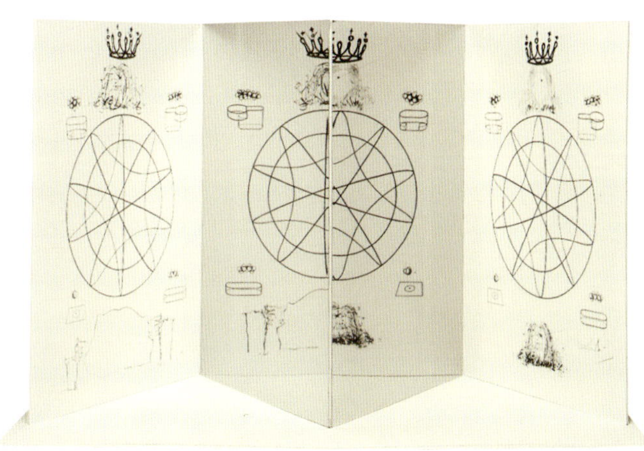

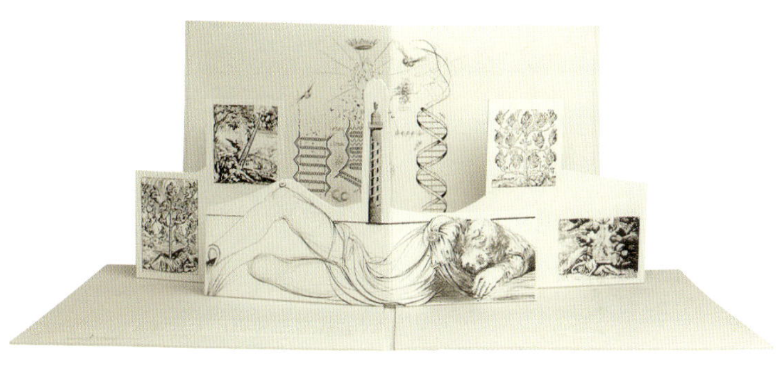

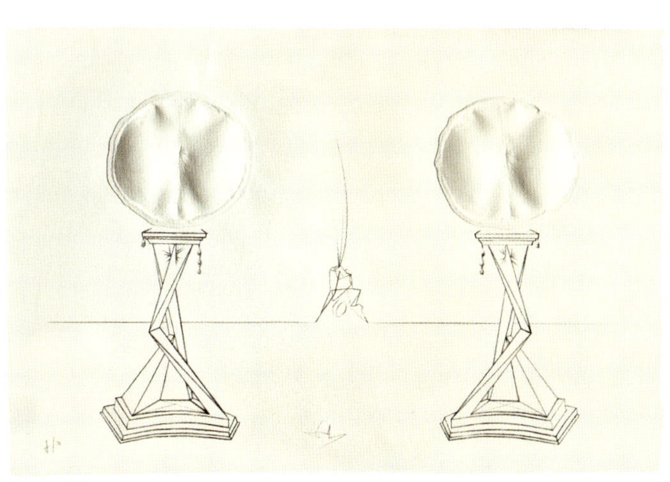

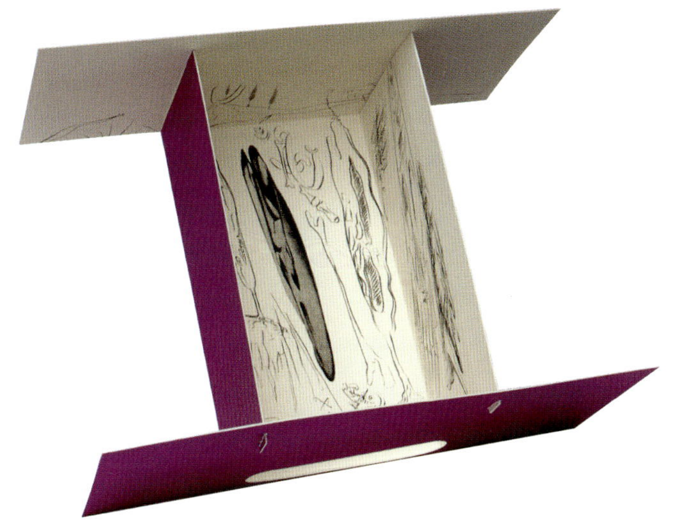

THE BRIDE STRIPPED BARE BY HER BACHELORS, EVEN
DAWN ADES

Duchamp started making notes towards the preparation of a major work in 1912. He began to construct the work in glass after moving to New York in 1915, and abandoned it, 'definitively' unfinished, in 1923. Although it is often referred to as *The Large Glass* or the *Glass*, its full title in French is *La Mariée mise à nu par ses célibataires, même*, which is generally rendered in English as *The Bride Stripped Bare by Her Bachelors, Even*. A selection of 94 facsimiles of Duchamp's handwritten notes was published in 1934, loose in a flat case, known as the *Green Box* (cat. 124).[1] Referring to this as an album, Duchamp commented: 'I wanted this album to go with the Glass and that one should consult it to see the Glass because, in my opinion, this shouldn't be looked at in the aesthetic sense of the term. It was necessary to consult the book and see them together. The conjunction of the two things removed the retinal side that I don't like.'[2] Duchamp unfavourably compared current painting, which he regarded as appealing solely to the eye, with the functions painting had had in the past: 'It could be religious, philosophical, moral....'[3] The problem was how to restore a function other than the purely retinal to painting. His notes are both a statement of the problem and a solution. Fragmentary, elusive and enigmatic, they draw on the new ideas that purport to give structure to our world – science, sex and energy – as well as some old myths, to provide the literary and poetic basis for the images in *The Large Glass*.

The English title *The Bride Stripped Bare by Her Bachelors, Even* cannot convey the pun in French between the adverb *même* ('even') and the pronoun and verb *m'aime* ('loves me'). Duchamp's interest in puns as a potential creative source was inspired by his visit in 1912 to Raymond Roussel's play *Impressions of Africa*, which used homonyms to generate very unusual object-assemblages. Although Roussel did not explain his system until much later, Duchamp, alert to linguistic games, intuited his method of construction. An early note of 1912,[4] in which Duchamp refers to a trip in the company of his friends the poet and critic Guillaume Apollinaire, Francis Picabia and Gabrielle Buffet-Picabia to the Jura mountains, at a time when he had not yet decided on the medium of his new work ('the pictorial matter of this Jura–Paris road / will be wood'), plays with (untranslatable) puns: 'the machine with five hearts' ('machine à cinq cœurs / cinq heures'); 'Enfant-phares / en fanfare', 'chef des cinq nus / chef des seins nus'.

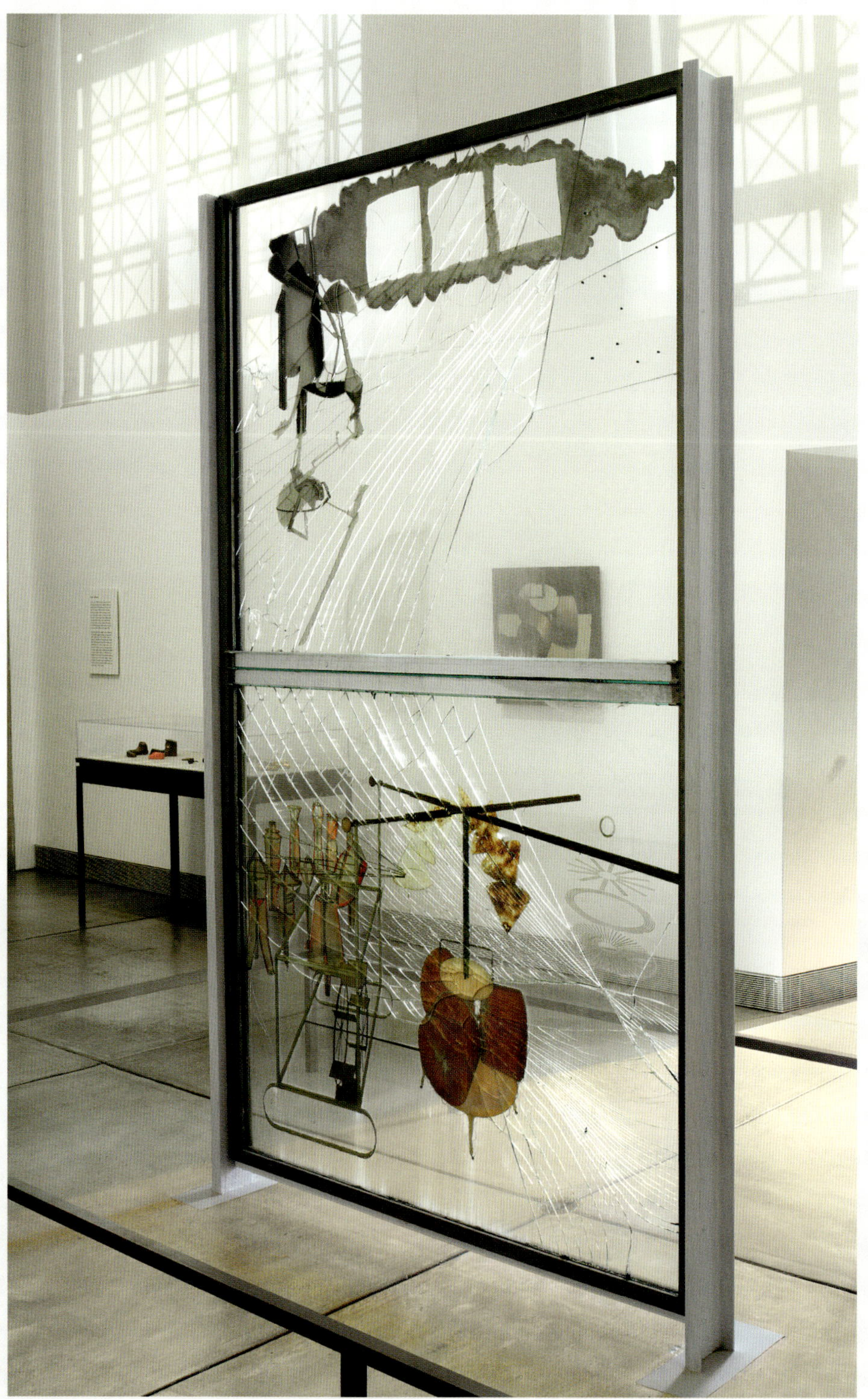

The notes are very various, comprising a scrap of paper with three or four words; careful calculations of elements in the *Glass*; algebraic equations; unclassifiable speculations related to physics, philosophy, perspective, gender and art; descriptions of the elements in the *Glass*; and, the longest text in the *Green Box*, a metaphorical account of the encounter between the Bride and her Bachelors. This last is a wonderfully graphic and poetic analysis of a sexual encounter powered through all kinds of mechanical operations, which include the internal combustion engine, 'love gasoline', electrical stripping and clockwork gears. The Bride strips and is stripped, the desire-motor bachelor-machine accelerates and climbs a slope in low gear... But it would seem from the evidence before our eyes that the encounter is doomed, the desire it embodies endlessly frustrated, because the two parts of *The Large Glass* are incompatible and their denizens can never meet.

The *Glass* is divided in two horizontally. The upper half is the domain of the Bride; the lower, of the Bachelors. These two domains are distinct in multiple ways (see also 'Perspective', pp. 168–71, and 'Measurement', pp. 172–77), with their male and female, earthly and heavenly and scientific and religious aspects taking various forms. The lower half is composed of quite precise machines and apparatuses: the Chocolate Grinder, the Water Mill, the Scissors and Sieves, with their suggestive functions, together with the Nine Malic Moulds, male-like, which are empty 'uniforms and liveries'. The Occulist Witnesses are the Peeping Toms of the sexual scenario. In the upper half the main elements from Duchamp's painting *Bride* (fig. 82) appear, suspended from a hook (the 'pendu femelle'), with an emanation of the Milky Way in a cloudy form beside her, indicating the heavenly realm, cut into by three 'draught pistons', squares distorted by the wind, one of several chance operations in the long production of the *Glass*.

André Breton was the first to respond to the 1934 *Green Box*; he had mentioned in the early 1920s 'the most beautiful legends' circulating about the glass picture, but now at last there were some clues to its meaning. In 'Phare de la mariée' he offers a reading that still holds alongside the many others that have subsequently been proposed: 'We find ourselves in the presence of a mechanistic and cynical interpretation of the love phenomenon: the passage of the woman from the state of virginity to the state of non-virginity as the theme of a strictly asentimental speculation – one might say a being from outer space trying to figure out this kind of operation.'[5] *The Large Glass*, Breton concluded, is a totally unprecedented work of art, which uniquely balances the rational and the irrational.

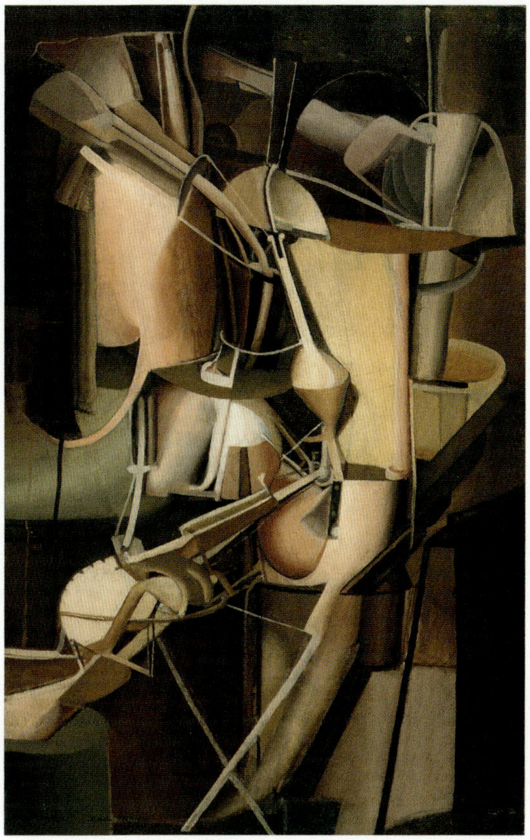

Subsequent commentaries have proposed sources in science, theories of the fourth dimension, alchemy, Classical myths and Christian iconography, and, in relation to the media themselves, photography, Bavarian glass paintings, glass palettes, windows, most of which are convincing. One of Duchamp's notes describes the work as a 'Delay in Glass'– 'a way of succeeding in no longer thinking that the thing in question is a picture...'.[6]

In 1926 *The Large Glass* was accidentally shattered in transit from an exhibition in Brooklyn (fig. 81). In 1936, its owner Katherine Dreier having finally brought herself to tell him, Duchamp painstakingly restored it, commenting that he felt the cracks completed it. The work is too fragile to leave its permanent home at the Philadelphia Museum of Art, but several replicas have been made, one of which (cat. 131) was constructed by Richard Hamilton for the 1966 Tate retrospective 'The Almost Complete Works of Marcel Duchamp'. On the back the inscription reads: 'R. Hamilton after M. D. Pour copie conforme Marcel Duchamp 1966.' The other one (cat. 130) was made for the Moderna Museet by Ulf Linde with Duchamp's authorisation and signature in 1961.

Opposite: Fig. 81
Marcel Duchamp, *The Bride Stripped Bare by Her Bachelors, Even* (*La Mariée mise à nu par ses célibataires, même*), known as *The Large Glass*, 1915–23. Oil, varnish, lead foil, lead wire and dust on two glass panels, 277.5 x 177.8 x 8.6 cm. Philadelphia Museum of Art, bequest of Katherine S. Dreier, 1952

Fig. 82
Marcel Duchamp, *Bride*, 1912. Oil on canvas, 94.3 x 60. Philadelphia Museum of Art. The Louise and Walter Arensberg Collection, 1950-134-65

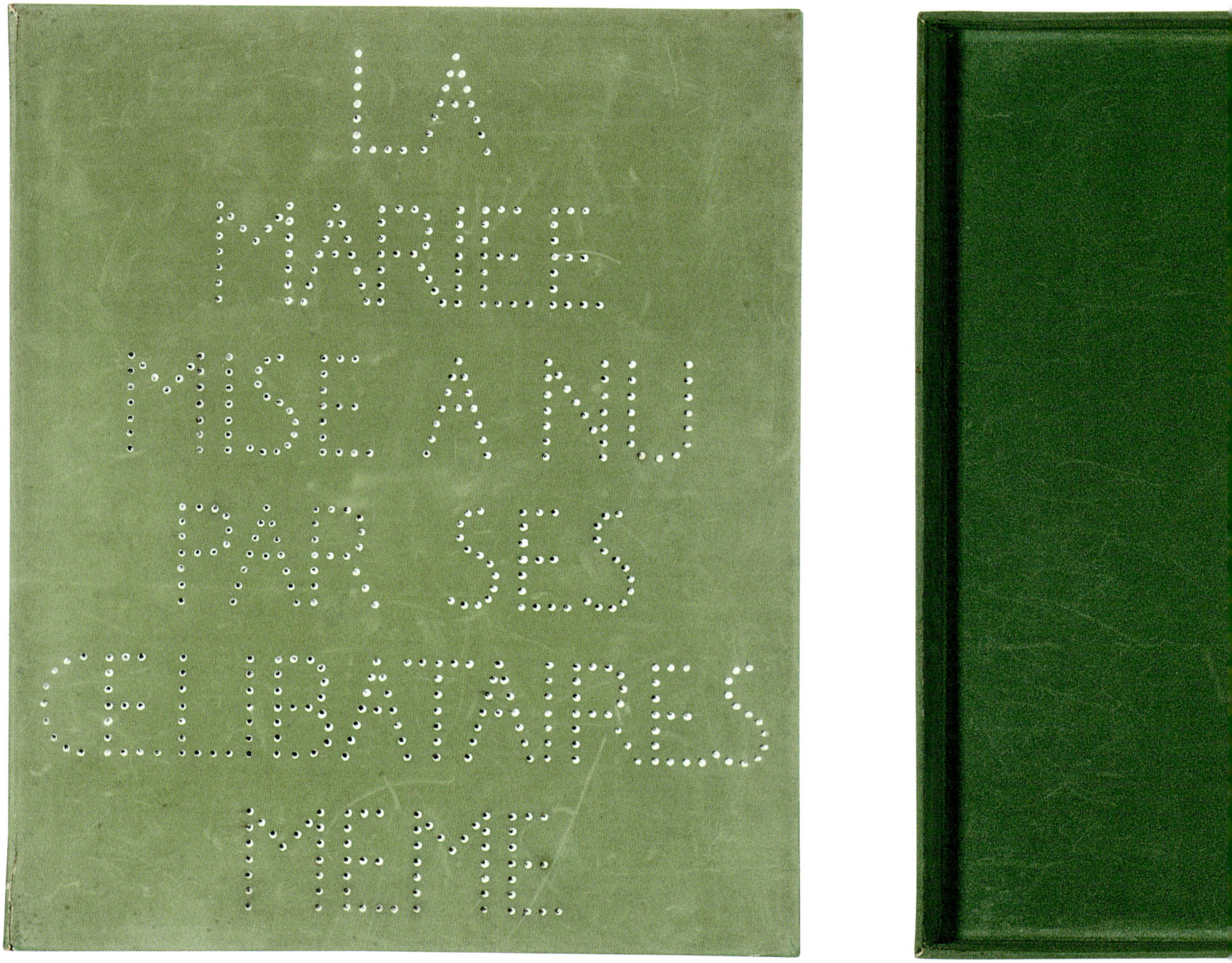

124
Marcel Duchamp
La Mariée mise à nu par ses célibataires, même (*The Bride Stripped Bare by Her Bachelors, Even*) known as *The Green Box*, 1934
Cardboard box, colour plate and 94 lithographs, collotypes and drawings in ink on paper, 33.3 x 27.9 x 2.5 cm
Tate: Purchased 2001

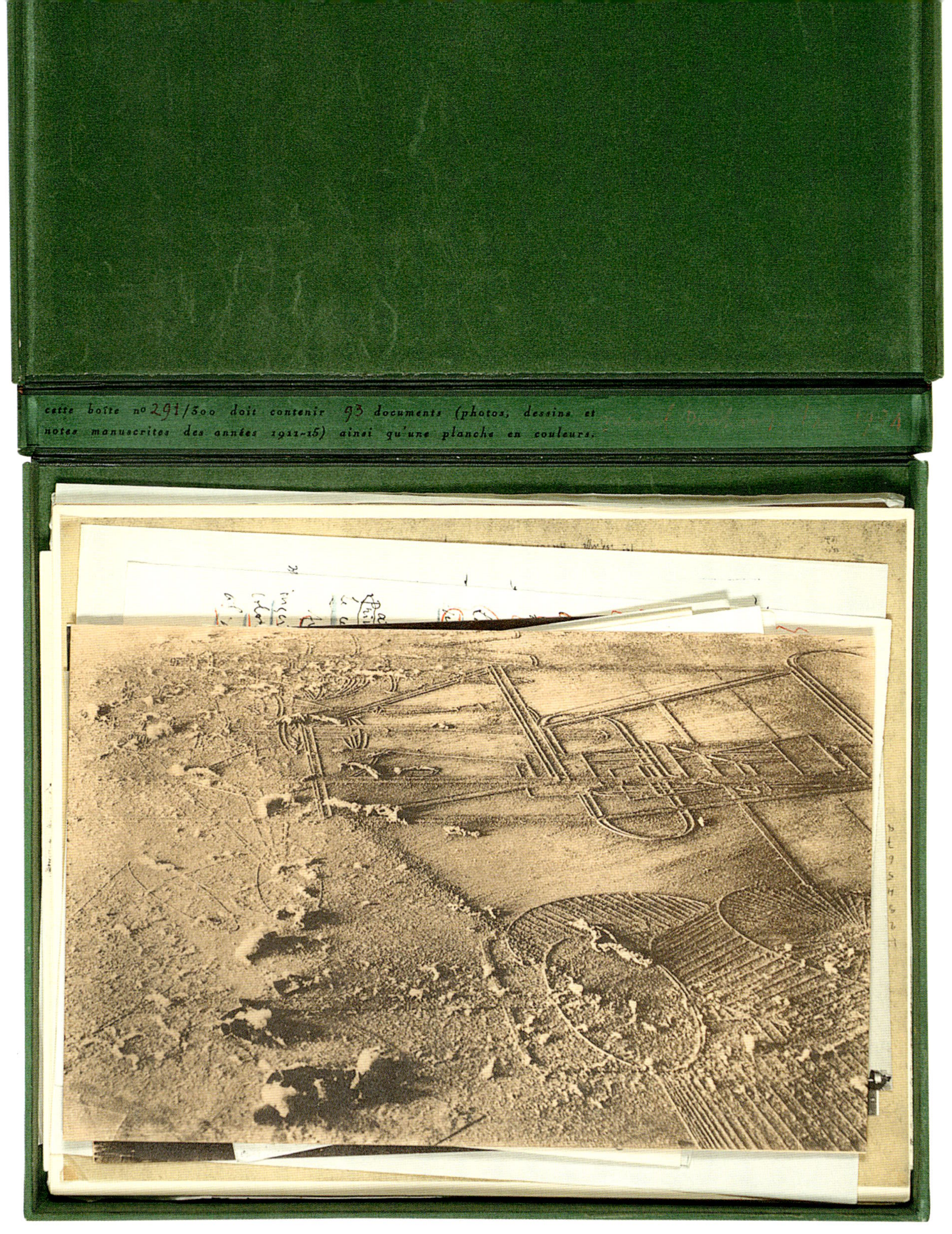

cette boîte no 291/300 doit contenir 93 documents (photos, dessins et
notes manuscrites des années 1911-15) ainsi qu'une planche en couleurs.

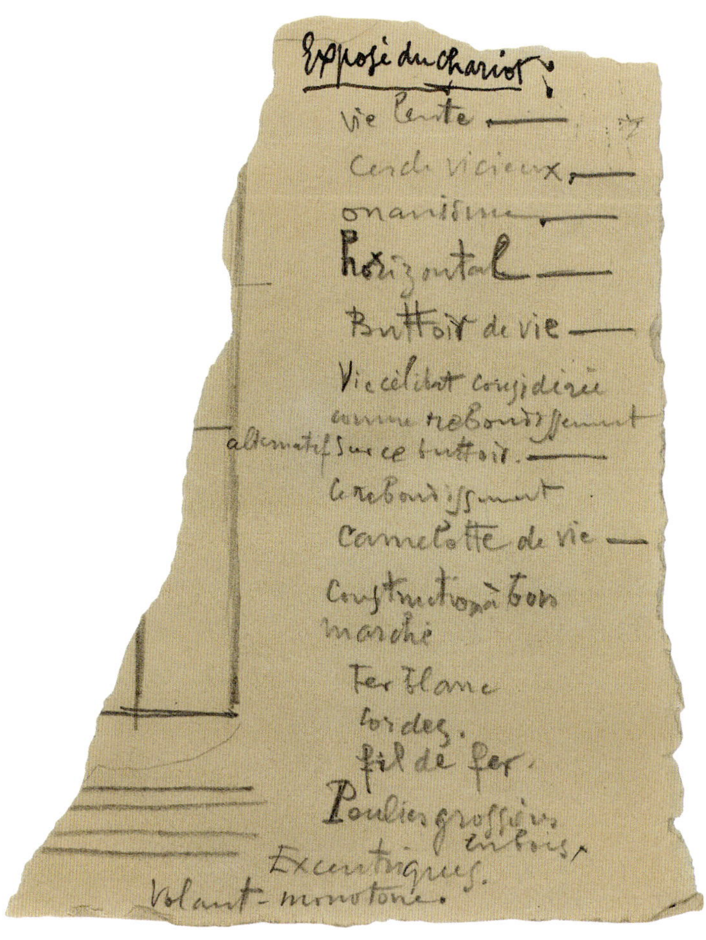

125
Marcel Duchamp
Note: *'Executer un tableau sur verre tel qu'il...'* ('Make a painting on glass so that it has neither front nor back nor up nor down'), date unknown
Ink on paper, 4.8 x 11.5 cm
Centre Pompidou, Paris. Musée national d'art moderne/Centre de création industrielle

126
Marcel Duchamp
Note: *'Exposé du chariot...'* ('Exposé of the carriage...') with list including 'onanism', date unknown
Black ink and pencil on paper, 12.5 x 9.6 cm
Centre Pompidou, Paris. Musée national d'art moderne/Centre de création industrielle

127
Marcel Duchamp
Note: *'L'imitation de la photographie...'* ('Imitation of photography/make it evident in the *pendu femelle*'), date unknown
Pencil on paper, 8.7 x 13 cm
Centre Pompidou, Paris. Musée national d'art moderne/Centre de création industrielle

128
Marcel Duchamp
Note: *'La vie a credit'* ('Life on credit'), date unknown
Pencil on paper, 6.1 x 13.1 cm
Centre Pompidou, Paris. Musée national d'art moderne/Centre de création industrielle

129
Marcel Duchamp
Note: *'Allegorie d'oubli'* ('Allegory of Oblivion'), date unknown
Black ink on paper, 7.1 x 9.2 cm
Centre Pompidou, Paris. Musée national d'art moderne/Centre de création industrielle

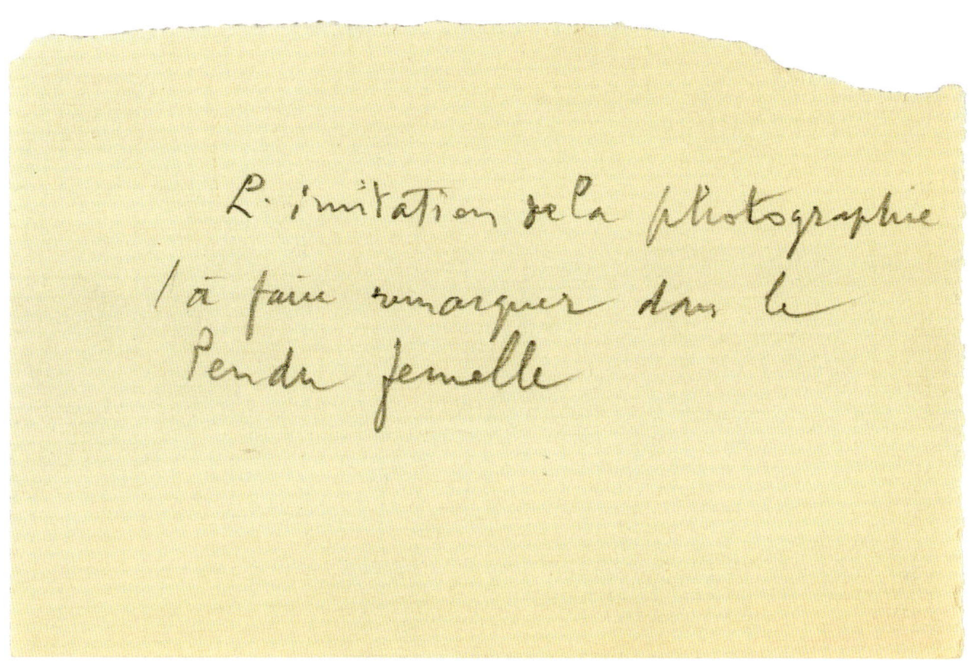

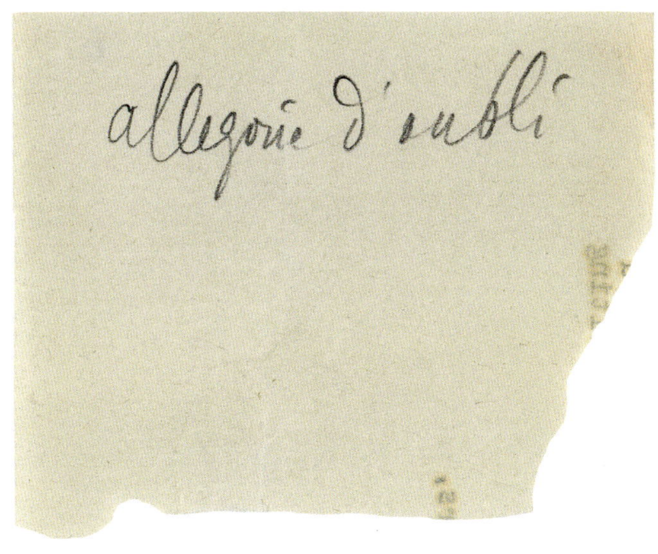

Page 166: 130
Marcel Duchamp
(reconstruction by Ulf Linde)
The Bride Stripped Bare by Her Bachelors, Even (*La Mariée mise à nu par ses célibataires, même*), known as *The Large Glass*, 1915–23 (reconstructed in 1991–92)
Oil and lead on glass in wooden frame, 321 x 204.3 x 111.7 cm
Moderna Museet, Stockholm
Florida only

Page 167: 131
Marcel Duchamp
(reconstruction by Richard Hamilton)
The Bride Stripped Bare by Her Bachelors, Even (*La mariée mise à nu par ses célibataires, même*), known as *The Large Glass*, 1915 (reconstructed in 1965–66 and 1985)
Oil, lead, dust and varnish on glass in metal frame, 277.5 x 175.9 cm
Tate: Presented by William N. Copley through the American Federation of Arts 1975
London only

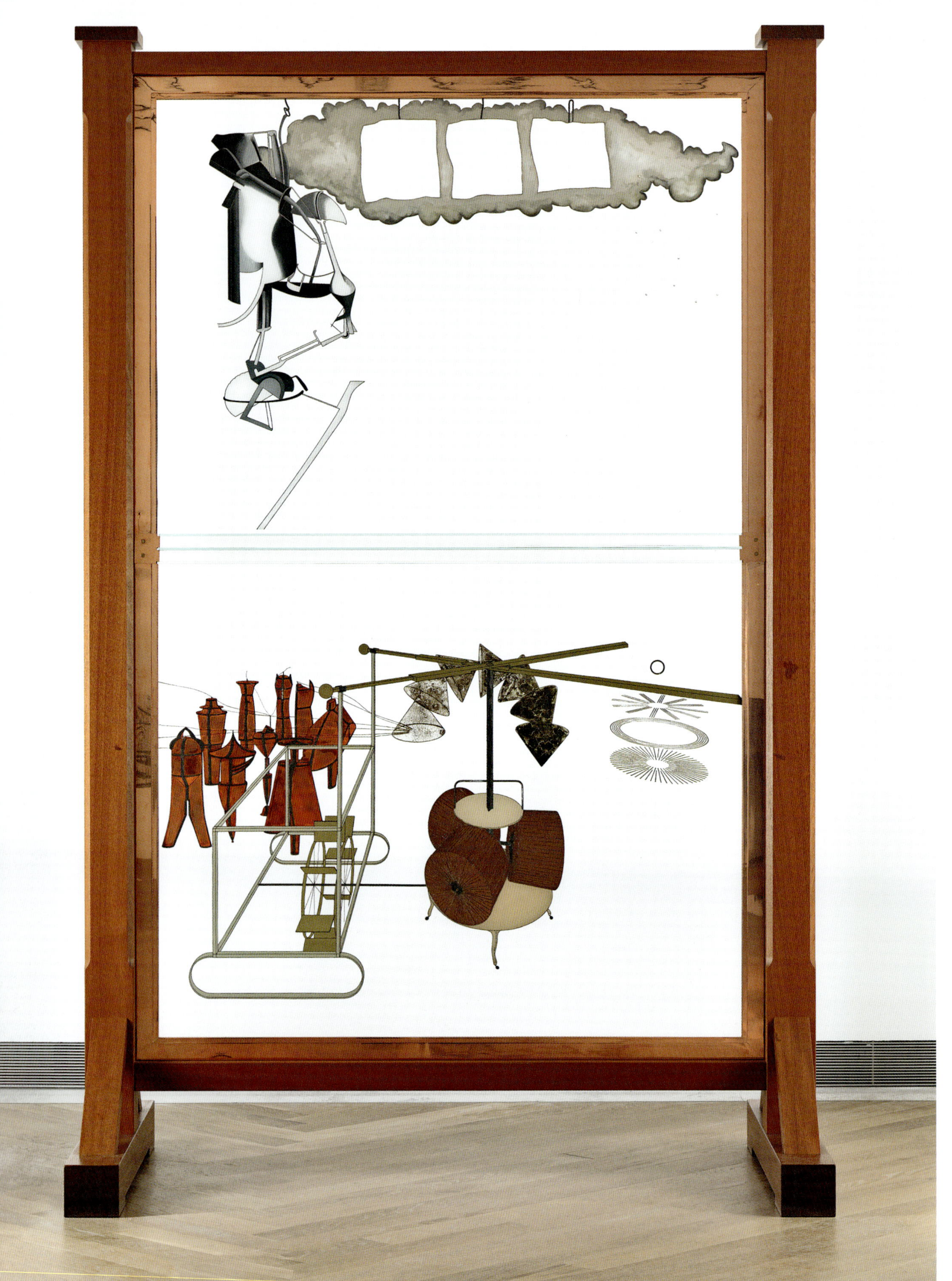

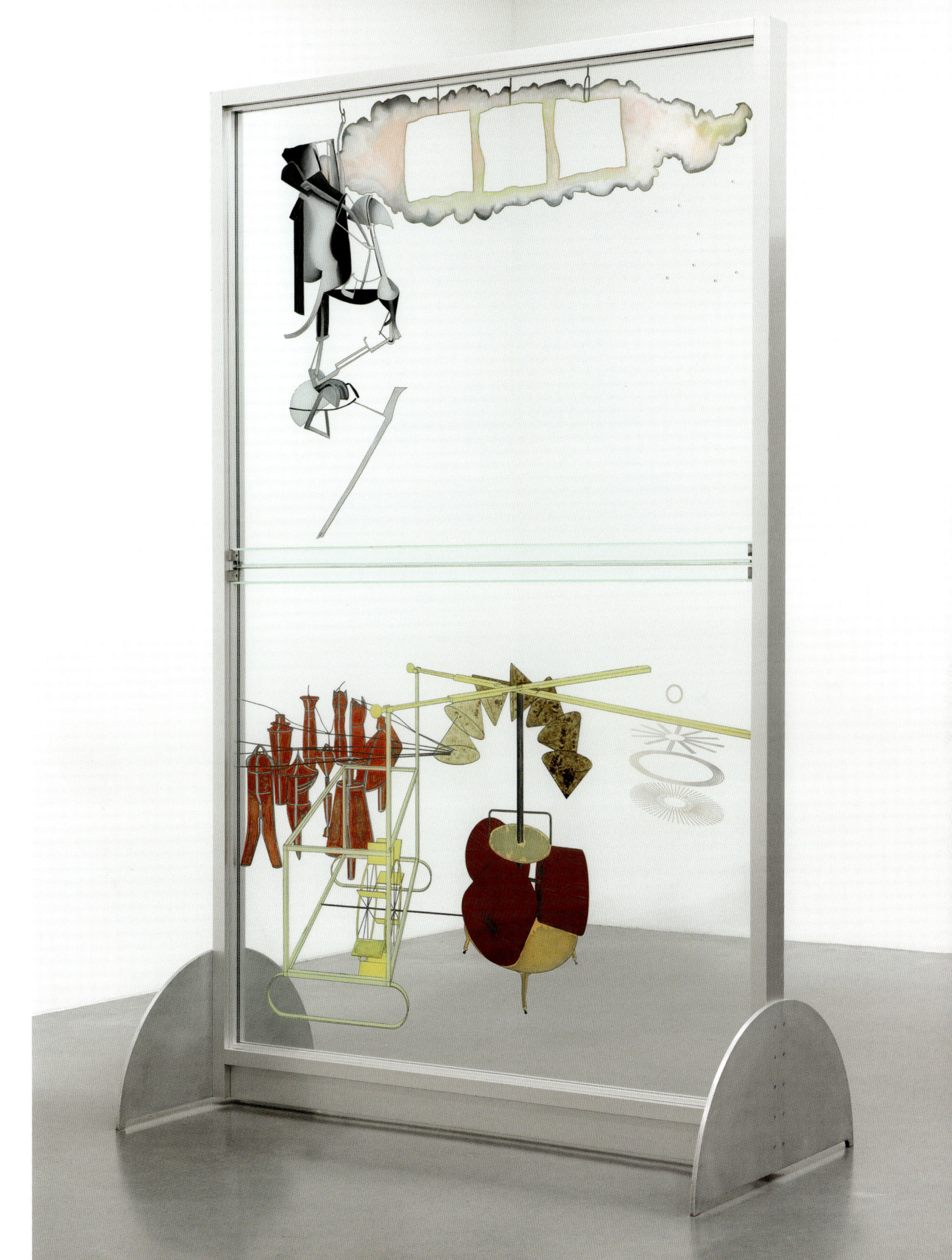

PERSPECTIVE
DAWN ADES

Going against the grain of modern art, Duchamp and Dalí were unusual in the importance they placed on perspective. Most twentieth-century artists had dispensed with this system of creating the illusion of a three-dimensional image on a two-dimensional surface, which had been a fundamental pictorial conquest of the early Renaissance. The new priorities centred on colour and form, which now acquired an autonomy that shifted the emphasis to the picture surface itself and away from the illusion of a real scene.

Neither Duchamp nor Dalí used perspective in conventional ways. Both stretched and questioned its potential functions and put them to unusual ends. For Duchamp perspective was, paradoxically, one of the ways he challenged the 'purely retinal' aspect of modern painting.

The two-part division of *The Large Glass*, the lower the domain of the Bachelors and their machines and the upper that of the Bride, corresponds not only to the separation of the terrestrial and aerial realms, which echoes images such as Titian's *Assumption of the Virgin* (fig. 83), with its different registers for Earth and Heaven, but also to different types of perspective. The *Glass*, Duchamp said, 'constitutes a rehabilitation of perspective, which had been completely ignored, despised. Perspective, for me, became absolutely scientific.'[1] The lower section of the *Glass*, the domain of the Bachelors, is the part of the work most obviously constructed according to the laws of perspective. The open framework of the Glider containing the Water Wheel is meticulously calculated according to a single-point perspective, with the vanishing point at the centre of the 'horizon' line or bar separating the upper and lower sections of the *Glass*, to which the central machine, the Chocolate Grinder with its three rollers, also conforms. The effect is to make these two structures appear to occupy the real space beyond the *Glass*. The nine Malic Moulds, clustered to the left of the Water Wheel, have their own notional layout depending on the *3 Standard Stoppages* (cat. 133), but this doesn't contradict the basic, solid perspectival grounding of the Bachelor Machines. The Occulist Witnesses are also laid out in perspective but have their own vanishing point. The principal forms of the Bachelor Machines are, Duchamp wrote in his Notes, imperfect, but measurable.

In the Bride's section (the upper part of the *Glass*), the forms of the 'Pendu femelle', the Wasp and other elements 'have lost all character of measurable position'.[2] They are 'freed forms', at least freed according to a given and known perspective. None of these images was conditioned by perspective, but this is nonetheless conceptually present. The 'Pendu femelle' originated in the 1912 painting *Bride*, and the draught pistons in Duchamp's experiments with a square of gauze. There is a hint of anamorphic perspective – that is, a form of distorted drawing of an object that can be resolved if the drawing or painting is seen from a particular viewpoint, as most famously in Holbein's *The Ambassadors* (1533; National Gallery, London). However, Duchamp pushes this idea further, trailing and perhaps mocking abstract forms, suggesting that if only we knew where to stand we could make sense of any given form:

> The Pendu femelle
> is the form
> in *ordinary perspective*
> of a Pendu femelle
> for which one could perhaps
> try to discover
> the true form

> This comes from the
> fact that any
> form is the perspective
> of another form
> according to a certain *vanishing point*
> and a certain *distance*[3]

This *reductio ad absurdum* of the notion of perspective takes its 'absolutely scientific' application theoretically way beyond logic. Perspective for Duchamp was both a rigorous method – with whose founding literature he was thoroughly familiar from his days as a librarian at the Bibliothèque Sainte-Geneviève, which has the best collection of early texts on the subject in the world – and a source for metaphysical and erotic speculation. The very material and proportions of the *Glass* are, as Jean Clair demonstrated, based on the diagrams in the treatises of Abraham Bosse and Jean Du Breuil.[4] The idea that the plane surface of the picture is analogous to a pane of glass – a window – through which the forms of the objects to be depicted are seen, as in Dürer's famous 1525 image of a draughtsman with female model, was suggestive. Duchamp's notes speculate about the ocular nature of desire, separation, frustration and consummation: 'The question of shop

On the whole, for Dalí perspective was 'a means to create not the illusion of a real scene but the reality of illusions'.[7] During the 1930s, as he most forcefully explained in his 1935 text *Conquest of the Irrational*, his aim in his paintings was to make his imagination, the product of his paranoiac-critical vision, as real, as 'persuasively, cognoscitively, and communicably thick as the exterior world of phenomenal reality'.[8] Perspective was crucial to Dalí's illusionism, but distorted or exaggerated, especially in the paintings of his early Surrealist period, where he makes use of 'the clever tricks of a paralysing foreshortening'.[9]

Dalí was fascinated by the anamorphic perspective in *The Ambassadors*, where death lurks invisibly in the foreground, a shapeless object when seen from the front, but taking its true form, a skull, when viewed from a sharp angle to the side of the canvas. Dalí's drawings and paintings of distorted skulls and elongated limbs or heads resemble the effects of anamorphosis – what he called 'anamorphic hysteria'.[10] One of his anamorphic objects consists of an unreadable configuration curved around a reflective

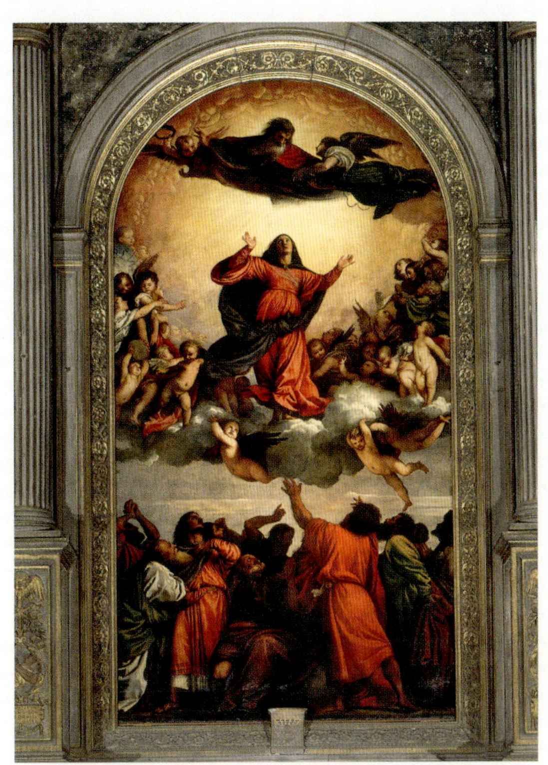

Fig. 83
Titian, *The Assumption of Virgin*, 1516–18. Oil on wood, 690 x 360 cm. Santa Maria Gloriosa de' Frari, Venice

Fig. 84
Salvador Dalí, *Study for Christ of St John of the Cross*, 1950–51. Gouache, watercolour and collage on card, 18.5 x 20.1 cm. Lent by Glasgow Life (Glasgow Museums) on behalf of Glasgow City Council

windows … hiding this coition through a sheet of glass.'[5] The two great works that emerged from the Notes, *The Large Glass* and *Étant donnés* (fig. 76), are exact opposites of each other, underlined by the various roles and effects of perspective. The *Glass* is a window-size manifestation of a diagram, with the protagonists determined by and separated by different aspects of perspective. Transparent, it is two-dimensional but can be walked round and viewed from all angles, while *Étant donnés* is fully three-dimensional, but can only be seen from one position: a fixed viewpoint whose vanishing point is that of the female sex.

Like Duchamp, Dalí was intrigued by the various perspective theories and by the imagery in which these were couched in seventeenth- and eighteenth-century treatises. He recognised that these theories of perspective were wrestling with the problem of marrying empirical observation of the natural world with belief in a world beyond it: 'I am like the alchemist trying to apprehend the non-measurable through the measurable, and the power of my paranoia-critical delirium will see me through.'[6]

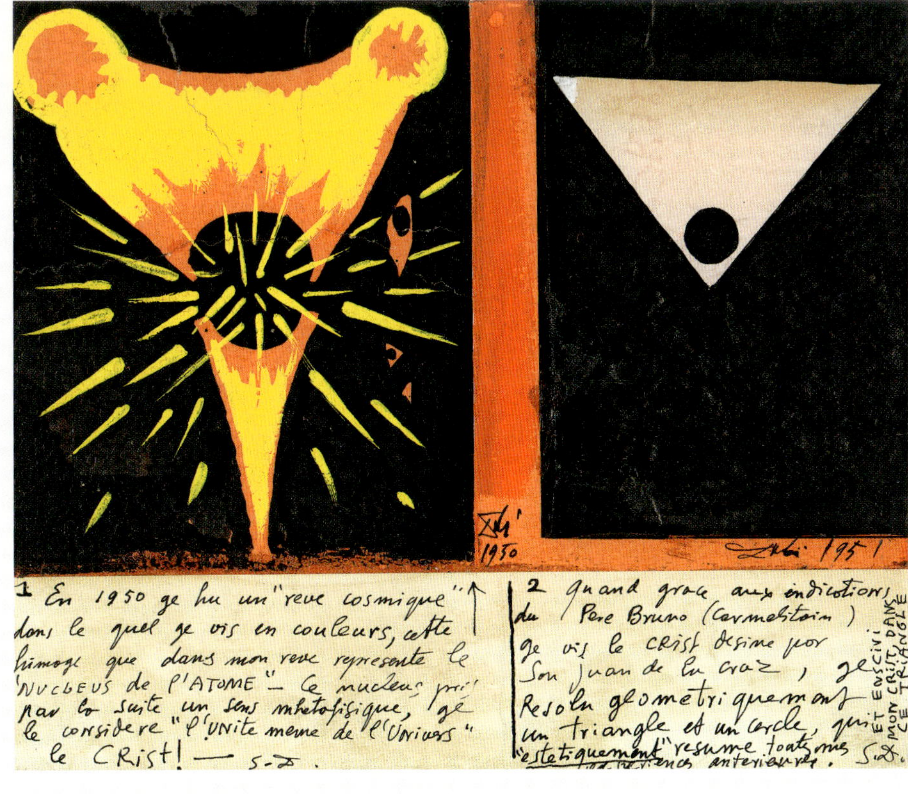

cylinder. In the reflection, the form resolves into a skull (cat. 146).

The dramatic foreshortening and unusual viewpoint of the body in *Christ of St John of the Cross* (cat. 132) were partially inspired by a drawing attributed to St John of the Cross (fig. 85), which Dalí had been shown by Bruno de Jesus-Marie, like St John a monk of the Carmelite order.[11] In both, the viewpoint is from above, which in the case of the drawing makes it look more like a devotional object, though legend has it that it was produced while the saint was in a state of ecstasy. The drawing, however, shows the cross obliquely, while Dalí's cross and figure are upright and symmetrical. As in *The Large Glass*, whose proportions are similar to those of Dalí's picture, the notional viewer is faced with two spatially incompatible scenes, in the upper and the lower parts of the picture, which represent different worlds. As Neil MacGregor commented, there is no place for you, the viewer, to be.[12] The lower part shows a real landscape: the bay outside Dalí's house at Portlligat, with the stone path winding around the shore, his yellow boat pulled up on the beach and two fishermen curiously dressed in antique costume, based respectively on a drawing by Velázquez and a Le Nain peasant. Christ's cross, however, hovers against blackness, receding downwards away from the viewer; this is presumably a mystical vision rather than a representation of the viewpoint of God. The angle from which it is seen resembles a diagram by Abraham Bosse from 1648 (fig. 86) although Bosse's 'cross' is simply there to demonstrate the system for constructing horizontal perspective. It is interesting that his plate is divided into two sections, with a 'horizon' between them, and a normal vanishing point. Just as one can see a model for *The Large Glass* in plates from perspective treatises by mathematicians such as Du Breuil, which are divided horizontally equally into two parts, the format of Dalí's *Christ* follows the proportions of Bosse's demonstration, in which the lower section is a third of the whole.

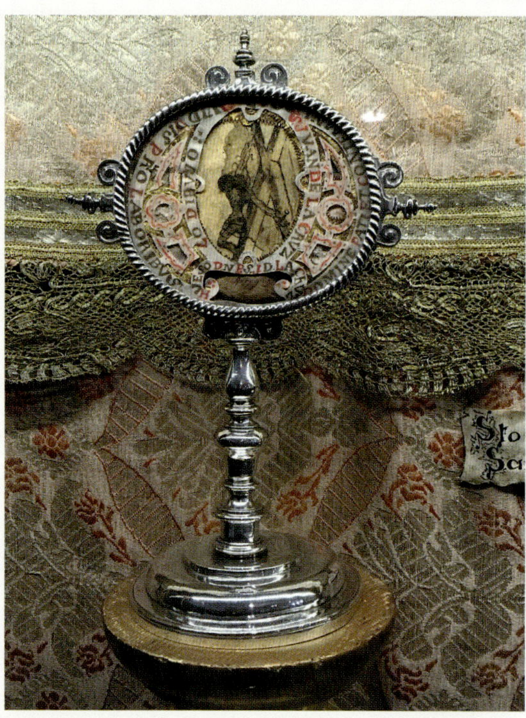

Fig. 85
St John of the Cross, *Crucifixion*, c. 1572–74. Pen and ink on paper, 5.7 x 4.7 cm, set within a reliquary. Monastery of the Incarnation, Ávila

Fig. 86
Abraham Bosse, 'Pour la Perspective horizontale'. Engraved illustration from Girard Desargues, *Manière universelle de M. Desargues, pour pratiquer la perspective par petit-pied, comme le géométral, ensemble les places et proportions des fortes et foibles touches, teintes ou couleurs, par A. Bosse...*, Paris, 1648, f.p. 165.
Royal Academy of Arts, London, 03/2820

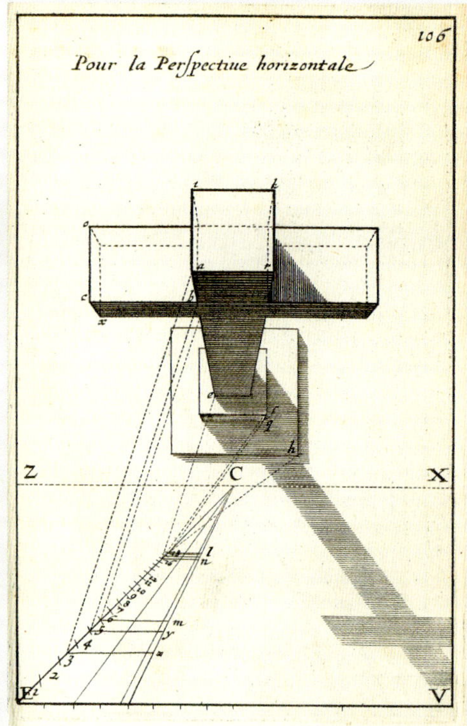

Opposite: 132
Salvador Dalí
Christ of St John of the Cross, c. 1951
Oil on canvas, 204.8 x 115.9 cm
Lent by Glasgow Life (Glasgow Museums) on behalf of Glasgow City Council

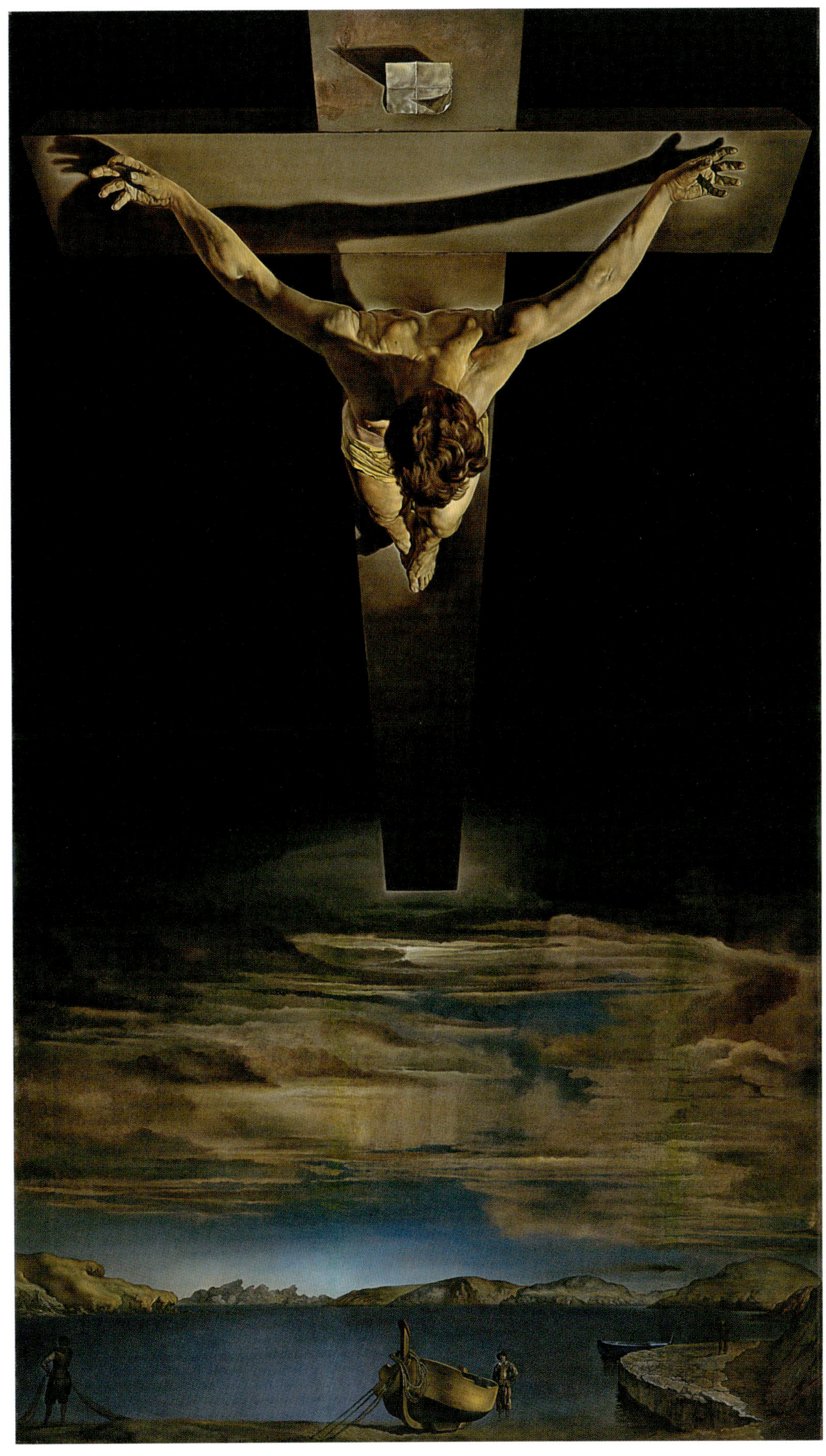

MEASUREMENT
DAWN ADES

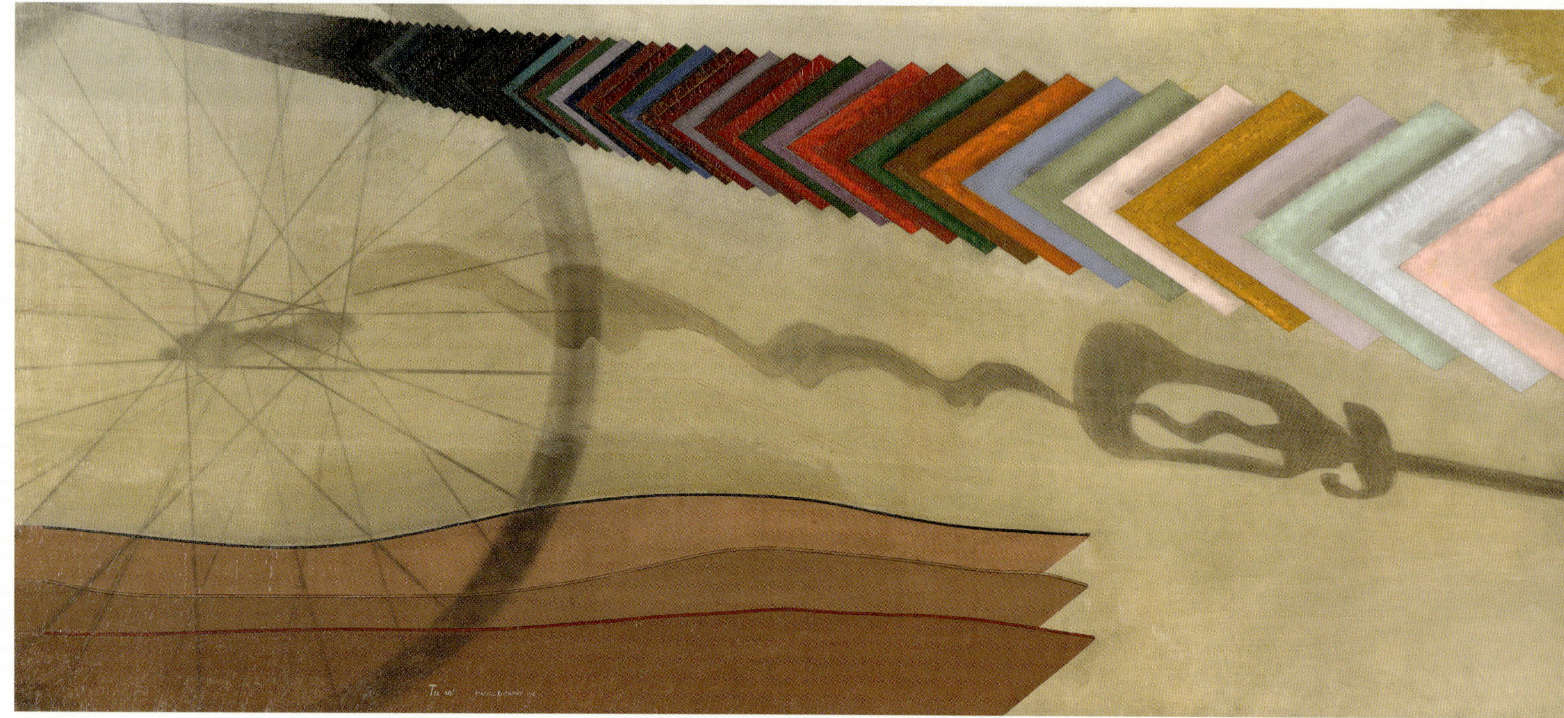

Duchamp's work *3 Standard Stoppages* (cat. 133) is both a humorous comment on the confidence of positivist physics and of mathematics to provide a system of accurate measurement based on the circumference of the globe, and a profoundly philosophical response to the way questions of measurement relate to problems of order, origin and generation. *3 Standard Stoppages* originated with the genesis of *The Bride Stripped Bare by Her Bachelors, Even* (*The Large Glass*; fig. 81). Although he did not begin *The Large Glass* until 1915 in New York, Duchamp had been planning it in detail for several years, with notes and diagrams, including speculations on measurement. A note from 1914, later published in the *Green Box*, reads:

> 3 Standard Stops =
>   canned chance
> 1914
>
> *the Idea of the Fabrication*
> If a [horizontal] thread one metre long falls
>   straight

from a height of one metre onto a horizontal plane
twisting *as it pleases* and creates
a new image of the unit of length.

Earlier notes had considered, in the same realm of 'playful physics', 'the phenomenon of stretching in the unit of length', but the experiment Duchamp chose to fabricate, the Standard Stoppages, produced not a stretched unit but 'the metre diminished', thus casting 'pataphysical doubt on the concept of a straight line as being the shortest route from one point to another'.[1]

In 1791 the French Academy of Sciences defined the metre as one ten-millionth part of the distance from the North Pole to the Equator.[2] Establishing a physical object as this absolute unit of measurement was later attempted: a platinum-iridium bar, with two engraved marks one 'standard metre' apart, is held at the Bureau International des Poids et Mesures at Sèvres, and is known as an 'étalon', after the French term *étalonner*, 'to calibrate'. Unfortunately, because the Earth is not a perfect sphere, the original 'standard metre' is a tiny bit shorter than it should have been: the planet's circumference is 40,0007,863 metres rather

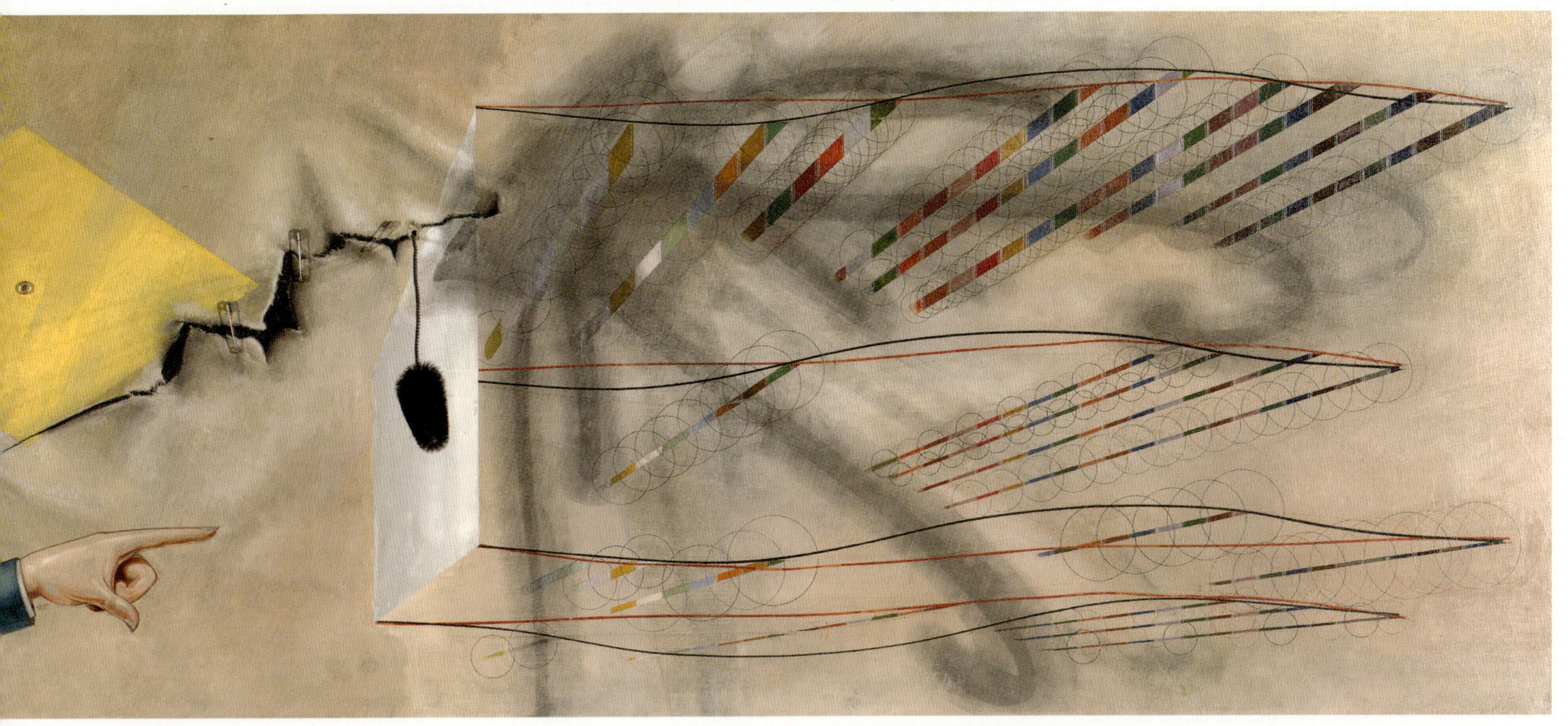

than 40,000,000. So despite its claim to be absolute, the étalon (standard metre) is essentially arbitrary.

The title of Duchamp's work is difficult to render in English: the term 'etalon' is used in English to mean a standard unit, while *stoppage* means 'invisible mending' in French. Duchamp settled on this latter term, which he noticed one day on a sign above a tailor's shop, because it seemed appropriate to his associated experiments with thread.

The work was made as follows: a metre-long thread was dropped from a height of one metre, and the procedure repeated twice. The resulting three new chance shapes Duchamp treated as different 'units of measurement'. He fastened the three dropped threads onto strips of blue-black canvas with tiny drops of glue. This technique was important, he told Richard Hamilton, because it anticipated the way he was later to make the outlines of objects on *The Large Glass*, with lead wires affixed to the glass with varnish.[3] *3 Standard Stoppages* as it now exists comprises three wooden slats, one edge of each shaped to match the curve of the dropped threads. These, with the threads on canvas (the *stoppages*), mounted on glass panels, are housed in a specially constructed

wooden box made to look like a case for a croquet set. However, the work seems not to have been thus assembled until 1936; the wooden templates were made for the painting *Tu m'* (fig. 87), Duchamp's last oil painting on canvas, which was commissioned by Katherine Dreier in 1918. Although Dreier had both the threads and the wooden templates in her possession in 1935, she had difficulty finding them when Duchamp asked her to send photographs for the reproduction he was planning for the *Boîte-en-valise*.[4] Recently a tiny gold stamp on each of the wooden slats, first noticed by Ulf Linde, has been identified as the trademark of the Société des Lunetiers, which manufactured 'a plethora of precision instruments for measuring, drafting, engraving etc',[5] including plane rulers one metre long.[6] Perhaps Duchamp took some of these 'metre units' with him to New York and carved one edge of them into templates for curves of the dropped threads in 1918. It seems that in the summer of 1936, while he was mending the shattered *Large Glass* at Dreier's home, Duchamp stuck the *stoppages* onto glass plates, and gathered everything into the wooden box. They should be seen horizontally rather than vertically, he said. The work was exhibited for the first

Fig. 87
Marcel Duchamp, *Tu m'*, 1918.
Oil on canvas, with bottlebrush, safety pins and bolt, 69.8 x 303 cm.
Gift of the Estate of Katherine S. Dreier.
Yale University Art Gallery, 1953.6.4

time at Alfred Barr's 'Fantastic Art, Dada, Surrealism', which opened at the Museum of Modern Art, New York, in December 1936, but it was not illustrated in the catalogue; a photograph was reproduced in the Surrealist journal *Minotaure* (1937), in which the work is seen among an array of strange and marvellous objects (fig. 88). The catalogue of the 1963 retrospective organised by Walter Hopps claimed, 'Today this manifestation of "canned chance" is the artist's favourite work.'[7]

3 Standard Stoppages is not just a playful intervention among the careful calculations of size, form and relationships for the Bachelor Apparatus in the lower half of *The Large Glass*, but a challenge to the whole apparently carefully calculated system of measurements and perspective, casting doubt on it by introducing chance. Duchamp's interest in chance anticipated that of the Dadaists, for whom it was a favourite strategy for renewing creativity as well as a convenient way to deny rational ordering systems. But his approach was distinctive. The characteristics of chance – spontaneity, ephemerality and the abnegation of conscious control – are tempered, or trapped, by his experiments, which acquire a personal character. *3 Standard Stoppages* was an experiment, he later commented, 'made in 1913 to imprison and preserve forms obtained through chance, through my chance'.[8] They not only disrupt the notion of rational measurement, but replace it with their own system: so the positions of the Nine Malic Moulds, the Bachelors, on *The Large Glass*, which had previously been calculated according to conventional geometrical models, such as rectangles, parallelepipeds, and so on (fig. 89), are now positioned according to the chance forms of the *Stoppages*.

The randomly formed shapes of *3 Standard Stoppages* have a curious relationship with a technique for measuring awkward shapes, for instance the contours of parcels of land whose borders are not properly geometric. A precision instrument that Duchamp may well have known, manufactured at the time by the Société des Lunetiers and resembling a pen with a rolling nib, enables measurement of such wandering shapes that can then be translated into 'proper' measures.[9]

Duchamp used his 'invisibly mended etalons' or 'standard invisible mendings' to determine the positions of the Nine Malic Moulds in *The Large Glass* by means of what he called 'capillary tubes'. In the painting *Network of Stoppages* (cat. 134) the new 'measures of length' are seen in plan, each 'diminished metre' repeated three times, with numbered circles indicating the positions of the Malic Moulds. These positions are based on a measurement that is given – even if by chance – and thus become fixed points in a universe otherwise determined by perspectives – that is things seen from a particular viewpoint. The wooden slats did not, however, exist at the date of this painting, so another method – perhaps paper torn

or cut to follow the curved line – must have been adopted to transfer the shapes onto the canvas.

Network of Stoppages is the third composition on its canvas. The first, *Young Girl and Man in Spring* (fig. 14), was the largest painting, at over six feet, that Duchamp had yet made, and was exhibited at the 1911 Salon d'Automne. In 1913 he painted black strips down both sides of the canvas to replicate the proportions of the planned *Large Glass*, and made a half-scale drawing of that work. The final painting, now horizontal, almost obliterates both. In appearance almost abstract, differing from both the precise style of technical representation of such works as *The Chocolate Grinder* (1914) or the plans for *The Large Glass* and from the Cubist inventions of *Bride* (fig. 82), it uncannily resembles diagrams of circuits from a much later form of technology.

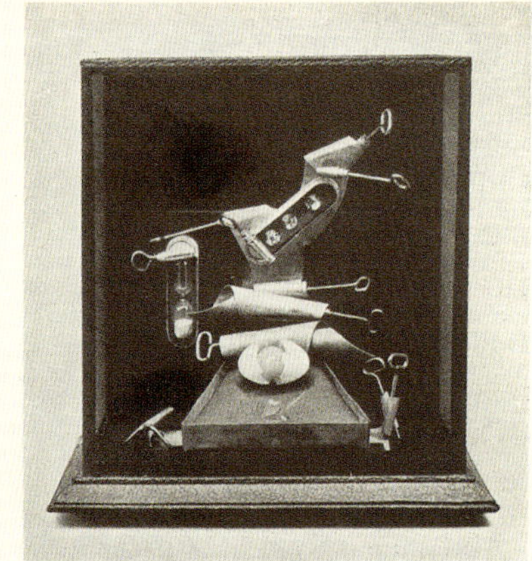

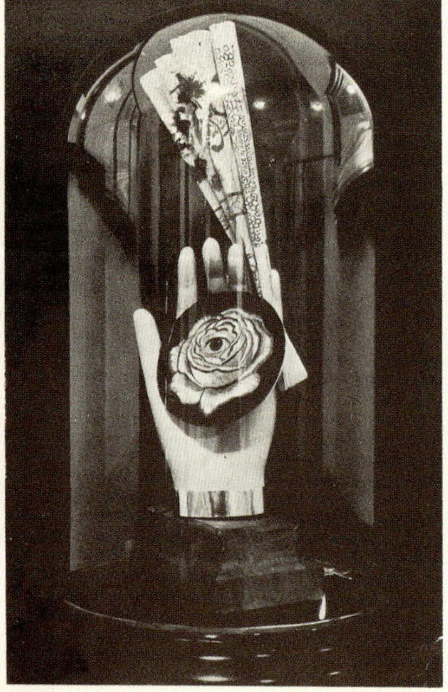

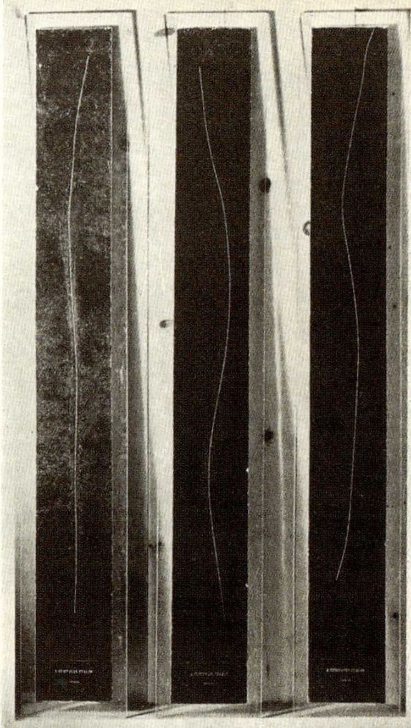

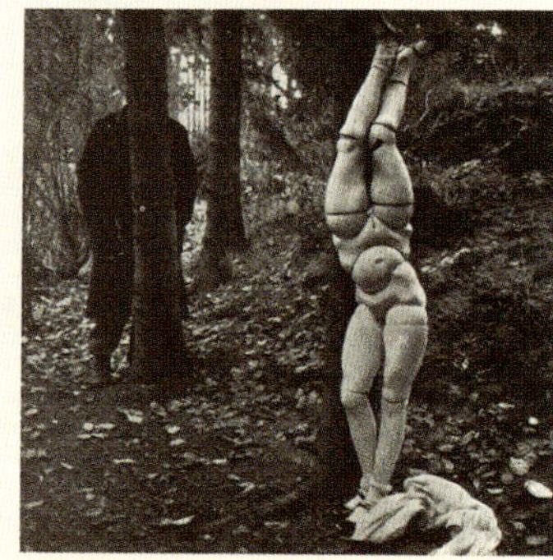

Fig. 88
Page from *Minotaure*, no. 10, Winter 1937. *3 Standard Stoppages* is shown top-right

Although it was never so directly implicated in the material character of Dalí's work, measurement quite literally pervades both his painting and his writing at a crucial period. In 'St Sebastian', a text published in 1927 that emerged from a dialogue with Federico García Lorca, Dalí elaborated what he called an 'aesthetics of objectivity', in which he conjured up a dream landscape littered with instruments and apparatuses indicating 'a new scale of precisions for unsuspected normalities'. One of these apparatuses was related to astronomy: the 'Heliometer for Deaf Mutes … an instrument of high physical poetry formed by distances and by the relations of those distances and those relations … expressed geometrically in some parts and arithmetically in others. In the centre,

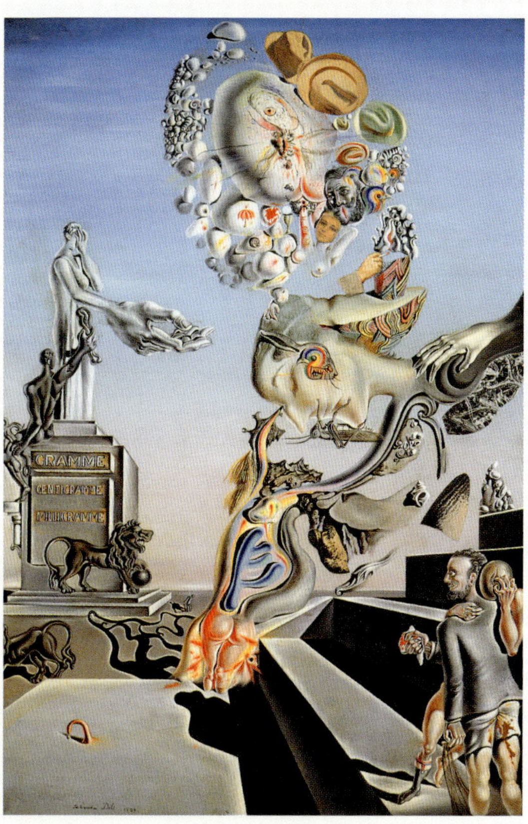

Unhappy Readymade. There is a stony, or perhaps crystalline, character to Dalí's aesthetics of objectivity; a highly personal resistance to the sentimental art-lover and to the art this 'putrefact'[11] loves, as well as to self-indulgent personal expression. His aesthetics of objectivity are a form of anti-art. Phrases from 'St Sebastian' illuminate such paintings as *Apparatus and Hand* (1927; Dalí Museum, St Petersburg, Florida): 'the exact instruments of an unknown physics were projecting their explicative shadows, and offered their crystals and aluminiums to the disinfected light.'[12] In *The Lugubrious Game* (fig. 90) the mammoth pedestal of the bisexual statue is inscribed 'Gramme, Centigramme, Milligramme' – but what exactly is being weighed and measured remains an enigma.

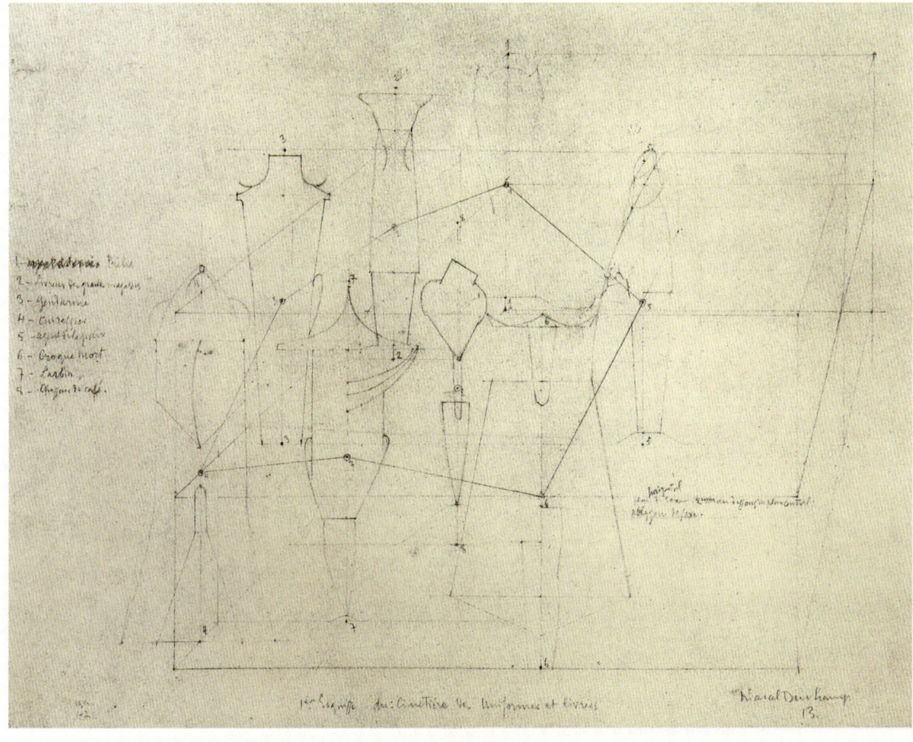

a simple gauge served to measure the agony of the saint. This mechanism was formed by a small dial of graduated plaster, in the centre of which a scarlet drop of coagulated blood, trapped between two slides of glass, served as a sensible barometer of each new wound.'[10] The notion of a scientific instrument, seemingly related both to the telescope and the microscope, whose purpose is to measure pain, is revealing concerning Dalí's notion of objectivity, and anticipates his Surrealist objects. This is not the rationalised order and measurement of Purism, admiring as Dalí was of Le Corbusier at the time, but an irrational and deliberately wayward invocation of the rational orders of physics and astronomy. In its yoking together of categories different in kind – science and martyrdom, precision instruments and suffering – there is some similarity with Duchamp's

Fig. 89
Marcel Duchamp, *Cemetery of Uniforms and Liveries* (1913; pencil on paper, 23.9 x 30.9 cm). Collotype 1940 produced for *Boîte-en-valise*, Series C (1958, cat. 62).
Collection Hummel, Vienna

Fig. 90
Salvador Dalí, *The Lugubrious Game*, 1929. Oil and collage on cardboard, 44.4 x 30.3 cm.
Private collection

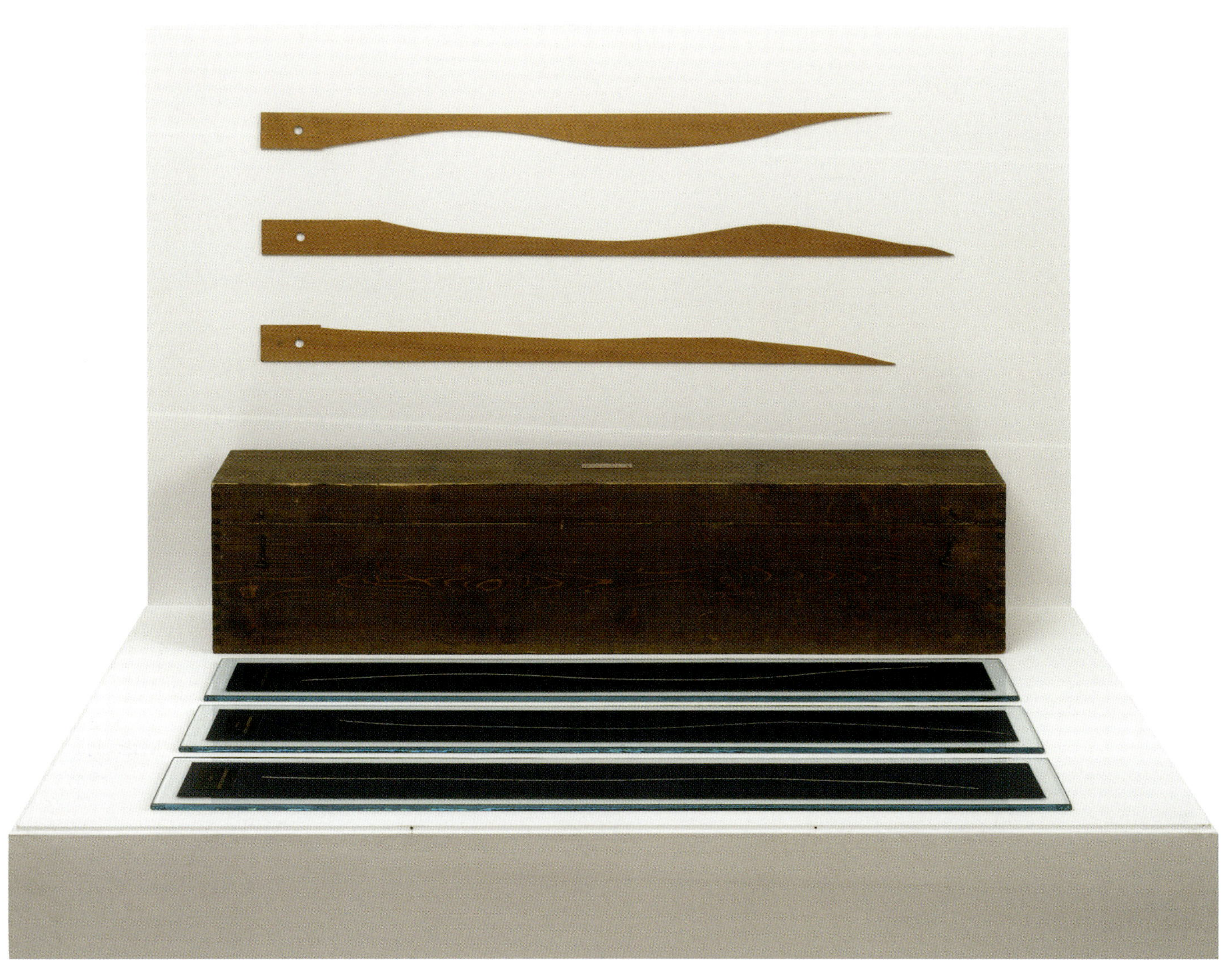

133
Marcel Duchamp
3 Standard Stoppages (*3 Stoppages étalons*), 1913–14 (1964 edition)
Wood, glass and paint on canvas,
40 x 130 x 90 cm
Tate: Purchased 1999

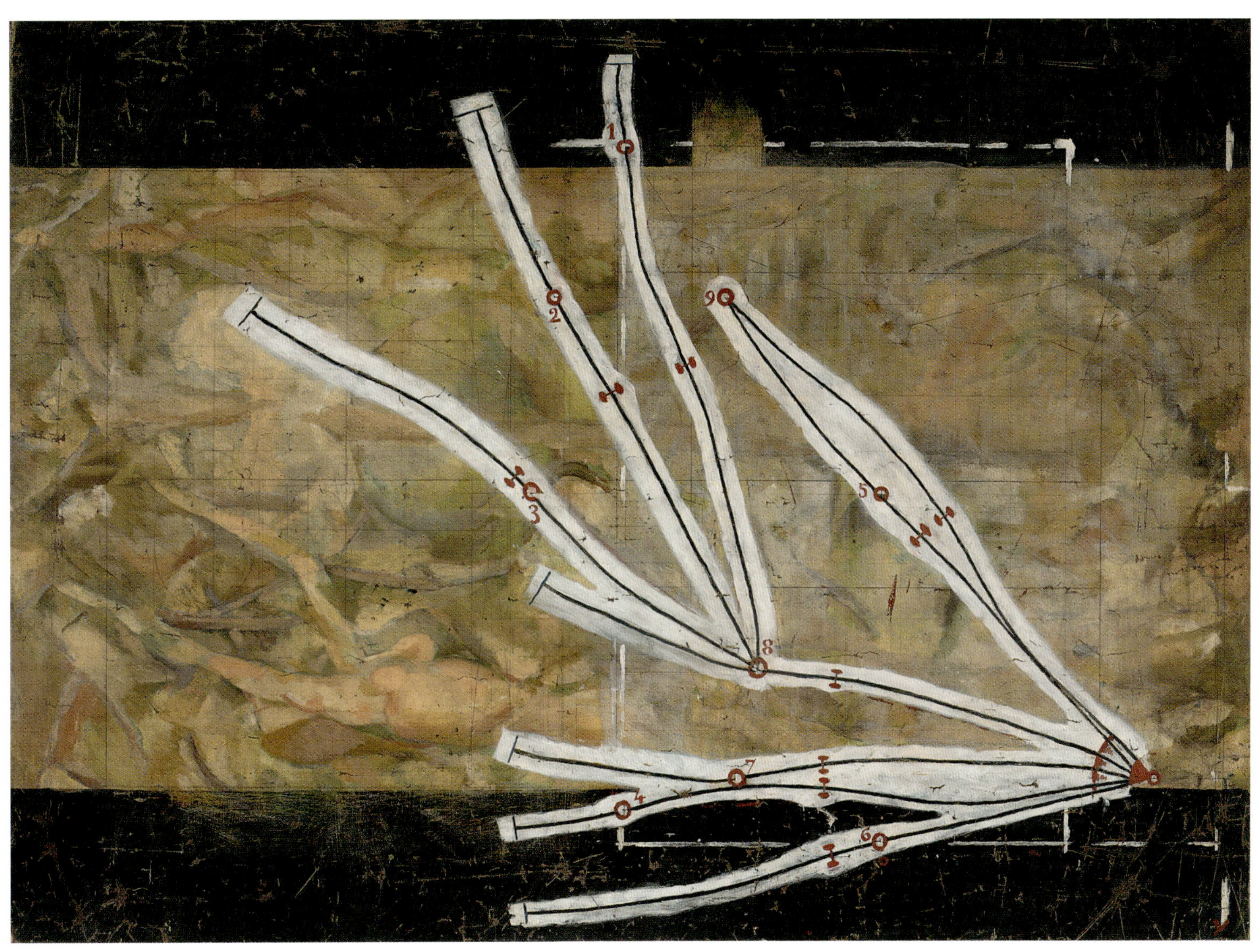

134
Marcel Duchamp
Network of Stoppages, 1914
Oil and pencil on canvas, 148.9 x 197.7 cm
The Museum of Modern Art, New York.
Abby Aldrich Rockefeller Fund and gifts
of Mrs William Sisler, 1970
London only

OPTICAL ILLUSIONS
DAWN ADES

Concurrently with their fascination with projecting or depicting the invisible, both Duchamp and Dalí pursued what seem to be the exact opposite: the ambiguities of perception and the powers of optical illusion – a paradox at the heart of their practices. Duchamp famously rejected what he called the 'retinal', the *frisson retinien* (retinal frisson) that he claimed had dominated painting since Courbet. However, this dislike did not stop him from exploring optical effects in mobile devices, stereoscopy and anaglyphs. These experiments were connected to his interest in film and photography as well as to his longstanding researches in perspective and movement. In 1918 he made the *Handmade Stereopticon Slide* (fig. 91). In 1920 he constructed the first elaborate machine, *Rotary Glass Plates (Precision Optics)* (fig. 93), a three-dimensional construction with five rectangular glass plates diminishing in size painted with circular lines mounted on an axle, which give the illusion when spinning of concentric circles in a single plane. The second machine was the *Rotary Demisphere* of 1925, commissioned in 1924 by the French collector Jacques Doucet. This time, black eccentric circles, which give the appearance of a spiral, were painted on a white wooden demisphere mounted on a black velvet disk. When the disk revolves, the lines appear to advance and recede. Duchamp and Man Ray tried to add a further illusion of depth when they attempted to make a stereoscopic film of the turning machine, of which only a couple of

frames survived. The following year Duchamp, Man Ray and Marc Allégret completed the short film *Anémic cinéma*: nine disks bearing puns alternate with ten discs inscribed with eccentric circles, which appear to pulsate when rotating.

In 1935 he carried these experiments a stage further with the *Rotoreliefs*: six cardboard disks printed on both sides with colour lithographs, to be 'played' on a gramophone spinning at 33⅓ rpm (like a long-playing record) and to be seen from above. Some of the lithographs were again purely optical, others were images of various objects such as a 'Japanese fish' and a 'Chinese lantern', which when turning appear to be 'real objects', i.e. three-dimensional. Duchamp hired a stand at the Concours Lépine, the inventors' fair in Paris, in September – October 1935 to market his *Rotoreliefs*, of which he had made an edition of 500, but he failed to sell any. Visitors in search of the useful showed no interest, Henri-Pierre Roché reported, and Duchamp with perfect good humour said, 'Error, one hundred per cent. At least it's clear.'[1] However, specialists in optics did take notice of his experiments.

Dalí, too, was fascinated by optical effects and the links between eye and brain, which he investigated in his paranoiac-critical method. In the 1970s, after Duchamp's death, he made numerous experiments in stereoscopy, producing pairs of canvases, sometimes on a very large scale, which when viewed together, using mirrors or special spectacles, merge to create the illusion of a three-dimensional image (cat. 135).

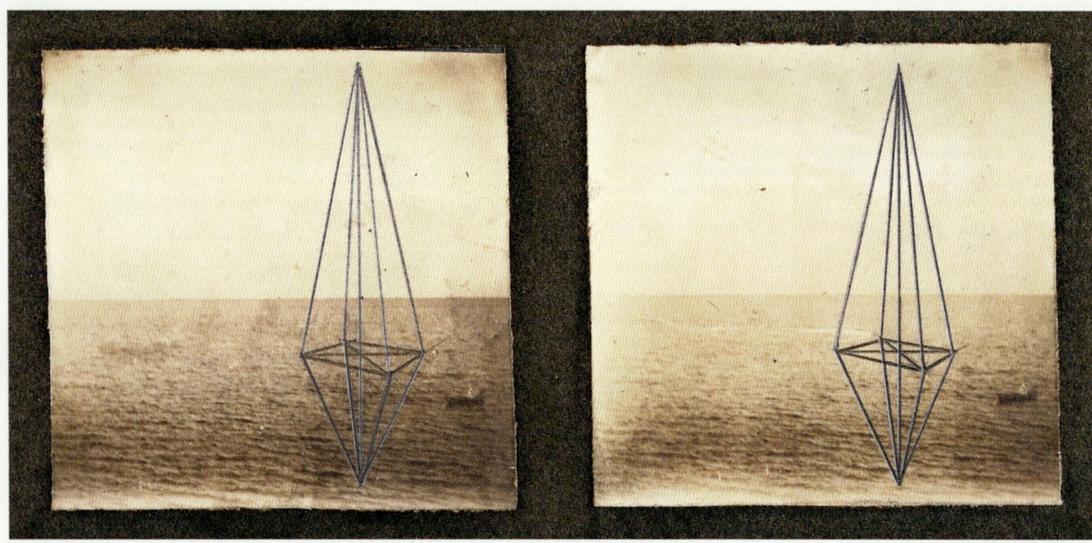

Fig. 91
Marcel Duchamp, *Handmade Stereopticon Slide*, 1918–19. Pencil on gelatin silver prints mounted on black-paper-surfaced board, 6.8 x 17.2 cm. Museum of Modern Art (MoMA), New York. Katherine S. Dreier Bequest. Inv. 152.195

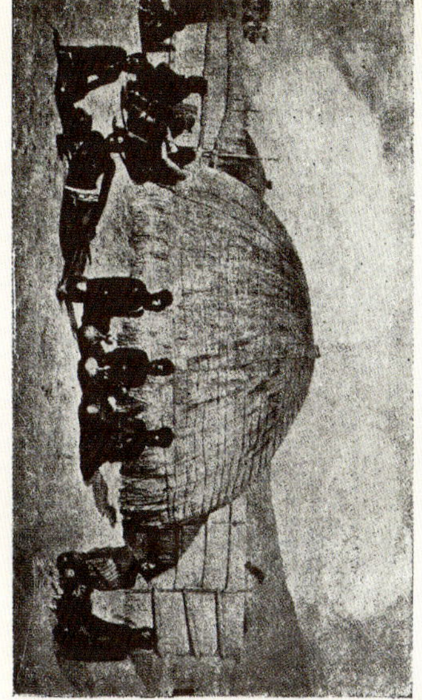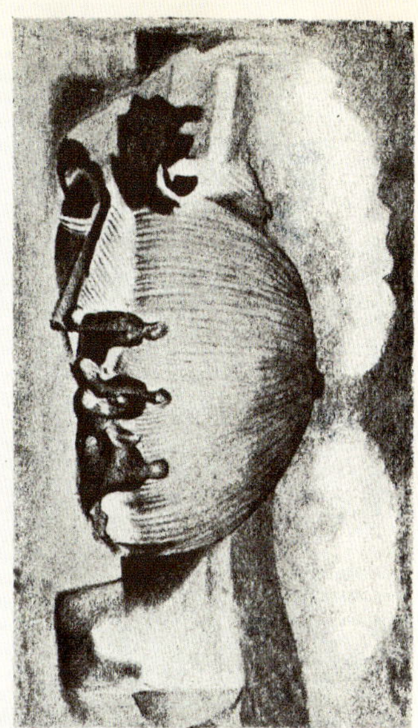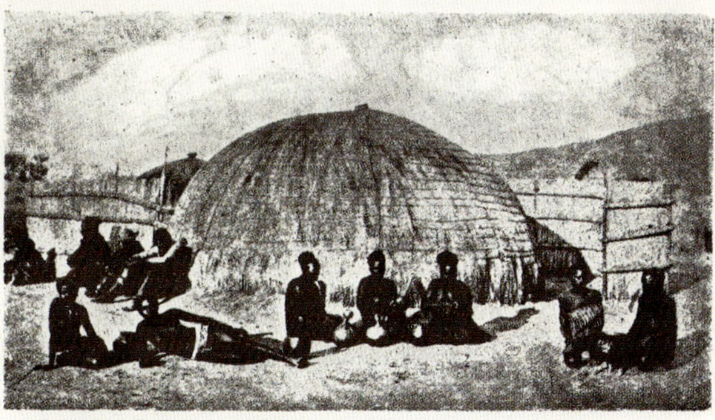

COMMUNICATION : Visage paranoïaque.

A la suite d'une étude, au cours de laquelle m'avait obsédé une longue réflexion sur les visages de Picasso et particulièrement ceux de l'époque noire, je cherche une adresse dans un tas de papiers et suis soudain frappé par la reproduction d'un visage que je crois de Picasso, visage absolument inconnu.

Tout à coup, ce visage s'efface et je me rends compte de l'illusion (?) L'analyse de l'image paranoïaque en question me vaut de retrouver, par une interprétation symbolique, toutes les idées qui avaient précédé la vision du visage.

André Breton avait interprété ce visage comme étant celui de Sade, ce qui correspondait à une toute particulière préoccupation de Breton quant à Sade.

Dans les cheveux du visage en question Breton voyait une perruque poudrée, alors que moi je voyais un fragment de toile non peinte, comme il est fréquent dans le style picassien.

Salvador DALI

Fig. 92
Salvador Dalí, 'Communication: Paranoiac Face', in *Le Surréalisme au service de la révolution (SASDLR)*, no. 3, December 1931

One of the etchings in *Ten Recipes for Immortality* (cat. 123) uses stereoscopic effects. Like Duchamp, Dalí had been intrigued as a child by optical machines like the zoetrope, and the popular stereoscopic devices, hand-held viewers in which pairs of photographs – like those used by Duchamp for his *Stereopticon Slide* – produce the illusion of a 'real scene'.

Dalí's interests in optics, perception and visuality brought his art into conjunction with science, but were also heavily influenced by psychology and his readings in psychoanalysis – subjects which did not interest Duchamp at all. Dalí described his paranoiac-critical method in texts published as *La Femme visible* in 1930, in which he emphasised it as an active process unlike the passivity, as he regarded it, of automatism: 'I believe the moment is at hand when by a paranoiac and active thought process it will be possible (simultaneously with automatism and other passive states) to systematise confusion and contribute to the total discredit of the real world.'[2] He based his idea on contemporary definitions of paranoia as a mental disturbance that involved interpreting the surrounding world according to an over-riding obsession, in a 'delirium of interpretation'.[3] He demonstrated the idea with 'Communication: Paranoiac Face' in *SASDLR*, 3, 1931 (fig. 92), and continued to refine the translation of such 'mis-readings' into his paintings. His double images are the visual equivalent of the Duchamp/Rrose Sélavy puns: the act of pronouncing the words with more than one meaning is like reading more than one image in a single configuration. *Apparition of Face and Fruit Dish on a Beach* (cat. 136) is one of the most complex of Dalí's paintings. In the foreground to the left is a kind of key, a form used by scientists testing the nature of perception: the object reads either as the head of a rabbit or of a duck, but not both simultaneously. The painting as a whole is a masterpiece of illusion. The plane in the foreground functions like a table in a still-life but melds into the landscape background. The fruit dish of pears becomes the forehead but also part of the body of a dog, whose eyes are a tunnel through the rocks and whose collar is an aqueduct. Just below the dog's muzzle is a cavalry scene reminiscent of Leonardo da Vinci, whose advice to 'see' scenes in the stains and moss on an old wall as an exercise of the imagination was often recalled by Dalí.

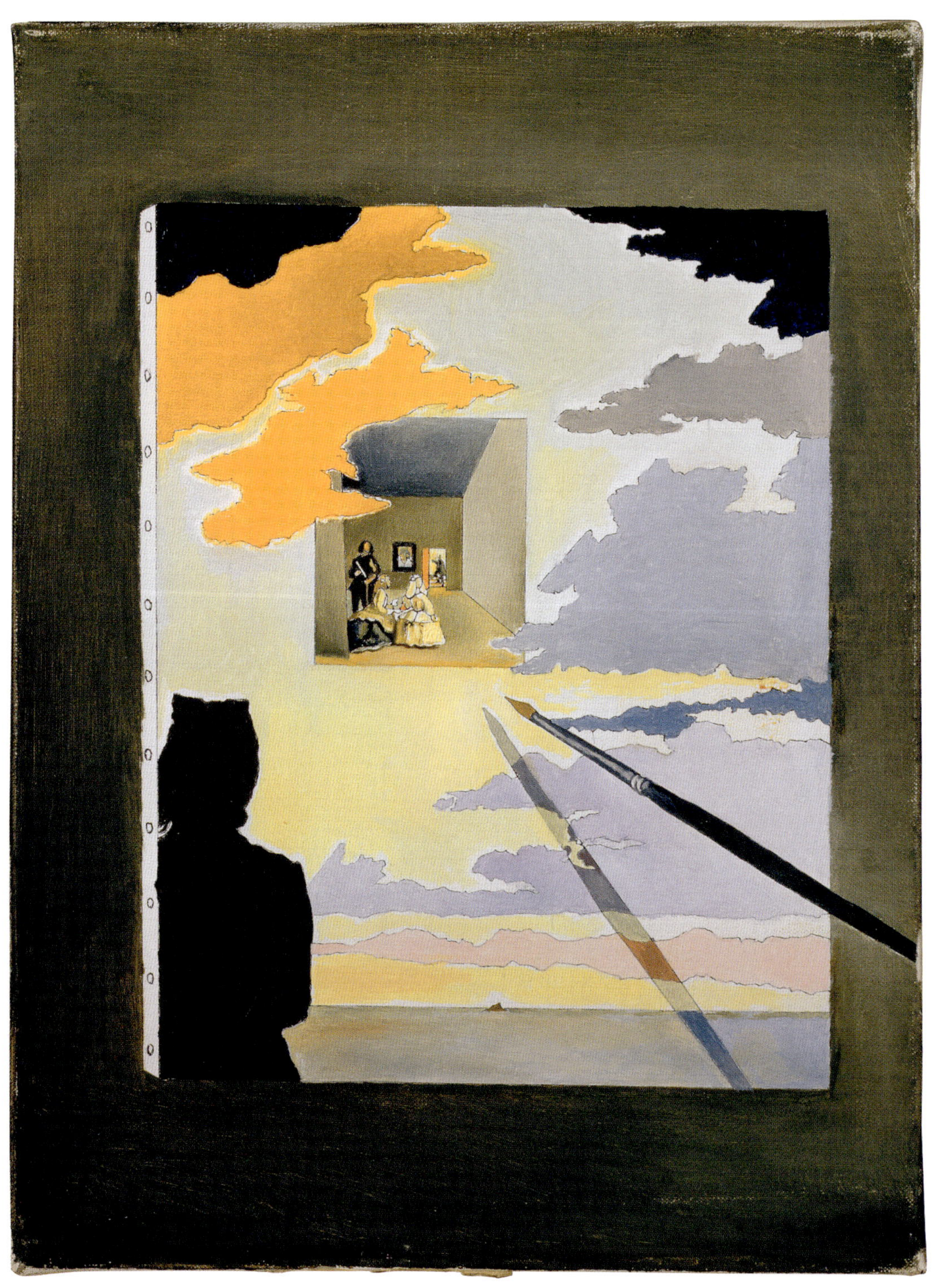

135
Salvador Dalí
Las Meninas, 1975–76
Stereoscopic work: oil on two canvases,
each 35.5 x 25 cm
Museo Nacional Centro de Arte Reina
Sofía, Madrid

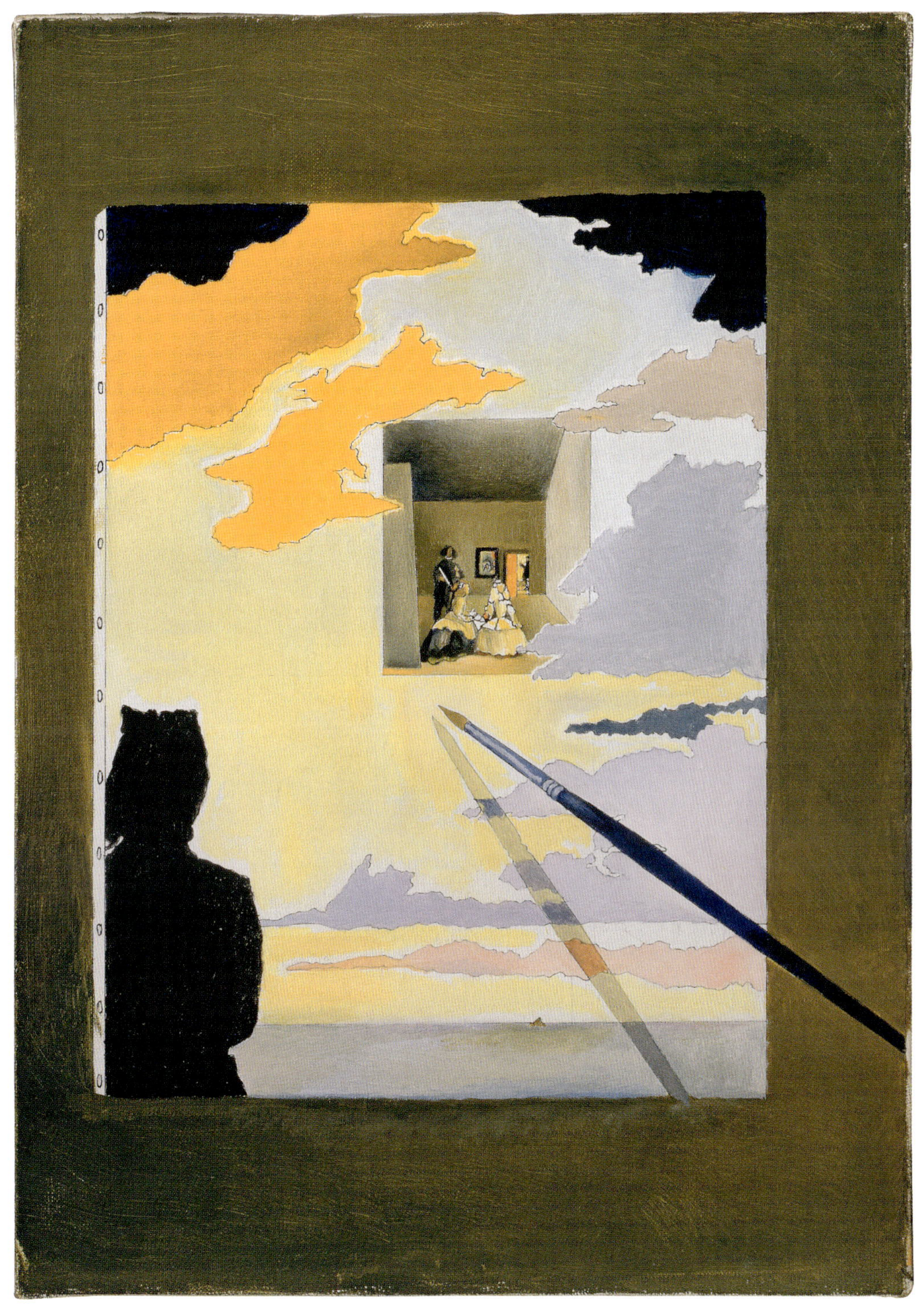

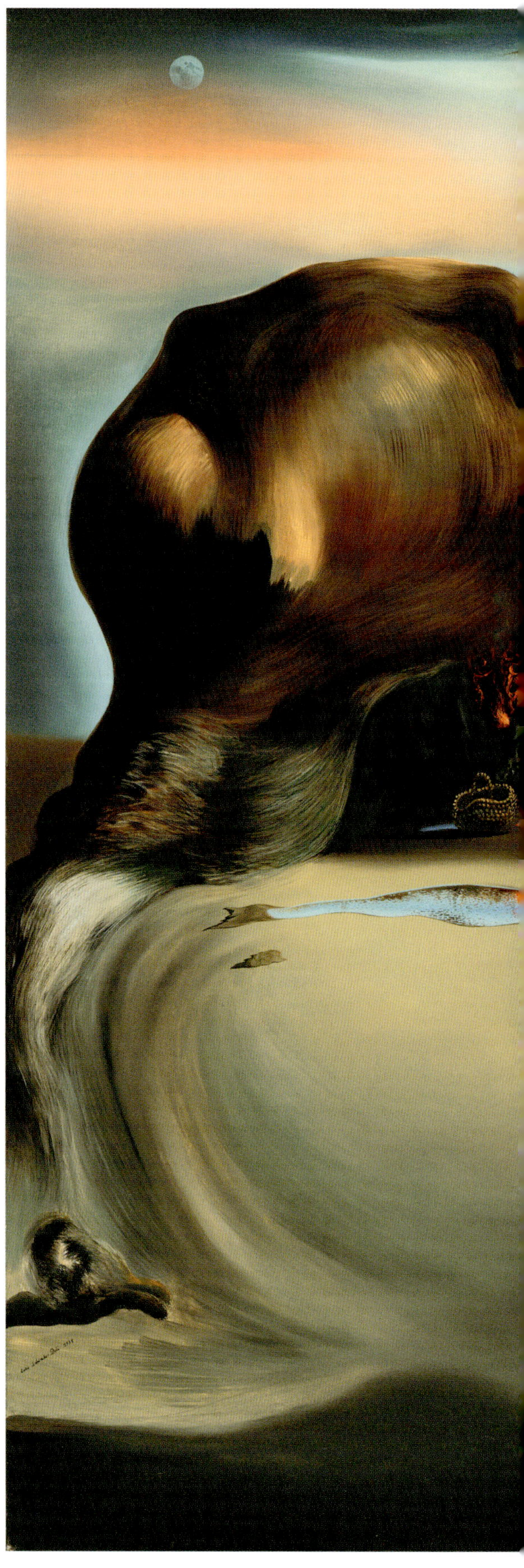

136
Salvador Dalí
*Apparition of Face and Fruit Dish
on a Beach*, 1938
Oil on canvas, 114.3 x 143.8 cm
Wadsworth Atheneum Museum of Art,
Hartford, CT. The Ella Gallup Sumner and
Mary Catlin Sumner Collection Fund

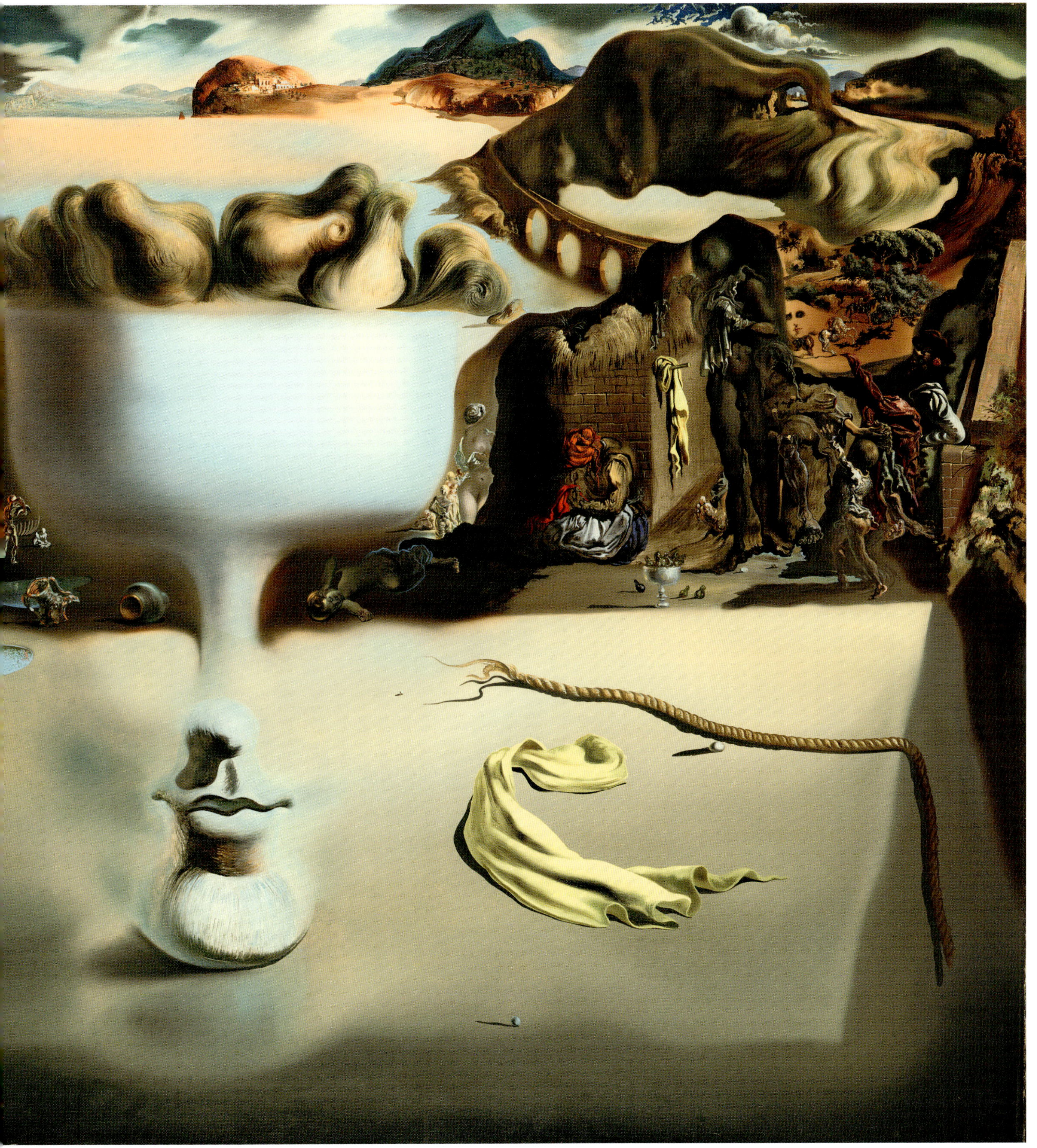

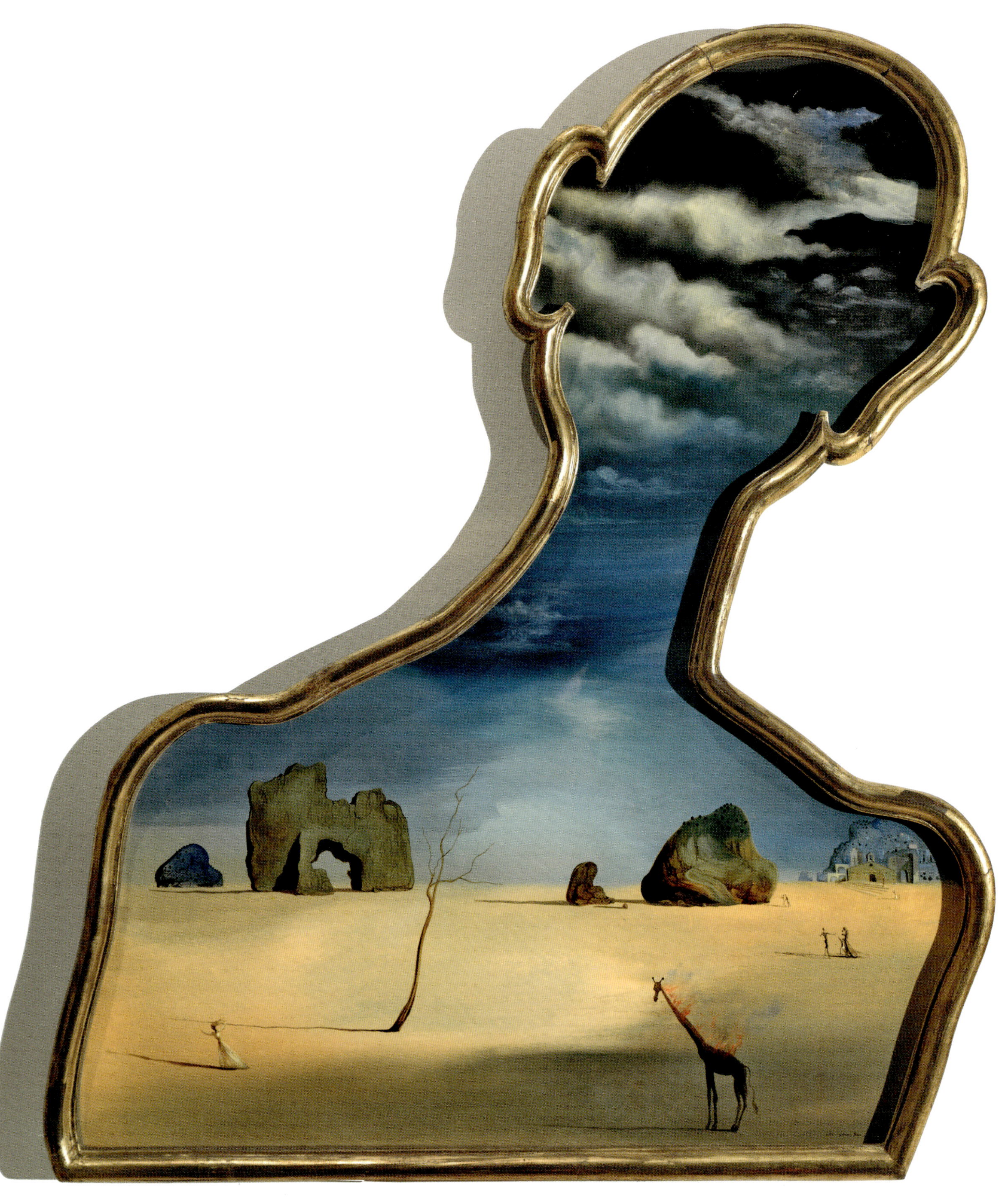

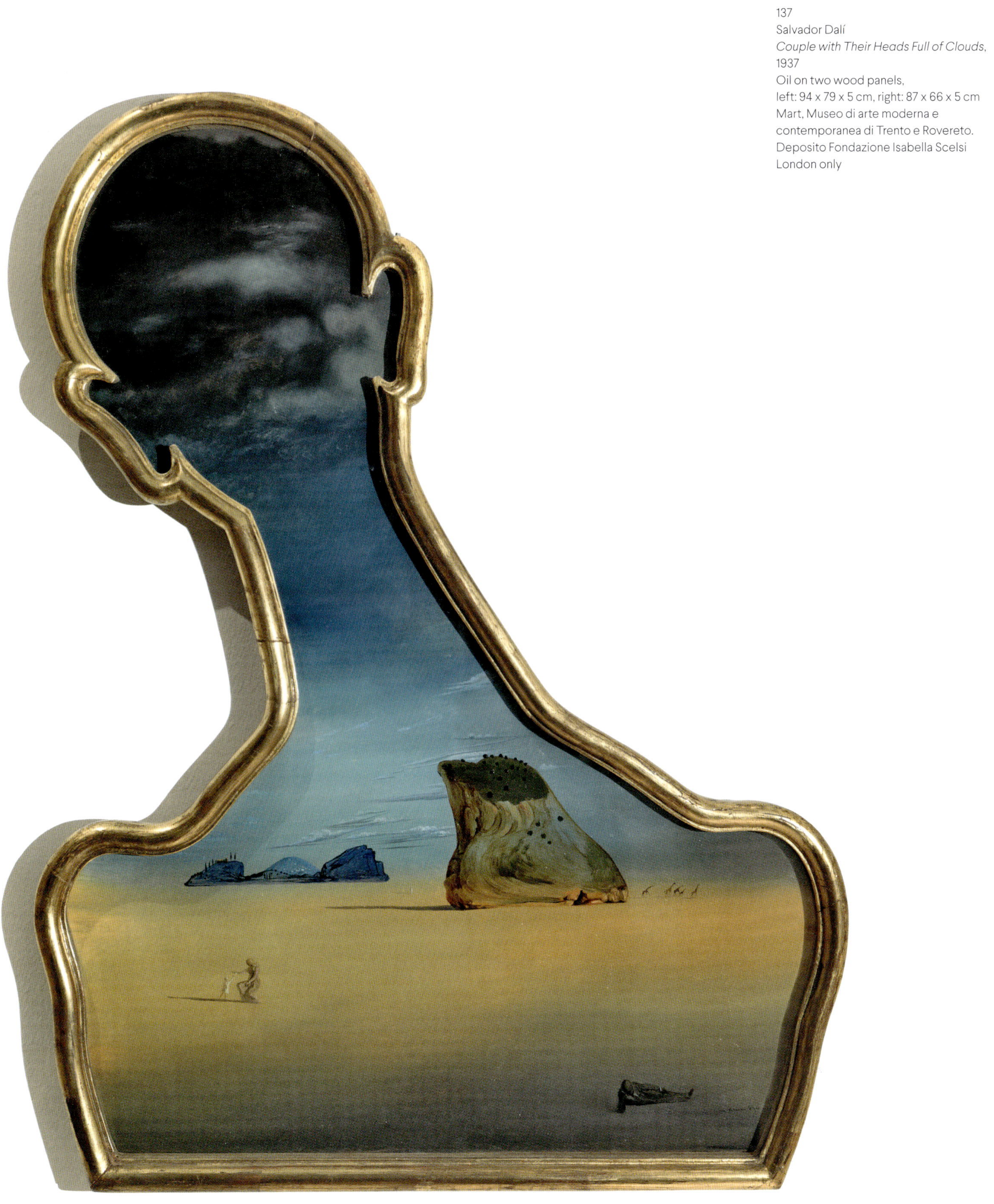

137
Salvador Dalí
Couple with Their Heads Full of Clouds,
1937
Oil on two wood panels,
left: 94 x 79 x 5 cm, right: 87 x 66 x 5 cm
Mart, Museo di arte moderna e
contemporanea di Trento e Rovereto.
Deposito Fondazione Isabella Scelsi
London only

WE DON'T EAR IT THAT WAY

Une exposition internationale du surréalisme se tient actuellement à New-York, galeries d'Arcy. Un événement aussi fâcheux qu'imprévisible en a marqué le vernissage. Nous apprenons en effet, de source indirecte, que Salvador Dali en personne y a été reçu avec les égards dus à un invité de marque. Ceci a été rendu possible par l'intrusion, parmi les toiles de l'exposition, d'une "Madone" (*) de sa façon sulpicienne, de dimensions considérables et d'exécution récente, qui ne pouvait y figurer à aucun titre.

Seul des quatre organisateurs : Marcel Duchamp, André Breton, Edouard Jaguer et José Pierre, le premier se trouvait sur place, fondé à prendre toute décision de dernière heure. Les trois autres ignorent à ce jour sous quelles pressions ou en raison de quelles considérations stratégiques il a pu se déterminer à faire à Dali, dans une entreprise qui nous est commune, cette part exorbitante.

Depuis longtemps nous honorons bien trop les ressources de son esprit pour lui faire l'outrage de penser qu'il ait pu, fût-ce un instant, être dupe de cette dialectique fallacieuse, selon laquelle c'est aujourd'hui le conformisme qui recèle le levain de la subversion.

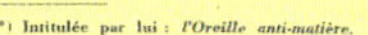

La conjoncture politique en France, dans ces premiers jours de décembre 1960, nous oblige à ne pas différer d'un instant la présente protestation. Moins que jamais à nos yeux l'aventure esthétique et ses "à-côtés" scandaleux à bon compte ne sauraient se suffire à eux-mêmes. Alors qu'ici les intellectuels qualifiés luttent en pleine conscience pour défendre ce qui reste de liberté d'opinion et d'expression, nous nous devons de rappeler que Dali a été exclu du surréalisme il y a plus de vingt ans et que nous n'avons cessé de voir en lui l'ancien apologiste d'Hitler, au demeurant le peintre fasciste, clérical et raciste, ami du Franco qui ouvrit l'Espagne comme champ de manœuvres à la plus abominable barbarie qui fut jamais.

An international exhibition of surrealism is now being held in New York at the D'Arcy Galleries. Its opening has been marked by a very unexpected and annoying event: Salvador Dali's appearance on the premises, his formal introduction with respects due to a high-ranking guest, and, most of all, the deliberate intrusion, amongst the other exhibits, of a portentous *Madonna* (*), painted in his most clerical manner, and which its large dimensions, added to its recent execution, should have excluded from such a gathering.

Of the exhibition's four promoters (Marcel Duchamp, André Breton, Edouard Jaguer and José Pierre) only the first was present on the spot, and able to take any last-minute decision as befitted the incident. The last three still ignore, at this very minute, under which pressures, on wich strategical motives he could concede Dali, in such a collective demonstration, this exorbitant part.

We respect him too much, we have too long respected the resources of his mind to believe he could yield, were it a second, to such deceptive dialectics following which conformism should provide nowadays the only yeast of subversion.

France's present political climate in these very first day of December 1960, make it at once imperious for us to issue this protest. Never less than now have the aesthetical adventure and its cheap, notorious *asides* appeared self-sufficient. At the particular moment when qualified intellectuals are consciously fighting for the defense of whatever freedom for thought and expression as is yet left to them, we remind everyone concerned that Salvador Dali, more than twenty years ago, was expelled from surrealism. More than ever do we see in this man, Hitler's former apologist, the fascist painter, the religious bigot, and the avowed racist, friend of Franco, who opened Spain as a drill-ground for the most abominable surge of barbary the world has yet endured.

(*) Intitulée par lui : *l'Oreille anti-matière.*

(*) Entitled by him: *The anti-matter ear.*

Robert BENAYOUN, Jean BENOIT, Guido BIASI, Vincent BOUNOURE, André BRETON, CORNEILLE, Adrien DAX, Gianni DOVA, Yves ELLEOUET, Roland GIGUÈRE, Radovan IVSIC, Edouard JAGUER, Alain JOUBERT, Jacques LACOMBLEZ, Juan LANGLOIS, Gérard LEGRAND, Julio LLINAS, E.L.T. MESENS, Mimi PARENT, José PIERRE, Carl-Fredrik REUTERSWÄRD, Jean SCHUSTER, Claude TARNAUD, Jean THIERCELIN, TOYEN.

Il a été tiré vingt-cinq exemplaires sur papier couché vert d'eau, adornés de quelques poils de la Vraye Moustache.

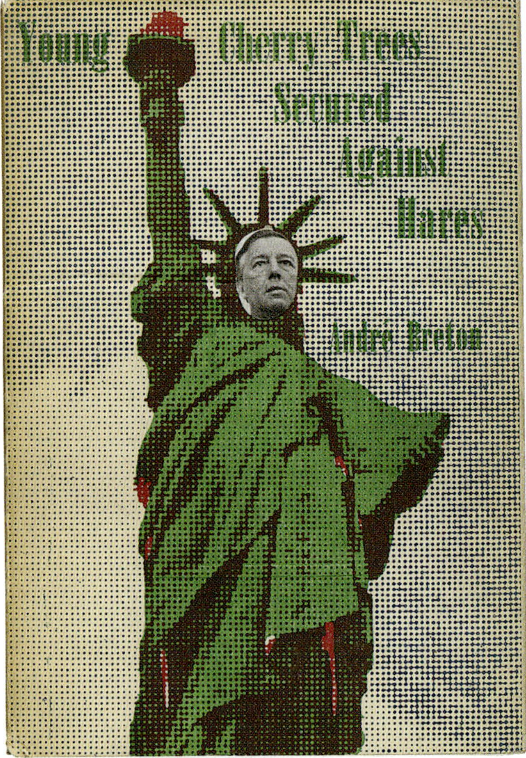

138
Robert Benayoun
'We Don't Ear It that Way', Surrealist
Manifesto, 1960
Printed ink on paper, 29.9 x 24 cm
Collection of The Dalí Museum Archives,
St Petersburg, Florida

139
'Young Cherry Trees Secured Against
Hares', text by André Breton, cover by
Marcel Duchamp, 1946
Book, 23.6 x 16 cm
Collection of The Dalí Museum Archives,
St Petersburg, Florida

Opposite: 140
Salvador Dalí
Madonna, 1958
Oil on canvas, 225.7 x 191.1 cm
Lent by The Metropolitan Museum of Art.
Gift of Drue Heinz, in memory of Henry
J. Heinz II, 1987
London only

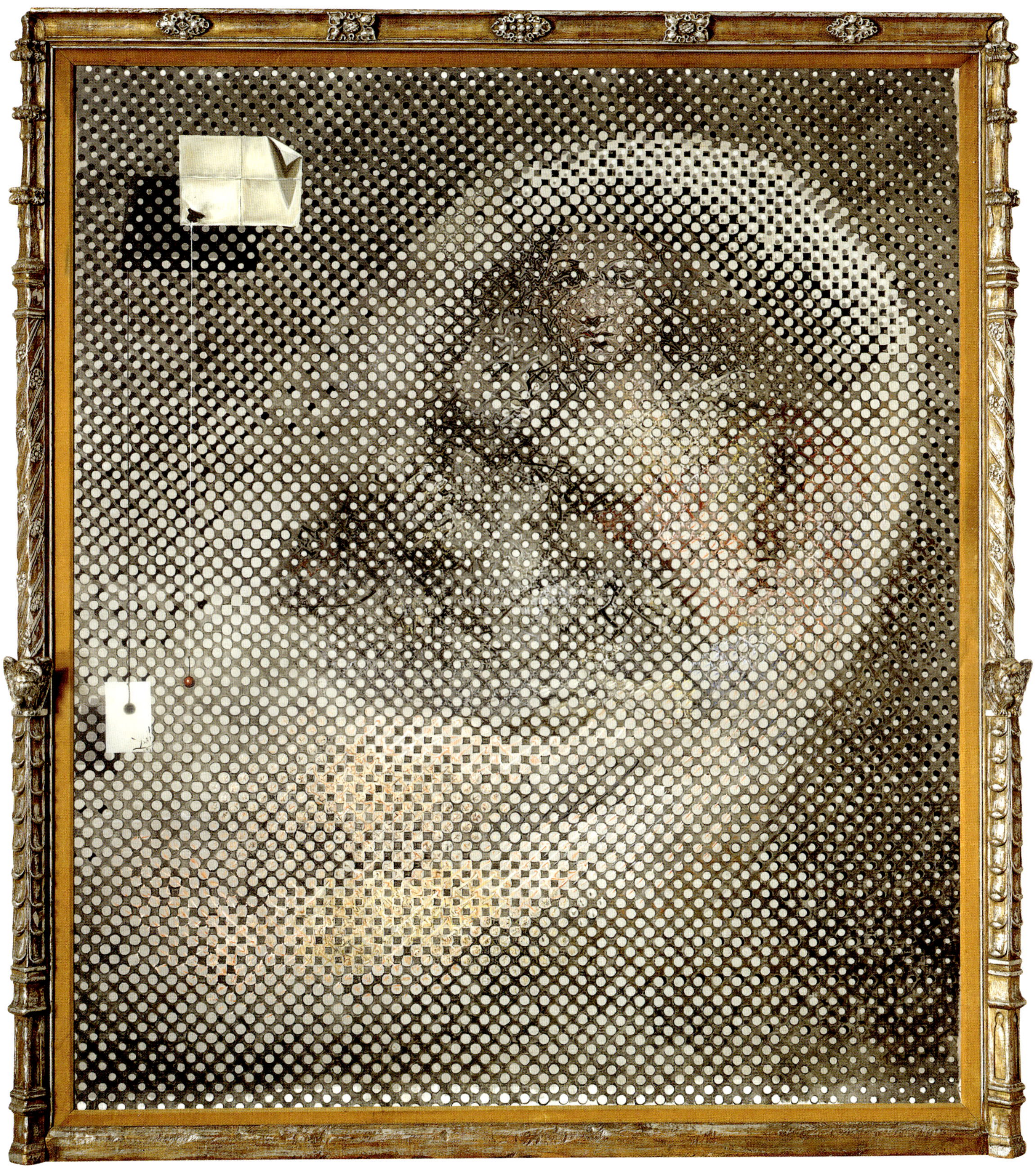

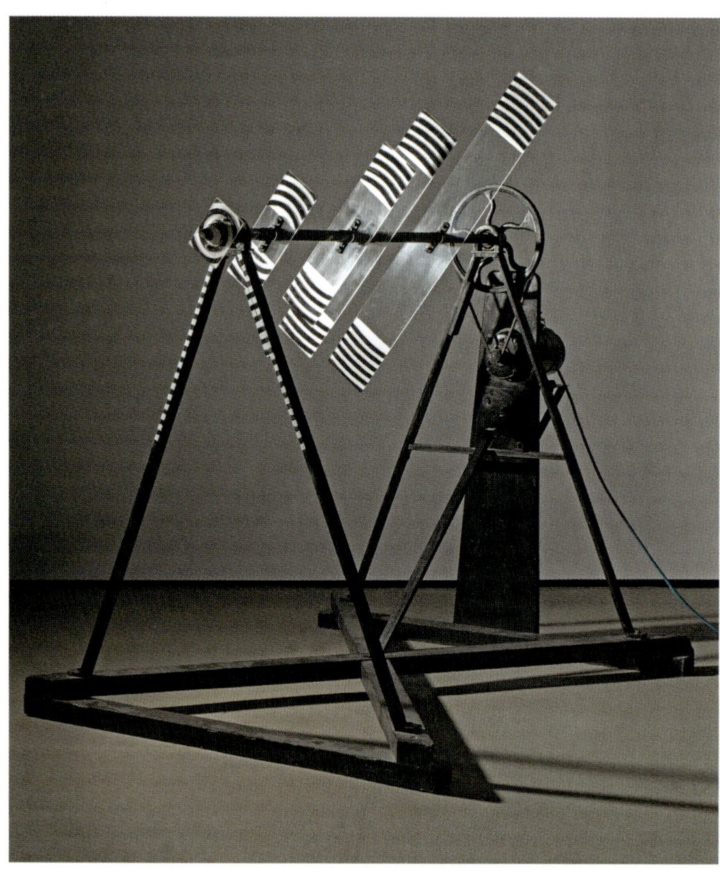

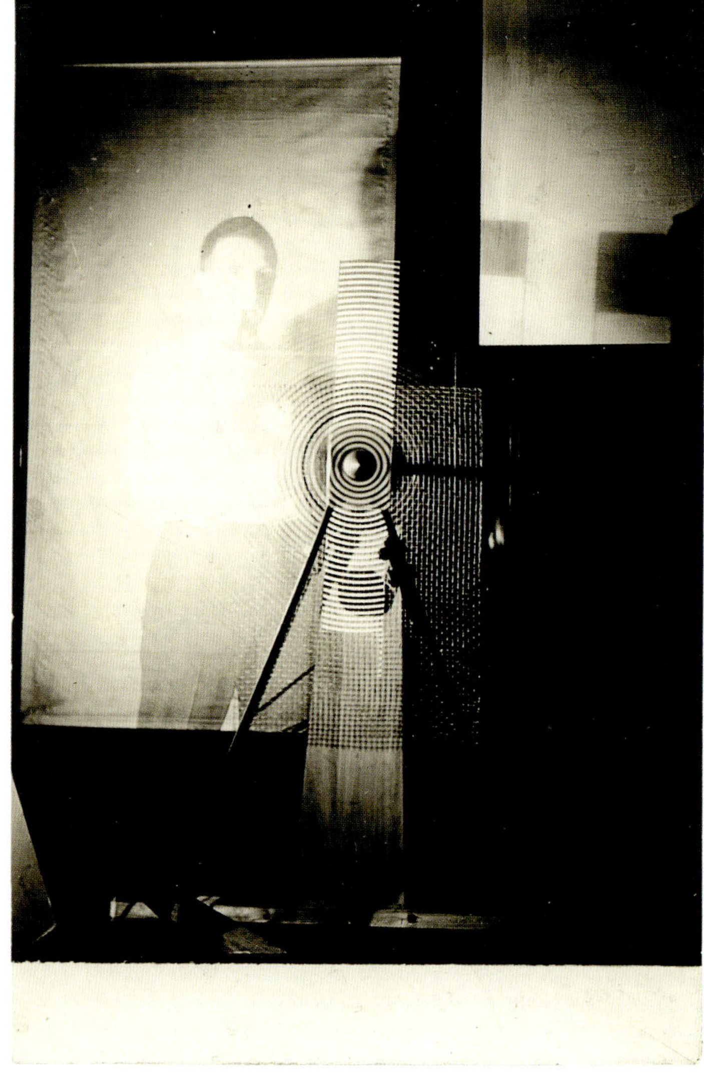

Above: fig. 93
Marcel Duchamp
Rotary Glass Plates, 1920 (1976 edition)
Plexiglas, paint, metal, wood,
electric motor, five plates of glass,
135 x 170 x 123 cm
Centre Pompidou, Paris. Musée national
d'art moderne/Centre de création
industrielle

141
Man Ray
*Duchamp behind the Rotary Glass
Plates*, 1920
Gelatin silver print, 8.7 x 13.6 cm
Private collection

Opposite: 142
Marcel Duchamp
Rotoreliefs (optical disks), 1935/1959,
(edition MAT, no. 21/100)
Printed cardboard, electric motor,
velvet, wire (steel), electric wire on
wood panel, d. 20 cm
Private collection

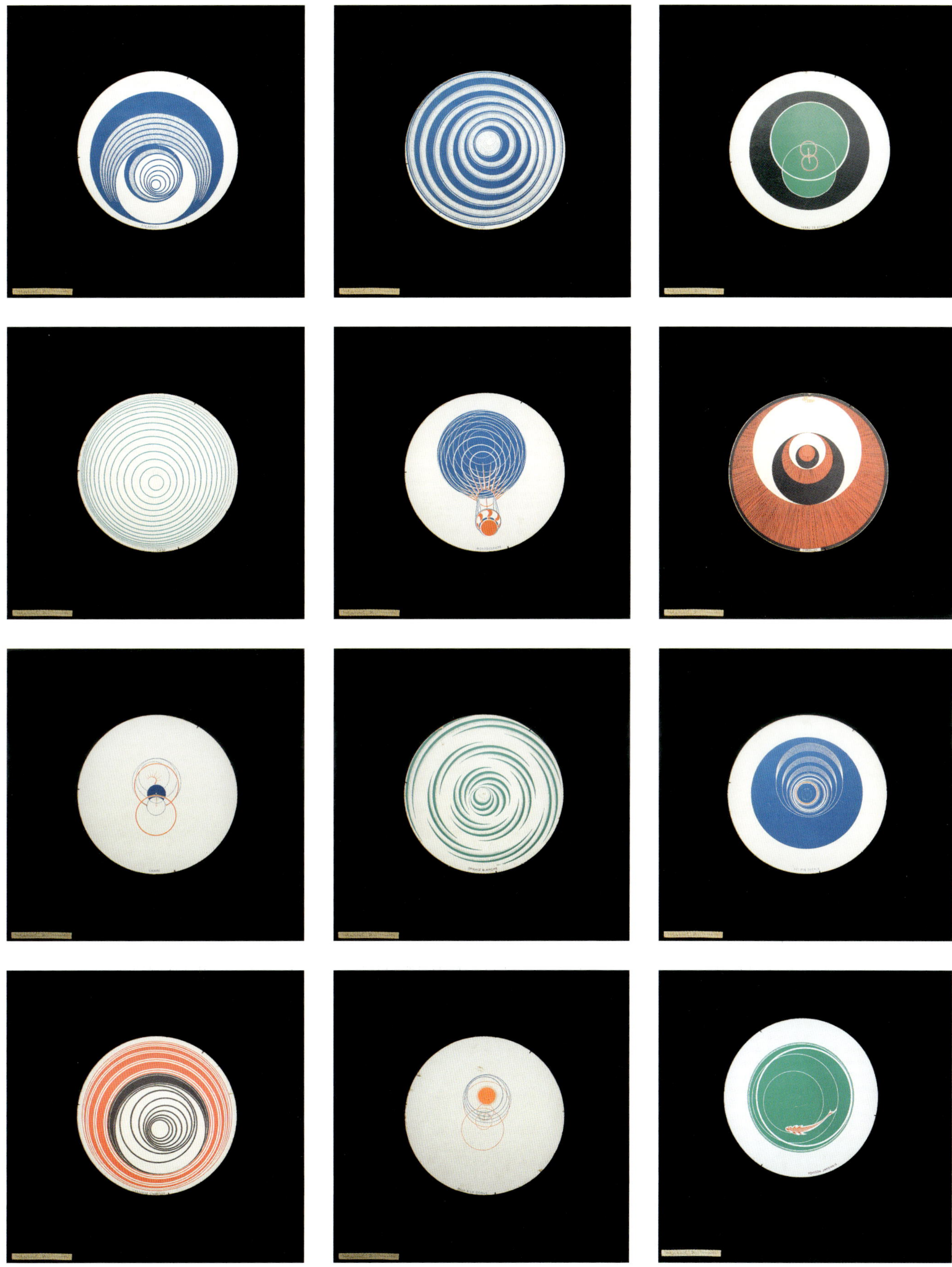

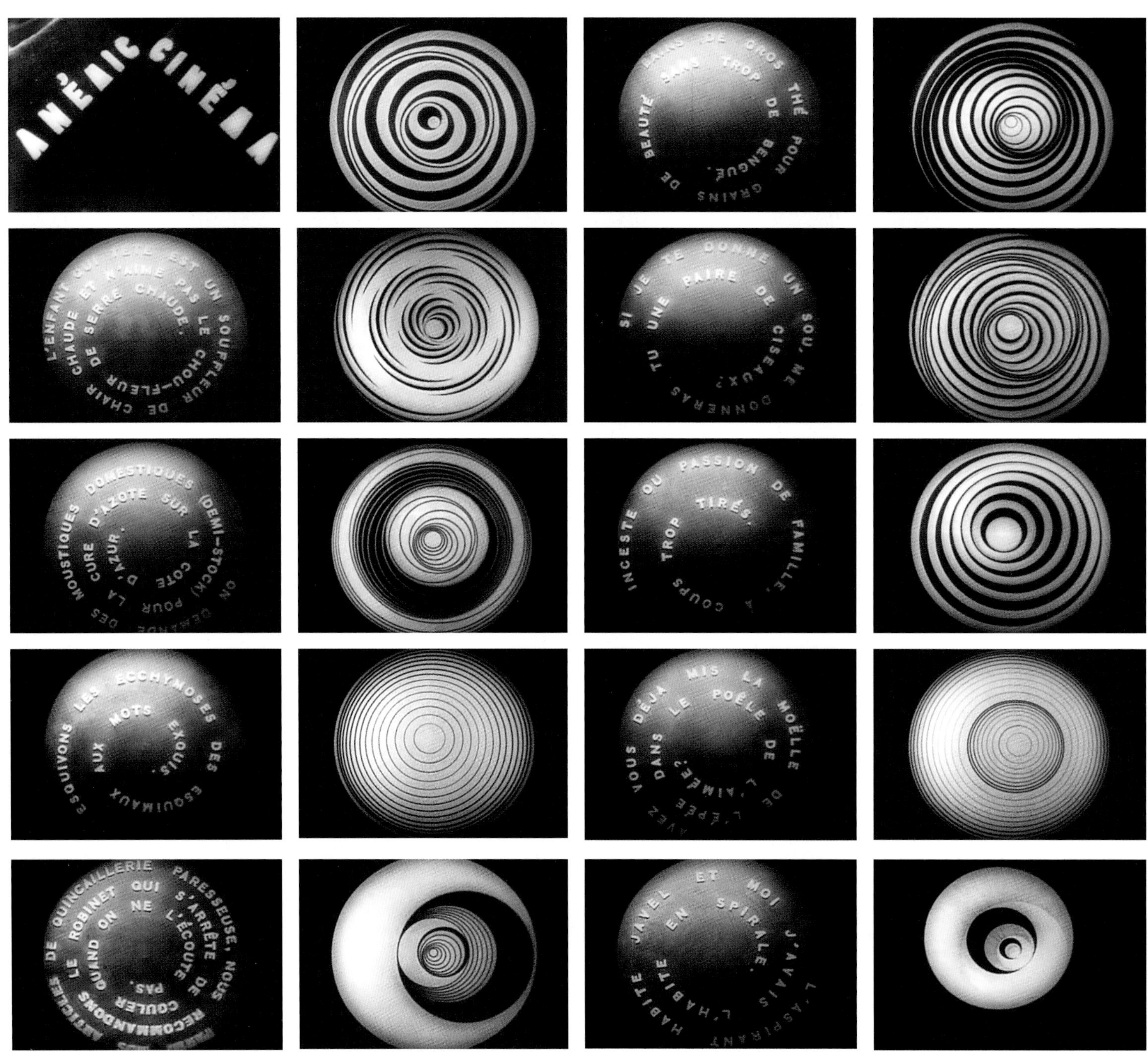

143
Marcel Duchamp (in collaboration
with Man Ray and Marc Allégret)
Anémic cinéma, 1926 (individual frames)
Digital transfer film, 7 minutes
Cinedoc Paris Films Coop, Paris

144
Salvador Dalí in front of one of the sets
for the film *Spellbound*, 1945
(Photographer unknown)
Harry Ransom Humanities Research
Center, University of Texas, Austin. David
O. Selznick Collection (box. 4538.6)

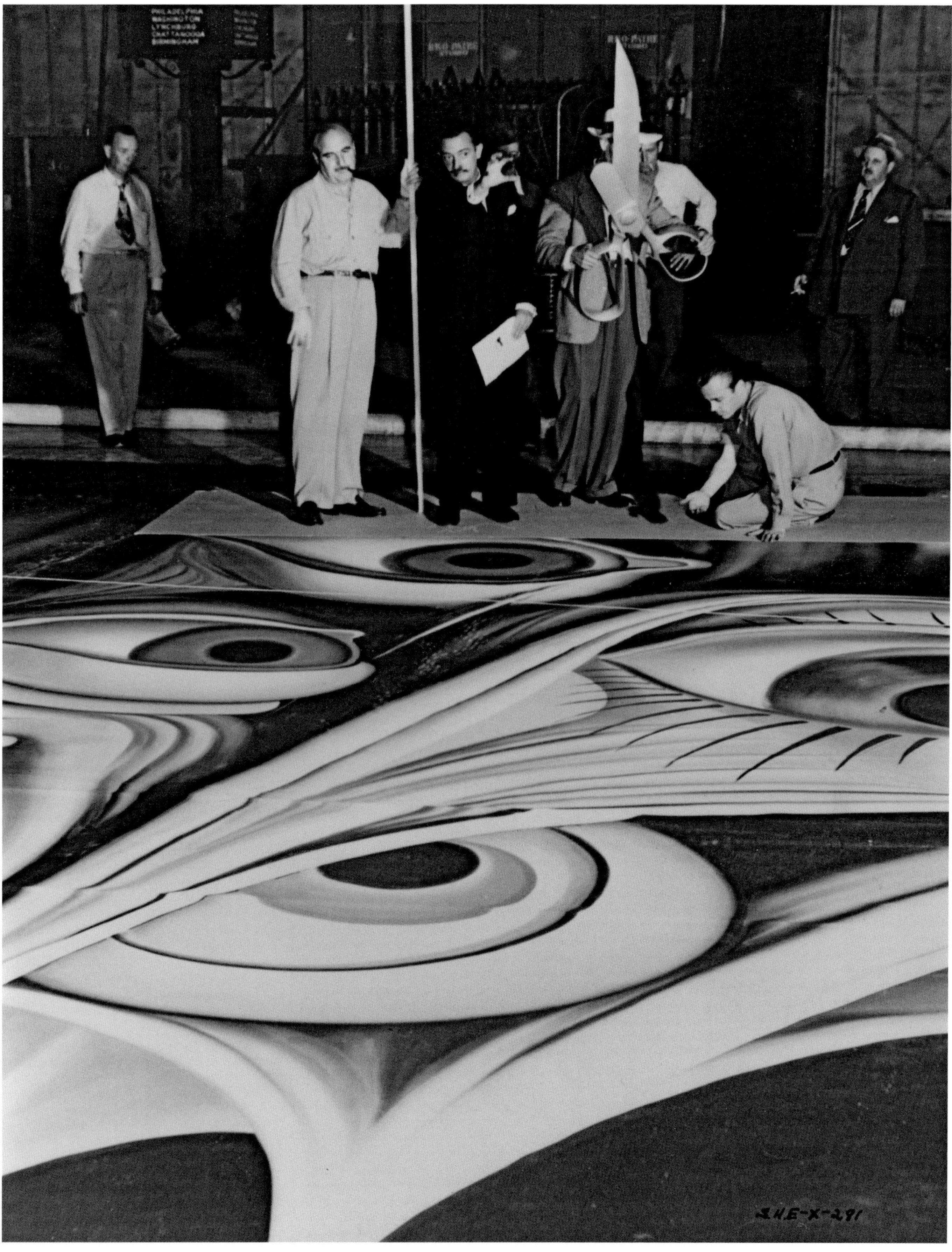
PHILADELPHIA
WASHINGTON
LYNCHBURG
CHATTANOOGA
BIRMINGHAM

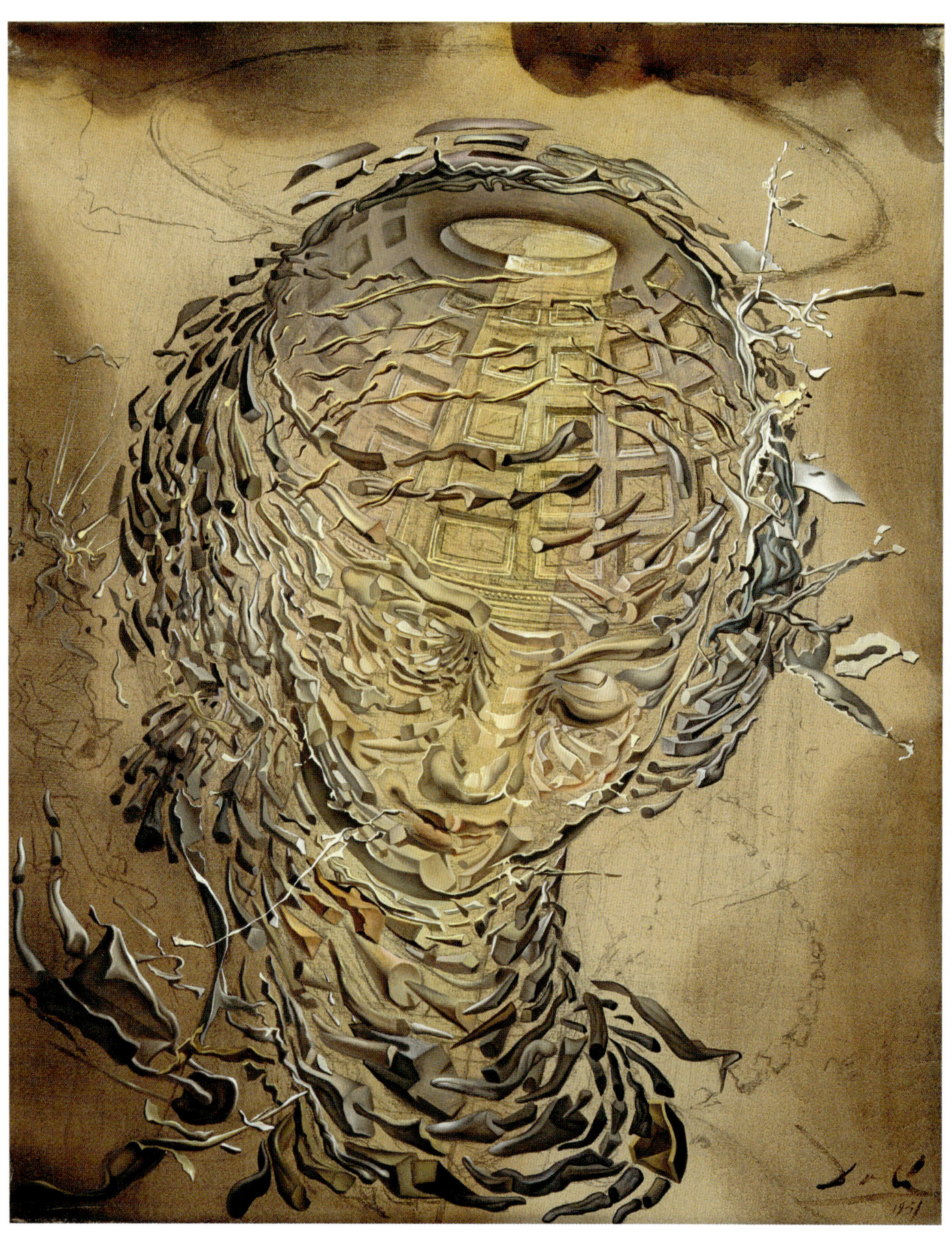

145
Salvador Dalí
Exploding Raphaelesque Head, 1951
Oil on canvas, 43.2 x 33.1 cm
National Galleries of Scotland.
Private collection

146
Salvador Dalí
Skull, 1972
Anamorphic object: coloured lithograph
and reflective cylinder, 25.4 x 8.9 cm
Collection of The Dalí Museum,
St Petersburg, Florida

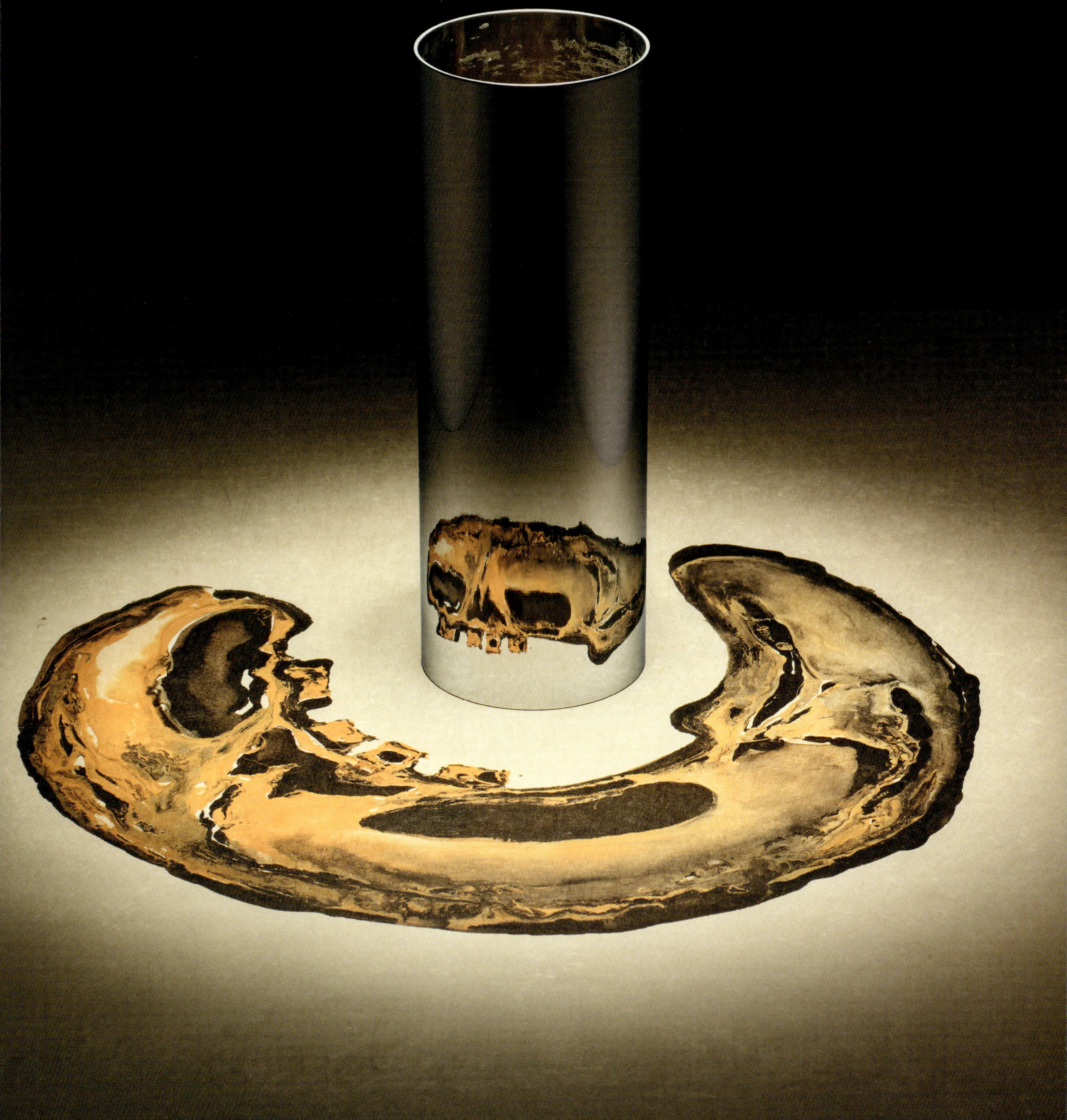

CHRONOLOGY
MONTSE AGUER TEIXIDOR AND CARME RUIZ GONZÁLEZ

Marcel Duchamp (1887–1968) and Salvador Dalí (1904–1989) had spaces in common, both physical and intellectual. From 1933, when they were together in Cadaques, until 1968, the year Duchamp died, the two artists were more than colleagues; their biographies were interwoven at various moments in their lives. Their backgrounds were similar, and their fathers were both notaries. They shared geographies: Paris and New York, but also Arcachon and Cadaqués. Both artists passed through various avant-garde styles at the beginning of the twentieth century, arriving at an anti-modernist position; Duchamp became associated with Dada, while Dalí was to affiliate himself to what was known among the Catalan avant-garde as 'anti-art'. The mutual influences are striking and extend beyond the death of Duchamp. This chronology examines the intersection of their lives and their art until Duchamp's death in 1968.

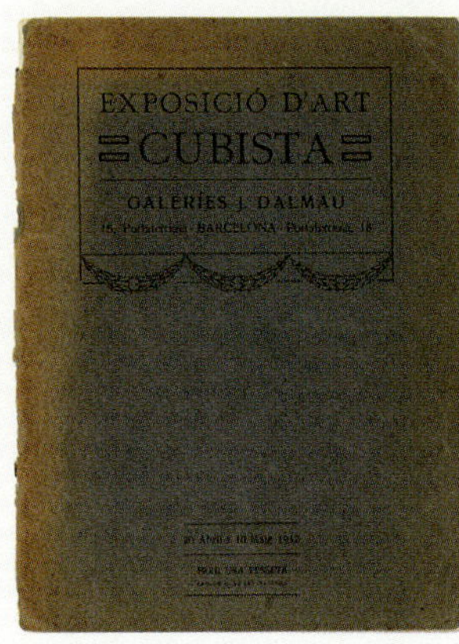
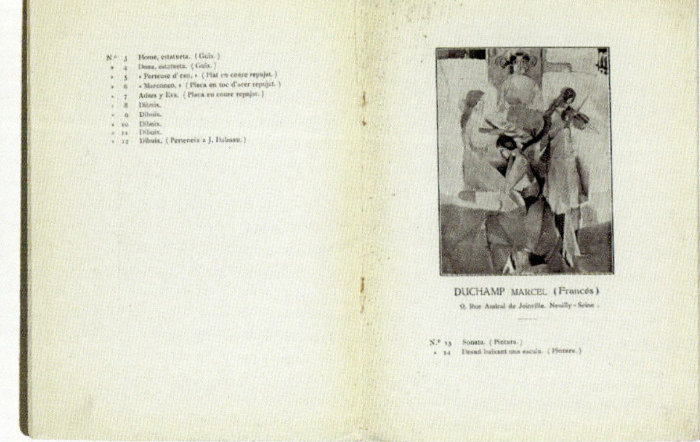

Fig. 94

1887

28 July: birth of Henri-Robert-Marcel Duchamp. His older brothers are also artists: Gaston (b. 1875), who adopts the name Jacques Villon, and Raymond (b. 1876), who assumes the name Duchamp-Villon. His sister Suzanne (b. 1889) is also a painter.

1904

Duchamp moves to Paris.
11 May: birth of Salvador Dalí.

1908

Birth of Anna Maria, Dalí's sister.

1912

Duchamp withdraws *Nude Descending a Staircase* from the Salon des Indépendants following demands from the Hanging Committee for the Cubist room that he either change the painting or the title (possibly because of its Futurist associations). The painting, together with *Sonata* (1911), is exhibited later that year at the 'Exhibition of Cubist Art' in Barcelona, organised by Josep Dalmau (fig. 94). Duchamp attends a performance of Roussel's play *Impressions of Africa* with Francis Picabia and possibly Guillaume Apollinaire. Over the summer, while in Munich, he paints *Bride*. In October a trip to the Jura Mountains with Picabia and Apollinaire prompts the first of the Notes that lead to *The Bride Stripped Bare by Her Bachelors, Even*. In November Duchamp begins to train as a librarian, in order to not have to earn his living as a painter in future.

1913

Duchamp mounts a bicycle wheel upside down on a stool as a distraction in his studio (cat. 77). *Nude Descending a Staircase* is exhibited at the Armory Show in New York and becomes the focus of attention, controversy and ridicule for its apparent unintelligibility. Duchamp sells all four of his paintings from the Armory Show, including *The King and Queen Surrounded by Swift Nudes* (cat. 46).

1914

Duchamp selects his first readymade, *Bottle Rack*, from the department store Bazar de l'Hôtel de Ville, Paris.

1915

Duchamp moves to New York, acquires two glass panels and starts work on *The Large Glass*. He meets Man Ray and buys more manufactured objects, including a snow shovel (cat. 103).

1916

January: Duchamp writes to his sister from New York explaining the concept of the 'readymade' and gifting her *Bottle Rack*, but it is too late, she has already thrown this and *Bicycle Wheel* away while clearing his Paris studio. Dalí spends periods on the outskirts of Figueres, at the Molí de la Torre estate owned by the Pichots, a family of intellectuals and artists; it is there, through the painter Ramon Pichot's collection, that he discovers Impressionism.

Fig. 94
Exhibition of Cubist Art, Barcelona, 1912. Catalogue for the exhibition at Galeries Dalmau, Barcelona, 20 April – 10 May 1912; cover and interior spread showing a reproduction of Marcel Duchamp, *Sonata* (1911).
Fundació Gala-Salvador Dalí, Figueres

1917

Duchamp arranges for a porcelain urinal to be submitted to the First Annual Exhibition of the Society of Independent Artists in New York, under the pseudonym R. Mutt and with the title *Fountain* (cat. 102). When it is rejected he resigns from the jury and publishes the second issue of his small magazine *The Blind Man* (cat. 101), which contains Stieglitz's photograph of *Fountain* and the first justification of the idea of the readymade.

1918

Duchamp paints his last oil on canvas, *Tu m'* (fig. 87), commissioned by his friend and patron Katherine Dreier to fit a space above a bookcase in her apartment. More than ten feet long and two feet high, it is a kind of inventory of his previous works, including shadows of *Bicycle Wheel* and *Hat Rack*. As the United States enters the First World War, Duchamp moves to Buenos Aires, where he plays chess avidly.

1919

Duchamp returns to Paris, where he stays with Picabia and makes contact with the Paris Dadaists, including André Breton, Philippe Soupault, Louis Aragon and Paul Éluard. He adds a moustache and a goatee beard to a reproduction of the *Mona Lisa*, entitling the result *L.H.O.O.Q.* (cat. 28), a word-play on *Elle a chaud au cul* (she has a hot ass). Dalí takes part in a group exhibition in the Municipal Theatre in Figueres (which years later becomes the Dalí Theatre-Museum).

1920

Duchamp returns to New York. Picabia publishes *L.H.O.O.Q.*, minus the beard, in his Dada review 391. Duchamp signs a work, *Fresh Widow*, as 'Copyright Rose Sélavy', the first use of his female alter ego. The following year he adds an extra 'R' to Rose, producing Rrose Sélavy, *Eros c'est la vie* (Eros, that's life).

1921

Duchamp edits and publishes *New York Dada* with Man Ray, whose photograph of him as Rrose Sélavy appears on the cover (cat. 32). Duchamp returns to Paris. July: his first word games are published in *391*. February: Dalí's mother dies. The next year, his father marries Catalina Domènech Ferrés, his sister-in-law.

1922

André Breton's first critical essay on Duchamp is published in *Littérature*. November: Breton lectures in Barcelona on the eve of the opening of Picabia's exhibition of watercolours at the Galeries Dalmau, praising 'the vigilance of Duchamp and Picabia' and heralding 'an art that is richer in surprises than painting'. Dalí takes part in the 'Students Original Artworks Competition Exhibition' of the Catalan Students' Association, held at Galeries Dalmau in Barcelona, where his work *Market* is awarded the university vice-chancellor's prize. In Madrid, he attends the Real Academia de Bellas Artes de San Fernando and lives at the Residencia de Estudiantes, where he makes friends with a group of young people who are to become leading intellectual and artistic personalities: Luis Buñuel, Federico García Lorca, Pedro Garfias, Eugenio Montes and Pepín Bello, among others.

1923

Duchamp abandons *The Large Glass*, leaving it unfinished. He spends most of the 1920s playing chess. Dalí is expelled for a year from the Academia de San Fernando for indiscipline.

1924

Duchamp is mentioned (among other artists) in a footnote to Breton's *Surrealist Manifesto*, as well as in the main text. Breton imagines meeting Duchamp for the first time in the hall of mirrors of a half-ruined castle where he dreams of living with his friends.

1925

May–June: Dalí takes part in the first Exhibition of the Iberian Artists Society in Madrid. November: Dalí's first solo show opens at the Galeries Dalmau in Barcelona.

1926

Dalí participates in several exhibitions in Madrid and Barcelona. In the company of his aunt and sister, he makes his first trip to Paris, where he meets Picasso and visits the Louvre. He is definitively expelled from the Academia de San Fernando after refusing to be examined in Theory of Art, declaring the examiners incompetent to judge him.

1927

Dalí holds his second individual exhibition at Galeries Dalmau in Barcelona and participates in the Second Autumn Salon at the Sala Parés Gallery, Barcelona. He does his military service at Sant Ferran castle in Figueres. With the publication of the article 'Sant Sebastià', dedicated to Lorca, Dalí's regular and extensive collaboration with the vanguardist journal *L'Amic de les Arts* begins, a relationship that continues until 1929.

1928

March: Dalí publishes the anti-art *Yellow Manifesto* with Sebastià Gasch and Lluís Montanyà. In autumn Dalí participates in the Third Autumn Salon at Sala Parés in Barcelona and in the 'Twenty-seventh International Exhibition of Paintings' in Pittsburgh, USA.

1929

Dalí and Luis Buñuel write the screenplay of *Un Chien andalou*, which is published in the final issue of the review *La Révolution surréaliste*. The film is screened in Paris. Dalí joins the Surrealist group and several

Surrealists including Paul Éluard, Éluard's Russian wife Gala and their daughter Cécile, Magritte and his wife Georgette, and the dealer Camille Goemans visit him in Cadaqués (fig. 95) that summer. Gala stays in Cadaqués and becomes Dalí's lifelong companion. The love affair scandalises Dalí's father, who throws his son out of the family house. November: Dalí has his first solo exhibition in Paris, at the Galerie Goemans, with a catalogue preface by Breton.

1930

March: both artists show in 'La Peinture au défi' ('A Challenge to Painting'; fig. 96), an exhibition of collages organised by Louis Aragon at the Galerie Goemans in Paris. July: Dalí publishes the first of several contributions to the journal *Le Surréalisme au service de la révolution* (SASDLR).[1] October: Duchamp publishes an extract on chess problems in *SASDLR* from his book *L'Opposition et les cases conjuguées sont reconciliées*.[2] 28 November: the film *L'Âge d'or* by Buñuel and Dalí is launched at Studio 28, Paris; Duchamp is on the guest list. Dalí buys a fisherman's shack at Portlligat (fig. 98), henceforth his home with Gala. Éditions Surréalistes publishes Dalí's first book, *La Femme visible* (*The Visible Woman*).

1931

Dalí publishes 'Objets surréalistes' in *SASDLR*, 3. He has a solo exhibition at Galerie Pierre Colle in Paris (3–15 June), where he exhibits *The Persistence of Memory*. He is included in the first Surrealist exhibition in the United States, held at the Wadsworth Atheneum in Hartford, with the title 'Newer Super-Realism'. His book *L'Amour et la mémoire* (*Love and Memory*) is published by Éditions Surréalistes, Paris.

1932

Dalí publishes the result of his investigations concerning the Surrealist object in the Surrealist number of *This Quarter*.[3] He quotes the commentary on Duchamp's *Why Not Sneeze Rose Sélavy?* from Breton's 1922 Barcelona lecture 'Characteristics of the modern evolution and what it consists of', in which Breton describes how Duchamp tricked his friends into trying to lift the birdcage apparently filled with sugarlumps; they find it unexpectedly heavy because the sugarlumps are in fact cubes of marble, sawn to order at considerable expense.[4] The same issue publishes for the first time extracts from Duchamp's 'large unpublished collection of notes which were intended to accompany and explain the "verre" (glass)', rendered in English by J. Bronowski. Dalí holds a second solo exhibition at Galerie Pierre Colle (26 May – 7 June), which may have been attended by Duchamp. Dalí's book *Babaouo* is published, in which he outlines his conception of cinema. In financial difficulties, Gala and Dalí, with the help of collectors and aristocratic patrons, set up the 'Zodiac' group to support the painter; as Gala explained in a letter to the Prince de

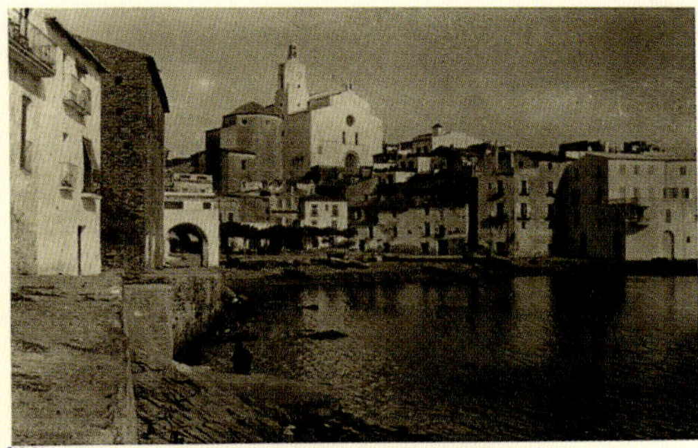

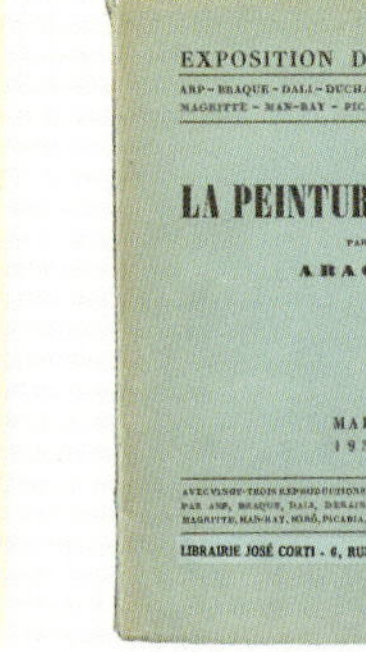

Fig. 95

Fig. 96

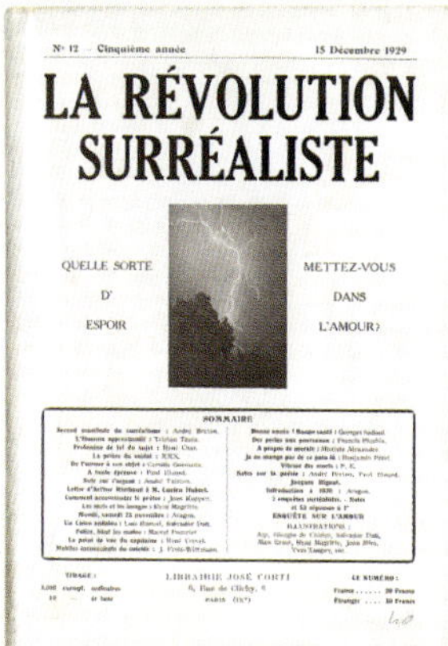

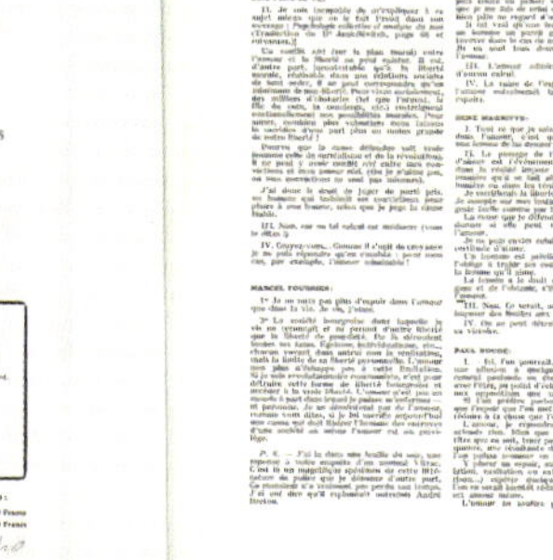

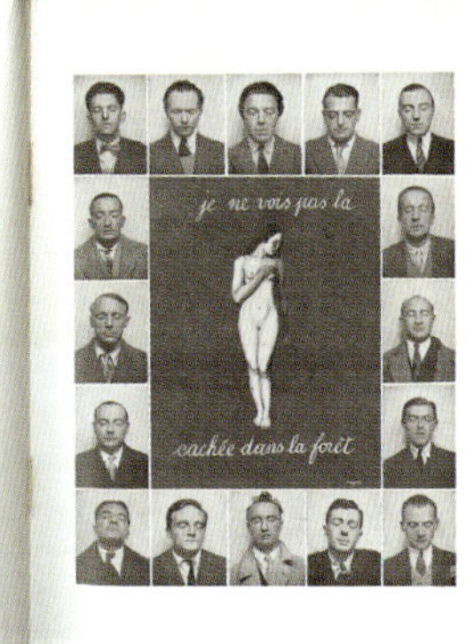

Fig. 97

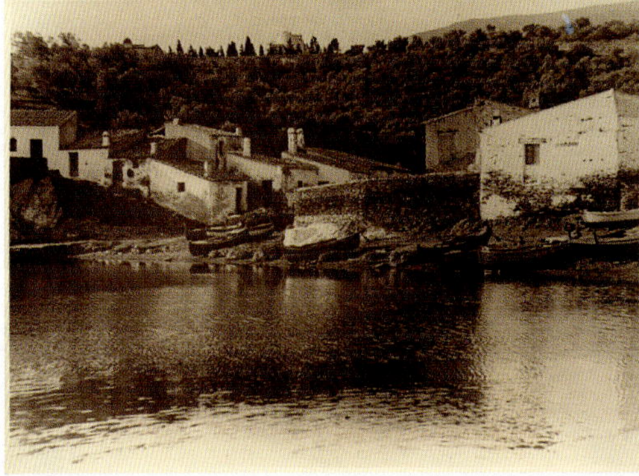

Fig. 98

Faucigny-Lucinge at the end of December, the twelve subscribers would pay 2,500 francs a year in monthly instalments, and receive a painting (either one large, or one small and two drawings).[5] On 28 December Dalí announces to one of the subscribers, his friend and patron the vicomte de Noailles, that his name was drawn in the ballot and he would thus be the first to choose a painting, in January.[6]

1933

15 May: Notes related to Duchamp's *Large Glass* and its first reproduction are published in *SASDLR*, 5; Dalí's article 'Objets psycho-atmosphériques-anamorphiques' appears in the same issue. Dalí's article 'Interprétation Paranoïaque-critique de l'image obsédante, *L'Angélus* de Millet' is his first contribution

Fig. 95
View of Cadaqués, 1920s.
Photograph by Carlos Santias.
Fundació Gala-Salvador Dalí, Figueres

Fig. 96
Louis Aragon, *La Peinture au défi*,
Paris, 1930 (cat. 147)
Exhibition catalogue, 19.5 x 14.5 cm
Collection of The Dalí Museum Archives,
St Petersburg, Florida

Fig. 97
La Révolution surréaliste,
December 1929 (cat. 148)
Journal, 29 x 20.1 cm
Collection of The Dalí Museum
Archives, St Petersburg, Florida

Fig. 98
Dalí's fishermen's hut, Portlligat, 1930.
Fundació Gala-Salvador Dalí, Figueres

Fig. 99
Salvador Dalí, Gala, an unidentified person
and Man Ray, 1933. Photograph by Man
Ray. Gelatin silver print, 4 x 6.6 cm.
Fundació Gala-Salvador Dalí, Figueres

Fig. 100
Salvador Dalí, *Le Phénomène de l'extase*,
1933. Photomontage published in
Minotaure, 3–4, December 1933.
Collection of The Dalí Museum Archives,
St Petersburg, Florida

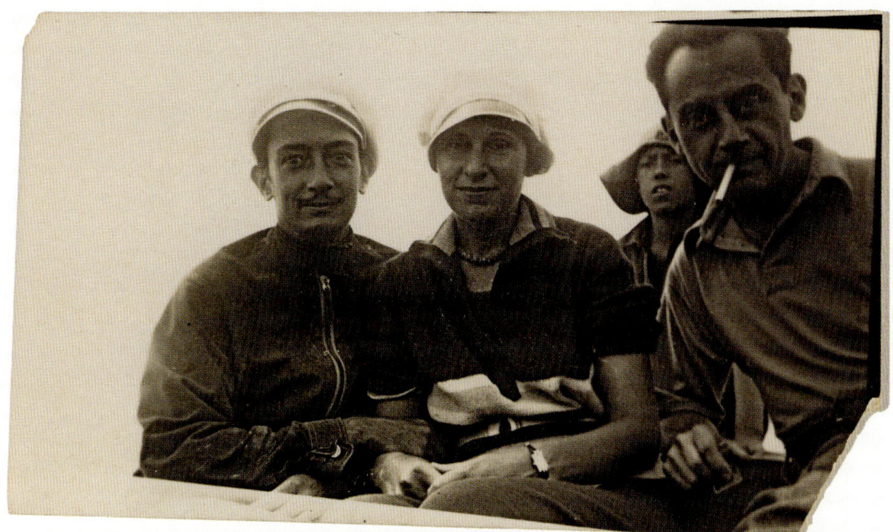

Fig. 99

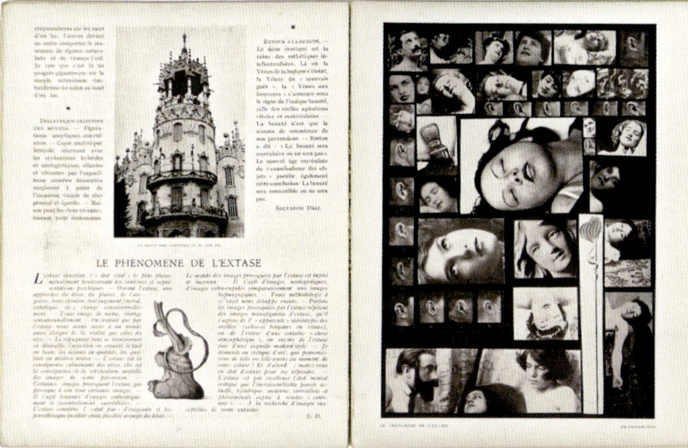

Fig. 100

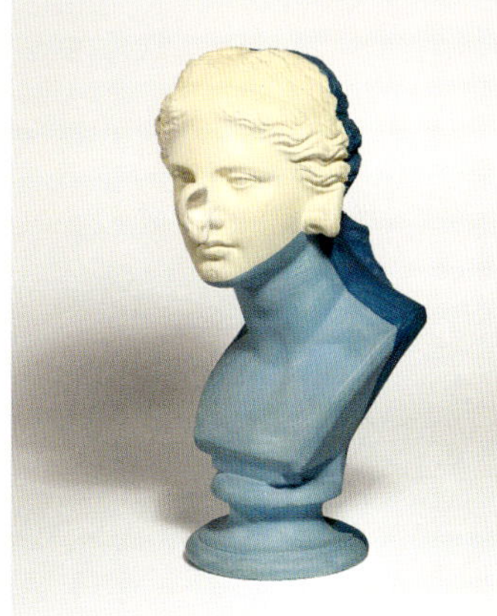

Fig. 101

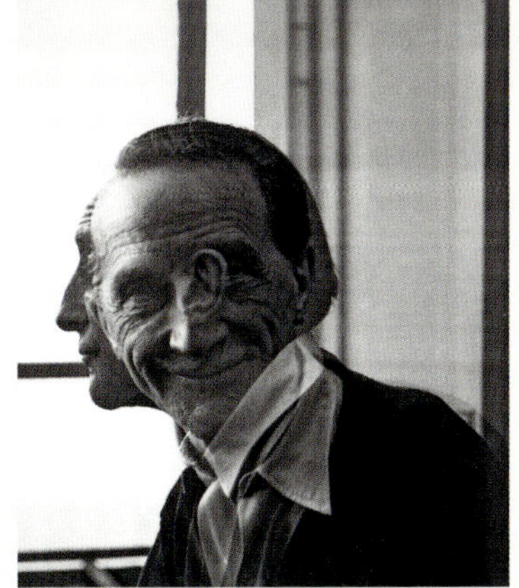

Fig. 102

Fig. 102
Victor Obsatz, *Portrait No. 29 (Double Exposure: Full Face and Profile)*, 1953.
Gelatin silver print, 25.2 x 20.3 cm.
Philadelphia Museum of Art. Gift of Jacqueline, Paul and Peter Matisse in memory of their mother Alexina Duchamp, 13-1972-9(292)

Fig. 101
Salvador Dalí, *Oto-rhinologic Head of Venus*, 1964.
Painted plaster, 61 x 35 x 28 cm.
Fundació Gala- Salvador Dalí, Figueres

to *Minotaure* magazine. 19–29 June: Dalí's third solo show at Pierre Colle; the preface to the catalogue is a letter from Dalí to Breton. August: Duchamp, who had visited Spain for the first time in 1929, returns for a summer holiday with his partner Mary Reynolds; they stay in Cadaqués, where they see Dalí and Gala almost daily. At Dalí's request, Duchamp writes to Man Ray to propose that he come to photograph Barcelona's art-nouveau architecture to accompany an article by Dalí that was scheduled to appear in the next issue of *Minotaure*. On 5 September Dalí writes to Man Ray himself, responding to his confirmation of a trip to Cadaqués, to which Gala adds a note: 'Dalí, meanwhile, is dreaming of the photographs of the Gaudí buildings in Barcelona for Minotaure.' In Portlligat, Man Ray photographs Dalí in various guises (fig. 99), and in Barcelona he photographs Gaudí's La Pedrera and Park Güell; Duchamp sends a postcard with an image of La Pedrera to Dalí at Portlligat, reporting their work and announcing his plans for returning to Paris. In early September Paul Éluard writes to Gala from Paris requesting that Dalí, still at Portlligat, produce his text as urgently as possible and he pleads for more photographic 'sculptures involuntaires', ideally by Man Ray, in addition to those already made by Brassaï, to be included in the next issue of the magazine; in 1932 Brassaï had photographed fragmentary objects assembled by Dalí – paper, soap, toothpaste, unconsciously rolled, folded, and shaped – 'readyfound' Surrealist objects.[7] Éluard also mentions the desirability of a contribution by Duchamp, as long as it is not about chess. Dalí's eventual article in *Minotaure*,[8] accompanied by Man Ray's photographs of Gaudí's architecture and other art-nouveau decorations, is preceded by six 'sculptures involontaires'. In his article Dalí proclaims that 'beauty would be edible or it would not be' ('La beauté sera comestible ou ne sera pas'); in the following issue of *Minotaure* (no. 5, 1934) Breton publishes his article 'La beauté sera convulsive'. The text sought from Duchamp was absent. Dalí's *Minotaure* article has as an epilogue 'Le phénomène de l'extase' (fig. 100), a short text on ecstasy and the way it helps to generate multiple images and realities, illustrated with a photo-collage by Dalí. Among the images forming the collage, ears – one of the body's erogenous zones – appear frequently and continue to be a persistent theme in the work of both artists (see figs 101, 102). November: Dalí's first solo exhibition at the Julien Levy Gallery, New York. Duchamp writes to him, having seen it: 'The exhibition was a great success and the sales not bad. If you take account of the stagnation in which the people find themselves here, you would be surprised, even more than in Paris, that they even think of buying anything. So congratulate yourself, even if the material result is less than what you expected. You can count on an "American market" as they say in cotton. Julien Levy tells me that he is ready to take one or two positions in the "set up of the Twelve".'[9]

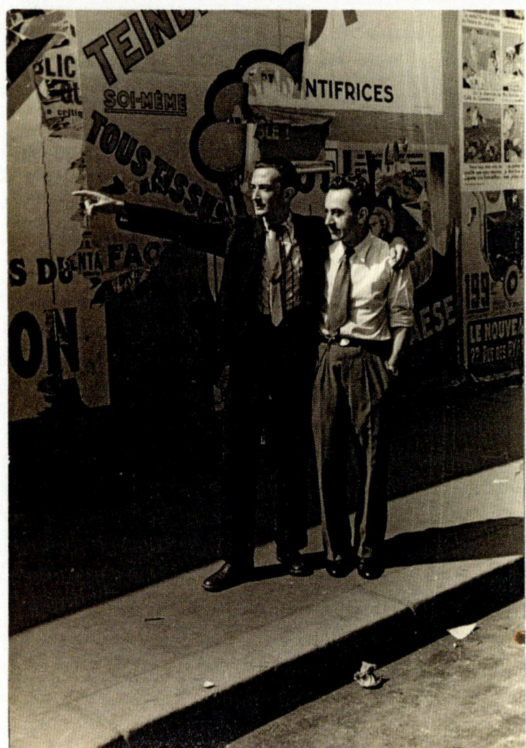

Fig. 103

1935

19 January: Dalí and Gala return to Europe. A family reconciliation takes place in March. Dalí contributes to the 'Systematic Cycle of Lectures on the most recent positions of Surrealism' to clarify the group's political position. According to the programme, he was to read an unpublished poem entitled 'Je mange Gala' ('I eat Gala'), 'suitably dressed while manipulating a living foreign body'.[12] This long text is written in a notebook filled with drawings, mostly erotic, with scenes of amorous cannibalism. Included are titles of paintings such as *Edible Portrait of Gala*, which must refer to *Portrait of Gala with Two Lamb Chops in Equilibrium upon Her Shoulder* (fig. 70). The first canto is dedicated to 'The Birth of Liquid Perversions', which is perhaps linked to the painting *The Birth of Liquid Desires* (1932; Peggy Guggenheim Collection, Venice). The second

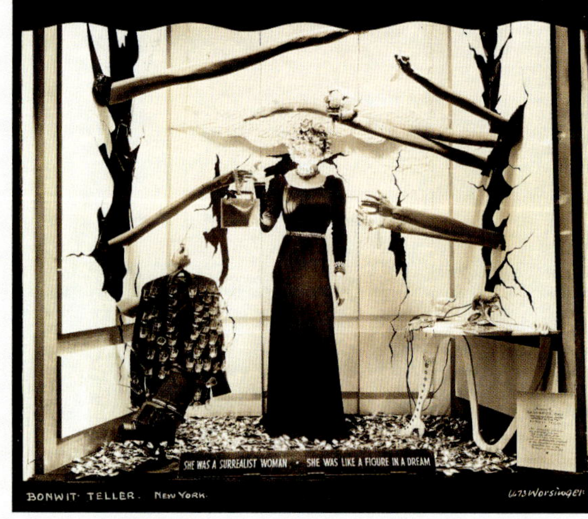

Fig. 104

1934

A year of frenetic activity for Dalí, which sees the first attempt to expel him from the Surrealist group, the realisation of his exhibitions in Paris, New York, Barcelona, London and Pittsburgh, several lectures, and the publication with Albert Skira of the Comte de Lautréamont's *Les Chants de Maldoror* with his illustrations. 30 January: The civil wedding of Gala and Dalí takes place. November: Dalí's first visit to the United States. Duchamp returns to Paris from New York and recommences his artistic activities, publishing facsimiles of a selection of the notes, drawings and photos for *The Large Glass* in the *Green Box* (Éditions Rrose Sélavy). The edition goes on for almost six years and consists of 300 copies. At some point, Duchamp gives Dalí no. 144 in the edition, which the painter keeps to the end of his life. In 'Les Nouvelles couleurs du sex-appeal spectral'[10] Dalí analyses and compares the morphology of the phantom with that of the spectre – recurrent images in his works of this period. He defines the phantom as a 'simulacrum of volume', while the spectre, on the contrary, represents decomposition. He urges the reader to discover which of his/her acquaintances is a phantom and which a spectre; according to Dalí, Duchamp and Gala belong to the latter category. Finally, he predicts the future of sex-appeal via the spectral beauty of the woman represented by means of the dismantling of her anatomy: 'La femme spectrale sera la femme démontable'.[11]

Fig. 105

Fig. 103
Salvador Dalí and Man Ray in Paris, 1934.
Photograph by Carl Van Vechten.
Silver gelatin print, 23.5 x 16.1 cm.
Fundació Gala-Salvador Dalí, Figueres

Fig. 104
Surrealist window at Bonwit Teller & Co.,
based on a sketch by Salvador Dalí, 1936.
Photograph by Photo Worsinger.
Gelatin silver print, 25.3 x 20.3 cm.
Museum of the City of New York,
New York

Fig. 105
Letter from Marcel Duchamp to
Salvador Dalí referring to Dalí's
exhibition at the Julien Levy Gallery,
11 December 1933 (cat. 149)
Ink on paper, 28 x 21.5 cm
Collection of The Dalí Museum,
St Petersburg, Florida

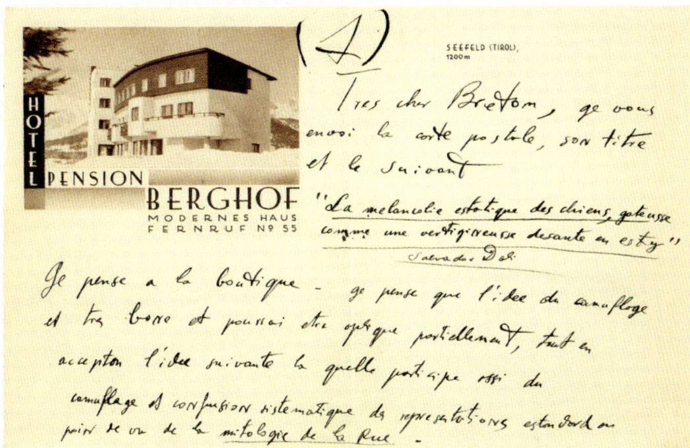

Fig. 106

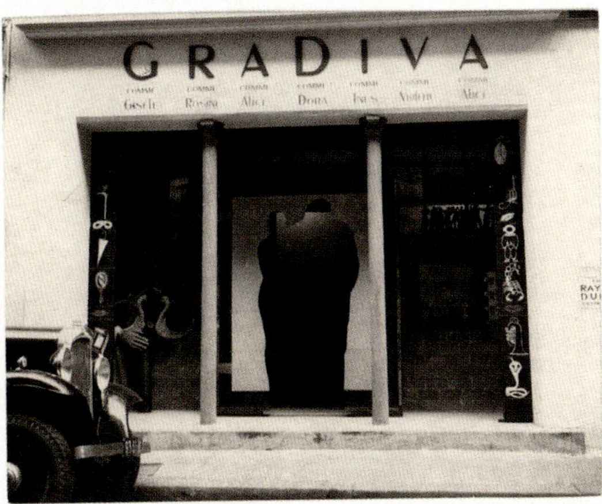

Fig. 107

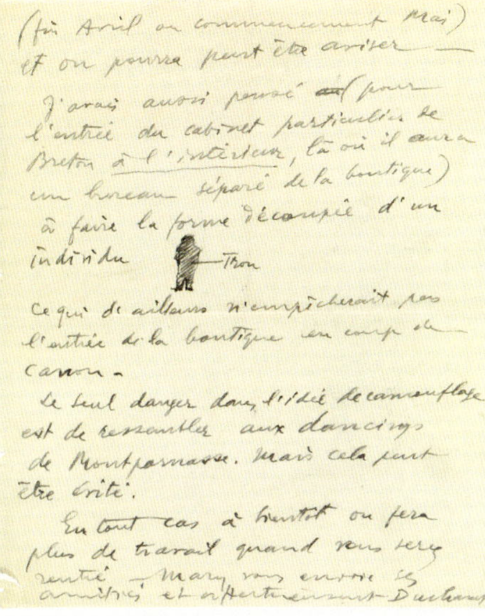

Fig. 108

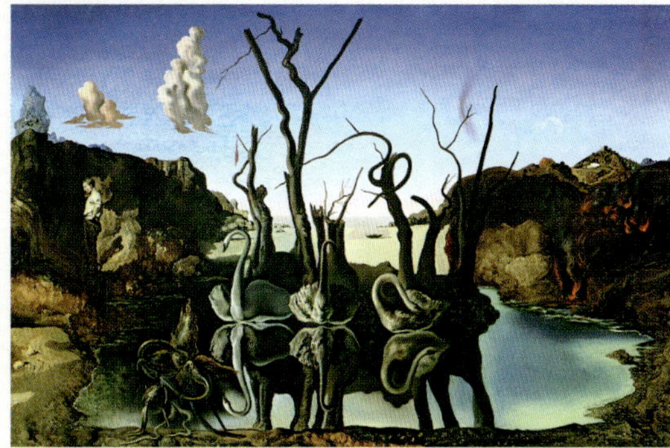

Fig. 109

Fig. 106
Letter from Salvador Dalí to André Breton discussing the Gradiva Gallery, 27 March 1937. Ink on paper, 14.6 x 22.3 cm. Fundació Gala-Salvador Dalí, Figueres

Fig. 107
Completed shop front of the Gradiva Gallery, 1937. Photograph, annotated '1938' by André Breton. Association Atelier André Breton

Fig. 108
Letter from Marcel Duchamp to Gala and Salvador Dalí, including a sketch of the silhouette to be used as an entrance at the Gradiva Gallery, 1937 (cat. 150) Ink on paper, 28.3 x 22.7 cm Fundació Gala-Salvador Dalí, Figueres

Fig. 109
Salvador Dalí, *Swans Reflecting Elephants*, 1937. Oil on canvas, 51 x 77 cm. Private collection

canto is entitled 'The Birth of Nutritious Perversions' and springs from an excursion to Cap de Creus in August 1933, which included Gala and Duchamp.[13] One sheet includes a sketch representing a sunburned Duchamp wearing a pith helmet (cat. 66). Breton publishes the first critical account of *The Large Glass*, 'Phare de la mariée', in *Minotaure*.[14]

March: Duchamp begins to plan a portable museum of 'approximately all his work'. The preparation of the miniature reproductions and the production of the different series of the *Boîte* (cat. 62) occupies him off and on for the rest of his life.

1936

The department store Bonwit Teller in New York commissions Dalí among other artists to decorate a 'Surrealist' shop window, in connection with the MoMA exhibition 'Fantastic Art, Dada, Surrealism'. The store commissions him again in connection with the New York World's Fair in 1939.

1937

February: André Breton is invited by an acquaintance, Louis Bomsel, to become director of an art gallery at 31 rue de Seine in Paris. Named in homage to Wilhelm Jensen and Sigmund Freud, the Galerie Gradiva is unsuccessful despite the energy Breton devotes to it. Duchamp is charged with the gallery's design. Dalí, too, sends Breton his ideas for the gallery: 'My idea is to call the shop Café, written as on café fronts (it could be "Café Gradiva", Café in large letters, Gradiva in small)… the exterior of the shop would correspond exactly with that of a "horse-butcher" with … fake marble and gilded horses' heads, from which would hang thick hair (but longer than usual) as at a hairdresser's…' He adds that he will also write to Duchamp because he thinks his theories might be useful for his conception of camouflage, and ends with the following affirmation: 'I haven't come across any better ideas than Duchamp's project, which seems to me the most lyrical and best adapted for the circumstances' (fig. 106).[15] 5 April: Duchamp replies to Dalí's letter, explaining that although he loves Dalí's proposal neither he nor Breton has the last word. He is planning the entrance to Breton's office inside the shop in the form of 'the cut-out profile of an individual', which would not interfere with the idea of camouflage for the entrance. The only danger of the camouflage idea, he continues, is that it might make the gallery look like a

Montparnasse nightclub. In the end, Duchamp designs the main entrance to the gallery in the shape not of an individual but a couple (fig. 107). Perhaps Duchamp's design was influenced by Dalí's shaped canvases of 1936 such as the *Couple with Their Heads full of Clouds* (cat. 137). Dalí paints *Swans Reflecting Elephants* (fig. 109), containing a portrait that could be indentified as Duchamp, which would testify to his admiration for the older artist.

1938

January – February: the 'International Exhibition of Surrealism' takes place at the Galerie Beaux-Arts in Paris (fig. 110). André Breton and Paul Éluard are organisers, Marcel Duchamp is 'générateur-arbitre', assisted by Claude Le Gentil. Max Ernst and Dalí are 'conseillers spéciaux'. Man Ray is responsible for the lighting and Wolfgang Paalen for the fountains. Besides showing several early works, Duchamp has the idea of hanging 1,200 coal sacks filled with paper from the ceiling of the central room; Dalí, Duchamp later said, was responsible for the pond. Part of the exhibition brings together 'the most beautiful streets of Paris', comprising a 'Surrealist street' populated with mannequins decorated by various artists. Duchamp dresses his in his hat and jacket. Besides *Rainy Taxi*, which opens the exhibition in the courtyard, Dalí presents six paintings, some objects and a number of drawings. His mannequin is covered with teaspoons, the head with a balaclava designed by Elsa Schiaparelli, with a bird's head as a hat. As a complement to the exhibition, the *Dictionnaire abrégé du Surréalisme* (fig. 102) is published, containing several definitions by Dalí. The painter's own entry defines him as a poet and Surrealist theorist since 1929.[16]

1939

16 March: Dalí breaks a window at the Bonwit Teller department store on Fifth Avenue in New York; angry that his installation of a model reclining in a bathtub has been changed, he pushes the bathtub, which smashes through the window, taking him with it. Taken in by the police, Dalí is later released without charge. Dalí is finally excommunicated from the Surrealist movement, just before construction of his 'Surrealist House', the Dream of Venus pavilion at the New York World's Fair. May: Breton marks the rupture in *Minotaure*, accusing Dalí of racism and fascist sympathies.[17] From then on, with one exception, Dalí is only represented in shows organised by the group with works predating 1939. Duchamp, by contrast, continues his active association with them. Dalí publishes his manifesto *Declaration of the Independence of the Imagination and the Rights of Man to His Own Madness*, in protest against the World's Fair committee for refusing permission for a reproduction of Botticelli's *Venus* with a fish head on the front of his pavilion. Dalí and Gala return to Paris just before the opening, leaving Edward James to finalise the display.

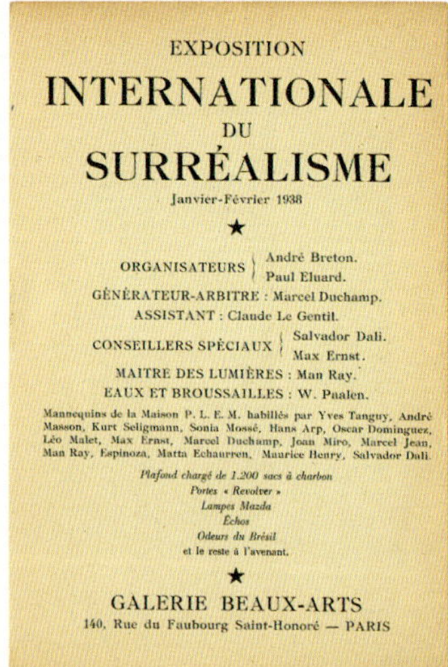

Fig. 110

Fig. 111

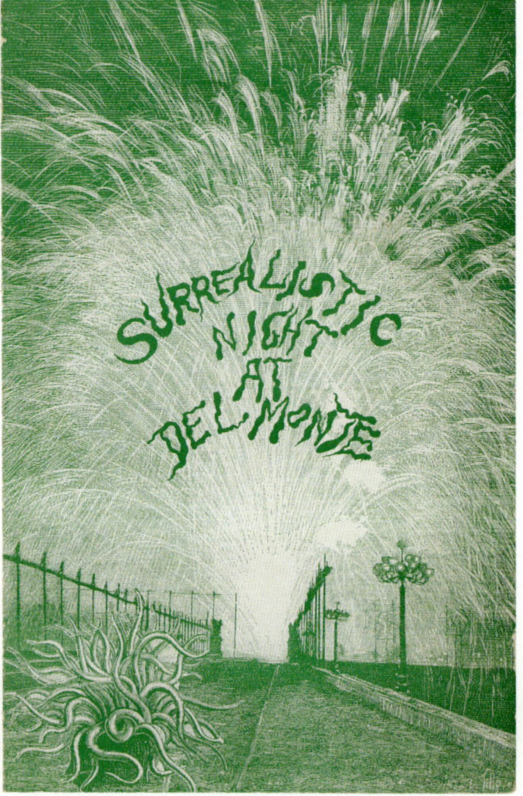

Fig. 112

1940

February: following the outbreak of the Second World War and mobilisation in France, Gala and Dalí move to Arcachon, in the southwest of France, where they find several friends including Duchamp, who is staying there with his sister Suzanne and her husband Jean Crotti. Dalí paints *Two Pieces of Bread Expressing the Sentiment of Love* (cat. 50), in which the chess pawn between the crusts of bread alludes to Duchamp. According to Dalí, 'In Arcachon Gala and Duchamp

Fig. 110
Poster for 'Exposition internationale du Surréalisme' ('International Exhibition of Surrealism'), Galerie Beaux-Arts, Paris, January – February 1938.
Fundació Gala-Salvador Dalí, Figueres

Fig. 111
André Breton and Paul Éluard (eds), *Dictionnaire abrégé du surréalisme* (*Abridged Dictionary of Surrealism*), Paris, 1938. Cover design by Yves Tanguy.
Fundació Gala-Salvador Dalí, Figueres

Fig. 112
Brochure for the Surrealistic Night at Del Monte, Hotel Del Monte, Pebble Beach, California, 2 September 1941.
Fundació Gala-Salvador Dalí, Figueres

Fig. 113
Presentation of *Arcane 17*, designed by Marcel Duchamp, at the Gotham Book Mart, New York, 1945.
Photograph by Maya Deren.
Association Atelier André Breton

Fig. 114
Dizzy Dalí Dinner, 1941 (cat. 151)
Film, 49 seconds
Paramount News. Footage provided by the Sherman Grinberg Film Library

played chess after midday every day, at the same time that I set about painting these pieces of bread. Sometimes things fell on the ground, such as pawns. One day ... one of the pawns landed in the middle of the model for my still life. Afterwards they had to find other pawns to continue the game, because I was using it....'[18] June: the Germans occupy Paris and advance to the southwest. Dalí and Gala leave France for Spain and then the United States, arriving in August.

1941

Duchamp's first 'portable museum', the *Boîte-en-valise* (strictly speaking the title only of the deluxe limited edition, of which there are 24), is signed in Paris. As well as the deluxe edition seven series of *Boîtes* are produced, from 1941 to 1968 (cat. 62). Duchamp obtains a pass as a cheese dealer to travel between the Occupied and Free zones in France, so that he can move the elements of the *Boîtes* to Marseille, whence they can be shipped to New York. Duchampian references appear in Dalí's work. 2 September: at the fancy-dress ball 'A Surrealistic Night in an Enchanted Forest' at the Hotel Del Monte, Monterey, California (fig. 112), Dalí transforms one room into a cave from whose ceiling hang 5,000 sacks, together with mannequins,[19] with the intention of depressing the guests (fig. 114).

1942

25 June: Duchamp arrives in New York, having finally obtained a visa. He designs the installation, using 'a mile' of string wound round the exhibits, for the 'First Papers of Surrealism' exhibition (14 October – 7 November). Duchamp's friend the architect Frederick

Fig. 114

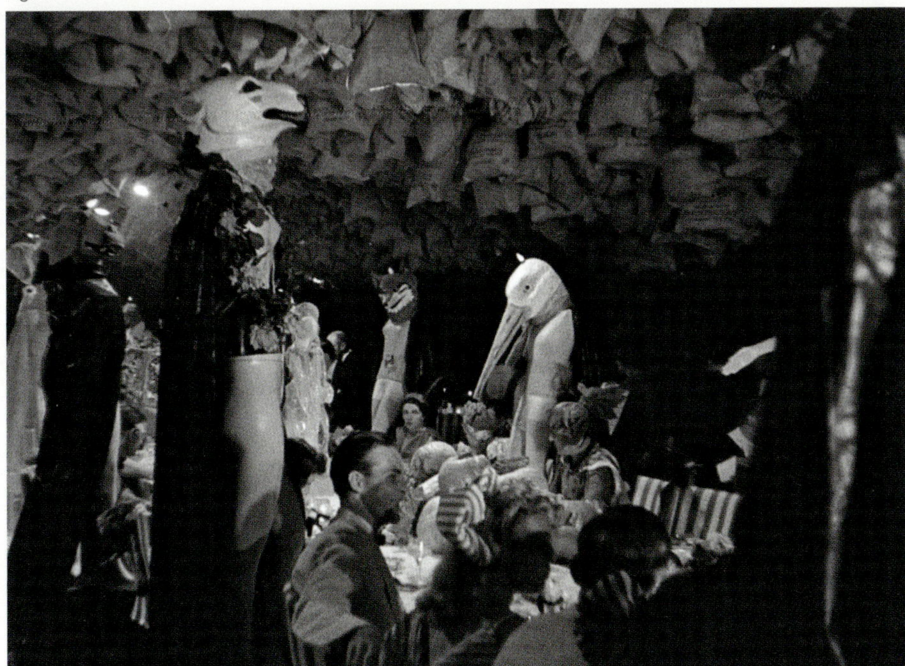

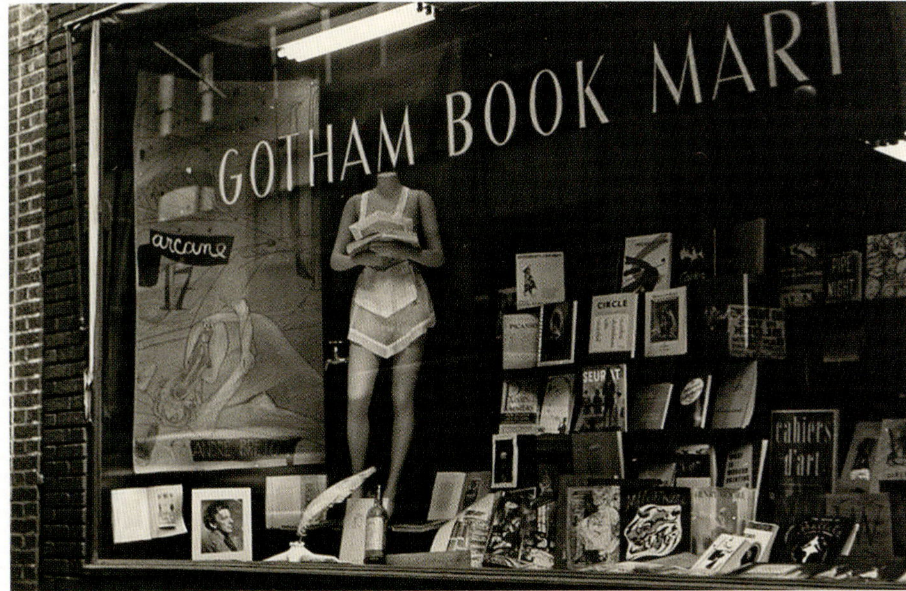

Fig. 113

Kiesler designs an installation at Peggy Guggenheim's new gallery Art of This Century for Duchamp's *Boîte*, seen through holes in a revolving disc that the viewer turns with a wheel.

1943

Duchamp and the Surrealist painter Kurt Seligmann decorate the window of Brentano's Bookstore on Fifth Avenue in New York for the publication of Denis de Rougemont's *The Devil's Share*, suspending open black umbrellas from the ceiling.

1945

April: Duchamp contributes a headless mannequin (fig. 113), naked except for a dainty maid's apron and with a tap in her thigh, for the window display at Brentano's, for the publication of Breton's *Arcane 17*. After protests by the League of Women, the installation is moved to Gotham Book Mart. In November Duchamp and Enrico Donati design another window display at Brentano's, for a new edition of Breton's *Surrealism and Painting*.

1946

Duchamp is on the jury for an art prize, for a painting on the theme of the Temptation of St Anthony, to promote the film *Bel Ami*, based on the novel by Guy de Maupassant. Dalí presents his painting *The Temptation of St Anthony*. The first prize goes to Max Ernst.

1948

July: Dalí and Gala return to Spain.

1950

November: Dalí shows two versions of the *Madonna of Portlligat* in his solo exhibition at the Carstairs Gallery, New York (27 November – 10 January 1951). This may be the exhibition visited by Duchamp (fig. 115).

201

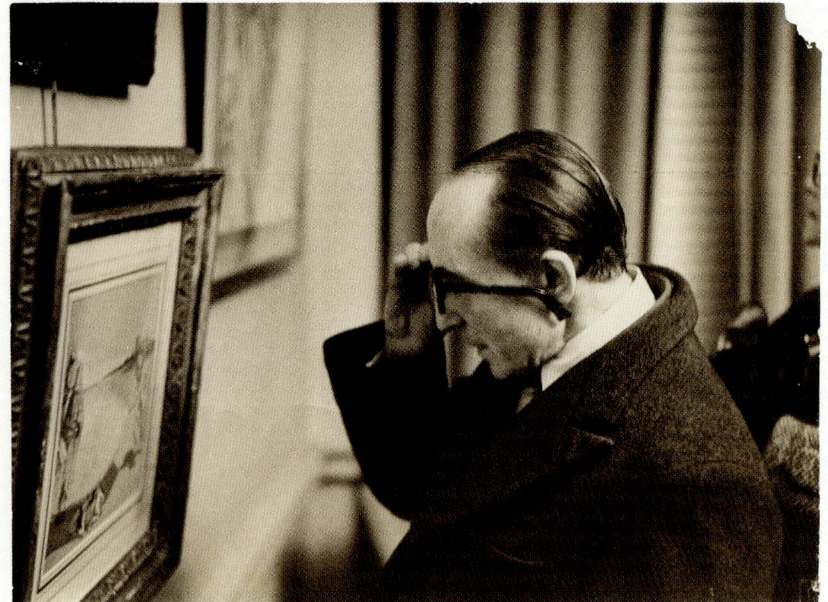

Fig. 115

1954

16 January: Duchamp marries Teeny Matisse (born Alexina Sattler) in New York. He commissions the Georgian poet Ilia Zdanevich to make a more solid packaging using a framework of wood and cardboard for the *Boîte* 'Series C'. Because of customs difficulties, it is not until 1958 that 30 examples of this *Boîte* are put together.[20]

1956

December: Dalí presents the oil *Nude Vibrations Dematerialising a Clothed Nude of Super-nude Vibrations* (1956; Art Hispania, Barcelona) at the Carstairs Gallery, New York – a reference to Duchamp.

1958

August: Duchamp spends the summer at Cadaqués, where his friendship with Dalí intensifies. Duchamp gives a signed *Boîte* from the recently completed 'Series C' to Gala and Dalí (fig. 118).[21]

1959

April: Dalí publishes 'The King and Queen Traversed by Swift Nudes' in *Art News*,[22] announced as follows: 'The master of melting watches pays homage to the master of *Nude Descending a Staircase*, on the occasion of a big Duchamp show in New York and the publication of his biography.'[23] The text comprises thirteen reasons for which Duchamp, in Dalí's opinion, has become 'one of the greatest of the painters and poets of our era'.

1960

Dalí refers to Duchamp in his video *Chaos and Creation*. 9 June: an official, typed letter from Duchamp, now President of the 'Arts Committee for American Chess', requests Dalí's collaboration as a member of the committee and asks for an artwork

as a gift. In a handwritten note in the margin Duchamp tells Dalí when he and Teeny will be arriving at Cadaqués (fig. 116). Dalí contributes a watercolour, which is sold in the auction held for the benefit of the American Chess Foundation in New York the next year. November: A crucial incident in the artists' friendship occurs, revealing their complicity. The occasion is the exhibition 'Surrealist Intrusion in the Enchanters' Domain' at the D'Arcy Galleries in New York,[24] curated by Duchamp and Breton, with the assistance of José Pierre and Edouard Jaguer (fig. 117).[25] The Galleries write to Breton enquiring about the possibility of securing works by Dalí and Picasso – names to conjure

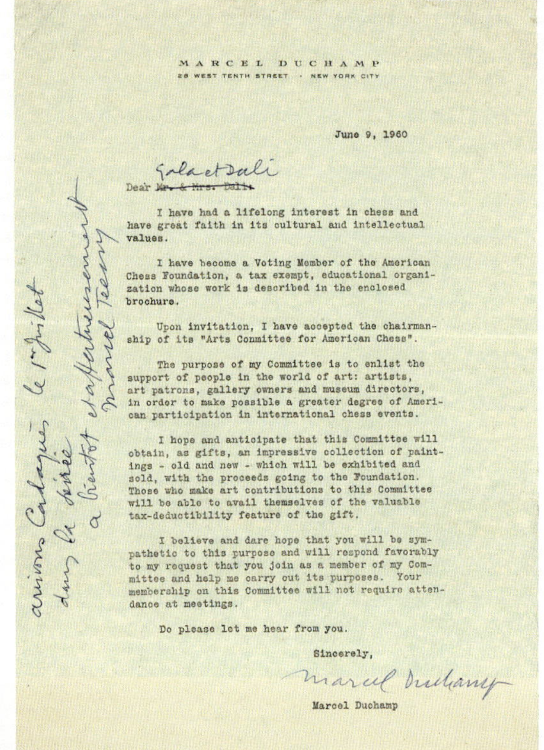

Fig. 116

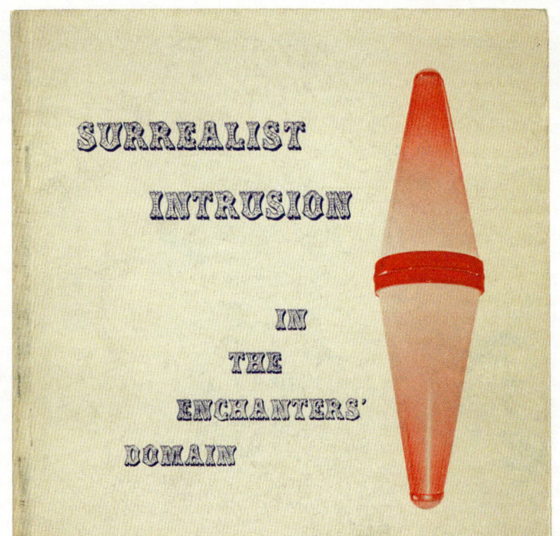

Fig. 117

Fig. 115
Marcel Duchamp at the Salvador Dalí exhibition in New York, *c.* 1950 (cat. 152)
Photograph by Marvin Koner
Silver gelatin print, 15.9 x 21.5 cm
Fundació Gala-Salvador Dalí, Figueres

Fig. 116
Letter from Marcel Duchamp to Salvador and Gala Dalí, 9 June 1960.
Type and ink on paper, 26.7 x 18.4 cm.
Fundació Gala-Salvador Dalí, Figueres

Fig. 117
Marcel Duchamp, catalogue cover for *Surrealist Intrusion in the Enchanters' Domain*, 'International Surrealist Exhibition', D'Arcy Galleries, New York, 29 November 1960 – 14 January 1961.
Fundació Gala-Salvador Dalí, Figueres

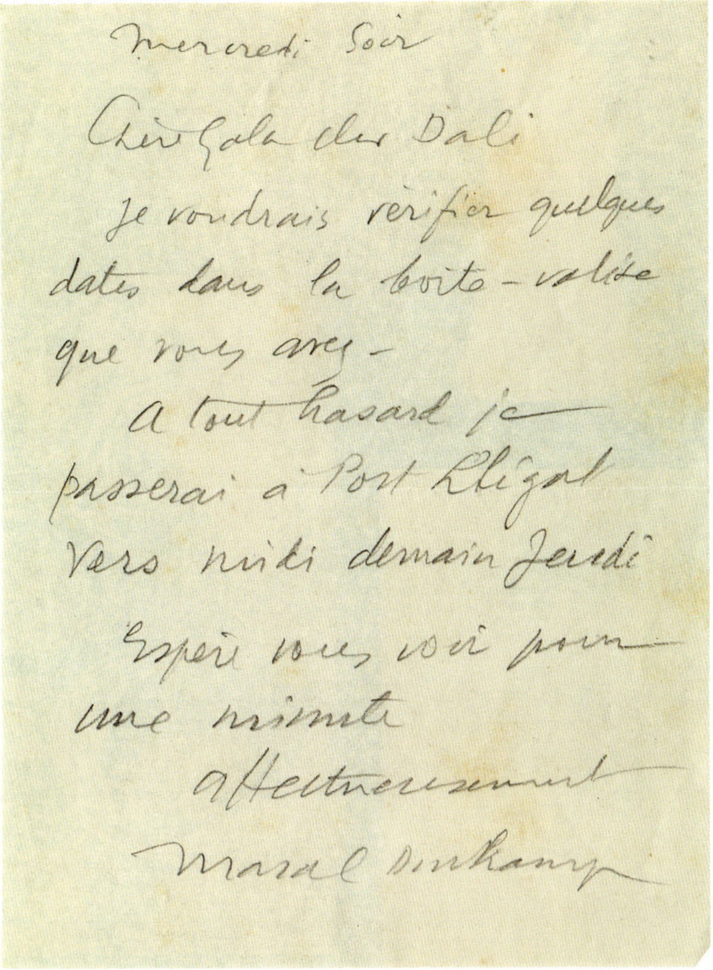

Fig. 118

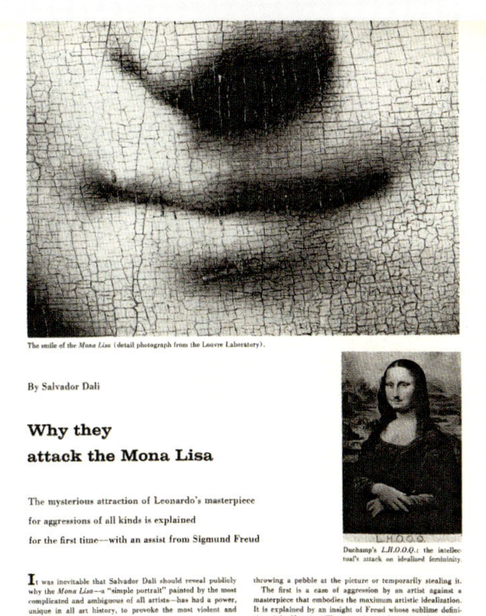

Fig. 119

Duchamp expresses regret that he agreed to organise the exhibition. December: Dalí inaugurates an exhibition at the Carstairs Gallery in New York (which coincides with the D'Arcy Galleries exhibition), where he shows *The Enigma of William Tell* (fig. 79). This painting, controversial at the time of its creation, had been one of the reasons for the Surrealist group's first attempt to exclude Dalí in 1934. Duchamp attends the exhibition.

1961

The friendship between the two artists is obvious in the joint drawing (fig. 56) they present to Leonard Lyons, a journalist at the *New York Post*, whose column 'The Lyons Den' harvested gossip about celebrities of the day.[28] 12 August: A bullfight is held at the Plaza de Toros, Figueres, in homage to Dalí (pp. 104–05). Jean Tinguely and Niki de Saint-Phalle participate at Duchamp's request, constructing an exploding bull.

1963

March: Dalí publishes 'Why They Attack the *Mona Lisa*' in *Art News* (fig. 119).[29] He feels the attacks can be explained with the help of Sigmund Freud, and are of two kinds: the intellectual, perpetrated by the Dada movement (Duchamp), and the primitive or naïve type of attack perpetrated anonymously. After explaining in detail this second type, Dalí ends with the words: 'Anyone who can offer different explanations of the attacks suffered by the *Mona Lisa* should cast his first stone at me; I will pick it up and go on with my task of building the truth.'

Fig. 118
Letter from Duchamp to Gala and Dalí concerning the *Boîte-en-valise*, 1960s (cat. 153)
Pencil on paper, 21.8 x 15.8 cm
Fundació Gala-Salvador Dalí, Figueres

Fig. 119
Salvador Dalí, 'Why they attack the *Mona Lisa*', *Art News*, vol. 62, no. 1, March 1963.
Collection of The Dalí Museum Archives, St Petersburg, Florida

with in New York – and asking whether Dalí could attend the opening, bringing the event huge publicity. Breton annotates the letter 'non'. Duchamp, who is present in New York, telephones Dalí and the result is the arrival of an enormous 1958 painting by him entitled in the catalogue *L'Oreille anti-matière* (*Anti-Matter Ear*): *Quasi-grey picture which, closely seen, is an abstract one; seen from two metres is the Sistine Madonna of Raphael; and from fifteen metres is the ear of an angel measuring one metre and a half; which is painted with anti-matter; therefore with pure energy* (known as *Madonna*; cat. 140).[26] For this painting Dalí used a 'dot-matrix based on an enlarged photograph of Pope John XXIII's ear printed in *Paris Match*'.[27] The painting is hung in a prominent place amid Duchamp's subtle Surrealist setting, next to a cupboard containing live hens. Dalí's presentation of the painting is badly received by the Surrealist group, which draws up the manifesto 'We don't EAR it that way' (cat. 138). In the text they recall that Dalí is 'Hitler's former apologist', describe him as 'the fascist painter, the religious bigot and the avowed racist' and express their incomprehension that Duchamp, whom they respect so highly, could concede Dalí this 'exorbitant part' in a collective enterprise. In a letter to Breton,

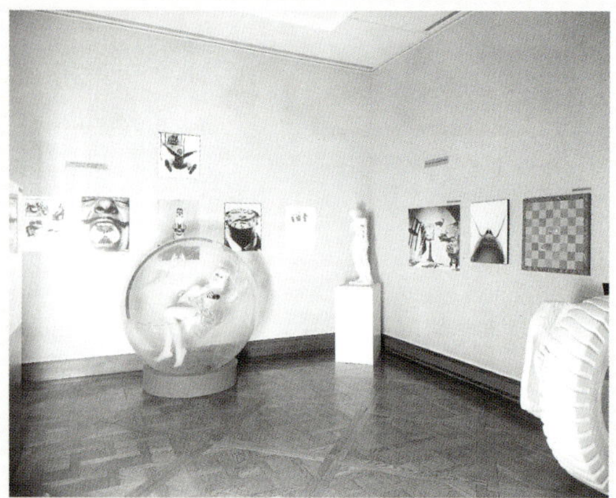

Fig. 120

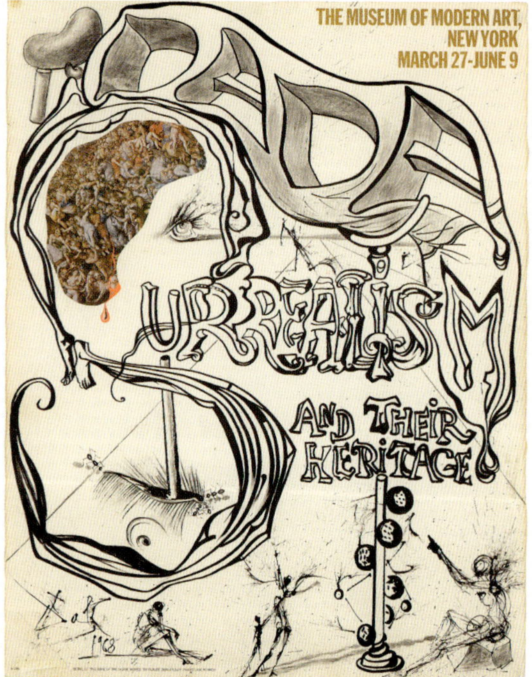

Fig. 121

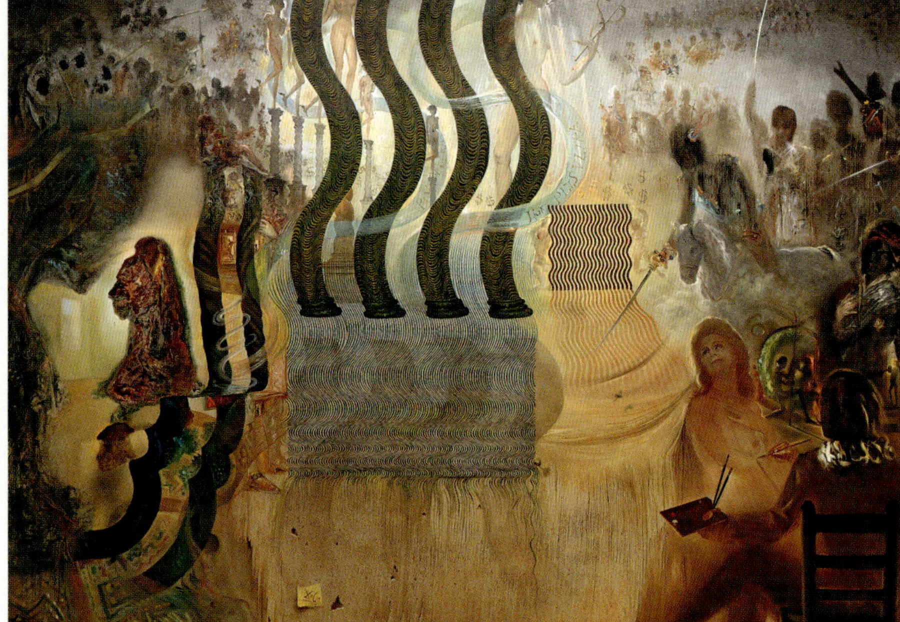

Fig. 122

Fig. 123

Fig. 120
Installation view of the Salvador
Dalí exhibition at the Gallery of
Modern Art, New York, 1965–66.
Photograph by Peter A. Juley and Son.
Peter A. Juley and Son Collection,
Smithsonian American Art Museum,
Washington DC

Fig. 121
After Salvador Dalí, Black castle from
chess set made in homage to Marcel
Duchamp, 1964. *c.* 1985 edition by Barclay
Gallery Ltd, for American Chess
Foundation (detail of cat. 7). 32 pieces
cast in polished light bronze and antique
dark bronze. Collection of The Dalí
Museum, St Petersburg, Florida

Fig. 122
Salvador Dalí, *Dalí painting Gala in
the Apotheosis of the Dollar*, 1965.
Oil on canvas, 400 x 498 cm.
Fundació Gala-Salvador Dalí, Figueres

Fig. 123
Salvador Dalí, Poster for 'Dada, Surrealism,
and Their Heritage', Museum of Modern
Art, New York, 1968. Poster, 81 x 62 cm.
Fundació Gala-Salvador Dalí, Figueres

1965

December: Dalí's 'Homage to Duchamp' is presented
at Dalí's 1910–65 retrospective at the Gallery of
Modern Art, New York (fig. 120). A chessboard
with a salt cellar and a pepper pot from the St Regis
Hotel (where Dalí and Gala stayed when in New York)
represented the white and black castles (fig. 121). Dalí
based the design of the other chess pieces on his own
fingers. For the king and queen, he used his thumbs
as the model, crowned with a tooth. Dalí also paints
Apotheosis of the Dollar, depicting Duchamp as
Louis XIV, to the centre-left of the work (fig. 122).

1966

February: the chess set (a prototype in plastic or
wax) is shown at the exhibition 'Homage to Caïssa',
organised by Duchamp for the American Chess
Foundation at the Cordier & Ekstrom Gallery, New
York.[30] 7 February: Duchamp reportedly plays a game
of chess with Dalí at the show's opening. In 1970 Dalí
presents his chess set in silver at a press conference,
in honour of Duchamp, and donates it to the American
Chess Foundation.[31] The two artists also appear
playing chess together in the film *Autoportrait mou
de Salvador Dalí* by Jean-Christophe Averty (1966).

1968

January: Dalí writes the preface for the English edition
of Pierre Cabanne's *Dialogues with Marcel Duchamp*;
the preface, on the theme of Duchamp and chess,
is entitled 'L'échecs, c'est moi' ('Chess, it's me').[32] March:
works by Duchamp and Dalí appear in the exhibition
'Dada, Surrealism and Their Heritage' at MoMA,
New York (fig. 123). In connection with this exhibition
Vogue asks Dalí to write an article entitled 'Who is

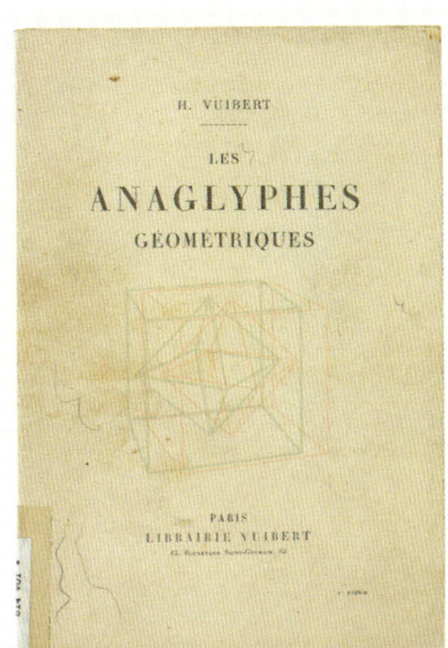
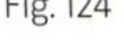

Fig. 124

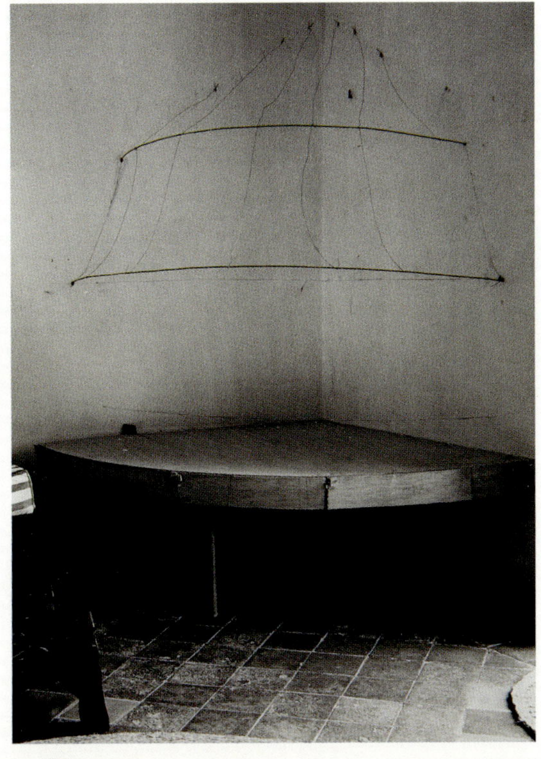

Fig. 125

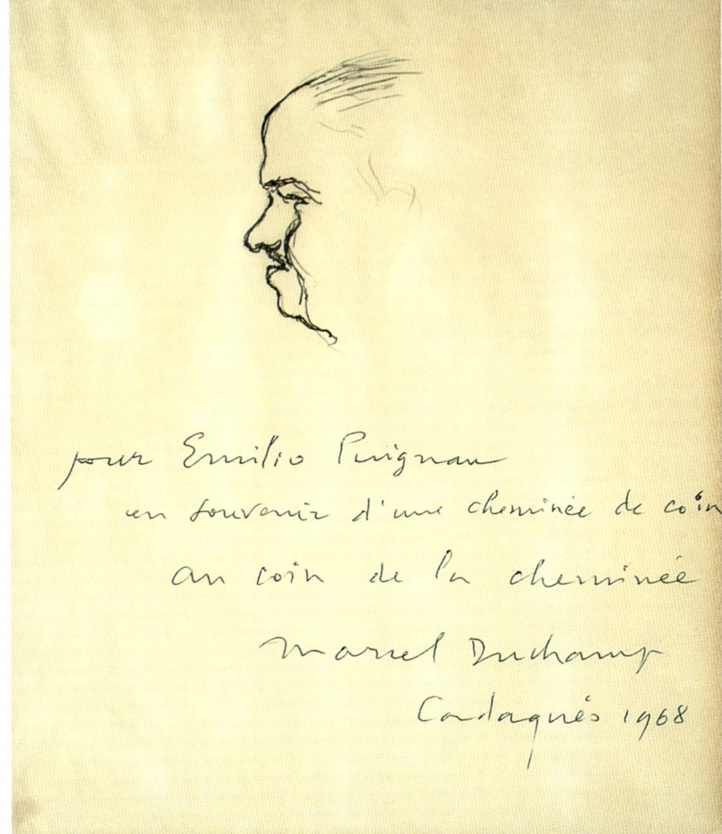

Fig. 126

Surrealism?'[33] The artist explains again his paranoiac-critical method in relation to his latest obsessions and ends by affirming: 'Modern art, the last result of the French Revolution, stands for the triumph of the bourgeoisie. "A good picture is like being seated in a good chair," said Henri Matisse. Dada was the first intellectual revolt against the bourgeoisie. The attitude of Duchamp was entirely aristocratic. The Surrealist archetype is the architect of Louis XVI, Claude-Nicolas Ledoux.'[34] The two artists shared a life-long interest in optical effects and Duchamp's last completed project, the chimney of his house at Cadaqués (fig. 125), which was built for him by Emilio Puignau (fig. 126), testifies to this. Both Dalí and Duchamp sought to break with monocular vision by means of stereoscopy and anamorphosis and Henry Vuibert's *Les anaglyphes géométriques* (fig. 124) was in both their libraries. In it Vuibert explains how to construct stereoscopes and anaglyphs, and Duchamp used the manual to design the chimney. Puignau, who was very close to Dalí, was also commissioned to extend Dalí's Portlligat house, collaborating closely with the artist.
2 October: Duchamp dies suddenly in Paris.

Dalí's admiration for Duchamp continues after Duchamp's death. From 1961 to 1974, the year of its inauguration, Dalí devotes most of his energy to his Theatre-Museum in his native town, Figueres (see pp. 206–07). He often describes it as a gigantic readymade, a work of art in itself, or like a text by Raymond Roussel, full of information but lacking any complete explanation. In Dalí's words: 'Let everyone draw from what they see conclusions linked inseparably to their own psychology and cosmogony.'[35]

Fig. 124
H. Vuibert, *Les Anaglyphes géométriques*, Paris, 1912.
Fundació Gala-Salvador Dalí, Figueres

Fig. 125
Man Ray, *The Last Work of Marcel Duchamp/Anaglyphic Chimney*, 1968.
Silver gelatin print, 18.4 x 12.7 cm.
Private collection, courtesy
Sean Kelly, New York

Fig. 126
Marcel Duchamp, *Emilio Puignau, Mayor of Cadaqués*, 1968.
Blue ink on paper, 24 x 19 cm.
Arxiu Pere Vehí, Cadaqués

THE DALÍ THEATRE-MUSEUM AS A READYMADE
MONTSE AGUER TEIXIDOR AND CARME RUIZ GONZÁLEZ

The Dalí Theatre-Museum at Figueres, the artist's last major creation, is an unusual museum in that it concerns itself with its creator's life and artistic trajectory as well as his concept of art. There are explicit references in the museum to Marcel Duchamp, who can be placed within Dalí's expanded concept of art – Dalí in his conceptual mode is close to Duchamp.

Duchamp was present at the time when the Theatre-Museum was in gestation, since he participated in the homage of the Surrealist Bullfight that Dalí received from his birthplace in 1961 (see pp. 104–05). Dalí later declared that the museum 'will be the museum of all my friends'.[1] When he made this statement, Duchamp was again undoubtedly in Cadaqués, during what was to be the last summer of his life. The Catalan painter wanted his future museum to be a meeting place for contemporary artists, and had aspirations for it to become the spiritual centre of Europe. An attentive walk through the rooms of the museum confirms that in the case of Duchamp, his intention was fulfilled.

In 1974 the museum was inaugurated, and Dalí included significant references to the last great exhibition in which he took part as a full member of the Surrealist group, the 'International Exhibition of Surrealism', which took place in 1938 at the Galerie Beaux-Arts, Paris, and in which both Dalí and Duchamp played key roles.[2]

By means of a homage to Duchamp's work *Étant donnés* (fig. 76), in the Mae West Room we discover the installation *Paradise* (fig. 127), a space situated behind the wall that forms part of the actress's face, in which, through two strategically situated orifices, one can view scenes that refer to the 1938 exhibition: a bed on which lies an ear surrounded with plants and animals, a small pool and a washbasin (fig. 128). It is lit in such a way that reality and fantasy are blurred, suggesting a dream world.

Leaving the Mae West Room and going up to the third floor we find the Room of Masterpieces (fig. 129) and 'Trajan Street'. In the first of these, together with some of his own paintings, Dalí placed works by other artists from his personal collection. In the centre, in a vitrine, the *Boîte-en-valise* given to him by Duchamp in 1958 occupies a prominent place, beside the drawing 'Preliminary Study of Gala' for the painting *One Hundred Thousand Virtual Virgins Reflected by a Number of Real Mirrors to be Determined by 'Étant donnés' Cybernetics* (1974), whose title is a clear

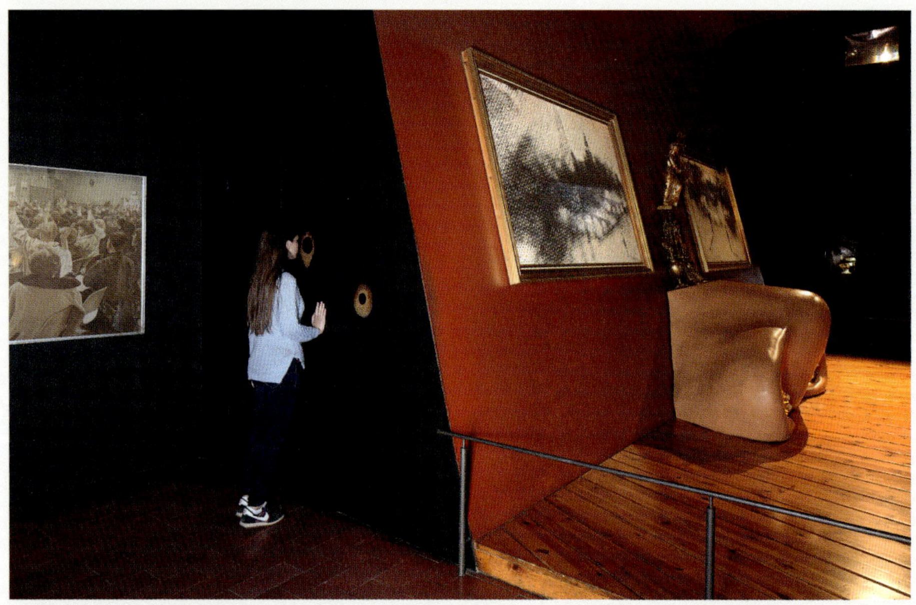

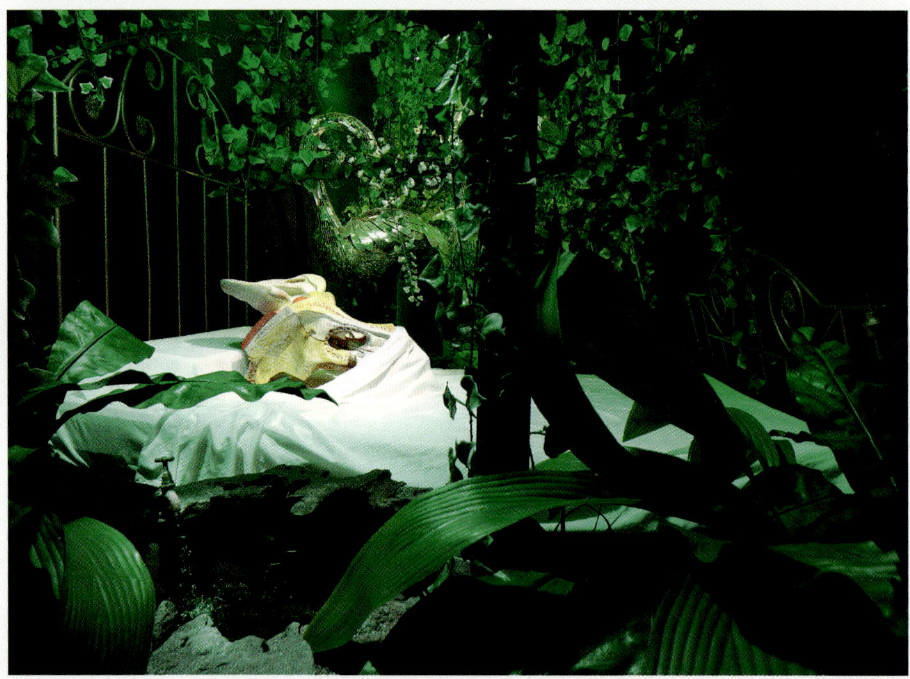

Fig. 127
Exterior view of Salvador Dalí's installation *Paradise* at the Dalí Theatre-Museum, Figueres, c. 1975.
Fundació Gala-Salvador Dalí, Figueres

Fig. 128
Interior view of *Paradise*, c. 1975.
Fundació Gala-Salvador Dalí, Figueres

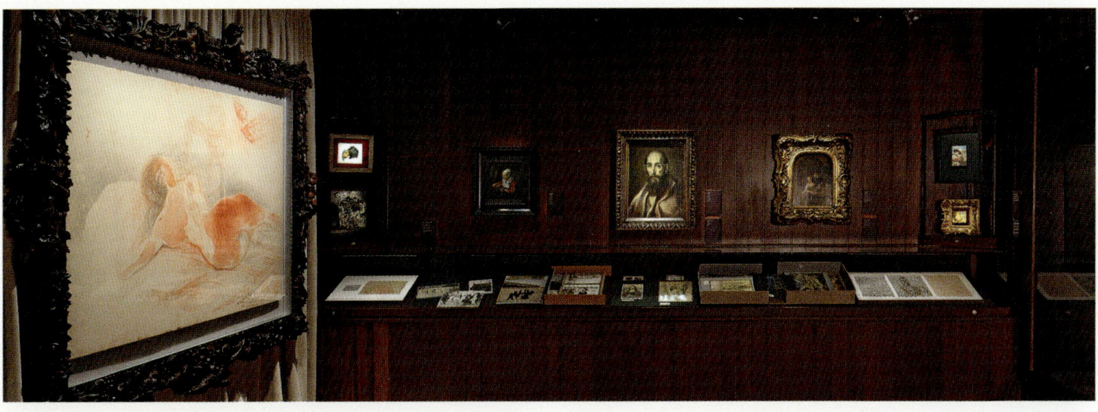

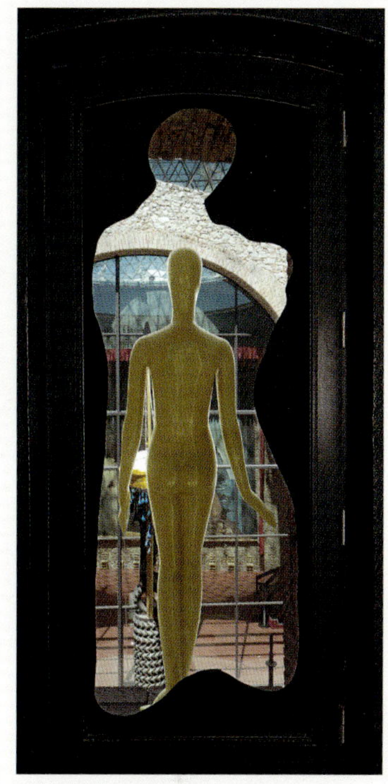

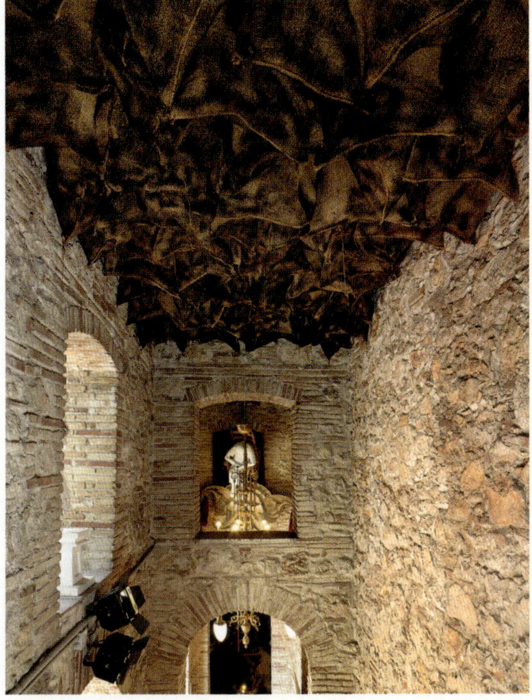

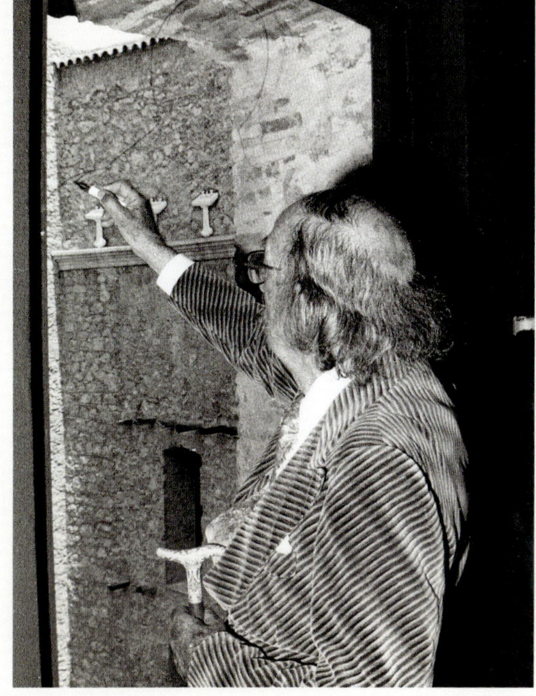

reference to Duchamp and their shared interest in optical effects. Leaving this room we enter a passage painted black. A street sign informs us that we are in Trajan Street, one of 'the most beautiful streets of Paris'.[3]

If we turn to the right, the last window brings us close to an installation in which the ceiling is covered with sacks painted black to resemble sacks of coal (fig. 131) – again an allusion to the 1938 Exhibition of Surrealism. If we retrace our steps and walk to the left, another window invites us to look out. However, the vista is not complete because a silhouette on the glass, like Duchamp's entrance to the Gradiva Gallery, determines our view of, in this case, the cupola and patio (fig. 130).

The opening of the Theatre-Museum in 1974 was the continuation of a great adventure that began in 1961 (fig. 132). From then and right up until 1988 Dalí constantly intervened and made additions to the museum, for instance, the upper part of an electricity pole, out of place and ennobled by being placed on one of the walls of the cupola stage, or *Rainy Taxi* on the patio, the most theatrical part of the museum, which startles the visitor just as it did when the first version was installed in the 1938 exhibition.

Dalí frequently described the museum as a readymade, as the largest Surrealist object in the world as well as a found object, and it is thus that we should see it. Dalí was interested in the museum as a total work of art, as the conceptualisation of the object as well as a Surrealist work of art. In fact, before its inauguration, he had declared that, even if no original works were on display, it would still be interesting to visit. What better homage to Duchamp?

Top left: Fig. 129
The Room of Masterpieces, *c.* 1975.
Fundació Gala-Salvador Dalí, Figueres

Top right: Fig. 130
The silhouetted window, 1973–75.
Black velvet on plywood, 195 x 69 cm.
Fundació Gala-Salvador Dalí, Figueres

Bottom left: Fig. 131
Salvador Dalí, *Coal-sack Ceiling* installation at the Theatre-Museum, Figueres, *c.* 1975.
Fundació Gala-Salvador Dalí, Figueres

Bottom right: Fig. 132
Salvador Dalí at the Theatre-Museum, Figueres, *c.* 1973. Photograph by 'Meli' (Melitó Casals), 23.6 x 17.2 cm.
Fundació Gala-Salvador Dalí, Figueres

EXHIBITIONS FEATURING WORKS BY DALÍ AND DUCHAMP

Compiled by the Centre for Dalinian Studies, Fundació Gala-Salvador Dalí, Figueres

Titles, descriptions and dates of works are listed as they appear in the respective catalogues. Dates of works are included where mentioned in the catalogue. In the case of Dalí's paintings titles and dates may not always correlate with the artist's catalogue raisonné. The list ends at 1968, the year of Duchamp's death.

'La Peinture au défi: Exposition de collages', Galerie Goemans, Paris, March 1930
Dalí: *Les Premiers Jours du printemps*
Duchamp: *L.H.O.O.Q.* (1919), *L.H.O.O.Q.* (1930), *Pharmacie* (1914), *Eau de Voilette*, *Roulette de Monte-Carlo*

'A Century of Progress: Exhibition of Painting and Sculpture', The Art Institute of Chicago, 1 June – 1 November 1933
Dalí: *The Shades of Night Descending* (1931)
Duchamp: *Nude Descending the Stairs* (1912)

'Exposition Surréaliste', Galerie Pierre Colle, Paris, 7–18 June 1933
Dalí: *Harpe invisible*, *Méditation sur la harpe*, *Planche d'associations démentielles*, *Chaise atmosphérique*, *Cuillère atmosphérique*, *Œufs sur le plat atmosphériques*, *Buste de femme rétrospectif*, *Académie atmosphérique*
Duchamp: *Pharmacie*

'Exposition Minotaure', Palais des Beaux-Arts, Brussels, May – June 1934
Dalí: *Guillaume Tell*, *Le Lever du jour*, *Le Grand Masturbateur*, *Peinture*, *Cannibalisme des objets*, *Buste de femme rétrospectif*
Duchamp: *Le Roi et la Reine traversés par les nus en vitesse*

'Modern Works of Art: Fifth Anniversary Exhibition', The Museum of Modern Art, New York, 20 November 1934 – 20 January 1935
Dalí: *Les Plaisirs Illuminés* (1929), *The Persistence of Memory* (1931)
Duchamp: *Disturbed Balance* (1918) [*To be Looked at (from the other side of the Glass), with One Eye, Close to, for Almost an Hour*]

'Exposición Surrealista', Ateneo de Santa Cruz de Tenerife, 11–21 May 1935
Dalí: *La libre inclinación del deseo*, *El reflejo craneano*, *Casa para erotómanos* [reproduced but not in catalogue list]
Duchamp: *Farmacia* (drawing), *Espiral*, *Por qué no estornudar?*, *Desnudos bajando una escalera*, *Virgen*, *El rey y la reina atravesados por desnudos rápidos*, *Testimonios oculistas* (photographs)

'Exposition Surréaliste d'Objets', Galerie Charles Ratton, Paris, 22–29 May 1936
Dalí: *Le Veston aphrodisiaque*, *Monument à Kant*
Duchamp: *Porte-bouteille* (1914), *Why not Sneeze?*, *La Bagarre d'Austerlitz* (1921)

'International Surrealist Exhibition', New Burlington Galleries, London, 11 June – 4 July 1936
Dalí: *The Dream* (1931), *Daybreak*, *Paranoiac Head* (1935), *Fantasy* (engraving), *The Horseman of Death* (drawing; 1934), *Retrospective Bust of a Woman Devoured by Ants* [not in all versions of the catalogue], *Poached Lion's Head* [not in all versions of the catalogue], *Aphrodisiac Jacket*, 4 studies for *Les Chants de Maldoror*, drawings
Duchamp: *The King and the Queen Crossed Rapidly by Nudes* (1912), *Chemist's Shop* (watercolour; 1914), Engraving, *About a Young Sister* (oil; 1911), *Roto Reliefs* (machine)

'Fantastic Art, Dada, Surrealism', The Museum of Modern Art, New York, 7 December 1936 – 17 January 1937
Dalí: *Illumined Pleasures* (1929), *The Font* (1930), *The Feeling of Becoming* (1930), *Andromeda* (ink, 1930), *Sun and Sand* (ink, 1930), *The Persistence of Memory* (1931), *Retrospective Bust of Woman* (photograph by Man Ray; 1933), *The Convalescence of a Kleptomaniac* (pencil and ink; 1933), *The Ghost of Vermeer of Delft, which Can Be Used as a Table* (1934), *Etching Paranoiac Face* (1935), *Paranoiac-critical Solitude* (1935), *Puzzle of Autumn* (1935), *City of Drawers* (1936), *Un Chien Andalou* (film, with Luis Buñuel; 1929)
Duchamp: *Coffee Mill* (1911), *The Bride* (1912), *The King and Queen Traversed by Swift Nudes* (1912), *Pharmacy* (1914), *The Bachelors (neuf moules mâlic)* (1914), '*Ready-made*' (photograph by Man Ray of a bottle-drying rack signed by the artist and sent to an exhibition; 1914), *Rotating Apparatus (Optique de precision)* (1920), *3 Stoppages-étalon* (wooden silhouettes), *Why Not Sneeze?* (1921), *Monte Carlo Share* (1925), *Anaemic Cinema* (film; 1938?) [Additional work included in catalogue via correction sheet: *Roto-Reliefs* (1934)]

'Surrealism', Cambridge University Arts Society, Gordon Fraser Gallery, Portugal Place, n.d. (1937)
Dalí: *Pastel* (1930), *La mélancolie de la plage* (drawing)
Duchamp: *La Mariée mise à Nu*, Documents, *Rotoreliefs*

Galerie Gradiva, Paris, 1937
(unspecified artworks)

'Surrealist Objects and Poems', London Gallery, London, 1937
Dalí: *Bust of Woman Devoured by Ants*
Duchamp: *Ready Made Object*

'Exposition Internationale du Surréalisme', Galerie Beaux-Arts, Paris, January – February 1938
Dalí: *Le Grand Masturbateur* (1929), *L'Homme invisible* (1930), *Naissance des désirs liquides* (1933), *Le Sommeil* (1937), *Plage enchantée* (1937), '*En bateï*' (1937), drawings and objects including *Telephone aphrodisiaque*.
Duchamp: *Pharmacie* (1914), *Neuf Moules mâlic* (1913), objects including *La Bagarre d'Austerlitz* (1921), *Rrose Sélavy et moi nous esquivons les ecchymoses des Esquimaux aux maux exquis* (1925), *Ready made* (1914)

'Old and New Trompe l'Œil', Julien Levy Gallery, New York, 8 March – 3 April 1938
Dalí: *Javanese Mannequin* (1934), *Aerodynamic Chair* (1936), *Femenine Figure in the Form of a Battle* (1936), *Double Profile* (1937), *Portrait of Joella* (1935)
Duchamp: *Bagarre d'Austerliz* (1935), *Rotos* (1935), *Spiral* (film)

'Exposition Internationale du Surréalisme', Galerie Robert, Amsterdam, Spring 1938
Dalí: *Le Bureaucrate moyen* (1932), *L'Omelette fines herbes* (1932), *La Chevelure* (1931), *Feuille d'étude, Eaux-fortes pour 'Les Chants de Maldoror' d'Isidore Ducasse*
Duchamp: *La Mariée mise à nu par ses célibataires même – livre-boîte*, *Couverture cigarettes* (1936), *colour photographs for Georges Hugnet 'La septième face du dé'*

'Contemporary Movements in European Painting', The Toledo Museum of Art, Ohio, 6 November – 11 December 1938
Dalí: *Ghost of Vermeer of Delft* (1934), *Puzzle of Autumn* (1935), *Shades of Night Descending* (1931)
Duchamp: *Nude Descending a Staircase* (1912)

'Exposición internacional del Surrealismo', Galería de Arte Mexicano, Mexico, January – February 1940
Dalí: *Momento sublime* (painting; 1938), *Soledad Mental* (drawing; 1935); 3 drawings
Duchamp: *Desnudo bajando de una escalera* (reproduction; 1911); *El Rey y la reina rodeados de desnudos veloces* (reproduction; 1912), *Trituradora de chocolate* (reproduction)

'Art of this Century: Objects, Drawings, Photographs, Paintings, Sculpture, Collages, 1910 to 1942', Art of This Century Gallery, New York, 1942
Dalí: *The Spectral Cow* (1926), *Woman Sleeping in a Landscape* (1931), *The Birth of Liquid Desires* (1932)
Duchamp: *Sad Young Man in a Train* (1912)

'20th Century Portraits', The Museum of Modern Art, New York, 9 December 1942 – 24 January 1943
Dalí: *Joella Lloyd* (1934), *Portrait of Gala (Mme Dalí)* (1935), *Dr Sigmund Freud* (1938), *Harpo Marx* (1939), *Soft Self-portrait* (1941)
Duchamp: *The Artist's Father* (1910), *The Sonata* (1911)

'15 Early Paintings. 15 Late Paintings', Art of This Century Gallery, New York, 13 March – 10 April 1943
Dalí: *The Birth of Liquid Desires* (1932), *Daddy Long Legs of the Evening, Hope* (1940), *Visage of War* (1941)
Duchamp: *Sad Young Man in a Train* (1912)

'Modern Drawings', The Museum of Modern Art, New York, 16 February – 10 May 1944
Dalí: *Cavalier of Death* (1934), *Studies* (1934), *Harpo Marx* (1937), *Figure of Drawers* (1937)
Duchamp: *Témoins Oculistes* (1920)

'Art in Progress: 15th Anniversary Exhibitions', The Museum of Modern Art, New York, 24 May – 15 October 1944
Dalí: *Impression of Africa* (1938), *Amor and Psyche, design for costumes* (1941), *Labyrinth, ballet design* (1941), *Designs for costumes Venus and Vulcan* (1941), *Design for six Paranoiac ballet costumes*
Duchamp: *The Large Glass (La Mariée mise à nu par ses célibataires, même)* (1915–23)

'European Artists in America', Whitney Museum of American Art, New York, 13 March – 11 April 1945
Dalí: *Tristan and Isolde* (1945), *Tristan fou* (1944), *Visage of War* (1940), *Chevalier de la mort* (1943), *Marsupial Figure* (1940), *Projets de costumes paranoïaques pour ballet*
Duchamp: *Boîte-en-valise* (1941–42), *Allégorie de genre* (1943)

'XXIV Biennale di Venezia: La Collezione Peggy Guggenheim', Padiglioni Stranieri, Venice, May – September 1948
Dalí: *Donna addormentata in un paesaggio* (1931), *Nascita di desideri liquidi* (1931)
Duchamp: *Giovane triste in treno* (1912)

'20th Century Art from the Louise and Walter Arensberg Collection', The Art Institute of Chicago, Chicago, 20 October – 18 December 1949
Dalí: *Agnostic Symbol* (1932), *Soft Construction with Boiled Beans; Premonition of Civil War* (1936)
Duchamp: *Head of Woman* (1910), *The Artist's Father* (1910), *Two Seated Figures* (1911), *The Bush* (1911), *The Sonata* (1911), *Yvonne et Magdeleine Torn in Tatters* (1911), *Portrait* (1911), *Study for the Chess Players* (1911), *Study for Nude Descending a Staircase* (1911), *Nude Descending a Staircase, Number 1* (1911), *Nude Descending a Staircase, Number 2* (1911), *Nude Descending a Staircase, Number 3* (1911), *Study for The King and the Queen* (1912), *Study for The King and the Queen* (two artworks with same title; 1912), *The King and Queen Surrounded by Swift Nudes* (1912), *Study for The Virgin* (1912), *The Bride* (1912), *Cemetery of Uniforms and Liveries* (1913), *Boxing Match* (1913), *Glider and the Water Mill* (1913–14–15), *Chocolate Grinder, Number 1* (1913), *Chocolate Grinder, Number 2* (1914), *Ready-made, Ball of Twine* (in metal frame; 1916), *Ready-made, Comb* (1916), *Ready-made, Girl with Bedstead (Apolinère Enameled)* (1916–17), *Témoins Oculistes* (1920), *Ready-made, Why Not Sneeze?* *Rrose Sélavy* (1921), *Sketch for Optique de Précision* (1925), *Bookbinding for Ubu Roi* (1935)

'Surréalisme + Abstraction: choix de la collection Peggy Guggenheim = Surrealisme + abstractie: keuze uit de verzameling Peggy Guggenheim', Palais des Beaux-Arts, Brussels and Stedelijk Museum, Amsterdam, 1951
Dalí: *La naissance des désirs liquides* (1932), *Femme endormie dans un paysage* (1931)
Duchamp: *Jeune homme triste dans un train* (1911), *Valise surréaliste, contenant la documentation de l'œuvre complète de l'artiste en format minimum* (1941)

'75 Œuvre du demi-siècle' Knokke-le-Zoute-Albert plage, Grande Salle des Expositions de 'La Réserve', 15 July – 9 September 1951
Dalí: *Gradiva* (1930)
Duchamp: *Document photographique: A Regarder d'un œil, de près, pendant presque un heure*, *Document photographique: Eau de Voilette*, '*Ready-made aidé*' (1921)

'Reality and Fantasy 1900–1954', Walker Art Center, Minneapolis, 23 May – 2 July 1954
Dalí: *Inventions of the Monsters* (1937), *Debris of an Automobile Giving Birth to a Blind Horse Biting a Telephone* (1938)
Duchamp: *Boîte-en-valise* (1941), *Le Reseau*

'Dichtende maler malende dichter', Kunstverein St Gallen, 3 August – 20 October 1957
Dalí: *Gedichtmanusrkipt mit Federzeichnungen*
Duchamp: *Rrose Sélavy* (1939), sketch for *Les joueurs d'échecs* (1911), study for *Nu descendant un escalier* (1911), 3 studies for *La Mariée mise à nu par ses célibataires, même* (1914), cover of the magazine *The Blind Man*, edited by Marcel Duchamp (1917), *Ready made: Porte bouteille* (1919), *Le domaine de Rrose Sélavy* (1921), text from *la Boîte verte* (1934)

'The Disquieting Muse: Surrealism',
Contemporary Arts Museum, Houston,
9 January – 16 February 1958
Dalí: *Phantasmagora* (1923), *Enigmatic Elements
in a Landscape* (1934), *Heavenly Disintegration*
(1950), *Living Flower* (1956)
Duchamp: *The Bachelors* (Study for *La Mariée
mise à nu par ses célibataires, même*, 1915–23)
(1914)

'50 ans d'art moderne', Exposition Universelle
et Internationale de Bruxelles, Palais
International des Beaux-Arts, Brussels,
17 April – 19 October 1958
Dalí: *Prémonition de la guerre civile.
Construction avec fèves bouillies* (1936),
La Tentation de saint Antoine (1946)
Duchamp: *Le Passage de la vierge à la mariée*
(1912), *Broyeuse de chocolat n° 2* (1914), *Réseaux
de stoppages-étalon* (1914)

'Exposition Internationale du Surréalisme,
Galerie Daniel Cordier, Paris, December 1959
– February 1960
Dalí: *Guillaume Tell* (1933)
Duchamp: *With My Tongue in My Cheek* (1959),
Dessin-sculpture

'Surrealist Intrusion in the Enchanters' Domain',
D'Arcy Galleries, New York, 28 November 1960
– 14 January 1961
Dalí: *Oreille anti-matière*, *The Spirit of the
Angelus of Millet*, *Costume design* (1939)
Duchamp: *Coin de chasteté* (1954), *Pharmacie
(Ready-Made)*

'Surréalisme et précurseurs', Palais Granvelle,
Besançon, 1961
Dalí: *Paysage* (1931), *La Tour* (1934), *Mystère
Surréaliste de New York* (1935), *Cannibalisme
des objets*
Duchamp: *Pharmacie* (1914), *Rotorelief* (1935),
Boîte-en-valise (1938), *La Mariée mise à nu par
ses célibataires, même* (1912), *Moulin à café*

'Paintings from the Arensberg and Gallatin
Collections of the Philadelphia Museum of
Art', The Solomon R. Guggenheim Museum,
New York City, 1961
Dalí: *Soft Construction with Boiled Beans;
Premonition of Civil War* (1936)
Duchamp: *Artist's Father* (1910), *The Sonata*
(1911), *Yvonne and Magdeleine Torn in Tatters*
(1911), *Portrait* (1911), *Portrait of Chess Players*
(1911), *Study for 'Nude Descending a Staircase'*
(1911), *Nude Descending a Staircase, n° 1* (1911),
Nude Descending a Staircase, n° 2 (1912), *Nude
Descending a Staircase, n° 3* (1916), *The King
and the Queen Surrounded By Swift Nudes*
(1912), *Chocolate Grinder, n° 2* (1914)

'Da Boldini a Pollock: pittura e scultura del XX
secolo', Mostra della Moda Stile Costume,
Museo Civico, Turin, 1961
Dalí: *Fontana di Roma* (1954)
Duchamp: *Boîte en valise* (1941–42), *Roto-relief*

'Art Contemporain', Grand Palais des
Champs-Élysées, Paris, 1963
Dalí: *Composition surréaliste* (1928),
Le Rêve (1932)
Duchamp: *Feuille de vigne feminine*

'Le Surréalisme: sources, histoire, affinités',
Galerie Charpentier, Paris, 13 April –
30 September 1964
Dalí: *Le Rêve* (1932), *Le Jeu lugubre* (1932),
Les Montres molles (1933), *Babaouo* (six glass
plates; 1932), *L'Heure triangulaire* (1933), *La
Vénus aux tiroirs*, *L'Illusion et la Fantaisie* (1932),
drawing for *'Le Somnanbule'*, poème de René
Laporte, *Les Atavismes impérials* (drawing;
1933), *Dédicace à Renée Laporte* (1933), *Dessin*

gouaché (1934), *Hommage à Kant* (1936),
Expérimentation surréaliste (Planche n° 1) ;
Books: *Babaouo* (1932), *Métamorphoses de
Narcisse* (1937)
Duchamp: *La Mariée mise à nu par ses
célibataires, même*. *'Le grand verre'* (1961),
Feuille de vigne femele (1958), *Boîte verte*,
Boîte en valise, *Coin de chasteté* (Bronze edition
5/8)

'A Selection of 20th Century Art of
3 Generations', Sidney Janis Gallery, New York,
November 24 – December 26, 1964
Dalí: *Illumined Pleasures* (1929)
Duchamp: *Bicycle Wheel* (1913)

'First International Biennale of Sculpture:
Panathenaia of World Sculpture', Philopappos
Hill, Athens, 8 September – 8 November 1965
Dalí: *Aphrodite with Drawers* (bronze; 1936
[1964])
Duchamp: *Roue de bicyclette*

'Poetry in Painting 1931–1949, from the
Collection of The Julien Levy Gallery,
New York', Richard Feigen Gallery, Chicago,
10 November – 18 December 1965
(unspecified artworks)

'L'Écart absolu', XIe Exposition Internationale
du Surréalisme, Galerie l'Œil, Paris, December
1965
Dalí: *Peinture* (1934), *La Mélancolie extatique
des chiens* (1931)
Duchamp: *Why not sneeze?* (1921), *Fresh Widow*
(1920), *Torture morte* (1962)

'The Other Tradition', The Institute of
Contemporary Art, University of Pennsylvania,
Philadelphia, Pennsylvania, 27 January –
7 March 1966
Dalí: *Un Œuf Sur le Plat sans le Plat* (193? [*sic*])
Duchamp: *Broyeuse de chocolat No. 1* (1913),
Neuf Moules Malic (Nine Malic Moulds)
(original 1937), *Porte-Bouteilles (Bottle Rack)*
(3rd version, 1961)

'Hommage à Caïssa', Cordier and Ekstrom
Gallery, New York, 8 – 26 February 1966
(unspecified artworks)

'Surrealism: A State of Mind 1924–1965',
University of California Art Galleries, Santa
Barbara, California, 26 February – 27 March
1966
Dalí: *Spectre du Soir* (1930), *Honey Is Sweeter
Than Blood* (1941), *Beach Scene* (1936),
City of Drawers (1936)
Duchamp: *Boîte-en-valise* (1938–42)

'Art in the Mirror', The Museum of Modern Art,
New York, 22 November 1966 – 6 February 1967
Dalí: *Portrait of Gala* (1935)
Duchamp: *Valise* (1943)

'The Enchanted Domain: Surrealist Art
at Exeter City Gallery and Exe Gallery',
Exe Gallery, Exeter, 25 April – 20 May 1967
Dalí: *À mon ami Paul Éluard* (1931), *Untitled
beach scene* (1935), *Victory* (1944), *Beach scene*
Duchamp: *Boîte-en-valise* (1938), *Rote-relief*
cover of *Minotaure* (1935), *Cœurs volants*, cover
of *Cahiers d'Art* (1936)

'Le Muse Inquietanti. Maestri del Surrealismo'.
Galleria Civica d'Arte Moderna, Torino,
November 1967 – January 1968
Dalí: *Gioco lugubre* (1929), *Nascita dei desideri
liquidi* (1932), *L'Angelo architettonico di Millet*
(1933), *Vestigia ataviche dopo la pioggia* (1934),
Il bacio (1929), *Venere con tiretti* (1936), *Il
Cavaliere della Morte* (c. 1935), *Donna con la
testa di rose* (1957), *Violette imperiali* (1938)

Duchamp: *Il grande vetro (acqueforti – secondo
stato)* (1923/66), *La sposa*, *L'Iscrizione in alto e i
nove colpi*, *Nove mole Malic*, *Scivolo con mulino
ad acqua*, *La Macina per cioccolato*, *I setacci*,
Testimoni oculari, *Il Grande vetro (con
l'aggiunta degli elementi mancanti quando fu
lasciato incompleto nel 1923)*, *Obbligazione per
la roulette di Montecarlo* (1925), *Alla maniera di
Delvaux* (1942)

'The Sidney and Harriet Janis Collection.
A Gift to The Museum of Modern Art',
The Museum of Modern Art, New York,
17 January – 4 March 1968
Dalí: *Illumined Pleasures* (1929), *Frontispiece
for Second Surrealist Manifesto* (1930)
Duchamp: *Bicycle Wheel* (1951)

'Schatten van het surrealisme = Trésors du
surréalisme', Casino Communal de Knokke –
Le Zoute, Brussels, June – September 1968
Dalí: *Danseuses, lion, cheval* (1930), *Le Rêve*
(1932), *L'Heure triangulaire* (1933), *Harpe* (1934),
Venus de Milo aux tiroirs (1964), *Cycle
systématique de conférences surréalistes*
Duchamp: *Boîte en valise* (1942)

'Dada, Surrealism, and Their Heritage', The
Museum of Modern Art, New York, 27 March
– 9 June 1968 / Los Angeles Country Museum
of Art, Los Angeles, 16 July – 8 September
1968 / The Art Institute of Chicago, Chicago,
19 October – 8 December 1968
The notation (NY), (LA), or (C) indicates that the
respective works were shown only in New York,
Los Angeles, or Chicago.
Dalí: *Senicitas* (1928), *Accommodations of
Desire* (1929), *The Great Masturbator* (1929),
Illumined Pleasures (NY) (1929), *Imperial
Monument to the Child-Woman* (unfinished) (c.
1929), *The Lugubrious Game* (NY) (1929), *The
Invisible Man* (1929–33), *The Persistence of
Memory* (LA, C) (1931), *The Specter of Sex
Appeal* (1934), *Six Objects (all that is left of a
tray of objects)* (1936), *The Venus de Milo of the
Drawers* (1964)
Duchamp: *The Bride* (NY, C) (1912), *The Passage
from Virgin to Bride* (1912), *Bicycle Wheel* (1964),
Chocolate Grinder n.1 (NY, C) (1913), *Bottlerack*
(1964), *Nine Malic Molds* (NY) (1914–15), *The
Bride Stripped Bare by Her Bacherlors, Even*
(1966), *Traveler's Folding Item* (1964), *Tu m'* (NY)
(1918), *Fresh Widow* (NY) (1920), *Rotary Glass
Plate (Precision Optics)* (NY) (1920), *Why Not
Sneeze?* (1964), *Rotoreliefs (Optical Disks)* (1935)

ENDNOTES

Salvador Dalí, Tenor Sax | Marcel Duchamp, Drums (pp. 10–13)

1 Julian Street, 'Why I Became a Cubist', *Everybody's Magazine*, 28, June 1913.
2 Bonnie Clearwater (ed.), *West Coast Duchamp*, Miami Beach, 1991, pp. 109–10.
3 Clearwater 1991, p. 110.
4 Clearwater 1991, p. 114.
5 Clearwater 1991, p. 121.

Introduction (pp. 14–19)

1 Salvador Dalí, 'The King and the Queen Traversed by Swift Nudes', Richard Howard (trans.), *Art News*, 58, April 1959.
2 Moira Roth and William Roth, 'John Cage on Marcel Duchamp', in Joseph Masheck (ed.), *Duchamp in Perspective*, Englewood Cliffs, 1975, pp. 151–61, quote p. 161.
3 Letter from Edward James to Salvador Dalí, undated and probably never sent. Edward James Archive, West Dean, Box 21.
4 Marcel Duchamp in conversation with Richard Hamilton, 1961, quoted in Anne d'Harnoncourt and Walter Hopps, *Etant donnés: I. la chute d'eau, 2. le gas d'éclairage: Reflections on a New Work by Marcel Duchamp*, Philadelphia, 1969, p. 40.
5 The Knoedler Gallery in New York offered Duchamp £10,000 a year in 1916 or 1917, probably the first of many attempts to lure him back into the market, but he refused.
6 Paul B. Franklin, 'Bottlerack', unpublished text.
7 Alfred Jarry, 'La Passion considérée comme course de côte', *La Canard sauvage*, April 1903.
8 Letter from Marcel Duchamp to Suzanne Duchamp, 15 January 1916, in Francis Naumann and Hector Obalk (eds), *Affectionately, Marcel: The Selected Correspondence of Marcel Duchamp*, Antwerp, 2000.
9 Duchamp wrote to Suzanne on 11 April 1917, 'One of my woman friends under a masculine pseudonym, Richard Mutt, had sent a porcelain urinal as a sculpture....' Admittedly an ambiguous statement, this has been misinterpreted to imply that Duchamp usurped the identity of a female artist. The *Fountain* episode was masterminded by Duchamp with the collaboration of his female friends Louise Norton, who wrote 'Buddha of the Bathroom', and Beatrice Wood, who wrote 'The Richard Mutt Case', for *The Blind Man*.
10 *The Blind Man*, 2, May 1917, n.p. See Marcel Duchamp, Henri-Pierre Roché, Beatrice Wood, *3 New York Dadas and The Blind Man*, London, 2013. Duchamp wrote to Suzanne on 11 April 1917, 'One of my woman friends under a masculine pseudonym, Richard Mutt, had sent a porcelain urinal as a sculpture....' Admittedly an ambiguous statement, this has been misinterpreted to imply that Duchamp usurped the identity of a female artist. The *Fountain* episode was masterminded by Duchamp with the collaboration of his female friends Louise Norton, who wrote 'Buddha of the Bathroom', and Beatrice Wood, who wrote 'The Richard Mutt Case', for *The Blind Man*.
11 André Breton, 'Marcel Duchamp', *Littérature*, 5, October 1922, in André Breton, *Les Pas Perdus*, Paris, 1924, p. 86.
12 Salvador Dalí, Sebastià Gasch and Lluís Montanyà, *Manifest Groc (Yellow Manifesto)*, Barcelona, March 1928, John London (trans.), in *Salvador Dalí: The Early Years*, exh. cat., Hayward Gallery, London, 1994, pp. 221–22.
13 Joan Miró quoted in Maurice Raynal, *Anthologie de la peinture en France de 1906 à nos jours*, Paris, 1927, p. 34.
14 William Copley, 'The New Piece', *Art in America*, 57, 4, 1969, p. 36, reprinted in Mashek 1975, p. 112.
15 André Breton, 'What Is Surrealism?', 1934, in Franklin Rosemont (ed.), *What Is Surrealism? Selected Writings*, New York, 1978, p. 136.
16 André Breton, *Second Manifeste de surréalisme*, 1929, p. 170. 'Harrar' is a reference to Arthur Rimbaud, who abandoned his life as a poet to become a tradesman in Africa.
17 Yves Peyré and Evelyne Toussaint, *Duchamp à la Bibliothèque Sainte-Geneviève*, Paris, 2014.
18 Harriet and Sidney Janis, 'Marcel Duchamp: Anti-Artist', *View*, 5, no. 1, 1945, p. 24.
19 Dalí 1959.
20 Michel de Montaigne, *The Complete Essays*, M. A. Screech (trans.), London, 1987, p. 563.
21 'Both Fascism and Communism are bent on regimenting people, robbing them of their individuality. It is no atmosphere in which creative art can thrive.' Interview with Duchamp in *Chicago News*, 1936, quoted in Robert Radford, '"There is No Art; There Are Only Artists": Salvador Dalí and Marcel Duchamp, Modernism and Individualism', *Étant donné*, 5, 2003, p. 56.
22 *Entretiens avec Georges Charbonnier*, Marseilles, 1994, p. 43. Quoted in Radford 2003, p. 56.
23 Letter from Salvador Dalí to André Breton, quoted in José Pierre, 'Breton et Dalí', in *Salvador Dalí: Retrospective, 1920–1980*, exh. cat., Centre Georges Pompidou, Paris, 1979, p. 137.
24 Salvador Dalí, *The Secret Life of Salvador Dalí*, Haakon M. Chevalier (trans.), London, 1968, p. 339.
25 Radford 2003, pp. 53–76, quote p. 57. See also Félix Fanés, *Salvador Dalí: The Construction of the Image 1925–1930*, New Haven and London, 2007, in particular Appendix 5, pp. 193–97: Salvador Dalí, 'For a Terrorist Tribunal of Intellectual Responsibilities', lecture given at the Ateneu Enciclopèdic Popular, Barcelona, 5 April 1934.
26 Salvador Dalí and André Parinaud, *The Unspeakable Confessions of Salvador Dalí*, Harold J. Salemson (trans.), New York, 1977, p. 131.
27 Marcel Duchamp, unpublished interview by Jean-Marie Drot, 'Jeu d'échecs avec Marcel Duchamp' (1963), quoted in Calvin Tomkins, *Duchamp: A Biography*, London, 1997, p. 93.
28 Luis Buñuel, Charles de Noailles, Jean-Michel Bouhours, Nathalie Schoeller, *L'Âge d'or: Correspondance Luis Buñuel-Charles de Noailles. Lettres et documents (1929–1976)*, Paris, 1993, p. 83.
29 Duchamp wrote to Pierre de Massot on 30 August 1933. 'Dalí est ici. – Nous nous voyons presque tous les jours; il habite à un kilomètre du village.' Naumann and Obalk 2000, p. 174.
30 Pierre Cabanne, *Entretiens avec Marcel Duchamp*, Paris, 1967, p. 74.
31 Marcel Duchamp interviewed by George Heard Hamilton and Richard Hamilton, BBC Third Programme, 6 March 1978.
32 Cabanne 1967, p. 66.
33 The uncanny ability of Duchamp's works and actions to speak to successive generations is true again now, when 'curating' dominates artistic activity; see, for example, Elena Filipovic, *The Apparently Marginal Activities of Marcel Duchamp*, Cambridge MA, 2016.

Repression in Painting (pp. 20–25)

1 The exhibition *Duchamp. La peinture, même*, directed by Cécile Debray (exh. cat., Centre Georges Pompidou, Paris, 2013), approached Marcel Duchamp from the angle of the artist as painter for the first time.
2 Entry for 11 July 1964, quoted in Jennifer Gough-Cooper, Pontus Hultén, Jacques Caumont, *Marcel Duchamp: Work and Life; Ephemerides on and about Marcel Duchamp and Rrose Sélavy: 1887–1968*, Cambridge MA, 1993.
3 Interview in the *Chicago Daily News*, 25 August 1936; entry for 25 August 1936, in Gough-Cooper et al. 1993.
4 See Thierry Dufrêne, 'Dalí préfère le mythe à l'histoire', in Montse Aguer, Jean-Michel Bouhours, Thierry Dufrêne and Jean-Hubert Martin, *Dalí*, exh. cat., Centre Georges Pompidou, Paris, and MNCARS, Madrid, 2012, pp. 222–23.
5 Salvador Dalí, 'Le Grand Masturbateur', in *La Femme visible*, Paris, 1930.
6 Salvador Dalí, 'I Defy Aragon', *Art Front*, vol. 3, no. 2, March 1937.
7 Salvador Dalí, 'Vive la guerre! Le surréalisme et Hitler', 1933–34, a French text unpublished at the time but included in Paris 2012, p. 329.
8 Salvador Dalí, 'Le Surréalisme au service de la révolution', text of a lecture given on 18 September 1931 in Barcelona, published in Paris 2012, pp. 317–18.
9 Calvin Tomkins, 'Not Seen and/or Less Seen: Marcel Duchamp', *The New Yorker*, 6 February 1965, pp. 48–50.
10 Alain Jouffroy, 'L'Idée de jugement devrait disparaître', *Arts, Lettres et spectacles*, Paris, 24 November 1954, reprinted in Alain Jouffroy, *Une Révolution du regard*, Paris, 1964, pp. 110–11.
11 Man Ray, *Autoportrait*, Paris, 1998, p. 321.
12 Letter from Marcel Duchamp to the restorer Mary Ann Adler, who was preparing to renew the painting's canvas, 6 June or July 1951. Paintings Documentation, Philadelphia Museum of Art.
13 Marcel Duchamp, 'A propos de moi-même', 1964, in Michel Sanouillet and Paul Matisse, *Duchamp du signe: suivi des Notes*, Paris, 2008, p. 206.
14 The piece entitled *Pharmacy* is an allusive illustration of the words of Laforgue: '...Tout s'allume! Beuglants, salons, tripots et bouges, / Et le pharmacien sur le blême trottoir / Fait s'épandre les lacs des bocaux verts ou rouges / Phares lointains de ceux qui s'en iront ce soir.' Jules Laforgue, 'Recueillement du soir', in *Œuvres complètes*, Paris, 1903.
15 Marcel Duchamp, in Pierre Cabanne, *Dialogues with Marcel Duchamp*, New York, 1987, p. 88.
16 Daniel Abadie, Pontus Hultén et al., *Salvador Dalí: Retrospective, 1920–1980*, exh. cat., Centre Georges Pompidou, Paris, 1979, pp. 16–17.
17 Paris 1979, p. 51.
18 Sanouillet and Matisse 2008, p. 167.
19 Salvador Dalí, 'Le Début de mon hommage à Fortuny...', *c*. 1962. Manuscript, Fundació Gala-Salvador Dalí, Figueres, published in Paris 2012, p. 355.
20 Duchamp's reply to Cloyd Head during a press conference at the Art Institute of Chicago, 19 October 1949. See Gough-Cooper et al. 1993, 19 October 1949. Quoted in Françoise Le Penven, 'Marcel Duchamp ou la pérennité des sources', *Etudes*, 397, December 2002, pp. 651–61, note 1.
21 Salvador Dalí, *Le Mythe tragique de l'Angélus de Millet*, Paris, 1963, quoted in Paris 1979, p. 322.
22 *Paris Match*, 500, 8 November 1958.
23 Edouard Jaguer, 'A propos d'un écart absolu de Marcel Duchamp (et de l'Exposition internationale du surréalisme de New York, 1960–61)', *Étant donné*, 5, 'Marcel Duchamp et Salvador Dalí', 2003, pp. 23–47.
24 André Breton, 'Des tendances les plus récentes de la peinture surréaliste', *Minotaure*, 12–13, May 1939, p. 17.
25 Salvador Dalí, 'The King and the Queen Traversed by Swift Nudes', Richard Howard (trans.), *Art News*, 58, April 1959.
26 Marcel Duchamp interviewed by James Johnson Sweeney, 1945. Tapescript. Archives of the Philadelphia Museum of Art.

Readymades, Sculptures, Objects: 'A Happy Blasphemy' (pp. 26–33)

1 Louis Aragon, *La Peinture au défi*, Paris, 1930, trans. as 'Challenge to Painting', in Lucy Lippard (ed.), *Surrealists on Art*, Englewood Cliffs, 1970, p. 50.
2 Duchamp, conversation with Jeanne Siegel 12 April 1967, broadcast WBAI, 18 May 1967.
3 Marcel Duchamp, *The Bride Stripped Bare by Her Bachelors, Even*, Typographic version of the *Green Box* [1934] by Richard Hamilton, George Heard Hamilton (trans.), Stuttgart, London and Reykjavik, 1976, n.p.
4 Interview with George Heard Hamilton, 19 January 1959, broadcast on the BBC Third Programme, 13 November 1959.
5 Letter to Jean Crotti, 8 July 1918, in Francis Naumann and Hector Obalk (eds), *Affectionately, Marcel: The Selected Correspondence of Marcel Duchamp*, Antwerp, 2000, p. 53.
6 William Camfield, *Marcel Duchamp: Fountain*, Houston, 1989, pp. 48–49, and Arturo Schwarz, *The Complete Works of Marcel Duchamp*, New York, 2000, p. 189. See also Anthony Shelton (ed.), *Fetishism: Visualising Power and Desire*, London, 1995.
7 Michel Sanouillet and Elmer Peterson (eds), *Salt Seller: The Essential Writings of Marcel Duchamp*, London and New York, 1975, p. 37.
8 Jean Wahl, 'L'Existence comme fracture et soudure (fragment)', *L'Usage de la Parole*, Paris, 1, 3, April 1940, pp. 44–45. Present author's translation.
9 André Breton, 'Crise de l'objet' (1936), in *Œuvres complètes IV*, Paris, 2008, p. 688, trans. Simon Watson Taylor as 'Crisis of the Object', in André Breton, *Surrealism and Painting*, London, 1972, p. 280.
10 Salvador Dalí, 'Derniers modes d'excitation intéllectuelle pour l'été 1934', *Documents 1934. No. spécial Intervention surréaliste*, Paris, nouvelle série 1, June 1934, pp. 33–35, and trans. in Haim Finkelstein (ed.), *The Collected Writings of Salvador Dalí*, Cambridge and New York, 1998, p. 254. See also Pilar Parcerisas, *Marcel Duchamp, 'Don't Forget': Una partida de ajedrez con Man Ray y Salvador Dalí*, exh. cat., Museo de Arte Contemporáneo, Santiago de Chile, 2014–15, p. 37.
11 Salvador Dalí, 'Objets psycho-atmospherique-anamorphiques', *SASDLR*, 6, 15 May 1932, pp. 45–48, trans. in Finkelstein 1998, p. 247.
12 Marcel Duchamp, Interview with Lawrence Steefel, September 1956, in Lawrence D. Steefel, *The Position of Duchamp's* Glass *in the Development of His Art*, New York, 1977, note 39, p. 312.
13 Michel Sanouillet and Elmer Peterson (eds), *Salt Seller: The Essential Writings of Marcel Duchamp*, London, 1975, p. 93.
14 Salvador Dalí, 'De la beauté terrifiante et

comestible de l'architecture *Modern Style*, *Minotaure*, Geneva, 3–4, December 1933, pp. 68–76.

15   'Exposition Dalí', Galerie Jacques Bonjean, Paris, 20 June – 13 July 1934.

16   Robert and Nicolas Descharnes, *Dalí: The Hard and the Soft: Spells for the Magic of Form. Sculptures and Objects*, Azay-le-Rideau, 2004, p. 31. The work was cast in bronze by Valsuani and painted white in an edition published by André-François Petit in 1973.

17   Salvador Dalí, 'Honneur à l'objet!', *Cahiers d'art*, 11, 1936, pp. 33–37; André Breton, 'Crise de l'objet', pp. 21–26.

18   'Cœurs volants' is a word play on 'Cœurs vaillants', the name of a Catholic children's newspaper founded in 1929. Bernard Marcadé, *Marcel Duchamp: La vie à crédit*, Paris, 2007, p. 334.

19   Gabrielle Buffet, 'Cœurs volants', *Cahiers d'art*, Paris, 11, 1–2, 1936, pp. 34–43, quotation p. 40.

20   Louis Aragon, *La Peinture au défi*, in Lippard 1970.

21   Paul Matisse (ed.), *Marcel Duchamp, Notes*, Paris, 1980, n. p., no. 172: 'Look for a Readymade/which weighs a weight/chosen in advance.'

22   Duchamp, conversation with Jeanne Siegel, 12 April 1967, broadcast WBAI, 18 May 1967.

23   Georges Charbonnier, 'Natural Art and Cultural Art: A Conversation with Claude Levi-Strauss', in Joseph Masheck, *Marcel Duchamp in Perspective*, Englewood Cliffs, 1975, p. 79.

24   André Breton, *Dictionnaire abrégé du surréalisme*, in his *Œuvres complètes II*, Paris, 1992, p. 837.

25   Breton 1992., p. 826.

26   André Breton, 'Introduction au discours sur le peu de réalité', dated 1924, published 1925; Breton 1992, pp. 263–80.

27   André Breton, *Dictionnaire abrégé du surréalisme*, in Breton 1992, p. 826.

28   Thomas McEvilley, *Sculpture in the Age of Doubt*, New York, 1999, in particular Chapter 3, 'Duchamp, Pyrrhonism, and the Overthrow of the Kantian Tradition', pp. 48–66; Arturo Schwarz, *The Complete Works of Marcel Duchamp*, New York, 2000, p. 33. For more precision on the editions available to Duchamp, see Yves Peyré and Evelyne Toussaint, *Duchamp à la bibliothèque Sainte-Geneviève*, Paris, 2014, pp. 48–53, 121–26.

29   Salvador Dalí, 'The King and the Queen Traversed by Swift Nudes', Richard Howard (trans.), *Art News*, 58, April 1959, pp. 22–25, trans. in Finkelstein, 1998, p. 368.

30   Salvador Dalí, Preface, 'L'échecs c'est moi' ('Chess, it's me'), in Pierre Cabanne, *Dialogues with Marcel Duchamp*, New York, 1971, pp. 13–14.

31   Marcel Duchamp, in Cabanne 1971, pp. 89–90.

32   James Johnson Sweeny, 'A Conversation with Marcel Duchamp' (January 1956), in Sanouillet and Peterson 1975, p. 181, and *The Writings of Marcel Duchamp*, trans. (1973), 1989, pp. 133–34.

33   Marcel Duchamp, in Schwarz 2000, p. 256.

34   Salvador Dalí, 'Psychologie non-euclidienne d'une photographie', *Minotaure*, 7, June 1935, pp. 56–57, trans. in Finklestein, 1998, p. 304.

35   Duchamp's correspondence with Robert Lebel (1953), in Paul Franklin (ed.), *The Artist and the Critic Stripped Bare. The Correspondence of Marcel Duchamp and Robert Lebel*, Los Angeles, 2016, pp. 132–33, and Cabanne 1971, p. 67.

36   Marcel Duchamp, quoted in Maurizio Lazzarato, *Marcel Duchamp et le refus du travail*, Paris, 2014, p. 29.

37   Marcel Duchamp, in Schwarz 2000, p. 41.

Systematising Confusion: Marcel Duchamp and Salvador Dalí, 'Writers' (pp. 34–39)

1   Robert and Nicolas Descharnes, *Salvador Dalí*, Charles Akin (trans.), New York, 1993, p. 35.

2   Marcel Duchamp, letter of 25 October 1958 to Marcel Jean, *Affectt Marcel. The Selected Correspondence of Marcel Duchamp*, Francis M. Naumann and Hector Obalk (eds), Jill Taylor (trans.), London, 2000, pp. 356–7, quotation on p. 357.

3   Marcel Duchamp, 'The Great Trouble with Art in This Country' (1946), in *Salt Seller: The Essential Writings of Marcel Duchamp* [1973], Michel Sanouillet and Elmer Peterson (eds), London, 1975, pp. 123–26, quotation on p. 126.

4   Marcel Duchamp, 'The Green Box' (1934), Sanouillet and Peterson 1975, pp. 26–71, quotation on p. 26.

5   This point is made by Haim Finkelstein in his introduction to Salvador Dalí, *The Collected Writings of Salvador Dalí*, Cambridge and New York, 1998, pp. 2, 7.

6   Dalí, 'Poem' (1928), in Finkelstein 1998, p. 27.

7   See the brief notice of the publication of Péret's *Le Grand Jeu* (1928) in 1929 by Dalí, Finkelstein 1998, p. 105.

8   Dalí, 'Love and Memory' (1931), in Finkelstein 1998, pp. 162–72, quotation on pp. 163–64.

9   See Dalí, 'Surrealist Objects' (1931) and 'The Object as Revealed in Surrealist Experiment' (1932) in Finkelstein 1998, pp. 231–34.

10   Dalí, 'The Rotting Donkey' (1930), in Finkelstein 1998, pp. 223–36, quotation on p. 223.

11   Marcel Duchamp, 'La mariée mise à nu par ses célibataires mêmes', *SASDLR*, 5/6, May 1933, pp. 1–2. Duchamp had already published a piece in the review on chess, and his fixation on the game goes a long way towards explaining his hiatus from activities associable with art: Marcel Duchamp, 'Formule de l'opposition hétérodoxe dans les domaines principaux', *SASDLR*, 2, October 1930, 18–19.

12   Duchamp, in Sanouillet and Peterson 1975, p. 51.

13   Dalí, 'Psychoatmospheric-Anamorphic Objects' (1933), in Finkelstein 1998, pp. 244–48, quotation on p. 247.

14   Margaret Cohen, *Profane Illumination: Walter Benjamin and the Paris of Surrealist Revolution*, Berkeley, Los Angeles, London, 1993, pp. 60–61.

15   Dalí, 'The Tragic Myth of Millet's *Angelus*: Paranoiac-critical Interpretation (excerpts)' (1963), in Finkelstein 1998, pp. 282–97, quotation on p. 288.

16   All notes are taken from Paul Matisse (ed.), *Marcel Duchamp, Notes*, Paris, 1980, n. p.

17   Salvador Dalí, 'The King and the Queen Traversed by Swift Nudes', Richard Howard (trans.), *Art News*, 58, April 1959, pp. 22–25, trans. in Finkelstein, 1998, pp. 367–69, quotation on p. 367.

18   For the 'convoluted language', 'meandering prose' and general obscurity of the texts in Dalí's book-object, see Elliott King, 'Ten Recipes for Immortality: A Study in Dalinian Science and Paranoiac Fictions', in Gavin Parkinson (ed.), *Surrealism, Science Fiction and Comics*, Liverpool, 2015, pp. 213–32, quotation on p. 220.

Photography and Film (pp. 40–47)

1   Francis Naumann and Hector Obalk (eds), *Affectionately, Marcel: The Selected Correspondence of Marcel Duchamp*, Antwerp, 2000, p. 109.

2   Anne d'Harnoncourt and Kynaston McShine, *Marcel Duchamp*, exh. cat., Philadelphia Museum of Art and Museum of Modern Art, New York, 1973, p. 256. From Duchamp's notes for a lecture, 'Apropos of Myself', 1964.

3   Duchamp gave the original notes to Walter Arensberg in 1915.

4   See Jean Clair, *Duchamp et la photographie*, Paris, 1977.

5   For a detailed discussion of Rrose Sélavy and of the 'soap man' see Dawn Ades, 'Duchamp's Masquerades', in Graham Clarke (ed.), *The Portrait in Photography*, London, 1992, pp. 94–114.

6   André Breton, 'Surrealism and Painting', in *Surrealism and Painting*, Simon Watson Taylor (trans.), New York, 1972, p. 32.

7   Breton 1972, p. 33.

8   *Littérature*, n.s., 5, 1 October 1922, facing p. 10.

9   Dawn Ades, 'Why Film?', in Matthew Gale (ed.), *Dalí and Film*, exh. cat., Tate, London, and Museum of Modern Art, New York, 2007, p. 26.

10   László Moholy-Nagy, *Painting, Photography, Film*, Bauhaus Book, vol. 8 (1925/27), London, 1969, p. 28. The English edition used the 1927 Bauhaus edition. Which Bauhaus edition Dalí owned is unknown.

11   Salvador Dalí, 'Documentary – Paris 1929 – 111', *La Publicitat*, Barcelona, 7 May 1929, *OUI*, p. 100.

12   Pierre Cabanne, *Entretiens avec Marcel Duchamp*, Paris, 1967, p. 126.

13   *G*, 5/6, April 1926, Hans Richter (ed.); facsimile Detlef Martins and Michael W. Jennings (eds), *G: An Avant-garde Journal of Art, Architecture, Design and Film*, Getty Research Institute, Los Angeles, 2010, p. 218. The caption beneath a reproduction of *Rotary Demisphere* read: 'Marcel Duchamp, le plus parisian [*sic*] used this device – a moving disk of concentric circles that produces spirals as it rotates – to record a short film.' This may have been the failed stereoscopic film.

14   Naumann and Obalk 2000, p. 94.

15   Naumann and Obalk 2000, note p. 101.

16   Cabanne 1967, p. 126.

17   Naumann and Obalk 2000, 15 November 1921, p. 102.

18   See Annette Michelson, '*Anémic-Cinéma*: Reflections on an Emblematic Work', *Artforum*, 12, 2, October 1973; Arturo Schwarz, *The Complete Works of Marcel Duchamp*, London, 1997, vol. 2, p. 710.

19   This is a version of the pun published in *Littérature* (5, October 1922) opposite the photograph 'The Domain of Rrose Sélavy: "Conseil d'Hygiène intime: Il faut mettre la moëlle de l'épée dans le poil de l'aimée' ('Intimate hygiene advice: you must put the marrow of the sword in the hair of the beloved').

20   Katrina Martin, 'Marcel Duchamp's Anémic-Cinéma', *Studio International*, January/February 1975, p. 60.

21   Georges Bataille, 'Oeil' ('Dictionnaire'), *Documents*, 5, September 1929, p. 218.

22   Salvador Dalí, 'Film-arte, film antiartístico', *Gaceta Literaria*, 1, 24, Madrid, 15 December 1927, p. 4.

23   Salvador Dalí, Lluis Montanyà and Sebastià Gasch, 'Cinema', *L'Amic de les Arts*, March 1928, p. 175.

24   This term of abuse, 'the putrefied', was invented by Dalí and Lorca to refer to the sentimental, picturesque and conventionally artistic: here, the 'putrified artistic cinema-tography' of Murnau, Gance and Fritz Lang.

25   Moholy-Nagy 1969, p. 122.

26   Dalí collaborated again with Buñuel, though to a much lesser degree, in the latter's next film, *L'Âge d'Or*, and continued for the rest of his life to write scenarios, plan film projects and occasionally contribute to Hollywood productions such as Hitchcock's *Spellbound*, as part of his polymorphous approach to the expression of his ideas. In 1960 he made what is arguably the first artist video, *Chaos and Creation*.

Dalí/Duchamp, A Chess Game (pp. 48–53)

1   Walter Benjamin, *Selected Writings*, vol. 4, 1938–40, Cambridge MA, London and Frankfurt, 2003, p. 389.

2   Michel Carrouges, *Les Machines célibataires*, Paris, 1954, p. 24.

3   *Billard* means billiards and *pillard* plunderer or looter. 'The white letters on the bands of old billiards' and 'The white letters on the bands of the old ruffian.'

4   Michel Foucault, *Raymond Roussel*, Paris, 1963.

5   Pilar Parcerisas (ed.), *Dalí, Elective Affinities*, Barcelona, 2004, pp. 113–89.

6   Pierre Cabanne, *Dialogues with Marcel Duchamp*, New York, 1971, p. 27.

7   Cabanne 1971, p. 27.

8   Cabanne 1971, p. 27.

9   Francis M. Naumann and Bradley Bailey, *Marcel Duchamp: The Art of Chess*, New York, 2009, p. 35.

10   *L'Echiquier*, November 1932.

11   Savielly Tartakower, *Les Cahiers de l'Echiquier français*, 33rd cahier, January–February 1933. Published in Raymond Roussel, *Comment j'ai écrit certains de mes livres*, Paris, 1963, pp. 155–60.

12   Henry Dupuy-Mazuel, *Le Joueur d'échecs*, Paris, 1926.

13   S. S. Van Dine, *Le Crime du Fou d'Échecs*, Paris, 1930: a French translation of *The Bishop Murder Case*, New York, 1929.

14   Nabokov was interested in chess problems. *The Defense*, the English translation of the novel by Nabokov and Michael Scammell, was published by Putnam's in 1964.

15   Naumann and Bailey 2009, p. 21.

16   On this trip Duchamp was accompanied by Mary Reynolds. Pilar Parcerisas, *Duchamp en España*, Madrid, 2009.

17   Pilar Parcerisas, 'Picasso and Dalí, Double Portrait in the Bullring of Art', lecture at The Dalí Museum, St Petersburg, Florida, February 2015.

18   Salvador Dalí, *Art News*, 58, April 1959.

19   Salvador Dalí, 'The King and the Queen Traversed by Swift Nudes', Richard Howard (trans.), *Art News*, 58, April 1959.

20   Dalí 1959.

21   Dalí 1959.

22   *Echec* in the sense of 'failure' or *échecs* meaning 'chess'.

23   Paul B. Franklin, 'Introduction to Salvador Dalí, "L'échecs, c'est moi' ('Chess, It's Me')', *Étant donné*, 5, 'Marcel Duchamp et Salvador Dalí', 2003, pp. 119–25.

24   André Breton, 'La beauté sera convulsive ou ne sera pas', *in Œuvres complètes*, vol. 1, Paris, 1988, quote on page 753.

25   Naumann and Bailey 2009, p. 21.

26   Pilar Parcerisas, in *Dalí, Duchamp, Man Ray, Una partida d'escacs*, exh. cat., Ajuntament de Cadaqués, Museu Municipal de Cadaqués, 2016, pp. 119–39.

27   A transcript of this text was published in *Art in America*, 57, 4, July–August 1969, p. 43.

28   Jean Ferry, *L'Afrique des Impressions*, Paris, 1967. First published in instalments in *Le Gaulois de Dimanche* in 1909.

29   Marcel Duchamp, lecture, 'The Creative Act', 1957.

CATALOGUE

Identity (pp. 58–60)

1 Duchamp letter to Man Ray, 21 August 1933, in Francis Naumann and Hector Obalk (eds), *Affectionately, Marcel: The Selected Correspondence of Marcel Duchamp*, Antwerp, 2000, p. 173.
2 Salvador Dalí and André Parinaud, *The Unspeakable Confessions of Salvador Dalí*, Harold J. Salemson (trans.), New York, 1977, p. 131.
3 Dalí and Parinaud 1977, p. 134
4 Gertrude Stein, *Everybody's Autobiography*, William Heinemann Ltd London and Toronto, 1938, pp. 12 and 16.
5 'Tableau Dada par Marcel Duchamp', *391*, March 1920, p. 1.
6 Salvador Dalí, 'New Limits of Painting', *L'Amic de les Arts*, 1928, p. 195, in *Oui: The Paranoid-Critical Revolution, Writings by Salvador Dalí 1927–1933*, Robert Descharnes (ed.), Yvonne Shafir (trans.), Boston, 1998, p. 40.
7 Interview with Richard Hamilton, 1959, in Marcel Duchamp, *The Creative Act*, Marc Dachy (ed.), Brussels, 1994 (CD).
8 Pierre Cabanne, *Entretiens avec Marcel Duchamp*, Paris, 1967, p. 118.
9 Elliott King, *Salvador Dalí, The Late Work*, exh. cat., High Museum of Art, Atlanta, 2010, p. 43.

Gender and Public Personae (pp. 68–69)

1 Salvador Dalí, 'Sant Sebastià', *L'Amic de les Arts*, 2, 16, 31 July 1927, pp. 52–54, quoted p. 52, trans. in Haim Finkelstein, *The Complete Writings of Salvador Dalí*, Cambridge, 1998, pp. 19–24, quoted p. 19.
2 Salvador Dalí, 'Why They Attack the Mona Lisa', *Art News*, New York, 62, 1, March 1963, pp. 36, 63–64, reprinted in Finkelstein 1998, pp. 369–70, quoted p. 370.
3 Marcel Duchamp, radio interview with Herbert Crehan on WBAI, New York, 1961, transcribed by Robert Cowan in 'Dada', *Evidence*, Toronto, 3, Fall 1961, pp. 36–38, and reprinted in Arturo Schwarz, *The Complete Works of Marcel Duchamp*, New York, 2000, p. 670.

Anti-Art and Modern Art (pp. 82–83)

1 Marcel Duchamp, interview on 19 January 1959 by Georges Heard Hamilton in New York and Richard Hamilton in London, broadcast over the BBC Third Programme in the series 'Art-Anti-Art', 13 November 1959.
2 Tristan Tzara, 'Proclamation without Pretension', from 'Seven Dada Manifestos', in Robert Motherwell, *Dada Painters and Poets*, New York, 1951, p. 82.
3 Tristan Tzara, 'Dada Manifesto 1918', in Motherwell 1951, p. 77.
4 Dora Vallier interview with Fernand Léger, 'La vie fait l'œuvre de Fernand Léger', *Cahiers d'art*, vol. 29, no. 3, 1954, p. 140, trans. and quoted in William A. Camfield, *Marcel Duchamp, Fountain*, Houston, 1989, p. 44.
5 Henri Pierre Roché, 'The Blind Man', *The Blind Man*, no. 1, 10 April 1917, p. 6.
6 Menno Hubregtse, 'Robert J. Coady's "The Soil" and Marcel Duchamp's "Fountain": Taste, Nationalism, Capitalism, and New York Dada', *RACAR: revue d'art canadienne / Canadian Art Review*, vol. 34, no. 2, 2009, pp. 28–42.
7 Quoted in Dawn Ades, 'Introduction', in Marcel Duchamp, Henri-Pierre Roché and Beatrice Wood, *3 New York Dadas and The Blind Man*, London, 2013, p. 20.
8 'The Richard Mutt Case', *The Blind Man*, no. 2, May 1917, n.p.
9 Roger Vitrac, 'André Breton n'écrira plus', *Le Journal du Peuple*, no. 7, vol. IV, 1923, and Roger Vitrac, 'Tristan Tzara va cultiver ses vices', *Le Journal du peuple*, no. 14, vol. IV, 1923. Texts reprinted in André Breton, *Œuvres complètes*, vol. I, p. 1215, and Tristan Tzara, *Œuvres complètes*, vol. 1, Paris, 1975, p. 623.
10 Maurice Raynal, *Anthologie de la peinture en France, de 1906 à nos jours*, Paris, 1927, p. 34.
11 Guillermo de Torre, *Literaturas europeas de vanguardia*, Madrid, 1925.
12 Louis Aragon, *La Peinture au défi*, Paris, 1930, trans. as 'Challenge to Painting', in Lucy Lippard (ed.), *Surrealists on Art*, Englewood Cliffs, 1970, p. 50.
13 Trans. in Lippard 1970, p. 41.
14 Interview with William C. Seitz, 'What's happened to Art?', *Vogue* (New York), no. 41, 15 February 1963, p. 113; quoted in Arturo Schwarz, *The Complete Works of Marcel Duchamp*, New York, 2000, p. 34.

The Ironic, the Comic and the Absurd (pp. 98–99)

1 Quoted in Anne d'Harnoncourt and Kynaston McShine, *Marcel Duchamp*, exh. cat., Philadelphia Museum of Art and Museum of Modern Art, New York, 1973, p. 251.
2 Pierre Cabanne, *Dialogues with Marcel Duchamp*, London, 1971, p. 29.
3 Cabanne 1971, p. 39.
4 Quoted in Calvin Tomkins, *Duchamp: A Biography*, London, 1997, p. 226.
5 Marcel Duchamp, in Michel Sanouillet and Elmer Peterson (eds), *Salt Seller: The Essential Writings of Marcel Duchamp*, London and New York, 1975, p. 30.
6 Mark Polizzotti, *Revolution of the Mind: The Life of André Breton*, New York, 1995, p. 332.
7 Quoted in Katherine Kuh, 'Marcel Duchamp', in *The Artist's Voice: Talks with Seventeen Modern Artists*, New York, 2000, pp. 81–93, quotation on p. 90.
8 André Breton, *Anthology of Black Humour* [1945], Mark Polizzotti (trans.), San Francisco, 1997, pp. 277–82, quotations on pp. 278, 281.
9 André Breton, 'Salvador Dalí', in Breton 1997, quotations on pp. 322, 323.
10 Duchamp in 1961 quoted in Francis Naumann, *The Art of Making Art in the Age of Mechanical Reproduction*, New York, 1999, p. 233.

The Surrealist Bullfight (p. 104)

1 Ramón Guardiola Rovira, *Dalí y su museo. La obra que no quisa bellas artes*, Figueres, 1984, pp. 53–76.
2 Manuel Del Arco, 'Dalí en el Parque Güell, Barcelona. Proyecto de "corrida surrealista"', *Revista*, Barcelona, 16 April 1953, reprinted in Ricard Mas (ed.), *La vida pública de Salvador Dalí a través de sus mejores entrevistas*, Barcelona, 2004, pp. 120–22.

Eroticism (pp. 108–109)

1 Pierre Cabanne, *Entretiens avec Marcel Duchamp*, Paris, 1967, p. 166.
2 Daniel Abadie, Pontus Hultén et al., *Salvador Dalí: Retrospective, 1920–1980*, exh. cat., Centre Georges Pompidou, Paris, 1979, p. 133.
3 Salvador Dalí, 'Rêverie', *SASDLR*, no. 4, 1931, pp. 31–36.
4 Salvador Dalí, 'Objets surréalistes', *SASDLR*, no. 3, 1931, p. 16.
5 Toni Stoos and Patrick Elliott, *Alberto Giacometti 1901–1966*, exh. cat., Scottish National Gallery of Modern Art, Edinburgh, and Royal Academy of Arts, London, 1996, p. 146. Also suggested as a source are the 'tusk-shaped metal horns made by the Toba group of the Batak people of Sumatra'.
6 André Breton, *Introduction to the Discourse on the Paucity of Reality* (written 1924, first published 1925), in Franklin Rosemont (ed.), *André Breton: What Is Surrealism? Selected Writings*, New York, 1978, p. 26.
7 Salvador Dalí and André Parinaud, *The Unspeakable Confessions of Salvador Dalí*, Harold J. Salemson (trans.), New York, 1977, p. 221. See also William Jeffett, *Dalí Doubled*, exh. cat., Dalí Museum, St Petersburg, 2010, pp. 264–69.
8 'Lexique succinct de l'érotisme', in *Exposition InteRnatiOnal du Surréalisme (EROS)*, exh. cat., Galerie Cordier, Paris, 1959–60, pp. 138–39.
9 Francisco Javier San Martín, *Dalí-Duchamp: una fraternidad oculta*, Madrid, 2014, p. 48.
10 The pun on 'même / m'aime', 'loves me', is lost in English.
11 'Lexique succinct de l'érotisme', in *Exposition InteRnatiOnal du Surréalisme (EROS)*, exh. cat., Galerie Cordier, Paris, 1959–60, p. 132.

Erotic Objects (pp. 114–15)

1 Salvador Dalí, 'Objets surréalistes', *Le Surréalisme au service de la Révolution*, Paris, 3, December 1931, pp. 16–17.
2 Salvador Dalí, 'Objets surréalistes', *Le Surréalisme au service de la Révolution*, Paris, 3, December 1931, pp. 16–17, trans. as 'Surrealist Objects', in Haim Finkelstein (ed.), *The Complete Writings of Salvador Dalí*, Cambridge, 1998, pp. 231–34.
3 André Breton, 'L'Objet fantôme, *SASDLR*, no. 6, 15 May 1932, pp. 20–22.
4 'Ann Temkin and Enrico Donati in Conversation, January 1997', in Dawn Ades, *Enrico Donati*, New York, 2015, p. 107.
5 Didier Ottinger, *Hypothèses élémentaires sur l'Origine du Monde: Courbet – Masson – Duchamp*, Paris, 2008. The Courbet painting had recently seen the light of day, having in 1955 been acquired by the psychoanalyst Jacques Lacan and his wife, the actress Sylvia Bataille (*née* Maklès).
6 Robert Descharnes in *D'après l'antique*, exh. cat., Musée du Louvre, Paris, 2000, p. 463. Descharnes recounts that Dalí repeatedly told of how Duchamp helped him in sourcing the model-maker for *Venus with Drawers*, even once in the presence of Duchamp (1966), and that the sculpture was exhibited twice in the 1930s privately at Dalí's residences (19 June 1936 and 2 February 1939). Otherwise it was not shown during the 1930s. The painted bronze was first shown in 'Le Surréalisme: sources, histoire, affinités' at the Galerie Charpentier, Paris, in 1964.
7 Lawrence D. Steefel, *The Position of Duchamp's Glass in the Development of His Art*, New York, 1977, p. 134.

The Tragic Myth of Millet's Angelus (p. 150)

1 Letter to Caresse Crosby, 1945, Caresse Crosby Collection, Morris Library, Southern Illinois University at Carbondale, USA. Documents reproduced by Marijke Peyser-Verhaar in *Salvador Dalí et le mécénat du Zodiaque*, unpublished PhD thesis, University of Utrecht, 2008. *The Tragic Myth of Millet's Angelus* was finally published in 1963. See also Dawn Ades 'Dalí: "The Tragic Myth of Millet's Angelus", SDM, St Petersburg, Avant-garde Studies, 'Vida Secreta, Palabra Oculta: Dalí as Writer', 2, Fall 2016.
2 Salvador Dalí, *Le conquête de l'irrationnel*, Paris, 1935, p. 19; trans. in Haim Finkelstein (ed.), *The Collected Writings of Salvador Dalí*, Cambridge and New York, 1998, p. 268.

3 Salvador Dalí, *Le Mythe tragique de l'Angélus de Millet*, Paris, 1963. English translation: *The Tragic Myth of Millet's Angelus*, Eleanor R. Morse (trans.), St Petersburg FL, 1986, p. 172.

Science and Religion (pp. 154–56)

1 Gabrielle Buffet-Picabia, 'Some Memories of Pre-Dada: Picabia and Duchamp', in Robert Motherwell, *The Dada Painters and Poets: An Anthology*, New York, 1951, p. 255.
2 Haim Finkelstein (ed.), *The Collected Writings of Salvador Dalí*, Cambridge and New York, 1998, p. 366.
3 Salvador Dalí, 'The Conquest of the Irrational', in Alain Bosquet, *Conversations with Dalí*, New York, 1969, p. 112.
4 Gavin Parkinson, *Surrealism, Art and Modern Science: Relativity, Quantum Mechanics, Epistemology*, New Haven and London, 2008, p. 214.
5 Salvador Dalí, *Mystical Manifesto* (1951), in Finkelstein 1998, p. 365.
6 Salvador Dalí, *The Secret Life of Salvador Dalí*, Haakon M. Chevalier (trans.), London, 1968, p. 400.
7 Salvador Dalí, letter to Paul Éluard, 1934, in Daniel Abadie, Pontus Hultén et al., *Salvador Dalí: Retrospective, 1920–1980*, exh. cat., Centre Georges Pompidou, Paris, 1979, p. 300.
8 Letter from Marcel Duchamp to Breton, 11 December 1960, in Francis Naumann and Hector Obalk (eds), *Affectionately, Marcel: The Selected Correspondence of Marcel Duchamp*, Antwerp, 2000, p. 370.
9 Mick Gold, *Private Life of an Easter Masterpiece: Christ of St John of the Cross*, (film), 2006.
10 Elliott King, *Salvador Dalí, The Late Work*, exh. cat., High Museum of Art, Atlanta, 2010, p. 32.
11 Salvador Dalí, 'Nuclear Mysticism', quoted in King 2010, p. 32.
12 King 2010, p. 258.
13 Quoted in Parkinson 2008, p. 32.
14 Linda Dalrymple Henderson, *Duchamp in Context*, Princeton, 1998, p. 19.
15 Salvador Dalí, 'The King and the Queen Traversed by Swift Nudes', Richard Howard (trans.), *Art News*, 58, April 1959.
16 Henderson 1998, p. 20.
17 Marcel Duchamp, *The Bride Stripped Bare by Her Bachelors, Even*, Typographic version of the *Green Box* [1934] by Richard Hamilton, George Heard Hamilton (trans.), Stuttgart, London and Reykjavik, 1976, n.p.; Michel Sanouillet and Elmer Peterson (eds), *Salt Seller: The Essential Writings of Marcel Duchamp*, London and New York, 1975, p. 42.
18 Duchamp 1934; Sanouillet and Peterson 1975, p. 43.
19 Interview with George Heard Hamilton, London, 1959, Marcel Duchamp *The Creatice Act* (DVD), Marc Dachy (ed.).
20 Parkinson 2008, p. 184.
21 Pierre Cabanne, *Entretiens avec Marcel Duchamp*, Paris, 1967, p. 68.

The Bride Stripped Bare by Her Bachelors, Even (pp. 160–61)

1 The Notes were published under the same title as the original work: *La Mariée mise à nu par ses célibataires, même*.
2 Pierre Cabanne, *Entretiens avec Marcel Duchamp*, Paris, 1967, p. 73. Author's transl.
3 Cabanne 1967, p. 74.
4 Marcel Duchamp, *The Bride Stripped Bare by Her Bachelors, Even*, Typographic version of the *Green Box* [1934] by Richard Hamilton, George Heard Hamilton (trans.), Stuttgart, London and Reykjavik, 1976, n.p.

5   André Breton, 'Phare de la mariée',
    Minotaure, 6, 1935, pp 45–49.
6   Duchamp 1934.

Perspective (pp. 168–70)

1   Pierre Cabanne, *Entretiens avec Marcel
    Duchamp*, Paris, 1967, p. 65.
2   Marcel Duchamp, *The Bride Stripped Bare
    by Her Bachelors, Even*, Typographic
    version of the *Green Box* [1934] by Richard
    Hamilton, translated by George Heard
    Hamilton, Stuttgart, London and Reykjavik,
    1976, n.p.
3   Duchamp 1934.
4   Jean Clair, 'Marcel Duchamp et la tradition
    des Perspecteurs', in Marcel Duchamp, Jean
    Clair, Jennifer Gough-Cooper, Jacques
    Caumont and Henri Pierre Roché, *Marcel
    Duchamp: abécédaire*, Paris, 1977.
5   Duchamp 1934.
6   Salvador Dalí and André Parinaud, *The
    Unspeakable Confessions of Salvador Dalí*,
    Harold J. Salemson (trans.), New York, 1977,
    p. 159.
7   Dawn Ades, *Dalí's Optical Illusions*, exh.
    cat., Wadsworth Atheneum Museum of Art,
    in association with Yale University Press,
    2000, p. 17.
8   Salvador Dalí, *The Conquest of the
    Irrational* (1935), Joachim Neugroschel
    (trans.), in Alain Bosquet, *Conversations with
    Dalí*, New York, 1969, p. 113.
9   Dalí 1935a, in Bosquet 1969, p. 113.
10 Dalí 1935a, in Bosquet 1969, p. 116.
11 Elliott King et al., *Salvador Dalí, The Late
    Work*, exh. cat., High Museum of Art, Atlanta,
    2010, p. 31.
12 Mick Gold, *Private Life of an Easter
    Masterpiece: Christ of St John of the Cross*,
    (film), 2006.

Measurement (pp. 172–75)

1   Anne D'Harnoncourt and Kynaston L.
    McShine (eds), *Marcel Duchamp*, exh. cat.,
    Museum of Modern Art, New York, and
    Philadelphia Museum of Art, 1973, p. 273.
2   See David J. Hand, *Measurement: A Very
    Short Introduction*, Oxford, 2016.
3   Arturo Schwarz, *The Complete Works of
    Marcel Duchamp*, New York, 1970, no. 595.
4   'When I made the panel *Tu m'*, I made from
    the *stoppages-étalons* 3 wooden rulers
    which have the same profile as the threads
    on the canvas.' Letter to Katharine Dreier,
    May 1935, quoted in Ecke Bonk, *Marcel
    Duchamp: The Portable Museum*, London,
    1989, p. 218.
5   Thomas Breitenstein Millroth and Paul B.
    Franklin, 'Rrosa Selavsdotter', *Étant Donné*,
    11, 2016, p. 209.
6   Personal communication with Ecke Bonk.
7   'Chronology: Certain Facts of and about
    Marcel Duchamp', in *By or Of Marcel
    Duchamp or Rose Sélavy*, exh. cat.,
    Pasadena Art Museum, 1963, n.p.
8   Philadelphia 1973, p. 273.
9   Personal communication with Antoine
    Monnier.
10 Dalí 'Sant Sebastià', *L'Amic de les Arts*, no. 16,
    31 July 1927, pp. 52–54. 'Saint Sebastian' John
    London (trans.), in *Dalí The Early Years*, exh.
    cat., Hayward Gallery, 1994, pp. 214–15.
11 Dalí and his friends in the student
    residencia, Madrid, used this term to refer
    to the bourgeois culture-lover, derived from
    their opposition between sentimentality
    ('putrefied') and objectivity/measurement.
    'We oppose Astronomy to Putrefaction',
    Letter from Dalí to Pepín Bello, December
    1925 see Dawn Ades, 'Morphologies of
    Desire', in *Dalí The Early Years*.
12 Dalí 1927a.

Optical Illusions (pp. 178–79)

1   Arturo Schwarz, *The Complete Works of
    Marcel Duchamp*, New York, 1970, no. 729.
2   Salvador Dalí, 'L'Âne pourri', *SASDLR*, 1, 1930,
    p. 9, subsequently published in *La Femme
    visible*, 1930, pp. 9–12.
3   See David Lomas, *The Haunted Self:
    Surrealism, Psychoanalysis, Subjectivity*,
    New Haven and London, 2000; and Dawn
    Ades (ed.), *Dalí's Optical Illusions*, exh. cat.,
    Wadsworth Atheneum, Hartford, 2000.

Chronology (pp. 194–205)

*We are grateful to Clara Silvestre of the
Centre for Dalinian Studies for her
assistance in the documentation and
research.*

1   Salvador Dalí, 'L'Âne pourri', *SASDLR*, 1, 1930,
    p. 9, subsequently published in *La Femme
    visible*, 1930, pp. 9–12.
2   Marcel Duchamp, 'Formule de l'opposition
    hétérodoxe dans les domaines principaux',
    SASDLR, 2, October 1930, pp. 18–19.
3   Salvador Dalí, 'The Object as Revealed in
    Surrealist Experiment', *This Quarter*, 5, 1,
    September 1932, pp. 197–207.
4   André Breton, *The Lost Steps* (1924), Mark
    Polizzotti (trans.), Lincoln NE, 1996
5   See Marijke Peyser-Verhaar, 'Salvador Dalí
    et le mécénat du Zodiac', *Les Cahiers du
    musée d'art moderne*, 121, Autumn 2012.
6   'La vie publique de Salvador Dalí', in Daniel
    Abadie, Pontus Hultén et al., *Salvador Dalí:
    Retrospective, 1920–1980*, exh. cat., Centre
    Georges Pompidou, Paris, 1979, p. 32.
7   A selection of these images was published
    the following year in *Minotaure* with
    captions written by Dalí. *Minotaure*, 3–4,
    December 1933, p. 68.
8   Salvador Dalí, 'De la Beauté terrifiante et
    comestible de l'architecture *Modern Style*',
    Minotaure, 3–4, December 1933, pp. 69–76.
9   This is a reference to the Zodiac group.
10 Salvador Dalí, 'Les Nouvelles Couleurs du
    sex-appeal spectral', *Minotaure*, 5, 12 May
    1934, pp. 20–22.
11 Dalí 1934, p. 22.
12 'Dalí, vêtu d'une manière appropriée, lira son
    poème inédit: Je mange Gala'. 'Systematic
    series of conferences on the most recent
    positions of Surrealism', June 1935.
13 The original manuscript, 'Naissance des
    perversions nutritives', is preserved at the
    Fundació Gala-Salvador Dalí, Figueres.
14 *Minotaure*, 6, 1935.
15 Letter from Salvador Dalí to André Breton,
    27 March 1937. Centre for Dalinian Studies,
    Fundació Gala-Salvador Dalí, Figueres.
16 The exact text reads: 'DALÍ (Salvador), né en
    1904. "Prince de l'intelligence catalane
    colossalement riche." Peintre poète et
    théoricien surréaliste depuis 1929.'
17 André Breton, 'Des tendances les plus
    récentes de la peinture surréaliste',
    Minotaure, 12 May 1939, p. 17.
18 *400 obras de Salvador Dalí de 1914 a 1983*,
    exh. cat., Obra Cultural de la Caixa de
    Pensions, Madrid, 1983, p. 148.
19 The ball was to benefit the Museum of
    Modern Art, New York, which was
    fundraising for refugee European artists.
20 See Ecke Bonk, *Marcel Duchamp, The
    Portable Museum*, London, 1989.
21 This is now installed in the Room of Master
    Works at the Dalí Theatre-Museum,
    Figueres. The dedication reads: 'Pour Gala
    et Salvador Dalí [...] de Cadaqués. Marcel
    Duchamp 1958.'
22 Salvador Dalí, 'The King and the Queen
    Traversed by Swift Nudes', Richard Howard
    (trans.), *Art News*, 58, April 1959.
23 The exhibition, probably in fact quite small,

of works by Duchamp took place in April
1959 at the Sidney Janis Gallery in New York,
coinciding with the publication in French
and English of the monograph by Robert
Lebel, *Sur Marcel Duchamp*, by the Trianon
Press, Paris and London, 1959, with texts by
Duchamp himself, Breton, Henri-Pierre
Roché and a catalogue raisonné of his work.
24 29 November 1960 – 14 January 1961.
25 Jaguer broke years of silence about this
    painful episode with his essay 'A propos
    d'un écart absolu de Marcel Duchamp (et
    de l'exposition international du surréalisme
    de New York, 1960–61)', in *Étant donné*, no.
    5, 2003. The phrase *écart absolu* ('absolute
    separation') was the title of the 1965
    'International Surrealist Exhibition' in Paris,
    the last before Breton's death.
26 This is the full title of the piece as printed in
    the 1958–59 Carstairs catalogue. The
    Metropolitan Museum of Art, New York,
    calls it simply *Madonna*.
27 Elliott King et al., *Salvador Dalí: The Late
    Work*, exh. cat., High Museum of Art, Atlanta,
    2010, p. 41.
28 They used the frontispice of Lebel's book on
    Robert Lebel, *Sur Marcel Duchamp*, Paris,
    1959 (published in English as *Marcel
    Duchamp*, London, 1959).
29 Salvador Dalí, 'Why They Attack the *Mona
    Lisa*', *Art News*, 62, 1, March 1963, p. 64.
30 Nat Finkelstein, 'Dinner with Dalí' and
    'Meeting Marcel', *Étant donné*, 5, 'Marcel
    Duchamp and Salvador Dalí', 2003, p. 83.
31 Dalí presented the set at a press conference
    in February 1971. Assured that the price
    would be $4,000, Douglas Cooper
    announced in an advert: 'We bet you've
    never seen a chess set quite like this before.
    The pieces are cast from Salvador Dalí's
    fingers in solid sterling silver. Dalí created
    the set in honour of his late friend, Marcel
    Duchamp, and in tribute donated it to the
    American Chess Foundation. F. J. Cooper
    was commissioned to produce a limited
    number of sets. Both the King and the
    Queen (the King is Dalí's thumb, the Queen
    is Madam Dalí's) wear a tooth as a crown. Mr
    Cooper, in a moment of unrestrained
    curiosity, asked Dalí why a tooth. Dalí
    fielded the question brilliantly and asked Mr
    Cooper why not a tooth. (Mr Cooper went
    on to other things.) As to the reason why Dalí
    created a set using his own fingers, he said, "I
    had a precise and yet symbolic concept. In
    chess, as in other forms of human alchemy,
    there is always the creator, above all, the
    artist as the creator. It is this that I wanted
    represented: the hand of the artist, the
    eternal creator. How better to express this
    vision than by sculpting my own hand, my
    own fingers?" Each piece is signed by Dalí.
    Each set is numbered (Dalí owns set number
    one) and comes in its own oaken chest. Four
    thousand dollars. Mail address: ... P.S. One
    collector we know bought a set and gave
    different friends different pieces. Now
    thirty-two people have a signed Dalí
    sculpture. Not a bad thought.'
32 See cat. 43.
33 The article was published on 15 April 1968.
34 Salvador Dalí, 'Who is Surrealism', *Vogue*,
    15 April 1968.
35 Antoni Pitxot, Montse Aguer, *The Dalí
    Theatre-Museum in Figueres*, Fundació
    Gala-Salvador Dalí, Figueres, Sant Lluís
    (Menorca), 2005, p. 7.

The Dalí Theatre-Museum as a Readymade (pp. 206–07)

1   The artist explained, concerning the future
    creation of the Theatre-Museum: 'My
    ambition is that it will not just be a Dalí

Museum, but the nucleus of Western and
European spirituality. Everyone who wants
to be up to date with what is happening in
Europe will have to come, inevitably, to
Figueres itself ... to eat delicious Catalan
sausage and see what is happening in the
world through The Dalí Museum, which will
be the museum of all my friends, and in
which, every month, there will be a different
exhibition, of Op, Pop, and all the
international isms.' 'Dalí reaffirms the
creation of the DALÍ museum', *Ampurdan*,
10 July 1968, Figueres.
2   There are references to this exhibition in
    other installations by Dalí such as the
    'Dream of Venus' pavilion at the New York
    World's Fair in 1939.
3   Another allusion to the 1938 Paris exhibition.
    The street is described as such on the
    invitation to the 1938 exhibition.

SELECT BIBLIOGRAPHY

Ades 1981
Dawn Ades, *Salvador Dalí*, London, 1981

Ades 1992
Dawn Ades, 'Duchamp's Masquerades', in Graham Clark (ed.), *The Portrait in Photography*, London, 1992

Ades 2004
Dawn Ades, 'Dalí and Duchamp', in Hank Hine, William Jeffett and Kelly Reynolds (eds), *Persistence and Memory: New Critical Perspectives on Dalí at the Centennial*, Milan, and St Petersburg FL, 2004

Ades 2013
Dawn Ades, 'Introduction', in Duchamp, Roché and Wood 2013

Ades, Cox and Hopkins 1999
Dawn Ades, Neil Cox and David Hopkins, *Marcel Duchamp*, London, 1999

Anon 1917
'The Richard Mutt Case', *The Blind Man*, 2, May 1917, n.p.

Atlanta 2010
Elliott King et al., *Salvador Dalí: The Late Work*, exh. cat., High Museum of Art, Atlanta, 2010

Barcelona 2004
Pilar Parcerisas (ed.), *Dalí, Elective Affinities*, exh. cat., Generalitat de Catalunya, Department de Cultura, Palau Moja, Barcelona, 2004

Bonk 1989
Ecke Bonk, *Marcel Duchamp: The Portable Museum*, London, 1989

Bosquet 1969
Alain Bosquet, *Conversations with Dalí*, New York, 1969

Breton 1922
André Breton, 'Marcel Duchamp', *Littérature*, 5, October 1922, pp. 7–10

Breton 1924
André Breton, *The Lost Steps* [1924], Mark Polizzotti (trans.), Lincoln NE, 1996

Breton 1929
André Breton, *Second Manifeste du Surréalisme*, Paris, 1929

Breton 1934
André Breton, 'What Is Surrealism?' [1934], in Rosemont 1978

Breton 1939
André Breton, 'Des tendances les plus récentes de la peinture surréaliste', *Minotaure*, 12–13, May 1939, p. 17

Breton 1945
André Breton, *Anthology of Black Humour* [1945], Mark Polizzotti (trans.), San Francisco, 1997

Breton 1972
André Breton, *Surrealism and Painting*, London, 1972

Breton 1992
André Breton, *Œuvres complètes II*, Paris, 1992

Buffet 1936
Gabrielle Buffet, 'Cœurs volants', *Cahiers d'art*, vol. 11, 1–2, 1936, pp. 34–43

Cabanne 1967
Pierre Cabanne, *Entretiens avec Marcel Duchamp*, Paris, 1967 (Published in English as *Dialogues with Marcel Duchamp*, New York, 1971)

Cadaqués 2016
Pilar Parcericas, *Dalí, Duchamp, Man Ray, Una partida d'escacs*, exh. cat., Museu Municipal de Cadaqués, 2016

Camfield 1989
William Camfield (introduction by Walter Hopps), *Marcel Duchamp: Fountain*, Houston, 1989

Casellas 2010
Joan Casellas, 'La vida secreta de Marcel Duchamp prop de Figueres', *L'Avenç*, 363, December 2010, pp. 31–39

Casellas 2015
Joan Casellas, 'Duchamp y Dalí: Una amistat codificada a les sales del Teatre-Museu de Figueres', *L'Avenç*, 413, June 2015, pp. 27–31

Clair 1977
Jean Clair, *Duchamp et la photographie*, Paris, 1977

Clearwater 1991
Bonnie Clearwater (ed.), *West Coast Duchamp*, Miami Beach, 1991

Dalí 1927a
Dalí 'Sant Sebastià', *L'Amic de les Arts*, no. 16, 31 July 1927, pp. 52–54

Dalí 1927b
Salvador Dalí, 'Film-arte, film antiartístico', *Gaceta Literaria*, 1, 24, Madrid, 15 December 1927

Dalí 1930a
Salvador Dalí, 'L'Ane pourri', *Le Surréalisme au service de la révolution (SASDLR)*, 1, 1930, pp. 9–12

Dalí 1930b
Salvador Dalí, 'Le Grand Masturbateur', in *La Femme visible*, Paris, 1930

Dalí 1931a
Salvador Dalí, 'Objets surréalistes', *SASDLR*, 3, 1931, p. 16

Dalí 1931b
Salvador Dalí, 'Rêverie', *SASDLR*, 4, 1931, pp. 31–36

Dalí 1932
Salvador Dalí, 'The Object as Revealed in Surrealist Experiment', *This Quarter*, 5, 1, September 1932, pp. 197–207

Dalí 1933
Salvador Dalí, 'De la Beauté terrifiante et comestible de l'architecture *Modern Style*', *Minotaure*, 3–4, December 1933, pp. 69–76

Dalí 1934
Salvador Dalí, 'Les Nouvelles Couleurs du sex-appeal spectral', *Minotaure*, 5, May 1934, pp. 20–22

Dalí 1935a
Salvador Dalí, *Le conquête de l'irrationnel*, Paris, 1935 (Published in English as *The Conquest of the Irrational*, New York, 1935)

Dalí 1935b
Salvador Dalí, 'Psychologie non-euclidienne d'une photographie', *Minotaure*, 7, June 1935, pp. 56–57

Dalí 1936
Salvador Dalí, 'Honneur à l'objet!', *Cahiers d'art*, 11, 1936, pp. 33–37

Dalí 1937
Salvador Dalí, 'I Defy Aragon', *Art Front*, 3, 2, March 1937

Dalí 1959
Salvador Dalí, 'The King and the Queen Traversed by Swift Nudes', Richard Howard (trans.), *Art News*, 58, April 1959

Dalí 1963a
Salvador Dalí, *Le Mythe tragique de l'Angélus de Millet*, Paris, 1963 (Published in English as *The Tragic Myth of Millet's Angelus*, Eleanor R. Morse [trans.], St Petersburg FL, 1986)

Dalí 1963b
Salvador Dalí, 'Why They Attack the *Mona Lisa*', *Art News*, 62, 1, March 1963, p. 64

Dalí 1968
Salvador Dalí, *The Secret Life of Salvador Dalí*, Haakon M. Chevalier (trans.), London, 1968

Dalí 1971
Salvador Dalí 'L'échecs, c'est moi' ('Chess, it's me'), preface to Pierre Cabanne, *Dialogues with Marcel Duchamp*, New York, 1971, pp. 13–14

Dalí, Gasch and Montanyà 1928a
Salvador Dalí, Sebastià Gasch and Lluis Montanyà, 'Cinema', *L'Amic de les Arts*, March 1928, p. 175

Dalí, Gasch and Montanyà 1928b
Salvador Dalí, Sebastià Gasch and Lluis Montanyà, *Manifest Groc (Yellow Manifesto)*, Barcelona, March 1928

Dalí and Parinaud 1977
Salvador Dalí and André Parinaud, *The Unspeakable Confessions of Salvador Dalí*, Harold J. Salemson (trans.), New York, 1977

De Diego 2004
Estrella de Diego, '"To Be a Painter" or "To Be a Duchamp"? Dalí, Warhol and Autobiographical Conflict in a Media Society' in *Dalí and Mass Culture*, exh. cat., Fundació La Caixa, Barcelona, 2004, pp. 254–59

Descharnes and Descharnes 1993
Robert and Nicolas Descharnes, *Salvador Dalí*, Charles Akin (trans.), New York, 1993

Descharnes and Descharnes 2004
Robert and Nicolas Descharnes, *Dalí: The Hard and the Soft: Spells for the Magic of Form. Sculptures and Objects*, Azay-le-Rideau, 2004

d'Harnoncourt and Hopps 1969
Anne d'Harnoncourt and Walter Hopps, *Étant donnés: I. la chute d'eau, 2. le gas d'éclairage: Reflections on a New Work by Marcel Duchamp*, Philadelphia, 1969

Duchamp 1930
Marcel Duchamp, 'Formule de l'opposition hétérodoxe dans les domaines principaux', *SASDLR*, 2, October 1930, 18–19

Duchamp 1933
Marcel Duchamp, 'La mariée mise à nu par ses célibataires mêmes', *SASDLR*, 5/6, May 1933, pp. 1–2

Duchamp 1934
Marcel Duchamp, *The Bride Stripped Bare by Her Bachelors, Even*, Typographic version of the *Green Box* [1934] by Richard Hamilton, George Heard Hamilton (trans.), Stuttgart, London and Reykjavik, 1976, n.p.

Duchamp 1967
Marcel Duchamp, *À l'infinitif*, typographic version of Duchamp's *White Box* [1967], trans. Richard Hamilton and Ecke Bonk, New York [n.d. and n.p.]

Duchamp et al. 1977
Marcel Duchamp, Jean Clair, Jennifer Gough-Cooper, Jacques Caumont and Henri Pierre Roché, *Marcel Duchamp: abécédaire*, Paris, 1977

Duchamp et al. 2012
Marcel Duchamp, Henri Pierre Roché, Scarlett Reliquet, Philippe Reliquet, *Correspondance Marcel Duchamp, Henri Pierre Roché: 1918–1959*, Geneva, 2012

Duchamp, Roché and Wood 2013
Marcel Duchamp, Henri-Pierre Roché, Beatrice Wood, *3 New York Dadas and The Blind Man*, London, 2013

Fanés 2007
Fèlix Fanés, *Salvador Dalí: The Construction of the Image 1925–1930*, New Haven and London, 2007

Filipovic 2016
Elena Filipovic, *The Apparently Marginal Activities of Marcel Duchamp*, Cambridge MA, 2016

Finkelstein 1998
Haim Finkelstein (ed.), *The Collected Writings of Salvador Dalí*, Cambridge and New York, 1998

Finkelstein 2003
Nat Finkelstein, 'Dinner with Dalí' and 'Meeting Marcel', in Franklin 2003a, pp. 76–89

Frankfurt 2011
Ingrid Pfeiffer and Max Hollein (eds), *Surreal Objects: Three-Dimensional Objects from Dalí to Many Ray*, exh. cat., Schirn Kunsthalle Frankfurt, 2011

Franklin 2003a
Paul Franklin (ed.), 'Marcel Duchamp and Salvador Dalí', special number of *Étant donné: revue de l'Association pour l'étude de Marcel Duchamp*, 5, 2003

Franklin 2003b
Paul Franklin, 'Introduction to Salvador Dalí, "L'échecs, c'est moi" ("Chess, It's Me")', in Franklin 2003a, pp. 119–25

Franklin 2016
Paul Franklin (ed.), *The Artist and the Critic Stripped Bare. The Correspondence of Marcel Duchamp and Robert Lebel*, Los Angeles, 2016

Girst 2014
Thomas Girst, *The Duchamp Dictionary*, London, 2014

Golding 1973
John Golding, *Marcel Duchamp: The Bride Stripped Bare by her Bachelors, Even* (Art in Context), London 1973

Gough-Cooper et al. 1993
Jennifer Gough-Cooper, Pontus Hultén, Jacques Caumont, *Marcel Duchamp: Work and Life; Ephemerides on and about Marcel Duchamp and Rrose Sélavy: 1887–1968*, Cambridge MA, 1993

Guardiola Rovira 1984
Ramón Guardiola Rovira, *Dalí y su museo. La obra que no quisa bellas artes*, Figueres, 1984

Hartford 2000
Dawn Ades, *Dalí's Optical Illusions*, exh. cat., Wadsworth Atheneum Museum of Art, Hartford CT, in association with Yale University Press, New Haven CT, 2000

Hill 1994
Anthony Hill (ed.), *Duchamp: Passim*, London, 1994

Hultén 1993
Pontus Hultén (ed.), *Marcel Duchamp: Work and Life*, Cambridge MA, 1993

Jaguer 2003
Edouard Jaguer, 'A propos d'un écart absolu de Marcel Duchamp (et de l'Exposition internationale du surréalisme de New York, 1960–61)', in Franklin 2003a, pp. 23–47

Janis and Janis 1945
Harriet and Sidney Janis, 'Marcel Duchamp: Anti-Artist', *View*, 5, 1, 1945

Jeffett 2010
William Jeffett, *Dalí Doubled: From Surrealism to the Self, A New Critical View of Dalí*, St Petersburg FL, 2010

Jouffroy 1964
Alain Jouffroy, *Une révolution du regard*, Paris, 1964

Judovitz 2010
Dalia Judovitz, *Drawing on Art: Duchamp and Company*, Minneapolis, 2010

Kachur 2001
Lewis Kachur, *Displaying the Marvelous: Marcel Duchamp, Salvador Dalí, and Surrealist Exhibition Installations*, Cambridge, 2001

Kuh 2000
Katherine Kuh, 'Marcel Duchamp', in *The Artist's Voice: Talks with Seventeen Modern Artists*, New York, 2000

Lazzarato 2014
Maurizio Lazzarato, *Marcel Duchamp et le refus du travail*, Paris, 2014

Lebel 1959
Robert Lebel, *Sur Marcel Duchamp*, Paris, 1959 (published in English as *Marcel Duchamp*, London, 1959)

Le Penven 2002
Françoise Le Penven, 'Marcel Duchamp ou la pérennité des sources', *Etudes*, 397, December 2002, pp. 651–61

Lippard 1970
Lucy R. Lippard (ed.), *Surrealists on Art*, Englewood Cliffs, 1970

London 1966
Richard Hamilton, *The Almost Complete Works of Marcel Duchamp*, exh. cat., Tate, London, 1966

London 1994
Dawn Ades, *Salvador Dalí: The Early Years*, exh. cat., Hayward Gallery, London, 1994

London 2007
Matthew Gale (ed.), *Dalí and Film*, exh. cat., Tate, London, and Museum of Modern Art, New York, 2007

McEvilley 1999
Thomas McEvilley, *Sculpture in the Age of Doubt*, New York, 1999

Madrid 1983
400 obras de Salvador Dalí de 1914 a 1983, exh. cat., Obra Cultural de la Caixa de Pensions, Madrid, 1983

Marcadé 2007
Bernard Marcadé, *Marcel Duchamp: La vie à crédit*, Paris, 2007

Martin 1975
Katrina Martin, 'Marcel Duchamp's Anémic-Cinéma', *Studio International*, January/February 1975

Mas 2017
Ricard Mas, *Dalí i Barcelona*, Barcelona, 2017

Masheck 1975
Joseph Masheck (ed.), *Marcel Duchamp in Perspective*, Englewood Cliffs, 1975

Matisse 1980
Paul Matisse (ed.), *Marcel Duchamp, Notes*, Paris, 1980

Michelson 1973
Annette Michelson, '*Anémic-Cinéma*: Reflections on an Emblematic Work', *Artforum*, 12, 2, October 1973

Montaigne 2003
Michel de Montaigne, *The Complete Essays*, M. A. Screech (trans.), London, 2003

Motherwell 1951
Robert Motherwell, *The Dada Painters and Poets: An Anthology*, New York, 1951

Murcia 2013
Pilar Parcerisas, *Marcel Duchamp: 'Don't Forget'. Una partida de Ajedrez con Man Ray y Salvador Dalí*, exh. cat., Museo Arqueólogico de Murcia, and Museo de Arte Contemporáneo, Santiago 2013

Naumann and Obalk 2000
Francis Naumann and Hector Obalk (eds), *Affectionately, Marcel: The Selected Correspondence of Marcel Duchamp*, Antwerp, 2000 (also published as *Affect' Marcel. The Selected Correspondence of Marcel Duchamp*, Jill Taylor [trans.], London, 2000)

New York 2013
Timothy Baum, *Dada and Surrealist Objects*, exh. cat., Di Donna Galleries, New York, 2013

Ottinger 2008
Didier Ottinger, *Hypothèse élémentaires sur 'L'origine du monde': Courbet, Masson, Duchamp*, Paris, 2008

Ottinger 2013
Didier Ottinger, *Dictionnaire de l'objet surréaliste*, Paris, 2013

Parcerisas 2009
Pilar Parcerisas, *Duchamp en España: las claves ocultas de sus estancias en Cadaqués*, Madrid, 2009

Paris 1959
André Breton, Marcel Duchamp, et al., *Exposition InteRnatiOnal du Surréalisme (EROS)*, exh. cat., Galerie Daniel Cordier, Paris, 1959

Paris 1979
Daniel Abadie, Pontus Hulten et al., *Salvador Dalí: Retrospective, 1920–1980*, exh. cat., Centre Georges Pompidou, Paris, 1979

Paris 2012
Montse Aguer, Jean-Michel Bouhours, Thierry Dufrêne and Jean-Hubert Martin, *Dalí*, exh. cat., Centre Georges Pompidou, Paris, and MNCARS, Madrid, 2012

Paris 2013
Cécile Debray, *Duchamp. La peinture, même*, exh. cat., Centre Georges Pompidou, Paris, 2013

Parkinson 2008
Gavin Parkinson, *Surrealism, Art and Modern Science: Relativity, Quantum Mechanics, Epistemology*, New Haven and London, 2008

Parkinson 2015
Gavin Parkinson (ed.), *Surrealism, Science Fiction and Comics*, Liverpool, 2015

Pasadena 1963
By or Of Marcel Duchamp or Rrose Sélavy, exh. cat., Pasadena Art Museum, 1963, n.p.

Peyré and Toussaint 2014
Yves Peyré and Evelyne Toussaint, *Duchamp à la Bibliothèque Sainte-Geneviève*, Paris, 2014

Philadelphia 1973
Anne d'Harnoncourt and Kynaston McShine, *Marcel Duchamp*, exh. cat., Philadelphia Museum of Art and Museum of Modern Art, New York, 1973

Philadelphia 2009
Michael Taylor, *Marcel Duchamp, Étant donnés*, Philadelphia, 2009

Polizzotti 1995
Mark Polizzotti, *Revolution of the Mind: The Life of André Breton*, New York, 1995

Radford 2003
Robert Radford, '"There is No Art; There Are Only Artists": Salvador Dalí and Marcel Duchamp, Modernism and Individualism', in Franklin 2003a, pp. 52–67

Ray 1963
Man Ray, *Autoportrait* (1963), Paris, 1998

Raynal 1927
Maurice Raynal, *Anthologie de la peinture en France de 1906 à nos jours*, Paris, 1927

Richter 1926
Hans Richter (ed.); *G*, 5/6, April 1926 (Facsimile: Detlef Martins and Michael W. Jennings [eds], *G: An Avant-garde Journal of Art, Architecture, Design and Film*, Getty Research Institute, Los Angeles, 2010)

Rosemont 1978
Franklin Rosemont (ed.), *André Breton: What Is Surrealism? Selected Writings*, New York, 1978

St Louis 2009
Francis M. Naumann and Bradley Bailey, *Marcel Duchamp: The Art of Chess*, exh. cat., St Louis University Museum of Art and Francis M. Naumann Fine Art, New York, 2009

St Petersburg 2000
William Jeffett, 'Masterpieces of Painting: 'A Challenge to Painting' in William Jeffett (ed.), *Masterpieces of Surrealism*, exh. cat., St Petersburg, 2000

San Martín 2014
Francisco Javier San Martín, *Dalí-Duchamp: una fraternidad oculta*, Madrid, 2014

Sanouillet and Matisse 2008
Michel Sanouillet and Paul Matisse, *Duchamp du signe: suivi des Notes*, Paris, 2008

Sanouillet and Peterson 1975
Michel Sanouillet and Elmer Peterson (eds), *Salt Seller: The Essential Writings of Marcel Duchamp*, London and New York, 1975

Schwarz 2000
Arturo Schwarz, *The Complete Works of Marcel Duchamp*, London and New York, 2000

Steefel 1977
Lawrence D. Steefel, *The Position of Duchamp's Glass in the Development of His Art*, New York, 1977

Stuckey 2005a
Charles Stuckey, 'The Persistence of Dalí', *Art in America*, 93, 3, March 2005, pp. 113–49

Stuckey 2005b
Charles Stuckey, 'Dalí in Duchamp-Land', *Art in America*, 95, 5, May 2005, pp. 148–55

Tomkins 1965
Calvin Tomkins, 'Not Seen and/or Less Seen: Marcel Duchamp', *The New Yorker*, 6 February 1965, pp. 48–50

Tomkins 1997
Calvin Tomkins, *Duchamp: A Biography*, London, 1997

Tomkins 2013
Calvin Tomkins, *Marcel Duchamp: The Afternoon Interviews*, New York and Cologne, 2013

Valencia 1998
Emmanuel Guigon, *El Objeto Surrealista*, exh. cat., IVAM – Institute Valencia d'Art Modern, Valencia, 1997

Washington 2015
Valerie J. Fletcher, *Marvelous Objects: Surrealist Sculpture from Paris to New York*, exh. cat., Hirshhorn Museum and Sculpture Gallery, Washington, and Delmonico Books/Prestel Verlag, Munich, London, New York, 2015

LENDERS TO THE EXHIBITION

Barcelona
MNAC. Museu Nacional d'Art de Catalunya, Barcelona

Cadaqués
Arxiu Pere Vehí

Archives Marcel Duchamp

Figueres
Fundació Gala-Salvador Dalí

Glasgow
Glasgow Life (Glasgow Museums) on behalf of Glasgow City Council

Philippe Halsman Archive

Hartford, CT
Wadsworth Atheneum Museum of Art

Horst Estate

London
Tate

Madrid
Museo Nacional Centro de Arte Reina Sofía

Milan
Collezione Prada

New York
The Metropoplitan Museum of Art

The Museum of Modern Art, New York

Ottawa
National Gallery of Canada

Paris
Centre Pompidou, Musée national d'art moderne/Centre de création industrielle

Emmanuel Boussard Library

Philadelphia
Philadelphia Museum of Art

Rome
Galleria Nazional d'Arte Moderna e Contemporanea

Rovereto
Mart, Museo di arte moderna e contemporanea di Trento e Rovereto, Deposito

St Petersburg, FL
The Dalí Museum

Sarasota, FL
The John and Mable Ringling Museum of Art, the State Art Museum of Florida,
Florida State University

Fondazione Isabella Scelsi

Stockholm
Moderna Museet

Vienna
Collection Hummel, Vienna

West Dean
West Dean College, Part of the Edward James Foundation

and others who wish to remain anonymous

PHOTOGRAPHIC ACKNOWLEDGEMENTS

All works of art are reproduced by kind permission of the owners. Every attempt has been made to trace the photographers of works reproduced. Specific acknowledgements are as follows:

Photographic Credits

Austin, Harry Ransom Center, The University of Texas, cat. 144

Avila, Monastery of La Encarnación. Photo Arturo Díaz: fig. 85

Barcelona, © Museu Nacional d'Art de Catalunya, Barcelona 2016. Photography: Jordi Calveras: cat. 10

Cadaqués, © Arxiu Pere Vehí. Photography Jordi Herms: cats 6, 18–21, 42, 54, 64, 65, 126

Edinburgh, © National Galleries of Scotland: cat. 145; fig. 39 (Photography: Antonia Reeve)

Figueres, © Fundació Gala-Salvador Dalí, 2017, cats 7, 12, 13, 22, 23, 29, 43, 50, 66, 67, 72–76, 114, 118, 150, 152, 153; figs 15, 70, 72, 94, 95, 98, 99, 101, 103, 106, 110–12, 116, 117, 122–24, 127–32

Florence, © 2017. Photo Scala, fig. 83

Glasgow, © CSG CIC Glasgow Museums Collection: cat. 132; fig. 84

Hartford, © Wadsworth Atheneum. Photography: Allen Phillips: cat. 136

Houston (TX), The Menil Collection. Photo Hickey-Robertson: fig. 64

Jerusalem, Photo © The Israel Museum, by Avshalom Avital: fig. 14

Kansas City (MO), The Nelson-Atkins Museum of Art. Purchase: acquired through the generosity of Mr and Mrs Louis Sosland, F73-53. Photo: Robert Newcombe: fig. 55

London, akg-images/Erich Lessing: fig. 109

London, Alamy Stock Photo: fig. 12 (Photo 12)

London, © Emmanuel Boussard Library: cats 14–17, 26, 97, 98

London, © Bridgeman Images: 4–5 (© Christie's Images); figs 90 (© Salvador Dalí, Fundació Gala-Salvador Dalí, Figueres, 2004)

London, © Getty Images: fig. 9 (Fred R. Dapprich/Condé Nast); 51 (Photo Eric Schaal/Pix Inc./The LIFE Images Collection)

London, Image courtesy of Photoplay Productions Ltd: fig. 48

London, © Tate, 2017: cats 44, 91, 124, 131, 133

Madrid, © Archivo fotográfico del MNCARS: cats 45, 56, 135

Madrid, Instituto de la Cinematografía y de Las Artes Audiovisuales, Filmoteca Española: fig. 71

Milan, courtesy of Arturo Schwarz: fig. 47

New Haven, CT, Yale University Art Gallery. Gift of the Estate of Katherine S. Dreier: fig. 87

New Jersey, courtesy Professor Lewis Kachur, Kean University: fig. 29

New York, John Ashbery via The Flow Chart Foundation: fig. 31

New York, © 2017. Image copyright The Metropolitan Museum of Art/Art Resource/Scala, Florence: cat. 140; fig. 16

New York, Image provided by The Metropolitan Museum of Art, New York, Thomas J. Watson Library: fig. 60

New York, The Museum of the City of New York/Art Resource: fig. 104

New York, © 2017. Digital image, The Museum of Modern Art, New York/Scala, Florence: cat. 134; figs 11, 80, 91

New York, © Private collection, courtesy Sean Kelly, New York: cats 36, 39; fig. 125

New York, Private collection; Courtesy Ubu Gallery: fig. 56

Ottawa, © National Gallery of Canada, cat. 77

Paris, © Centre Pompidou, MNAM-CCI, Dist. RMN-Grand Palais: cover (right image), cats 90, 127; figs 26, 27; 25 (Bibliothèque Kandinsky); cats 92–96 (Photography: Guy Carrard); cats 3, 125; fig. 65 (Photography: Jacques Faujour); cats 1, 30, 85, 126, 129 (Photography: Georges Meguerditchian); cats 49, 84, 86 (Photography: Philippe Migeat); cats 8, 99, 128 (Photography: Jean-Claude Planchet)

Paris, © Man Ray Photographic Library/Telimage: fig. 28

Paris, © Musée d'Orsay, Dist. RMN-Grand Palais. Photography: Patrice Schmidt, fig. 17

Paris, © Fonds de dotation Jean-Jacques Lebel: cat. 58

Philadelphia, © Philadelphia Museum of Art: cats 11, 46, 48; figs 13, 23, 24, 32, 37, 38, 62, 76, 78, 81, 82, 102

Rome, © National Gallery of Modern and Contemporary Art. By permission of Ministero dei Beni e delle Attività Culturali e del Turismo: cats 101–03, 106 (Photography: Schiavinotto Giuseppe); cat. 105

Rovereto, © Archivio Fotografico e Mediateca Mart: cat. 137

St Petersburg (Florida), © Collection of The Dalí Museum: cats 2, 4, 7, 9, 25, 34, 47, 51–53, 59, 60, 78, 82, 83, 88, 89, 107, 115–17, 119, 120–23, 138, 139, 146–49; figs 21, 35, 57, 59, 63, 100, 119

Sarasota, © Ringling Museum of Art: cats 24, 108–10

Stockholm, Kent Belenius; photo courtesy Carl Fredrik Reuterswärd Art Foundation: fig. 19

Stockholm, © Moderna Museet: cat. 130, fig. 79 (Photography: Albin Dahlström), cat. 113

Vienna, Collection Hummel. Photography: © Gisela Erlacher: cats 41, 57, 62, 68–71; figs 20, 46, 89

Washington D.C., © Peter A. Juley & Son Collection, Smithsonian American Art Museum: fig. 120

West Dean, © West Dean College, part of the Edward James Foundation: cat. 61

© Descharnes & Descharnes sarl / Photo12 2017, fig. 12

© 2016. Christie's Images Limited, cat. 55

Association Atelier André Breton, www.andrebreton.fr: figs 107, 113

Additional Copyright

Image Rights of Salvador Dalí reserved. Fundació Gala-Salvador Dalí, Figueres, 2017

Hans Bellmer, © ADAGP, Paris and DACS, London 2017, fig. 88

Denise Bellon, © Denise Bellon–les films de l'équinoxe, figs 18, 30, 36

Brassaï, © Estate Brassaï – RMN-Grand Palais: cat. 83, 100

André Breton © ADAGP, Paris and DACS, London, 2017, fig. 113

© Melitó Casals 'Meli'/Fundació Gala-Salvador Dalí, Figueres, 2017, cat. 65, 132

Joseph Cornell, © The Joseph and Robert Cornell Memorial Foundation/VAGA, NY/DACS, London 2017, fig. 88

Salvador Dalí, © Salvador Dalí, Fundació Gala-Salvador Dalí, DACS 2017: cats 2, 7, 9, 10, 22, 23, 25, 29, 43, 45, 47, 50, 51, 52–56, 59, 61, 64, 66, 67, 72–76, 78, 82, 83, 88, 89, 115–23, 135–37, 140, 144, 145, 146; figs 9, 13, 18, 21, 24, 25, 26, 42–44, 56, 57, 59, 61, 63, 70, 72, 73, 76a, 76b, 80, 84, 90, 92, 95, 100, 101, 106, 108, 109, 119, 120, 122, 123, 127–30

Salvador Dalí, © CSG CIC Glasgow Museums Collection: cat. 132

Robert Descharnes, © Descharnes & Descharnes sarl 2017: cats 18–21, 42; figs 12, 69

Oscar Domínguez, © ADAGP, Paris and DACS, London 2017, fig. 88

Marcel Duchamp, © Succession Marcel Duchamp/ADAGP, Paris and DACS, London 2017: cover (right image). cats 1, 3, 4, 8, 11, 12, 18, 24, 26, 28, 30–36, 38, 39, 41, 44, 46–49, 57, 58, 60, 62, 68–71, 77, 79–81, 84, 85, 86, 87, 91, 99, 101–13, 124–31, 133, 134, 139, 141–43, 149, 150, 151, 153; figs 3–5, 9, 10, 13, 14, 19, 20, 21, 22, 26, 28–30, 32, 36, 37, 38, 39, 41, 45, 46, 47, 50, 55, 56, 62, 65, 76a, 76b, 77, 78, 82, 87, 89, 91, 93, 94, 107, 113, 116, 117, 125, 126, 131

Philippe Halsman, © Philippe Halsman Archive: cat. 27

Horst P. Horst © Condé Nast: cat. 40

Georges Hugnet, © ADAGP, Paris and DACS, London 2017, cat. 34

Marvin Koner, © The Estate of Marvin Koner, cat. 152

René Magritte, © ADAGP, Paris and DACS, London 2017, cat. 148

André Masson, © ADAGP, Paris and DACS, London, 2017: fig. 29

Roberto E. Matta, © ADAGP, Paris and DACS, London, 2017, fig. 107

Victor Obsatz, © Victor Obsatz c/o Moeller Fine Art, New York 2017, cat. 47; fig. 102

Francis Picabia © ADAGP, Paris and DACS, London 2017: cat. 26

Man Ray, © Man Ray Trust/ADAGP, Paris and DACS, London 2017: cover (right image), cats 13, 31, 33, 39, 47, 90, 92–98, 141, 143; figs 19, 24–28, 41, 125

Narcís Sans, © Ajuntament de Girona. CRDI (Narcís Sans Prat), cat. 63

David O. Selznick, © Selznick Collection, cat. 144

Yves Tanguy, © ARS, NY and DACS, London 2017, fig. 111

Carl Van Vechten, Library of Congress © Van Vechten Trust: fig. 103

Andy Warhol, © 2017 The Andy Warhol Museum, Pittsburgh, PA, a museum of Carnegie Institute. All rights reserved: figs 1–2

Julian Wasser, ©1963 Julian Wasser, cat. 41

INDEX

All references are to page numbers; those in **bold** type indicate catalogue plates and those in *italic* type indicate essay illustrations

391 (magazine) 60, 195

Abraham 150
Abstract Expressionism 22, 51
African sculpture 28
L'Âge d'or (film) 18, 24, 196
Ali, Muhammad 12
Allégret, Marc
  Anémic cinéma (film) 46, 178, **190**
'The Almost Complete Works of Marcel Duchamp', London (1966) 161
American Chess Foundation 202, 204
L'Amic de les Arts (journal) 37, 44, *44*, 47, 68, 83, 195
anamorphic perspective **168**, *169*
Anémic cinéma (film) 45, 46, 60, 178, **190**
anti-art 15, 17, 44, 83
Apollinaire, Guillaume 35, 50, 160, 194
Aragon, Louis 17, 18, 27, 31, 83, 195, 196, *196*
  Paris Peasant 45
Arcachon 51, 201
Arensberg, Mr and Mrs Walter *16*, 46
Argentina 28
Armory Show, New York (1913) 16, 194
Art News 52, **87**, 156, 202, 203
Art of This Century, New York 201
Arts Committee for American Chess 202
automata 49
Autoportrait mou de Salvador Dalí (film) 52, **81**, 204
automatism 45, 179
Averty, Jean-Christophe 52, **81**, 204

Barcelona 19, 30, 58, 197
Barr, Alfred 173–74
Bataille, Georges 18, 46–47
Bauhaus 44
Bazar de l'Hôtel de Ville, Paris 194
Bel Ami (film) 201
Bellevue, Switzerland 140–41
Bello, Pepín 195
Benayoun, Robert
  'We Don't EAR It that Way' **186**, 203
Benjamin, Walter 50
  On the Concept of History 49
Bernard, Raymond 50
Bible 19
Bibliothèque Saint-Geneviève, Paris 18, 36, 168
The Blind Man (journal) 16, 42, 82, **132**, 195
Bloc Obrer I Camperol (Workers' and Peasants' Bloc) 18
Böcklin, Arnold 23–24
  Island of the Dead 24
Bomsel, Louis 199
Bonwit Teller & Co., New York *198*, 199, 200
Bosse, Abraham 168, 170
  'Pour la Perspective horizontale' *170*
Botticelli, Sandro
  Venus 200
Brancusi, Constantin 82
Brassaï 30, 197
Brentano's bookstore, New York 201
Breton, André 21, 27, 38, 42–43, 52, 53, 83, 195, *199*
  Communist criticism of 38
  'Contre-attaque' 18
  on Duchamp 17, 18
  eroticism and erotic objects 108, 114, 115
  exhibitions 31–32
  Galerie Gradiva 199–200
  and the *Green Box* 161
  and humour 99
  'International Exhibition of Surrealism' 24
  on *The Large Glass* 199
  lectures 196
  Abridged Dictionary of Surrealism (Dictionnaire abrégé du Surréalisme) 32, 200, *200*
  Anthology of Black Humour 99
  Arcane 17 201, *201*
  'La beauté sera convulsive' 197
  'Crisis of the Object' 29, 31
  Manifesto of Surrealism 195
  'Second Manifesto' 18
  Surrealism and Painting 201
  Le Surréalisme, même 42, *43*
  'Surrealist Intrusion' exhibition 203
  What is Surrealism? 18
  'Young Cherry Trees Secured Against Hares' **187**
Bronowski, J. 196
Brooklyn Museum, New York 141
Bruno de Jesus-Marie 170
Buenos Aires 28, 83, 195
Buffet-Picabia, Gabrielle 35, 154, 160
  'Cœurs volants' 31
bullfight, Surrealist 104, *104–105*, 203
Buñuel, Luis 144
  L'Âge d'or 18, 24, 196
  Un Chien andalou 37, 45, 47, 108–109, 195
Bureau International des Poids et Mesures, Sèvres 172

Cabanne, Pierre 45, 50
  Dialogues with Marcel Duchamp 52, **81**, 204
Cadaqués 15, 18–19, 25, 30, 46, 51, 58, *65*, *66–67*, 144, 196, *196*, 197, 202, 205
Cage, John 15, 99
Cahiers d'Art 31, **137**
Camino, Paco 104
Cap de Creus 51, 58, 108, 110, 199
Capote, Truman 50
Carmelite order 170
Carrouges, Michel 49, 155
Carstairs Gallery, New York 202, 203
Catalan Students Association 195
Catalonia 17, 58, 144
Catherine II, Empress of Russia 49
Catholic Church 24, 25, 108, 154
'celibate machines' 49, 50
Centre Georges Pompidou, Paris 23
Chanel, Coco 51
Chaplin, Charlie 47
chess 49–53, 69
Chexbres, Switzerland 140–41
Un Chien andalou (film) 37, 45, 46–47, 108–109, 195
Christ 150, 154–56
Christianity 155, 156, 161
Clair, Jean 168–70
Coady, Robert 82, *82*
Cocteau, Jean 58
Cohen, Arthur A. 52
Cohen, Margaret 38
Colle, Edgard 83
Communist Party 18, 21–22, 38, 144, 150
Concours Lépine, Paris 178
Constructivism 45
'Contre-attaque' 18
Copley, William 17
Cordes, Paul *52*
Cordier & Ekstrom Gallery, New York 204
Costa Brava 141
Courbet, Gustave 19, 178
  Origin of the World 114
Cranach, Lucas the Elder 23
Crick, Francis 154
Crotti, Jean 45, 82, 201
Cubism 16, 19, 22, 23, 35, 50
Cubo-Futurism 51

Dada 15, 17, 22, 27, 44, 51, 52, 82–83, 98, 174, 195, 203, 205
'Dada, Surrealism, and Their Heritage', New York (1968) 204, 205
Dalí, Anna Maria 194
Dalí, Gala 58, *65–67*, 114, **129**, **130**, 197, *197*
  in Dalí's paintings 25, 68, *109*, 144, 198, *204*
  plays chess 51, *51*, 53, 201
  relationship with Dalí 18–19, 108, 110, 144, 196, 198
  in Second World War 200–201
  'Zodiac' group 196
Dalí, Salvador 10, 52, *64–67*, **79**, **128–29**, *146*, *191*, *197*, *198*, *204*
  anamorphic objects 169
  'anti-art' 15, 17, 44, 83
  as artist-celebrity 15
  and chess 49, 51–53, *51*, 69, **81**
  and Duchamp's *Étant donnés* 141, 144
  early life 58, 194
  Ed Ruscha on 12–13
  eroticism and erotic objects 22, 60, 108–109, 110, 115
  friendship with Duchamp 15, 39, 51, 58
  and Gala 18–19, 108, 110, 144, 196, 198
  gender and public persona 68–69
  humour 98–99
  iconography 19, 25
  and identity 58–60
  letter to Breton *199*
  measurement 174–75
  as notary's son 58, 68
  optical illusions 19, 24, 178–79
  and painting 21–25
  paranoiac-critical method 18, 21, 38, 50, 52–53, 144, *144*, 150, 154–56, 179, 205
  perspective 168, 169–70
  photography and film 41, 43–45, 46–47, 60, 69
  and scepticism 18
  science and religion 23, 154–56
  sculptures and objects 29–33
  and Surrealism 15–18, 21–22, 37–38, *39*
  Surrealist bullfight 104, **104**, *105*, 203
  'Surrealist object with symbolic function' 16–17
  Theatre-Museum, Figueres 19, 205, 206–207, *206–207*
  titles of works 13, 31
  and William Tell legend 144
  as a writer 35, 36–39
  10 Recipes for Immortality 19, 39, *159*, 179
  50 Secrets of Magic Craftsmanship 18, 19
  L'Âge d'or (film) 18, 24, 196
  Anamorphosis of Anamorphoses and all is Hologrammorphosis 159
  Anthropomorphic Beach 68, **92**
  Anti-Matter Ear 203
  Aphrodisiac Jacket 30, *30*
  Apotheosis of the Dollar 204, *204*
  Apparatus and Hand 37, 175
  Apparition of Face and Fruit Dish on a Beach 179, **182–83**
  Atmospheric Chair 30
  Atmospheric Spoon 30
  The Average Fine and Invisible Harp 99
  The Basket of Bread 23, **91**
  The Bather **92**
  The Birth of Liquid Desires 198–99
  Board of Demented Associations 30
  Catalan Bread 108, **121**
  Chaos and Creation (video) 202
  Chess set made in homage to Marcel Duchamp **53**, 204, *204*
  Un Chien andalou (film) 37, 45, 46–47, 108–109, 195
  Christ of St John of the Cross 155, 169–70, *171*
  Couple with Their Heads Full of Clouds **184–85**, *196*
  Cubist Self-portrait **85**
  The Enigma of William Tell 21–22, 69, 144, *145*, *146*, 203
  The Enigma of William Tell with the Apparition of a Celestial Gala **147**
  Exploding Raphaelesque Head **192**
  Figure in Flames **71**
  The First Days of Spring 17, 27, 45, 60, 68, 83, **96–97**
  Fishermen in the Sun **93**
  Fishermen in the Sun, preparatory drawing **93**
  frontispiece to *La Femme Visible* 69
  Gangsterism and Goofy Visions of New York 99, *99*
  Gradiva **148**
  The Great Masturbator 98–99
  Honey is Sweeter than Blood 37
  Hysterical and Aerodynamic Female Nude 30
  Illumined Pleasures 144
  Immortality of Castor and Pollux 159
  Immortality of Genetic Imperialism 159
  Impressions of Upper Mongolia: Homage to Raymond Roussel (film) 43–44
  The Lane to Portlligat with View of Cap de Creus 61
  Lobster Telephone 32, 99, **101**
  The Lugubrious Game 175, *175*
  Madonna 24, **186**
  Madonna of Portlligat 202
  Mannequin 26
  Market 195
  Meditation on the Harp 150, **151**
  Memory of the Child Woman 68
  Las Meninas **180–81**
  Minotaure cover **124**
  Monument to Kant 30–31, *30*, 33
  Morphological Echo **158**
  Nude Vibrations Dematerialising a Clothed Nude of Super-nude Vibrations 202
  Object 30
  One Hundred Thousand Virtual Virgins Reflected by a Number of Real Mirrors to be Determined by 'Étant donnés' Cybernetics 206–207
  Oto-rhinologic Head of Venus 197
  Paradise 206, *206*
  The Persistence of Memory 154, *154*, 196
  Please Touch 108
  Portrait of Gala with Two Lamb Chops in Equilibrium upon Her Shoulder *109*, 198
  Portrait of My Father 58, **62**
  Portrait of Pablo Picasso in the Twenty-first Century 51
  Premonition of Civil War 16
  Rainy Taxi 31, 200, 207
  Retrospective Bust of a Woman 30
  Surrealist Object Functioning Symbolically – Gala's Shoe 99, 114, **117**
  The Secret Life of Salvador Dalí 18
  Skull **193**
  Skull with Its Lyric Appendage Leaning on a Bedside Table which Should Have the Exact Temperature of a Cardinal's Nest 98, 99
  Spectre ornamental de l'érection 30
  The Spectre of Sex-Appeal 108, **111**
  Stereoscopic and Stereochemical Immortality of Monarchy 159
  Still Life – Fast Moving **157**
  Study for Christ of St John of the Cross 169
  Swans Reflecting Elephants *199*, 200
  The Temptation of St Anthony 201
  Two Pieces of Bread Expressing the Sentiment of Love 51, **90**, 201
  Untitled (c. 1928) **93**
  Untitled (Erotic scene) (c. 1932) **113**
  Untitled (Erotic scene) (1960s) **113**
  Untitled (Female nude, erotic scene) **113**
  Untitled (Multiple erotic scenes) **113**
  Untitled (Note to Leonard Lyons) *59*, 60
  Untitled (St Sebastian) **70**
  Venus de Milo with Drawers 108, 115, **125**
  William Tell 99
  William Tell and Gradiva **149**
  William Tell Group **147**
  writings:
  Love and Memory 37–38, 144, *144*, 196
  'Anti-Matter Manifesto' 39, 154
  Babaouo 50, 196
  'Birth of nutritious perversions' 108, 110, 199
  'Communication: Paranoiac Face' 179, *179*
  The Conquest of the Irrational 39, *39*, 150, 154, 169
  'Daydream' 38
  Declaration of the Independence of the Imagination and the Rights of Man to His Own Madness 200
  'Documentaries' 45
  'L'échecs, c'est moi' ('I am Chess') 52, **81**, 204
  The Visible Woman 37, *69*, 179, 196
  Giraffes on Horseback Salad 99
  'The Great Masturbator' 22
  'Honour to the Object' 31
  'I defy Aragon' 22
  'I eat Gala' 108, **110**, 198
  'The King and the Queen Traversed by Swift Nudes' 51, 52, 156, 202
  'Latest Intellectual Excitement for the Summer' *29*
  Manuscript for 'Freud et la Gioconda' **73**
  The Metamorphosis of Narcissus 39
  Mystical Manifesto 39, 154–55
  'Les Nouvelles couleurs du sex-appeal spectral' 198
  'Objets psycho-atmosphériques-anamorphiques' 196
  'Le Phénomène de l'extase' 197, *197*

'Picasso and I' (lecture) 51
'Poem' 37
'Psychoatmospheric-Anamorphic Objects' 38
'Rêverie' 108, 150
'The Rotting Donkey' 38
'St Sebastian' 175
'Salvador Dalí Reveals the Mona Lisa Secret' 69
'Sant Sebastià' 68, 195
The Secret Life of Salvador Dalí 39
Studium 37
'Surrealist Objects' 108, **114**, 196
'The Terrifying and Edible Beauty of "Modern Style" Architecture' **122**
The Tragic Myth of Millet's Angelus, A Paranoiac-critical Interpretation 19, 39, 150, **150**, 154, 196
'Vive la guerre! Le surréalisme et Hitler' 22
'Who is Surrealism?' 205
'Why They Attack the Mona Lisa' 68, 203–204, 203
Yellow Manifesto 17, 83, 83, 195
Dalí Cusí, Salvador 144–45
Dalí Theatre-Museum, Figueres 19, 58, 195, 205, 206–207, 206–207
Dalmau, Josep 194
D'Arcy Galleries, New York 203
De Kooning, Willem 52
Desargues, Girard
    Manière universelle de M. Desargues 170
Descharnes, Michèle 67
Descharnes, Nicolas 35
Descharnes, Robert 35, 52, 65–67, 69, **81**, 104
Deville, Jean 50
Dictionnaire abrégé du Surréalisme 32, 200, 200
Diehl, Gaston
    The Moderns: A Treasury of Painting Throughout the World 13
Dizzy Dalí Dinner (1941) 201
Documents (magazine) 47
Domènech Ferrés, Catalina 195
Domínguín, Luis Miguel 104
Donati, Enrico 114, 201
d'Ors, Eugenio 144
Doucet, Jacques 178
Dreier, Katherine S. 35, 161, 173, 195
Du Breuil, Jean 168, 170
Duchamp, Marcel 10, 15, 32, 64–67, **126**, **146**, 202
    anaglyptic and stereoscopic works 25, 46
    'anti-art' 15, 17, 23, 82, 178
    'celibate machines' 49, 50
    as chess player 15, 17, 18, 25, 49–53, 50, 60, 69, **80**, **81**, 83
    death 52, 205
    early life 58, 194
    Ed Ruscha on 11–12, 13
    eroticism and erotic objects 22–23, 108, 109, 114–15
    exhibitions 11, 16, 27, 30–32
    friendship with Dalí 15, 39, 51, 58
    gender and public persona 68–69
    humour 98–99
    iconography 25
    and identity 58–60
    infra-mince 39
    'International Exhibition of Surrealism' 24
    letters to Dalí 198, 199, 202, 203
    measurement 172–74
    'meta-realism' 22
    on modern art 19
    multiple editions 12
    as notary's son 58, 68
    optical illusions 19, 24, 25, 178, 179
    and painting 21–25
    perspective 168–69
    photography and film 41–43, 45–46, 60, 69
    puns 46, 160
    readymades 15, 16–17, 19, 27–33, 36, 52, 82, 98, 99, 114
    representation of movement 41, 45
    as Rrose Sélavy 17, 32, 42, 43, 46, 60, 68, **74–75**, 179, 195
    and scepticism 18, 33
    science and religion 154, 156
    and Surrealism 15–18, 19, 38
    Surrealist bullfight 104, 105, 203
    and the Theatre-Museum, Figueres 206–207
    titles of works 13, 31, 35
    as a writer 35–36, 38–39

3 Standard Stoppages 42, 98, 99, 168, 172–74, 174, **176**
Anémic cinéma (film) 45, 46, 60, 178, **190**
Beautiful Breath: Veil Water 27, 27, 68
The Bec Auer **112**
Bicycle Wheel 16, 28, 45, 60, 82, 98, 114, **116**, 194, 195
Boîte-en-valise 19, 28, 39, 51, 69, 98, **102–103**, 173, 199, 201, 202, 206
Bottle Rack 16, 28, 30, 30, 31, 32, 60, **95**, 98, **136**, 194
The Brawl at Austerlitz 31, 32
The Bride 161, 161, 168, 174
The Bride Stripped Bare by Her Bachelors, Even (The Large Glass) 17, 19, 21, 22, 23, 28, 31, 35–36, 38, 39, 41, 42, 43, 50, 52, 98, 99, 108, 109, 140, 141, 155, 156, 160–61, 160, **166–67**, 168–69, 170, 172–74, 194, 195, 196, 198
Brie 194
The Bush 21, 22
Cahiers d'Art cover **137**
The Chess Players 45, **89**
The Chocolate Grinder 60, 174
Cemetery of Uniforms and Liveries 175
Coal-sack Ceiling 32, 33, 200
'Cœurs volants' 31
Coffee Mill **84**
Comb 36
'Couple of Laundress's Aprons' from Mimi Parent, Boîte alerte **127**
Couverture-cigarettes **123**
Dart Object 25, 109, 114, **120**
Emilio Puignau, Mayor of Cadaqués 205
Étant donnés 19, 21, 25, 51, 53, 109, 114, 140–41, 140–41, **143**, 144, 168–69, 206
Female Fig Leaf 25, 42, 109, 114–15, **119**, **123**
Fountain 16, 23, 24, 28–29, 42, 82, **133**, 195
Frames from an Uncompleted Stereoscopic Film 47
Fresh Widow 195
Green Ray 40, 42
Handmade Stereopticon Slide 178, 178, 179
Hat Rack 29, **132**, 195
In Advance of the Broken Arm 36, **134**
The King and Queen Surrounded by Swift Nudes 24–25, 35, 39, 51, 53, **86–87**, 115, 156, 194
Landscape study for Étant donnés **142**
The Large Glass see The Bride Stripped Bare by Her Bachelors, Even
L.H.O.O.Q. 15, 22, 23, 27, 52, 60, 68, 69, **73**, **76**, 83, 98, 115, 150, 195
Mannequin (Rrose Sélavy) 32
Marcel Duchamp Cast Alive 52, 53
Monte Carlo Bond 27, 29, 42, 68, **76**
Moustache and Beard of L.H.O.O.Q. **76**
Network of Stoppages 174, **177**
The Non-Dada 42, 42
Not a Shoe 115, **123**
Nude Descending a Staircase (No. 2) 11, 16, 16, 41, 41, 45, 51, 194, 202
Paris Air 98, **139**
The Passage from Virgin to Bride 35
Pharmacy 22, 27, 28, 30, 32, **94**
Photograph of Shadows Cast by Readymades **131**
Please Touch 25, 114, **124**
Pocket Chess Set 51
Portrait of the Artist's Father 58, **63**
Portrait of Chess Players **88**
Ready-made (Hat Rack) 29
Rendez-vous of Sunday 6 February 1916 36, 36
Rotary Demisphere (Precision Optics) 45, 46, 46, 178
Rotary Glass Plates 45, 178, **188**
Rotoreliefs 178, **189**
Rrose Sélavy **75**
Rrose Sélavy (booklet) **100**
Sad Young Man on a Train 98
St Sebastian 68, **71**
Selected Details after Courbet **112**
Selected Details after Cranach and 'Relâche' **112**
Selected Details after Ingres I **112**
Selected Pieces 25
Shaved L.H.O.O.Q. **76**
Sink Stopper 12, 12, **134**
Sonata 194, 194
'Study for the Bride in Étant donnés' 141, **142**

The 36
Tonsure 78
Torture-morte 99, 99
Traveller's Folding Item (Underwood Cover) **138**
Travelling Sculpture 28, 28
Tu m' 16, 41, 58, 172–73, 173, 195
Unhappy Readymade 175
Untitled (Note to Leonard Lyons) 59, 60
Wedge of Chastity 25, 109, 114, 115, **118**
Why Not Sneeze Rose Sélavy? 17, 30, 31, 115, **135**, 196
With Hidden Noise 36, **138**
'Young Cherry Trees Secured Against Hares' cover **186**
Young Girl and Man in Spring 22, 23, 174
Yvonne and Magdeleine Torn in Tatters 98, 98
writings
    The Box of 1914 36, 42, 42
    Dialogues with Marcel Duchamp 39
    Green Box 22, 36, 38, 140, 156, 160–61, **162–63**, 172, 198
    Manual of Instructions for the Assembly of Étant donnés 141
    Marchand du Sel: écrits de Marcel Duchamp 35, 39
    Notes 31, 41–42, 109, **164–65**, 194, 196
    Note: 'Un rayon de lumière…' **38**
    Note: 'Rrose Sélavy born in 1920 in N.Y….' **74**
    Note: 'Study for Knight: Pocket Chess Set 1943' 53
    L'Opposition et les cases conjuguées sont reconciliées 50, 51, 52, 196
    White Box 22, 36
Duchamp, Suzanne 16, 45, 194, 201
Duchamp, Teeny 51, 65–67, 115, 202
Duchamp-Villon, Raymond 58, 194
Dufresne, Isabelle (Ultra Violet) 12
Dullin, Charles 49
Dupuy-Mazuel, Henry 50
Dürer, Albrecht 51, 53, 168

Easter Island 108
Éditions Surréalistes 37, 196
Eilshemius, Louis Michel 23
Einstein, Albert 154, 155
Éluard, Cécile 196
Éluard, Paul 17, 18, 31–32, 150, 195–96, 197, 200
    Abridged Dictionary of Surrealism 32, 200, 200
Empiricus, Sextus
    Les Hipotiposes; ou, Institutions Pirroniennes de Sextus Empiricus 18
Ernst, Max 200, 201
erotic objects 114–15
eroticism 108–10
L'Esprit nouveau 17
'Exhibition of Cubist Art', Barcelona (1912) 194
'Exhibition of Surrealist Objects', Paris (1936) 30–31, 30–31
Exposición de Arte Cubista, Barcelona (1912) 194
Exposition InteRnatIonal du Surréalisme (EROS), Paris (1959–60) 108, 127
'Exposition Surréaliste', Paris (1933) 29–30, 30

'Fallas', Valencia 104
'Fantastic Art, Dada, Surrealism', New York (1936) 173–74, 199
fascism 18, 21–22, 24
Faucigny-Lucinge, Prince de 196
Fauvism 19, 22, 23
Ferry, Jean 52
Field, Albert 52
Fifth Avenue Cinema, New York 46
Figueres 19, 58, 104, 194, 195, 203, 205, 206–207
film 41–47, 60
'The First Papers of Surrealism', New York (1942) 51, 201
First World War 28, 82, 195
Foucault, Michel 50
Fox News 47
Franco, General Francisco 18
Franklin, Benjamin 49
Franklin, Paul B. 16
French Academy of Sciences 172
French Revolution 205
Freud, Sigmund 22, 51, 83, 144, 154, 155, 199, 203
    Leonardo da Vinci and a Memory of His Childhood 52
Futurism 16, 17, 28, 82

G (magazine) 45, 45
La Gaceta Literaria 37
Galerie Beaux-Arts, Paris 32–33, 200, 206
Galerie Charles Ratton, Paris 30–31, 30–31
Galerie Charpentier, Paris 115
Galerie Cordier, Paris 108
Galerie Goemans, Paris 27, 83, 196
Galerie Gradiva, Paris 199–200, 199, 207
Galerie Jacques Bonjean, Paris 30
Galerie Maeght, Paris 41
Galerie Pierre Colle, Paris 29–30, 196–97
Galeries Dalmau, Barcelona 194, 195
Gallery of Modern Art, New York 204, 204
Garfias, Pedro 195
Gasch, Sebastià 17, 195
    Yellow Manifesto 83, 83
Gaudí, Antoni 197
gender identity 68–69
Ghyka, Matila 154
Giacometti, Alberto
    Disagreeable Object 108
    Suspended Ball 114
Girón, Curro 104
Gleizes, Albert 16
Goemans, Camille 196
Goethe, Johann Wolfgang von 82
Gotham Book Mart, New York 201, 201
Greece, ancient 155
Griswold, J. F.
    'Seeing New York with a Cubist: The Rude Descending a Staircase (Rush Hour at the Subway)' 17
Guardiola, Ramón 104
Guggenheim, Peggy 201

Halberstadt, Vitaly
    Opposition and Sister Squares are Reconciled 50, 52
Halsman, Philippe 68
    A Paragon of Beauty from 'Dalí's Mustache' **73**
Hamilton, Richard 15, 161, **167**, 173
Hawking, Stephen 154
Heisenberg, Werner 53, 154, 155
Hermitage of St Sebastian, Cadaqués 68
Herms, George 12
Hitler, Adolf 21, 22, 203
Holbein, Hans the Younger
    The Ambassadors 168, 169
'Homage to Caïssa', New York (1966) 204
Hopps, Walter 11, 174
Horst, Horst P.
    Portrait of Dalí **79**
Hotel Del Monte, Pebble Beach, California 200, 201
Hugnet, Georges
    'Marcel Duchamp' **76**
Hugo, Valentine 114
Hultén, Pontus 21–22, 144
humour 98–99

Iberian Artists Society 195
'The Imagery of Chess', New York (1944) 51
Impressionism 19, 22, 23, 194
Impressions of Upper Mongolia: Homage to Raymond Roussel (film) 43–44
Independents Exhibition, New York (1917) 16, 24, 82
Informalism 51
International Exhibition of Paintings, Pittsburgh (1928) 195
'International Exhibition of Surrealism', New York (1960–61) 24, 60, 202, 203
'International Exhibition of Surrealism', Paris (1947) 41, 42, 109, 114
'International Surrealist Exhibition', Paris (1938) 19, 31–32, 32–33, 200, 200, 206, 207

Jaguer, Edouard 24, 203
James, Edward 15, 200
    Lobster Telephone **101**
Jarry, Alfred 49, 156
    'The Passion Considered as an Uphill Bicycle Race' 16
Je ne vois pas… (photomontage) 18
Jean, Marcel 35
Jeaurat, Edme-Sébastien
    Traité de perspective à l'usage des artistes 170

Jensen, Wilhelm 199
Gradiva 144
John XXIII, Pope 24, 203
John of the Cross, St 169–70
Crucifixion 170
Le Joueur d'échecs (films) *49*, 50
Julien Levy Gallery, New York 51, 109, 197, *198*
Jura Mountains 35–36, 160, 194

Kafka, Franz 49
Kant, Immanuel 30–31, 33
The Critique of Judgement 31
Keaton, Buster 47
Kempelen, Wolfgang von 49, *49*, 50
Kiesler, Frederick 42, 201
King, Elliott 155
Kline, Franz 52
Kodak 42

Lacan, Jacques 22
Laforgue, Jules 22
Langdon, Harry 47
Lautréamont, Comte de
Les Chants de Maldoror 49, 198
Le Corbusier 17, 175
Le Forestay waterfall 140–41
Le Gentil, Claude 200
Le Nain 170
League of Nations 24
League of Women 201
Lebel, Robert 39
Marcel Duchamp 60
Ledoux, Claude-Nicolas 205
Léger, Fernand 82
Ballet mécanique 47
Leiris, Michel 35
Lenin, Vladimir 21, 22, 144
Leonardo da Vinci 179
Mona Lisa 52, 60, 68, 69, **76**, 115, 150, 195, 203–204, *203*
Virgin and Child with St Anne 150
Lévi-Strauss, Claude 31
Levy, Julien 197
Linde, Ulf 173
Littérature (magazine) 17, 43, 46, 195
Londe, Albert 23
Lorca, Federico García 37, 58, 68, 175, 195
Losfeld, Eric 35
Louvre, Paris 195
Lumière 42
Lyons, Leonard *59*, 60, 203

McEvilley, Thomas 33
MacGregor, Neil 170
machines célibataires ('celibate machines') 49, 50
Madrid 37, 58, 154
Magritte, Georgette 196
Magritte, René 196
Mallarmé, Stéphane 22
Marey, Étienne-Jules 41
Maria Theresa, Empress 49
Marseille 201
Martin, Katrina 46
Marx, Harpo 99
Marx, Karl 155
Mathieu, Georges 52
Matisse, Henri 22, 205
Maupassant, Guy de
Bel Ami 201
measurement 172–75
Meissonier, Ernest 23
Portrait of Napoleon 24
Milhaud, Darius 11
Millares 52
Millet, Jean-François
The Angelus 19, 24, *25*, 30, 32, 39, 144, 150
Minotaure (journal) 19, 30, 39, **124**, 150, 174, *174*, 196, 197, 199, 200
Miró, Joan 17, 83
Sculpture 114
Modern Style architecture 24
Moderna Museet, Stockholm 22, 69, 144
Moholy-Nagy, László 45
Painting Photography Film 44, *44*, 47
Molí de la Torre estate, Figueres 194
Monnier, Bernard *67*
Monnier, Jacqueline Matisse *67*

Montaigne, Michel de 18
Essays 18
Montanyà, Lluís 17, 195
Yellow Manifesto 83, *83*
Montes, Eugenio 195
Multiple Portrait of Marcel Duchamp 15
Munich 194
Municipal Theatre, Figueres 195
Murillo, Fermín 104
Museum of Modern Art (MoMA), New York 52, 173–74, 199, 205
'Mutt, R.' 16, 27, 195
Muybridge, Eadweard 41

Nabokov, Vladimir
La Défense Loujine 51
Napoleon I, Emperor 49
neo-Hegelianism 29
New York 16, 69, 201
New York Dada 17, *74*, 195
The New York Evening Sun 17
New York Post 60, 203
New York World's Fair (1939) 199, 200
'Newer Super-Realism', Hartford (1931) 196
Nietzsche, Friedrich Wilhelm 155
Nkisi sculpture 28
Noailles, Vicomte de 196
Nouveaux Réalisme 104

Obsatz, Victor
Portrait No. 29 197
Oedipus myth 24, 144, 150
Old Masters 25
Olivier, Fernande 18
optical illusions 19, 24, 25, 178–79
Ozenfant, Amédée 17

Paalen, Wolfgang 200
Pacioli, Luca
De divina proportione 155
Parent, Mimi
Boîte alerte **127**
Paris Match 24, 203
Parkinson, Gavin 154
Pasadena Art Museum 11, *80*
'La Peinture au défi', Paris (1930) 18, 27, 83, 196, *196*
Péret, Benjamin 37
Perlmutter, Bronia **126**
perspective 168–70
Philadelphia Museum of Art 140, 161
photography 41–47, 60, 69
Picabia, Francis 27, 31, 35, 49, 60, **72**, 154, 160, 194, 195, *391*
L'Oeil cacodylate 60
Picasso, Pablo 17, 18, 31, 51, 83, 195, 203
Pichot, Ramon 194
Pichot family 194
Pierre, José 24, 203
Pierre Colle Gallery, Paris *30*
Pittsburgh 195
Plexiglas 141
Poe, Edgar Allan 49
'Maelzel's Chess Player' 49
Pointillism 23, 24
Pop Art 39
Portlligat 18, *19*, 25, 58, 60, 141, 170, 196, *196*, 197, 205
Pradier, James 30
La Publicitat (newspaper) 83
Puignau, Emilio 205, *205*
Purism 175
Puteaux 45
Pyrenees 58
Pyrrho of Elis 18, 33

Radford, Robert 18
Raphael
Sistine Madonna 24, 203
Ray, Man 27, 45, 58, *66*, *77*, 194, *196*, *198*, 200
on Dalí 22
on Duchamp 52
films 46, 47, 178
and *Minotaure* 19, 30, 197
New York Dada 17, 195
photographs *30–32*, 42, 43, 69, 197
and Rrose Sélavy 43, 60, 68, **74**
Adam and Eve **126**
Anémic cinéma (film) 46, 178, **190**

Dalí drapé series **128**
Dalí tête renversée **128**
Duchamp behind the Rotary Glass **188**
Female Fig Leaf **123**
Gala and Dalí **129**
Gala with a Surrealist Sculpture **130**
Gala with Surrealist Sculptures **130**
The Last Work of Marcel Duchamp/ Anaglyphic Chimney 205
Marcel Duchamp as Rrose Sélavy **74**
Le Monde des échecs 50
This is the Domain of Rrose Sélavy, View from an Aeroplane (Dust Breeding) 43, *43*
Real Academia de Bellas Artes de San Fernando, Barcelona 195
religion 154–56
Renaissance 168
Residencia de Estudiantes, Madrid 154, 195
La Révolution surréaliste (journal) 17–18, 37, 195, *196*
Reynolds, Mary 18, *66*, 197
Richter, Hans 45, *45*
Roché, Henri-Pierre 16, 82, 178
Romanticism 108
Rouen 58
Rougemont, Denis de
The Devil's Share 201
Roussel, Raymond 22, 35, 36, 49–50, 52–53, 205
Comment j'ai écrit certains de mes livres 50
Impressions of Africa 35, *35*, 50, 52, 160, 194
'Mat du fou et du cavalier' 50
Rutherford, Ernest 156
Ruttman, Walter
Berlin: Symphony of a City 47

Sacher-Masoch, Leopold von
Venus in Furs 115
Saint-Martin, Veules-les-Roses 68
Saint-Phalle, Niki de 104, 203
St Regis Hotel, New York 12, 52, 204
Sala Parés, Barcelona 195
Salon d'Automne, Paris 58, 174
Salon des Indépendants, Paris 16, 21, 58, 194
Salon de la locomotion aérienne, Paris 82
San Francisco Museum of Art 11
Sanouillet, Michel 35, 39
Saturn 150
Schiaparelli, Elsa 200
Schrödinger, Erwin 154, 155
Schwarz, Arturo 33, 115, 141
science 154–56
Sebastian, St 68
Sebond, Raymond 18
Second World War 200–201
Sélavy, Rrose (Duchamp's alter ego) 17, *32*, 42, 43, 46, 60, 68, **74–75**, 179, 195
Seligmann, Kurt 201
Seurat, Georges 24
Sheeler, Charles 42
Sidney Janis Gallery, New York 39
Sirine, W.
La Défense Loujine 51
Skira 150
Skira, Albert 198
Société Anonyme 35
Société des Lunetiers 173, 174
Society of Independent Artists, New York 195
A Soft Self-Portrait (film) 52, **81**, 204
The Soil (magazine) 82, *82*
Soupault, Philippe 195
Spanish Civil War (1936–39) 18
Spellbound (film) **191**
Steefel 115
Stein, Gertrude 58
Stettheimer family 45
Stieglitz, Alfred 16, 41, 42, 195
Stockholm 22, 69, 144
Stravinsky, Igor 17
Studio 28, Paris 196
'Succinct Dictionary of Eroticism' 108, 109
Surrealism
automatism 45, 179
Breton and 83
Un Chien andalou 46–47
Dalí and 15–18, 21–22, 37–38, 39
Duchamp and 15–18, 19, 38
eroticism and erotic objects 108, 114–15
exhibitions 31–32

machines célibataires 49
objects 28, 29, 31–32
and science 154, 155
Surrealist bullfight 104, *104–105*, 203
word games 50
La Surréalisme au service de la révolution (*SASDLR*, journal) 37, 38, *50*, 114, 150, 179, *179*, 196
Le Surréalisme en 1947, Paris 41, 42, 109, 114, **124**
Le Surréalisme, même (journal) 42, *43*
'Surrealist Intrusion in the Enchanters' Domain', New York (1960–61) 24, 60, *202*, 203
Switzerland 35, 140–41
Symbolism 22, 108
'Systemic Cycle of Lectures' 198

Tapiés, Antoni 52
Tartakower, Savielly 50–51
Raymond Roussel et les échecs dans la Littérature 50
Tate Gallery, London 161
Tell, William 19, 21, 22, 68, 144–45, 150
Théâtre Antoine, Paris *35*, 50
Theatre-Museum, Figueres *see* Dalí Theatre-Museum
This Quarter (journal) 196
Thom, René 154
Thompson, D'Arcy
On Growth and Form 154
Tinguely, Jean 104, 203
Titian
The Assumption of the Virgin 154–56, *169*
Torre, Guillermo de 83
Tzara, Tristan 17, 83
Dada Manifesto 82

Ultra Violet (Isabelle Dufresne) 12

Valencia 104
Van Dine, S. S.
Le Crime du fou d'échecs 50–51
Vanity Fair 42
Varèse, Edgard
Little Gioconda Collage: Dalí à Paris **77**
Velázquez, Diego Rodríguez de Silva y 51, 170
Venus de Milo 115, **125**
Verne, Jules 50
Villon, Jacques 58, 194
Vogue 205
Vuibert, Henry
Les Anaglyphes géométriques 205, *205*

Wadsworth Atheneum, Hartford 196
Wahl, Jean 29
Warhol, Andy
Screen Test: Marcel Duchamp 10
Screen Test: Salvador Dalí 10
Wasser, Julian
Chess Match at the Pasadena Museum **80**
Watson, James D. 154
Weissberg, Will **146**
Whitelaw Reid mansion, New York 51
Wood, Beatrice 16, 82
Wright, Frank Lloyd 11

Yugoslavia 108

Zdanevich, Ilia 202
Znosko-Borovsky, Eugene 83
'Zodiac' group 196
Zurbarán, Francisco 108
Zweig, Stefan
Chess Story (The Royal Game) 51